Fundamental Concepts of Educational Leadership and Management

Educational Leadership Policy Standards and Functions: ISLLC 2008 Addressed by Chapter

ISLLC Standards and Functions: 2008	Chapter 1	Chapter 2	Chapter 3
An education leader promotes the success of every student by:			
1. facilitating the development, articulation, implementation, and stewardship of a vision of learning that is shared and supported by all stakeholders.	X	X	X
A. Collaboratively develop and implement a shared vision and mission	X	X	X
B. Collect and use data to identify goals, assess organizational effectiveness, and promote organizational learning	X	X	X
C. Create and implement plans to achieve goals	X	X	X
D. Promote continuous and sustainable improvement	X	X	X
E. Monitor and evaluate progress and revise plans	X	X	X
2. advocating, nurturing, and sustaining a school culture and instructional program conducive to student learning and staff professional growth.	X		
A. Nurture and sustain a culture of collaboration, trust, learning, and high expectations	X		X
B. Create a comprehensive, rigorous, and coherent curricular program	X		X
C. Create a personalized and motivating learning environment for students	X		X
D. Supervise instruction	X		
E. Develop assessment and accountability systems to monitor student progress	X	X	X
F. Develop the instructional and leadership capacity of staff	X	X	X
G. Maximize time spent on quality instruction	X		
H. Promote the use of the most effective and appropriate technologies to support teaching and learning	X		X
I. Monitor and evaluate the impact of the instructional program	X	X	X
3. ensuring management of the organization, operation, and resources for a safe, efficient, and effective learning environment.			
A. Monitor and evaluate the management and operational systems	X	X	X
B. Obtain, allocate, align, and efficiently utilize human, fiscal, and technological resources	X	X	X
C. Promote and protect the welfare and safety of students and staff	X		X
D. Develop the capacity for distributed leadership	X	X	X
E. Ensure teacher and organizational time is focused to support quality instruction and student learning			X
4. collaborating with faculty and community members, responding to diverse community interests and needs, and mobilizing community resources.	X	X	X
A. Collect and analyze data and information pertinent to the educational environment	X	X	X
B. Promote understanding, appreciation, and use of the community's diverse cultural, social, and intellectual resources	X	X	X
C. Build and sustain positive relationships with families and caregivers	X	X	X
D. Build and sustain productive relationships with community partners	X	X	X
5. acting with integrity, fairness, and in an ethical manner.	X		
A. Ensure a system of accountability for every student's academic and social success	X		X
B. Model principles of self-awareness, reflective practice, transparency, and ethical behavior	X		
C. Safeguard the values of democracy, equity, and diversity	X		
D. Consider and evaluate the potential moral and legal consequences of decision making	X		
E. Promote social justice and ensure that individual student needs inform all aspects of schooling	X		X
6. understanding, responding to, and influencing the political, social, economic, legal, and cultural context.	X		
A. Advocate for children, families, and caregivers	X		
B. Act to influence local, district, state, and national decisions affecting student learning	X	X	X
C. Assess, analyze, and anticipate emerging trends and initiatives in order to adapt leadership strategies	X	X	X

Source: The Interstate School Leaders Licensure Consortium (ISLLC) Standards were developed by the Council of Chief State School Officers (CCSSO) and member states. Copies may be downloaded from the Council's website at www.ccsso.org.

Council of Chief State School Officers. (2008). *Educational Leadership Policy Standards: ISLLC 2008 as Adopted by the National Policy Board for Educational Administration.* Washington, DC: Author.

Chapter 4	Chapter 5	Chapter 6	Chapter 7	Chapter 8	Chapter 9	Chapter 10	Chapter 11	Chapter 12	Chapter 13	Chapter 14
X		X			X					X
X	X	X	X		X	X	X		X	X
X		X	X	X	X	X				X
X		X					X	X	X	X
X		X	X	X	X	X	X	X	X	X
X		X	X	X					X	X
X					X	X		X		X
X	X	X			X	X	X	X	X	X
X					X		X	X		X
X	X	X			X			X		X
X					X			X		X
X		X	X	X	X			X		X
X			X		X	X	X	X	X	X
X					X			X		X
X					X	X	X	X		X
X		X	X	X	X			X		X
X					X	X		X		X
X		X	X	X	X	X		X		X
X	X	X			X	X	X	X	X	X
X					X	X		X		X
X	X		X		X	X	X	X	X	X
X				X	X	X		X		X
X		X				X				X
X		X	X	X	X	X				X
X	X	X			X	X	X			X
X	X	X				X	X			X
X		X				X	X			X
X			X			X		X		X
X		X	X	X	X	X		X		X
X	X		X			X		X		X
X	X		X			X	X	X		X
X			X			X		X		X
X	X		X			X		X		X
X			X		X	X		X		X
X		X	X		X	X		X		X
X		X	X	X		X		X	X	X
X			X	X	X	X	X	X	X	X

THIRD EDITION

Fundamental Concepts of Educational Leadership and Management

Taher A. Razik
State University of New York at Buffalo

Austin D. Swanson
State University of New York at Buffalo

Allyn & Bacon

Boston   New York   San Francisco
Mexico City   Montreal   Toronto   London   Madrid   Munich   Paris
Hong Kong   Singapore   Tokyo   Cape Town   Sydney

Executive Editor and Publisher: Stephen D. Dragin
Series Editorial Assistant: Anne Whittaker
Marketing Manager: Amanda Stedke
Production Editor: Paula Carroll
Editorial Production Service: Connie Strassburg, GGS
Composition Buyer: Linda Cox
Manufacturing Buyer: Megan Cochran
Electronic Composition: GGS Higher Education Resources
Cover Coordinator: Elena Sidorova

Library of Congress Cataloging-in-Publication Data

Razik, Taher A.
    Fundamental concepts of educational leadership and management / Taher A. Razik, Austin D. Swanson.—3rd ed.
    Rev. ed of : Fundamental concepts of educational leadership. 2nd ed. © 2001; 1st ed. © 1995.
        p. cm.
    Includes bibliographical references and index.
    ISBN-13: 978-0-13-233271-2
    ISBN-10: 0-13-233271-X
    1. School management and organization—United States. 2. Educational leadership—United States. I. Swanson, Austin D. II. Razik, Taher A. Fundamental concepts of educational leadership. III. Title.

LB2805.R29 2010
371.200973—dc20

                                                2008051056

10 9 8 7 6 5 4 3 2 1 HAM 12 11 10 09

ISBN-10: 0-13-233271-X
ISBN-13: 978-0-13-233271-2

About the Authors

Taher A Razik and Austin D. Swanson are Professors Emeritus at the State University of New York at Buffalo. While co-teaching an introductory course in educational administration, they sought in vain to find an appropriate text that would be comprehensive in coverage, yet of sufficient depth to lead students to a fundamental understanding of the basic issues. They wanted a text that was eclectic in approach, not ideological, and that would emphasize an action-research perspective compelling readers to consider critically the theoretical underpinnings of current educational practice and to motivate them to seek practical alternative approaches to solving both common and unique problems. Not finding such a text, they set out to create their own; *Fundamental Concepts of Educational Leadership and Management* was the result. Widespread acceptance of the first edition led to a second edition, and now to a third.

"Retirement" from teaching has allowed the authors to devote greater attention to their research, writing, and consultancies. Professor Razik's research interests and scholarship are in communication theory, characteristics of leadership, teacher education, and the application of general systems theory to curriculum development and the uses of media in teaching and learning. Specific issues addressed by his scholarship include evaluating internal efficiency of school systems, strategies of change in curriculum planning and development, teacher preparation, evaluation as a component of instruction, and educational planning.

Professor Swanson's research interests relate to the economics of education and school finance and the governance and politics of education. Specific issues that his scholarship address include equity and social justice, alternative governance structures for schooling (e.g., choice among public schools, charter schools, vouchers, school governing boards, teacher empowerment), efficiency of allocation of resources within schools (e. g., whole school reform, labor intensiveness of schooling, use of technology in instruction and management, cost-benefit and cost-effectiveness analysis), and alternative means of allocating monies for schooling purposes (e. g., full state funding, the role of the federal government in school finance, school-based budgeting, and the "money following the child" concept).

To complement their knowledge and understanding of American education systems gained from working with and within schools, districts, and state and federal agencies, both authors have had extensive international experience enabling them to view the American education scene with a global perspective. Professor Razik has held two appointments with UNESCO in Paris as well as numerous contracts to conduct research for that agency. He has also contracted with foreign governments, especially those in the Middle East, to evaluate and design elements of their educational systems. He received the highest civilian decoration for non-Omanis from the government of Oman. He also received an outstanding recognition award for his work in systems research and cybernetics from the International Institute for Advanced Studies, Baden-Baden, Germany.

Professor Swanson has conducted comparative and longitudinal studies of the school systems of the United States, England, and Australia. The home base for his field studies in England was at the University of London, Institute of Education where he held successive honorary Visiting Scholar appointments. His initial visit to Australia was supported in part by a Fulbright Senior Scholar Award and a Visiting Research Fellowship from the University of Melbourne which served as the base for his field studies there. He has also lectured at Alvan Ikoku College of Education, Nigeria; Beijing Teachers College, China; and at several Israeli universities sponsored by the Zold Institute, Jerusalem.

Professor Razik's graduate studies were done at Ohio State University where he was awarded the M. A. and Ph. D. degrees. In addition to his faculty appointment at SUNY Buffalo, he was Director of its Instructional Communications Center for several years. Besides his UNESCO appointments, other international positions include: Executive Advisor to the Minister of Education, Oman; Member of the Foundation Committee for the Establishment of Oaboos University, Oman; Senior Expert, Education Section, Ministry of Planning, Iraq; and member of the three person team charged with planning, developing and implementing the United Arab Emirates University.

Professor Swanson's doctoral and master's degrees were earned at Teachers College, Columbia University. A Fellowship in Educational Research sponsored by the U. S. Department of Education enabled post-doctoral study at Stanford University. While at Columbia, he held appointments as Research Associate in the Institute of Administrative Research and, subsequently, Executive Secretary of the Central School Boards' Committee for Educational Research. Positions held at SUNY Buffalo concurrently with his faculty appointment included nine years as chair of departments housing programs in educational administration and Executive Director of the Western New York Educational Service Council.

Contents

Part V   Implementation of Systemic Change   345

Preface

Perspective

If there was ever a time when educational institutions required effective leadership, it is now. This is the first time in the history of the United States and other economically advanced nations that the quality of the education provided for their citizens has been recognized politically as being strategically linked to national survival and economic success. Educational issues are among the major concerns of voters; therefore, not surprisingly, they are debated vigorously by candidates for public office at all levels of government and are covered regularly on the front pages of major newspapers and by other media.

Educational quality and content are concerns not only at the collective, governmental levels but also of most families. While in the past, parents routinely enrolled their children in the neighborhood public or parish school, many are now asking, What is the best educational experience for our children? Is the local school able to provide our children with the necessary skills to live a happy and productive life? Should we take advantage of the public choice options within our school district beyond the neighborhood school to secure the kind and quality of education we desire for our children? Should we move to another community where the schools are reported to be better? Should we make the economic sacrifice to send our children to a private school? Should we assume the responsibility for our children's education ourselves and school them at home?

In a time of high educational expectations and professional accountability, today's educational leaders need to possess a broad variety of skills that enable them to function comfortably and effectively in changing environments and under highly politicized conditions. Under these circumstances, change is the only constant. The mission of this book is to foster understanding of this reality among those preparing for administrative and managerial careers in precollegiate educational institutions and to help them develop skills necessary for working competently within those institutions.

For better or for worse, this is a dynamic and exciting period in human history. Because of the fluidity of the situation, it is a period of unparalleled opportunity and of potential danger. Capitalizing on the opportunities and minimizing the dangers demands extraordinarily wise leadership in all sectors and in all enterprises, including education.

While pervasive social change affects persons in every walk of life, there is bound to be greater impact on those in positions of great social visibility and concern—such as those holding administrative and managerial responsibilities in educational organizations. Society has a right to expect proficient performance from people in those positions; in a climate of change, expert leadership cannot be a matter of copying conventional behavior. To advance education, there is a clear need for educational leaders to have and exercise: the ability to comprehend the dynamics of human affairs as a basis for relevant action under novel conditions, an understanding of issues and processes in educational institutions, and originality and collaboration in designing strategic policies. Their approach to the opportunities and problems confronting them must remain hypothetical and open ended so that more may be learned by what is done.

Past assumptions used by educators in designing schools and school curricula no longer hold across the board. Children are less likely to come from majority backgrounds, they are more likely to be members of nontraditional families, and they are more likely to be poor. Education through high school and beyond is essential if graduates are to be employed in other than menial jobs and to enjoy comfortable standards of living. Well-paying employment opportunities increasingly require sophisticated intellectual skills. Educational leadership is being challenged to design new curricula that recognize the multicultural nature of students, provide institutional support for those at risk, and link schooling to employment and citizenship. Solving our "educational" crises will also require coordination of schools' efforts with those of other social agencies in the community.

Not only will school leaders of the future be working with a student body markedly different from that of the past, but also the organizational structures and professional and political relationships will be quite different as well. These changes will produce a new climate for school organizations that demands transformational rather than hierarchical leadership. Parents and community members are likely to have greater influence on the organization and operation of schools through membership on school councils or because of increasing opportunities for parental choice among schooling options. The relationships between teachers and administrators are likely to be collegial, not authoritarian. Principals and teachers are likely to have greater professional discretion as many decisions formerly made at the district, state, and federal levels are left to schools. Nevertheless, local, state, and federal authorities will increasingly set and monitor standards while progressively divesting themselves of operational detail. We can expect states in particular, with the encouragement of the federal government, to set achievement standards, to design curricula to meet those standards, and to administer examinations to identify schools failing to meet those standards.

Pedagogy

Fundamental Concepts of Educational Leadership and Management, Third Edition is designed for graduate students beginning their studies of educational administration. It is comprehensive in coverage yet of sufficient depth to lead students to a fundamental understanding of basic issues. It is eclectic in approach, not ideological, and emphasizes an action-research perspective that encourages readers to consider critically the theoretical underpinnings of current educational practice and to seek practical alternative approaches for solving both common and unique problems.

The careful reader will quickly detect that we do not subscribe entirely to any particular philosophy. We attempt to report effective practice that has been validated by research and external evaluation regardless of the underlying paradigm and orientation. We view the study of leadership as a multiple-perspective activity. Theories of leadership are not viewed as competing with one another in the quest for the one best view. Each approach, each theory, has inherent strengths and weaknesses. Each theory is better able to illuminate and explain particular aspects of each concept rather than the whole; however, taken together, a more complete understanding of a concept is possible through the power of triangulation of perspectives made possible by accessing the insights provided by multiple theories.

It is common to elevate "leadership" and to denigrate "administration" and "management." We believe that this is a mistake. While it may be possible to be an effective administrator or manager without strong leadership skills, it is not possible to be an effective leader without good administrative and management skills. When "leaders" administer to the needs of schools, what appears superficially to be managerial can be transformed into opportunities for exerting leadership by communicating meaning and purpose within the context of the routine and mundane.

In organizing the content of the text, we have taken a systemic approach as is illustrated in Figure P.1. At the core is the goal of facilitating the development of visionary leadership for educational institutions. At the periphery are the social, political, economic and cultural contexts within which leaders must function, chapter 1. Chapter 2, the second ring, describes systems theory, which is the overarching theory shaping the structure of the book and used to unify the many concepts of educational leadership that are discussed in subsequent chapters. The third ring, chapter 3, describes schools, the primary functional

FIGURE P.1

Systemic conceptualization of *Fundamental Concepts of Educational Leadership and Management*

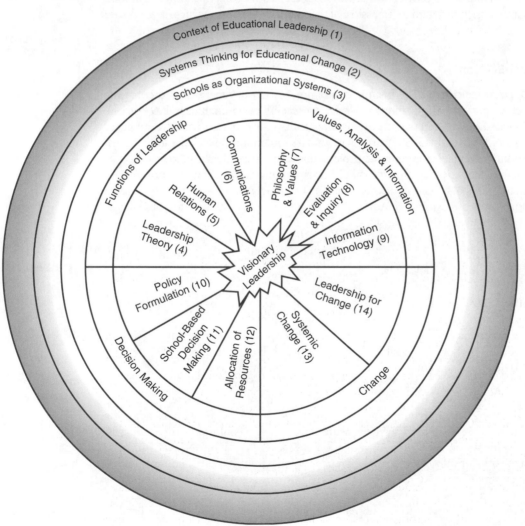

unit of education systems, the way we see them through the lens of organizational theories. The first three chapters make up part I of the book. The fourth ring represents the bulk of this book, addressing specific aspects of educational leadership. It is divided into four parts, parts II through V. Part II deals with characteristics of leadership and includes presentations of theories and definitions of leadership in chapter 4, of human relations in chapter 5, and of communications in chapter 6. Part III focuses on values and philosophies and their influence on behavior, decisions, research, and how we interpret information. Chapter 7 examines philosophy and values; chapter 8, evaluation and research; and chapter 9, information technology. The focus of part IV is on decision making as it takes place at four levels (school, district, state, and national). Chapter 10 centers on policy development at the three higher levels, while chapter 11 centers on the operational level, the school. Chapter 12 is devoted specifically to human and economic resource allocation decisions made at all four levels. Part V looks toward the future with chapter 13 discussing how we might get there through systemic change. Chapter 14 synthesizes the highlights of the previous13 chapters and projects what the emerging structure of education might look like. The chapter concludes with a discussion of the implications of the structure for future school leaders.

New to This Edition

Keying to ISLLC Standards. The first major attempt to arrive at general agreement at the national level on performance standards for school leaders was initiated in 1994 by the Interstate School Leaders Licensure Consortium (ISLLC), a program of the Council of Chief State School Officers (CCSSO). Involved in the undertaking were personnel from 24 state education agencies and relevant professional and university associations such as the National Association of Secondary School Principals, the National Association of Elementary School Principals, the American Association of School Administrators, the National Council of Professors of Educational Administration, the American Association of Colleges for Teacher Education, and the University Council for Educational Administration (CCSSO, 1996; Murphy, Yff, & Shipman, 2000). The result was what has become known as the "ISLLC Standards," first published by the CCSSO in 1996 under the title *Standards for School Leaders* and revised as *Educational Leadership Policy Standards: ISLLC 2008* (CCSSO, 2008).

While the ISLLC standards were available as the second edition of *Fundamental Concepts* was in preparation in 2000–2001, they were still being debated widely, and the extent of their acceptance was uncertain. Because of this, we saw no compelling reason for linking that edition to them, although the standards themselves were discussed.

By 2003, however, the education community was beginning to coalesce around the ISLLC standards (Murphy, 2003). They were being used by approximately 40 states as the platform for thinking about school administration, and several of those states were requiring universities to align their preparation programs with the standards. Most states adopting ISLLC standards have also revised their licensure regulations to conform to the standards. Further, the National Council for the Accreditation of Teacher Education (NCATE) adopted the ISLLC standards for the accreditation of preparatory programs in school administration, causing all such programs in NCATE institutions in approximately 45 states to fall under the professional and state-policy umbrella of the standards. Finally, the ISLLC contracted with the Educational Testing Service to develop an examination for principals (School Leaders

Licensure Assessment [SLLA]) and one for superintendents (School Superintendent Assessment [SSA]). The SLLA is required by 14 state licensing boards to measure the knowledge and skills needed to perform competently on the job of entry-level school professionals aspiring for certification as principals and other school leadership positions. Only Missouri requires the SSA for superintendent certification (http://www.ets.org, accessed July, 6, 2007).

The ISLLC standards are not without their severe critics (e.g., Anderson, 2001; English, 2000, 2003; Keeler, 2002). Nevertheless, the influence of the ISLLC standards has become ubiquitous and should not be ignored in a textbook prepared for aspiring school administrators.

The ISLLC model is a parsimonious one, consisting of only six standards. The essence of each standard, however, is illustrated by several associated functions. The 2008 version of the Standards is presented in Table P.1 along with their accompanying Functions (CCSSO, 2008). The table on page ii and iii of this book shows the coverage of each Standard and Function chapter by chapter. Competent on-the-job performance is most effectively developed through coaching and mentoring during clinical experiences that normally come toward the end of preparatory programs for aspiring administrators. The case studies and activities included within the chapters in this book, however, provide an introduction to the intensive clinical experiences likely to follow in a student's program. Each case study reports the standard or standards to which it is most closely related. Each activity identifies the ISLLC standards and functions to which it is most relevant.

Fundamental Concepts. As part of the summary section for each chapter, we have included a list of the fundamental concepts discussed in the chapter, designating the ISLLC standards and functions to which each concept is relevant. These are summarized in the table on ii and iii.

Instructional Aids. Activities have been embedded in boxes in the text of each chapter at appropriate spots instead of at the end of the chapter as in previous editions. Case studies follow at the end of several chapters as in previous editions. Table P.2 lists all activities and case studies and indicates for which ISLLC standards and function each activity is relevant.

Internet Resources. Numerous valuable Internet resources are brought to the reader's attention. This usually takes place through the activities but occasionally in the text itself.

Updating and Realignment. The third edition continues to set forth principles undergirding the knowledge base of educational leadership, updated throughout to address new and evolving thinking, learning, and organizational paradigms that are in a significant period of transformation. It maintains the thorough coverage of relevant theory of the first two editions but is more consistent in relating that theory to practice.

To eliminate redundancy, four chapters have been combined into two. Chapters 7 and 12 in the second edition have been consolidated into chapter 7 in the third edition, and chapters 10 and 13 in the second edition have been consolidated into chapter 11 in the third edition.

Chapter 8 contains a new section on evaluation and accountability that reports on and analyzes the efforts by states and school districts to raise student academic achievement

TABLE P.1

Educational Leadership Policy Standards: ISLLC 2008

An education leader promotes the success of every student by:

1. *facilitating the development, articulation, implementation, and stewardship of a vision of learning that is shared and supported by all stakeholders.*
   A. Collaboratively develop and implement a shared vision and mission
   B. Collect and use data to identify goals, assess organizational effectiveness, and promote organizational learning
   C. Create and implement plans to achieve goals
   D. Promote continuous and sustainable improvement
   E. Monitor and evaluate progress and revise plans

2. *advocating, nurturing, and sustaining a school culture and instructional program conducive to student learning and staff professional growth.*
   A. Nurture and sustain a culture of collaboration, trust, learning, and high expectations
   B. Create a comprehensive, rigorous, and coherent curricular program
   C. Create a personalized and motivating learning environment for students
   D. Supervise instruction
   E. Develop assessment and accountability systems to monitor student progress
   F. Develop the instructional and leadership capacity of staff
   G. Maximize time spent on quality instruction
   H. Promote the use of the most effective and appropriate technologies to support teaching and learning
   I. Monitor and evaluate the impact of the instructional program

3. *ensuring management of the organization, operation, and resources for a safe, efficient, and effective learning environment.*
   A. Monitor and evaluate the management and operational systems
   B. Obtain, allocate, align, and efficiently utilize human, fiscal, and technological resources
   C. Promote and protect the welfare and safety of students and staff
   D. Develop the capacity for distributed leadership
   E. Ensure teacher and organizational time is focused to support quality instruction and student learning

4. *collaborating with faculty and community members, responding to diverse community interests and needs, and mobilizing community resources.*
   A. Collect and analyze data and information pertinent to the educational environment
   B. Promote understanding, appreciation, and use of the community's diverse cultural, social, and intellectual resources
   C. Build and sustain positive relationships with families and caregivers
   D. Build and sustain productive relationships with community partners

5. *acting with integrity, fairness, and in an ethical manner.*
   A. Ensure a system of accountability for every student's academic and social success
   B. Model principles of self-awareness, reflective practice, transparency, and ethical behavior
   C. Safeguard the values of democracy, equity, and diversity
   D. Consider and evaluate the potential moral and legal consequences of decision making
   E. Promote social justice and ensure that individual student needs inform all aspects of schooling

6. *understanding, responding to, and influencing the political, social, economic, legal, and cultural context.*
   A. Advocate for children, families, and caregivers
   B. Act to influence local, district, state, and national decisions affecting student learning
   C. Assess, analyze, and anticipate emerging trends and initiatives in order to adapt leadership strategies

Source: The Interstate School Leaders Licensure Consortium (ISLLC) Standards were developed by the Council of Chief State School Officers (CCSSO) and member states. Copies may be downloaded from the Council's website at www.ccsso.org.

Council of Chief State School Officers. (2008). *Educational Leadership Policy Standards: ISLLC 2008 as Adopted by the National Policy Board for Educational Administration.* Washington, DC: Author.

TABLE P.2

Instructional Aids: Case Studies and Activities Showing Related ISLLC 2008 Standards and Functions

Chapter/Activity/ Case	Standards and Functions
Chapter 1. Context for Leadership	
Activity 1.1, p. 5	1B, 2B, 4A, 6
Activity 1.2, p. 10	1B, 2E, 3A, 4A, 5A, 6
Activity 1.3, p. 24	2A, 3B, 3C, 4, 5, 6
Activity 1.4, p. 28	3B, 4C, 4D, 5, 6
Activity 1.5, p. 28	3B, 5, 6
Chapter 2. Systems Thinking	
Case Study, p. 50	1, 2, 6
Activity 2.1, p. 39	1A, 6C
Activity 2.2, p. 43	1A, 3B, 6C
Activity 2.3, p. 49	6C
Chapter 3. Schools as Organizations	
Case Study, p. 74	All
Activity 3.1, p. 59	All
Activity 3.2, p. 66	All
Activity 3.3, p. 71	1, 2, 3, 6
Chapter 4. Leadership Theory	
Case Study, p. 100	1, 2, 3, 5, 6
Activity 4.1, p. 85	1, 2, 3, 4, 5
Activity 4.2, p. 97	All
Activity 4.3, p. 99	All
Chapter 5. Human Relations	
Case Study, p. 127	All
Activity 5.1, p. 115	3
Activity 5.2, p. 119	1, 2, 3, 4
Chapter 6. Communications	
Case Study, p. 155	All
Activity 6.1, p. 136	All
Activity 6.2, p. 147	All
Activity 6.3, p. 154	All
Chapter 7. Impact of Values on Decisions	
Case Study, p. 185	2, 4, 5
Activity 7.1, p. 163	5
Activity 7.2, p. 165	5
Activity 7.3, p. 176	5C, 5E, 6
Activity 7.4, p. 177	1A, 2, 3C, 3D, 3E, 6
Chapter 8. Evaluation	
Case Study, p. 216	All
Activity 8.1, p. 198	1, 2, 3, 4
Activity 8.2, p. 203	1, 2, 3, 4
Activity 8.3, p. 208	1, 2, 3, 4
Chapter 9. Information Technology	
Activity 9.1, p. 227	1B, 1E, 2E, 2H, 3A, 3B, 3D, 4A, 5A, 6
Activity 9.2, p. 230	2, 3D, 4A, 5A, 6C
Activity 9.3, p. 231	1B, 2B, 2C, 2H, 4A, 6C

(Continued)

TABLE P.2 (Continued)

Instructional Aids: Case Studies and Activities Showing Related ISLLC 2008 Standards and Functions

Chapter/Activity/ Case	Standards and Functions
Chapter 10. Policy Formulation	
Activity 10.1, p. 259	All
Activity 10.2, p. 264	6
Activity 10.3, p. 268	All, but especially 6
Activity 10.4, p. 271	All
Activity 10.5, p. 273	1, 3, 6
Chapter 11. Decision Making	
Activity 11.1, p. 299	1, 3
Activity 11.2, p. 301	4, 6
Activity 11.3, p. 302	3A, 3B, 5C
Chapter 12. Allocation of Resources	
Activity 12.1, p. 309	1B, 3A, 4A, 6C
Activity 12.2, p. 314	1B, 3A, 4A, 5C, 5D, 6C
Activity 12.3, p. 316	1B, 3A, 3B, 4A, 6
Activity 12.4, p. 329	1B, 2, 5A
Activity 12.5, p. 333	2A, 2B, 2C, 3A, 3B
Activity 12.6, p. 337	2H, 3B, 5C, 6B
Activity 12.7, p. 337	2H, 2I, 3A, 3B
Activity 12.8, p. 339	1C, 2B, 3B, 3E, 6
Chapter 13. Systemic Change	
Case Study, p. 368	1, 2, 3, 4, 6
Activity 13.1, p. 351	1, 2, 3, 6
Activity 13.2, p. 356	1, 2, 3, 6
Activity 13.3, p. 365	All
Chapter 14. Educational Leadership for Reform	
Activity 14.1, p. 385	All
Activity 14.2, p. 385	All

through high-stakes testing programs and the federal No Child Left Behind Act. Chapter 10 contains a new section on the impact of collective negotiations with employee unions on policy formation.

The alignment of parts and chapters has been modified to improve the logical flow of information.

REFERENCES

Anderson, G. L. (2001). Disciplining leaders: A critical discourse analysis of the ISLLC national examination and performance standards in educational administration. *International Journal of Leadership in Education*, 4(3), 199–2116.

Council of Chief State School Officers. (1996). *Interstate School Leaders Licensure Consortium: Standards for school leaders*. Washington, DC: Author.

Council of Chief State School Officers. (2008). *Educational leadership policy standards: ISLLC 2008 as adopted by the National Policy Board for Educational Administration on December 12, 2007*. Washington, DC: Author.

English, F. W. (2000). Pssssst! What does one call a set of non-empirical beliefs required to be accepted on faith and enforced by authority? [Answer: a religion, aka the ISLLC standards]. *International Journal of Leadership in Education*, 3(2), 159–167.

English, F. W. (2003). "Functional foremanship" and the virtue of historical amnesia: The AASA, the ELLC standards, and the reincarnation of scientific management in educational preparation programs for profit. *Teaching in Educational Administration*, 10(1), 5–6.

Keeler, C. M. (2002). Exploring the validity of standards for school administration preparation. *Journal of School Leadership*, 12(5), 579–602.

Murphy, J. (2003). *Reculturing educational leadership: The ISSLC standards ten years out.* Fairfax, VA: National Policy Board for Educational Administration.

Murphy, J., Yff, J., & Shipman, N. (2000). Implementation of the Interstate School Leaders Licensure Consortium Standards. *Leadership in Education*, 3(1), 17–39.

Acknowledgments

We are especially indebted to Dr. Bruce Hilyard, Professor Emeritus at Genesee Community College, Batavia, New York, and lecturer at State University of New York Empire State College for specific contributions to several chapters, including literature searches, editing, and critiquing as well as for his valuable suggestions in general.

For their valuable input, we wish to thank our reviewers: Stacey Edmonson, Sam Houston State University; Bonnie Fusarelli, North Carolina State University; Lance Fusarelli, North Carolina State University; Ron Nanney, Gardner-Webb University; Mary Ann Walko, Kean University; and George Watson, Marshall University.

Taher A. Razik
Austin D. Swanson
Buffalo, New York
2009

The Context of Educational Leadership

For the past three decades, education in the United States has been going through a sustained period of reform and restructuring. Old certainties have been shaken by the multiplicity of new demands placed on schools, while new certainties are yet to form, although strong trends are becoming apparent. One thing is clear: the educational structure and practices of the 20th-century industrial era will not meet the educational needs of the United States in the information age of the 21st.

To guide human organizations effectively, leaders must possess an understanding of the context in which leadership is exercised. As with other human organizations, educational institutions function in and are shaped by a web of external and internal expectations and forces. The reality of the environment in which educational leaders will have to maneuver skillfully now and in the immediate future is one of complexity and change.

In part I, we build a foundation for the study of educational leadership and management. Chapter 1 examines the social, political, economic, and cultural contexts within which leaders must function. The impact of the revolutionary forces of the information age and globalization on schools is described in some detail. Chapter 2 explains systems theory, the overarching theory shaping the structure of this book, and is used to unify the many concepts of educational leadership that are discussed in subsequent chapters. Chapter 3 extends the discussion of systems theory to schools, the primary functional unit of education systems, describing them the way the authors see them through the lens of organizational theories.

Chapter 1: The Imperative for Education Reform. The global social, economic, and political forces that impact educational institutions and the causes for concern over public education as it exists today are described. Special attention is given to the persistent academic achievement gaps among ethnic and economic groups and to the social and economic consequences for students if those gaps are continued. The unacceptable level of academic achievement by U.S. students is examined along with the decline in their relative standings internationally. Data are presented documenting claims that the conditions under which many schools operate are becoming more difficult because the populations they serve are increasing in ethnic diversity, in variation of family structures, and in the proportion of children coming from impoverished homes. We briefly look at the political and professional responses to the criticisms (i.e., the educational reform movement) and the historical roots of current dilemmas.

Chapter 2: The Power of Systems Thinking for Educational Change. A modified version of systems theory is presented for perceiving the many facets of leadership and as a framework for understanding their interrelationships. It traces the history of systems theory and describes its frameworks and properties in general terms. The discussion includes the implications of a systems perspective for schools and school districts and speaks to issues surrounding the modern paradigm.

Chapter 3: Schools as Organizational Systems. Organizational theory and practice relating to educational enterprises is examined. Depending on one's view, organizational activity may be linked to values, effectiveness, integration, and more. Metaphors are examined to help the reader envision the broad nature of how we think about, use, and evaluate organizational performance today.

The Imperative for Education Reform

This chapter appraises evidence supporting the need for fundamental reform of educational systems to meet contemporary conditions. While we focus on the case for the United States, the forces with which we are dealing are global, and similar cases could (and have been) developed for other nations. Our reality is dominated by pervasive social, economic, and technological change, and educational leaders have no choice but to reconstitute the ways in which we prepare our youth to be happy, productive citizens in this new environment of globalization and rapid change. Reflecting on his distinguished 40-year career as an educator, Theodore Sizer (2004) concludes,

> Americans have run out the string on "school" as it has evolved over the past century. Tinkering with it, testing it, belittling it, pouring money into it as it is makes even less sense. The painful work of reconstituting what we mean by "school" . . . is no longer avoidable. (p. 115)

In this chapter, we describe the forces bringing about these megachanges and their impact on educational institutions. We highlight the resulting causes for concern over public education as it exists today. Special attention is given to the persistent achievement gaps between ethnic and economic groups and the social and economic consequences if the gaps are allowed to continue. The unacceptable level of academic achievement by U.S. students is examined along with the decline in their relative standings internationally. Data are presented documenting claims that the conditions under which many schools operate are becoming more difficult because the populations they serve are increasing in ethnic

diversity, in variation of family structures, and in the proportion of children coming from impoverished homes. We briefly look at the political and professional responses to the criticisms (i.e., the educational reform movement).

Adapting to a Global Society

If there was ever a time when educational institutions require intellegent, informed, imaginative, creative, and effective leadership, it is now. Since the nation's founding, its leaders have recognized the importance of an educated citizenery to the success of a democratic state; however, this is the first time in our history that the *quality* as well as the *quantity* of the education of the nation's citizens is being linked strategically to national economic success and survival. As a result, many demands are being made for structural and substatantive reforms, but these demands are not limited to educational institutions. Rather, they reflect worldwide changes in social, economic, political, and technological relationships that are impacting all social institutions.

Toffler (1980, 1990) dubbed such changes the "third wave" and subsequently the "powershift era." Naisbitt (1982) and Naisbitt and Aburdene (1990) identified them as "megatrends." Drucker (1989) referred to their amalgam as the "postindustrial society," the "postbusiness society," and the "information age." Friedman (2006) described their consequence as the "flattened world." Whatever they are called, the age we have entered is different from the one that preceded it and for which our historic social and political institutions were designed. The magnitude of the shift has been likened to the shift from feudalism to capitalism or from an agriculturally based economy to industrialization. All institutions must make appropriate adjustments to survive in this new environment, and educational institutions are no exception.

This is a time of shifting paradigms (Kuhn, 1996). Social and economic structures are in a state of flux. Many of the world's totalitarian governments have fallen along with the Berlin Wall and the Soviet Union. In other nations, near anarchy prevails. While there has been a decline in overt hostility among the most powerful nations of the world, there is growing conflict among ethnic and religious groups and violent regional rivalries. The Cold War has been succeeded by the War on Terror.

Reasons for both optimism and concern exist in this new millennium. Naisbitt and Aburdene (1990), building on Naisbitt's (1982) successful predictions of a decade earlier, see the triumph of the individual and the demise of the collective. With newfound freedom, they predict a global economic boom, a renaissance in the arts, and a growing interest in things spiritual. According to them, a new free-market socialism will become the dominant socioeconomic structure, and the welfare state will be privatized. Women increasingly will assume leadership roles, and global lifestyles and cultural nationalism will emerge. Biology will dominate the sciences, and Pacific Rim nations will dominate economic relationships.

According to Freidman (2006), the flattening of the world was brought about by "connecting all the knowledge centers of the planet together into a single global network, which—if politics and terrorism do not get in the way—could usher in an amazing era of prosperity, innovation, and collaboration, by companies, communities, and individuals" (p. 8). In addition,

> The flat-world platform is the product of a convergence of the personal computer (which allows every individual suddenly to become the author of his or her own content in digital form) with fiber-optic cable (which suddenly allowed all those individuals to access more and more digital content around the world for next to nothing) with the rise of work flow software (which enabled individuals all over the world to collaborate on the same digital content from anywhere, regardless of the distances between them). (pp. 10–11)

However, the "amazing era of prosperity, innovation, and collaboration, by companies, communities, and individuals" to which Freidman refers is conditional on making appropriate adaptations to the "flat-world platform." For individuals, success will depend on skills and attitudes shaped in part by their educational experiences—some of which are similar to those offered by existing institutions but others quite different. The success of communities (e.g., nations) will depend on the cumulative success of individuals. In a "flat world," companies can seek their skilled labor worldwide, no longer hampered by traditional national boundries, and there are likely to be both winners and losers.

Not everyone is as optimistic about the future as are Friedman and Naisbitt and Aburdene. Galbraith (1992), for example, sees a growing disparity between the haves and the have-nots in the United States and predicts that eventually the have-nots will rise in rebellion. The disparity is growing, according to Galbraith, because for the first time in U.S. history, the "contented" constitute the majority of the population and are in complete control of government. The contented do not support social legislation that redistributes wealth through higher taxes on the rich and greater services for the poor. Galbraith argues that it was the social legislation engineered by George early in the 20th century that saved British capitalism during the years between the two world wars and, similarly, that it was the social legislation of Franklin Roosevelt that saved capitalism in the United States during the Great Depression. In each instance, the legislation was opposed by the contented, who lost; but now that the contented are firmly in the majority, there is little hope of government enacting legislation to bridge the gap between the haves and the have-nots. (The shift in power at the national level brought about by the 2008 elections *may* weaken the grip of the contented to the point where improved services for the poor may again become possible.)

The growing gap between the haves and the have-nots in the United States has been documented in the report of the New Commission on the Skills of the American Workforce (2007), which also proposes sweeping changes for the educational establishment that the commission sees as necessary to close the gap and to maintain the nation's

ACTIVITY 1.1

Map of the Future Forces Affecting Education

Addresses ISLLC Standards and Functions: 1B; 2B; 4A; 6

Visit http://www.kwfdn.org/map/map.aspx

This interactive site forecasts the forces that are likely to affect K–12 learning over the next decade and organizes them into five categories: drivers of change, impact areas, trends, hot spots, and dilemmas. The dilemmas category addresses the question "How do schools maintain academic standards while also taking a more personalized approach to teaching and learning?" Users then can participate in or simply read discussion forums about these topics and see resources related to them. This site is a useful tool to be consulted before writing or revising a district's strategic plan. It is a collaborative effort by the KnowledgeWorks Foundation and the Institute for the Future.

economic and political viability. In describing the educational requirements of the world into which we are entering, the commission writes,

> This is a world in which a very high level of preparation in reading, writing, speaking, mathematics, science, literature, history, and the arts will be an indispensable foundation for everything that comes after for most members of the workforce. It is a world in which comfort with ideas and abstractions is the passport to a good job, in which creativity and innovation are the key to the good life, in which high levels of education—a very different kind of education than most of us have had—are going to be the only security there is. . . . The core problem is that our education systems were built for another era, an era in which most workers needed only a rudimentary education. It is not possible to get where we have to go by patching that system. (pp. xviii–xix)

For better or for worse, this is indeed a dynamic and exciting period in human history. Because of the fluidity of the situation, it is a period of unparalleled opportunity and potential danger. To capitalize on the opportunities and to minimize the dangers demands extraordinarily wise leadership in all sectors and in all enterprises, including education.

In short, our reality is pervasive social, economic, and technological change. Although these changes affect persons in all walks of life, there is bound to be greater impact on those in positions demanding wide social visibility and concern, such as persons holding administrative and supervisory responsibility for educational institutions and systems. Society has a right to expect competent performance in those positions. Under these circumstances, competent leadership cannot be a matter of copying conventional behavior. To advance education, there is a clear need for educational leaders to have the ability to comprehend the dynamics of human affairs as a basis for relevant action under novel conditions, the need for better understanding of issues and processes in educational institutions, and the need for greater originality and collaboration in designing strategic policies. The approach that these leaders take in response to such opportunities and problems needs to remain hypothetical and open ended so that more may be learned by what is done. No silver-bullet solutions exist.

Causes for Concern

International Comparisons of Academic Achievement

Since the 1960s, the United States has been involved in developing and conducting cross-national assessments that have resulted in significant advances in their scope and technical sophistication. Currently, the United States participates in four international assessments: the Progress in International Reading Literacy Study, which assesses reading performance in grade 4; the Program for International Student Assesment, which assesses the reading, mathematics, and science literacy of 15-year-olds; the Trends in International Mathematics and Science Study, which assesses mathematics and science performance in grades 4 and 8; and the Adult Literacy and Lifeskills Survey, which assesses the adult literacy and numeracy skills of the

16–65 age-group (National Center for Education Statistics [NCES], 2006). Table 1.1 summarizes the comparative performance of U.S. students and the population in the latest round of assessments in reading, mathematics, and science.

Students in the United States perform relatively well in relation to their peers in other nations in reading, even those in the 15-year-old cohort. Fourth and eighth graders also do relatively well with respect to mathematics and science, but 15-year-olds' average scores fall in the bottom third of nations. This is part of the evidence supporting national concern over the curriculum and structure of secondary education in the United States. The assessments of adult literacy and numeracy are limited to six countries, but the results correspond to the poor performance of the 15-year-old cohort. Adults in the United States scored significantly below adults in Norway, Bermuda,

Canada, and Switzerland on both assessments; only Italy scored lower.

National Assessment of Educational Progress Trends

The National Assessment of Educational Progress (NAEP) has assessed the mathematics abilities of students in grades 4, 8, and 12 in both public and private schools since 1990 and reading abilities since 1992. The assessment of science achievement began in 1996. Assessments of writing abilities were made in 1998 and 2002 and assessments of performance in history and geography in 1994 and 2001. Results are reported by scale scores ranging from 0 to 500 for reading and mathematics and from 0 to 300 for science and by achievement levels (basic, proficient, and advanced) that identify what students should

TABLE 1.1

U.S. Performance on International Assessments of Mathematics, Science, and Reading Relative to Other Countries

Subject and Grade or Age		Number of Countries[1]	Number of Countries with Average Score Relative to the United States		
			Significantly Higher	Not Significantly Different	Significantly Lower
Reading					
Fourth-graders	(2001)	34	3	8	23
15-years-olds	(2000)	30	3	20	7
Mathematics					
Fourth-graders	(2003)	24	11	0	13
Eighth-graders	(2003)	44	9	10	25
15-years-olds	(2003)	38	23	4	11
Science					
Fourth-graders	(2003)	24	3	5	16
Eighth-graders	(2003)	44	7	5	32
15-years-olds	(2003)	38	18	9	11
Adult literacy					
Age 16–65	(2003)	5	4	0	1
Adult numeracy					
Ages 16–64	(2003)	5	4	0	1

[1]Includes those countries with approved data appearing in reports. Total excludes the United States.

Source: International Association for the Evaluation of Educational Achievement Progress in International Reading Literacy Study, 2001; Trends in International Mathematics and Science Study, 2003; Statistics Canada and Organization for Economic Cooperation and Development (OECD), Adult Literacy and Lifeskills Survey, 2003; OECD, Program for International Student Assessment, 2003, previously unpublished tabulation (October 2005). The table is published in NCES (2006).

know and be able to do at each grade. The NAEP results are reported for the total population and by ethnic group, gender, and other educational, social, and economic classifications. Results also permit state-level comparisons of the student abilities in public schools (NCES, 2006).

Reading. Table 1.2 reports the percentage of students in grades 4, 8, and 12 at each level of achievement in reading for various years from 1992 through 2005. Despite three decades of reform efforts, the reading results show remarkable stability. The percentage of fourth graders at or above proficient (indicating solid academic achievement) increased between 1992 and 2002 (from 29% to 31%) and has remained steady since then. Thirty-one percent of eighth graders were at or above proficient in 2005. The percentage of

eighth graders at or above basic has increased since 1992, but there has been a decrease in the percentage since 2002. The assessment for grade 12 shows a decline in the percentage of students scoring at or above basic and proficient levels and an increase in the percentage scoring below basic. A reasonable goal is to bring virtually all children to at least a proficient level of achievement; it is a matter of serious national concern that after three decades of attempting to improve the level of achievement in reading, less than one-third of the student population has reached the level of proficiency.

Mathematics. Unlike for reading, achievement in mathematics has improved significantly since 1990. In 2005, the national average mathematics scale scores of fourth and eighth graders were higher than

TABLE 1.2

Percentage of Students at Each Reading Achievement Level, by Grade: Various Years, 1992–2005

Grade and Achievement Level	1992[1]	1994[1]	1998[1]	1998	2000	2002	2003	2005
Grade 4								
Below basic	37.9	39.5	37.6	40.4	40.5	36.1	36.6	35.8
At or above basic	62.1	60.5	62.4	59.6	59.5	63.9	63.4	64.2
At or above proficient	28.6	29.6	30.8	29.3	29.4	31.5	31.5	31.5
At advanced	6.4	7.4	7.3	7.1	6.9	7.1	7.7	7.5
Grade 8								
Below basic	30.5	30.4	25.9	26.6	—	24.5	26.2	27.4
At or above basic	69.5	69.6	74.1	73.4	—	75.5	73.8	72.6
At or above proficient	29.2	29.5	33.2	32.3	—	32.6	32.2	30.8
At advanced	2.9	2.8	2.7	2.6	—	2.8	3.2	3.0
Grade 12								
Below basic	20.3	25.5	23.0	23.7	—	26.3	—	—
At or above basic	79.7	74.5	77.0	76.3	—	73.7	—	—
At or above proficient	40.2	36.3	40.2	40.1	—	36.0	—	—
At advanced	3.9	4.2	5.7	5.6	—	4.5	—	—

— not available.

[1]Testing accommodations (e.g., extended time, small-group testing) for children with disabilities and limited-English-proficient students were not permitted.

Note: The 2005 National Assessment of Educational Progress (NAEP) assessment included a 12th-grade component, but these data were not available at the time of this analysis. Beginning in 2003, the NAEP national sample was obtained by aggregating the samples from each state rather than by obtaining an independently selected national sample. As a consequence, the size of the national sample increased, and smaller differences between years or between types of students were found to be statistically significant than would have been detected in previous assessments.

Source: U.S. Department of Education, National Center for Education Statistics, NAEP, various years, 1992–2005 Reading Assessments, previously unpublished tabulation (November 2005). The table is published in NCES (2006).

in all previous assessments. The latest results available for 12th graders at publication were for 2000, which also showed gains over 1990.

Table 1.3 reports the percentage of students in grades 4, 8, and 12 at each level of achievement in mathematics for various years from 1990 through 2005. The percentages at each achievement level (basic, proficient, and advanced) were also higher in 2005 than in all previous assessments. The percentage of students at or above proficient increased from 13% to 36% during this period in grade 4 and from 15% to 30% in grade 8. The percentage of students at or above basic increased from 50% to 80% in grade 4 and from 52% to 69% in grade 8. By 2000, the percentage of 12th graders scoring at or above

proficient increased from 12% to 17%, and those scoring at or above basic rose from 58% to 65%. While the improvements in mathematics achievement are encouraging, even with these gains, as for reading, less than one-third of the students have reached the proficient level. For 12th graders, it is less than one-fifth.

Science. Between 1996 and 2005, the national average fourth-grade science scale score increased from 147 to 151; there was no measurable change in the eighth-grade score, and the 12th-grade score decreased from 150 to 147. The percentages of fourth and eighth graders at or above the proficient level were not measurably different from 1996 to

TABLE 1.3

Percentage of Students at Each Mathematics Achievement Level, by Grade: Various Years, 1990–2005

Grade and Achievement Level	1990[1]	1992[1]	1996[1]	1996	2000	2003	2005
Grade 4							
Below basic	50.1	41.1	35.8	36.7	34.5	22.8	19.7
At or above basic	49.9	58.9	64.2	63.3	65.5	77.2	80.3
At or above proficient	12.7	17.9	21.3	20.8	23.8	32.5	36.3
At advanced	1.2	1.7	2.3	2.2	2.5	3.9	5.0
Grade 8							
Below basic	48.2	42.5	37.6	39.0	36.6	31.9	30.9
At or above basic	51.8	57.5	62.4	61.0	63.4	68.1	69.1
At or above proficient	15.3	20.9	23.8	23.3	25.7	28.8	29.8
At advanced	2.0	3.1	3.8	3.7	4.7	5.4	6.0
Grade 12							
Below basic	41.9	36.3	30.8	34.2	35.0	—	—
At or above basic	58.1	63.7	69.2	65.8	65.0	—	—
At or above proficient	11.9	14.7	16.3	16.0	16.8	—	—
At advanced	1.4	1.6	1.9	2.0	2.3	—	—

— not available.

[1]Testing accommodations (e.g., extended time, small-group testing) for children with disabilities and limited-English-proficient students were not permitted.

Note: The 2005 National Assessment of Educational Progress (NAEP) assessment included a 12th-grade component, but at the time of this analysis, these data were not available. Beginning in 2003, the NAEP national sample was obtained by aggregating the samples from each state rather than by obtaining an independently selected national sample. As a consequence, the size of the national sample increased, and smaller differences between years or between types of students were found to be statistically significant than would have been detected in previous assessments. See supplemental note 4 for more information on testing accommodations, achievement levels, and NAEP.

Source: U.S. Department of Education, National Center for Education Statistics, NAEP, various years, 1990–2005 Mathematics Assessments, previously unpublished tabulation (November 2005). The table is published in NCES (2006).

2005, while the percentage of 12th graders at or above this achievement level decreased. In 2005, 29% percent of fourth and eighth graders and 18% of 12th graders were at or above the proficient level.

Table 1.4 reports the percentage of students in grades 4, 8, and 12 at each level of achievement in science for 1996, 2000, and 2005. Again, the science assessment results are discouraging given the concerted effort exerted over the past three decades to raise the level of student achievement in the science subjects. As with reading and math, less than one-third of fourth- and eighth-grade students have reached a proficient level, and less than one-fifth (as for mathematics) of 12th graders have reached that level.

Other Subjects. The NAEP assessed the performance of fourth, eighth, and 12th graders in public and private schools in writing in 1998 and 2002. Average scale scores increased at grades 4 and 8 over the period. In contrast, no significant change was detected at grade 12 (NCES, 2004).

In 2002, 28% of fourth graders, 31% of eighth graders, and 24% of 12th graders performed at or above the proficient level in writing. The percentages of fourth graders at or above basic and proficient and eighth graders at or above proficient were higher in 2002 than in 1998. The percentage of 12th graders at or above basic decreased over the period. Although only 2% of students in each grade performed at the advanced level in 2002, at all three grades the percentage represented an increase. As with reading, mathematics, and science, less than one-third of students are writing at or above a proficient level, and the 12th graders are performing relatively more poorly than students at the lower grades.

The NAEP assessed the performance of fourth, eighth, and 12th graders in U.S. history and geography in 1994 and 2001. Average scale scores for history increased for fourth and eighth graders from 1994 to 2001; there was no significant change in the scale score of 12th graders over the period. In 2001, 18% of fourth graders, 17% of eighth graders, and 11% of 12th graders performed at or above the proficient level in history. The percentage of fourth graders performing at or above the basic level was higher in 2001 than in 1994. For history, at grade 8, the percentages of students at or above the basic level, at or above the proficient level, and at the advanced level were higher in 2001 than in 1994. At grade 12, no significant changes were detected in the percentages of students performing at each level over the period (NCES, 2003).

The average scale scores for geography of fourth and eighth graders increased from 1994 to 2001 (from 206 to 209 and from 260 to 262, respectively), while there was no change in the scale score at grade 12 (285). In 2001, 21% of fourth graders, 30% of

TABLE 1.4

Percentage of Students at Each Achievement Level in Science, by Grade: 1996, 2000, and 2005

Achievement Level	Grade 4			Grade 8			Grade 12		
	1996[1]	2000	2005	1996[1]	2000	2005	1996[1]	2000	2005
Below basic	37	37	32	40	41	41	43	48	46
At or above basic	63	63	68	60	59	59	57	52	54
At or above proficient	28	27	29	29	30	29	21	18	18
At advanced	3	3	3	3	4	3	3	2	2

[1]Testing accommodations (e.g., extended time, small-group testing) for children with disabilities and limited-English-proficient students were not permitted on the 1996 science assessment.

Source: Grigg, Lauko, and Brockway, (2006), figures 1 and 17 and previously unpublished tabulation (January 2006). Data from U.S. Department of Education, National Center for Education Statistics, National Assessment of Educational Progress, 1996, 2000, and 2005 Science Assessments. The table is published in NCES (2006).

eighth graders, and 25% of 12th graders were at or above the proficient level. At grades 4 and 8, the percentage of students below basic decreased from 1994 to 2001. At grade 12, no significant changes were detected in the percentages of students performing at any of the achievement levels (NCES, 2003).

The consistent pattern established in reading, mathematic, science, and writing continues in history and geography, with less than one-third of students reaching a level of proficient mastery.

The Achievement Gap. While the general pattern of achievement is disturbing, it becomes heart wrenching when achievement patterns among ethnic groups are examined. A primary purpose of the federal Elementary and Secondary Act (ESEA), enacted in 1965, was to close the gap in achievement between minority and majority students. Instead, by high school graduation, the gap remains equivalent to two grade levels. The most recent reauthorization of the ESEA, the No Child Left Behind Act, retains the objective but changes the strategy. Table 1.5 reports data showing the persistent achievement gaps between white majority students and minority African American, Hispanic, and Asian/Pacific Islander students.

Table 1.5 reports the average scale scores on NAEP tests of achievement in mathematics, reading, and science for the first year in which an assessment was administered and in 2005 made by fourth- and fifth-grade students categorized by ethnic group and parent education level. All ethic groups improved their scores in all three subjects over the years. For mathematics, however, the gap between the averages for white students and African American and Hispanic students actually grew. For reading, the gap shrunk slightly between both minority groups and white students but remained substantial. For science, the gap remained the same for African Americans at the fourth grade but grew slightly at the eighth grade. For Hispanic students, the gap declined at the fourth grade but grew at the eighth grade. The average for Asian students was above that for whites in mathematics and only slightly below in reading and science.

When compared to group averages according to education level of parents, Asian and white students consistently averaged above the students whose parents had completed some college and nearly equaled those whose parents had completed a bachelor's degree or higher. The average for African American students was consistently below that of students whose parents had less than a high school education. Hispanic students' average scores consistently fell between the averages of those students whose parents had less than a high school education and those who were high school graduates. Similar gaps exist in writing, history, and geography (NCES, 2003, 2004, 2006).

ACTIVITY 1.2

Comparing Student Achievement among States, Districts, and Schools

Addresses ISLLC Standards and Functions: 1B; 2E; 3A; 4A; 5A; 6

1. Visit the National Center for Educational Statistics (NCES) Web site (http://nces.ed.gov/) and search for information on the performance of children in your state on the NAEP assessment examinations. How does the performance of the children in your state compare with the national average? With your neighboring states?

2. Collect statistics on the achievement of students in a nearby school or school district. Compare them with those of regional, state, and national norms and with those collected by other members of your class. Hint:

Many school districts and schools have their own Web sites that provide such information. In addition, information on a school's average performance on state examinations is frequently posted on its state education department's Web site, as is financial information for the school district. What are the implications of your findings for school, district, state, and national policy? For schools and districts studied by members of your class, look for relationships between pupil achievement and demographic characteristics, expenditure levels, quality of teaching staffs, and facilities.

TABLE 1.5

Average Achievement in Mathematics, Reading, and Science for Fourth and Eighth Graders by Ethnicity and Education of Parents

Subject, Years, and Student Characteristic	Grade 4		Grade 8	
	1990/1992/1996[1]	2005	1990/1992/1996[1]	2005
Mathematics (1990/2005)				
Race/ethnicity				
White	220	246	270	289
Black	188	220	237	255
Hispanic	200	226	246	262
Asian/Pacific Islander	#	251	#	295
Parents' education				
Less than high school	NA	NA	242	259
High school diploma or equivalent	NA	NA	255	267
Some college	NA	NA	267	280
Bachelor's degree or higher	NA	NA	274	290
Reading (1992/2005)				
Race/ethnicity				
White	224	229	267	271
Black	192	200	237	243
Hispanic	197	203	241	246
Asian/Pacific Islander	216	229	268	271
Parents' education				
Less than high school	NA	NA	243	244
High school diploma or equivalent	NA	NA	251	252
Some college	NA	NA	265	265
Bachelor's degree or higher	NA	NA	271	272
Science (1996/2005)				
Race/ethnicity				
White	158	162	159	160
Black	120	129	121	124
Hispanic	124	133	128	129
Asian/Pacific Islander	144	158	151	156
Parents' education				
Less than high school	NA	NA	NA	128
High school diploma or equivalent	NA	NA	NA	138
Some college	NA	NA	NA	151
Bachelor's degree or higher	NA	NA	NA	159

NA - not available.

- too few cases.

[1]Testing accommodations (e.g., extended time, small-group testing) for children with disabilities and limited-English-proficient students were not permitted.

Note: The 2005 National Assessment of Educational Progress (NAEP) assessment included a 12th-grade component, but at the time of this analysis, these data were not available. Beginning in 2003, the NAEP national sample was obtained by aggregating the samples from each state rather than by obtaining an independently selected national sample. As a consequence, the size of the national sample increased, and smaller differences between years or between types of students were found to be statistically significant than would have been detected in previous assessments. See supplemental note 4 for more information on testing accommodations and NAEP.

Source: U.S. Department of Education, National Center for Education Statistics, NAEP, 1990 and 2005 Mathematics Assessments, previously unpublished tabulation (November 2005). Table is composed of data published in NCES (2006).

Links between Education and Economic Considerations

Economic Threats Posed by the Global Economy. Following a comprehensive analysis of the challenges of global competition to the economic welfare of the United States, the New Commission on the Skills of the American Workforce (2007) concluded that if we are to maintain our standard of living, we must maintain our worldwide leads in technology and research and expand our ability to apply imaginatively newfound knowledge to practical applications. To ensure that the workforce possesses those qualities in sufficient quantities, the commission determined that the United States must design a pre-K–12 educational system that prepares almost all its graduates for college. The commission identified the problem as the existing education and training systems that were built for an industrial era in which most workers needed only a rudimentary education. This observation is consistent with the NAEP achievement data already presented showing that less than one-third of the K–12 population in the United States is prepared for college-level work (performing at a proficient level or above by the time of high school graduation). Pointing out that there will be no net growth of native-born Americans in the U.S. workforce for a long time to come, the commission reports that

> to maintain our standard of living, every working person must be much more productive than our generation has been, and the children of our immigrants will have to be vastly more productive than their parents.
>
> If we do not do a far better job of educating these immigrants and our other low-income minority populations than we have done up to now, we can confidently expect the knowledge and skill of our workforce to decline precipitously at the very time we desperately need the opposite to happen. And this has to happen at the same time we are doing a much better job of educating the native born [majority]. (pp. 40–41)

The commission's recommendations for reforming the system of education in the United States are discussed in subsequent chapters.

Charles Kolb (2006), president of the Committee for Economic Development, has issued a similar warning that if we do not improve our performance in educating minority students, the average education level of the American workforce in 2020 will be lower than it is today.

The National Innovation Initiative (NII) (2005), composed of 15 prominent business organizations in the United States, has set a goal to double the number of science, technology, engineering, and mathematics graduates with bachelor's degrees by 2015. The NII believes that this is necessary if the United States is to remain the world's scientific leader. In supporting their arguments, the NII refers to the fact that the number of engineering graduates in the United States is down 20% from its peak in 1985 at a time when more than 50% of the current science and engineering workforce is approaching retirement. Further, more than half of all doctoral degrees in engineering awarded by American universities have been to foreign nationals at a time when security concerns are reducing the number of foreign students available to study and work in the United States and the opportunities for them to study and work in their home countries and other nations are increasing. The NII projects that by 2010, more than 90% of all scientists and engineers in the world will be living in Asia, concluding that "one of the pillars of American economic prosperity—our scientific and technological superiority—is beginning to atrophy even as other nations are developing their own human capital" (p. 5).

The NII (2005) points out that past state and national efforts to improve math and science achievement clearly demonstrate that such efforts cannot be isolated from the need to improve the overall quality and results of the entire U.S. education system, pre-K through 16. Toward this end, the national business community has supported efforts to bring about high-quality early childhood education, supporting the No Child Left Behind Act, improving high schools, addressing the high school dropout problem, closing the achievement gap, expanding charter schools, and improving access to and completion of higher education.

Education and Domestic Economic Equity. The purchasing power of average weekly earnings for all workers in the United States regardless of education level declined greatly between 1972 and 1992 and has leveled off since 1999. This long-term trend has not impacted all workers equally, however. Figure 1.1 shows the trend in median weekly earnings of full-time workers categorized by level of education in inflation-adjusted dollars from 1979 to the present. Those with less than a high school education have lost about 20% of their purchasing power since 1979, and the earnings of those who have acquired a high school diploma or had some college have stagnated. Only persons holding bachelor's and graduate degrees have experienced significant increases in their real wages.

Figure 1.2 shows that the education advantage applies to all ethnic groups. College graduates in 2005 earned more than twice as much as high school dropouts. The disparity for African Americans between college graduates and high school dropouts in average weekly earnings was $828 to $372, respectively, and for Hispanics $866 to $388. Nevertheless, both minority groups earned less within each education-level category than did whites and Asians. The degree of inequity among groups was least at the high school dropout level and greatest at the college/graduate school level.

A report by the U.S. Census Bureau (Jones & Weinberg, 2000) identifies the roots of the growing inequities in the distribution of national income as follows:

> Researchers have tied the long-run increase in income inequality to changes in the U.S. labor market and household composition. More highly-skilled, trained, and educated workers are at the top and experiencing real wage gains, while those at the bottom are experiencing real wage losses making the wage distribution considerably more unequal. Changes in the labor market in the 1980s included a shift from goods-producing industries (that had disproportionately provided high-wage opportunities for low-skilled workers) to technical service industries (that disproportionately employ college graduates) and low-wage industries, such as retail trade.

But within-industry shifts in labor demand away from less-educated workers are, perhaps, a more important explanation of eroding wages than the shift out of manufacturing. Other factors related to the

FIGURE 1.1

Median weekly earnings of full-time workers by level of education: 1979–2005 (in constant 2005 dollars)

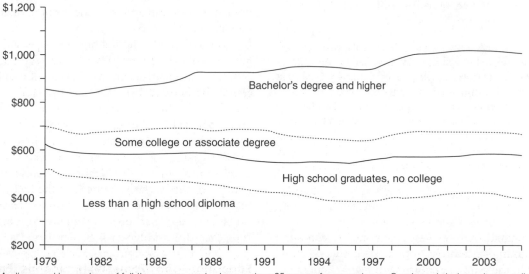

Note: Median weekly earnings of full-time wage and salary workers 25 years of age and over. Earnings data have been adjusted using the CPI-U-RS research series. Beginning in 1992, data were based on highest diploma or degree received, prior to 1992, data were based on years of school completed.

Source: Business of Labor Statistics.

FIGURE 1.2

Median weekly earnings of full-time workers 25 Years of age and over by ethnicity: 2005

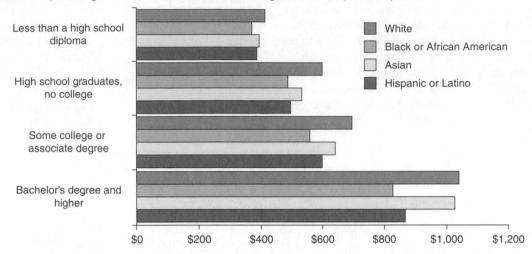

Source: Business of Labor Statistics.

downward trend in wages of less-educated workers include intensifying global competition and immigration, the decline in the proportion of workers belonging to unions, the decline in the real value of the minimum wage, the increasing need for computer skills, and the increasing use of temporary workers.

At the same time, changes in living arrangements have occurred that tend to exacerbate differences in household incomes. For example, increases in divorces and separations, increases in births out of wedlock, and the increasing age at first marriage may have all led to a shift away from traditionally higher-income married couple households and toward typically lower-income single-parent and non-family households. Also, the increasing tendency for men with higher-than-average earnings to marry women with higher-than-average earnings may have contributed to widening the gap between high-income and low-income households. (p. 10)

Other factors, such as the ability to find employment and general health, contribute to the relationship between education level and earnings. In 2005, 54% of youth 16 to 19 years of age not in school and without high school diplomas were not working. Of those in the same age-group with high school diplomas, only 13% were not working or pursuing further education (U.S. Department of Commerce, Census Bureau, 2005).

The National Center for Health Statistics conducts annual surveys of people concerning their health. In 2001, it found that better-educated persons were more likely to report that they were in excellent or very good health than persons with less education. Among adults age 25 and older, 78% of those with a bachelor's degree or higher reported being in excellent or very good health. This is in comparison with 66% of those with some education beyond high school, 56% of high school completers, and 39% of high school dropouts (U.S. Department of Health and Human Services, National Center for Health Statistics, 2003).

The Making of an Underclass. Both the achievement and the earnings data presented here suggest that the United States is facing the real possibility of developing a structural underclass, and many believe that the nature of the public school system is a primary cause and a potential instrument for solving the problem. These fears are also supported by findings from the 2000 and earlier U.S. censuses. Data from the 2000 census indicate that more people were living in poverty than a decade earlier and that the middle class shrank while the number of rich increased. Inequity in distribution of the nation's income among families has steadily become greater since

1968 (Jones & Weinberg, 2000). The purchasing power of the average weekly earnings for U.S. workers has dropped by about 20% since 1969, as reported in the previous section. But the hardship has not been borne equally by all Americans. The highest quintile of U.S. families in earnings has increased its share of national aggregate income from 41.3% in 1969 to 48.0% 30 years later, while the other four quintiles lost aggregate share. The share for the lowest quintile dropped from 5.7% in 1969 to 4.1% in 1999, the second quintile from 12.1% to 9.8%, the middle quintile from 17.3% to 15.3%, and the fourth quintile from 23.6% to 22.8% (McNeil, 2000). The highest quintile in income consists mainly of professional and technical workers, usually graduates of 4-year colleges and graduate schools who are prospering, while frontline workers have seen their real wages shrink year after year. The impact is proportionally greatest on the two lowest quintiles.

The problems created by the increasing numbers of children coming from the ranks of poverty is compounded by changes in family structures, as was suggested by the census study by Jones and Weinberg (2000) quoted previously. Characteristics of households are reported in Table 1.6 for the period 1980 through 2005. During that period, the characteristics of U.S. families continued to move away from the traditional two-parent, two-children configuration; married couples with children dropped from 31% of all households in 1980 to 23% in 2005. Households with children headed by single women remained steady over the period at 7% of all households; households with children headed by men doubled from 1% to 2% of all households. More than two-thirds of households have no children at all, a fact that makes funding of public schools by locally levied property taxes exceedingly difficult where such levies require voter approval. Children being raised by single mothers will have about one-third as much family spending on their needs than children being raised by two parents (Hodgkinson, 1991). About one-quarter of American children are living in households below the poverty level (Forum for Education and Democracy, 2008).

The proportion of public school enrollment represented by minority groups (those most likely to be ravaged by poverty) is on the rise. In 1972, minorities represented 22% of elementary and secondary enrollment, rising to 43% in 2004. Correspondingly, white majority students have decreased proportionally from 78% to 57%. The changes are due more to immigration than to differences in fertility rates. African American students have increased only 1%, from 15% of total enrollment in 1972 to 16% in 2004. Over the same period, Hispanics increased from 6% to 19%, now outnumbering African Americans as the nation's largest minority group. Other minority groups, including Asians, have increased from 1% to 7%. The minority population is not evenly distributed across schools and districts, however, being concentrated in urban core cities, while the white majority is concentrated in urban fringe and rural areas. Nearly two-thirds of white students attend majority white schools (NCES, 2006).

In addition to being three times as likely to be impoverished, minority children are more likely to encounter other "risk" factors, such as coming from a single-parent household, having limited English proficiency, and having a parent or sibling (or both) who has dropped out of school. Minority children are 3.5 times as likely to have two or more of these risk factors as are white children. The effect is also intergenerational; 62% of children under age 6 who are below the poverty level have parents who did not complete high school. If one parent completed high school, the rate drops to 26%, and if one parent had some schooling beyond high school, it drops to 7% ("Poverty and Education," 1992).

Family and Peer Influences on School Success

Coleman's (1966) finding that school inputs independently explained very little of the variations in pupil achievement came as a shock to educators and policymakers. School people had confidently claimed that, given adequate resources, they would close the achievement gap between children from poor families and those from middle-class families. In 1965, a year before the release of the Coleman study, Congress began investing billions in new resources for just that purpose through the ESEA (whose

TABLE 1.6

Numbers of U.S. Households by Characteristics: 1980–2005

Characteristic	1980 # Households	1980 % Households	1990 # Households	1990 % Households	2000 # Households	2000 % Households	2005 # Households	2005 % Households
All households	80,776,000	100%	93,347,000	100%	112,000,000	100%	113,146,000	100%
Family households	59,550,000	74%	66,090,000	71%	72,025,000	64%	77,010,000	68%
Married couples	49,112,000	61%	52,317,000	56%	55,311,000	49%	58,109,000	51%
Married couples without children	24,115,000	30%	27,780,000	30%	30,062,000	27%	31,929,000	28%
Married couples with children	24,961,000	31%	24,537,000	26%	25,248,000	23%	26,180,000	23%
Single female head with children	5,445,000	7%	6,599,000	7%	7,571,000	7%	8,305,000	7%
Single male head with children	616,000	1%	1,153,000	1%	1,786,000	2%	2,034,000	2%
People living with relatives	1,150,000	1%	2,403,000	3%	2,984,000	3%	3,444,000	3%
People living with nonrelatives	360,000	0%	534,000	1%	571,000	1%	518,000	0%
People living alone	18,296,000	23%	22,999,000	25%	26,724,000	24%	29,859,000	26%

Source: U.S. Census Bureau (2007).

successor is the No Child Left Behind Act). The Coleman study, published as *Equality of Educational Opportunity*, had been authorized by the Civil Rights Act of 1964, a part of President Lyndon Johnson's "War on Poverty"as was the ESEA. More than 40 years later, poverty is still with us, and so is the achievement gap, as was documented in a previous section. The two are interrelated. As a society, we will not close the achievement gap until the ill effects of poverty have been eliminated, and poverty will not be eliminated until we close the achievement gap (A Broader, Bolder Approach to Education Task Force, 2008; Forum for Education and Democracy, 2008).

Coleman found that the best predictor of student achievement was the socioeconomic status of a child's family, which explained about two-thirds of the variance among students in achievement. In the ensuing years, numerous studies reinforced Coleman's findings. Reflecting on his 40-year career as an educator and a student of education, Sizer (2004) states in no uncertain terms that

> the best predictor of a child's educational success always has been and still is the economic and social class of his family rather than the school that he or she happens to attend. The schools as they presently function appear, save at the well-publicized margins, rarely to countervail the accidents of family, wealth, and residence. "Success," as conventionally defined, and ultimately graduation thus depend largely on the chance of birth and income, embarrassing a democracy that pretends to offer equal educational opportunities for all. (p. xii)

The Curriculum of the Home. School consumes only about 13% of the waking hours of a person's first 18 years of life (Walberg, 1984). Children receive their initial instruction in the home and in the community, albeit informally, and children whose parents are well educated usually come to school better prepared to function efficiently in an environment of abstract learning than do children whose parents are less well educated. Schools composed of children who already have developed good learning skills can begin their instruction at a more advanced level than can schools where most of the children enter with poor learning skills.

An NCES-sponsored study, the Early Childhood Longitudinal Study of Kindergarten Class of 1998–99, collected information on a cohort of children who began kindergarten in the fall of 1998 and followed them through the spring of 2004, when most had completed grade 5 (Rathbun & West, 2004). Table 1.7 reports some of the findings of the study through the third grade. The scale scores were higher in both reading and mathematics for white children and for children living in families with no risk factors on entrance to kindergarten than for minority children and for children living in families with risk factors. The gap had increased by the end of third grade, especially for African American children. Risk factors include living below the poverty level, having a home language other than English, one's mother being a high school dropout, and living in a single-parent household.

Research in the United States on the impact of a family's socioeconomic status on the achievement of its children has been clouded by the issue of racial and ethnic group membership. Despite the minority focus, low socioeconomic status has emerged as the dominating detracting factor from achievement, with little, if any, effect being explained independently by minority-group membership. This is not to deny that racial-minority children experience discriminatory situations that have an additional negative impact on the development of self-concept and realistic aspirations and expectations. Some social scientists refer to the treatment of minorities in the United States as functioning more like a caste system than like socioeconomic differentiation (Brown, 1990). As such, minorities quickly learn their castelike status and develop adaptive behaviors in order to survive socially and psychologically in schools and elsewhere (Allport, 1958; Myrdal, 1962; Ogbu, 1978; Shade & Edwards, 1987).

Socioeconomic status is only a proxy for *interactions* within a family that *tend* to be related to socioeconomic status. Home environment predicts academic learning twice as well as socioeconomic status of families (Walberg, 1984), but it is much more difficult and expensive to measure for research purposes. The "curriculum of the home" for children under age 2 includes being read and told stories, being sung to, being taken on errands, playing peekaboo, and playing outside. Table 1.8 reports the extent to which young children are involved in such

TABLE 1.7

Children's Reading and Mathematics Mean Scale Scores from Kindergarten Through Third Grade, by Selected Characteristics: Fall 1998, Spring 1999, Spring 2000, and Spring 2002

Characteristic	Fall kindergarten	Spring kindergarten	Spring first grade	Spring third grade	Total gain from fall kindergarten to spring third grade
			Reading		
Total	27	39	69	108	81
Race/ethnicity[1]					
Asian/Pacific Islander	30	43	75	111	81
Black	25	34	61	98	73
White	28	40	71	112	84
Hispanic	24	36	65	105	81
Number of family risk factors[2]					
Zero	29	41	73	113	84
One	25	36	65	105	79
Two or more	22	32	58	95	73
			Mathematics		
Total	22	32	55	85	63
Race/ethnicity[1]					
Asian/Pacific Islander	23	34	56	88	65
Black	18	26	47	73	55
White	23	34	58	89	65
Hispanic	19	29	52	82	63
Number of family risk factors[2]					
Zero	24	34	59	89	65
One	20	29	51	81	61
Two or more	17	25	47	74	57

[1]Black includes African American, Pacific Islander includes Native Hawaiian, and Hispanic includes Latino. Racial categories exclude Hispanic origin.

[2]Family risk factors include living below the poverty level, primary home language was non-English, mother's highest education was less than a high school diploma/GED, and living in a single-parent household, as measured in kindergarten.

Note: Detail may not sum to totals because of rounding. Estimates reflect the sample of children assessed in English in all assessment years (approximately 19% of Asian children and approximately 30% of Hispanic children were not assessed). The Early Childhood Longitudinal Study, Kindergarten Class of 1998–99 (ECLS-K) reading and mathematics assessments were not administered in spring 2001, when most of the children were in second grade. Although most of the sample was in third grade in spring 2002, 10% were in second grade, and about 1% were enrolled in other grades.

Source: Rathbun and West (2004), tables A-4 and A-5. Data from U.S. Department of Education, National Center for Education Statistics, Early Child Longitudinal Study, Kindergarten Class of 1998–99 (ECLS-K), Longitudinal Kindergarten-First Grade Public-Use data file and Third Grade Restricted-Use data file, fall 1998, spring 1999, spring 2000, and spring 2002.

TABLE 1.8

Percentage of Children Under 2 Years of Age Who Engage in Selected Activities with a Family Member Daily in a Typical Week, by Family Characteristics: 2001–2002

Child and Family Characteristic	Read Stories	Told Stories	Sung To	Taken on Errands	Played Peekaboo	Played Outside
Total	33	27	74	64	68	47
Race/ethnicity[1]						
American Indian	18	23	64	75	64	46
Asian/Pacific Islander	26	25	71	38	73	43
Black	23	24	73	63	61	45
White	41	31	75	65	72	47
Hispanic	21	21	70	64	64	48
Poverty status						
Poor	22	24	67	64	64	48
Nonpoor	36	28	75	64	70	47
Mother's education						
Less than high school	22	22	66	64	65	50
High school diploma or equivalent	27	25	72	67	70	44
Some college	35	29	78	65	69	44
Bachelor's degree or higher	48	33	79	59	70	48
Family type						
Two parents, with other siblings	31	25	71	63	65	46
Two parents, without other siblings	38	32	78	62	75	48
One parent, with other siblings	24	25	72	62	65	46
One parent, without other siblings	29	27	73	71	70	48
Primary language spoken in the home						
English	36	29	75	65	70	46
Other than English	18	19	67	57	63	49
Mother's employment						
35 hours or more	29	26	73	59	67	41
Less than 35 hours	36	27	75	66	69	46
Unemployed	27	26	75	68	71	50
Not in labor force	34	28	73	65	68	51
Number of family risk factors[2]						
Zero	41	31	77	64	70	46
One	25	25	73	64	67	47
Two or more	20	20	65	63	64	51

[1] American Indian includes Alaska Native, Black includes African American, Pacific Islander includes Native Hawaiian, and Hispanic includes Latino. Race catagories exclude Hispanic origin unless specified.

[2] Family risk factors include living below the poverty level, living in a household where the primary language was not English, having a mother whose highest education was less than a high school diploma or equivalent, and living in a single-parent household.

Note: While the Early Childhood Longitudinal Study, Birth Cohort (ECLS–B) was designed to collect information on children about 9 months of age (i.e., 8–10 months), children were assessed as young as 6 months and as old as 22 months. Seventy-two percent of the children were between 8 and 10 months at the time of the assessment, and 84% were between 8 and 11 months.

Source: U.S. Department of Education, National Center for Education Statistics, Early Childhood Longitudinal Study, Birth Cohort (ECLS–B), Restricted-Use File (NCES 2004–093), previously unpublished tabulation (January 2005). Table was published in NCES (2006).

activities by family characteristics. Such involvement is less for low-socioeconomic-class families than for middle-class families.

Table 1.9 reports the extent of involvement of children ages 3 to 5 in home literacy activities, such as being read to; told a story; taught letters, words, or numbers; and/or taught songs or music. Nonpoor families, well-educated parents, white and Asian families, and small families were more likely to involve their children in these activities than corresponding categories of parent characteristics. It is encouraging to note that all families had increased participation in 2005 when compared to data for 1993.

The curriculum of the home for school-age children includes informed parent–child conversations about everyday events, encouragement and discussion of leisure reading, monitoring and joint analysis of television viewing, expressions of affection and interest in children's academic and personal growth, deferred gratification to accomplish long-range goals, time management, and discipline–reward patterns. In reality, the home environment varies markedly among families with similar financial backgrounds, and many children from families of low socioeconomic status do succeed in school when the home environment is supportive. Mark (1993), in a study of high-achieving African American children from low-income, single-parent families, found that the parents who nurtured these children had high expectations for their children and good communication with them, had high regard for reading, monitored television programs watched by the children, maintained structured households, and established a system of rewards and punishments for the children. The parents were fully aware of their precarious position in society but possessed a sense of conviction in their own abilities and a determination to have their children mature into high-achieving adults.

A study by the W. T. Grant Foundation Commission on Work, Family and Citizenship (1988), published as *The Forgotten Half* (those high school graduates not going on for further education), found that young people want and need adult support. According to the study's findings, teenagers constantly point to their parents as the most influential adults in their lives. A full 70% of high school seniors share their parents' views of what they should do with their lives; and the activity that young people most enjoy sharing with their parents is "just talking." Yet typical American adolescents spend only about 5 minutes per day alone with their fathers and 40 minutes alone with their mothers.

Other environmental factors have a direct relationship with a child's potential success in school. For example, nearly half of all infants are born with one or more factors that mark them for potential school failure later (National Education Goals Panel, 1993). These include late or no prenatal care; a mother who smoked, used drugs, or drank alcohol during pregnancy; and low maternal weight gain. Nearly 37% of all 2-year-olds have not been fully immunized for childhood diseases. Further, each year more than 1 million children experience the divorce of their parents, and 60% of today's 5-year-olds will live in a single-parent family before they reach the age of 18. Children from single-parent families are less likely to be high achievers; they are consistently more likely to be late to school, truant, and subject to disciplinary action; and they are more than twice as likely to drop out of school (Eitzen, 1992).

Even some privileged families can provide only uneven support for their children's school experiences. Real or perceived economic pressures force most parents to work long hours or at more than one job simply to keep the family's finances on track. More than 50% of mothers with children under the age of 6 work outside the home, and about 70% of mothers with children between the ages of 6 and 17 do so. As a result, more children are being raised in families in which the parents have less time for them. This also means that more school-age children are spending more time without adult supervision (latchkey children) and that more preschoolers are being cared for by adults who are not their parents.

Peer Influences on Student Achievement.
Relationships with peer groups within and outside school also have a strong and direct impact on student achievement (Coleman & Hoffer, 1987). The norms and sanctions generated by fellow students (i.e., youth culture) influence how students respond to the instructional opportunities offered by a school; in designing those experiences, prevailing

TABLE 1.9

Percentage of Prekindergarten Children Ages 3 to 5 Who Participated in Home Literacy Activities with a Family Member Three or More Times in the Preceding Week, by Selected Child and Family Characteristics: 1993 and 2005

Child or Family Characteristic	Read To[1]		Told a Story		Taught Letters, Words, or Numbers		Taught Songs or Music	
	1993	2005	1993	2005	1993	2005	1993	2005
Total	78.3	85.7	43.0	53.7	57.7	76.6	41.0	54.4
Race/ethnicity[2]								
White	84.8	91.9	44.3	53.3	57.2	75.7	40.2	52.1
Black	65.9	78.5	39.0	54.3	62.7	80.6	48.9	56.4
Hispanic	58.2	71.8	37.7	49.8	53.9	74.3	38.7	59.1
Asian/Pacific Islander	68.8	84.4	52.1	64.5	61.8	75.2	35.9	46.9
Parents' primary home language								
Both parents speak English	81.1	88.8	43.6	55.0	58.1	77.8	41.6	54.4
One parent speaks English	65.1	76.4	48.7	56.3	57.0	70.8	35.2	61.9
Neither parent speaks English	40.3	64.6	33.0	43.8	51.6	68.9	32.9	53.0
Parents' education[3]								
Less than high school	54.4	62.7	34.1	42.6	54.6	67.8	37.3	49.0
High school diploma or equivalent	73.0	79.9	40.5	46.9	57.9	76.8	42.6	56.7
Some college, including vocational/technical	81.8	86.4	42.4	56.5	58.3	79.7	41.3	56.9
Bachelor's degree	88.9	92.2	47.7	56.4	57.3	75.8	36.7	53.8
Graduate/professional degree	88.5	94.4	52.0	60.7	58.2	76.1	42.7	50.1
Mother's employment[4]								
35 hours or more per week	77.9	83.2	42.7	52.0	55.7	74.7	41.9	54.8
Less than 35 hours per week	81.5	89.3	45.0	54.1	57.7	78.8	40.2	50.5
Looking for work	70.9	89.4	42.9	57.6	65.8	81.0	49.2	54.5
Not in the labor force	78.9	85.1	42.5	54.9	58.3	76.4	40.0	56.4
Family type								
Two-parent household	81.1	86.5	43.8	53.4	57.1	76.1	39.9	53.6
One-parent or guardian-only household	70.8	82.8	40.7	54.9	59.1	78.3	43.9	57.2
Poverty status[5]								
Poor	67.5	78.4	39.1	50.8	59.6	76.0	45.2	53.7
Near poor	75.5	82.4	42.5	53.6	58.1	78.0	39.4	59.2
Nonpoor	86.8	90.2	45.6	55.0	56.2	76.2	39.5	52.5

(Continued)

TABLE 1.9 (Continued)

Percentage of Prekindergarten Children Ages 3 to 5 Who Participated in Home Literacy Activities with a Family Member Three or More Times in the Preceding Week, by Selected Child and Family Characteristics: 1993 and 2005

Child or Family Characteristic	Read To[1]		Told a Story		Taught Letters, Words, or Numbers		Taught Songs or Music	
	1993	2005	1993	2005	1993	2005	1993	2005
Number of children under age 18 in the home								
One	80.9	85.8	45.9	56.5	65.0	77.8	44.0	56.5
Two to three	78.7	85.9	43.1	53.0	55.8	76.8	39.7	52.8
Four or more	72.4	84.6	38.3	53.8	56.8	74.1	43.3	60.0

[1]In 1993, respondents were asked about their reading frequency in one of the two versions of the survey questionnaire. The percentages presented in the table are for all the respondents who answered three or more times on either version of the questionnaire.

[2]Black includes African American, Hispanic includes Latino, and Pacific Islander includes Native Hawaiian. Race categories exclude Hispanic origin unless specified. Other race/ethnicities are included in the total but are not shown separately.

[3]Parents' education is based on the highest level of education attained by either parent.

[4]Estimates do not include children without mothers (birth, adoptive, step, or foster) residing in the household.

[5]"Poor" is defined to include those families below the poverty threshold, "near poor" is defined as 100% to 199% of the poverty threshold; and "nonpoor" is defined as 200% or more than the poverty threshold.

Source: U.S. Department of Education, National Center for Education Statistics, School Readiness Survey of the 1993 National Household Education Surveys Program (NHES) and Early Childhood Program Participation Survey of the 2005 NHES, previously unpublished tabulation (October 2005). Table published in NCES (2006).

student attitudes need to be taken into account, especially at the secondary level.

A pupil's achievement is strongly related to the educational backgrounds and aspirations of the other pupils in the school; this is particularly true for at-risk children (Coleman, 1966; Mayeski & Beaton, 1975; NCES, 2006). Peer groups can provide incentives to high achievement or distractions and disincentives; they determine whether the associations and casual discussions outside the classroom support or undermine the educational mission of the school. Indeed, when parents and educators think of a "good" school, the criterion most frequently used is the nature of the student body, college bound and high achieving being the most preferred.

According to Coleman and Hoffer (1987), in some schools nearly all student social relationships beyond the family revolve around the community of youth in the school. With a high degree of closure, these social relations constitute extensive social capital for the formation of norms and sanctions that can positively shape student behavior. In other schools, students develop most of their social relationships with others the same age outside the school in the neighborhood, in gangs, at work, or elsewhere. In these schools, there is little social capital that school personnel can rely on to support their educational mission.

Since the 1960s and 1970s, there has been a steady decline in the strength of the youth communities in schools, a decline manifested in the decreased interest in such school events as interscholastic sports, an increase in the proportion of students holding part-time jobs, and an increase in attention to phenomena that cut across schools, especially popular music and clothing styles. The reduced focus of students on others within the school reduces the social capital in the youth community of the school and thus reduces the potential of schools to change the students' attitudes and behaviors. As a principal might put it, there is "less to work with" (Coleman & Hoffer, 1987, pp. 236–237).

With respect to the nature of the social culture of a school, the norms and sanctions of the peer group may reward athletic prowess, delinquent activities such as drug use and vandalism, social attractiveness, or academic achievement. The effect of the nature of peer values on achievement of educational goals is great when the culture is positive. If the culture supports educational goals, overall academic achievement is enhanced, but if the culture demeans academic achievement, the performance of all pupils is likely to be reduced below potential.

Coleman and Hoffer (1987) drew two implications for school personnel with respect to these possibilities: to develop a student body sufficiently integrated and cohesive that it constitutes social capital that can be a positive force in the lives of students and to direct that force toward educational objectives. The first goal can best be achieved through collective events in which the entire school is involved, events that compensate for the individualistic nature of the educational process. Interschool competitions are an effective way of doing this, usually taking the form of interscholastic sports. The school cohesion that is developed around athletics, however, needs to be deliberately and effectively broadened to include other educational objectives.

Pupil–teacher relationships can also be a powerful force in shaping peer values. As cited previously, the W. T. Grant Foundation (1988) reported survey evidence that, despite popular belief to the contrary, young people want—and need—adult support. A nationwide study of outstanding middle schools reported that students who feel valued by teachers show respect for their schools (George & Oldaker, 1985). A study by Corcoran, Walker, and White (1988) found that many urban teachers want better relations with their students but that their efforts are hampered by disciplinary problems, large class sizes, lack of time for individual interaction, busing policies, and lack of student participation in extracurricular activities. Many of these inhibitors can be addressed through school policy and wise leadership.

Thus, past assumptions used by educators in designing school curricula no longer hold across the board. Children are less likely to come from majority backgrounds. They are more likely to be members of nontraditional families and more likely to be poor and non–English speaking. Education through high school and beyond is essential if graduates are to be employed in other than menial jobs and to enjoy comfortable standards of living. Well-paying employment opportunities increasingly require sophisticated intellectual skills.

ACTIVITY 1.3

Alternative Delivery Systems for Publicly Financed Education

Addresses ISLLC Standards and Functions: 2A; 3B, 3C; 4; 5; 6

Describe alternative possible systems for coordinating the delivery of publicly financed social services (including educational services) to a child and his or her family. What are the advantages and disadvantages of each design?

Educational leadership is being challenged to design new curricula that recognize the multicultural nature of students, provide institutional support for those at risk, and link schooling and employment. At the same time, school officials must respect the strong influence of families on their students' achievement and attitudes and work closely with parents. Further, solving our "educational" crisis will require coordination of schools' efforts with those of other community agencies, including health care, housing, transportation, and social welfare.

The Education Reform Movement

The report of the National Commission on Excellence in Education (1983), *A Nation at Risk: The Imperative for Educational Reform*, is generally credited with triggering the school reform movement that continues today. The commission was appointed by President Ronald Reagan and is an excellent example of the "bully pulpit" powers of the federal government. The federal government provides only about 8% of the funding for public elementary and secondary schools, yet, because of the categorical nature of its aid and its access to the media, the federal influence over education is far greater than that level of financial support might suggest.

Analysts of the time were increasingly recognizing that all was not well with the nation's school system. Only a year before *A Nation at Risk*, Adler (1982), on behalf of the members of the Paideia

Group, had written *The Paideia Proposal: An Educational Manifesto*, a sweeping indictment of the failures of the public school system with recommendations for reforming it to bring all students to a level of academic achievement that would qualify them to do college-level work. Although largely ignored at the time, the *Paideia Proposal* takes on a new relevancy today. Rather, *A Nation at Risk*, full of rhetoric and with little substance with respect to policies that might successfully address the crisis it effectively articulated, grabbed the attention of the American public and policymakers and launched the current educational reform movement. Twenty-five years later, the Forum for Education and Democracy (2008) issued a report claiming that "two decades later, we are further away from the goals that emerged from *A Nation at Risk* than we were when they were announced" (p. 1).

Waves of Educational Reform

Response to the crises confronting public education has been portrayed as coming in three waves. The first wave, beginning in the mid-1980s, focused on raising student performance and teacher quality. States raised expectations for students and teachers through increased high school graduation and teacher certification requirements. Policymakers and state education departments also initiated longer school days and years, competency tests, standardized curricula, and promotion criteria for students. These policies did little to alter the prevailing ideas about teaching and learning and did not involve teachers directly in the reform process (Smith & O'Day, 1991).

A second wave of reform began in the late 1980s that called for a fundamental rethinking of the schooling process. This wave viewed schools as the basic unit of educational productivity and made them the focus for improvement. Change efforts at the school level emphasized capacity building, especially through the professional development of teachers, and governance changes that brought teachers, parents, and other members of the immediate community into the decision process (Ladd & Hansen, 1999). Decentralized decision making did bring new ideas and energy to the schools. However, many of the issues addressed at the school level, including higher expectations for student performance, were universal and could be addressed more effectively at state and national levels. Addressing universal issues at the school level did not provide sufficient coherence for a highly complex system to function well in a multifaceted society.

The third and current wave is *systemic reform*, characterized by two themes: comprehensive change that focuses on many aspects of the system and policy integration and coordination around a clear set of outcomes (Fuhrman, Elmore, & Massell, 1993). Greater professional discretion is being allowed at the school site under the umbrella of centralized coordination.

To bring focus to the educational reform movement, the state governors joined with President George H. W. Bush in 1989 through 1990 and articulated six national goals for public education to be realized by 2000 (which became eight with the passage of the Educate America Act in 1994). In 1991, the National Council on Educational Standards and Testing was established by Congress to consider whether and how to develop new standards and tests (Ravitch, 1993). The council recommended the establishment of voluntary national standards in key subject areas and a national system of achievement tests. (The debate over these issues continues.) The work of the National Council of Teachers of Mathematics (NCTM) in developing national standards in mathematics (published in 1989) served as a model for doing this. Following the NCTM model, the federal government funded an effort by the National Academy of Sciences to develop standards in science. Similar arrangements were negotiated with other professional groups to develop standards in history, the arts, civics, geography, English, and foreign languages. Operating under the principle that federalism does not mean the supremacy of the federal government but rather a careful balancing of interests of the different levels of government, the projects were not to create a national curriculum but to describe what all children should know and be able to do in a particular field. In this case, it meant steering a course between two extremes: the familiar

pattern of complete local control—in which there were no standards or widely different standards from district to district—and the imposition of a federal one-size-fits-all program (Ravitch, 1993). No national standards exist today, though these initiatives were helpful to the states as they established their educational standards.

Although the White House changed hands in 1992 with the election of Bill Clinton, there was little change in overall strategy. It should be recognized that this has been a bipartisan effort from the beginning and that President Clinton was influential in shaping the America 2000 design as the 1989 chair of the National Governors Association when he was governor of Arkansas.

A National Education Goals Panel was authorized by the 1994 Educate America Act to monitor progress being made toward the goals articulated in the law and to coordinate efforts of state and national organizations, but bipartisanship broke down at this point, and the panel was never activated. The issue that divided the two parties was disagreement over the level of government to establish and monitor the standards-setting process. The Republicans felt that such authority should remain with the states, whereas the Democrats preferred to have it placed with the federal government. In much the same way, the development of national tests to measure progress in meeting the goals stalled.

Although the reform movement experienced an unusual amount of voluntary coordination to this point at the national level, most of the action took place at the state, school district, and school levels. Charter schools, which are public schools freed from many of the policies that apply to district-operated schools as specified in their charters, have been legalized in 40 states and are attended by more than 1 million students. Florida, along with six other states, has authorized a statewide system of educational vouchers, although the Florida law was declared unconstitutional by the Florida Supreme Court in January 2006. Minneapolis and Cleveland were authorized by their respective states to operate limited voucher programs allowing children from low-income families to attend secular and religious private schools supported by public monies (these programs have been upheld by the United States Supreme Court). Site-based decision making and management are in vogue, and increasingly states and school districts are allowing family choice of schools and school-based budgeting. A voluntary national certification program for teachers is in place.

The private sector is becoming more involved in the running and support of public schools. The New American Schools Development Corporation was formed by U.S. business leaders in July 1991 at the request of President George H. W. Bush. The purpose of the corporation was to underwrite the design and implementation of a new generation of "break-the-mold" schools. It raised millions of dollars from private sources to finance the effort. In response to its initial call for proposals, 686 design teams responded, and 11 of them were selected to be supported financially for further development over a 5-year period. The overriding criterion for selection was the likelihood that a design would enable all students to reach the national education goals and attain "world-class" standards (Kearns, 1993; Mecklenburger, 1992). Several of the resulting whole-school reform models were included in the list of exemplary reform models that schools may emulate to qualify for grants under the bipartisan Comprehensive School Reform Demonstration Program, passed by Congress and signed into law in 1997. Although most partnerships are organized at the local level, in 1996 a summit meeting of the National Governors Association and leading business executives focused exclusively on reform at the state level.

Members of the private sector are also working in other ways to promote and to profit from school reform. Their efforts range from school–business partnerships to creating foundations and trusts to outright entrepreneurial initiatives. The most ambitious of the latter type of initiatives was launched by Tennessee businessman and media magnate Chris Whittle. His Edison Project, which was originally intended to be a network of private schools, has developed a design for a network of publicly chartered and contracted schools operating in urban areas across the country.

In 2001, a new president assumed residency in the White House, George W. Bush. As former governor of Texas, he brought with him many of the reform ideas that seemed to have worked reasonably well there, along with the former superintendant of the Houston Independent School District, Rod Paige, to serve as education secretary. This led to the enactment in 2001 with strong bipartisan support the No Child Left Behind Act (a 6-year reauthorization of the ESEA). This legislation took a standards-based approach to reform linked to test-based accountability (David & Cuban, 2006). The standards and the tests are to be developed by each state. While initially welcomed by governors and educators alike, the inflexibility and ambiguity of the law (or possibly its interpretation in the process of implementation [Rudalevige, 2003]) has led to widespread criticism and discontent.

Within 2 years of the law's enactment, educators, state and federal legislators, governors, and even entire states (including Arizona, Connecticut, Hawaii, New Hampshire, New Mexico, Utah, Vermont, and Virginia) mobilized in rebellion against it. Strong support for the general intent of the law remained—to raise the level of academic achievement of all children to acceptable levels—but concern over technical issues were intense, including underfunding by the federal government, restrictive definitions of teacher qualifications, treatment of disabled and limited-English-proficient students, definition of "adequate yearly progress," and measuring student achievement by standardized tests alone (Wood, 2004).

Critics charged further that No Child Left Behind Act had dictated school practices to an unprecedented degree, "maintaining a compliance-and-control regulatory approach that holds the bulk of the system in place, trapping most schools within the constraints of a factory model designed a century ago for another purpose" (Forum for Education and Democracy, 2008, p. iv). The Forum for Education and Democracy sought support not only for school programs for high-need students but also for out-of-school learning supports, such as high-quality preschool, health care, and nutrition, to ensure that children come to school ready and able to learn.

The Broader, Bolder Approach to Education Task Force (2008), convened by the Economic Policy Institute, noted a half century of research showing a powerful association between social and economic disadvantage and low student achievement, yet education policy has been crafted around the assumption that schools alone can offset the full impact. The task force finds no evidence supporting such an assumption. On the other hand, there is strong evidence that policies directed at education-related social and economic disadvantage can improve school performance and student achievement. While encouraging the continuation of school improvement efforts, the task force called for increased investment in early childhood and preschool education, in health services, and in out-of-school programs to close the achievement gap between at-risk and other children.

In 2007, when the legislation was to be reauthorized, Congress found itself in gridlock, unable to agree on the changes to be included. The task was left to the new Congress to be elected in 2008 and to take office in 2009.

Emerging Patterns of Reform

Much concern exists over the adequacy of our educational system and the implications it has for our societal well-being, including a strong and genuine desire to close the achievement gaps between ethnic and income groupings. Much debate and experimentation has taken place. The issue of national goals, for example, raises a myriad of related controversial issues, such as national standards, a national curriculum, national assessment, and national teacher certification. Issues of balance exist as well, such as between federal, state, and local governments; between political and professional authorities; and between public and private sectors, as does the issue of balance between the rights and responsibilities of parents and those of the public. These issues strike at the heart of American social beliefs and traditions.

The challenge we face is not so much a function of the deteriorating quality of public education in its traditional format as it is the result of global social and economic changes that have made irrelevant much of what the system was designed to do. The solution requires realignment or redesign of the system, enabling educators to prepare graduates to live and work successfully and happily under new conditions.

Through nearly 30 years of rigorous debate and experimentation, a pattern of consensus appears to be building as to what to do and the means for doing it. The pattern calls for establishing and monitoring content and performance standards by central authorities and designing and implementing instructional systems by school authorities. For the first time in the history of this nation, schools are called on to bring all students to high levels of academic performance—essentially, to be prepared to do college-level work.

Policymakers in many nations now recognize that there is no single reform that will fully meet the challenges of school improvement. No single reform is a panacea, yet most are sold as if they were (David & Cuban, 2006). The third and current wave of reform in the United States is a broader systemic reform effort than were the prior movements. Although the seeds of this movement were sown early in the 1990s (Smith & O'Day, 1991), the policy changes blended with those of the prior excellence and restructuring movements. In this emerging systemic reform, a coordinated set of policy initiatives include *centralized* goal setting and accountability via standards, curricula, and testing programs; *decentralized* reforms via school-site decision making involving teachers, administrators, staff, parents, and community members; and *family choice* of schooling within the public sector through charter schools and across public and private sectors through vouchers for low-income families. The direction of this systemic reform movement is clearly focused on improving school and student performance through standards-based curricula and assessments:

> This systemic strategy operates alongside the second wave of school reform; it emphasizes state (and to a lesser degree federal) actions to complement school and district restructuring by creating a more coherent environment within which successful schools can thrive and by creating external pressure for change when it does not emerge spontaneously. The linchpin in the system is the development of content standards expressing shared understandings about what students need to know and be able to do, with which other elements of the educational system (school curricula, assessments, teacher education and professional development, and accountability) can be aligned. (Ladd & Hansen, 1999, p. 156)

While there is much agreement as to the general pattern of reform, there is still little agreement on the details of implementation. Achieving such agreement is a political process taking place in schools as they reconstitute themselves and in school districts, state legislatures, Congress, and state and federal courts.

Systems thinking reminds us to be cognizant of the importance of environmental influences. Schools cannot raise the achievement of all students and close achievement gaps among groups of students by themselves. They must work closely with the families of their students and with the other social agencies that serve those families. This will require a new level of cooperation and coordination among social service agencies (which includes schools) to which all are unaccustomed (A Broader, Bolder Approach to Education Task Force, 2008; Forum for Education and Democracy, 2008).

Because of the multifaceted nature of reform, educational leaders must be skilled at bringing together these facets into coherent systems. They must be designers and inventors. Even in applying a "scientifically evaluated" whole-school reform model, the model needs to be restructured to fit the uniqueness of a school's students, its staff, its traditions, and its community. To aid in the development of such leadership, this book emphasizes systems theory, systems design, and systems thinking.

School leaders of the future will be working with a student body markedly different from that of the past, and the organizational structures and professional and political relationships are likely to be different as well. The relationships between teachers and administrators are likely to be collegial rather than authoritarian.

ACTIVITY 1.4
Assessing School Reform Proposals

Addresses ISLLC Standards and Functions: 3B; 4C, 4D; 5; 6

Select one of the school reform proposals from the following list; study its pros and cons and make a recommendation concerning its acceptance or rejection and under what circumstances:

1. School-site management
2. Parental choice of schools
3. Raising high school graduation standards
4. Year-round schooling and/or longer school day or week
5. State or national assessment
6. National teacher certification
7. State or national curriculum

From a systems standpoint, which reform proposals would you cluster together? Why?

ACTIVITY 1.5
Impact of Alternative Reforms on Expanding Diversity in Schools

Addresses ISLLC Standards and Functions: 3B; 5; 6

Discuss the advantages and disadvantages of the following alternative arrangements for expanding diversity in schooling options:

1. The current arrangement of free publicly financed and operated schools with direct aid to private schools prohibited but allowing supporting services that benefit children attending private schools
2. Educational vouchers, with options among public and private schools
3. Tax deductions for tuition and other expenses incurred in public and private education
4. Tax credits that rebate the cost of tuition up to a specified amount
5. Direct aid to private schools
6. Open enrollment among public schools without public aid for private schools

Principals and teachers are likely to have greater professional discretion. School will be more open and transparent to its immediate community. As a result, acceptable leadership styles and strategies will be altered in the future from what they have been in the past.

SUMMARY AND FUNDAMENTAL CONCEPTS

This chapter began with a discussion of the global forces that combine to make the reconstitution of the American school system imperative if the standard of living of Americans is to be preserved. The specific causes for concern were discussed. Evidence was presented showing that more than two-thirds of the clients of public schools are achieving below a proficient level as defined by the NAEP. In part, this is attributable to the failure of schools to adapt to a changing school population that is poorer, less likely to speak English at home, and from nontraditional family structures. Attempts to address these issues were summarized.

In designing new schools and their curricula, the nature and influence of families and peer characteristics on behavior and achievement must be accommodated. The social climate in which education professionals practice in the 21st century are different from that experienced in the 20th, demanding a new kind of leadership that is transformational and collegial rather than hierarchical.

Fundamental Concepts

The fundamental concepts that follow have been discussed in this chapter. The citations that conclude each concept indicate the Interstate School Leaders Licensure Consortium (ISLLC) standards and their associated functions related to the concept. The Arabic numeral refers to the ISLLC standard, and the letters refer to functions as presented in the table found inside the front cover.

- Our reality is pervasive social, economic, and technological change. (1B, 1D; 2B, 2H; 3B; 4A; 5A; 6)
- Our educational systems were designed for another era and need to be reconstituted to meet the needs of a new era. (1B, 1D; 2B, 2H; 3B; 4A; 5A; 6)
- Educational leaders need to have the ability to comprehend the dynamics of human affairs as a basis for relevant action under novel conditions. (1D; 2A, 2C, 2F; 3D; 4A, 4B; 5; 6)
- Educational leaders need to display originality and be able to collaborate with others in designing strategic policies. (1; 2A, 2F; 3D; 4B)
- Educational leaders need to approach the problems and opportunities confronting them openly and

hypothetically so that more may be learned by what is done. (1B, 1D, 1E; 2A, 2F, 2I; 3A, 3D; 4A; 5A; 6)
- We will not close the achievement gap between majority and minority students until the ill effects of poverty have been eliminated, and poverty will not be eliminated until the achievement gap is closed. (2, 4, 5, 6)
- The best predictor of a child's educational success is the economic and social class of his or her family, embarrassing a democracy that pretends to offer equal educational opportunities for all. (2, 4, 5, 6)
- School officials must respect the strong influence of families on their students' achievement and attitudes and work closely with parents and with community agencies serving their students' families. (4, 5, 6)
- The norms and sanctions generated by fellow students (i.e., youth culture) influence how students respond to instructional opportunities offered by the school. (2A, 2C; 3C; 4B; 5E)
- Educational leadership is being challenged to design new curricula that recognize the multicultural nature of students, provide institutional support for those at risk, and link schooling to employment. (2; 4B; 5E; 6)

REFERENCES

A Broader, Bolder Approach to Education Task Force. (2008). *A broader, bolder approach to education.* (www.boldapproach. org, accessed June 11, 2008.)

Adler, M. J. (1982). *The paideia proposal: An educational manifesto.* New York: Macmillan.

Allport, G. (1958). *The nature of prejudice.* Garden City, NY: Doubleday.

Brown, F. (1990). The language of politics, education and the disadvantaged. In S. L. Jacobson & J. A. Conway (Eds.), *Educational leadership in an age of reform* (pp. 83–100). New York: Longman.

Coleman, J. S. (1966). *Equality of educational opportunity.* Washington, DC: Office of Education, U.S. Department of Health, Education, and Welfare.

Coleman, J. S., & Hoffer, T. (1987). *Public and private high schools: The impact of communities.* New York: Basic Books.

Corcoran, T. B., Walker, L. J., & White, J. L. (1988). *Working in urban schools.* Washington, DC: Institute for Educational Leadership.

David, J. L., & Cuban, L. (2006). *Cutting through the hype: A taxpayer's guide to school reforms.* Mount Morris, IL: Education Week Press.

Drucker, P. F. (1989). *The new realities: In government and politics, in economics and business, in society and world view.* New York: Harper & Row.

Eitzen, D. S. (1992). Problem students: The sociocultural roots. *Phi Delta Kappan, 73,* 584–590.

Forum for Education and Democracy. (2008). *Democracy at risk: The need for a new federal policy in education.* Washington, DC: Author.

Friedman, T. L. (2006). *The world is flat: A brief history of the twenty-first century.* New York: Farrar, Straus and Giroux.

Fuhrman, S. H., Elmore, R. F., & Massell, D. (1993). School reform in the United States: Putting it into context. In S. L. Jacobson & R. Berne (Eds.), *Reforming education: The emerging systemic approach* (pp. 3–27). Thousand Oaks, CA: Corwin Press.

Galbraith, J. K. (1992). *The culture of contentment.* Boston: Houghton Mifflin.

George, P. S., & Oldaker, L. L. (1985). A national survey of middle school effectiveness. *Educational Leadership, 42,* 81.

Grigg, W. S., Lauko, M. A., & Brockway, D. M. (2006). *The Nation's Report Card: Science 2005* (NCES 2006-466). U.S. Department of Education Statistics, National Center for Education Statistics. Washington, DC: U.S. Government Printing Office.

Hodgkinson, H. (1991). Reform versus reality. *Phi Delta Kappan, 73,* 9–16.

Jones, A. F., Jr., & Weinberg, D. H. (2000, June). The changing shape of the nation's income distribution: 1947–1998. In U.S. Department of Commerce, Census Bureau, *Current Population Reports.* Washington, DC: U.S. Census Bureau.

Kearns, D. T. (1993). Towards a new generation of American schools. *Phi Delta Kappan, 74,* 773–776.

Kolb, C. E. M. (2006). The cracks in our education pipeline. *Education Week, 25*(42), 45, 56.

Kuhn, T. S. (1996). *The structure of scientific revolutions* (3rd ed.). Chicago: University of Chicago Press.

Ladd, H. F., & Hansen, J. S. (Eds.). (1999). *Making money matter: Financing America's schools.* Washington, DC: National Academies Press.

Mark, D. L. H. (1993). *High achieving African-American children in low income single parent families: The home learning environment.* Unpublished doctoral dissertation, State University of New York at Buffalo.

Mayeski, G. W., & Beaton, A. E. (1975). *Special studies of our nation's schools.* Washington, DC: Office of Education, U.S. Department of Health, Education, and Welfare.

McNeil, J. (2000). *Shares of income received by quintiles when equivalent income is used as the measure of income.* Washington, DC: Housing and Household Economics Statistics Division, U.S. Census Bureau.

Mecklenburger, J. A. (1992). The breaking of the "break-the-mold" express. *Phi Delta Kappan, 74,* 280–289.

Myrdal, G. (1962). *The American dilemma: The Negro problem and modern democracy* (Vols. 1 & 2). New York: Harper & Row.

Naisbitt, J. (1982). *Megatrends: Ten new directions transforming our lives.* New York: Warner Books.

Naisbitt, J., & Aburdene, P. (1990). *Megatrends 2000: Ten new directions for the 1990s.* New York: Morrow.

National Center for Education Statistics. (2003). *The condition of education 2003.* Washington, DC: Institute of Education Science, U.S. Department of Education.

National Center for Education Statistics. (2004). *The condition of education 2004.* Washington, DC: Institute of Education Science, U.S. Department of Education.

National Center for Education Statistics. (2006). *The condition of education 2006.* Washington, DC: Institute of Education Science, U.S. Department of Education.

National Commission on Excellence in Education. (1983). *A nation at risk: The imperative for educational reform.* Washington, DC: U.S. Government Printing Office.

National Education Goals Panel. (1993). *National education goals report: Vol. 1. The national report.* Washington, DC: U.S. Government Printing Office.

National Innovation Initiative. (2005). *Tapping America's potential: The education for innovation initiative.* Washington, DC: Council on Competitiveness.

New Commission on the Skills of the American Workforce. (2007). *Tough choices or tough times.* San Francisco: Wiley/Jossey-Bass.

Ogbu, J. (1978). *Minority education and caste.* New York: Academic Press.

Poverty and education. (1992). *Education Week, 11*(16), 5.

Rathbun, A. & West, J. (2004). *From kindergarten through third grade: Children's beginning school experiences* (NCES 2004-007). Washington, DC: National Center for Education Statistics.

Ravitch, D. (1993). Launching a revolution in standards and assessments. *Phi Delta Kappan, 74,* 767–772.

Rudalevige, A. (2003). No Child Left Behind: Forging a congressional compromise. In P. E. Peterson and M. R. West (Eds.), *No Child Left Behind? The politics and practice of school accountability.* Washington, DC: Brookings Institution Press.

Shade, B. J., & Edwards, P. A. (1987). Ecological correlates of the educative style of Afro-American children. *Journal of Negro Education, 86,* 88–99.

Sizer, T. R. (2004). *The red pencil: Convictions from experience in education.* New Haven, CT: Yale University Press.

Smith, M. S., & O'Day, J. O. (1991). Systemic school reform. In S. H. Fuhrman & B. Malen (Eds.), *The politics of curriculum and testing: The 1990 Politics of Education Association yearbook* (pp. 233–267). New York: Falmer.

Toffler, A. (1980). *The third wave.* New York: Bantam Books.

Toffler, A. (1990). *Powershift: Knowledge, wealth, and violence at the edge of the 21st century.* New York: Bantam Books.

U.S. Department of Commerce, Census Bureau. (2005). *Current Population Survey: Annual social and economic supplement, 2005.* Washington, DC: Author.

U.S. Department of Health and Human Services, National Center for Health Statistics. (2003). *National Health Interview Survey, 2001.* Washington, DC: Author.

W. T. Grant Foundation Commission on Work, Family and Citizenship. (1988). *The forgotten half: Pathways to success for America's youth and young families.* Washington, DC: Author.

Walberg, H. J. (1984). Families as partners in educational productivity. *Phi Delta Kappan, 65,* 397–400.

Wood, G. (2004). Introduction. In D. Meier & G. Wood (Eds.), *Many children left behind: How the No Child Left Behind Act is damaging our children and our schools.* Boston: Beacon Press.

The Power of Systems Thinking for Educational Change

In chapter 1, we discussed a variety of causes for concern about the current state of the educational system. We reviewed a number of attempts at reform and noted that piecemeal approaches to reform have not been effective. A systemic approach based on whole-school reform was recommended as more effective for the problems discussed. Assuming that schools and school districts are open social systems, understanding systems thinking can greatly enhance the effectiveness of school leaders.

This chapter presents a modified version of systems theory as a framework for identifying and understanding the interrelationships of the many facets of leadership. It traces the history of systems theory, including significant detail about systems frameworks and properties. The discussion includes organizational implications of a systems perspective for schools and school districts, addressing issues surrounding the postindustrial paradigm.

Current reform efforts in the U.S. school system offer a rich setting for the use of systems theory. Schools are composed of critical subsystems, such as administration, instruction, finance, and transportation. In addition, as administrators seek methods to implement multifaceted school improvement programs, a systems perspective can empower an administrator to emerge as a visionary or a problem solver instead of merely a manager. Educational administrators have been using systems analytic methods for more than 40 years. A clearer understanding of educational systems can occur as the practitioner begins to observe and think in terms of system interactivity, interdependence, and integration of critical school systems and subsystems.

Systems thinking has proven to be particularly helpful in identifying variables and organizing processes associated with schooling. It is time to consider which aspects of the systems paradigm are being enriched and which are being ignored.

Definitions of systems are widely available; as definitions multiply, clarity about systems can be lost amid the host of approaches. The definition and power of popularized versions of Bertalanffy's original *general systems theory* have been misconstrued frequently in academic literature. As a result, systems thinking suffered from ill-informed use and therefore had less-than-optimal impact. In this chapter, we more clearly characterize general systems theory to help educators gain a greater understanding about the power of systems thinking.

Systems thinking in the past several decades in school systems has been too dependent on the management science of the industrial age. As a result, educators often are unaware of the role that general systems theory can play in understanding how schools function. Ashmos and Huber (1987) and Salisbury (1990) have indicated that relatively few systems concepts have been researched and put into operation. These findings indicate both an untapped potential in the general systems paradigm and a lack of risk taking in the application of general systems concepts. Still, the use of systems ideas is now worldwide. For example, global ecological–environmental cooperation and many new business practices can be traced to general systems theory.

Understanding how theory and practice interrelate is crucial to administrators as they lead school organizations. However, offhand practice, sometimes demanded by the constant pressures within a school organization, may seem more expedient or practical than reflection about theory that could provide a basis for change. Without a broad base of knowledge from which to act, an administrator may be doomed to making immediate decisions that may damage the long-run well-being of the organization. Systems theory has evolved a wide range of concepts to enable the knowledgeable administrator to take appropriate short- and long-term action to promote the overall growth of all elements of the school organization.

Conceptualizing Systems

The Development of Systems Thinking

In the past century, the physical sciences dominated scientific endeavor. Many scientific minds were engaged in establishing a predictive system of laws. On the other hand, other disciplines were uncovering problems that were unsolvable by classical scientific methods. Many of these were problems posed by organized complexity; that is, the entire entity under study could not be broken into discrete elements without losing its essence. Bertalanffy (a theoretical biologist) and others called for the development of new conceptual models to facilitate the study of complex biological and social phenomena.

Bertalanffy (1968) began incorporating into his own work concepts from physical chemistry, kinetics, and thermodynamics. He expressed the germ of this theory as early as 1937. As the theory developed, he viewed it as having the character of a basic science. Its correlate, as an applied science, is now known as *systems science*. Systems science has since emerged as operations research, systems engineering, cybernetics, organizational theory, infomatics, and other sciences that use systems theory, concepts, and methodologies.

In 1954, Bertalanffy and some colleagues agreed to collaborate as cofounders of a society for general systems thinking and research. They agreed on goals that would seek to encourage the development of theoretical models, to standardize the efforts across disciplines, to promote the unity of science through greater communication, and to investigate the correspondence of concepts, models, and laws in various fields. Over time, they built a theoretical bridge across scientific disciplines and diminished the fragmentation that once limited cross-disciplinary exchanges and contributions (Emery, 1970). Their contributions to the development of a metalanguage and the advancement of the study of holism have enabled scientists and practitioners to think about and design new investigative strategies.

Systems Definitions

Critics comment that the very idea of a "system" loses efficacy because everything can be viewed as a system. Proponents of general systems theory find systems existing in all "shapes and flavors," but an aggregate of units does not constitute a system. An often-cited example is an unorganized and inactive pile of marbles (see Figure 2.1). Similarly, a work group of individuals does not possess the same

FIGURE 2.1

Aggregate Thinking

An aggregate is a collection that does not demonstrate a purpose or relate system activity. Although the diagram at the right demonstrates one view of communication in an organization, it does not exhibit the many other ways that communication takes place. Both demonstrate aggregate thinking that does not thoroughly explain system activity.

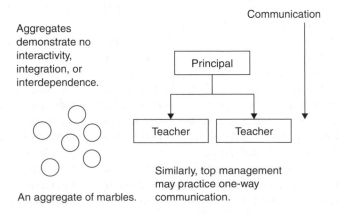

Aggregates demonstrate no interactivity, integration, or interdependence.

An aggregate of marbles.

Similarly, top management may practice one-way communication.

capacities as a self-directed project team. Some form of organizing agent is needed to "motivate" these aggregates to create and further understand system interactivity.

Differentiation between aggregates and systems is important since systems are sometimes treated as if they were aggregates. Practitioners often incorrectly assume that a top-down model of organizational communications implies that each unit or person is insulated from interaction with other units or persons inside or outside the organization (see Figure 2.1). This incomplete view presumes that no other systems (whether interpersonal, organizational, family, or community) are functioning.

Corporate mergers, acquisitions, or divestitures may exemplify aggregate rather than systems thinking. If managers perceive people as noninteracting aggregates and imply that other values are more important, they may forget to consider the plight of the human components. Similarly, relocation of teachers or students from one school to another or hair-trigger decisions to expel troublesome students regardless of their home situations are examples of aggregate thinking. The aggregate mentality is additive. It assumes that aggregate units can be added or subtracted at will without damage to the larger aggregate called the company, school, or office. Politically, the aggregate mentality may even encourage the aggression of large nations against small nations, with nearby additions of territory, people, and resources presumed to have no or negligible effect on the social system. In truth, disturbance in one part of a system creates ripple effects that are unsettling for the entire system, often for extraordinarily long periods of time. Systems thinkers can anticipate this, knowing that multisystem interactions are inevitable.

Aggregate nonsystems are closely associated with the idea of system closure. In a closed system, all energy is drawn from within the system, all events occur within the system, and all products are used by and within the system. Nothing is imported or exported. This is a recipe for system deterioration and demise since the closed system exhausts itself in repeated cycles of self-consumption.

The closed system is largely a theoretical construct, as it is unlikely that an example of a totally closed system can be found. Theorists more commonly speak of relative closure or openness. Relatively closed systems need new energy as input, which is the system justification for medical or spiritual intervention in the case of human illness or, in the case of organizational disorder, the justification for hiring a consultant or new executive or seeking additional training or learning. All such interventions are aimed at overcoming entropy in the relatively closed system.

Similarly, the completely open system is a conceptual convenience. When systems theorists speak of open systems, they are referring to degrees of openness. The relatively open system remains exposed to many interventions; an open system may also reach beyond its boundaries to exert external influence. The extent to which any system and its subunits allows incoming and outgoing communication and other exchanges determines its degree of boundary permeability.

Relative closure of systems can be psychologically comforting to many people since in a closed system, unwanted intrusions can be prevented or derailed. On the other hand, excitement and benefit can be enjoyed in relatively open systems. In open systems, self-regulatory devices are established to monitor boundary exchanges and the effects these exchanges have on parts of the system, the entire system, and the environment.

For a school administrator, maintaining a relatively open system involves regulating school enrollment, making learning enjoyable for all, monitoring downstream entry of students into work life, anticipating growth in school populations, and more. Administrators cannot be oblivious to the potential variety and potential value conflicts in the environment.

Once it is clear that systems are not aggregates and are relatively closed or open, other system characteristics become evident. By definition, a system denotes a connection between parts and wholes. For example, Ackoff's (1974) definition is: "A system is a set of two or more interrelated elements of any kind; for example, concepts (as in the number system), objects (as in a telephone system or human body), or people (as in a social system)" (p. 13). From the beginning of general systems theory, interrelationship, interaction, and interdependence have defined the characteristic elements of systems.

Many definitions of systems refer to organization as a condition that enables parts to work together on behalf of the whole. Thus, the ideas of interrelationship and interdependency migrate into the broader concepts of organized complexity and holism (Hodge & Anthony, 1988; Kast & Rosenzweig, 1972). Internally, schools may be viewed as being composed of administration, instruction, and learning. These may even form our primary definition. But schools must equally be understood in combination with their external environments, including the school districts and state and federal governments.

Systems Frameworks

Systems literature treats the general characteristics of systems in several ways. Authors may initially discuss the elements of a system and then describe their functions. They may undertake system model building that seeks to incorporate all pertinent variables and processes, or they may begin with taxonomies that categorize systems and their variables in thought-provoking ways. Most theorists conceptualize a vertical dimension to systems that allows them to speak of hierarchies of systems, hierarchies within systems, or hierarchical levels of abstraction. In this fashion, the theorist or practitioner can observe a system's embeddedness (see Figure 2.2). A horizontal dimension to systems thinking and practice is also prevalent that allows researchers to model the

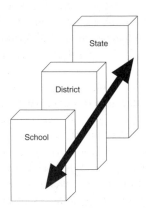

FIGURE 2.2

Hierarchy of Systems

A hierarchy of systems demonstrates level of embeddedness and potential system activity.

system of interest with x and y types of coordinates (i.e., intersections of horizontal and vertical dimensions varying according to different assigned values). Yet vertical or horizontal references do not represent all the dimensions inherent in systems. Systemic thinking may require a third axis, "z," that exhibits the multidimensionality of a system or systems concept over time. Characteristically, then, a hierarchy of systems demonstrates embeddedness, the vertical dimension captures system interactivity, and a time dimension captures movement or flow.

Theoretical systems and systems constructs may be arranged in an ascending order of complexity. This yields rich insights about organized complexity, and serves well as an invitation to rethink systems.

Another way of framing systems thinking is to identify broad categories and then develop functional classifications. For example, abstract systems are composed of interrelated symbols, ideas, concepts, and principles. Concrete systems are composed of interrelated physical and material resources. Real systems are observable (i.e., they are "visual–tactile" systems falling within the compass of human sensory experience). Human systems add interrelated organic and psychological dimensions and embody elements of abstract, concrete, and real systems. Cybernetic systems steer organizations through turbulence toward stability. Organizations include all these systems, and each must be accorded its own value.

The functional behavior of these systems could be classified as state maintaining, goal seeking, multigoal seeking, and purposeful (Hodge & Anthony, 1988). A *state-maintaining system* wants to continue in a customary pattern. A *goal-seeking system* moves toward a different but highly specified outcome. A *multigoal-seeking system* pursues several outcomes that are not mutually exclusive. A *purposeful system* has a clear sense of mission in a broad, value-laden sense. School organizations, from the district to the individual classroom units, exhibit qualities of all four system behaviors.

Simon (1970) spoke of a "system of systems" in hierarchical arrangement, and some scientists have decided that there are also systems of systems theory—a metasystem. Immegart and Pilecki (1973) constructed five theoretical approaches to understanding these metasystems: comprehensive system theories of wholes and components; subsystem or process theories, with microscopic analysis of input processing; feedback and system control theories, with cybernetics as a prominent contender; theories of system properties that help formulate longitudinal, evolutionary systems analyses; and output theories and output analysis (i.e., results of system activity). Operations research was a primary example of the latter.

Discussions of applied systems thinking often consider two organizing ideas—dynamics and complexity—and two influential metaphors—mechanical and biological. Dynamics studies the behavior of systems in a state of change. It is the source of chaos theory, which is concerned with systems that exhibit change behavior so that long-range prediction is not possible. Complexity includes complex and complex adaptive systems. They consist of many interacting stakeholders whose goals are often in competition. Complex systems are self-adapting. Study of complex and complex adaptive systems generally considers ways in which elements of the system following relatively simple rules of behavior can produce emergent complexity and unpredictable behavior. Also considered in the study of such systems are the adaptive agents within the system, feedback, and self-organization.

The mechanical metaphor for systems considers them as machines made up of interacting parts and subsystems. The biological metaphor views systems as living and evolving, made up of parts and subsystems that are also living and evolving.

To many, systems thinking is a mix of positivistic and naturalistic, or nomothetic and idiographic, points of view (Kimbrough & Nunnery, 1988; for further discussion, see chapter 11). For the systems scientist, this is as it should be. By definition, general systems theory organizes and subsumes widely divergent scientific views and methodologies. Systems thinking requires a synthesizing, "both–and" perspective rather than the piecemeal exercise of serial "either–or" judgments.

Because systems are viewed as wholes, their structures and functions are also studied as a dynamic and ongoing process rather than as subsets of analytical interest. For scientists who have

escaped the rigid cause-and-effect line of thought, other criteria of science not only are possible but also hold more promise. Naturalistic inquiry, for example, has enormous potential for translating observations of systems at work into scientific probabilities and challenging bodies of knowledge. The qualitative research that has resulted and been applied in numerous academic areas has demonstrated new part–whole variables that may prove valuable.

Systems approaches that rely heavily on either analytical or conceptual modeling are unable to express all the existing relationships among systems. Presumed causes cannot always account for observed effects in complex systems, and neither quantitative nor qualitative studies provide all the answers. Consequently, whatever approach is used still contains the danger of oversimplifying organizational relationships. Using multiple points of view to study organizations may initially yield overwhelming amounts of data, some of which may conflict with other data, but from this muddle, new and testable hypotheses arise. It takes complex science to study complex systems.

Systems Properties Explored

The simple input–throughput–output model for system activity has been the source of theory building and the metaphoric bane of systems thinkers. It represents an oversimplified version of systems inquiry that can lead to the very rigidity and scaling down of ideas that systems thinking seeks to avoid. Graphically, the model overemphasizes analytical, procedural, and directional properties of systems, casting them in a "systematic" stepwise mold. When this model is all that is visible, the systematic approach is taken for the whole of general systems theory. This belies the system's actual, "lived" dynamism and diversity. The simplified input–throughput–output model prevents the systems thinker from observing the system's full energy, interactivity, and interdependence.

Paradoxically, this otherwise regrettable simplicity helps newcomers to general systems theory identify important system elements from which more systemic ideas and models are constructed. As an example, management and instructional design models can often be seen as more systematic and

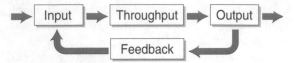

FIGURE 2.3

Input–Throughput–Output Model

procedural than systemic and functional. These models are frequently used in this text, but they should be viewed as an enlargement of a particular component of an implied embracing system. In simplest graphic form, Figure 2.3 represents a systematic (procedural) model. Inputs are transformed through system activity to outputs.

By placing an environment around the model and representing boundaries between the system and the environment as permeable, this representation of the system becomes more useful (see Figure 2.4). In this fashion, then, the model begins to represent a holistic nature as it illustrates more thorough knowledge and understanding about the system.

The social, economic, and political milieu in which schools and school districts exist often determines their survival. This interactivity is representative of the new energy, information, material resources, and people from the environment moving into the system as inputs, providing new "raw materials" for system activity. Other sources of new input activity may include feedback about the input the system has consumed and feedback about the outputs the system has produced. For example, a more specific input activity could be family impact on the student, community job availability, state and federal mandates, or local and regional economic conditions. Multiple forms of input are utilized or transformed by the system into output. Transformation

processes in the educational context might include instruction, various forms of decision making and problem solving, or actual thinking by the student. Throughput (the transformation) can take many forms. Outputs may be products, services, energy, damages, or any combination of these. For example, a systems solution to environmental damage might be to capture toxic emissions or substances (outputs) and reuse (input) them in some ecologically sound way. In school systems, capturing dropouts and carefully "recycling" their energies is an appropriate systems solution to educational waste. Outputs can thus become new inputs for the same system as well as inputs for other systems.

As outputs are realized, forms of information are fed back by the system to enable the system to realize its full potential. Instructional content, lesson objectives, and other resources (inputs) are used to instruct the student. The outcome of this process, knowledge acquisition in some form, is evaluated and fed back as changes that may or may not provide necessary further control. In this fashion, feedback is utilized to monitor and change the systems activity as further iterations occur.

Feedback loops may be considered as having two forms: positive (self-reinforcing) and negative (self-correcting or balancing) (Galbraith, 2001; Hudson, 2000). Positive, or self-reinforcing, feedback loops are those that increase deviation within the system. They do this by adding iterations of the deviation together (e.g., 1, $1+1=2$, $1+2=3$, and so on), driving the system toward greater variation and possible eventual change. Negative, or self-correcting, feedback loops are those that decrease deviation within the system or hold it to a particular level (e.g., 1, $1+1=2$, $1+(-1)=1$, and so on). A negative feedback loop tends to maintain equilibrium within the system.

FIGURE 2.4

Simplifed Systems Model

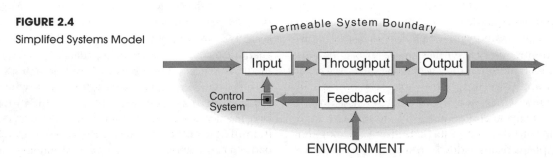

Installing a cybernetic control device in the feedback loop to show regulation and self-correction of the system completes the basic model. At this point, the organized complexity of systems may be present but can scarcely be inferred from the diagram. Considerable variation is apparent here as the system becomes dynamic. Even in an "assembly-line" transformation, inputs and processes can vary from one "batch" to another. In modern organizations, the application of increasingly more standardization cannot cope with the vast complexity that arises as input continues to vary and grow exponentially. This is particularly evident today in the information age, when system complexity is fueled by greater information availability.

Environment generally refers to the collections of systems that lie outside the system under study. Environments are not controllable by the system but can be selectively responsive to the system's behavior. Environments may be stable, dynamic, or even chaotic. Churchman (1979) suggested that analysis of a system ought to determine whether influences on the system are environmental, systemic, or neither, for such influences are potential growth and survival factors. Strategically, the organization (i.e., the school) must know of the existence of resources, employ managerial talent to import and organize their use, and then call on organizational intelligence to make sure that the entire system, including its environments, is well served.

Other Properties of Systems

Other system properties are important to the understanding of general systems theory. These additional features help the new practitioner comprehend the full extent of evolving systems beliefs and practices.

1. *Synergy, or the presence of synergism.* Synergy is a process equivalent to structural holism, wherein structural components (e.g., bricks and mortar, classrooms, libraries, offices, and gyms) become more than the sum of the parts. Together, these concepts aptly describe part–whole relationships in general systems theory: the whole is structurally, functionally, and synergistically greater than (and other than) the sum of its parts. Team teaching, for example, creates added synergistic features to enhance instruction. Content can be made more relevant as people interact to provide a more profound level of instruction and learning.

2. *Functionalism, or system activity.* Similar to synergy, functionalism has implications concerning system processing. Parsons (1960), an early supporter of the pattern-and-function view of systems, urged a systemic examination of structures, processes, and functions. Just as the openness of a system is perceived to lie somewhere on a continuum between open and closed, so too the functionality of a system lies on a continuum between optimal functioning and complete dysfunction. The system that functions well has dynamic properties; the system that becomes dysfunctional or "neurotic" suffers from static processes and relationships (Hodge & Anthony, 1988; Kets de Vries & Miller, 1989). In a classroom, the need for standardized control mechanisms coexists with a particular teacher's need for more flexibility in the classroom. These dichotomies exist everywhere.

3. *Leading parts.* Which parts of a system act as its leading parts: the static components or the dynamic components? Administrators may "switch the lineup" or change the dysfunctional components from static to dynamic. In small-group behavior, leading parts may be individuals who emerge when needed or when prepared to do so. Larger organizations display this same flexibility and potential for emergence of unexpected leading parts. The adoption of a dramatic and new teaching method may raise achievement, shared decision making may allow teachers and administrators to balance standardization and flexibility more effectively, or the school band may ignite pride throughout the school. This may be the very pulse of innovation, and systems thinking invites this perception. Leading parts and emergence are interdependent concepts; both are situational rather than positional. School administrators are defined by their positions as leaders, but this neither guarantees that they are leading parts nor excludes them from that status. Other leading parts may emerge at critical times to help a school become more functional—for example, an energetic new teacher, a lead teacher, a student opinion leader, or someone from the external environment. Perhaps the leading part is a new computer system or a new building.

4. *Dynamic homeostasis.* In a cybernetic sense, leading parts help "steer" the organization toward relative equilibrium, a condition that allows the organization to grow and change in a stable way. Systems need the fresh inputs of leading parts as well as the information–communication regulatory systems to enhance helpful forces and minimize destructive ones wherever they may be found.

5. *Isomorphism.* A system may have structures that show correspondence to structures in another system. This means that structurally the parts correspond to each other one to one. What is learned about one structure (even if it is an abstract structure like a concept) is applicable to its isomorph. Therefore, looking for isomorphism is a way to infer knowledge from one organization that may hold true in a second organization. For example, can we utilize business practices or knowledge in school settings? One caution is needed: while all isomorphisms are analogies, not all analogies are isomorphisms. The difference is that analogies do not have to meet the condition of one-to-one correspondence (Schoderbek, Schoderbek, & Kefalas, 1990).

6. *Differentiation and specialization in a system.* Most systems contain internal elaboration processes between their subsystems and their influence relationships. This can account for system symbiosis, a situation in which one subsystem becomes so differentiated that it cannot perform certain functions for itself and thus must "live off" another subsystem. If one of the symbiotic pairs is self-sufficient, the relationship is unipolar; if each has something vital to offer the other, the relationship is bipolar. Another type of differentiation occurs in redundant subsystems where design and functioning are duplicated as a backup to other subsystems. An example is central database duplication and access at more than one location of a school. Hodge and Anthony (1988) identified still another kind of subsystem—a decomposable one—a "short-run independent" system that has many internal sustaining interactions. A project group might exemplify the decomposable subsystem.

7. *Principle of progressive mechanization.* This principle, postulated by Bertalanffy (1968), implies that control functions can be decentralized when subsystem routines proceed to the point that regulation is more easily managed at that level. Progressive inclusion and progressive centralization indicate system tendencies to centralize and become more and more integrated and complex. These properties of systems may cyclically emerge and recede, depending on how system variety is managed (Willis, 1977). Progressive segregation refers to the subdivision of systems parts into recognizable, separate subsystems.

8. *Goals and adaptation.* According to Bertalanffy, one cannot talk about organisms, behavior, and society without taking into account the concepts of goals and adaptation toward those goals. Consequently, the property of teleology (desired "end states") has a critical role in systems thinking. All systems, living and non-living, may have directedness or purposiveness, but human systems clearly have purposes. For example, businesses create profit, schools educate, and students learn. Identifying this property leads naturally to the idea of equifinality, where a system may reach equal–final goals by means of different paths and strategies. Clearly, businesses achieve profit in varying ways, and different schools educate using a variety of different but successful methods.

9. *Negentropy (negative entropy).* Katz and Kahn (1966) reported this property of open systems, the system's defense against decline. Negentropic inputs (feedback) keep a system healthy. The system's dilemma is to determine which of many possible inputs will be most beneficial. Feedback is the mechanism that allows the system to self-correct. Vocal parents demand change, teachers evaluate performance, and administrators review resource utilization. Each of these self-correcting mechanisms changes the system in fundamental ways.

The properties of organized complexity, holism, teleology, emergence, synergy, isomorphism, and leading part activity are often given short shrift when predictive or quasi-predictive systems analysis methods are used. When more qualitative approaches are taken, these properties become vital to the analysis. The cybernetic and adaptive aspects of systems receive much attention from scientists, although some writers have suggested that organizational inertia interferes with the notion of adaptability (e.g., Carroll, 1988).

Complex Systems

Complex systems are systems of many parts that are linked in nonlinear fashion. They are more than the sum of their parts because of their nonlinearity. They have mutually interactive dynamic parts. Because of their complexity, input does not lead to completely predictable output, nor is output necessarily proportional to input. Examples of complex systems include cells, living things (including humans), the brain, and human organizations.

Complex systems demonstrate specific features. They are nonlinear open systems, sensitive to their environments and working to maintain dynamic equilibrium through the use of both negative and positive feedback loops. Nonlinearity in a complex system means that a small change within the system may have a large effect (sometimes called the butterfly effect), a proportional effect, or no immediate effect at all. In a linear system, the effect is always directly proportional to the cause. Nonlinear systems may be made up of smaller complex systems that may be nested or contained within the larger complex system. Their boundaries are often difficult to define and may be a result of a decision by the observer.

Bar-Yam (2000) has identified a set of characteristics and issues related to complex systems. He argued the following: (a) Multiscale descriptions are necessary to understand complex systems. (b) Small inputs may affect large-scale behavior. (c) Patterning is a characteristic of complex systems. (d) Small disturbances to the system may lead to recovery of the original state, but large disturbances can lead to significant change in the system. (e) The systems are complex both in structure and in behavior that responds to their environments. (f) The systems demonstrate emergence so that the leading part or parts may change as conditions change. Therefore, they must be studied in action rather than analyzed in stasis. (g) New complex systems may be formed by recombination of parts of existing complex systems. (h) The complexity of a system's responses is governed by the complexity of the controlling or leading part. With a single controlling or leading part, complexity of output will be restricted. (i) Complex systems may be modeled and so studied

effectively as long as the model is appropriately structured.

Complex adaptive systems are those complex systems that have the following properties: primitive components called "agents," nonlinear interactions among the agents and their environment, unanticipated global behaviors resulting from those interactions, agents that adapt their behavior to other agents and to the environment, and systemic evolution over time resulting from those adaptations. (Krivov, Dahiya, & Ashraf, 2002). Ecosystems, economies, and social systems are examples of complex adaptive systems. Schools, school districts, and education in general fall within those models.

Organizational Implications of Systems Thinking

Groundbreaking: Early Organizational Theories

Organizational theory has not totally ignored the impact of systems theory. Educational institutions that prepare school administrators cannot sensibly ignore the impact of systems thinking in other disciplines, nor have they done so. Taking a systems view frees administrators from single-cause analysis, narrow interpretations of what systems are and do, and misunderstandings about the meaning of isolated events. Systems thinking can also add a more thorough cultural perspective to institutional history, to present concerns, and to projections of the future. Chin, Bennis, and Benne (1961) reported that systems approaches serve as major operating frameworks for physical as well as social sciences.

ACTIVITY 2.1

The Workplace as a System

Addresses ISLLC Standards 1A and 6C

Consider the organization in which you work. What is its environment? What are its goals? Is it primarily a closed or open system? Is it a complex adaptive system? What are its major elements in systems terms?

Bertalanffy's (1968) experimental approach to inter-disciplinary "parallelism" has become everyday reality. Cities now depend on systems thinking to plan urban renewal and transportation, NASA launches spaceships replete with systemic environments, and global economies are understood to be interdependent and synergistic.

Changes in Management Roles and Contexts

Systems thinking has brought new capacities to management over time. Boundaries of systems are continually redefined by events in the system or the environment. For example, school district reform and restructuring efforts parlay bureaucratic systems against site-based management systems. An emerging function of management, in addition to combating entropy, is to manage those boundary shifts successfully.

Exploring various management philosophies can readily demonstrate the extent that management beliefs have changed over time. Such changes include those seen in traditional hierarchical, human relations, and contingency models and to the current models evident today.

A taxonomy of six analytical models, including mechanistic/bureaucratic, human relations, individual behavior, technological, economic, and power, has been discussed by Hodge and Anthony (1988). All these models proceed from several assumptions: the organization exists to satisfy environmental needs; the organization's work system mobilizes to meet objectives that will in turn meet environmental needs; the organization structures itself to facilitate the work system activity; the design of power and authority relationships, system differentiation, and delegation are dedicated to work facilitation; and renewal and change processes are mandatory for survival and effectiveness. These models are significant in that they explicitly seek to investigate organizational management from a systemic point of view. The models explore the management of organizations in light of their reality: as open and dynamic systems and subsystems, as interrelated across functional boundaries, as interactive combinations, and as integrative processes. The models specifically

demonstrate the necessity for interdependence; one system or subsystem cannot and does not act individually but does always act in concert with other systems or subsystems. Management, then, cannot simply justify singular problem solving confined in individual, local, or larger arenas. Analysis must become holistic.

Although the literature on the organization of schools borrows from all the foregoing theories, there was initially no specific body of literature that linked systems theory to school organizations. Nevertheless, systems concepts have continually been applied in analyses of schools.

Organizational Change

To help assess organizational change across time, Grenier (1972) identified five organizational dimensions: organizational age, size, stage of evolution, stage of revolution, and industry growth rate. In one view, organization growth stages enable the practicing manager to understand related, systemic organizational needs as development continues. At times during a cycle of growth, organizations can be seen as evolutionary, progressive, or striving to change. At other times in the cycle, problematic issues arise as the organization confronts internal crisis and strives to continue its existence. These periods are revolutionary. With organization growth, differing managerial styles are needed.

1. *Evolutionary creativity leading to a leadership crisis.* At this stage, technical and entrepreneurial competence become insufficient. Managers have to be created or imported.

2. *Directed evolutionary growth leading to an autonomy crisis.* Here, communication is often lacking as people become frustrated and alienated. Management begins to share decision making.

3. *Growth through delegation leading to a control crisis.* Subsystems appear to be too independent. Situations develop that trigger centralization. Other problems emerge as a result.

4. *Growth through coordination, leading to a crisis in bureaucracy.* The organization becomes rigid, inflexible, rule bound, and inefficient.

5. *Collaboration leading to a crisis of unknown origin.* At this organizational stage, the organization has presumably matured enough to be able to assess its risks and act accordingly.

Characteristics of organizations that have successfully managed change have been identified in a range of studies. McLagan (2003) summarized the characteristics of organization with an inbuilt capacity for change as follows: (a) Linking present and future: able to see the current situation as an extension of the past and a precursor to the future. (b) Making learning a way of life: finding, spreading, and managing knowledge as an expected activity for all. (c) Actively supporting and encouraging day-to-day improvements and changes. (d) Ensuring diversity in teams that encourages openness to new ideas and change. (e) Encouraging mavericks: mavericks are risk takers, often uncomfortable with business as usual. Their search for change often makes others uncomfortable and creates resistance to change, but it is becoming increasingly clear that in order to have a focus on transformation, an organization must encourage and respond to mavericks. (f) Sheltering breakthroughs: organizations by their nature tend to try to maintain the status quo. In order to be flexible enough to adapt to new conditions, there must be a shelter and support for new ways of doing things—a separate department, that is, an independent unit with its own goals and operating systems—some structural shelter that nurtures the new approach and gives it a chance to succeed. (g) Integrating technology: technology is a vehicle to change, but it must be a means to an end, not an end in and of itself. (h) Broadening and deepening trust: people will see proposed changes as legitimate and support them when they trust those around them and those leading the effort, but without that trust, they are more likely to resist or ignore the new idea.

Movements toward change tend to fail under certain identifiable conditions. These include placing too much emphasis on the initial steps toward change and not providing long-term leadership and support, assuming that introducing change means that it will be accepted and implemented, assuming that everyone in the organization has the same goals and interests, and failing to see the change and the organization broadly enough—an example of failed systems thinking (McLahan, 2002).

Contingency Theory

Contingency theory says that there is no one best way of managing to reach organizational goals. The best management style is based on a variety of internal and external conditions. Therefore, a leadership style that is appropriate in one situation may not be appropriate in another. Contingency theory links with the Grenier (1972) model discussed previously since structural forms and managerial characteristics are contingent on the phase in which the organization is functioning. Each successive growth stage corresponds to a managerial style. Other aspects of contingency theory are long-range structural adaptation within the system (Darwinian) and within the environment (Singerian). Familiarity with the environment, willingness and ability to change, and information acquisition and feedback response are all prerequisites for change (Schoderbek et al., 1990).

Contingency theory also builds on the concept of systems equifinality; there is no one best way to reach systems goals. Initial inputs do not determine the extent of goal achievement, and outputs may vary even when the inputs are consistent (Kimbrough & Nunnery, 1988). The latter feature may be one reason why systems thinking has been overlooked in circles that espouse scientific management models. Yet the concept of equifinality provides answers to problems in organizations. The nonlinear approach can promote a manager's ability to cultivate an environment for creative problem solving and change. Problem solving, therefore, takes the shape of multifaceted intervention.

Misconceptions about Systems Thinking

While general systems theory and systems thinking as concepts have had broad appeal and have been under discussion for half a century, practical applications in some areas such as public health have been slower in coming than was anticipated. Two misconceptions about systems thinking have been problematic. (a) Systems thinking has been seen by some as a rejection of traditional scientific views that are linear, reductionist, mechanical and framed by spatial, temporal, or mechanical metaphors. (b) Some have seen systems thinking as lacking in scientific rigor. Opponents have pointed out that most of the techniques used in systems thinking and modeling are based on mathematics and the physical, biological, and social sciences and have been used to conduct rigorously controlled experiments.

Sometimes there are attempts to apply a systems approach inappropriately. General systems thinking has sometimes been applied in situations that did not call for that depth of approach and where direct line cause-and-effect thinking would have been adequate to the task. Sometimes, they also noted, individual behavior, values, decision-making processes, or elements of the systems model being developed are not adequately considered, creating blind spots in the overall view of the system and leading to what Senge (1990) called "fixes that fail." Mulej et al. (2003) identified systems thinking applied only partially and failure of the current model of teaching specialized sciences to allow for teaching of systems thinking as problems in developing successful systems applications.

Unintended consequences are another issue in applications of systems thinking. It is a misconception to assume that approaching an issue from the nonlinear systems perspective will produce linear results. Because systems are by definition complex and adaptive as described previously, they can be expected to behave in unpredictable ways. Unintended consequences within and external to the system should be expected (Chapman, 2005). Chapman described some ways to anticipate and perhaps forestall such consequences: analyze the system from as many aspects as possible, identify as many of the operating feedback loops as possible, identify which operating feedback loops will be affected by the planned change, and envisage the system operating with the planned adjustment in place so as to try to identify as many outcomes and impacts as possible.

Systemic Interventions

Marney and Smith (1964) provided an intervention model citing four major determinants of system change: feedback, organizational memory learning (refined and developed over time), change capacity, and system–environmental relations. For example, a system can choose to change or not. If the decision is to change, resources and energies must be marshaled accordingly. Change is costly, however, and the system needs to balance its immediate fiscal position against long-range survival needs. Change requires continuous feedback, a capacity to learn from feedback, and knowledge of how to design mechanisms that allow change to occur. In any case, the system must be cognizant of its environmental relations.

Feedback Requirements

Like their counterparts in business and industry, educational administrators need to sense organizational signs of decline and assess the cost of system disruptions. A built-in and ongoing feedback system can act against system decline by identifying regulatory and maintenance necessities.

The importance of feedback from within as well as from outside the organization cannot be overemphasized. It nourishes the self-regulatory processes, allows the system to evaluate its viability and contributions, and detects needed changes in the communication system. Systems require specific mechanisms, both formal and informal, for receiving, manipulating, and using the data gained from feedback.

In his review of a feedback classification system developed by Carlson and others, Hearn (1958) outlined various types of feedback. Continuous feedback allows a controlled amount of feedback to be monitored regularly. Mechanized continuous feedback, non–labor intensive, can provide continuous, valuable self-correction. Security systems are an example. Intermittent feedback arrives at specified intervals or, on some occasions, unexpectedly. Open-door office hours, regular meetings, or regular classroom observations are examples of intermittent feedback mechanisms. Proportional feedback designates feedback that is controlled by the amount and type of information that the system needs. For example, if an administrator is out of touch with faculty, students, staff, or constituents or unaware of how others perceive him or her, feedback needs tend to be higher. Proportional feedback can also be targeted feedback, as it is capable of prioritizing informational needs.

Relay feedback refers to an "on" or "off" flow of information: feedback is relayed only if and when it is requested. Continuous and intermittent feedback usually incur high costs. Relay feedback loses data or promotes other inefficiencies. Proportional feedback has the most value, but it is time consuming and time bound. A combination of relay and proportional feedback allows timeliness to become less of an issue. In the *informed organization*, however, feedback may be generated quickly via electronic mail and quickly analyzed by computer programs designed for that purpose.

Looking Toward the Future

Unrest in Organizations

Systems theory can be applied in many ways to organizational theory and practice. For systems thinkers, this is an exciting time, marked by a convergence of naturalistic inquiry, general systems theory, and any number of auxiliary paradigms. The research that management systems scientists have offered is now being recognized as only a preview of what systems science can do. Bertalanffy's (1968) interdisciplinary energy is being reinfused to encourage businesspeople, educators, and scientists to read widely outside their own disciplines. A part of this new energy is being generated by common recognition that old ways of thinking about and doing things simply are not responsive to all that is happening in system environments. This new state of affairs in organizations has often been described as *chaos, turbulence*, or *permanent white water*.

Harmon (1989) called for the integration of three current trends: technological revolutions in communications, a demand by employees for more complete and meaningful work, and the rising pressure for efficiency, fueled by fast-paced and increasingly global competition. Traditional organizations are suffering acute stress because of the struggle to fit these trends into an organizational design created for a disappearing world.

Toffler (1990) said that "survival of the fastest" will be the hallmark of the 21st century. The "fastest" are those with the ability to shorten development times, to move products and services faster and closer to consumers, and to use information almost instantaneously. Toffler envisioned a new and accelerated role of knowledge in the creation of wealth. Imagination, values, images, and motivation will be components of this knowledge. He suggested that there will be a new economic significance of free expression, "as governments that were closed begin to open the valves of public discussion."

Schein (1989) identified holographic, multigoal, heterarchical, coordinational, informed systems designed for controlled diversity or for harmonies of dissimilar elements as systems forms being considered. He believed that they may be the beginning of a major organizational revolution. Organizations need covenantal relationships, according to DePree (1989), who viewed contractual relationships as stifling and having nothing to do with reaching human potential of any kind. In his view, the advantages of covenantal relationships are that they induce freedom, not paralysis; rest on shared commitments; fill deep needs and make work meaningful; reflect unity and poise; enable organizations to be hospitable to the unusual person and unusual ideas; and tolerate risk and forgive errors.

At the international level, Ohmae (1990) described an economic system that "follows its own logic and develops its own webs of interest, which rarely duplicate the historical borders between nations" (p. 183). In a borderless world, any small movement in any economy affects all economies. Pluralism is a fact of life, not a generous concession to other nations. Another economist (Carroll, 1988) believes that entire organizations will be selected or replaced in the future as some organizational forms become obsolete and others become more viable. He views adaptation as severely constrained by existing forms. Carroll insists that organizational ecology demands that organizations and environments move toward isomorphism. An empirical correspondence should exist between environmental change and patterns of organizational founding and mortality.

Systems theorists are studying the realities of functioning at the edge of chaotic environments (Brown & Eisenhardt, 1998). As the speed of change heightens, as connectivity broadens information availability, and as intangible features of the contingent environment multiply, educational organizations need to rethink organizational change (Davis & Meyer, 1998). Reacting to change or even merely adapting to change may not provide adequate methods for keeping the educational system in tune with cultural, political, and economic environments. System interventions must be rethought.

In the highly volatile environment that exists today, educational administrators and practitioners need to learn to promote newfound leadership tactics: creating new learning and instructional methods that raise the bar, launching new programs regularly, raising the standards of excellence and performance, redefining learner needs and expectations, and increasing the pace at which all of education ensures its viability (Brown & Eisenhardt, 1998).

One of the most profound lessons to be learned is how to build our interventions and strategies on the basis of future scenarios. System interventions and strategies are built from events and circumstances relevant to a current and historical environment. Scenario planning and plotting is a new strategic process that holds the potential to revise how educational practitioners create change. Being able to deal with problems associated with some future scenario is wholly different from dealing with existing circumstances from a current or historical frame of reference.

Regulating Variety in Organizations

Conflict emerges in organizations when the need for variety is unappeased. As Ackoff (1974) suggested, "Few have tried to redesign education in broad interactive terms. To do so requires recognizing that the current system is a Machine Age product of reductionist, analytic, and mechanistic thinking. We need

a system that is the product of expansionist, synthetic, and teleological thinking" (p. 74). How much formal educational systems have learned since then about adaptation and reconfiguration is still to be determined. In practical terms, this suggests that the "products" of our mechanistic schools are not highly adaptable or able to meet the educational needs of our society. A cursory glance at current political and business claims about the ineffectiveness of our schools reinforces this concern.

Beer (1974) felt that there are only two ways to provide the requisite variety to keep organizations alive: reduce the variety generated by the system in order to match the available regulatory variety (variety attenuation) or amplify the variety of the system's regulatory part (variety amplification).

From Beer's perspective, if administration cannot handle the amount of variety existing in the system, the administrator lessens the variety and everyone follows the rules. That is one way of regulating. The other way is to increase the variety in the regulatory systems. This can be done by deciding how to deal with more information from the system and/or by passing on regulatory responsibility to the lowest levels. The law of requisite variety, an organizing rule for systems, has important implications for educational administrators. Human need for autonomy and internal locus of control is a psychological equivalent of self-regulation in systems theory.

Gleick (1987) saw evolution as chaos with feedback. Chaotic variety becomes organized when feedback is available, pertinent, and psychologically usable by the receiver. Feedback, so often depicted as linear, in reality is multidirectional. Those in charge generally have the most intimate knowledge of how decisions made elsewhere affect the rest of the organization. Leaders should be encouraged to organize their feedback for use throughout the organization. The rank and file enjoy requisite variety when, acting as feedback senders, they select the most important data to be diffused.

Davis and Meyer (1998) believe the added exposure and access that variety breeds adds significant new capacity to learners' and instructional providers' abilities. This added capacity increases the likelihood that our educational systems will act in concert with current and future trends. This technique is used internationally in business and military planning and has applications for educational planning as well.

Metaphor and System Modeling in Educational Administration

Metaphors have been in vogue primarily in natural and social sciences as a means of describing complex phenomena. Poets use metaphor as a means of capturing and sharing multidimensional human experiences that are unique and universal simultaneously.

Clancy (1989) stated that in a world of "endemic complexity," metaphors help sort out and classify phenomena, helping humankind understand and express one phenomenon in terms of another. Although metaphor is not the thing in itself and does not enable users to grasp the entire implied experience, as Clancy argued, a metaphor can shape views of experience. "It is important to recognize that metaphor is an integral part of our thought process. We use metaphor much as we breathe; we cannot avoid its use or its consequences" (p. 13).

Metaphors of heroic journey, games, and wars furnished business with its self-perceptions. The journey elicits images of ships, captains, and even ships of fools. The game metaphor is associated with players, playing fields, and winning or losing. The metaphor of war engenders visions of soldiers receiving and giving marching orders. These are not particularly systemic metaphors; instead, they call up visions of heroic life and heroic death. Educators have always resisted these as images for schooling even as they adopted some of the philosophical underpinnings.

Another set of metaphors is closer to Boulding's (1964) system of system structure: the machine, the organism, and society. The spirit of the machine metaphor remains in organizations in the form of *Taylorism*, the term for unreconstructed "scientific management." The mechanical metaphor implies systems that are ultimately predictable, rational, and deterministic. People are cogs in the machinery, and the leader is an omniscient machine operator. The organism metaphor retains traces of determinism: there is a "genetic" fate in the evolution of the system that must grow and adapt even in the face of complexity and ambiguity. The society metaphor, which

educational administration theories have often embraced, is built on and may overemphasize culture, stakeholders, rituals/myths/symbols, shared values, and meaningful leadership.

Systems thinkers can accept part or all of the organism and society metaphors but still find them insufficient for the future. The metaphors of journey, game, and war can be associated with three paradigms that have had limited success: journey, wealth, and the institution. Much of the organizational literature has been concerned with wealth and institutionalization.

A new eclectic paradigm needs to be merged with these metaphors in order to see the future. One approach is the prototype of the "market fair," a medieval convenience that allowed craftspeople, sellers, and clients to conduct their affairs anywhere. The watchword of this paradigm is extreme flexibility; the most important role is that of the "shape changer," a leader whose role and work shifts constantly according to need.

Developing new metaphors and models in any field can be risky since the new forms may elicit commitments to new roles, policies, and an organizational life that changes continually. One of the most profound changes notable in society today evolves from the variety of metaphors associated with the information age. Davis and Botkin (1994) have cited numerous examples showing that the speed at which educational practitioners change may be directly associated with the speed at which new forms and structures of education develop. Information availability and transfer are readily available to a variety of users, including schooling-at-home users, new organization forms and partners, and more.

The metaphor of the "learning organization" (i.e., the organization that learns [Kiechel, 1990]) has not received as much credence as hoped for in educational institutions (Senge, 1990). The difference is that organizations are not for learners but rather *of* and *about* learners. Yet no organizational member should be exempt from universal, systemwide continuous learning (Senge, 1990).

Throughout this discussion, references have been made to the unrealized potential of systems thinking in all fields, educational administration being no exception. But what can a systems-literate administrator plunged into the district, the school, or the principal's office achieve in practical terms?

He or she can think differently and approach organizational issues, positive or negative, differently. The practice of conceptual modeling should become second nature, allowing the administrator to devise maps and diagrams that help organize and question data and that enable system members to choose alternatives and enact them. Every case of variety out of control needs this decisive thought: can this variety producer contain the means of self-regulation, or must regulation be imposed from outside? This mandates an administrators' clear understanding of energy sources and drains in a school system.

Literature on school administration over the past several decades reveals a marked influence of nomothetic biases. Nevertheless, idiographic themes have persisted and seem to be coming into their own in the present state of organizational turmoil. After all, nomothetic planning and evaluation has not yielded what educators or businesspeople seek—the sense of productive, quality, enjoyable work. The place to begin to change the systems of the world is in the minds of the new thinkers in that world. All that may be required is a return to ancient metaphors of what it is to learn. Ironically, these are systems metaphors.

One example of an ancient metaphor in new dress is provided by Engleberg's (1991) discussion of integrative study. Integrative study is a curriculum that cuts across discipline lines, combining two or more to provide in-depth study of a particular theme or issue. Ross and Olsen (1993) identified five models for implementation in the middle and high schools: single subject integration, which presents content from one curriculum in relation to real life; the coordinated model, which links two or more teachers teaching different disciplines to the same students separately but cooperatively; the integrated core model, which has one teacher working with the same students for two or more periods, teaching one content area in the context of another (e.g., language in the context of science); the integrated double core model, which has two or more teachers teaching the same students within two integrated cores (e.g., math

in the context of science and language in the context of social studies); and the self-contained core model, which has one teacher with multiple-subject credentials working with one group of students all day, teaching all skills and content within one or more contexts.

Engleberg (1991) insisted that acute social and political problems cannot be solved by specialists because resolution of these problems lies at the integrative level. Integrative study takes place in the here and now, among those we live with, and exerts a benign influence on the community in which it takes place. A more cogent belief statement in support of lowering walls between schools and the communities they serve could hardly exist. Engleberg added that everyone is capable of some level of integrative study. Integration implies participation in schooling by teachers, parents, students, and all other stakeholders. It is intrinsically democratic.

Bredeson (1985), however, found that in only one out of five schools studied were parents highly involved in a formal sense. "In fact, one principal indicated that there were problems in having parents in the schools because they often do not understand many things that are occurring. Therefore, parental involvement was more often viewed as supportive and tangential as opposed to a rich source of expertise and knowledge" (p. 44). Structures for parental involvement were bounded by predetermined roles, much like the roles of all other school stakeholders.

Aside from the implications for less "bounded" schools, the notions of integrative study deserve closer inspection for their systemic version of curriculum. Engleberg believes that since living systems can be understood only by reference to their transformations over time, the objects of integrative study are narratives (histories, case histories, works of literature, and so on). Specialists can function only as long as there is an integrative matrix in which they can find a place. The occupants of the realm of wholes create and maintain these matrices. Engleberg (1991) called for educators to "face away" from their specializations, which have been so powerfully developed and researched by the "realm of parts." He suggested that educators fear facing "nothingness" when they turn away from the disciplines, but instead they will find themselves *facing life*. The challenge then becomes the difficulty of sharing wisdom without imposing dogma that accentuates fragmentation. This implies a new vision of teachers and administrators as facilitators of learning, not mere sharers of facts.

Engleberg assumed that language exists to facilitate integrative study, carrying learners forward through an integration of differences in which differences are maintained and preserved. While integrative study sessions require a moderator and rules of discourse, their object should be works of art, dense in information, rich in meaning. "Framework statements" (i.e., "a cumulative repository of insights") are the specified outcomes. Correlative outcomes are personal and social integrations. Extending Engleberg's thesis logically, competency-based (specialist) education may be no more than part sensitive, able to function only if whole-sensitive integrative studies provide the matrices on which the carefully honed parts can hang without fragmentation.

The old metaphors invoked may be "liberal arts," "great books," storytelling, or even mythmaking. Speaking of the qualitative uses of mythmaking in organizational development, Boje, Fedor, and Rowland (1982) identified the development of myths with the development of specific organizational situations. When a myth is guiding decision making and strategy successfully, it is a developing myth. When the myth and the organization have become completely intertwined, it is a solid myth. Myth split occurs when groups in an organization begin to develop competing myths in order to encourage renewal or survival. Myth shift occurs when reformulation and perhaps new leadership of the organization is imminent. Although this is reminiscent of Kuhn's (1962) discussion of paradigm shifts, it is obvious that new metaphors and myths appear with every "scientific revolution" and that sometimes older metaphors and myths are reinstated in contemporary, more acceptable forms.

Bredeson (1985) referred to the influence of studies in general semantics that called attention to the importance of metaphors as a mediator of reality. Bredeson said that the very words or analogies used may limit one's view of phenomena and the world. Aristotelian logic is seen as having drawn researchers in the Western world into a habit of "two-valued"

thinking, accompanied by broad sets of fundamental and pervasive silent assumptions and premises. Thus, thought is governed by perceptions of "either–or" rather than "both–and" or, even more sensibly, "many and all." On this basis, educators imagine ultravariability in systems with difficulty if at all. Unchanged semantic traditions may prevent administrators from handling diversity and welcoming the "chaos" of accommodating many simultaneous "truths" and interpretations.

Bredeson (1985) cited a number of authors and their uses of prevailing metaphors about the nature or the role of school administrators: the principalship as a "constellation of positions" (Knezevich, 1975) and the principal as consummate manager, organizational change agent, educational/curricular leader, applied philosopher, school manager, behavioral scientist, politician, gamesman, broker, facilitator, missionary, and gardener (Blumberg & Greenfield, 1980; Kmetz & Willower, 1982; Lipham & Hoeh, 1974; Martin & Willower, 1981; Sergiovanni, Burlingame, Coombs, & Thurston, 1980; Wayson, 1971). Bredeson believed that such topologies are inadequate to represent any school leader and that, instead, a composite imagery is needed. Further, he suggested that metaphors of purpose might be more instructive. If the perceived purpose of the principalship is to behave like a chief executive officer, command center behavior will follow, and the principal will rarely leave the office. If the perceived purpose is student control (disciplinarian), that will be the principal's modus operandi. If the perceived purpose is to ensure that a school survives in a tight economy, that will engender another set of behaviors. These prevailing metaphors result, systemically, in a maintenance function that occupies more than three-fourths of an administrator's time and energy, overriding any vision or holistic view of the present an administrator might otherwise have.

Bredeson (1985) suspected that the expectations of education administration students skew their preparation toward specific skills development that will help them survive immediately in new administrative appointments. This, he says, may help create, foster, and maintain a culturally standardized image of the school principalship that reinforces metaphoric themes and old myths, all of which can stand in the way of change. The obvious solution is to teach skills and theory, with course work geared toward reflective, theory-based, systemic considerations. Two-valued thinking will not suffice in schools of the 21st century.

Conway (1985) called for a rediscovery of values in schools that would parallel current efforts to rediscover values in business organizations. He felt that society asks schools to restructure themselves and their culture, to go through an organizational learning of the most difficult type. Efforts to control time spent on tasks or to extend the school year represent a linear, unitary approach to change that Conway associates with single-loop learning. In contrast, Argyris and Schön (1978), and Bateson (1972) have envisioned a more complex approach called, respectively, double-loop learning, deuterolearning, and reconstructive learning. Conway (1985) noted that culture change will not take root without appropriate reconstructive learning. The way beliefs are ordered and linked in a psychological framework can be an analogy of the way organizations believe or disbelieve. He asked, What are the structural connections that map the organization? Can new information enter to reorganize beliefs, revise ideology, and repattern paradigms? How does the organization view time? If there is a fixation on a given time period, for example, the system tends toward closure. The closure is effected through a "narrowing" process that may include denigration of the past, dissolution of future-oriented functions such as planning, or institutionalizing of a "now" attitude to the exclusion of other time frames. The excluded frames then represent disbelief regions. Conway reported that in his own experience, certain indicators of structural closed-openness conditions have surfaced: knowledge disavowal (it cannot be true), belief avoidance (silence), and the relative time perspective that can either expand or truncate organizational memory.

Hoy and Ferguson (1985) attempted to create a model for assessing school effectiveness across such variables as innovation, student achievement, cohesiveness, and organizational commitment. They borrowed Steers's (1977) argument that the goal model of school effectiveness and the systems model are complementary. This supports the synthesis of the two models that resulted in the dimensions or variables used in Hoy and Ferguson's (1985) study. The researchers chose these dimensions specifically because they addressed Parsons's (1960) imperative for social organizations: adaptation, goal attainment, integration, and latency (creation and maintenance of motivational and value patterns). They sought to draw on the perceptions of different groups in the schools they assessed. Notable for its absence was any effort to sample student perceptions. Although their empirical analysis was considered reasonably successful, the researchers believed that an expanded model could be developed to allow more focused comparative study of schools on both rational systems and subjective dimensions. This would imply the use of a variety of methodologies.

Liberating Systems Theory: The Critical Stance

Earlier in this chapter, the systems paradigm was described as currently being merely surface minded and transported far from its origins. Flood (1990) produced a detailed, reasoned argument for a complementarist theoretical position that is open and conciliatory, overcoming the theoretical fortress mentality that has developed in the various streams of systems thinking. Subservience of any of these streams to another, he stated, is a distortion of what systems thinking represents. Certainly, such subservience has kept systems thinking from realizing its full potential. Flood (1990) felt that those who seriously consider the system's epistemological ideal cannot help but conclude that beyond the positivistic (objectivist, or a belief that sense perceptions are the only admissible basis for human knowledge) and the interpretivistic (hermeneutic, or the study of theories of interpretation of texts) ideals of science, the emancipatory force of critical self-reflection is necessary. He is concerned that managers tend to hide behind the facade of common interests, claiming to have surveyed opinion and reached consensus when, in fact, only a narrow band of interests are being served. The critical approach has the potential to destroy the facades of rationality and objectivity that allow decision makers to defend their own interests on grounds of rationality.

Further, whereas much of management and systems literature applauds convergence and universality, Flood (1990) argued for divergence and multiple truths, reminding us that it is anticritical to expect that we can work toward a view we all feel comfortable with. In the interests of social conservatism, he noted, ideological positions are ignored and objectivist research is preferred. However, in the critical inquiry framework, debates over soft versus hard systems research are irrelevant since the choice is not between nonreflective positivistic and nonreflective interpretivistic research positions but between nonreflection and critical self-reflection. It is conceptual reflexivity, those self-confirming and self-perpetuating aspects of systems science, that has constrained system thinking. This has ensured that the abstract, paradigmatic richness of the word system is hidden under an avalanche of desolate labels for such things as "hair-replacement systems," "school systems," and "information systems," which have no metatheoretical connection. What Flood demanded is antiprovincialism, a thinking between paradigms, a mapping of the intellectual world of systems thinking, in order to embark in new directions.

Greatly oversimplified, Flood's (1990) map includes positivistic, interpretivistic, and critical–reflective (complementarist) regions of systems theory. He placed Herbert Simon squarely in the positivistic region, with Ackoff (1979), and Checkland (1981) belonging to the interpretivistic region. Jackson and Keys (1984) occupy the complementarist region along with Flood (1990). The first two regions are isolated by their methodologies, whereas those oriented to critical reflection view all theories and methodologies as complementary. What the complementarists see as necessary is a way to break through the "colonized" territory ruled by traditional management and operations research scientists and also through the paradigmatic isolation of competing worldviews into the openness and "emancipation" of critical systems theory.

Such a breakthrough would allow researchers to deal with such issues as employee empowerment, workplace diversity, cultural anomalies, coercion, ideologies, and ownership of values in a deliberately normative way. Subjective inquiry would be openly acknowledged, not as antithetical to systems science but as part of its legitimate discourse.

Postulating a role for critical systems theory immediately removes most of the "two-value" constraints that have plagued systems literature on educational administration. "Machine" images as metaphors for social systems, those associated with management by objectives, management information systems, accountability, control, efficiency, competencies, and performance objectives (Sergiovanni et al., 1980), can be complemented by contextual analysis and "getting the drama right" (Bolman & Deal, 1991). Surely in an era that speaks incessantly about the need for liberation and empowerment, control must be imagined differently.

Orton and Weick (1990) argued that researchers (and practitioners) must continue to transform methodology to serve theory and not the other way around. DeGreene (1990) also admitted that the theory and practice of management must change with the dynamic reconfiguration in the environment. In addition, the approaches and tools that appeared to be well adapted to more "linear" times may be counterproductive during today's epoch of massive structural change. Robb (1990) noted that "getting a better tailor" to alter organizations will not work, for it is necessary to enter into states of disorder from which new orders can emerge.

If schooling is to flower in the future, if integration is to democratize institutions and nations, systems thinking is, indeed, a wave of the future. The study of systems thinking in this chapter carries implications for the reader's reflection on both organizational life and the research that examines that life. Both avenues for reflection lead to new questions and, furthermore, to a questioning of the conventional

ACTIVITY 2.3

Organizational Future

Addresses ISLLC Standard 6C

Consider the organization within which you work. What do you consider the future of that organization to be in the next 5 years? The next 10 years? In what ways are the concepts and issues discussed in this chapter a part of that future as you see it? Why? In what ways are they not? Why not?

established two-dimensional focus of schooling and positivistic research. At no other time in the history of formal education has such questioning been more needed than it is today.

SUMMARY AND FUNDAMENTAL CONCEPTS

General systems theory was developed initially as a method of understanding complex biological and social phenomena. Based on the work of Bertalanffy (1968) in biology, systems theory has developed a wide range of proponents and applications. Systems thinking has untapped potential to be a significant basis for current reforms in education. It can help a leader understand the structures and operations of organizational life, both generally and more specifically in schools and school districts.

Systems may be seen as closed or open. They differ from aggregates in that they share certain characteristics, including internal and external environments, input, throughput, output based on teleological behavior, communication, processes, feedback, identification of leading parts, dynamic homeostasis, and negentropy, among others. Schools and school districts may be seen as open systems. Whether (or to what extent) they are complex adaptive systems as defined in this chapter is a matter of discussion and debate.

Organizations are constantly in a state of change because the environments in which the organizations exist and the expectations of those organizations change. This is true of educational organizations as well as of organizations in general. Looking ahead, systems thinking can be the basis for understanding the current perspectives on educational organizations and the metaphors under which they function and for developing new metaphors leading to greater understanding and more effective change. Developing and articulating those metaphors and overseeing the changes that result are the tasks of an effective leader.

Fundamental Concepts

The fundamental concepts that follow have been discussed in this chapter. The citations that conclude each concept indicate the Interstate School Leaders Licensure Consortium (ISLLC) Standards and Functions related to the concept. The Arabic numeral refers to the ISLLC standards, and the letters refer to the functions as presented in the table found inside the front cover.

- Systems thinking is scientifically based and interdisciplinary. (1A; 6C)
- Systems are not aggregates. (1A; 6C)

- Systems may tend toward openness or closedness. (1A; 6C)
- Systems are state maintaining, goal seeking, purposeful, and dynamic. (1A; 6C)
- Systems models vary from simple to complex. (1A; 6C)
- Systems have a variety of characteristics that allow them to seek goals, respond to their environments, grow and change, and maintain their individual identities. (1; 2E; 2F; 2I; 3A, 3B, 3D; 4; 6B, 6C)
- Complex adaptive systems are those that have the ability to adjust to changes in the environment, in goals and objectives, and in their own component parts while maintaining their integrity. (1; 2E; 2F; 2I; 3A, 3B, 3D; 4; 6B, 6C)
- A variety of theories apply systems thinking to organizations and their management, including educational organizations. (1A; 6C)
- Systems thinking is a useful tool in managing operations and change in organizations, including schools and school districts. (1A; 6C)
- Metaphors can be useful tools for modeling complex evolving systems. (1A; 6C)
- Systems thinking will be a significant tool for managing educational systems in the 21st century. (1; 2E; 2F; 2I; 3A, 3B, 3D; 4; 6B, 6C)

Chapter 3 expands on the application of systems thinking to education in general and schools in specific. It will introduce the construct of the "learning organization" and endorse it as the most appropriate organizational model for educational endeavors. The nature of the educational system and of schools, of change, and of the nature of leadership that can produce effective change is central to the discussion.

Case Study

Systems Thinking: The Case of Karen Avery

Addresses ISLLC Standards 1, 2, and 6

Karen Avery is a new department chair in a/an (rural/suburban/urban school district—select one for this exercise). The district is relatively traditional in the operation of its schools. During the past year, Karen has participated in a task force created to devise a new strategic agenda for the school district. The national mood to discredit schools, educational practices, and school administration had settled abruptly in her community 14 months ago. There are issues of budget, parental support, student performance, and changing external expectations on the part of the community, the state, and the nation to be considered, to name a few.

A variety of subgroups to the task force met over the past year to study and recommend rigorous improvements, actions, and changes. One subgroup recommended adoption of total quality management to assess outcomes on a continuous basis and act on the findings. Another subgroup recommended a service management–based program to include better strategic planning, decentralization of control, more flexibility, and consistency—all designed to release the intrinsic motivation in administrators, teachers, and students alike. A third subgroup recommended "a return to basics": stronger discipline, greater expectations, more definitive rules, and structure. Karen's subgroup was locked in controversy and had not provided its own solutions.

At the end of the year as she reflected on these events, Karen realized that the task force had offered only piecemeal solutions to problems that appeared unmanageable.

During the summer break, Karen attended a series of seminars at a national education convention held in her community. She elected to attend several seminars dealing with systems theory as applied to the schools.

At the first fall meeting of her subgroup, Karen explained the rudiments of what she had learned about systems thinking. Her ideas interested the group and helped them focus on some recommendations for a new school model.

Karen's group proposed a new school structure. In their system, teachers would become guides, advisers, motivators, and managers rather than content disseminators and disciplinarians. New resources, including interactive computers, videodisks, peer tutors, projects, and learning laboratories, would be employed to transfer knowledge to the student. A guide would advise, motivate, and manage students and also coordinate the efforts of other new elements in the system, such as inexpensive assistants, apprentice guides, senior citizens, parents and peer tutors, well-designed projects, discussion groups, learning laboratories, and resource people. Parents in particular would help decide instructional goals in conjunction with their guides and the individual students. A student's development in the physical, social, moral, psychological, and intellectual domains would be considerations. The traditional classroom environment would disappear. A guide and student or small groups of students would work together to attain agreed-on developmental goals. A guide would be responsible for each student through one of the four developmental stages within K–12, about 4 years per student per development stage.

Each student's educational goals would be matched to uniquely suited educational resources orchestrated by the guide and other assistants.

The guide would not work independently but would be integrated into a cluster of three to six guides. The guides would participate in decision making and exert control over a particular cluster. In each cluster, all guides would be responsible for cluster success. Clusters themselves would create and meet goals. A master guide would also serve in the cluster as an instructional leader. The success of each cluster would depend on parent and student satisfaction. As clusters succeeded in meeting the specified developmental goals, parents would elect the very best clusters. Effective clusters would survive as a result of incentives and rewards and financial support from the school district.

As goal achievement occurred and students passed through developmental stages, new student goals would become more specific. Learning laboratories would provide specialized expertise in traditional, discipline-oriented, and cross-disciplinary areas. Students' progress in their clusters would earn them the privilege of attending a variety of learning labs. These labs would operate independently of the clusters but cooperatively.

Questions

1. From a systems perspective, what factors do you believe contributed to the marginal results obtained by the various subgroups within the task force?
2. Identify and discuss instances of an aggregate mentality at work in this case.
3. Would Karen today describe her school or school system as relatively open or relatively closed? Why? Classify the new model as open or closed. Why?
4. Discuss the feedback mechanisms that exist in the new school model.
5. Does the new school model appear to invite chaos or amplify variety? Discuss why.
6. In what ways does the new school model apply the following systems concepts?
   a. Input–throughput–output
   b. Synergy
   c. Leading part and emergence
   d. Dynamic homeostasis
   e. Equifinality
   f. Negentropy
7. Karen's group has proposed an extensive revision of the traditional approach to the operation of schools. If her group is to function as a lead part of the school system in the effort to deal with its problems, what

steps might it take to move the district toward their vision? What might help her group function as a lead part in the effort? What might impede her group's effectiveness? How might impedances be dealt with?

REFERENCES

Ackoff, R. L. (1974). *Redesigning the future*. New York: Wiley.

Ackoff, R. L. (1979). The future of operational research is past. *Journal of the Operational Research Society, 30*(2), 189–199.

Argyris, C., & Schön, D. A. (1978). *Organizational learning*. Reading, MA: Addison-Wesley.

Ashmos, D. P., & Huber, G. P. (1987). The systems paradigm in organization theory: Correcting the record and suggesting the future. *Academy of Management Review, 12*(4), 607–621.

Bar-Yam, Yaneer. (2000). *Overview: The dynamics of complex systems—Examples, questions, methods, and concepts.* Retrieved April 18, 2006, from http://necsi.org/guide/index.html

Bateson, G. (1972). *Steps to an ecology of mind.* New York: Ballantine Books.

Beer, S. (1974). *Designing freedom*. New York: Wiley.

Bertalanffy, L. von. (1968). *General system theory: Foundations, development, applications.* New York: Braziller.

Blumberg, A., & Greenfield, W. (1980). *The effective principal: Perspectives of school leadership.* Boston: Allyn & Bacon.

Boje, D. M., Fedor, D. B., & Rowland, K. M. (1982). Myth-making: A qualitative step in O.D. interventions. *Journal of Applied Behavioral Science, 18*(1), 17–28.

Bolman, L. G., & Deal, T. E. (1991). *Reframing organizations.* San Francisco: Jossey-Bass.

Boulding, K. E. (1964). *The meaning of the 20th century: The great frustration.* New York: Harper & Row.

Bredeson, P. V. (1985). An analysis of the metaphorical perspectives of school principals. *Educational Administration Quarterly, 21*(1), 29–50.

Brown, S. L., & Eisenhardt, K. M. (1998). *Competing on the edge: Strategy as structured chaos.* Boston: Harvard Business School Press.

Carroll, G. R. (Ed.). (1988). *Ecological models of organizations.* Cambridge, MA: Ballinger.

Chapman, J. (2005). Unintended consequences. *Nursing Management, 12*(4), 30–34.

Checkland, P. B. (1981). *Systems thinking, systems practice.* Chichester: Wiley.

Chin, R., Bennis, W. G., & Benne, K. D. (1961). *The planning of change.* New York: Holt, Rinehart and Winston.

Churchman, C. W. (1979). *The systems approach.* New York: Dell.

Clancy, J. J. (1989). *The invisible powers: The language of business.* Lexington, MA: D. C. Heath.

Conway, J. A. (1985). A perspective on organizational cultures and organizational belief structure. *Educational Administration Quarterly, 21*(4), 7–25.

Davis, S., & Botkin, J. (1994). *The monster under the bed: How business is mastering the opportunity of knowledge for profit.* New York: Simon and Schuster.

Davis, S., & Meyer, C. (1998). *Blur: The speed of change in the connected economy.* Reading, MA: Addison-Wesley.

DeGreene, K. B. (1990). Nonlinear management in technologically induced fields. *Systems Research, 7*(3), 159–168.

DePree, M. (1989). *Leadership is an art.* New York: Doubleday.

Emery, F. E. (Ed.). (1970). *Systems thinking.* Harmondsworth: Penguin Books.

Engleberg, J. (1991). On integrative study. *Systems Research, 9*(1), 5–17.

Flood, R. L. (1990). *Liberating systems theory.* New York: Plenum Press.

Galbraith, P. (2001). *Systems thinking: A lens and scalpel for organizational learning.* (ERIC Document Reproduction Service No. ED453186)

Gleick, J. (1987) *Chaos: Making a new science.* New York: Penguin Books.

Grenier, L. E. (1972, July–August). Evolution and revolution as organization grows. *Harvard Business Review,* 37–46.

Harmon, F. G. (1989). *The executive odyssey.* New York: Wiley.

Hearn, G. (1958). *Theory building in social work.* Toronto: University of Toronto Press.

Hodge, B. J., & Anthony, W. P. (1988). *Organization theory.* Boston: Allyn & Bacon.

Hoy, W. K., & Ferguson, J. (1985). A theoretical framework and exploration of organizational effectiveness of schools. *Educational Administration Quarterly, 21*(2), 117–134.

Hudson, C. G. (2000). At the edge of chaos: A new paradigm for social work? *Journal of Social Work Education, 36*(2), 215–228.

Immegart, G. L., & Pilecki, F. J. (1973). *An introduction to systems for the educational administrator.* Reading, MA: Addison-Wesley.

Jackson, M. C., & Keys, P. (1984). Toward a system of system methodologies. *Journal of the Operational Research Society, 35,* 473–486.

Kast, F. E., & Rosenzweig, J. E. (1972). The modern view: A systems approach. In J. Beishon & G. Peters (Eds.), *Systems behavior* (pp. 11–28). New York: Harper & Row.

Katz, D., & Kahn, R. L. (1966). *The social psychology of organizations.* New York: Wiley.

Kets de Vries, M. F. R., & Miller, D. (1989). *The neurotic organization.* San Francisco: Jossey-Bass.

Kiechel, W., III. (1990). The organization that learns. *Fortune, 121*(6), 133–136.

Kimbrough, R. B., & Nunnery, M. Y. (1988). *Educational administration: An introduction* (3rd ed.). New York: Macmillan.

Kmetz, J. T., & Willower, D. J. (1982). Elementary school principals' work behavior. *Educational Administration Quarterly, 18*(4), 62–78.

Knezevich, S. J. (1975). *Administration of public education.* New York: Harper & Row.

Krivov, S., Dahiya, A. & Ashraf, J. (2002). From equations to patterns: Logic-based approach to general systems theory. *International Journal of General Systems, 31*(2), 183–205.

Kuhn, T. S. (1962). *The structure of scientific revolutions.* Chicago: University of Chicago Press.

Lipham, J. M., & Hoeh, J. A., Jr. (1974). *The principalship: Foundations and functions.* New York: Harper & Row.

Marney, M. C., & Smith, N. M. (1964). The domain of adaptive systems: A rudimentary taxonomy. *General Systems, 9,* 113.

Martin, W. J., & Willower, D. J. (1981). The managerial behavior of high school principals. *Educational Administration Quarterly, 17*(1), 69–90.

McLagan, P. A. (2002). *Change leadership today.* ERIC EJ655036.

McLagan, P. A. (2003). *The change-capable organization.* ERIC EJ663955.

Mulej, M., Bastic, M., Belak, J., Knez-Riedl, J., Pivka, M., Potocan, V., et al. (2003). Informal systems thinking or systems theory. *Cybernetics and Systems: An International Journal, 34,* 71–92.

Ohmae, K. (1990). *The borderless world: Power and strategy in the interlinked economy.* New York: HarperCollins.

Orton, J. D., & Weick, K. E. (1990). Loosely coupled systems: A reconceptualization. *Academy of Management Review, 15*(2), 203–223.

Parsons, T. (1960). *Structure and process in modern societies.* New York: Free Press.

Robb, F. F. (1990). Morphostasis and morphogenesis: Contexts of design inquiry. *Systems Research, 7*(3), 135–146.

Ross, A., & Olsen, K. (1993). *The way we were . . . the way we CAN be: A vision for the middle school through integrated thematic instruction* (2nd ed.). Kent, WA: Books for Educators.

Salisbury, D. F. (1990). General systems theory and instructional system design. *Performance and Instruction, 29*(2), 1–10.

Schein, E. (1989, May). Corporate teams and totems.*Across the Board, 26,* 12–17. (Reprinted from *Sloan Management Review,* Winter 1989).

Schoderbek, P. P., Schoderbek, C. G., & Kefalas, A. G. (1990). *Management systems: Conceptual considerations.* Boston: BPI/Irwin.

Senge, P. (1990). *The fifth discipline: The art and practice of the learning organization.* New York: Currency Doubleday.

Sergiovanni, J. J., Burlingame, M., Coombs, F. D., & Thurston, P. W. (1980). *Educational governance and administration.* Upper Saddle River, NJ: Prentice Hall.

Simon, H. A. (1970). *The science of the artificial.* Cambridge, MA: MIT Press.

Steers, R. M. (1977). *Organizational effectiveness: A behavioral view.* Santa Monica, CA: Goodyear.

Toffler, A. (1990) Toffler's next shock. *World Monitor, 3*(11), 34–44.

Wayson, W. W. (1971). A new kind of principal. *National Elementary Principal, 50*(4), 9–19.

Willis, V. J. (1977). *Emergent–devolvent synchrony in general systems: Creativity as a special case.* Unpublished doctoral dissertation, State University of New York at Buffalo.

Schools as Organizational Systems

In chapter 2, we discussed systems thinking as a means of approaching leadership in organizations as well as systems theory and the nature of organizations. In this chapter, we explore the enduring parameters of schools as organizations today. Classical, humanistic, and systemic constructs are discussed, and, additionally, the integrating elements that unite organizational thought are investigated. Using metaphor, we look at schools as organizations. In addition, current school issues are identified and related to the metaphors discussed. We also discuss schools for tomorrow as grounded in quantum and other new science theories.

Ways of Thinking about Organizations

Organizations can be conceptualized in a variety of ways: through definition, through one's perception of reality, and through theoretical constructs, even metaphorically, as in terms such as *turbulence* or *chaos*. Organizations may be defined as associations of several to many people who are attempting to fulfill a common goal. Etzioni (1964) saw organizations as social units that are deliberately constructed and reconstructed to seek previously defined objectives.

Shafritz and Ott (1992) specified the basic elements of an organization: implicit or explicit purposes, the ability to attract participants, the ability to acquire and allocate resources to accomplish goals, an internal structure that is used to divide and coordinate activities, and reliance on a member or set of members to lead and manage others. Banner and Gagne (1995) developed a parallel list that included goal direction, relatively identifiable boundaries, social interaction, deliberately structured activities, and a culture common to the members.

Organizations are deliberate creations. There must be a reason for the construction of an organization. However, Colapinto (1994) pointed out that any human organization will contain both formal and informal structures. Formal structures are those that are often defined in writing and serve as a frame of reference for interaction among those within the organization and for those interacting with the organization from outside. Informal structures are generally unwritten and often become the more real centers of authority and responsibility.

Some view organizations as having life cycles. These may be characterized by specific types of behavior. Although the behaviors may exist at the same time within an organization, one is likely to be dominant. In the initial developmental stage organizations may emphasize innovation and creativity. In the next stage emphasis may be on informal communication, structure, and development of a sense of family, on solidifying the organization. Next may come emphasis on efficiency, production, and observation of rules and procedures. Finally, in the full maturity of the organization, the emphasis may be on monitoring the external environment, self-renewal, and expansion of the organization's domain.

Weber (1947) devised the term *bureaucracy* to represent tightly controlled organizations. Organizations were understood to be well-oiled machines. Specialized parts of the machine were differentiated by function and combined through an authority-based, hierarchical structure. Rules, policy, and procedures enabled the specialized parts to achieve maximum effort. Woodward (1981), on the other hand, described organizations through their technology, a combination of processes or functions that were the result of technological operations. Individuals, in turn, are identified in relation to a technology component. Thus, organizations are conceived through a convergence/divergence lens. The principal effect on specialized organizations is the differentiation of activities so as to integrate the organization with its common purpose(s). This rational deterministic view maintained primacy for many years. Then other theorists began to question the relevance of this "things or events" focus. Today, many visualize organizations as being much more ubiquitous and complex (Barnard, 1938; Drucker, 1987; Mintzberg, 1983; Ouchi, 1981; Peters, 1992). They perceive organizations as instruments to maximize efficiency, a deterministic view that gives greater credence to the "science of work" and management and their applicability to the human component.

Taylor's (1947) work concentrated on the concept of scientific management. His five principles of work design advocated the following: shift work responsibility to management (managers plan and design work, while workers implement), use scientific analysis to devise precise worker actions, select the best workers for a given job, train workers effectively, and monitor work and worker performance (Morgan, 1986). Frank and Lillian Gilbreth (Spreigel, 1953) tested Taylor's principal contributions studying human motion through work study analysis of performance. In his discussion of management, Fayol (1949) provided a comprehensive explanation of organizations. The functions of management, he said, are planning, organizing, directing, coordinating, and controlling. By and large, Fayol's perspective is seen in most discussions of organization today. Although Taylor and Fayol are not viewed as human relations pioneers, their work led to further studies of the human component in organizations. Their scientific analysis, combined with Weberian classical structure, has had a profound effect on the structuring of organizations as they exist today.

Others viewed organizations as systems of interdependent human activities, as human beings were considered another essential resource required to achieve specific organizational purposes. Numerous authors and theorists viewed the human component as special in regard to the organization, not only as a resource for the organization to consume but also as an element whose behavior affects both the structure and the function of an organization. To these writers, people were the organization. For Mayo (1945), the major task of management was to organize the people in the organization and to secure the commitment of individuals to achieve ends for the organization. Mayo's work addressed the importance of communication to successful management as managers succeeded or failed based on their acceptance or disapproval by workers. McGregor (1985) postulated further that managers exhibit beliefs about human behavior in two broad categories of assumptions: theory X, viewing employees as untrustworthy, lazy, and in need of careful controlling, or theory Y, a more positive view of the employee. Similarly, Likert (1987) questioned why units in organizations with low efficiency ratings tended to have job-centered supervisors, whereas supervisors with the best performance records appeared employee centered. Both Likert and McGregor consider building supportive relationships an ideal supervisory practice.

"The manager's job is to foster attitudes and behavior which promote efficient performance, stimulate and use creativity, generate enthusiasm for experimentation and innovation, and learn from interaction of others," said Pugh and Hickson (1989, p. 183). Blake and Mouton (1988) supported an analogous approach. Their managerial grid identified behaviors they believed can be taught and learned. Other human behaviorists have examined a variety of aspects of human components in organizations. Herzberg (1968) found distinctively different factors associated with job satisfaction and job dissatisfaction. Theorists who simply maintain that being more supportive is sufficient must recognize further that job enrichment brings about more effective utilization of people in organizations and increases job satisfaction.

As described by Bolman and Deal (1997), the human resource perspective takes the view that organizations can be energizing, productive, and rewarding to their participants. They identified basic assumptions of the human resource model as follows: organizations exist to serve human needs rather than the reverse; people and organizations need each other; when the fit between individual and system is poor, both suffer; and a good fit profits both the individual and the organization. Bolman and Deal (1997) went on to say that an effective human resource model of organization includes specific practices that enhance the fit between the individual and the organization. These practices include hiring right and rewarding well, providing security for employees, promoting from within, providing training and education for employees, and sharing organizational wealth with the workers.

Schein (1985) extended assumptions about the human aspects of organization beyond the rational, social, and needs-based models. His complex model recognized that life events and development drive individual motives and that these motives vary across situations and time. Management therefore simply cannot be coordination and control or even largely supportive but must include a diagnostic component whereby managers learn and react to both individual employees and organizational expectations. This added level of understanding of people enables the organization to cope with internal and external realities, adapting to the external and integrating the internal.

Argyris, Putnam, and Smith (1985) developed a strikingly similar diagnostic view. In organizations, people are often confronted with built-in contradictory elements. These contradictory elements cause people to adhere to stability-producing conformance mechanisms and, in the next instant, be penalized for lacking initiative, aggressiveness, or adaptability. Different norms are needed in organizations, norms that decree openness in communication, openness to action, and openness to learning.

For those concerned with the human relations model of organizations, the organizational climate is significant. Cornell (1955) initiated the use of the term *organizational climate*, defining it as a blend of the perceptions of the members of the organization about their roles and the roles of others in the organization. Tagiuri and Litwin (1968) specified that consideration of an organization's climate must distinguish the objective from the subjective environment, persons from situations, the aspects of the organization appropriate to the issue under consideration, and the structures and dynamics of the organization appropriate to the issue under consideration.

To this point, organizations have been viewed as structure, as management, and as human relations. While each of these perspectives provides valuable data to use in understanding organizations, another approach to organizations is provided by systems theorists. Ultimately, in this view, organizations are organic entities or seen as sets of processes that interact with an environment. In the traditional rational/deterministic, scientific, and human relations perspectives, theorists attempted to constrain uncertainty in the organization. With the advent of systems theory, organization study addressed uncertainty across various boundary conditions. The input–throughput–output–feedback model became the cornerstone of organizational inquiry.

In the earliest studies of organizations using systems methodology, environment, boundaries, variety, feedback, and other elements were treated as another set of scientific variables with which to contend. School systems' environments were thought to include the school, the school district, the state, and the federal government. Others added the community, parents, businesses, and various professional and educational associations. In the mechanistic organization, problems were resolved in various specialized departments. As change, innovation, and uncertainty continued to grow, the organization became incapable of handling the ensuing variety. In the short term, the organization's communications broke down from the maze of problems that were encountered, and this breakdown may be inevitable.

Lawrence and Lorsch (1986) maintained that the additional requirement of the organization to interact with its environment complicates organization thinking processes even further. By advocating a contingency approach, they addressed the issue of integration and differentiation in the organization's internal environment and externally within the organization's suprasystem. In the organization's attempt to integrate and differentiate effectively, conflict resolution founded in compromise and competence balances organizational functioning. Thompson (1967) termed this an *alignment function*, where structure, technology, and environment interact.

Other authors further expand systems thinking as applied to organizations. Understanding organizations in terms of biology and evolution, Hannan and Freeman (1988) proposed a population ecology perspective of organizations. They attempted to explain the replacement of outmoded forms of organization with newer forms. Some organizations prosper and survive, whereas others die out. Silverman (1971) saw all organizational study as inadequate and conceptualized an "action" frame of reference. This approach views organizations as outcomes of the interaction of motivated people who are attempting to resolve their problems and pursue their needs.

The traditional organizational viewpoints focus principally on a series of impersonal elements to explain organizations' functions, while the human relations viewpoint focuses on a relationship orientation. To understand organizations further, we need to think about organizations as they occur in reality. Hypothesizing about either the traditional or the human relations focus serves only to limit our true understanding of the reality within and surrounding organizations.

Systems Thinking and Learning Organizations

Systems Thinking in Education

Brown and Packham (1999) have applied a systems model to organizations, focusing on critical systems thinking and systemic learning. They defined critical systems thinking as a way of thinking about the world as constructs rather than objective realities. Such constructs assist in problem solving. The basic themes of critical systems thinking are critical awareness, improvement, and methodological pluralism.

Critical awareness is the examination and reexamination of taken-for-granted assumptions and interpretations of the conditions that gave rise to their creation. Critical awareness helps maintain awareness of the need to consider a variety of views in defining problems. *Improvement* in the sense of the social constructivist is central to critical systems

thinking, according to Brown and Packham (1999). *Methodological pluralism* implies equifinality, a characteristic of systems theory that indicates that a variety of avenues may be available to reach the same goal. The appropriate avenue may be defined by the current circumstances.

Brown and Packham (1999) observed that systemic learning is the basis for action research. It embodies both the finding of new information and the taking of action as a result of the discovery. *Organizational learning*, according to Brown and Packham, is a social construction through a reflective process that transforms acquired cognition into knowledge. It becomes organizational learning when accountability assigned by the organization is accepted by a person and is acted on.

When considering organizational improvement that comes from critical systems thinking and systemic learning, Brown and Packham (1999) identified five possible approaches: action learning, in which improvement is based on disclosure of thoughts to colleagues in group settings and then action is taken; metaphors, in which one or more metaphors are used to gain insights into problems; scenarios, in which models of possible futures are developed to inform strategic planning; storytelling, in which a recounting of the past is used to assist in problem solving and planning; and dialogue, in which conversation is analyzed to determine the thinking that lies beneath it.

In education, systems thinking can be applied in a wide variety of ways, both as a means of solving problems and as a means of avoiding problems that arise from taking a narrower perspective. It can be applied in both administrative and instructional circumstances.

An example of systems thinking in education is the Cecil County, Maryland, School District. In 2001, the Maryland State Department of Education offered grants to support schools willing to use the Baldrige Criteria for Excellence in Education to study and apply systems thinking. The Baldrige National Quality Award is given by the president of the United States to a business, educational, or health care organization that has demonstrated that it is outstanding in seven areas: leadership; strategic planning; customer and market focus; measurement, analysis, and knowledge management; human resource focus; process management; and results (National Institute of Standards and Technology, 2005). The Cecil County School District became involved. Although the state grant ran out before the district could come fully to grips with its commitment, it continued and implemented two major initiatives: systems thinking for leadership and classroom systems for learning. In the former case, all mid- and top-level leaders received formal training in systems thinking using the Baldrige criteria. A standing committee monitors the school leaders' implementation of the systems approach, and school and department plans are now developed on the Baldrige model. In the latter case, during the period 2003–2005, approximately 25% of the district's 1,300 teachers have been trained in the use of classroom learning systems. Summer training programs for teachers are supported by follow-up training and sharing, and each of the district's 29 schools has staff coaches to provide support in implementing the programs (Roberts, 2006). As of 2006, the district's goals were to move toward training of 100% of the teachers, to continue to assess the effectiveness of the program in the classroom, and to seek external consultants who could evaluate the effectiveness of the overall effort.

Classroom teachers leave their profession at a very high rate in the United States. Recruitment and replacement efforts are very costly and have a major impact on the budgets of individual schools, districts, and the system overall.

Minarik, Thornton, and Perrault (2003) joined others in ascribing the high dropout rate to a combination of causes, including inadequate preparation, lack of principal support, feelings of isolation, low economic rewards, unsafe work environments, and student discipline and motivation problems. They went on to say that the current approach to the problem—identify the vacancy and hire anew—deals with the symptom of the underlying problem, not the problem itself. To get to the root of the problem, they said that systems thinking, which can approach a complex issue in ways that traditional thinking cannot, is necessary. In this case, they proposed five interrelated strategies for improving teacher tenure: developing effective principal leadership of the school, transforming the school and the district to an employer of choice, hiring appropriate teachers, enhancing relationships within the educational community, and promoting connectedness with the larger community. Taking this multipronged approach, they suggested, would be a more effective means of extending teacher retention.

Direct applications of systems thinking to classroom learning are also described by Rosenthal (2003) in a discussion of teaching systems thinking through courses in environmental art at the college level, Gulyaev and Stonyer (2002) in a discussion of using general systems theory as an approach to tertiary science education in New Zealand, and d'Apollonia, Charles, and Boyd (2004) in a discussion of the positive effects of teaching evolutionary theory used complex systems thinking as a frame of reference. Moving beyond the individual classroom, Jenks (2004) has recommended that public schools' present curricula would be improved by teaching systems thinking to students. This curriculum revision would be based on four overall themes: competencies and attitudes needed to understand and engage in systems thinking in both the natural world and social organizations; development of self-knowledge, self-mastery, sensitivity to others' points of view and the ability to interact and cooperate with others; understanding of the connectiveness of knowledge and the ability to interconnect concepts from various disciplines in solving problems; and ability to evaluate information for usefulness and credibility when making decisions and applications in personal and group life.

Learning Organizations

In learning organizations people continually expand their capacity to create results, new and expansive patterns of thinking are nurtured, collective aspiration is set free, and people are continually learning to see the whole.

Learning organizations are distinguished from other organizations by mastery of certain basic disciplines called component technologies. Senge (1990) mentioned five keys to initiating a learning organization: systems thinking, personal mastery, mental models, building a shared vision, and team learning.

Systems thinking is the discipline that draws other disciplines together, creating a coherent body of theory, according to Smith (2006). He noted that Senge saw systems theory's ability to address the whole and to examine the relationships among the parts as key to integrating the other disciplines.

Learning organizations share certain characteristics. They provide continuous learning opportunities for members, use learning to reach organizational goals, link the performance of individual members to the overall performance of the organization, foster inquiry and dialogue and make it safe for members to share openly and take risks, embrace creative tension as a source of organizational energy and renewal, and are continuously aware of and interacting with the organizational environment.

Members of a learning organization experience two types of learning, according to Giesecke and McNeil (2004). Maintenance learning is finding better ways to do current work. It helps ensure that procedures and processes are efficiently done. It is short term and may not be sensitive to changes in the organizational environment. Anticipatory learning is the acquisition of new knowledge and building the new knowledge into the organization so that goals and objectives can be met in a changing environment. In a learning organization, both types of learning are vital.

A number of reasons make it desirable for an organization to become a learning organization. Farago and Skyrme (1995) noted that many of the initiatives for organizational improvement, such as total quality management and business process reengineering, have not met initial expectations. What is needed in addition to the previous models, they said, is the ability to cope with rapid and unexpected change, flexibility in meeting changing situations, and freeing up frontline staff to respond to identified needs rather than constraining them with routine processes. These conditions can be provided by learning organizations, according to Farago and Skyrme.

How is a learning organization created? According to Giesecke and McNeil (2004), there are a series of identifiable steps to take. First, there must be a commitment to change, and this must be led from the top.

Then managers need to connect learning to the organization's operations. Learning for learning's sake is not the goal; learning for the sake of useful applications is. Assessment must be made of how well the organization can address the five disciplines that are characteristic of learning organizations. The vision of a learning organization must be communicated throughout the membership. Organizations must demonstrate and model a commitment to learning. Bureaucracy and red tape must be reduced so that cooperative activities and communication are encouraged. Learning must be rewarded and then shared. Continuous learning and adaptation to change are necessary for creating of a learning organization. A learning organization is neither static nor a fixed condition. It is created and defined by its actions.

Concern has arisen that educational systems—schools and districts—have not shown themselves to be learning organizations in the sense discussed here. It should be a given that schools are learning organizations. However, there is a gap between the idea and the reality. Even Senge expressed doubts about schools being able to function as learning organizations in the sense that he has recommended. He saw most teachers as constrained by conforming to rules, goals, and objectives. From Senge's point of view, schools are focused on passive intake of information, and their systems are often fragmented and layered. Moving schools to the Senge model would be no easy task given their bureaucratic, hierarchical structure and emphasis on maintaining their current state.

ACTIVITY 3.1

Participating in a Learning Organization

Addresses ISLLC Standards 1, 2, 3, 4, 5, and 6

Consider the organization in which you work. Is it a learning organization as discussed here? In what ways is it so; in what ways is it not? What could be done to move the organization toward becoming a learning organization?

One can identify a school that is a learning organization by responding to a series of questions based on a list developed by Brandt (2003):

1. Does the school have an incentive structure that encourages adaptive behavior?

2. Does the school have challenging but achievable goals?

3. Can members of the school organization accurately identify the school's stage of development?

4. Does the school gather, process, and act on information in ways best suited to the school's goals?

5. Does the school have an institutional knowledge base and processes for creating new ideas?

6. Does the school exchange information frequently with relevant external sources?

7. Does the school get feedback on its activities and services?

8. Does the school continuously review and refine its processes?

9. Does the school have a supportive organizational culture?

10. Is the school an open system, sensitive to the external environment, including social, political, and economic conditions?

Internal Processes of Organizations

In this section, we examine briefly four internal processes of organizations that are developed more fully in other chapters: decision making, leadership, communications, and change.

Decision Making

One school of thought maintains that decision making is the key to understanding organizational effectiveness. Organizational effectiveness is thought to reside principally in managerial actions. For decision theorists, all managerial action is decision making. In older theories, rationality is thought to be a cornerstone of decision making. The decision maker rationally determines a best course of action from a multitude of variables to maximize organizational functioning. Simon (1977) replaced the rational-economic person, who maximizes decisions, with the administrative person, who merely satisfices. *Satisficing* is defined as a situation in which the manager does not take the time to seek optimal resolution of a problem but rather settles for one that is satisfactory, one that "will do." Organizational action is based individually or organizationally on selection of satisfactory alternatives using a few comparatively relevant factors with which the person is capable of dealing.

In this viewpoint, organizations should necessarily strive to create situations in which unprogrammed decision contexts become programmed. Using these contexts, such as habits, routines, standard procedures, structure, and culture, allows the decision maker and the organization to function effectively. Both March (1988) and Simon (1977) believed the decision maker capable of a *bounded rationality*. Through negotiation and bargaining, the organization progresses to an organizational limit.

Organizations rarely resolve conflict completely because they avoid uncertainty by creating acceptable decision making. Accepting this short-term view results in the need to search for more satisfying alternatives. Over a period of time, this process leads to organizational learning based on a reactive stance. March (1988) contended any "garbage can" full of decision rules and action alternatives will suffice if the organization persists in the short-term action environment. Mintzberg (1989) postulated that individuals as decision makers fall into four patterns: the entrepreneur, who leads and determines new purpose; the disturbance handler, who resolves others' problems; the resource allocator, who disperses financial resources; and the negotiator, who seeks compromises.

Lindbloom (1980) termed his version of the decision-making process *disjointed incrementalism*, or the "science of muddling through." It is nearly impossible, according to Lindbloom, to find a rational/deterministic model of decision making in use in most organizations. At best, decision making in organizations may suffer from too much reactiveness, too few long-term horizons, and little effective control.

Tannebaum (1968) held a different view. While many believe that effective control in organizations is and should be concerned primarily with how managers use a particular decision-making model or process, Tannebaum, argued that decision making as a process should be shared with a wider variety of players. This provides a greater volume of realistic alternatives from which to satisfice. In Tannebaum's studies, people in organizations are interested not in exercising more control than others but simply in exercising more control themselves. Organizations would be wise to consider diminishing the slope of hierarchies to some degree and restricting their attention to who exercises power. Then the organizations should institute processes or models that allow members to increase the volume of decision making. This shared responsibility firmly moves organizational thinking away from its machine connotations to a shared decision-making perspective.

The organizational function of decision making is discussed more fully in part IV.

Leadership

Theorists, authors, and practitioners alike have sought to find links between leadership and other dimensions of organizations. Leadership is often confused with management in this regard. Some authors choose to emphasize similarities between leadership and management, others emphasize differences, while still others remain oblivious to these issues (Rost, 1991). Leadership and management are both processes and necessary elements of organizations. In the humanistic frame of reference, the behavior of the leader or manager also becomes a point of relevance. As processes and behaviors that have been discussed over time, however, neither is clearly understood. Mintzberg (in Rost, 1991) lamented that he and his counterparts have yet to understand leadership thoroughly or to define it adequately. Similarly, most authors and theorists have not been able to state leader or manager definitions succinctly (Rost, 1991).

However, much has been uncovered. We know a lot about what constitutes leadership and what does not. Leadership in the human context is behavioral and situational (Bass, 1990; Yukl, 1989). Leadership can also be viewed from a functional orientation: as a set of relationships, as influence, as change, as motivation, as communication, as conflict, or as growth and development (Knezevich, 1989). Similarly, leadership

can be a set of personality traits, a particular formal position, or a status. In each regard, leadership has been recognized as an imprecise concept. It can be rooted in values, action, or power. Above all, it is indeterminate and variable across numerous contexts.

As we continue to attempt to define leadership in this human context, we will undoubtedly continue to find leaders who are "all of the above." In this regard, Rost's (1991) definition seems highly appropriate. "Leadership is an influence relationship among leaders and followers who intend real changes that reflect their mutual purposes" (p. 98). But as we look to larger issues in an organization, leadership takes on a greater focus. In this respect, Davis and Davidson's (1991) perspective on leadership is insightful. "Leadership is defined in terms which relate a vision of the future to strategies for achieving it, which are capable of coopting support, compliance, and teamwork in its achievement and serve to motivate and sustain commitment to its purpose" (p. 201).

According to Damme (1995), leadership development falls into several models. These include integrated models, in which actual work problems are reviewed in order to learn from experience; nonintegrated models, in which a link is not made between theory and practice; and individual personal development models, in which an integrated model is applied at several levels: organizational, psychological, and experiential. A strong trend exists toward integrating action and learning, personal and professional development, and leadership and organizational development in order to support organizational change, according to Damme.

The concept of leadership is developed more fully in chapter 4.

Communications

A great portion of our communication takes place in organizations, and, as Etzioni (1964) said, we spend a great deal of time in different kinds of organizations. Monge and Eisenhart (1987) cited three frames of reference that enable us to view organizations and communication conveniently. In the traditional era, the positional frame of reference viewed communication up, down, and laterally through set positions in the bureaucratic hierarchy. In a more modern era, the relational frame sees communication as occurring naturally through relationships between participants. The organization is shaped and given meaning through these interactions. In another view, the cultural frame stresses the importance of stories, rituals, and work among its members and determines from these how the organization communicates. The real organization in this sense emerges from daily actions of members in their work.

Communication develops into organizational networks. Social, structural, and functional channels are the essence of communication in organizations. As an example, in a school these channels might involve communication of faculty with faculty, administration and parents; administration with faculty/staff, administration, and district; and district with school administration, faculty, and staff.

These ideas about communications are developed more fully in chapter 6.

Change

Over time, organizations of all styles begin, mature, and decline. The life cycle of organizations is thus considered through various maturity–decline and change models. In general, organizations spend a great deal of time in periods of stability punctuated by brief transition periods. Ecologists term this phenomenon *punctuated equilibrium*. Others call it *metamorphosis* or *dynamic equilibrium* (Schön, 1987; Starbach, 1981). These life cycle models usually address formation, development, maturity, and decline. Hannan and Freeman (1988) see a founding and disbanding sequence. Faced with crisis, organizations tend to either move to a next stage of development or develop renewal or revitalization mechanisms. Depending on internal and external environmental factors, organizations may choose strategies of renewal or revitalization. In other contexts, organizations may adopt a particular model of change based on a shift in strategic alignment.

Lewin's (1951) three-stage model of unfreezing, change, and refreezing helps explain these shifts in vision. *Unfreezing* involves overcoming natural defense mechanisms or discontinuities by scanning the environment for available change parameters. *Change* then

demands creating a willingness to step into a new environment, a shift of mind-sets. *Refreezing* involves vigorous pursuit of the new vision. In this process, people shed old frameworks and understand and implement new ones. In small, simple firms, this can be a relatively easy task, but as organizational size increases, the change process becomes exponentially more difficult to invoke and keep on track.

Empirically based change strategies are structured on a systems management perspective. Setting new goals, monitoring change, and holding individuals accountable reflect a typical methodology. From the organizational development perspective, empirically based change seeks to focus on individual motivations for change. From a power perspective, empirically based change seeks to reduce conflict, bargain, and negotiate preference. In contrast, theory-based change seeks to derive change in other ways. The innovation management model focuses on developing factors that improve the probability of successful implementation. The social or cultural model focuses change directly at values held in the organization's domain and seeks change through development of different value sets (Schein, 1985). The organizational learning model focuses change on learning how to learn. Dysfunction and defensiveness are replaced by creating new ways of thinking about future states (Argyris et al., 1985). Finally, the constructionalist model emphasizes social meaning. Change involves creating and realizing new behaviors, symbols, and activities (Deal & Kennedy, 1982).

Conner (1992) suggested that nine steps were central to effecting successful change: peer group consensus must be recognized as the major influence on willingness to change and acceptance of change, two-way trust related to change is necessary, change should be thought of as skill building developed from training, time must be allowed for the change to take hold, a committed person should be placed in charge of the change, change must be proposed as response to a real threat from outside the organization, transition rituals should be made the pivotal elements of the change, training should be provided in the new values and behaviors, and tangible symbols of the new directions must be provided.

The concept of organizational change is treated more fully in chapter 13.

Other Characteristics of Organizations

In this section, we examine several other characteristics of organizations that affect their functions and/or structures: power; culture; size, structure, and complexity; and organizational health.

Power

Thinking about organizational decision making leads to discussions about power in organizations. Individual, unit, or organizational decisions are based on interests, an orientation to act in one manner or another. Power in organizations relates directly to how these interests are pursued and defined and the variety of ways in which individuals position and perceive their interests. Various agendas collide as different players defend their interests. Power in organizations results as systems simultaneously compete and collaborate. Up and down the traditional organization, power is a mechanism by which the organization resolves conflict.

Sources of power in organizations are numerous (Morgan, 1986). In the Weberian tradition, power is derived from legitimate authority. The right to rule is a recognized tradition in most organizations, as formal authority is typically associated with position or command structure. Some organization members can gain power from control of scarce resources. Dependence must be established for this source of power to provide control. Structure and policy or regulation also is a source of power and another form of control in organizations. Bureaucratic regulation, plans, promotion requirements, and other regulatory rules give power potential to various controllers. The ability to influence decision making through these structural mechanisms is most often seen in the control of decision making, whether controlling decision agendas, actual decision making, or organizational objectives. The control of knowledge and information and the determination of what receives attention are also of vital importance. Key actors often resort to information and knowledge control, whether weaving a pattern of dependency via structure, change, gatekeeping, or limiting information or knowledge capability. Boundary management also is a source of power. Control of integrating mechanisms can promote progress, while isolation can limit progress. Other sources of power include networks, control of power relations, alliances, control of technology, coping with uncertainty, managing meaning, and gender management (Morgan, 1986).

Recognizing and understanding these sources of power enables the practitioner to cope with power's many political milieus. In a complex pluralistic society, power is viewed as inevitable. The questions become how to compete, how to collaborate, how to avoid, how to accommodate, or how to compromise (Thomas, 1977). While radical views pit factions against each other or unitary views integrate interests, in the pluralistic view the nature of the traditional organization is checked by the free interplay of various interest groups that have a stake in the organization.

In our society, the play of power creates numerous organizational forms. Organizations are constantly pulled by contending concepts and typically yield in a singular direction. As an organization adapts to a single purpose, power molds a modified political system. New images of the organization then form: as good management, quality or excellence, service, or information. The new image affects organizational action in various ways, depending on the current power structure in the organization. In the work unit and functional divisions, these power sources create, sustain, and support values and interests. They become the latest agenda. As the organization adopts these agendas, the organization transforms itself to this new value-interest system.

Organizational hierarchy breeds formation of new agendas. As career-focused persons become more specialized, the organization loses its ability to function effectively as careerists override new interests in favor of their own developed specialties. The organization tends toward superficiality as it loses its ability to know real necessities. Various power sources continue to act out their own agendas in lieu of pursuing substantive work. Consensus development abounds as individual sources seek support and favor for their interests (Bergquist, 1993). In this light, the ideology of the dominant political forces can become the ideology of organization and lead to entropy. In the end, understanding the "political" image of organizations allows us to understand the real limits that exist in the sociopolitical organization.

These ideas are developed further in chapter 10.

Culture

If power in organizations is as ubiquitous as it seems, it certainly appears that its presence can also become ingrained. In a similar fashion, other elements of the organization can also become habitual. Organizational theorists, sociologists, anthropologists, and managers have long recognized this trait in organizations. From an anthropologist's perspective, culture is a complex system that includes knowledge, beliefs, arts, morals, laws, customs, and other habits acquired by people in society (Sackmann, 1991). Culture can be characterized by breadth and depth. Breadth of culture is the range of values that are agreed to. Depth is the number of committed members and the strength of agreement on cultural norms (Freeman, 2006). In this respect, a cultural study of organizations has become a means to study the components of an organization. Whether uncovering mainstay principles, realizing hidden mental constructions, or identifying how members' personalities are determined or represented within the organization, cultural study in the organizational context has become the study of the conditions that create the ability of organizations to function and behave more effectively. The study of culture in organizations thus becomes a holistic integration mechanism whereby theorists and consultants study ways of thinking, feeling, and reacting that individuals and organizations have acquired and that somehow have been stored and transmitted through some form of symbolism. As a product of action, a shared system of meaning that incorporates the way people live and work in the organization, culture becomes a method to codify, modify, and control the organization (Sackmann, 1991). Schein (1985) stated that as the culture integrates an organization internally and adapts the organization externally, it defines the valid, correct way to inculcate new members. Phillips (1984) added that these products of action may become so typical that they become tacit.

The metaphor of organizations as culture offers an ideological view of the organization. As the organization's values and interests become the norm, they become symbols, rituals, meanings, and interpretations that openly or tacitly govern how the organization interacts internally and externally. No longer is the organization a collection of individuals or agendas; rather, it is an interdependent collection of shared meanings and circumstances. For example, American culture is one of individualism and separateness, while Japanese traditional culture is embodied in self-respect through service to a larger system. In an individualist culture, organizations reward individuals for "being first." In Japanese culture, the organization seeks commitment and loyalty to the collective.

Perhaps the greatest reason for studying organizational culture is that it allows us to observe the organization as it truly exists. The integration, fragmentation, and differentiation perspectives are all available to the researcher/observer. This approach offers us a crucial illustration of the organization's *ethos*: its historical purpose, power shaping, motivations, beliefs, informal settings, symbolic expression, visual data, and more. These norms, rituals, or symbols are open to scrutiny using various methods of inquiry (Jermier, 1991).

Thompson (2006) has argued that reculturing schools to produce a culture of trust, openness, and collaboration is a central issue in educational leadership. While there is no single universal approach for accomplishing this, Thompson has identified several useful strategies, including establishing a "no excuses" philosophy, developing a widely owned philosophy of teaching and learning, building trust and encouraging risk taking, shifting the focus of central administration from monitoring schools for compliance to active support, basing decisions on data rather than politics or favoritism, establishing shared accountability focused on results, and fostering a culture of continuous learning.

Size, Structure, and Complexity

The implications of size, structure, and complexity in organizations was best addressed by Mintzberg (1983, 1989). In his detailed analysis of design in organizations, Mintzberg identified five general structural configurations. The key differentiating feature in the design occurs as the result of some dominant part in each. In the simple structure, the upper echelon dominates and pulls the organization to centralize, utilizing direct supervision. In the machine bureaucracy, the technostructure dominates and causes standardization of work processes. In the professional bureaucracy, the *operating core* rules and causes the organization to professionalize through standardization of skills. In the divisionalized form the "middle line" dominates by coordinating and standardizing outputs. Finally, the adhocracy form coordinates the *support staff* and causes mutual adjustment in the organization.

The structure of the entrepreneurial organization (a simple structure) is characterized by little or no staff, a loose division of labor, and a small hierarchy. As its size is small, complexity also tends to be negligible. As an organization, the entrepreneurial firm tends to be informal, flexible, and responsive and operates with a sense of distinct purpose. Activities generally revolve around the owner or chief executive. As simple organizations mature, they tend to work toward the machine bureaucracy or professional bureaucracy.

In the machine bureaucracy, formal procedures, specialization, differentiation, and extreme hierarchy are common. A powerful support staff and middle management are needed for regulation control through standardization of the work. The organization is stable, consistent, and efficient in relatively stable environments. In unstable environments, it tends toward inflexibility and can then change only through long, drawn-out planning processes. As the size of the organization increases, the machine bureaucracy tends to become more and more controlled, to the point of redundancy. Decentralization usually occurs as the organization develops into a divisionalized form. Loosely coupled, autonomous divisions are subjected to performance controls in the form of standardized output, as directed from a central or corporate headquarters. This form is generally also the largest and most mature of the Mintzberg configurations.

The professional bureaucracy is a decentralized form of machine bureaucracy. The organization is characterized by autonomous and democratic professional work groups, typically subject to controls

of a profession. A large support staff functions as an administrative arm for the professional core. Complexity becomes extreme in this organization because various autonomous individuals or groups share allegiances to the organization and to external professional groups. As size increases, the professional bureaucracy becomes more and more difficult to operate.

Finally, Mintzberg (1983) postulated an *adhocracy*: a fluid, organic, and selectively decentralized organization. As the organization is characterized by autonomy and democracy, it is also the most innovative of the Mintzberg structures. Experts in teams typically work in highly dynamic and complex environments to carry out demanding and rapidly changing requirements. The organization appears to thrive on complexity. Size is a detriment.

More recently, Mintzberg (1989) added a sixth structure, the missionary organization. This organization is characterized by a rich system of values and beliefs and a strong sense of mission. This organization thrives because of the standardization of norms, reinforced by selection, socialization, and indoctrination. These organizations are typically highly decentralized and complex, as they enact complicated norms steeped in ideology.

In thinking about organization, authors and theorists have had to recapitulate regularly. For example, Blau (1977) defined structure as "the distribution, along various lines, of people among social position that influence role relations among these people" (p. 12). In this example, structure implies a division of labor, position, rules, and behavior. Structure uses power to achieve results. These organizations attempt to maintain a status quo. But as authors and theorists begin thinking beyond Weberian and, more recently, Japanese examples, they note that change may be the essence of organizations today. Thus, understanding how structure, size, and complexity affect organizations has been critical in the past, but today our focus must include how organizations change.

Organizational Health and Effectiveness

Organizations are part of a system of interlacing, interacting systems that are in a constant dynamic state. They may be construed as existing in various stages of health. Characteristics of healthy organizations include but are not limited to the following: defining themselves as systems; strong sensing systems for receiving current information on all parts of the system and its interactions; a strong sense of purpose; work to be done defines the structures and mechanisms of the organizations; information-driven team management; decisions made at the operational level; communication relatively open within the system; reward systems congruent with the work; operating in a learning mode; and high tolerance for different styles of thinking and ambiguity.

Crazy Bull and Prue (2003) emphasize the point that a healthy organization has a clear mission that all members of the organization can articulate and that is the basis of decisions. In such an organization, the members support one another, are committed to the organization's goals, and are realistic about the challenges that they face, leading to more innovative approaches to the organization's tasks. Creating and sustaining such an organization calls for the leadership to develop a clear process to achieve and maintain organizational health.

Roufa (1990) argued that organizational health is related to *person–environment fit*, defined as congruence in goals between the individual and the organization, resulting in the individual meeting the needs of the organization and the organization meeting the needs of the individual. The less congruent the goals, the more stress is generated and ill health results for both the individual and the organization.

Bush and Middlewood (2005) supported the position that people are the most significant element of any organization and that what distinguishes effective from less effective organizations are the quality and commitment of the people employed. This, they say, is even more significant an issue in situations where resources are scarce.

Defining organizational effectiveness as the result of the organization's pursuing its goals adequately, Ricotta (1992) posited that effectiveness would be affected by organizational life cycles. These include the entrepreneurial stage, where emphasis is on resource acquisition; the collectivity stage, where emphasis is on informal communications and structure; the formalization and control stage, where

---

ACTIVITY 3.2

Organizational Culture

Addresses ISLLC Standards 1, 2, 3, 4, 5, and 6

Describe the culture in the organization in which you work. Is it healthy in the terms discussed in this chapter? Is it effective in the terms discussed in this chapter? Why or why not? What could be done to improve the health and effectiveness of the organization in which you work?

---

organizational stability dominates; and the elaboration of structure stage, where the emphasis is on self-renewal and expansion of the organization's domain. These models are competing for preeminence in the organization. As each of these stages dominates, the organization must shift goals, resource allocation, and activities to remain in a state of good health.

Early in this chapter, organizations were investigated from traditional perspectives. In the following section, the reader is asked to think about organizations metaphorically. Since organizations are complex and paradoxical and no one viewpoint is absolutely relevant, metaphors can allow us to see differences not otherwise visible.

Images of Organizations

The use of metaphor to comprehend organizations is a common practice. Morgan (1986) and others (Bergquist, 1993; Clegg, 1990) have highlighted the process. In effect, it is a method of reducing complexity to manageable dimensions when considering the nature and functions of a system. Metaphors take a wide variety of forms, from the inorganic machine to the organic organism. Some of these metaphors are discussed next.

The Machine Metaphor

Classical management theory emphasized broad-based planning, coordinating, controlling, directing, and organizing (Fayol, 1949; Weber, 1947). Organizations whose major features resemble descriptions from the classical era abound, from the moderately large manufacturing firms or service firms to nearly every educational institution. As the machine metaphor implies, these organizations largely resemble the machine: efficient, hierarchical, highly centralized, planning oriented, highly regulated, highly organized, and tightly controlled (Mintzberg, 1983, 1989). Productivity is, to a large degree, the most vital measure of success and effectiveness. In addition, these organizations are deterministic, as demonstrated by the development of simple schedules or plans to larger, more encompassing strategic plans (Mintzberg & Quinn, 1988). Machine organizations move slowly and deliberately.

Machine organizations are highly rational. Tasks are straightforward, and precision is usually at a premium. These organizations create consistency and maintain stable environments. They are mass-production oriented. Differentiation of function and specialization of task are primal. Organizations whose primary purpose is to produce manufactured goods tend to take on a machine format. As manufacturing becomes less important in the economics of highly developed nations, the machine organization is becoming rarer. The machine organization positions the human component at two very different extremes: management controls, and subordinates are controlled. As a result, political conflict between functions occurs as power is sought to control resources, but informal mechanisms are developed whereby those lower in the hierarchy or with less power can contribute to decision making. Even though communication tends to be straightforward or top down, it also tends to be slow, as numerous levels of hierarchy need to be traversed for decision making and problem solving.

Early management theorists believed that they had discovered the "one best way," the productive organization (Morgan, 1986). However, many if not all of these theorists' machine principles are the basis of organizational problems today. Understanding organizations from a rational or technical point of view underscores the lack of attention to human components. It also creates organizations that adapt to changing environments slowly, are often mindless and unquestioning, and place organizational and other goals at a premium at the expense of human concerns. In many instances, the humans in the machine organization become complacent and unmotivated and lose their commitment to the organization. In the end, the organization may work at divergent purposes, in direct opposition to its organizational goals.

The Organism Metaphor

The study of organizations as open systems has brought new light to a variety of issues compounded during the machine age. Bertalanffy (1968), the lead theorist and researcher of the systems movement, felt that viewing parts of an organization does not allow us to gain a holistic understanding of that organization. Inquiry into separate functions of an organization cannot realize patterns of interactions, interdependence, or the integration that occurs in the entire organization. Organizational elements are not independent but, rather, interdependent as they interact within the organization and with various boundary environments. As with all other living things, constant interaction, interdependence, and integration occur. General systems theory attempts to explore organizations and their environments to seek explanations that can enhance understanding of the organization.

This image of organization has been maintained primarily in the human resources and organizational development perspectives. The systems movement has been labeled an "it depends" movement. Regardless of one's philosophical beliefs, however, key organic ingredients do provide a different way of thinking about organizations.

In the organic view, the interaction of subsystems in an organization takes on vital importance. This process largely explores communication links between and within these subsystems and the system environment. The input–throughput–output–feedback model provides the methodology. As a system, an organization is internally connected to its environment through the importation of resources. These resources can be from internal feedback mechanisms or from the larger suprasystem. Each external source, whether it be customers, clients, the community, or the government, has a dramatic bearing on the organization. As the organization realizes and utilizes its true input resources, fundamental change takes place within the organization. No longer can separate functional units act without external consideration as well.

In the organic metaphor, the organization measures output differently, not simply from the production line or through cost/revenue parameters but through quality, effectiveness, and satisfaction measures. These new measures become part of the organization's feedback systems in the form of new internal inputs. Self-renewal becomes consistent and constant. In this organization, the questions become what technology is being used, what kinds of people are needed, what the culture of the organization is, and how management philosophies relate to this new configuration (Morgan, 1986). Answers to these questions are the strengths found in the organic organization: openness, a process orientation, needs satisfaction, interactiveness, and a wide range of options both internally and strategically.

A key limitation of this metaphor is its reliance on adaptation. Many organisms in real life can make choices, but the organic model of organizations tends to create a marginal view whereby organizations can only hope to adapt to the environment. This may undermine the ability of the organization to control or change its own destiny. In addition, organizations have historically been incapable of promoting harmony within. Although some organizations have created harmonious interaction, others cannot manage the levels of interaction necessary. Many organizations are still too "tall." Organizational adaptation may thus not be a possibility for many as long as their change mechanisms remain incremental.

The Brain Metaphor

Another view of organizations is to see them as models of the brain. In practice, there are few organizations that have the capacity to become systemic. In these organizations, the requisite task is the organization's ability to foster self-renewal and self-organization (Morgan, 1986). These models stem from other authors (Argyris et al., 1985; Senge, 1990 for example). In contrast to the machine and organic views, this image implies almost complete change in the conception of the organization. The organization increases variety through a redundancy of function instead of a redundancy of parts. In this new part–whole schema, the whole is greater than the sum of its parts. For example, as is true of the brain, each activity in the organization is created in a separate part. This reduces the direct need for redundancy of parts in the organization. Second, as opposed to the machine, this new image through redundancy in function encourages all members of the organization to think in congruent terms. The machine organization restricts thinking in this regard as political systems develop to control. As a result, boundaries become more difficult to navigate internally and externally. The brain organization encourages decentralization in structure and, at the same time, increases levels of activity among various agents in a decentralized core. Boundaries between activities and between the organization and the environment become permeable. Third, whereas the machine organization develops structure to maintain accountability, rewards the accountable, and punishes the unaccountable, the brain image of organizations reduces and manages defensive structures and, as a result, approaches new activity from a learning-to-learn emphasis. The brain organization explores differences in individual and organizational theories of action and exposed theories (Argyris et al., 1985). As a result, the organization seeks to face uncertain conditions from a whole-organization perspective. The organization self-renews and self-organizes. In the long term, problems and decisions are brought to the forefront of organizational analysis rather than hiding issues or, worse, being unaware of them.

Significant differences also occur between this brain image and the organic image. The brain image more fully realizes implications of general systems theory. Whereas the manifestations of the organic organization have gravitated toward systematic implementation in organizations (modeling), brain organizations are more systemic (fluid). The redundancy in function enables self-renewal and self-organization fed by requisite variety and enabled by minimal specification (Morgan, 1986). While the organic form adapts, this newer form learns to learn. While the organic form encourages openness, this form encourages openness coupled with reflectivity. As the organic form maintains structural foundations iterated in the input–output model, this form creates its own organization in an "on the spot" fashion.

The brain image is configured to action. It utilizes the full realm of theory, praxis, and practice in recognition of its norms and values and at the same time questions these symbols to generate further learning (Hodgkinson, 1991). In this sense, the brain image encourages inquiry and criticism. A broader range of unit and strategic goals is explored, understood, and acted on. From this systemic format, new attitudes and values emerge: activeness over reactiveness, autonomy over dependence, flexibility over rigidity, collaboration over competition, openness over closeness, and democratic over authoritative.

The brain form of organization is extremely difficult to imagine in practice. The questions become how to create this form and how to penetrate the older paradigms. These are difficult questions to answer, but metaphors of "new science" (i.e., quantum theory, field theory, and class theory) are very helpful in making the transition. We discuss them next.

Metaphors of New Science

We must focus our thinking about organizations and schools for tomorrow. In this process, we must consider whether the Newtonian tools and techniques most familiar to us are appropriate or whether the body of developing knowledge centered in quantum science can affect our understanding of organization. Schrödinger's illustration of the cat in the box can help us define the major distinctions between these two thinking styles (Zohar, 1990). The problem as described by Zohar is as follows. Place a live cat in a box with solid walls. No one is able to see into the box. A triggering device at some point is set to release, with equal probability, either poison or food. At some point, the cat meets its fate, and the box is opened to determine what the cat's fate has been. In the Newtonian world, since our organizations are deterministic, we will look for facts, variables, and parts in an attempt to be objective, calculative, and find the truth. Our organizations are built on these same premises as we seek solidarity, identity, distinctiveness, singularity, and rational solutions to issues. We will measure the box, the food, and the poison or

seek environmental clues and hypothesize about everything. In the quantum world, however, the problem in the cat story is not a problem. Before observation, the fate of the cat is only a set of probabilities, not to be decided until we physically open the box. What we see is what we get.

In this exercise, the role of the observer is critical. In organizations, we confine humans, students, and others to Schrödinger boxes. Organizations daily make these attempts at objectivity. In the quantum science world, however, objectivity is constructed at the moment of observation. As observers, we may really be participants in only a set of potentials. Herein lies one of the keys to effective quantum thinking about organizations. As participants in today's organizations, we often restrict who gets to "have a say." A senior management official interprets and decides, followed by a reinterpretation by middle management and then supervisors. This limits the possibilities, but, in reality, each member of the organization is part of the potential of the organization. An organization that builds the capacity to utilize all interpretations swims in a sea of rich data that then can be discussed, combined, and built on. Becoming wiser in this sense and more participative also effects true ownership as the organization builds a capacity to be flexible and responsive to ideas and then promote further action. Participation, ownership, and subjective data enrich relationship construction and further cement ownership.

Maturana and Varela (1980) argued that organizations may be like closed, autonomous biological systems. This view is in contrast to the organic view, which sees living systems as open and in constant interaction with their environment. In describing organizations as closed and autonomous, the authors aimed to illustrate why organizations always attempt to strive toward stability. In this closed system view, internal circular interactions are built, maintained, and renewed in the effort to maintain stability. Any change in the system changes the entire system. Maturana and Varela's view does not represent a fully closed system view, as the organization still interacts with its environment, but does close itself in order to maintain and regulate its functioning. To study the organization, we need to study the nature of these patterns of circularity and how this circularity promotes growth for the system and balances the system. Senge (1990) termed these *circles of causality*. These circular systems usually change from within as well as a consequence of random internal disorder that leads to new patterns of order and change. Prigogine and Stengers (1984) termed this change *dissipative structure*. Some believe that human ideas and practices may develop similarly, accomplishing change when "critical mass" is achieved. Thus, organizational systems may shape their own futures through self-referential patterns.

Circles of causality incorporate positive and negative feedback loops that possess the potential to reveal patterns of relations. These patterns of relations not only reveal relationships but also can be used to leverage change. In the organizational context, we constantly see relationships whose patterns can reveal both the internal and the external organizational "ways we do business." The entire dynamic of an organization can be mapped and provide a richer picture of the system. As an example, a representation can be made of how individuals within an organization communicate—and with whom—outside the formal channels.

This is not to imply that circles of causality are the only form of interpretation available to us. We have grown accustomed largely to a view of organization that seeks understanding by looking at opposites, through dialectical analysis. Growth and decline, wealth and poverty, and industrialization and unionization are all dialectic viewpoints that often cause us to take sides. By understanding these dialectic forces, we can learn their importance and determine which of the forces are primary causes and which are superficial and secondary. By combining self-producing systems, circles of causality, and dialectic analysis, we can better understand the logic of change as it unfolds rather than deal with change in our normal piecemeal fashion.

Self-Organizing Organizations

Self-organizing organizations provide a new view. Instead of viewing the organization through its system structures, contemplation of its system dynamics, form, and function become important. We often incorporate understanding the role of negative feedback as a revitalizing source but neglect the essence and the importance of positive feedback. Positive feedback can be disruptive if it is taken on blind faith, leading to disorganization and disequilibrium and compromising the integrity of the organization. When considered thoughtfully, positive feedback can be a source of organizational change as well. Positive feedback is merely the variety that already exists in the organization. Disturbance, then, is a consequence that the organization ultimately responds to, as added neglect builds until the system must respond. In the quantum world, this disintegrity system can build a new vital system. Thus, disorder creates a new order. Over time, if we view the entropic system long enough, we would possibly capture its orderly striving to become something new.

Managing this disorder, as De Pree (1987) wrote, is in one instance "roving leadership" and points to the emergent qualities of the organization, using its indispensable people, who always seem to make a difference. These indispensable members create *fields of action* in the organization in response to necessities generated on the spot. You can sense this in many organizations: a feeling of good customer service that pervades the organization or a feeling that "learning is going on here."

We have described a developing view of organizational thinking derived from new science whose foundational assumptions are the opposite of those on which Newtonian sciences and traditional organizational theory are based. How does this translate to future school models that are emerging?

The virtual school, using metaphors of the new science, is composed of a partnership among the teacher, student, and learning. As the importance of these new participative relationships is realized and the school organization settles into creating its future, the school can draw new and necessary fields of skills and knowledge. The ongoing administration of the school system would occur within and be self-regulating. Delivery systems can vary according to the needs and expectations created within an organization. Processes to deliver can expand and incorporate new delivery contexts. Partners outside the school, such as parents, the community, and state and federal agencies, become supportive and facilitative. A virtual school model is described in chapter 9.

ACTIVITY 3.3

Organizational Metaphors

Addresses ISLLC Standards 1, 2, 3, and 6

Consider the organization in which you work. What metaphors are currently used in discussing or managing the organization and its functions? Are those metaphors helpful or harmful in achieving organizational goals? What metaphors could be used in the next few years that would be helpful in achieving organizational goals?

Reflections on Organizational Theory and Practice

Conflicts between Theory and Practice

Historically, schools as organizations have been nearly perfect portraits of larger organizations in industrialized society. The influence of scientific management is prevalent throughout all schools and school systems (Owen, 1987). Traces of Taylor, Fayol, Weber, and others are readily perceptible in school organizations. School districts mandate efficiency through standardization of work processes, audit school adherence with control and measurement mechanisms, and certify minimum proficiency of the products. Much reflection has taken place on how to understand the fundamental problems of schools and how to address them. In too many cases, repeated calls for renewal and revitalization have resulted in patching the system. Similarly, as the human relations movement garnered attention for the development and use of more favorable human resource models, the revitalization too often became still another set of poorly conceived or enacted sets of one-dimensional spot solutions.

As school achievement and performance ratings have failed to meet expectations in recent decades, there are continued calls for new criteria for excellence: schools need good management and leadership, and schools need to understand and confront their cultures and the cultures of their students. Some have claimed that schools need to create their own distinctiveness as they decouple from mainstream organizational thought (Cohen, March, &

Olsen, 1972). In this context, schools' purposes and definitions become fleeting, fuzzy, and even fluid, or they become reconstituted elements of more highly refined leadership studies, strengthening their core competencies and devising better communication mechanisms. For others, schools are viewed as systems in an effort to capture elements of the systems movement. The administrator or the supervisor at the school level is understood to be an integrative element to upper management, the community, teachers, staff, and students. As early as 1957, Getzels and Guba took the social behavioral view of education, proposing that the entire social system of education, comprised of the school, roles and expectations of various members, and various individual personalities and needs, interacts with tools, techniques, and curriculum in a sociotechnical arrangement seeing schools as dynamic organisms existing within numerous contexts.

Intertwined with the evolution of education as organization are other integrating elements. Hodgkinson (1991) outlined the historical purpose of schools from Greek liberal educational foundations to the Roman tradition of administration and governance to religious and moral reflections of the Protestant ethic. Additionally, he cited the effects of the agrarian and industrialized eras that gave rise to mass education as it generally exists today. Our democratic system of education exists largely to protect the democratic rights of its citizens. As the scientific era spawns productive efficiency, schools find themselves engaged in creating social efficiency (Kowalski & Reitzug, 1993). Schools as well as industries devise methods to control, coordinate, plan, direct, and organize themselves; hence, administration continues its development around scientific and human resource principles. The parade of leadership and management literature crossed boundaries easily as education mirrored industry.

Sergiovanni and Moore (1989) distinguished between transactional and transformational leadership viewpoints. Leaders in a traditional sense manage the consequences of an exchange process and ensure that behaviors of various subordinate actors remain within established norms. In contrast, the transformational leader manages more intrinsic, moral consequences, building shared commitment, distributing and facilitating power, building the capacity in other members, and instigating awareness of self in order to crystallize a more thorough commitment to responsibility and accountability.

In education, teaching professionals mediate conflicting demands across the entire school environment (Sergiovanni & Moore, 1989). While teachers aspire to maintain their own professional responsibilities, the school and school administration ask them to work in a factory environment. The professional role is difficult to maintain in this situation and gives rise to the "informal organization." The autonomous teacher now lives, on the one hand, profoundly tied to practice and expertise taught in a profession and, on the other, tied to the realities of a bureaucratic school environment. But success in this political environment is hard to guarantee and requires that leaders and professionals collaborate to tap the strengths evident in both the informal and the formal environment.

In the transitional periods of the past several decades, schools have functioned as rational-objective organizations. They examine their training methodologies, strategies for change, financial controls, and model new curriculums. Structure and audit remain, but frontline teacher and student expectations are often voiced and not heard. Often empirical reviews present new personnel practices for consideration. But these reviews crumble when confronted with the realities of the school's political structure. Although these transitional periods tout change, new leadership, or revised culture, in practice they do not have a broad, long-lasting impact. Even with the realization that schools are multicultural, followed by demand for appropriate organizational changes, schools still find themselves mired in the traditional rational-objective structure. School culture and climate are expressed as an environment of learning but also as restricted, confining, objective laden, and out of touch with current teacher, student, and societal needs. Educational improvement requires more than a change of pencils and papers; it requires direct change in patterns of human interdependencies, collaboration, and commitment.

In the true transformational sense, schools need to be viewed as living and dynamic. Schools can be natural environments that demonstrate all desirable traits: social justice, freedom, responsibility, and maturing. Self-renewal may best be a process of enactment and alignment and accomplished more effectively at the local level (the school or school district). Learning to cope with crisis over the longer term can result in a school or school system that shows steady progress and achievement. But those who attempt to manage crisis usually address only symptoms and not root causes (Senge, 1990). Through organizational development formulas, schools can change if they have direction, if they show progress, and if all players become involved. Administration must learn to command and control less and facilitate and encourage participation more (Hoy & Miskel, 1987). Leadership is more than just management or administration. Leaders in schools today must possess a clear sense of the true and evolving purpose(s) of education and, equally evident, its ambiguities.

A Fruitful Field for Further Study

The organization of schools and schooling today should be largely organic or, ideally, brainlike. But on closer inspection, we find a mixture of organic and bureaucratic school forms. Magnet schools are a good example of this blending ("Schools That Work," 1991). Conceived during the 1980s, many of these elite public schools have achieved dramatic results. As schools of excellence, they embody significant educational reforms. Magnet schools thrive on interactiveness and interdependence and integrate much of the best that is known about educational practice. Generally, they are intimate learning environments emphasizing personal contact, teacher designed and controlled, interactive with numerous partners in the community and region, and small in size, and they have clear purpose. However, they also can resemble the bureaucratic environment of the past and suffer from similar consequences. Across most traditional measurement categories, the organizational differences between successful schools and those that are still failing are significant. Even more curious, these "preferred schools" feel different. The sense that education is ongoing is powerful. In response to the organizational differences between them, understanding the organic nature of education and educational administration could be highly useful. Understanding how an organic school organization works in practice can be very instructive. Organic thinking requires seeing beyond aggregates of inspection, development, and implementation to create useful knowledge. Excellence in education is more than an outstanding list of issues (Eisner, 1991), more than steps in a total quality focus (Glasser, 1990), more than relating trends and forecasts (Cetron & Gayle, 1990), and more than a demonstration of how the best of the best perform (Gatto, 1990). Even the professionalization of schools requires more than better teacher preparation, better follow-up, in-service training, and certification. Still attached to our previous educational paradigms, we view needed variety as complexity, leadership as management, higher test score results and low costs as efficiency, newness as inappropriate change, and autonomy as loss of control. However, these elements are necessary paradoxical components of equifinality, or differing ways to arrive at the same goals. Reform in the organic brain sense demands added variety, creation of more usable products, greater autonomy as a means of control, and structure that reverts to fluid forms. We have not really adopted the organic brain view in our thinking and action but only adapted it as a response to the strength of various existing power and political forces, or learned paradigms.

Organizational theory continues to be a fruitful area of further study. A need exists for the generation of broader theoretical perspectives, an acceptance of equifinality and variety, and new tools for inquiry. The future holds many new organizational hybrids.

Summary and Fundamental Concepts

Education systems are in a constant state of flux. Responsive to multiple stakeholders, filling the dual roles of cultural conservator and societal change agent, they are subject to constant simultaneous pressures to change, stabilize, meet the needs and desires of the many and the few, and be able to adjust swiftly. In many communities, the public education system is the most expensive service provided at taxpayer expense. The high cost of education, combined with a sense that entrusting the young to the system implies entrusting the future to the system, only intensifies concern and debate over what educational systems should do and how and why.

In this chapter, a variety of ways of conceptualizing organizations were discussed, and systems thinking was applied to educational systems. Internal processes and characteristics of organizations were considered, as were metaphoric images of organizations. Conflicts between theory and practice in educational systems was noted, and reform of educational systems based on extensive public debate over the past several decades was recommended.

Fundamental Concepts

The fundamental concepts that follow have been discussed in this chapter. The citations that conclude each concept indicate the Interstate School Leaders Licensure Consortium (ISLLC) standards and functions related to the concept. The Arabic numeral refers to the ISLLC standards, and the letters refer to the functions as presented in the table found inside the front cover.

- Organizations are deliberate human creations and can be seen and analyzed in a variety of ways. (1A, 6C)
- It is desirable for organizations to become learning organizations in the sense described by Senge. (1A, 6C)
- To their detriment, educational systems are, in general, not learning organizations in Senge's sense. (1A, 6C)
- Significant internal processes of organizations include decision making, leadership, communication, and changes resulting from their life cycles. (1A, 6C)
- Other characteristics of organizations that affect their functions and structures include development and uses of power; the culture of the organization; its size, structure, and complexity; and the organization's health and effectiveness. (1A, 6C)
- Metaphoric images of organizations include the machine, the organism, the brain, and metaphors developed from new science: the quantum perspective and closed and open systems. (1A, 6C)
- Schools as organizations reflect the organizations of the larger society. (1A, 6C)
- A conflict exists between theories of schools as organizations and the reality. (1A, 6C)
- These conflicts have rendered attempts to improve educational organizations to "spot solutions" rather than overall reform. (1A, 6C)
- To truly reform educational organizations, we need to break from the psychic prisons resulting from our unconscious images, ideas, thoughts, and actions and see the issues in a new and freer way. As that happens, new approaches to organizations and to education will emerge. (1A, 6C)

Leadership of the complex educational system is challenging, as will be seen in chapter 4. While all systems need managers who work to ensure effective systemic function, management is not enough if an educational system is to meet the multiple challenges placed before it. Leadership, the ability to see not only what is necessary in the present but also what will be most advantageous in the future and to change the system to meet future need, is vital.

Case Study

The Case of the National Commission Study

Addresses ISLLC Standards 1, 2, 3, 4, 5, and 6

You are a person who has long been interested in education. You are a parent. You have served as a teacher, local school district administrator, state-level education administrator, and consultant on educational issues. Because of your background and interests, you have been invited to serve on a presidentially appointed national commission to study the American education system and recommend ways to improve it. You have accepted the offer.

The commission consists of a wide range of leaders from education, government, business, and industry as well as parental representatives and representatives from the general public. The commission is given 2 years to complete its study and to make recommendations, which, it is expected, will then become the basis for a national debate. Supporters of the commission's efforts anticipate that this will produce major changes in the American educational structure and operation, but there is no question that some of those proposed changes will create controversy.

In preparation for their task, the members of the commission have been familiarized with a number of earlier studies and proposals concerning the American educational system. One of the more recent is a study by the National Center on Education and the Economy (2007) titled *Tough Choices or Tough Times*, which focuses on the commission's charges to prepare an effective national workforce and to participate in the global economy. This study cites America's increasing difficulty in competing in the global marketplace because other nations are outstripping American efforts at producing an educated and flexible workforce and a consequent danger of lowering the American standard of living. The study makes a series of recommendations intended to remedy the situation:

Make education a national rather than a state or local responsibility

Restructure the national educational system so that students would test out of high school into community colleges in the 10th grade or, if they scored high enough, could continue in high school until the 12th year, then test out for direct admission to a university or a 4-year college, thereby providing a college education for most persons

Recruit, train, and employ a teaching force from the top third of the nation's high school students

Build a high-quality early childhood education system for all 3- and 4-year-old children

Provide additional direct support for disadvantaged students

Develop state standards, assessments, and curricula appropriate for national needs, current and future

Fund reeducation for all members of the workforce who are currently employed and do not meet the testing standards for high school students outlined previously

Provide lifetime retraining funds for all members of the workforce that would assist them in meeting changes and increasing demands in the job market

Questions

1. If the National Commission pursues the model proposed in *Tough Choices or Tough Times*, how would that change American educational organizations on the national, state, and local levels?
2. Using systems thinking, how would you describe the proposed model of educational organization?
3. If the proposed model were to be implemented, what aspects of the current American educational system are likely to be retained? What components are likely to be eliminated? Why?
4. This chapter discussed several aspects of organizations, including decision making, leadership, communication, development and uses of power, and organizational culture. In what ways would these aspects be changed if the proposed model were adopted?

References

Argyris, C., Putnam, R., & Smith, D. M. (1985). *Action science: Concepts, methods, skills for research and intervention.* San Francisco: Jossey-Bass.

Banner, T. K., & Gagne, T. E. (1995). *Designing effective organizations: Traditional and transformational views.* Thousand Oaks, CA: Sage.

Barnard, C. (1938). *The functions of the executive.* Boston: Harvard University Press.

Bass, B. M. (1990). *Bass and Stogdill's handbook of leadership* (3rd ed.). New York: Free Press.

Bergquist, W. (1993). *The post modern organization: Mastering the art of irreversible change.* San Francisco: Jossey-Bass.

Bertalanffy, L. von. (1968). *General system theory: Foundations, development, applications.* New York: Braziller.

Blake, R. R., & Mouton, J. S. (1988). *Executive achievement: Making it at the top.* New York: McGraw-Hill.

Blau, P. M. (1977). *Inequality and homogeneity.* New York: Free Press.

Bolman, G., & Deal, T. (1997). *Reframing organizations: Artistry, choice, and leadership* (2nd ed.). San Francisco: Jossey-Bass.

Brandt, R. (2003). Is this school a learning organization? *Journal of Staff Development, 24*(1), 1–5. Retrieved June 16, 2006, from http://www.nsdc.org/library/publications/jsd/brandt241.cfm

Brown, M., & Packham, R. (1999). *Organizational learning, critical systems thinking, and systemic learning* (Centre for Systems Studies Research Memorandum 20). Hull: University of Hull.

Bush, T., & Middlewood, D. (2005). *Leading and managing people in education.* Thousand Oaks, CA: Sage.

Cetron, M. J., & Gayle, M. E. (1990, September–October). Educational renaissance: 43 trends for U.S. schools. *Futurists,* 33–40.

Clegg, S. R. (1990). *Modern organizations: Organization studies in the postmodern world.* Newbury Park, CA: Sage.

Cohen, M., March, J., & Olsen, J. (1972). A garbage can model of organizational choice. *Administrative Science Quarterly, 17*(1), 1–19.

Colapinto, S. J. (1994). *The impact of organizational structure on implementing change: A comparison of implementation effectiveness in functional and product line health care organizations.* Unpublished dissertation, California School of Professional Psychology, Los Angeles.

Conner, D. R. (1992). *Managing at the speed of change: How resilient managers succeed and prosper where others fail.* New York: Villard Books.

Cornell, F. G. (1955, March). Society perceptive administration. *Phi Delta Kappan,* 36(6).

Crazy Bull, C., & Prue, A., Sr. (2003). Wellness in the workplace: Building a more productive institution. *Tribal College Journal, 14*(4), 10–14.

Damme, S. R. (1995). *Discovering an organization's theories-in-use about leadership and proposal for incorporating action science into leadership development.* Unpublished doctoral dissertation, University of Minnesota, Minneapolis.

d'Appolonia, S. T., Charles, E. S., & Boyd, G. M. (2004). Acquisition of complex systemic thinking: Mental models of evolution. *Educational Research and Evaluation, 10*(4–6), 499–521.

Davis, S. M., & Davidson, D. H. (1991). *20–20 vision.* New York: Simon and Schuster.

Deal, T. E., & Kennedy, A. A. (1982). *Corporate culture: The rites and rituals of corporate life.* Reading, MA: Addison-Wesley.

De Pree, M. (1987). *Leadership is an art.* East Lansing: Michigan State University Press.

Drucker, P. F. (1987). *The frontiers of management.* New York: Harper & Row.

Eisner, E. (1991). What really counts in schools? *Educational Leadership, 48*(5), 10–11, 14–17.

Etzioni, A. (1964). *Modern organizations.* Upper Saddle River, NJ: Prentice Hall.

Farago, J., & Skyrme, D. (1995, October). The learning organization. *Insight, 3,* 1–7. Retrieved June 13, 2006, from http://skyrme.com/insights/31morg.htm

Fayol, H. (1949). *General and industrial management.* Paris: Pitman.

Freeman, L. N. (2006, June 15). Organizational culture guides practice performance. *Ophthalmology Times,* 58–59.

Gatto, J. (1990, September–October). Our children are dying in our schools. *New Age Journal,* 62–64.

Getzels, J., & Guba, E. (1957). Social behavior and administrative process. *School Review, 65,* 423–441.

Giesecke, J., & McNeil, B. (2004). Transitioning to the learning organization. *Library Trends, 53*(1), 54–67.

Glasser, W. (1990, February). The quality school. *Phi Delta Kappan,* 424–435.

Gulyaev, S., & Stonyer, H. R. (2002). Making a map of science: General systems theory as a conceptual framework for tertiary science education. *International Journal of Science Education, 24*(7), 753–769.

Hannan, M. T., & Freeman, J. (1988). *Organizational ecology.* Boston: Harvard University Press.

Herzberg, F. (1968). One more time: How do you motivate employees? *Harvard Business Review, 46*(4), 53–62.

Hodgkinson, C. (1991). *Educational leadership: The moral act.* Albany: State University of New York Press.

Hoy, W., & Miskel, C. (1987). *Educational administration: Theory, research and practice* (3rd ed.). New York: Random House.

Jenks, C. L. (2004). Missing links in the public school curriculum: Four dimensions for change. *World Futures, 60,* 195–216.

Jermier, J. M. (1991). Critical epistemology and the study of organizational culture: Reflections on street corner society. In P. J. Frost, L. F. Moore, M. R. Louis, C. C. Lundberg, & J. Martin (Eds.), *Reframing organizational culture* (pp. 223–233). Newbury Park, CA: Sage.

Knezevich, S. J. (1989). *Administration of public education: A sourcebook for the leadership and management of educational institutions* (4th ed.). New York: Harper & Row.

Kowalski, T. J., & Reitzug, U. C. (1993). *Contemporary school administration: An introduction.* New York: Longman.

Lawrence, P. R., & Lorsch, J. W. (1986). *Organization and environment.* Boston: Harvard University Press.

Lewin, K. (1951). *Field theory in social science.* New York: Harper.

Likert, R. (1987). *New patterns in management.* New York: Garland.

Lindbloom, C. E. (1980). *The policy-making process* (2nd ed.). Upper Saddle River, NJ: Prentice Hall.

March, J. G. (1988). *Decisions and organizations.* New York: Blackwell.

Maturana, H., & Varela, F. (1980). *Autopoiesis and cognition: The realization of living.* London: Reidl.

Mayo, E. (1945). *The social problems of an industrial civilization.* New York: Ayer.

McGregor, D. (1985). *Human side of enterprise.* New York: McGraw-Hill.

Minarik, M. M., Thornton, B., & Perrault, G. (2003). Systems thinking can improve teacher retention. *The Clearing House, 76*(5), 230–234.

Mintzberg, H. (1983). *Structure in fives: Designing effective organizations.* Upper Saddle River, NJ: Prentice Hall.

Mintzberg, H. (1989). *Mintzberg on management: Inside our strange world of management.* New York: Free Press.

Mintzberg, H., & Quinn, J. B. (1988). *The strategy process: Concepts, contexts, cases.* Upper Saddle River, NJ: Prentice Hall.

Monge, P. R., & Eisenhart, E. M. (1987). Emergent communication networks. In F. M. Jablin, L. L. Putnam, K. H. Roberts, & L. W. Porter (Eds.), *Handbook of organizational communication: An interdisciplinary perspective* (pp. 304–342). Newbury Park, CA: Sage.

Morgan, G. (1986). *Images of organization.* Newbury Park, CA: Sage.

National Center on Education and the Economy. (2007). *Tough choices or tough times: The report of the New Commission on the Skills of the American Workforce.* Washington, DC: Jossey-Bass.

National Institute of Standards and Technology. (2005, November 22). *Frequently asked questions about the Malcolm Baldrige National Quality Award.* Retrieved October 30, 2006, from http://www.nist.gov/public_affairs/factsheet/baldfaqs.htm

Ouchi, W. A. (1981). *Theory Z: How American business can meet the Japanese challenge.* Reading, MA: Addison-Wesley.

Owen, R. (1987). *Organizational behavior in education* (3rd ed.). Upper Saddle River, NJ: Prentice Hall.

Peters, T. J. (1992). *Liberation management: Necessary disorganization for the nanosecond nineties.* New York: Knopf.

Phillips, M. E. (1984). *Industry as a cultural grouping.* Unpublished doctoral dissertation, University of California, Los Angeles.

Prigogine, I., & Stengers, I. (1984). *Order out of chaos.* New York: Random House.

Pugh, D. S., & Hickson, D. J. (Eds.). (1989). *Writers on organization.* Newbury Park, CA: Sage.

Ricotta, M. C. (1992). *The application of the organizational life cycles and shifting criteria of effectiveness framework to a health professional organization.* Unpublished doctoral dissertation., University of Buffalo, Buffalo, NY.

Roberts, C. D. (2006, May). A daily dose of continuous improvement. *School Administrator, 63*(5), 55.

Rosenthal, A. T. (2003). Teaching systems thinking and practice through environmental art. *Ethics and the Environment, 8*(1), 153–168.

Rost, J. (1991). *Leadership for the twenty-first century.* New York: Praeger.

Roufa, S. A. (1990). *An investigation into the superintendency: The relationships between fit-to-profession and organizational health.* Unpublished doctoral dissertation, University of Buffalo, Buffalo, NY.

Sackmann, S. A. (1991). *Cultural knowledge in organizations: Exploring the collective mind.* Newbury Park, CA: Sage.

Schein, E. (1985). *Organizational culture and leadership.* San Francisco: Jossey-Bass.

Schön, D. (1987). *Educating the reflective practitioner: Toward a new design for teaching and learning in the profession.* San Francisco: Jossey-Bass.

Schools that work. (1991, May 27). *U.S. News and World Report,* 58–66.

Senge, P. (1990). *The fifth discipline: The art and practice of the learning organization.* New York: Doubleday/Currency.

Sergiovanni, T. J., & Moore, J. H. (Eds.). (1989). *Schooling for tomorrow: Directing reform issues that count.* Boston: Allyn & Bacon.

Shafritz, J., & Ott, S. (1992). *Classics of organizational theory.* Pacific Grove, CA: Brooks/Cole.

Silverman, D. (1971). *The theory of organizations.* New York: Basic Books.

Simon, H. A. (1977). *The new science of management decision.* New York: Harper & Row.

Smith, M. K. (2006, April 26). Peter Senge and the learning organization. *Infed,* 1–18. Retrieved June 13, 2006, from http://www.infed.org/thinkers/senge.htm

Spreigel, W. R. (1953). *The writings of the Gilbreths.* Homewood, IL: Irwin.

Starbach, W. H. (1981). A trip to view elephants and rattlesnakes in the garden of Aston. In A. H. de Van & W. F. Joyce (Eds.), *Perspectives on organizational design and behavior* (pp. 167–197). New York: Wiley.

Tagiuri, R., & Litwin, G. H. (Eds.). (1968). *Organizational climate: Explorations of concepts.* Boston: Harvard University Press.

Tannebaum, A. S. (1968). *Control in organizations.* New York: McGraw-Hill.

Taylor, F. W. (1947). *Scientific management.* New York: Harper & Row.

Thomas, K. W. (1977). Toward multi-dimensional values in teaching: The example of conflict behaviors. *Academy of Management Review, 12,* 484–490.

Thompson, J. D. (1967). *Organizations in action.* New York: McGraw-Hill.

Thompson, S. (2006). The importance of "reculturing." *Education Week, 25*(25), 31–44.

Weber, M. (1947). *The theory of social and economic organization.* New York: Free Press.

Woodward, J. (1981). *Industrial organization: Theory and practice* (2nd ed.). Oxford: University Press.

Yukl, G. A. (1989). *Leadership in organizations* (2nd ed.). Upper Saddle River, NJ: Prentice Hall.

Zohar, D. (1990). *The quantum self: Human nature and consciousness defined by the new physics.* New York: Macmillan.

Schools as Learning Organizations

art II begins our examination of educational leadership by reviewing theories of leadership and considering the leader's role as a communicator and responsibilities for developing wholesome working relationships among the members of the organization.

Chapter 4: Leadership Theory. Theories of leadership are presented, displaying leadership's many dimensions. Transformational leadership and other current theoretical models demonstrate the complexity and variety of components of leadership.

Chapter 5: Human Relations. The study of human relations seeks to identify ways of bringing people together in a way that allows them to work together productively and cooperatively. This chapter broadens the understanding of teamwork and team learning applications and explains how mental states affect the human component of educational enterprises. Each individual's ability to work harmoniously and to understand the educational organization is a key to organizational effectiveness.

Chapter 6: Communication: The Breath of Organizational Life. Communications, a key ingredient of effective leadership, is the conduit for inquiry that develops understanding within and across environments. As the information age progresses, competent communication skills become increasingly important. This chapter explores communication concepts as applied to social systems, with particular emphasis on educational systems.

Leadership for Learning Organizations

Leadership or Management

In chapter 3, we considered schools and school districts as learning organizations. Taking a systems perspective, we discussed the difficulties in making change in educational organizations and looked ahead to changes that might be made in the 21st century. We identified problems that could call for specific leadership approaches. A variety of those approaches is discussed here.

In this chapter, we examine leaders and managers and the problems they face, especially leadership and management in education. Educational institutions today are in crisis, but is the offender the individual leader or the manager? Too often our principals, superintendents, and teachers are scapegoats for larger institutional, societal, and even global problems. Often the performance of these individuals is labeled inadequate before there is a thorough review of the educational systems and their subsystems or a review of the suprasystems where educational practice is conceived. Educators have long believed that they can perform only within that system—within its processes, activities, and membership. However, the face of educational practice is changing, and thus so are our views about what constitutes leadership.

Leadership and management have been studied extensively. This has provided greater understanding for practitioners, and theories and models of the same have enlightened us, but there is no scholarly consensus about what distinguishes leadership from management, what defines each, or how they will change. Leadership and management are different, but the reasons for that difference have not been

fully investigated, nor have we arrived at plausible interpretations to explain those differences. So what is leadership? What is management? Are leaders and managers different? How does leadership or management occur within this educational environment? Do we have a firm grasp of the meaning of leadership and management? Does it matter in the new millennium?

Conceptualizing Leadership

Background

In the 1980s, leadership (or the lack of it) became the named excuse for myriad national problems. According to Rost (1991), leadership in the United States was at fault for our decline in the global economy while being the vehicle to restore our lost power and prestige. Bennis and Nanus (1985) asserted that "a chronic crisis of governance—that is, the pervasive incapacity of organizations to cope with the expectations of their constituents—is now an overwhelming factor worldwide" (p. 2). Burns (1978) maintained that "the crisis of leadership today is the mediocrity or irresponsibility of so many men and women in power" (p. 1).

In the 1990s, new thinking was emerging about leadership. The world was entering an unprecedented period. Never were so many changes ongoing; the rise of global competition, increased complexity and change, and the demise of hierarchy and position power were creating broad new challenges (McFarland, Senn, & Childress, 1994). Leaders were needed who could envision differing responses to a changing world. Such changes were driving the need for a different quality of education—teaching and learning that could help us transform leadership in businesses, government, and education itself with newer skills, abilities, and values.

Definitions of leadership endure for about 20 years. When research uncovers deficiencies in the theories, new perspectives for studying leadership are identified. The complexity of modern organizations suggests that leadership paradigms may change rapidly as we begin the 21st century. This raises several questions for students who will assume leadership positions in the future. How will leadership paradigms need to change as leaders and followers are observed in new roles and contexts? How do and will future organizational contexts affect current theories of leadership and lead to new conceptual frameworks about leadership?

Leadership Trait Theories

Early studies on leadership were based on the assumption that individuals possessed certain physical characteristics, personality traits, and intellectual abilities that made them natural leaders (Yukl, 1989). Using correlational statistics, these studies compared successful leaders with unsuccessful leaders to see if the possession of specified traits might be a prerequisite for effective leadership. Organizational theorist Stogdill (Bass, 1981), however, contended that leadership cannot be explained only in terms of the individual or group but must take into account the interaction of leadership traits with situational variables. The belief that people possessing leadership traits can be effective regardless of the situation, therefore, is no longer supportable (Gardner, 1990). Smith and Peterson's (1989) review of trait research also criticized trait studies that provide too little uniformity in design. Bennis and Nanus (1985) discounted the Great Man theory of leadership, which attributes power to character and limits the number of potential leaders based on birthright. Their research also refutes the idea that great events can transform ordinary people into great leaders.

Behavioral Theory

Behavioral theorists attempt to determine what effective leaders do by identifying both the behavior of leaders and the effects that leader behavior has on subordinate productivity and work satisfaction. Studies of leader behavior at the University of Iowa (White & Lippitt, 1990) examined the effect on subordinate attitudes and productivity as leadership style is varied. Leaders were trained to demonstrate three leadership styles: democratic, authoritarian, and laissez-faire. Individual leaders demonstrated behavior attributes consistent with each leadership style from complete control to near-complete freedom of choice.

White and Lippitt's study (1990) determined that workers preferred democratic leadership to autocratic leadership. Democratic situations showed more group mindedness, friendliness, and efficiency. Subordinates demonstrated aggressive or apathetic behavior in response to authoritarian leaders. Productivity was slightly higher with an authoritarian leader than with a democratic leader, but subordinates exhibited more dependence and less individuality with authoritarian leaders. Although the Iowa studies were highly criticized, they are still considered a classic research effort on the effects of leadership styles on subordinates' attitudes and productivity (Lunenburg & Ornstein, 1991).

Leadership studies were also carried out at Ohio State University. Two dimensions of leadership were identified: consideration and the ability to initiate structure (Stogdill & Coons, 1957). Consideration was defined as the leader's expression of trust, respect, warmth, support, and concern for subordinates' welfare. The capacity to initiate structure defined the leader's attention to organizational goals, the organization and assignment of tasks, the delineation of superior–subordinate relationships, and the evaluation of task performance (Lunenburg & Ornstein, 1991). The Ohio State leadership studies formulated a two-dimensional model (see Figure 4.1) identifying four leadership behaviors: low structure, high consideration; high structure, low consideration; low structure, low consideration; and high structure, high consideration. Correlations were established between initiating structures and consideration and between subordinate work satisfaction and performance or productivity as demonstrated by the leaders' behavior. Causality between leader behavior and subordinate performance could not be substantiated (Yukl, 1989). This behavioral approach to leadership analysis, however, did demonstrate

FIGURE 4.1

Two-dimensional leadership model

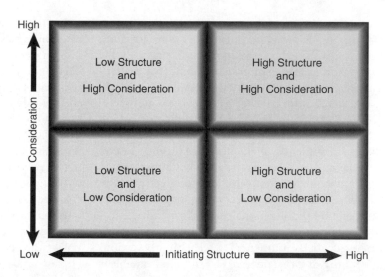

that leadership behaviors may be quantifiable and observable. Subordinate satisfaction and productivity may be improved by leaders who demonstrate high-initiating and high-consideration behaviors (Lunenburg & Ornstein, 1991).

Leadership studies done at the University of Michigan attempted to identify the relationships among leader behavior, group processes, and group performance. These studies showed three leadership styles: task-oriented behavior, relationship-oriented behavior, and participative leadership (Likert, 1961). Preliminary research indicated that productive work groups have leaders who are relationship oriented rather than task oriented. Inconsistency in research findings, however, later led researchers to conclude that effective leaders are both task and relationship oriented. Group effectiveness is determined by the quality of the leadership present in the group rather than by task differentiation.

Likert's (1961) four leadership styles (see Figure 4.2) are exploitative authoritative, benevolent authoritative, consultative, and participative

(democratic). Likert demonstrated that in situations in which leaders used consultative or participative leadership, there was evidence of trust, collaborative goal setting, bottom-up communication, and supportive leader behavior. In organizational situations where exploitative authoritative or benevolent authoritative leadership was utilized, organizations were characterized by threats, fear, punishment, top-down communication, and centralized decision making and control. These characteristics were used to elicit subordinate conformity to organizational goals and productivity standards. Likert also suggested that leaders who utilize participative decision procedures are more effective. Likert's continuum is still referred to frequently by leadership analysts because it provides systematic understanding of concepts that can often be applied to cross-organizational studies.

In an attempt to identify one leadership style that is optimal in all circumstances, various studies on theories of universal leadership (Blake & Mouton, 1981; Likert, 1961, 1967) concluded that effective leaders are supportive and task oriented. In these cases the value orientation, rather than the behavior pattern

FIGURE 4.2

Likert's four leadership styles

System 1	System 2	System 3	System 4
Exploitative Authoritative	Benevolent Authoritative	Consultative	Participative (Democratic)

Low ← ——————————————————— → High

Degree of Trust

of the leader, becomes the salient theoretical concept. Further studies postulated that leader behavior and trait research should be combined. The contention was that traits and leadership qualities influence leader behavior (Mazzarella & Grundy, 1989).

Research emphasizing a behavioral approach seeks to identify the behaviors and skills that could be taught to potential leaders. Research efforts have attempted to identify elements of leadership, based on social and task behaviors, and to rate them on a continuum to determine leadership effectiveness. Behavior research, however, does not take into consideration the situational factors (i.e., task differentiation, group composition, and environmental variables) that influence leadership behavior (Lunenburg & Ornstein, 1991). Behavioral variables cannot be treated but must be examined as interrelating factors (Smith & Peterson, 1989). It is important to note that these studies were first criticized for their leadership research but later resulted in efforts to explain leadership from a more systemic view.

Power Influence

Other studies attempt to understand leadership behavior from a power-influence perspective. Power relationships may be one of the more influential components surrounding our understanding of leadership. It may be one of those areas where leadership is

changing dramatically, too. Power is "a force that determines behavioral outcomes in an intended direction in a situation involving human interaction" (Abbott and Caracheo, 1988, p. 241). They limited the treatment of power to an organizational context and argued that there are two bases of power: authority and prestige. Power based on authority is derived from the leader's established position within a social institution's hierarchy and is delegated by the institution. Prestige power is based on the leader's possession of natural (honesty) or acquired (expertise) personal characteristics that are valued by others. This power must be earned by the leader through demonstration of these characteristics. The exercise of "institutional power, the potential to elicit intended behaviors from others . . . takes the form of either coercion or persuasion" (Abbott & Caracheo, 1988, p. 243). They argue that reward and coercive power are not the bases of power, as French and Raven (1968) purported, but ways in which power is exercised in an institutional environment based on authority, prestige, or both.

Abbott and Caracheo (1988) stated that legitimate power, derived from followers' conceding legitimacy to those who rule, is based on authority in institutional environments. They view referent and expert power as two of the elements that may constitute prestige power in an institutional setting. They postulated five bases for power: reward, coercion, legitimacy, reference, and expertise (see Table 4.1).

TABLE 4.1

Five Bases of Power

Basis of Power	Types of Influence
Reward	• The leader is capable of providing the reward. • The follower finds the reward desirable. • The follower perceives the leader's offering rewards as legitimate.
Coercive	• The follower perceives that the leader is capable of administering punishment for nonconformity to influence attempts.
Legitimate	• It arises from internalized values or norms in the follower that legitimize the leader's right to influence the follower and obligate the follower to accept this influence. • It can be derived from cultural values, acceptance of social structure, and designation by a legitimate agent.
Referent	• The follower perceives oneness and identification with the leader.
Expert	• The follower believes that the leader has some superior knowledge or expertise in a specific area and that this power is limited to this area of expertise.

Yukl (1989) defined power as an agent's capacity to influence one or more persons. To "influence" in this sense means to have an effect on the target's attitudes, perceptions, and/or behavior. Yukl claimed that the power to influence, which can be exerted downward, laterally, or upward, stems from three sources: position power, personal power, and political (or referent) power.

1. *Position power.* Followers are motivated to comply with and perceive the legitimacy of the leader and recognize the scope of authority and control over resources, rewards, punishments, and information in the physical environment and organizational subsystems.

2. *Personal power (expert and charismatic).* Expert power requires followers to recognize and submit to the leader's special skills. Charismatic power uses the leader's ability to identify followers' needs and values and thereby to motivate commitment.

3. *Referent power.* Power is developed slowly through symbolic actions that demonstrate the leader's consideration of followers and their reciprocity

through task compliance and the formation of similar attitudes toward the organization.

A leader's power base may be increased through political power or the means of controlling decision-making processes, coalescing parties to obtain desired results, and increasing the commitment of others to decisions through participation in the decision-making process (cooptation). Alternative ways to view power are summarized in Table 4.2.

Blake and Mouton (1961) defined power relationships using a power spectrum within which social power is distributed to accomplish a task. They identified three areas—competition, collaboration, and powerlessness—and built a power continuum that can be applied to decision making. They concluded that as a power relationship becomes balanced, work satisfaction and feelings of responsibility become optimal. Thus, mutual sharing of decision-making responsibilities may lead to the highest balance of satisfaction and responsibility between superiors and subordinates.

The strategic contingencies theory of Hickson, Hinings, Lee, Schneck, and Pennings (1971) proposes that the use of problem-solving skills in critical

TABLE 4.2
Power-Influence Studies of Leadership

Representatives	Study Concerns
French and Raven (1968)	Reward power, coercive power, legitimate power, referent power, expert power
Abbott and Caracheo (1988)	Authority power, prestige power
Yukl (1989)	Directions: downward, lateral, upward; Sources: position, personal, political
Blake and Mouton (1961)	Power situations: competition, collaboration, powerlessness
Hollander (1979)	Power processes: gain and loss
Hickson, Hinings, Lee, Schneck, and Pennings (1971)	Contingent variables: ability to cope with problems, centrality of function, degree of uniqueness
Salancik and Pfeffer (1977)	Utilization: shared power; Variables: scarcity, criticality, uncertainty
Shetty (1978)	Situational variables: managerial, subordinate, organizational
Bennis (1986)	Transformative power
House (1984)	Charisma, authority, expertise, political power
Smith and Peterson (1989), Gardner (1990)	Social- and culture-based power

situations that require unique expertise will lead to increased subunit power and authority over strategic decision making. They asserted that power is contingent on specific variables (ability to cope with important problems, centrality of function within the organization, and degree to which expertise is unique). As these variables are altered by changes in the internal and/or external environment, once-critical subunits may lose power to subunits that have newly acquired ability, responsibility, and power to perform critical functions. However, their theory does not explain how organizational subunits no longer in critical positions in some instances do maintain their power (Yukl, 1989).

In another strategic contingency model of power, Salancik and Pfeffer (1977) proposed that the political power of noncritical subunits is used to protect and maintain the subunits' position even though their expertise is no longer required. They maintained that power is shared in organizations not because of a belief in organizational development or participatory democracy but because one person cannot control all the critical activities. Three variables that affect the use of political power are scarcity, criticality, and uncertainty. Thus, power becomes institutionalized and protected by the power holder's ability to establish permanent structures and policies that ensure the power holder's position and influence.

Shetty (1978) contended that three situational variables may affect the type of power that leaders choose to employ. The variables affecting approaches to power are characteristics of the manager (authoritarian, self-confident, and training), the subordinate's characteristics (professionalism, need, cultural background, and training), and the organizational characteristics (task definition, visibility of task performance, organizational structure, and environmental conditions). These variables determine which characteristics of power may be appropriate in specific situations. Although most managers revert to authority or legitimate power when problems occur, Shetty states that managers might better "broaden their power bases in order to effectively respond to different demands" (p. 185).

According to Bennis (1986), leadership involves managing internal and external relations.

As organizations find themselves in an environment where stakeholders (public and organizational) desire a voice in decision making concerning problems that have an impact on diverse, sometimes conflicting societal groups, decision making becomes more complex and ill defined. Power is diffused over a broad base, creating a new power relationship. Bennis contended that transformative power requires leadership that "knows what it wants, communicates those intentions successfully, empowers others, and knows when and how to stay on course and when to change" (p. 66).

Transformative power is not based on organizational structures or management functions. Its source of power is the leader's ability to raise consciousness, build meanings, and inspire human intent. Vision, purposes, and beliefs embedded in the organization's culture empower participants to excel as meaning is found in routine actions uniting individuals and the organization in a symbiotic relationship (Bennis, 1986).

Although the foregoing views of power in organizations are instructive, Smith and Peterson (1989) asserted that there is an "implicit assumption that leaders are valued and constructive members of their organizations" (p. 126). They challenged French and Raven's (1968) five bases of power and House's (1984) four typologies of power, stating that a "leader's exercise of power resides in the ability to transmit influence by way of a network of meanings which constitutes the organization's culture" (p. 130), not in qualitative descriptions of power bases.

Power is the capacity to bring about certain intended consequences in the behaviors of others, Gardner (1990) observed. He proposed that only the power to accomplish specific objectives and not a generalized power functions in a pluralistic society such as the United States. Sources of power can be varied widely (property, position, personality, expertise, persuasiveness, and motivational abilities). Possession of one source may provide accessibility to other sources. Within human systems (organizations and institutions), organizational power is given to those possessing key positions that constitute the most common source of power in the modern world. Although a belief system firmly embedded in cultures may significantly legitimize leaders and validate their acts, any belief system usually places constraints on those trying to uphold the belief system, eventually diminishing the leader's power.

A significant question is whether a leader can have influence without having power. Sotarauta (2002) held that a leader needs power at some level in order to have influence. In order to have influence, however, a leader must be able to negotiate multiple interests and aims. Skills and abilities that enable leaders to gain and exercise influence, according to Sotarauta, include the ability to cooperate, encourage others, create an innovative environment, create the future, and create new knowledge.

According to Sotarauta (2002), the ability to cooperate is based on working effectively with others, creating working networks based on the needs of the actors rather than those of the administration, building trust, creating teams, listening to others, and looking for latent potential wherever it may be found. The ability to encourage others is based on creating an innovative environment that encourages others to innovate and function competitively. The ability to create the future is based on foreseeing the future without being too rigidly linked to plans and to develop the big picture without becoming lost in detail. Finally, the ability to create new knowledge is based on taking advantage of situations that are unclear, creating an enthusiastic atmosphere, and knowing how to use narratives, metaphors, and images effectively in communicating.

Given the complexity of leadership roles as described here, Sotarauta (2002) felt that the most efficient leaders employ a combination of several leadership models and styles, depending on the circumstances.

Leadership Styles

Leadership style is the pattern of behaviors of a person who assumes or is designated to a position of influence in an organization. The ways that leaders perceive workers and interpret their actions affect the leader's behavior toward the workers. Establishing relationships with subordinates is a critical factor in their work as leaders. People react to what they think they see in others. The degree of accuracy of perception determines the appropriateness of

---

ACTIVITY 4.1

Power and Authority

Addresses ISLLC Standards 1, 2, 3, 4, and 5

1. What is power?
2. What is authority?
3. Consider a school district as an open general system including the state legislature, the state department of education, the local legislature, local taxpayers, parents, the local school board, the superintendent of schools, a school building principal, teachers, and students. In each of the following situations, where does authority lie? Where does power lie? Under what circumstances might conflict arise?
   a. Developing the local school budget for the coming year
   b. Negotiating a raise for the teachers for the coming year
   c. Determining what textbooks to buy for the coming year
   d. Meeting state testing standards for students
   e. Developing a unit of instruction for use in a class
   f. A parent disapproves of a teacher's handling of his or her child and confronts the teacher on the issue
   g. A community group disapproves of a book that is in the school library and that is also used in a class and wants the book banned from the school

---

those actions taken. This is a mutual leader–follower behavior.

McGregor (1990a, 1990b) presented two perspectives that leaders use in dealing with workers: theory X and theory Y. Theory X is based on three assumptions: human beings dislike work inherently and try to avoid it (management must counteract this natural tendency); people must be coerced, controlled, directed, and threatened in order to achieve organizational goals (rewards will not lead to achievement; only external coercion, control, and threats will); and human beings are irresponsible, want to be controlled, are lazy, and are searching for security.

Theory Y is based on quite different assumptions: people work voluntarily when conditions are appropriate, workers will achieve organizational goals to which they are committed, commitment to organizational goals is based on the rewards of goal achievement, workers will seek responsibility when conditions are appropriate, many workers possess the ability to solve organizational problems, and human intellectual potential is not fully utilized in organizations.

Theory Y, allegedly founded in human growth, development, and selective adaptation rather than direct control, implies that leaders may create constraints that impede workers from achieving their potential in the organizational setting. Thus, theory Y challenges many of the routine actions and beliefs of leaders that operate from theory X assumptions.

The central principle of theory X, the scalar principle, is based on the belief that followers need direction and control through the exercise of authority (McGregor, 1990a). Theory Y's central principle, the integration principle, is based on the belief that workers can achieve their goals best by working toward organizational success. In some organizations, theory X characteristics are so firmly ingrained that it is difficult for members to adopt a theory Y viewpoint. In such cases organizational requirements often supersede individual needs. However, the principle of integration proposes that organizations can be successful only if they adjust to workers' needs and goals. In this way, the needs of both the organization and the individual are recognized.

A third theory combining elements of theories X and Y has been developed that offers ways to improve relationships between workers and leaders. Ouchi's (1981) theory Z provides different strategies and perspectives for organizing human effort, focusing on consensual decision making and a team approach to organizational processes and change. Unlike theories X and Y, theory Z defines the leader's style according to the ability to create an organizational culture where open communication, trust, and commitment to organizational goals are fostered. Consensual decision making "provides for the broad dissemination of information and of values within the organization, and it also serves the symbolic role of signaling in an unmistakable way the cooperative intent of the firm" (p. 66).

Long before Ouchi's theory Z, Likert (1961) developed four management systems that resemble some of the conceptual frameworks that have subsequently emerged in theories X, Y, and Z. Likert proposed that his four-system management model of participative management approaches an ideal state. Three key factors of this system were supportive relationships, group decision making, and high managerial performance goals. Likert believes that workers perform best when they function as members of effective work groups, not as individuals. The significance of Likert's system is that it acknowledges worker behavior as a leadership goal and as a factor in modifying leadership behaviors. McGregor's theories X and Y, Ouchi's theory Z, and Likert's four management systems illustrate that the perspective lens through which leaders view workers' characteristics and the subjective validity system developed for those characteristics determine what leadership style, strategies, and procedures will be employed.

Goleman, Boyatzis, and McKee (2004) viewed leadership style through a slightly different lens. They saw good leaders as effective because they were able to tune in to others' feelings and move them in a positive direction. They termed this the ability to create resonance. Resonance can be created in six ways based on six leadership styles. In the visionary style the leader believes in his or her own vision and moves people to a shared vision by explaining how their efforts contribute to the goal. The style is appropriate when a new vision or a clear change of direction is needed. In the coaching style the leader listens, counsels, helps, and delegates. This connects what the person wants with the organization's goals. The style is appropriate to help competent, motivated persons improve their performance. In the affirmative style the leader is empathetic and promotes harmony by solving conflicts. The style is appropriate when there is need to heal a rift or to motivate during stressful times. In the democratic style the leader is a listener, team worker, and collaborator, valuing others' input and getting commitment through participation. The style is appropriate when there is need to build cooperation and consensus. In the pacesetting style the leader has a strong drive to achieve challenging goals. He or she may be low on empathy and collaboration, micromanaging, and number driven. The style is appropriate when there is need to get high-quality results from highly motivated and competent persons. Finally, in the commanding style the leader is direct and tightly controlling. The style may reduce fear by giving clear direction in emergency conditions but otherwise may be threatening and a cause of conflict. The style may be appropriate when there is a crisis or urgent need for change or when working with problem persons.

Contingency Theories and Models

Contingency theories of leadership effectiveness focus on the leader's immediate work environment. Early contingency models focused on leader emergence by studying how the group's tasks and norms (situation) determine the leadership skills and values that would be effective in the group and acceptable to the subordinates (see Table 4.3).

Fiedler's (1967) research represents the first attempt to study leadership by examining the situation, its people, tasks, and organization. Fiedler (Lunenburg & Ornstein, 1991; Rost, 1991; Smith & Peterson, 1989; Yukl, 1989) hypothesized that leaders can improve their effectiveness by modifying situations to fit their leadership styles. Fiedler identified three situational factors that influence leader effectiveness: the quality of leader–subordinate relations, the leader's position power, and the degree of task structure (Smith & Peterson, 1989).

As a result of Fiedler's (1967) work, leadership styles are no longer rated as good or bad. Rather, styles are defined according to their effectiveness in specific situations. Fiedler's research recognized that leadership results from the interaction between leadership style and situational variables. This view

TABLE 4.3

Contingency and Situational Theories and Models

Theory	Situational Variables	Leadership Styles
Fiedler's (1967) contingency theory	Quality of leader–subordinate relations Leader's position power Degree of task structure	Task oriented Relationship oriented
House's (1971) path–goal theory	Subordinates Environment	Directive Supportive Participative Achievement
Hersey and Blanchard's (1952–1955) situational leadership theory	Subordinate maturity	Task Relationship
Blake and Mouton's (1978) managerial grid	All situations	Participative
Kerr and Jamier's (1978) substitute theory	Substitutes Neutralizers	
Vroom and Yetton's (1973) decision model	Decision quality importance Leaders' possession of relevant information Degree of structure contained in problem Importance of subordinates' acceptance of the decision Probability that subordinates will accept the leader's decision Importance of shared purpose and goals Amount of conflict among subordinates	Autocratic consultative Group

opened the door to subsequent research that describes leadership behaviors holistically.

During the 1970s, leadership theories reflected this more descriptive flair. For example, House's (House, 1971; House & Dressler, 1974) path–goal theory of leadership is based on the expectancy theory of motivation. House focused on the leader's ability to analyze the task environment and choose behaviors that maximize subordinates' ability and desire to achieve organizational goals. To accomplish this analysis, leaders examine situational variables such as the subordinates (personal qualities and skills, locus of control, and needs and motives) and the environment (work group, authority system, and task structure) and then select one of four leadership styles (directive, supportive, participative, and achievement oriented) to apply in the situation specified (see Figure 4.3).

Descriptive leadership theories that emerged in the 1980s served to illuminate a range of variables.

Hersey and Blanchard's (1988) situational leadership theory asserted that leader behavior is based on two dimensions of leadership: task behavior and relationship behavior. These dimensions are influenced by one environmental variable: subordinate maturity (Blanchard, Zigarmi, & Zigarmi, 1987; Rost, 1991; Smith & Peterson, 1989; Yukl, 1989).

Behavior variables in leaders (directive/supportive) interact with behavior variables in group members (high/low commitment and high/low competence). As the group members pass through various stages of commitment and competence, the leader varies the amount of direction and support given. The leader plays various roles of directing, coaching, supporting, and delegating as individuals and the group mature and become able to perform activities. Group maturity depends on individual maturity.

Yukl (1989) felt that Hersey and Blanchard's (1988) situational leadership theory needed further

FIGURE 4.3

House's path–goal theory

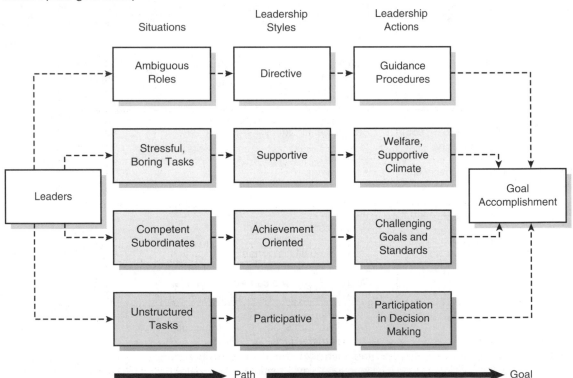

testing but felt that it emphasized the effectiveness of a flexible, adaptive leadership style that varies treatment of subordinates according to maturity levels in the same work environment and in varied work situations.

Blake and Mouton (1978, 1981, 1982a, 1982b, 1990) reexamined leadership theory using a two-factor framework in which concern for production and concern for people are interdependent but uncorrelated (see Figure 4.4). Their managerial grid provided a schematic behavioral science framework for comparing nine theories of interaction between production and human relationships (Blake & Mouton, 1978). Each variable was delineated on a 9-point scale in which 1 represented minimum and 9 maximum concern. The model developed five management styles and nine theories of how production and people can be integrated to accomplish organizational goals. Based on the belief that concerns for production and relationship are conflictual, Blake and Mouton (1978) posited that three management

FIGURE 4.4

Leadership grid

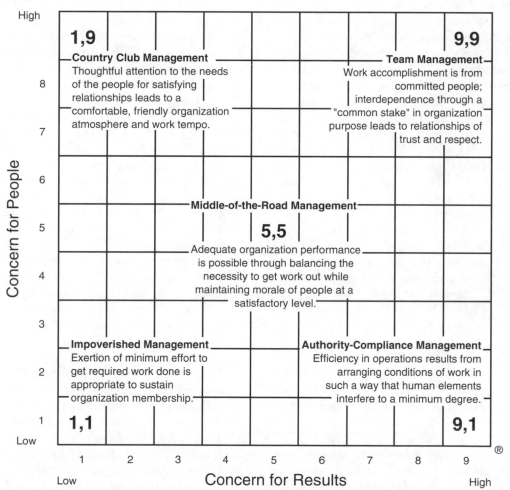

Source: The Leadership Grid® figure for *Leadership Dilemmas—Grid Solutions,* by Robert R. Blake and Anne Adams McCanse (formerly the Managerial Grid figure by Robert R. Blake and Jane S. Mouton). Houston. TX: Gulf Publishing Company, 1991. p. 29. Copyright 1991 by Scientific Methods, Inc. Reproduced by permission of the owners.

theories evolve: task management (9,1), where the focus is on attainment of production goals and where human beings are viewed as machines; country club management (1,9), where the focus on relationships dominates to the extent of compromising production goals; and impoverished management (1,1), where the focus is on avoidance of conflicts between production and relationships by ignoring or withdrawing from such situations.

The theories of Blake and Mouton (1978, 1981, 1982a, 1982b, 1990) represent a situational approach to leadership. Researchers assume that concerns for production and relationship building will conflict and therefore must be viewed more systemically or risk being compromised. In practice, the systemic nature of this model is accomplished by alternating styles that focus on each concern (1,9 and 9,1), by providing for both concerns through separate organizational structures (management–production and personnel–relationships), or by perceiving each factor as a separate concern that can be dealt with exclusively. Because production and relationship concerns are evident in all management situations, Blake and Mouton contended that the team management theory is the only style that can effectively integrate both production and relationship concerns. All members of the team plan for production and deal with conflict openly.

Vroom and Yetton's (1973) earlier model examined how the decision-making process is affected by the leader, subordinates, and situation to enhance decision quality, decision commitment, and decision satisfaction. The model analyzed decision situations and prescribed feasible decision procedures. Vroom and Yetton evaluated seven questions dealing with power sharing and participation in the decision-making process and their impact on the leadership style or amount of participation prescribed for each decision situation.

Using a decision tree, Vroom and Yetton (1973) analyzed problems using seven questions to assess the following: decision quality importance, leader's possession of relevant information, degree of structure contained in the problem, importance of subordinates' acceptance of the decision, probability that subordinates will accept the leader's decision, importance of shared purposes and goals in decision making,

and amount of conflict among subordinates that may result from the decision. After the leader moves through the decision tree and answers the seven questions, he or she can identify either one or several feasible alternative ways of dealing with the problem. These alternatives are classified in five leadership styles: two autocratic, two consultative, and one group.

Although Vroom and Yetton's (1973) model is complex and may require computer assistance for data analysis, it does provide information that can lead to precise, reliable, and effective decision-making procedures (Smith & Peterson, 1989). Further studies of Vroom and Yetton's model have substantiated its validity and reliability. Its focus on specific behaviors and meaningful intervening variables lends credence to its use as a situational leadership model.

However, Vroom and Yetton's (1973) narrow focus on only one situational leadership behavior, decision making, and their assumption that leaders possess the necessary skills and ability to use this skill and diagnose situations weakens the model. As a theory-to-practice model, the Vroom–Yetton model also has some deficiencies. The model indicates only what a leader should not do instead of what a leader should do. It gives no guidance for choosing alternatives when the process results in multiple alternatives, and it assumes that all seven factors can be delineated by clear "yes" or "no" responses. The model also fails to address such situational variables as the amount of information needed by subordinates in decision making, time constraints for reaching decisions, and the ability of all necessary participants to be present at decision time. Like many models for leadership, the strengths and weaknesses of the Vroom–Yetton model illustrate the complexity of modern organizations and the consequent intensified complexity of the leadership role.

Vroom and Jago (1988) revised the Vroom–Yetton model to address its deficiencies. In addition to the original five decision processes for group problems, two processes (one group and one delegative) were added to address individual problems of decision making. To evaluate problems and decision processes according to decision quality, decision commitment, time, and subordinate development, equations were developed to determine decision effectiveness. These equations also accounted for the trade-offs incurred when the size of a decision-making group varied. Because of the use of mathematical equations and the employment of computers, the Vroom–Jago model is capable of weighing answers to the situational factors (now including time, geographical, and motivational constraints—expanded from 7 to 12) along a 5-point continuum instead of using simple "yes" and "no" answers. The new model's use of continuous rather than dichotomous responses, the use of mathematical functions, and expanded situational factor consideration may result in greater validity of the decision-process decisions reached with the model's use.

Situational Determinants Theories and Models

Situational determinants theory defines leader behavior as determined by situational characteristics (role expectation, group mission and tasks, and flexible role definition) and leader traits and qualities. Leaders' personalities and values may bias their perceptions of their roles, causing role conflict. The theory suggests that leaders' expectations of behavioral outcomes influence their behavior choice (Nebecker & Mitchell, 1974).

The study of leadership remains complex, as seemingly different situations tax theorists' analysis capabilities. For many decades leadership theorists have attempted to integrate theories under the crush of increasingly complex situations for analysis. Koestenbaum's (1991) leadership model was one attempt to integrate leadership research strategies—traits, behaviors, contingencies, and situational determinants—into one model. The theory looked beyond the individual or traits and immediate work environment or behavior and contingency and examined the interactions of leader traits and behavior with the macro internal and external environment. Leadership was viewed as a mind-set and a pattern of behaviors. Koestenbaum contended that leadership can be learned and taught; therefore, leaders should empower and support subordinates to develop their own leadership potential. He also believes that a majority of a leader's time and energy should be used to facilitate skill development in frontline people in dealing with the organizational

system and with the external environment. Koestenbaum equated leadership with greatness and emphasized emotional appeal as a qualification for leadership. This, however, perpetuated the mistaken belief that leaders are superhuman.

Transformational and Transactional Leadership

Burns (1978) examined leadership in a political context by studying distinctions among power, leadership, transactional leadership, and transformative leadership. He believed that "power over other persons is exercised when potential power wielders, motivated to achieve certain goals of their own, marshal in their power base resources (economic, military, institutional, or skill) that enable them to influence the behavior of respondents by activating motives of respondents relevant to those resources and to those goals" (p. 18). Burns defined leadership as "the reciprocal process of mobilizing, by persons with certain motives and values, various economic, political, and other resources, in a context of competition or conflict, in order to realize goals independently or mutually held by both leaders and followers" (p. 425). This implies that the purpose of such a power wielder is to achieve goals whether or not the followers share in those goals (see Figure 4.5).

Burns (1978) differentiated between transactional and transformative leadership. He argued that in transactional leadership, persons engage in a relationship for the purpose of exchanging valued things. They are conscious of each other's power, usually pursue their own purposes and goals, and form temporary relationships. In transformative leadership, "one or more persons engage with others in such a way that leaders and followers raise one another to higher levels of motivation and morality" (p. 20). In such a relationship, purposes are fused, power bases are linked, and leadership becomes moral as leaders and followers unite to achieve higher goals. Burns based his general theory of leadership on a hierarchy of human needs, structure of values, and stages of moral development. The role of the leader is to help followers transcend the levels of need and stages of moral development to achieve mutually held higher purposes. For Burns, the test of a leader is the ability

FIGURE 4.5

Transformational versus transactional
leadership

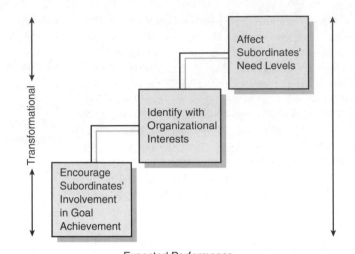

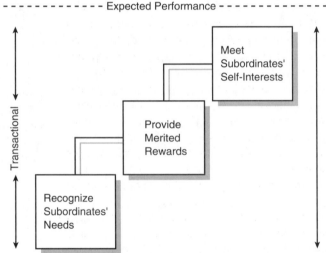

to achieve significant change that represents the mutual interests of followers and leaders.

Bass's (1985) conceptualization of leadership differs from Burns's (1978) in three areas: Bass included the idea of expanding subordinates' array of needs and wants in addition to Burns's emphasis on raising subordinates' need levels, Bass eliminated the moral implication of transformational leadership that Burns believes is a requirement (Burns considers all transformative leaders to be good, not evil), and although Burns viewed transactional and transformative leadership as opposite ends of a continuum, Bass argued that leaders exhibit both types of leadership, depending on the situation.

Bennis and Nanus (1985) argued that transformative leadership is the ability of leaders to shape and elevate followers' motives and goals to achieve significant change through common interests and collective energies. Leaders define a vision that is congruent with followers' key values and construct a social architecture, or an organizational culture, that provides shared meanings where followers can pursue tasks and strive for success. To accomplish this, leaders must be able to create a vision, communicate the vision through symbolic actions and shared meanings, exercise integrity through persistent pursuit of that vision, recognize their own strengths and weaknesses, evaluate ability in relation to job requirements, and focus on positive goals.

A key ingredient of transformative leadership for Bennis and Nanus (1985) is empowerment, which is the ability of leaders through an active and creative exchange of power to encourage followers to achieve a vision and realize goals. Leaders empower followers by bringing significance, competence, community, and enjoyment to leader–follower work relationships, where extraordinary efforts are perceived as the means to realizing vision and achieving goals. Bennis and Nanus focused their interpretation of transformational leadership on the behavior and skills of the leader.

Speaking of the transformational leader, Homrig (2001) identified several characteristics. He said that authentic transformational leadership builds genuine trust between leaders and followers. Transformational leaders focus on terminal values such as integrity and fairness. They are aware of their responsibility for the organization's development and impact on society. Transformational leaders increase the awareness of what is right, good, important. They move followers to move toward higher levels of self-actualization and to go beyond their self-interests to the good of the organization or society. The truly transformational leader seeks the greatest good for the greatest number and sets that example. Moral justification exists for the transformational leader's behavior. The roles of leader and follower in a transformational environment are based more on work relationships centered on common purposes than on positional authority. Finally, transformational leaders show a capacity for self-management, commitment, and courage.

Judge and Piccolo (2004) analyzed transformational, transactional, and laissez-faire leadership models. They tested the validity of transactional and transformational leadership against follower leader satisfaction, follower job satisfaction, follower motivation, rated leader effectiveness, leader job performance, and group/organizational performance. Their results showed transformational leadership as having the highest overall validity. Leader effectiveness and follower satisfaction with the leader were shown as stronger with the transformational leader. Laissez-faire leadership was least strong in relation to follower job satisfaction, follower satisfaction with the leader, and leader effectiveness.

Multiple Approaches to Leadership

Interest has increased in multiple approaches to leadership. Similar to contingency or situational approaches to leadership, this approach suggests that good leaders understand that they need to adjust their styles to cope with changing conditions. Flexible leadership was the goal of Yukl and Lespinger (2004), who argued that leaders must balance a variety of interactions over time that often involve competing demands and that they must assess the impact of their decisions and respond to that impact as part of the ongoing process. By developing the multiple approaches, effective leaders work toward finding solutions that will benefit both individuals and the overall organization.

Sorum (2007) presented a similar perspective. Taking the Goleman et al. (2004) perspective on multiple leadership styles, Sorum posited that the best leaders can use four or more of Goleman's styles in fulfilling their roles. Considering the context in which leadership is exercised, Sorum suggested that in a situation where the group has few resources and limited time to meet a goal, a top-down directive approach by the leader is most effective. In a situation where there is more time and/or resources, a mixed directive approach involving affiliative or democratic styles mixed with a directive approach may be useful. In a situation where change is planned over a long period of time and adequate resources are available, a developmental directive style of leadership involving pacesetting and coaching could bring the most positive results in meeting goals while achieving follower satisfaction.

Leadership within a Cultural Context

As shown by the previous discussion, theories about leadership are multidimensional. No one theory has embraced all the necessary variables to define satisfactorily the complexity of the leadership role or to predict best-case leadership scenarios. Some researchers suggest a total reconceptualization of the leadership problem. Among these are Sergiovanni and Corbally (1986), who argued that to change we must move "from a conception of leadership where effectiveness is defined as accomplishing objectives to one of building identity, increasing understanding, and making the work of others more meaningful" (p. 14).

Sergiovanni (1986) defined quality leadership as a balance between tactical leadership (achieving objectives effectively and efficiently) and strategic leadership (obtaining support for policies and purposes and devising long-range plans). Tactical leadership, in which evaluation is quick and success is based on short-term accomplishments, has been the focus of Western societies. Sergiovanni contended that in a cultural perspective of leadership, "cultural aspects of organization are being offered as better able to account for the artificial purposive, and practical aspects of organizational life" (p. 106). Organizations are viewed not as systems but as cultural entities, where meanings derived from actions are more important than the specific actions.

Schein (1985) defined culture as "a pattern of basic assumptions—invented, discovered, or developed by a given group as it learns to cope with its problems of external adaptation and internal integration—that has worked well enough to be considered valid, and therefore, to be taught to new members as the correct way to perceive, think, and feel in relation to those problems" (p. 8).

As discussed by Sergiovanni (1986), leadership as cultural expression relies on the analysis of the complex interplay of tactical leadership skills (management skills) and strategic antecedents and meanings within a framework of principles that form a cognitive map for quality leadership. To achieve leadership excellence, antecedents and meanings are needed to provide a basis for and direction to leadership skills. Antecedents are defined as perspective, principle, platform (operational framework), and politics (influencing others to achieve desired goals). These are required to guide the leader's decisions, actions, and behavior. Meaning develops in a belief system through purposive reflection (giving meaning to ordinary activities), planning (articulating purpose), persisting (creating climate through attention to issues, goals, or outcomes), and matching people to organizational goals and objectives. Sergiovanni felt that from the interaction of these components, a culture emerges that defines what is important and governs behavior. Organizational patriotism, commitment, and loyalty to a shared set of common beliefs and governing behavior create a strong bond among organizational members and give the organization unique meaning. These actions require leadership behavior (see Figure 4.6).

FIGURE 4.6

Leadership as cultural expression

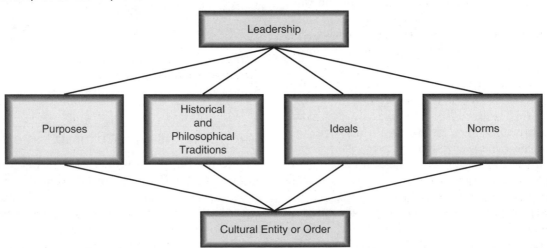

Sergiovanni's (1986) model appears to represent his interpretation of Burns's (1978) transactional and transformational leadership in one model where quality leadership is achieved by the leader's ability to move beyond the tactical skills component (transactional leadership) to the integration of antecedents and meanings (transformational leadership), achieving a quality leadership model. The leader here oscillates between the roles of transactional and transformational leader as the situation changes. In this respect, Sergiovanni's perception of leadership is closer to that of Bass than that of Burns.

Smith and Peterson (1989) contended that leadership as an aspect of organizational behavior can best be studied in a social context, not as an influence relationship within the leader–follower dyad. From a global perspective, organizational leadership is seen as comprising two aspects—task and relationship—within a team structure. Assignment of meanings to leadership acts derives from the cultural context of the group or organization. In assimilated cultures, attribution of meaning may be more consensually shared than in Western individualistic, pluralistic societies. Rather than searching for one best type of leadership, this theory implies that there may be one best organizational culture that can be created through a hierarchical structure. The hierarchy can develop shared meanings for organizational activities and events and thus foster shared visions and strategies for achieving organizational goals, a cultural form of control.

Schein (1985) said that creating, managing, and sometimes restructuring organizational culture may be one of the most decisive functions of leadership. Viewing culture as the element that most strongly affects how members of human systems think, feel, and act, he refuted the assumption of some leadership theorists that culture can easily be changed to suit one's purposes.

Because environmental conditions are constantly changing, leadership must be able to manipulate the organizational culture to ensure the system's ability to adapt to and survive in the environment through the evolution of new cultural assumptions. Leadership in practice verbalizes its assumptions and "embeds them gradually and consistently in the mission, goals, structures, and working procedures of the group" (Schein, 1985, p. 317). Leaders need to know how an organization's culture can help or hinder a mission's accomplishment. Leaders need to provide the impetus to implement the intervention strategies necessary to adapt the culture for organizational survival. Although leaders are responsible for replacing or redefining discarded assumptions, organizational members should be involved in the change process to ensure their renewed insight and motivation to achieve the new organizational mission.

Significant groups of authors have recently created and implemented a new empowerment model of leadership. In this era of rapid change, complexity, and globalness, further pursuits of building anew or remodeling the hierarchical organization have met with considerable resistance (McFarland et al., 1994). Rigid hierarchies or leadership in isolation are no longer possible. A more common view today places leadership in the hands of those closest to the situation and nearest to those capable of handling issues. More voices, creativity, innovation, and shared decision making may be akin to stronger organization in these functional systems. Bill Gates believes that "empowering leadership means bringing out the energy and capabilities that people have, and getting them to work together in a way they wouldn't do otherwise" (in McFarland et al., 1994, p. 68). That requires that they see the positive impact they can have and sense the opportunities.

Women in Authority

Additional differences in leadership and management styles can be discerned when reviewing the literature on women in positions of authority. With the advent of greater numbers of women in top leadership positions, it is possible to detect some distinctive ways that men and women differ in leadership roles.

Fitzpatrick (1983) described a competent communicator as one who can accurately perceive the environment and create and understand messages based on subsequent interpretation. His goals for communication were getting the job done, avoiding damage to the relationship between sender and receiver of the message, and projecting the desired image while communicating. According to Fitzpatrick, males generally operate from a problem-solving, aggressive, and focused routine and suppress strong emotion. On the other hand, females tend to give and expect to receive rewarding responses and are inclined to emphasize relational goals in interactions.

From this base comparison, Fitzpatrick (1983) conceptualized three models of organizational communicators. The first, or *masculine*, model focuses on task goals and impression management to the exclusion of relational goals. The second, or *feminine*, model emphasizes relational goals to the exclusion of task goals. The third, or *androgynous*, model blends the previous two styles. Androgynous communicators can be assertive and dominant, as is typical of task behaviors, or they can be warm and nurturing, reflecting relational behaviors.

While some argue that successful women do not necessarily lead differently than successful men, others, such as Carroll (1989), have found that women have a more sharing style of leadership than that of men and claim that women tend to give more recognition and create an empowering team atmosphere. In replicating a study by men in leadership roles (Mintzberg, 1973), Helgeson (1990) found distinct differences in leadership style. The women in her study worked at the same pace and under similar conditions as the men in Mintzberg's study but were less likely to feel controlled by the work schedule, thereby reducing job stress. More time was spent with people, and there was emphasis on sustaining good working relationships. By maintaining a more complex network of relationships both on and off the job, the women were less likely to feel isolated. In Helgeson's view, female leaders were more likely to feel themselves at the center of things instead of viewing themselves at the top, as the men in the study did.

In another context, decision making for men and women also showed distinctiveness. Putnam (1983) identified differences in ways that the two groups deal with conflict. Males are apt to arrive at a settlement using bargaining techniques, logical arguments, and anger in an effort to resolve the conflict. Women tend to work to understand others' feelings, handling conflict by smoothing over and playing down differences and emphasizing similarities. The male focus on independence, competitiveness, and autonomy often creates a win/lose scenario, whereas the female focus on interdependence can produce a win/win scenario.

Shakeshaft (1987) argued that research finding no distinctions between men and women in managing schools is faulty in that conceptually it is based on the white male model. Under these circumstances, successful women match successful men. However, when the additional motives and approaches of women are factored in, they can be seen to perform not only as well but also as differently. She argues that the work of female leaders in schools has five major elements: relationships with others are central to all actions of women administrators, teaching and learning are the major foci of women administrators, building community is an essential part of the female administrator's style, women administrators are constantly made aware of their marginality or status, and the line separating the public and private lives of women administrators are being blurred far more than for men.

Based on a survey of women's opinions conducted by the Australian Virtual Centre for Leadership in Women, Rodgers-Healey (2003) outlined a number of insights into women's perspectives on women as leaders. She perceived that most women believe that the potential to be a leader is developed incrementally over time within oneself and is focused though life experiences. Most women envision developing themselves and helping others develop. They define leadership as empowering others to achieve their visions and potential. But they feel that the percentage of women who, having achieved leadership roles, assist other women to become leaders is relatively small. They believe that if leadership by women is to be encouraged in workplaces, education, training, and formal and informal support from people who have achieved leadership will be vitally important.

ACTIVITY 4.2
Choice of Leadership Model

Addresses ISLLC Standards 1, 2, 3, 4, 5, and 6

Consider a school district as an open general system including the state legislature, the state department of education, the local legislature, local taxpayers, parents, the local school board, the superintendent of schools, a school building principal, teachers, and students.

You are the superintendent of schools in this district. Given the discussion of leadership models and styles in this chapter, in each of the following situations, what model of leadership would you choose to exercise? Why? Under what circumstances might you choose to shift your model of leadership? What shift might you make? Does making a shift make you a more or less effective leader from the point of view of others involved in the situation?

1. Developing the local school budget for the coming year
2. Negotiating a raise for the teachers for the coming year
3. Determining what textbooks to buy for the coming year
4. Meeting state testing standards for students
5. Developing a unit of instruction for use in a class
6. A parent disapproves of a teacher's handling of his or her child and confronts the teacher on the issue
7. A community group disapproves of a book that is in the school library and that is also used in a class and wants the book banned from the school

Leadership for Sustainable Change

Organizations by nature are confronted by change, both internal and external. One aspect of effective leadership is the ability to manage change while keeping the organization moving toward goals over time. This is true in educational organizations as well as generally.

This ability to manage change over time has been identified as "sustainable leadership." Rather than leadership by single charismatic individuals, it is leadership that "spreads across people over long periods of time . . . [and] benefits many schools and many children, not just a few schools that are bright exceptions in odd or eccentric places" (Hargreaves, 2005). Principles of sustainable leadership, according to Hargreaves, are that it creates and sustains learning, ensures success over time, depends on preparing both successors to the leader and those around the leader, exhibits thrift without being cheap, focuses on systems thinking and social justice, is self-sustaining, and promotes diversity and the capacity to share excellence.

A leader can follow 12 steps to build support for change that will sustain, according to Maurer (2006): identify stakeholders, what is needed from each, and what support can be provided for them; make the case

for change; identify strategies that will allow continuing to make the case for change throughout the process; determine who will lead the change effort and who will participate in the planning; consider sources and types of potential resistance; plan for and follow steps that can and will reduce problems; create and communicate a vision for where the group is to go; develop a plan for accomplishing the vision; develop measures of success and time lines; keep the change alive and work to energize the change effort over time; develop contingency plans; and celebrate achievement of milestones and of the overall goal.

Leading change that sustains over time rather than leading change that is short lived calls for a series of steps on the part of the leader, according to Covington (2007). These steps include the following: create a sense that change is needed and will in the long run benefit as many of the members of the organization as possible; ensure that the management team is actually supporting the proposed changed and not simply providing lip service; develop a clear vision of the expected outcome; communicate the vision of the expected outcome actively and effectively; set up an action plan in consultation with those persons who will be charged with implementing the change; build in a short-term win, creating encouragement by designing points of short-term gain and communicating those results energetically; and work toward making the change a matter of organizational culture, a known and understood way of doing things.

Fullan (2005), in *Leadership and Sustainability*, has taken a detailed look at sustainable change as it applies to the school, district, and system levels of education:

> The starting point is to observe that nothing tried so far really works . . . autonomy, whether it is the "let a thousand flowers bloom" variety or site-based management within a framework of external accountability, does not produce results on any scale; the command control, and support strategy of informed prescription takes us some distance, but it is still surface stuff without any likelihood of lasting. . . . Any solutions must be efficient, sophisticated, powerful, and amenable to action. (p. 13)

Fullan (2005) identified sustainability as an adaptive challenge that contains eight elements: public service with a moral purpose, commitment to changing the context of the system at all levels, lateral capacity building through networks, intelligent accountability and vertical relationships encompassing both capacity building and accountability, deep learning that examines new facts and ideas critically, dual commitment to short- and long-term results, cyclical reenergizing, and leadership that mobilizes and reinforces the other seven elements.

According to Fullan (2005), exercised at the school level, leadership of sustainable change in education involves effective assessment for learning that builds a clearer understanding of student performance and the condition of the system in which they learn, changing school shared values and beliefs (cultures) to support the effort being made, and establishing and maintaining effective links with parents and the community. At the district level, it involves leading with a compelling conceptualization; conveying a collective moral purpose; identifying and enlisting appropriate leaders and participants in the change effort; building capacity to maintain the change; building capacity to network in support of the change; encouraging online learning by the participants about the progress of the effort; understanding, accepting, and working with constructive conflict; generating and supporting a demand for competence; seeking

out and linking with external partners; and securing resources sufficient to support the effort. At the system level, it involves reality testing to ensure that ideas for change could actually be put into practice, ensuring moral purpose for the effort, getting the basics of literacy and numeracy right, communicating the overall purpose and plan for the effort, providing opportunities for local persons and groups to influence the overall picture and plan, establishing intelligent and intelligible systems of accountability, providing incentives for collaboration and lateral capacity building, exercising leadership by establishing standards and means for potential leaders to assume that role, emphasizing leadership development, providing opportunity and expectation for every teacher to become a leader in some aspect of the effort, providing consistent opportunities for questioning and reviewing the change effort, and ensuring sufficient funds to support the change effort.

Implicit in these discussions of managing sustainable change is the expectation that the leader will establish a vision, plan for and communicate the vision, direct and monitor the change process, and recognize successes and the need for improving the change process when it arises. To discharge these roles, the leader must be not only a leader in the sense in which the term is usually construed but also a teacher. To articulate a goal but not be sufficiently grounded to support and tutor those who are moving toward the goal would be visionary but not necessarily successful.

The need for developing a thoughtful approach to sustainable change has never been more apparent than now in the information age, when change and technology are the norm rather than the exception in organizations. Leadership in the information age calls for recognition of internal, external, and technological forces pressing for change, the human elements within the change process, and the danger of the leader being unconsciously a guardian of the status quo rather than a leader of change (Mackenzie, 2007). Further discussion of these issues is found in chapter 9.

Leading sustainable change also implies preparation for succession of leadership. No leader, regardless of how charismatic or effective, has permanent tenure. Succession will take place. Therefore, preparation should be made in advance for the succession. That

ACTIVITY 4.3
Leadership for Sustainable Change

Addresses ISLLC Standards 1, 2, 3, 4, 5, and 6

As the superintendent for the Lakeland School District, you have instituted an innovative curriculum for the high school. As part of the process of implementing the new approach to curriculum, you have just brought in Waldren DeLaney as principal. DeLaney was a principal in your previous district, and you share an interest in innovative approaches to education.

You both see the current administrative assignments are stepping-stones to advancement. You are interested in moving to a state-level position, and Waldren is interested in moving up to a superintendency. Because of these goals, you both plan to move on within the next 4 to 5 years. At the same time, you both believe strongly in the innovative curriculum that you have instituted.

1. What can you and Walden do over the next 2 or 3 years to strengthen the possibility that the innovative curriculum will persist beyond your stewardship?
2. What difficulties can you anticipate in your efforts to build a sustainable change?
3. What influences can you anticipate that could help you in your efforts to build a sustainable change?
4. Outline an action plan for yourself, Waldren, and the Lakeland district that will improve the chances of sustaining the new curriculum approach assuming that you and Waldren move on professionally as you plan.

said, to seek persons who will simply maintain the organizational status quo would be a disservice to the organization in the long run. The new leader must be a person with leadership vision, capable of sustaining the benefits of the current change as well as finding new directions for the organization as they are needed.

A New Paradigm for Leadership

Rost (1991) proposed that most theories of leadership reflect an industrial paradigm that is no longer acceptable or applicable to leadership needs for the 21st century. He felt that a paradigm shift is necessary so that leadership theory and practice can relate to the needs of a postindustrial world. He defined leadership as "an influence relationship among leaders and followers who intend real changes that reflect their mutual purposes" (p. 102). This is in contrast to management, which he defined as an authority relationship. He maintained that four elements must be present for a relationship to be considered a leadership relationship: a relationship based on influence, leaders and followers who are participants in the relationship, both parties intending that real changes are to take place, and both parties developing mutual purposes. He reinterpreted transformational leadership as the

involvement of "active people, engaging in influence relationships based on persuasion, intending real changes to happen, and insisting that those changes reflect their mutual purposes" (p. 213). Therefore, leadership is seen as a relationship involving multiple followers and multiple leaders who engage in shared or collaborative leadership. The roles, styles, and power influence of leaders and followers are not etched in stone but can shift.

In the new millennium our most important challenge will be to build new leadership capabilities through changes to the way we have educated our future leaders and followers. Higher education will be responsible for these dramatic changes, including the following:

1. Continuing to establish a world-class education system that is responsive to effective preparation of our future workforce.

2. Broader in-house or intraorganizational capabilities to train one's own.

3. Training new leaders in the art of building learning organizations. Perhaps our most important tasks will revolve around assimilating responses to these questions:
   a. How committed are we to lifelong learning and personal growth?

b. How is leadership training and education supported in my organization?

c. Do we collaborate across our communities to enhance our ability to function in the new millennium?

SUMMARY AND FUNDAMENTAL CONCEPTS

This chapter presented a brief compilation of the important leadership research that has been accomplished to date. It is important to build a framework that can serve as a guide to further reflection about educational and organizational leadership in the future. It is also evident that leadership research has not stood the tests of time well. Numerous authors have commented about leadership theory deficiencies. Theory ought to inform practice, as will be evident throughout the remainder of this book. Although progress is always evident, too little of value has occurred in leadership arenas. We sorely need combinations across disciplines and dimensions of intellectual thought before we can begin to be comfortable with leadership today.

Fundamental Concepts

The fundamental concepts that follow have been discussed in this chapter. The citations that conclude each concept indicate the Interstate School Leaders Licensure Consortium (ISLLC) standards and functions related to the concept. The Arabic numeral refers to the ISLLC standards, and the letters refer to the Functions as presented in the table found inside the front cover.

- To be successful, organizations need effective leadership. In many situations, that effective leadership is lacking. (1, 2, 3, 4, 5, 6)
- There is a wide variety of definitions and models of leadership, none universally applicable. (1, 2, 3, 4, 5, 6)
- Theories of leadership that have been discussed include the following:
  Leadership traits, which considers the characteristics of leaders
  Behavioral theory, which considers what leaders do
  Power influence, which considers how leaders exercise power and influence
  Leadership styles, which considers how leaders relate to tasks and to their subordinates
  Contingency and situational theories, which consider how the circumstances influence leadership
  Transformational and transactional leadership, which consider how leaders interact with others to accomplish goals

Multiple approaches to leadership
Leadership within a cultural context
Gender-based leadership styles. (1, 2, 3, 4, 5, 6)

- To sustain change over time, leaders must establish a vision, plan for and communicate the vision, direct and monitor change processes, and recognize and need for improvement where appropriate. (1A, 1B, 1C, 1D, 1E; 2D, 2E, 2F, 2H, 2I; 3A, 3D, 3E; 3A, 4B, 4C, 4D; 5A; 6A, 6B, 6C)
- Movement to the information age increases the emphasis on change and technology in education. (2H; 3B; 6C)
- A need exists to focus on training leaders in new ways to meet the coming new challenges. (2F; 3D; 5B; 6C)
- Preparations must be made in advance for leadership succession. (2F; 3D; 5B; 6C)

Chapter 5 discusses human relations as a fundamental issue in effective leadership, both in the context of a school community and generally.

Case Study

Leadership: The Case of the Invisible Principal

Addresses ISLLC Standards 1, 2, 3, 5, and 6

John Alvarez was a superior teacher who was known throughout the school district for his intellectual ability; stimulating classes; popularity with students, colleagues, and administrators; and problem-solving techniques. No one was surprised when John was appointed principal of one of the district's secondary schools. What was astounding were complaints that began to come from the chairpeople, faculty, building personnel, and students that nothing was really being accomplished. Department chairs were particularly vocal about John's insistence on knowing every detail of their decisions before permitting them to move forward. They also complained about their inability to arrange meetings with John and his lack of communication. Days would pass without any word from him about decisions. Teachers, building personnel, and students also found it difficult to arrange for personal communication with their principal.

Although acknowledging John's superior teaching ability, successful student management, and creative problem solving, several of the department chairs, faculty, and other building personnel questioned whether John would ever be a leader or even understand the difference between classroom responsibilities and those of building leadership.

John responded that his classroom abilities were the type of leadership that the school needed. He believed that if intelligent people were doing their jobs they did not need close personal contacts with their leaders. John viewed leadership as an extension of his classroom abilities and was amazed that some of his faculty, building personnel, and students were doubtful of his contribution. He could hardly believe that they labeled him their "invisible leader."

Questions

1. How is John defining leadership? How is it being defined by others?
2. What is meant by John's statement that "classroom abilities are the type of leadership that the school needs"? How is leadership in the classroom exercised? Is that model appropriate for a building principal to use?
3. If it is necessary, is it possible for John, the faculty, other building personnel, and students all to come to agreement about what leadership is and what is needed in this situation? How might that be done? What if it cannot be done?
4. Consider the work situation that you are in (or the most recent school situation that you were in). Given the discussion that you have read in this chapter, what model of leadership was demonstrated there? Was it effective? Why or why not?
5. If you were a building principal, what model of leadership do you feel that you would develop? Why? How?

REFERENCES

Abbott, M., & Caracheo, F. (1988). Power, authority and bureaucracy. In N. J. Boyan (Ed.), *Handbook of research on educational administration* (pp. 239–257). New York: Longman.

Bass, B. M. (Ed.). (1981). *Stogdill's handbook of leadership*. New York: Free Press.

Bass, B. M. (1985). *Leadership and performance beyond expectations*. New York: Free Press.

Bennis, W. (1986). Transformative power and leadership. In T. J. Sergiovanni & J. E. Corbally (Eds.), *Leadership and organizational culture* (pp. 64–71). Urbana: University of Illinois Press.

Bennis, W., & Nanus, B. (1985). *Leaders: The strategies for taking charge*. New York: Harper & Row.

Blake, R. R., & Mouton, J. S. (1961). How power affects human behavior. In J. Hall (Ed.), *Models for management: The structure of competence* (2nd ed., pp. 113–120). The Woodlands, TX: Woodstead Press.

Blake, R. R., & Mouton, J. S. (1978). *The new managerial grid*. Houston: Gulf.

Blake, R. R., & Mouton, J. S. (1981). Management by grid principles or situationalism: Which? *Group and Organization Studies, 6*(4), 439–455.

Blake, R. R., & Mouton, J. S. (1982a). How to choose a leadership style. *Training and Development Journal, 36*, 38–47.

Blake, R. R., & Mouton, J. S. (1982b). Theory and research for developing a science of leadership. *Journal of Applied Behavioral Science, 18*(3), 275–291.

Blake, R. R., & Mouton, J. S. (1990). The developing revolution in management practices. In J. Hall (Ed.), *Models for management: The structure of competence* (2nd ed., pp. 422–444). The Woodlands, TX: Woodstead Press.

Blanchard, K., Zigarmi, D., & Zigarmi, P. (1987). Situational leadership: Different strokes for different folks. *Principal, 66*, 12–16.

Burns, J. M. (1978). *Leadership*. New York: Harper & Row.

Carroll, S. (1989). Cited in Strategies for women in academe. *Academic Leadership, 5*(2).

Covington, J. (2007). Leading successful, sustainable change. *Course and Direction: The Path to Strategic Success*. Chesapeake Consulting, Inc. Retrieved June 11, 2007, from http://www.strategyletter.com

Fiedler, F. E. (1967). *A theory of leadership effectiveness*. New York: McGraw-Hill.

Fitzpatrick, M. A. (1983). Effective interpersonal communication for women of the corporation. In J. Pilotta (Ed.), *Women in organizations* (pp. 73–84). Prospect Heights, IL: Waveland Press.

French, J., & Raven, B. (1968). The bases of social power. In D. Cartwright & A. Zander (Eds.), *Group dynamics: Research and theory* (pp. 259–269). New York: Harper & Row.

Fullan, M. (2005). *Leadership and sustainability*. Thousand Oaks, CA: Corwin Press.

Gardner, J. W. (1990). *On leadership*. New York: Free Press.

Goleman, D., Boyatzis, R. E., & McKee, A. (2004, March). *Primal leadership: Learning to lead with emotional intelligence*. Cambridge, MA: Harvard Business School Press.

Hargreaves, A. (2005, Winter). Sustainable leadership. *Independent School 64*(2). Retrieved June 11, 2007, from http://library.genesee.edu:2061

Helgeson, S. (1990). *The female advantage: Women's ways of leadership*. New York: Doubleday/Currency.

Hersey, P., & Blanchard, K. H. (1988). *Management of organizational behavior* (5th ed.). Upper Saddle River, NJ: Prentice Hall.

Hickson, D., Hinings, C., Lee, C., Schneck, R., & Pennings, J. (1971). A strategic contingencies theory of intra-organizational power. *Administrative Science Quarterly, 16*, 216–229.

Homrig, M. A. (2001, December 21). *Transformational leadership*. Retrieved September 23, 2007, from http://leadership.au.af.mil/documents/homrig.htm

House, R. J. (1971). A path–goal theory of leader effectiveness. *Administrative Science Quarterly, 16*, 321–339.

House, R. J. (1984). *Power in organizations: A social psychological perspective.* Unpublished paper, University of Toronto.

House, R. J., & Dressler, G. (1974). The path–goal theory of leadership: Some post-hoc and a priori tests. In J. Hunt & L. Larson (Eds.), *Contingency approaches to leadership* (pp. 29–55). Carbondale: Southern Illinois University Press.

Judge, T. A., & Piccolo, R. F. (2004). Transformational and transactional leadership; A meta-analytic test of their relative validity. *Journal of the Applied Psychological Association, 89,* 755–768.

Kerr, S., & Jermier, J. (1978). Substitutes for leadership: Their meaning and measurements. *Organizational Behavior and Performance, 22,* 375–403.

Koestenbaum, P. (1991). *Leadership: The inner side of greatness.* San Francisco: Jossey-Bass.

Likert, R. (1961). *New patterns of management.* New York: McGraw-Hill.

Likert, R. (1967). *The human organization: Its management and value.* New York: McGraw-Hill.

Lunenburg, F. C., & Ornstein, A. C. (1991). *Educational administration: Concepts and practices.* Belmont, CA: Wadsworth.

Mackenzie, M. L. (2007, April/May). Leadership in the information age: A culture of continual change. *Bulletin.* Silver Spring, MD: American Society for Information Science and Technology. Retrieved September 23, 2007, from http://www.asis.org/Bulletin/Apr-07/mackenzie.html

Maurer, R. (2006, Spring). 12 steps that can build support for change. *Journal for Quality and Participation.* Retrieved October 28, 2008 from http://findarticles.com/p/articles/mi_qa3616/is_200604/ai_n17172793

Mazzarella, J., & Grundy, T. (1989). Portrait of a leader. In S. Smith & J. Piele (Eds.), *School leadership: Handbook for excellence* (pp. 9–27). Eugene: ERIC Clearinghouse on Educational Management, University of Oregon.

McFarland, L. J., Senn, L. E., & Childress, J. R. (1994). *21st century leadership: Dialogs with 100 top leaders.* New York: Leadership Press.

McGregor, D. (1990a). Theory X: The traditional view of direction and control. In J. Hall (Ed.), *Models for management: The structure of competence* (2nd ed., pp. 11–18). The Woodlands, TX: Woodstead Press.

McGregor, D. (1990b). Theory Y: The integration of individual and organizational goals. In J. Hall (Ed.), *Models of management: The structure of competence* (2nd ed., pp. 19–27). The Woodlands, TX: Woodstead Press.

Mintzberg, J. (1973). *The nature of managerial work.* New York: Harper & Row.

Nebecker, D., & Mitchell, T. (1974). Leader behavior: An expectancy theory approach. *Organizational Behavior and Human Performance, 11,* 355–367.

Ouchi, W. (1981). *Theory Z: How American business can meet the Japanese challenge.* New York: Avon Books.

Putnam, L. Z. (1983). Lady, you're trapped: Breaking out of conflict cycles. In J. J. Pilotta (Ed.), *Women in organizations.* Prospect Heights, IL: Waveland Press, pp. 39–53.

Rodgers-Healey, D. (2003, March 8). *12 insights into leadership for women.* Australian Virtual Centre for Leadership for Women. Retrieved September 23, 2007, from http://www.leadershipforwomen.com.au/questionnaire/12insights1.htm

Rost, J. C. (1991). *Leadership for the twenty-first century.* New York: Praeger.

Salancik, G., & Pfeffer, J. (1977). Who gets power—and how they hold on to it: A strategic contingency model of power. *Organizational Dynamics, 5,* 3–21.

Schein, E. H. (1985). *Organizational culture and leadership: A dynamic view.* San Francisco: Jossey-Bass.

Sergiovanni, T. J. (1986). Leadership as cultural expression. In T. J. Sergiovanni & J. E. Corbally (Eds.), *Leadership and organizational culture* (pp. 105–114). Urbana: University of Illinois Press.

Sergiovanni, T. J., & Corbally, J. E. (Eds.). (1986). *Leadership and organizational culture.* Urbana: University of Illinois Press.

Shakeshaft, C. (1987). *Women in educational administration.* Newbury Park, CA: Sage.

Shetty, Y. (1978). Managerial power and organizational effectiveness: A contingency analysis. *Journal of Management Studies, 15,* 176–186.

Smith, P. B., & Peterson, M. F. (1989). *Leadership, organizations and culture: An event management model.* London: Sage.

Sorum, A. (2007, June 20). *Better leaders employ the use of multiple management methods.* Retrieved September 12, 2007, from http://businessmanagement.suite101.com/article.cfm/utilize_varied

Sotarauta, M. (2002). *Leadership, power, and influence in regional development: A tentative typology of leaders and their ways of influencing.* Stockholm: Nordrigeo.

Stogdill, R., & Coons, A. (Eds.). (1957). *Leader behavior: Its description and measurement.* Columbus: Bureau of Business Research, Ohio State University.

Vroom, V., & Jago, A. (1988). *The new leadership: Managing participation in organizations.* Upper Saddle River, NJ: Prentice Hall.

Vroom, V., & Yetton, P. (1973). *Leadership and decision making.* Pittsburgh, PA: University of Pittsburgh Press.

White, R., & Lippitt, R. (1990). Leader behavior and member reaction in three "social climates." In J. Hall (Ed.), *Models for management: The structure of competence* (2nd ed., pp. 146–172). The Woodlands, TX: Woodstead Press.

Yukl, G. A. (1989). *Leadership in organizations.* Upper Saddle River, NJ: Prentice Hall.

Yukl, G., & Lespinger, R. (2004). *Flexible leadership: Creating value by balancing multiple challenges and choices.* Hoboken, NJ: Wiley.

Human Relations: The Base for Educational Leadership

Calls for strong educational leadership have increased in recent years. Faith in the power of leadership and its potential to make a difference in schools underlies much of the literature on leadership for educational excellence. The literature reveals that leaders in competent schools are skilled in managerial, instructional, and interpersonal tasks. In this era of excellence, more demands exist: school leaders must shape values, develop vision, create meanings, and develop unique culture based on their moral values (Sergiovanni, 1984, 1991, 1992). Like other organizational domains, school leadership must not only "do the things right" but also "do the right things." In goal-driven organizations, complex human interactions necessitate that educational constituencies, superintendents, principals, teachers, students, and community partners alike have a clear understanding of human nature and human behavior patterns—hence the necessity to understand human relations.

In chapter 4, we discussed the nature of leadership from a variety of perspectives. Transformational leadership and other theoretical models were explored. In this chapter, we focus on leadership as related to human relations and the development of skills necessary for professional growth and the ability to work in within the overall educational environment.

The Development of Human Relations Concepts

Although human relationships have existed since the beginning of time, the art and science of trying to deal with them formally in the work setting is relatively new. Not until the second half of the 19th century did researchers turn their attention to workers' needs. The evolution of the main concepts of human relations occurred in six stages: classical thinking, systematic development, teaching and practice, refinement, decline, and evolving (Davis, 1967; Sanford, 1977).

The Stage of Classical Thinking (Pre-1930s)

This stage is characterized by classical economic theory and the scientific management movement. The proponents of the theory of economic man believe that human behavior is determined by economic needs and economic goals. Human relations is a matter of establishing an incentive that contributes to the necessities of life and replenishment of the workforce. The scientific management movement focuses on increasing efficiency and productivity while drawing attention to the importance of people in the work situation. Taylor (1911), the father of scientific management, was one of the first to call attention to people in the work situation as an important factor in the quest for efficiency in production. In his view, human problems are what stand in the way of greater productivity. Taylor called for the scientific selection and development of the worker. Although some scholars (Dennison, 1931; Frankel & Fleisher, 1920; Gantt, 1916; Ure, 1835) emphasized individual human psychological and social needs, their ideas were accepted slowly or not at all. Effective and efficient organizations were characterized as if they were machines. Workers were perceived from an efficiency perspective or as productivity resources.

The Stage of Systematic Development (1930–1950)

Most of the foundation of modern human relations theory and practice developed during this stage. As an early reaction to mechanistic interpretation of organization, Follett (1930) spoke out on the dignity and value of satisfied workers. The works of Mayo (1933) and Roethlisberger and Dickson (1939) at the Hawthorne plant also sparked an early interest in human relations. Findings from the Hawthorne studies indicated that productivity concerned social and psychological interactions among human resources. Further studies showed that workers in continuous and close contact create informal social structures that may influence their productive behavior. Various iterations of the Hawthorne studies marked the beginning of the end of reliance on economic concepts as the primary explanation of work motivation and behavior. The study of organizations as social systems in which social needs are the most important motivator of workers became a focus.

The Stage of Teaching and Practice (1950–1960)

After the conclusions of the Hawthorne research were disseminated, human relations concepts began to be applied on a significant scale. As a result of the Hawthorne studies, the focus of human relations practice shifted from an economic emphasis to a sociopsychological emphasis. Worker need satisfaction was seen to lead to greater productivity, and the social and psychological needs of the worker were seen as significant determinants of behavior. The expectation was that worker productivity would increase if human relations activity in the organization were attended to and manipulated. Workers would derive greater social and psychological satisfaction as a result.

It was also believed that social satisfaction demands freedom to socialize on the job. Psychological satisfaction could be fulfilled by allowing workers to participate in managerial decisions. This, in turn, would result in greater need satisfaction, resulting in increased performance and higher productivity. Morale, a related concept, also became an interesting research topic. All these concepts reflected an optimistic view of human nature.

As this stage continued, Argyris (1964); Blake and Mouton (1964); Fiedler (1967); Herzberg, Mausner, and Snyderman (1959); Likert (1961); Maslow (1954); McGregor (1960); Porter and Lawler (1968); Tannebaum and Schmidt (1958); and Vroom (1964) were among the most important scholars. They elaborated on human aspects of organization as well as individual needs and motivation.

The Stage of Refinement (1960–1970)

Efforts continued in several arenas, including the development of better theory and improvement in the practice, resulting in a synthesis of human relations theories. Three major theory modifications include Miles's (1975) human resources model, Likert's (1967) supportive model, and Tosi and Hamner's (1974) contingency model.

Miles's human resource model assumed that work is not inherently distasteful and that people want to contribute to meaningful goals. For Miles, the most important matter in organizations is how to make use of untapped human resources. Likert's supportive model emphasized the supportive climate of the organizational life. A supportive climate ensures that members in an organization will feel a sense of personal worth and importance in all their interactions and relationships with the organization. Tosi and Hamner's contingency model required that we explore the organization as a system or unit of behavior composed of subsystems or subunits that have identified boundaries within the system. The behavior of one unit is dependent on its environmental relationship to other subunits and has some control over the consequences desired by the subunit. Individual and group behavior are contingent on four related elements: psychological determinants, organizational determinants, internal organizational characteristics, and environmental characteristics.

The Stage of Decline (1970–1980)

Research in human relations declined after the 1970s as researchers became interested in other factors. A majority of the theoretical studies in this period focused on leadership roles with reference to leaders rather than on the workers themselves. Models developed in this period focused on studies of various parts of the leadership process (e.g., communication, planning, decision making, and evaluation). No significant attempts were made to construct an integrative framework of human relations.

The Stage of Evolving (1980–Present)

Today it seems apropos to study the phases of successful Japanese management performance and "evolve" through the various applications of Japanese human relations concepts. This period looks critically at the human side of organizations. Ouchi's (1981) theory Z, which includes quality of work life, collective decision making and responsibility, lifetime employment, implicit control, and quality circles, reflects concepts being explored in the human relations paradigm (Kossen, 1987). Ouchi is credited with having drawn substantial attention during the 1980s to the differences between Japanese and North American styles of management. His models conceptualize organizations that maintain formal and explicit control mechanisms and believe in formal planning, management by objectives, and sophisticated information and accounting systems. Quality circles—groups consisting of rank-and-file workers who exchange information for mutual improvement—began the revival of managerial concern back to workers.

Conceptualizing Human Relations Theories

While the previously discussed stages help us trace the human relations movement, it is also important to understand the conceptual underpinnings of the movement. The human relations movement emphasizes the important roles of human factors in organizations.

Definitions of Human Relations

Efforts have been made to conceptualize human relations from different perspectives. Saltonstall (1959) viewed human relations as the "study of people in action" (p. 3). Saltonstall also saw human relations as the study of people at work, "not only people as individuals but people as members of informal work groups, people as executives in management, people as union members, and people as members of organizations with economic goals" (p. 4).

From the management perspective, Scott (1962) defined human relations as effective motivation of individuals in a given situation to achieve a balanced objective that yields greater satisfaction and helps accomplish organization goals. Concern with human relations promises higher productivity, greater organizational effectiveness, and satisfied employees.

Realizing the complexity of human organizations, Davis (1977) explained that the term *human relations* applies broadly to the interaction of people in all types of endeavor—in business, government, social clubs, schools, and homes. The human interactions developed at work are called *employee human relations* or *organizational human relations*. Therefore, human relations is the study of human behavior at work and an effort to take action in operating situations in order to produce better results.

Optimistic Assumptions of Human Nature

Classical studies tend to adopt the pessimistic view of human nature. Human beings are portrayed as rebellious, greedy, aggressive, and uncooperative. In contrast, human relations embraces an optimistic view. Proponents of this view believe that it is natural for human beings to be self-motivated and self-controlled, although behavioral reactions are influenced by the treatment received from others (Knezevich, 1984).

The optimistic view of human nature emphasizes four aspects: individual differences, the whole person, caused behavior, and human dignity (Davis, 1967, 1977). Davis and others held that although people have much in common, each person in the world is also individually different. Individual differences require therefore that justice and rightness be determined on a case-by-case basis and not statistically. Davis also maintained that a person's various traits may be studied separately, but in the final analysis all are part of one system making up a whole. Similarly, a person's emotional condition is not separate from one's physical condition. Each affects the other.

Clinical and Ethical Dimensions

The study of human relations can also be viewed from two other dimensions: a clinical dimension and an ethical dimension. From the clinical dimension, human relations uses tools and data to solve concrete human problems in situations where they occur. From an ethical dimension, ideas pertaining to personal freedom and the preeminence of individual action and an affirmation of the value of human collaboration and solidarity are considered (Scott, 1962).

Theoretical Perspectives of Human Relations

Research from various disciplines has contributed to the development of numerous usable human relations concepts, but most human relations concepts result from findings in industrial experiments and organizational psychology. Relevant human relations studies and their relation to leadership are summarized into four categories—human nature, human motivation, morale in organizations, and informal organizations—and are examined in the following sections. It should be noted that these studies use the terms *management* (managers) and *leadership* (leaders) interchangeably.

Human Nature

Theory X and Theory Y

Psychological studies indicate that, for the most part, our perception of others determines how we will treat others and respond to them. Our perception is the lens by which we judge and see others (Hall, 1980; Hammond, 1966). McGregor (1960) categorized two distinct lenses that managers use: theory X and theory Y. Theories X and Y contrast the perceptions that classical managerial and human relations thinkers espouse.

Theory X, representing the traditional mechanistic view, assumes the following: the average human being has an inherent dislike of work and will avoid it if he can; because of this human characteristic, most people must be coerced, controlled, directed, and threatened with punishment to get them to put forth

adequate effort to achieve organizational objectives; and the average human being prefers to be directed, wishes to avoid responsibility, has relatively little ambition, and wants security above all. McGregor (1960) argued that although theory X provides an explanation of some human behavior in organizations, there are many readily observable phenomena that are not consistent with this view of human nature.

Theory Y, representing the human relations view, provides a distinctly different assumption regarding human nature. It maintains the following: the expenditure of physical and mental effort in work is as natural as play or rest; external control and the threat of punishment are not the only means for bringing about effort toward organizational objectives (people will exercise self-direction and self-control in the service of objectives to which they are committed); commitment to objectives is a function of the rewards associated with their achievement; the average person learns, under proper conditions, not only to accept but also to seek responsibility; the capacity to exercise a relatively high degree of imagination, ingenuity, and creativity in the solution of organizational problems is widely, not narrowly, distributed in the population; and under the conditions of modern industrial life, the intellectual potential of the average person is only partially utilized.

Theory X offers a rationalization for ineffective organizational performance and the nature of the human resource. In contrast, theory Y suggests that the ineffectiveness of organizational behavior lies in different organizational contexts and processes. The central principle of organization evident in theory X is direction and control. The principle derived from theory Y demands that the needs of both the organization and the individual be recognized. McGregor (1960) stated that since external control and direction are appropriate means under certain circumstances, assumptions in theory Y do not deny the appropriateness of those of theory X. Theory Y simply shows that theory X does not apply in all cases.

Pygmalion Leadership

The selection of an appropriate style of management is a crucial task for managers. The style provides the basis for interpreting our own experiences. This exerts a powerful influence, as workers may be caught in a self-fulfilling prophecy, or Pygmalion effect (Berlew & Hall, 1966; Merton, 1948; Rosenthal, 1974; Rosenthal & Jacobson, 1968). Thus, when managers treat their subordinates as creative, committed, competent people, as in McGregor's theory Y, both the manager and the subordinates will reap the rewards of the self-fulfilling prophecy. When managers vacillate and treat their subordinates as incapable people, subordinates are less likely to perform at their full potential (Duchon, Green, & Taber, 1986; Eden, 1990a; Scandura, Graen, & Novak, 1986). Four factors that mediate the Pygmalion effect are socioemotional climate, feedback, input, and output (Brophy, 1985).

Leadership plays an important role in mediating the effects of self-fulfilling prophecy in organizations (see Figure 5.1). Pygmalion leadership is the consistent encouragement, support, and reinforcement of high expectations of followers. Pygmalion leadership, according to Eden (1990b), is an approach that leaders may adopt in order to lead their followers toward excellence.

Evaluating followers' performances and letting them know where they stand are leadership acts that make followers aware that someone is observing and monitoring activities. The Pygmalion leader can use many opportunities in day-to-day interactions to comment on followers' performances, either as compliments or as corrections. Positive feedback maintains good work performances, while negative feedback encourages performance improvement (Komaki, 1986). Giving workers opportunities to show what they can do fosters high performance both by expressing high expectations and by allowing excellence to occur (Eden, 1990b).

Pygmalion leadership is effective only when it functions in all four interrelated dimensions, as shown in Figure 5.1. A leader providing continuous feedback to followers will guide them in the right direction with confidence. A leader showing enthusiasm in worker training will find that workers progress well. Thus, increases in expectations become possible. The result of a supportive climate in the organization will be mutual respect between leader and followers. This mutual respect enables the followers to put more effort into the job. A leader wishing to provide more challenging tasks can examine the potential of the workers, which is often not fully realized. Challenging tasks upgrade workers' performances and facilitate high expectations.

FIGURE 5.1

Pygmalion leadership

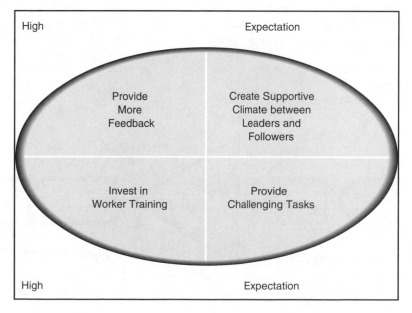

Human Motivation

Human Motivation and Human Behavior

Human relations thinkers see the terms *motivation* and *behavior* as closely related because human behavior occurs as a result of motivation. Motivation and behavior are connected through needs and wants (desires) (see Figure 5.2). Needs create tensions that are modified by one's culture or situations to cause certain wants (desires). These wants are interpreted in terms of positive and negative incentives to produce a certain response or action. The action is directed toward the accomplishment or the satisfaction of the needs (Davis, 1967; Halloran, 1978; Sanford, 1977).

Not all needs create tension and result in behavior. At any given point, people have some needs that are relatively well satisfied or at least partially satisfied as well as some unsatisfied needs. The satisfied needs do not motivate; the unsatisfied needs are the ones that create tension and motivate behavior.

Motivation Models

Students of human behavior and human motivation have identified two basic types of theoretical models that deal with human motivation in organizations: process models and content models (J. D. Campbell & Pritchard, 1983). Process models explore how and why motivation generally works. Content models deal with what specifically motivates people.

Process Models. Among the several different process models of motivation are the expectancy model, the behaviorist model, and the social learning model.

Expectancy Models. Expectancy models are derived principally from Tolman's (1932) cognitive theory and Lewin's (1951) field theory. Expectancy models suggest that the motivation to perform a task is a function of a person's expectations or beliefs about effort, performance, and outcomes. Vroom's expectancy model and the Porter and Lawler model are two widely used expectancy models that explain human motivation.

Vroom (1964) contended that motivation is a function of three factors: the strength or desirability of the goal, the perceived ability to exhibit the required behavior, and the perceived probability that the behavior will result in goal achievement.

Motivation is the product of how strongly one desires something and one's perception of the probability that certain strategies or instrumentalities are likely to fulfill those desires. Vroom called the intensity of the personal desire *valence* and the achievement probability by pursuing a given strategy *expectancy*.

Vroom's expectancy model has been replicated and refined numerous times (Dachler & Mobley, 1973; Feldman, Reitz, & Hiterman, 1976; Porter & Lawler, 1968). Porter and Lawler developed a more complete and complex expectancy model by investigating the relationship between satisfaction and productivity.

FIGURE 5.2

Motivation and behavior

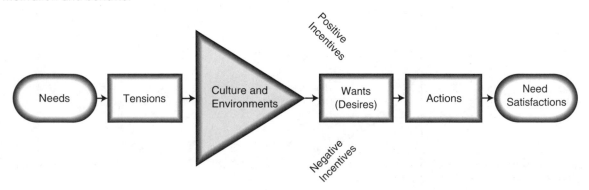

They suggested that the effort a person puts into work depends on the value one places on the expected reward and the likelihood that the reward actually will be received if the effort is made.

This process is completed in a sequence of steps (see Figure 5.3). First, the worker assigns some value to the possible reward for performing work. Based on this performance, the person expects to receive a fair reward and is then rewarded either intrinsically or extrinsically. Finally, this process is completed with two feedback loops. One results from the person's perception of the likelihood that effort will actually yield the expected reward and the other from the person's judgment as to the value of the rewards obtained. The Porter and Lawler model suggests that performance leads to satisfaction and that the level of satisfaction obtained shapes future effort to perform (Owens, 1987).

Path–goal theory is a leadership theory that utilizes the expectancy model. Path–goal theory includes four differing behavioral styles influencing employee satisfaction, the employees' acceptance of the leader, and employee beliefs that effort can result in performance and that performance will result in deserved rewards.

The four styles of leadership derived from expectancy theory are directive, supportive, participative, and achievement oriented. Path–goal theory assumes that leaders are capable of exhibiting more than one of those styles, depending on the circumstances. In whatever situation, the exhibition of the leadership style should recognize and arouse employee needs and attempt to increase the payoff to employees for successful performance when it occurs, attempt to influence subordinates' expectancy beliefs by assisting with the accomplishment of difficult tasks

FIGURE 5.3

Porter–Lawler model of motivation

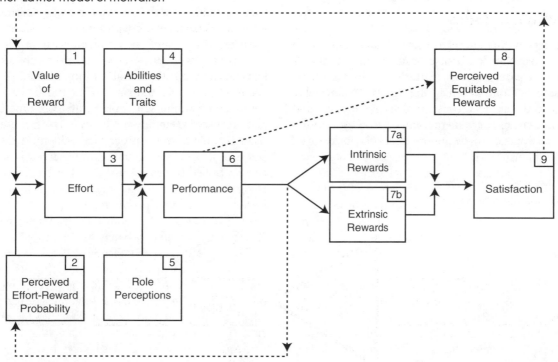

Source: L. W. Porter, and E. E. Lawler, *Managerial attitudes and performance* (p. 165). Homewood, IL: Irwin, 1968. Copyright 1968 by Richard D. Irwin. Reprinted by permission.

and clarifying vague task assignments, and make the distribution of rewards contingent on the successful accomplishment of work.

Behaviorist Models. Origins of the behaviorist model can be traced back to 1910 and the behavioral approach advocated by Watson. Watson (1930) limited the behaviorist approach to acts that can reliably be observed, what a person says or does. The model, elaborated by Skinner (1953, 1971, 1974), in use today follows that tradition. The behaviorist model is based on two simple assumptions. First, behavior is essentially determined by the environment through basic reinforcement processes: environmental stimuli, behavioral responses, and outcomes (S-R-O). Second, human behavior, like the behavior of physical and chemical elements, is subject to certain laws. Human behavior can be modified through reinforcement.

Behaviorist models question the concept of internal motivation that implies internal causal force that cannot be observed directly. Instead, according to behaviorists, people are motivated by external events called *reinforcers* and through positive and negative reinforcement processes (Skinner, 1974). Both positive and negative reinforcements strengthen the probability that a behavior is likely to occur. Positive reinforcement increases behavior frequency by the application of some circumstances, while negative reinforcement decreases behavior frequency by the removal of some circumstances that were previously part of the environmental context. By definition, negative reinforcement is not punishment. It aims at decreasing, not increasing, behavior occurrence. Behaviorist models indicate that the timing of rewards is often more important than their magnitude. Immediate rewards can affect performance more effectively than larger delayed rewards, while variable reinforcement can maintain high levels of effort more effectively than can mixed rewards (Reitz, 1987; Skinner, 1974).

The application of behaviorist models by management assumes that employees' desires for the rewards of positive reinforcement and recognition will, in large measure, motivate them to perform satisfactorily in anticipation of such rewards. Leadership in this model then requires the leader to inform subordinates concerning which behaviors are desirable and are rewarded and which behaviors are not rewarded; provide continuous feedback to employees regarding the nature and quality of their work; recognize employees for good work; ensure that employees receive immediate, unscheduled reinforcement during or immediately after strong performance; and reward differently depending on the performance level (Hamner & Hamner, 1976).

Social Learning Models. A third process model of human behavior in organizations is the social learning model. Developed by Bandura (1968, 1976, 1977), Mahoney (1974), Mischell (1973), and Staats (1975), it combines features of the cognitive and reinforcement approaches to help explain human behavior. It places emphasis on learning from other people (i.e., social learning).

Social learning is based on the principles of behaviorism and stresses the importance of reinforcement in explaining behavior. However, the social model maintains that the role of the environment in shaping behavior is mediated by cognitive processes. These processes are depicted in social learning models by adding one element to the basic S-R-O reinforcement model: cognitive processes (C) mediate the effects of environmental stimuli (S) on behavioral responses (R), which then are followed by outcomes (O). The social learning model is then S-C-R-O (Bandura, 1977).

Modeling and self-control are two types of behaviors that exemplify the social learning process. *Modeling* refers to the process by which a person learns a behavior by imitating an observed model. Self-controlled behavior is exhibited by the person's recognition of the external limits. Research in social learning reveals that people tend to reproduce the actions, attitudes, and emotional responses exhibited by models in modeling behavior (Bandura, 1969; Bandura & Walters, 1963; Flanders, 1968). Whether events or circumstances become reinforcing depends partly on observing or modeling the reinforcing or punishing outcomes of other people's behavior. People are motivated not only by their direct experience of response outcomes but also by observing the consequences of other people's behavior.

One of the most important implications of social learning is that leaders need to be especially aware of their own behavior. Leaders who have one set of expectations for their followers but then behave differently themselves may be setting themselves up for disappointment. It may be true that most effective leaders lead by example. A second implication of social learning is that both formal and informal organizational structures are of vital importance to leadership. Leaders may find that the best insights into the informal organization result from observing actions.

The behavioral and social learning models provide a means to further develop leadership skills. The efficacy of this approach has been demonstrated directly over the past few decades by women and minorities who have sought leadership roles. As more women and members of minority groups have ascended to leadership ranks, they have provided increasing opportunities for mentoring and role modeling. This has steadily increased access to leadership positions for these groups.

Process Models and Motivation. Two concepts implied by process models deserve leadership consideration: motivation to work harder versus motivation to work smarter and positive motivation versus negative motivation.

Motivating people to work harder means encouraging them to apply more physical energy to their work. Motivating people to work smarter means encouraging them to think and work creatively and to develop better ways of doing things. The first approach offers only limited increase in output and probably a decrease in satisfaction. The second approach is likely to offer greater reward without the necessity of harder work because new and better ways of work can be developed to replace the old ones. In addition, leaders can use positive and negative reinforcement at their disposal. Positive motivation involves the cultivation of a cooperative attitude among followers so that organizational goals can be accepted and achieved. Stimulating action through fear is the foundation of negative motivation. Negative motivation forces a person to select between undesirable alternatives. Most leaders use both. In light of the trend toward better employee education and greater independence, leaders need to reduce negative leadership and increase the positive. Followers need to cultivate working smarter.

Content Models. Process models describe how motivation works in general terms. In application, managers need to know more about how models work and what specifically rewards or reinforces human behavior. Content models help leaders understand human behavior further. Content models of motivation can be classified into two schools based on their research concerns. One focuses on common human needs and the second on human motivation at work.

The Importance of Human Needs. Psychological studies of human relations indicate that most human behavior is caused by a person's need structure. Behavior can be influenced by motivating people to fulfill their needs as they see them. People are motivated not by what others think ought to motivate them but by what they themselves want. As classical management study has determined, people cannot survive for long without the primary needs, such as food, drink, sleep, and air to breathe, being met. Yet classical management thought also demonstrated that secondary needs are equally important. We are eager to feel secure, to be with other people, to be respected, and to fulfill our potential. Since these human needs arise from the biological and sociopsychological makeup of individuals, they are significant elements of human behavior.

Psychologists working on content models of motivation have identified scores of different rewards and reinforcers and have arranged them into categories to aid understanding. Cognitive psychologists and psychoanalysts have further refined these categories into classes of needs and motives.

Maslow's Need Hierarchy. The most widely known classification of needs was compiled by Maslow, who described human motivation as arising from five categories of needs. Maslow (1954) conjectured that while different cultures satisfy these needs in different ways, the needs themselves remain the same. He identified five categories of needs: physiological needs, such as hunger, thirst, respiration, and sex; safety needs, such as shelter, orderliness, consistency, protection from threat and danger, and predictability in one's environment; social needs, such as needs for friendship, love, and affiliation; esteem needs, including self-esteem and the esteem of others; and self-actualization, or the need to fulfill one's potential, to test one's limits, and to become whatever one can become.

According to Maslow (1954), these five categories of needs form a hierarchy. Each level of need has to be gratified to some extent before the next level in order assumes importance. Lower-order needs do not become unimportant, but higher-order needs achieve greater significance for the person as basic needs become satisfied.

The first two levels of needs (lower-order needs) are satisfied primarily through economic behavior; the other three (higher-order needs) are satisfied primarily through symbolic behavior of psychic and social content. In light of these five basic needs, the classical economic-man concept can be considered incomplete in that it applies largely to lower-order needs. Self-actualization needs are the highest order of needs and may rarely be satisfied by most people. An important feature of self-actualization needs is that they express themselves through different behaviors in different people. Moreover, unlike other levels of needs, the satisfaction of self-actualization needs tends to increase their importance rather than reduce it (Maslow, 1962).

In practice, behavior by any given person during any given time probably is the result of more than one need or class of needs. Most acts are influenced by all five classes of needs, with one of the levels having a greater effect in the specific case.

Porter's Needs Hierarchy. Porter (1961) reformulated Maslow's original needs hierarchy slightly. He assumed that few people are motivated by such basic physical needs as thirst and hunger and instead, after self-esteem, have a need for autonomy. *Autonomy* refers to individuals' needs to participate in making decisions that affect them, exert influence in controlling the work situation, have a voice in setting job-related goals, and have authority to make decisions and latitude to work independently.

Alderfer's Three Categories of Needs. In an attempt to reconcile Maslow's theory with research on human needs in work settings, Alderfer (1969, 1972) proposed three categories of needs: existence, relatedness, and growth. Alderfer argued that these three categories of needs are primary and that they

are innate to human nature rather than learned. *Existence* refers to basic needs for survival, similar to Maslow's physiological and security needs. These needs often relate to scarce resources. According to Alderfer, Maslow's concept of social needs, love, self-esteem, and belonging are equally important. All people require interaction with others and the development of meaningful relationships with others. Alderfer refers to this category of needs as *relatedness. Growth* needs suggest that people need to develop their own skills, abilities, and self-esteem. This is similar to Maslow's need for self-esteem and self-actualization. While Maslow saw self-actualization as consisting of the fulfillment of an innate potential, Alderfer's growth needs consist of desires to interact successfully with one's environment. As the person's environment changes, so will the expression of growth needs. Although Alderfer's three categories cover roughly the same domains as Maslow's, he did not maintain that preceding needs have to be fulfilled before others can influence behavior.

McClelland's Social Motives. McClelland (1955, 1975) identified three important social motives: achievement, power, and affiliation. The *achievement* motive is the strongest common human need. Achievement refers to the desire of people to compete against a standard of excellence (McClelland, 1961, 1987; Steers & Spencer, 1977). Realizing this characteristic, leaders can promote excellence. The need the need for *power* or *dominance* represents a desire to influence others and to control one's environment. For leaders, power motives can take two forms: personalized power and socialized power. People who seek personalized power attempt to dominate others without regard to greater objectives. Those who have a socialized need use their power to work with and through others to accomplish objectives. To them, power is important but as a means to an end rather than as an end in itself. *Affiliation* is the need for positive relationships with other people. A major aspect of the affiliation motive is the need for communication. People with a high need for affiliation tend to take jobs characterized by a high amount of interpersonal contact. They tend to perform better when given supportive feedback.

According to McClelland (1975, 1976), those managers with a high need for socialized power are often excellent leaders. On the other hand, a high need for achievement can be detrimental. Similarly, a high need for affiliation leads to indecisiveness. Instead, McClelland (1976) found that power-oriented managers, when truly concerned about the organization as a whole, provide the structure, drive, and support necessary to facilitate goal-oriented group behavior.

Ardrey's Territorial Theory. Another description of common human needs is derived from cultural anthropologists. According to Ardrey (1966), people have three types of basic needs: identity, security, and stimulation. People strive for identity, not anonymity; stimulation, not boredom; and security, not anxiety. Ardrey believed that property or territory is one of the prime concepts that satisfies these needs; therefore, much individual behavior is directed toward acquiring property or defending territory. Property and territory refer to a range of things, running from real property to a favorite and customary seat in the classroom.

Leadership Considerations

Despite the criticisms, some implications suggested by theories and models of common human needs are significant for leadership. Study of common human needs reveals that it is unrealistic for leaders to think that they can satisfy all needs through entitlement. This economic-man concept may apply only to lower-order needs. Higher-order needs are satisfied primarily through symbolic behavior of psychic, social, and cultural content. It is also necessary for leaders to recognize that normally gratified needs are no longer highly motivating. Employees are more enthusiastically motivated by their own achievements than by needs that normally would have been satisfied.

Motivation at Work

There are almost as many theories of work motivation as there are writers on the subject of motivation. Their works commonly focus on the connection between motivation and work-related behavior. Two significant models are presented here: Herzberg's motivator–hygiene theory and Shamir's collectivistic motivation.

Studies in collectivistic motivation represent a new trend in work motivation. Although the models described earlier help us understand worker motivation to perform, their usefulness in everyday organizational contexts is limited. Leaders become confused when they try to apply these theories to workers in practice. If all people have changing needs, how can leaders or managers attempt to motivate an entire workforce? What the practicing leader or manager needs is an answer to the question, What will motivate most of the people most of the time? Herzberg and Shamir sought to provide practical representations to answer the question.

Herzberg's Motivator–Hygiene Theory. Herzberg's motivator–hygiene theory is one of the most recognized and most practical models. Herzberg and his associates aimed to determine what affects worker motivation and productivity in organizations (Herzberg, 1966, 1968; Herzberg et al., 1959). The theory assumes that employees are motivated to produce at high levels when they perceive satisfactory results. Herzberg proposed that the opposite of satisfaction and motivation is not dissatisfaction but simply no job satisfaction. The opposite of dissatisfaction, in turn, is not job satisfaction but simply the absence of dissatisfaction. The distinction between job satisfaction and dissatisfaction becomes clear when the two are related to levels of performance. A neutral point exists in performance levels where employees are not dissatisfied with their jobs, but neither are they experiencing job satisfaction. At this point, employees simply perform at the minimum acceptable level necessary to maintain their jobs and employment. Eliminating sources of dissatisfaction does not mean that the reduction is motivating to the worker or will lead to job satisfaction. Rather, job satisfaction and dissatisfaction are affected by different sets of factors and have different effects on employee motivation and performance. One set of factors, *hygiene*, tends to affect dissatisfaction and performance below acceptable levels, while a second set of factors, *motivator*, tends to affect job satisfaction, motivation, and performance above acceptable levels.

Herzberg (1968, 1981) found that hygiene factors such as company policy, types of supervision, status, job security, salary, working conditions, and interpersonal relations keep employees from being dissatisfied, although they do not necessarily motivate employees. Motivating factors such as achievement, recognition, the work itself, responsibility, growth, and advancement appear to motivate people and are associated with job satisfaction. To motivate an employee, Herzberg claimed that those factors originally identified as motivators must be built into an employee's job. The content of the work rather than the setting in which it is conducted is the important factor. The work must be enriched in such a way that it allows a person opportunities to feel achievement and recognition and provides for advancement and meaningful responsibility.

Shamir's Collectivistic Work Motivation. All models of motivation to this point are individually and rationally oriented because of their derivation from psychological and economic paradigms. These paradigms assume that people are motivated to satisfy their own personal needs. Recent studies, however, have shown that not all human motivations can be explained on the basis of individualistic or hedonistic considerations (Shamir, 1990). This is particularly evident given the individual contributions to collective work efforts in most organizational life.

In his study, Shamir (1990) pointed out that many collective entities in such organizations as government agencies, schools, and hospitals cannot be explained on purely individualistic and economic grounds, termed *calculative* by Etzioni (1961). Shamir maintained that "in order to understand individuals' contributions to such collective actions we have to consider both the calculative and the normal dimensions of the person's motivation simultaneously" (p. 314). Shamir proposed that understanding individual contributions to collective work efforts should be approached from three aspects simultaneously: calculative considerations, moral- or value-based considerations, and expression and maintenance of identities (see Figure 5.4).

A person's motivation to contribute to collective efforts can be explained, in part, by calculative considerations in terms of self-efficacy, collective efficacy, social rewards and sanctions, and social linkage between collective outcomes and individual rewards. *Self-efficacy* (i.e., expectancy) refers to the likelihood

FIGURE 5.4

Shamir's collectivistic work motivation

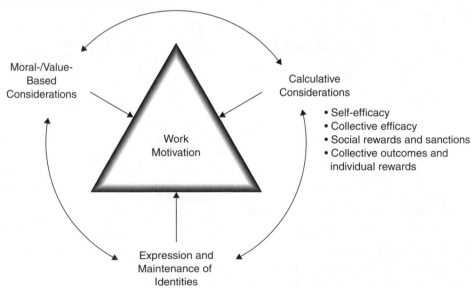

that a person's contribution will increase group performance. *Collective efficacy* refers to a person's subjective probability that collective efforts will result in collective accomplishment. Social rewards, such as social acceptance and social recognition or status, and social sanctions, such as pressure to conform, social rejection, and loss of status, influence a person's effort at collectivistic work motivation.

The relationship between collective outcomes and individual rewards is twofold. On the one hand, collective outcomes can be translated into individual rewards in terms of profits consumed by individuals. On the other hand, many outcomes of collective work efforts constitute a common good, such as improved equipment or a better technology, which cannot be consumed individually. The two dimensions have equally important impacts on individuals' efforts at collective work motivation.

Shamir (1990) proposed that in order to increase collective cohesiveness (members' attraction to the collectivity and their identification with the collectivity), leaders should try to establish the symbolic environment in ways that emphasize the unique identity of the organization or suborganization and increase

organizational identity salience in members' self-concepts. Leaders need to instill norms of cooperation and contribution in an organization. Leaders also need to engage frequently in attempts to show organizational members the link between organizational actions and members' cherished values.

Morale in Organizations

Morale is an emotional attribute, providing energy, acceptance of leadership, and cooperation among members of an organization. Morale has been conceptualized from three perspectives: physiological, psychological, and social. From the physiological point of view, satisfaction of the basic human need of survival is the prime morale factor. From the psychological perspective, morale is determined by a continual satisfaction of higher-order needs. From the social approach, morale can be considered a social phenomenon caused by people's strong desire to be associated with their peers.

In reality, morale is better described by the combination of the three perspectives. Morale is the atmosphere created by the attitudes of the members

---

ACTIVITY 5.1

Maintaining Motivation

Addresses ISLLC Standard 3

You are the principal of a small elementary school. This year a new teacher, Bob Fletcher, came in to teach the fifth grade. This is Bob's first teaching job. He served a tour in the army and then went to a local college, completing a bachelor's degree and his provisional certification to teach under the GI Bill. He is married and has two young children.

Within a few weeks it became apparent that Bob is very highly motivated to do well as a teacher. He comes into the building as soon as it opens in the morning and often does not leave until late in the afternoon. During lunch breaks he frequently works with students, and when he does take lunch, he generally strikes up conversations with more experienced teachers seeking to find ways to manage his classes more effectively. He is very popular with his students and with the other teachers.

In January, Bob signed up for a graduate class at a nearby university, beginning work on a master's degree that will lead to permanent teaching certification.

All seemed to be going well until mid-March, when Bob became ill. He was out for 2 weeks. He had contracted mononucleosis brought on by exhaustion. Talking with him on his return, you find that he is spending as much time in the evenings as he can with his young family, retiring with them about 10:00 p.m. and habitually rising about 3:00 a.m. to work on class preparations and paper correction.

Bob shows great promise as a career teacher, but he also shows great potential for burnout. How can you help Bob maintain his motivation while finding a better balance between his professional life and his personal life?

of an organization and is more likely to be revealed by groups than by individuals (Benge & Hickley, 1984). Morale is influenced by how employees perceive the organization and its goals in relation to themselves and in terms of their physical, psychological, social, and cultural background.

Major Morale Factors

The attitudes of employees are influenced significantly by the ways in which they perceive a number of important factors: the organization itself, their own activities, their self-concept, the nature of their work, their peers, the satisfaction of their needs, and leadership (Kossen, 1987). The organization significantly influences employees' attitudes toward their jobs. Higher employee morale results when an organization has a favorable reputation. An employee of a public agency encountering reduced public financial support might experience poor morale. Employees' personal lives may also affect their attitudes on the job. Relationships with families and friends, as part of their total environment, influence employees' morale in their working environment. Employees' self-concepts also tend to influence their attitudes toward organizational environments. Therefore, individuals who lack self-confidence or suffer from poor physical or mental health frequently develop morale problems. In addition, employees' current values and education lead them to expect considerably more from their work than just material prosperity. However, characteristics of many types of jobs, such as uniform pacing, repetition, large impersonal organizational structures, and vague as well as unattainable goals, seem to lead to boredom and obsessive thinking. These characteristics are likely to lower employee morale.

The informal system and actions of leaders in an organization also affect morale significantly. As a member of a group, an employee's attitude toward a working condition could be swayed by the collective attitudes of his or her cohorts. High rates of turnover often indicate ineffective leadership.

How employees' personal needs are satisfied can influence their morale. Salary and employee benefits are two examples that help to satisfy personal needs. While increases in pay do not necessarily motivate employees to increase productivity, poor pay can be a source for poor morale, especially when compared to the pay of employees doing similar work (Kossen, 1987; Reitz, 1987).

Morale, Job Satisfaction, and Productivity

Morale and Productivity. Morale is one of the important concepts of the human relations school. Morale, a concept closely related to motivation and satisfaction, refers to the atmosphere created by the attitudes of the members of an organization (Reitz, 1987). The human relations school believes that there is a relationship between productivity and morale. Under conditions of poor morale, favorable output is difficult to sustain for long periods. However, good morale does not necessarily cause high productivity. It is merely one influence on total productivity. For high morale to affect productivity favorably, it must be accompanied by reasonable direction and control.

Morale is closely connected with the satisfaction that a person hopes to derive from work. Whereas work satisfaction is the result of various attitudes by an individual employee at a given time, morale is the result of the total satisfaction of the employees in an organization. Low morale is often accompanied by high rates of absenteeism, tardiness, and high turnover.

Morale is also related to productivity. Some feel that there tends to be a direct relationship between high productivity and high morale. However, the nature of the relationship between morale and productivity is inconclusive. Others see an inverse, circular, or even reciprocal relationship between productivity and morale. The morale–productivity relationship can therefore be perceived as situational.

Approaches to Studying Morale

At least three approaches have been developed to study employee morale: analyzing organizational records for changes in resignations, tardiness, absenteeism, productivity, and complaints; interviewing employees using prepared questions or allowing employees to respond in an unstructured format; and administering unsigned questionnaires and then report morale indices (Benge & Hickley, 1984). The three approaches are complementary and can be conducted simultaneously. To be effective, studies of morale should be conducted periodically, not just once.

Diagnostic approaches to studying morale can be grouped into three categories. (Fitability Systems, 2000) These are measurements of attitudes toward work, measurements of organizational commitment, and measurements of organizational climate. Measurements of attitudes toward work consider employee's perceptions of job satisfaction, role clarity, role conflict, autonomy, participation in decision making, and job involvement. Measurements of organizational commitment consider employees' perceptions of job security, loyalty, trust in management, identification, alienation, and helplessness. Measurements of organizational climate consider employees' perceptions of fairness, safety, support, communication, tolerance for risk, flexibility, and continuous learning.

The Quality of Work Life

Regardless of the real relationship between productivity and morale, high morale remains an important organizational goal. However, morale frequently is not noticed unless it is poor. Far too often, leaders do not recognize how badly morale has deteriorated until they are faced with serious crises. Leaders must continually be alert to clues revealing the state of morale, such as absenteeism, tardiness, high turnover, strikes and sabotages, and lack of pride in work.

The number one reason that people leave their jobs, according to Smith (2000), is that they feel that they are not recognized and appreciated for their work. Other causes for low employee morale, according to Schuler (2004), are a bad relationship with an immediate superior, personal problems outside the workplace, either overly heavy workloads over an extended period of time or too little work to provide a challenge, negativity and gossip mongering in the workplace, and lack of opportunity (or the will) to develop positive relationships with fellow workers. The more affluent and better-educated workforces of today expect a higher quality of work life (O'Toole, 1981). Quality of work life refers to how effectively the job environment meets the personal needs and values of employees and consists of seven components: adequate and fair compensation, safe and healthy work conditions, opportunity for continued growth and security, a feeling of belonging, employee rights, work and total life span, and social relevance of work life (Greenberg & Glaser, 1983).

Several methods have been developed for leaders to improve the quality of work life, including job rotation, job enlargement, job enrichment, and sociotechnical systems (Aldag & Brief, 1979; Champagne & McAfee, 1989; Hackman, 1983; Hellriegel & Slocum, 1976; Lawler, 1992; Pinder, 1984; Plous, 1987; Reitz, 1987).

Job rotation is the practice of training a worker in several different tasks and rotating that worker through those tasks in a given time period, thereby reducing boredom and fatigue from endless repetitions of a task. Workers can also acquire a broader set of skills and knowledge, increasing efficiency during periods of absenteeism. Job enlargement increases the scope of a job, reducing boredom and fatigue and increasing the number of tasks a worker performs within a given job. It also allows for performance of a greater number and variety of skills, more decision making about work methods, and more responsibility. Job enrichment involves the worker in more than just the performance of a task. Employees are provided with greater work content that requires advanced skills and new knowledge. The worker is more autonomous and responsible for planning, organizing, and evaluating the work as well as carrying it out, providing personal growth and meaningful work experience.

It is important to note that job enlargement and job enrichment do not merely call for adding more low-level tasks to a worker's job. This may be demotivating. Four criteria exist in deciding whether a job can be enlarged or enriched. Any addition to the job should increase responsibility, increase worker autonomy, permit the worker to do the complete task, and provide feedback to the worker.

Sociotechnical systems design jobs around groups of workers rather than individuals. In this approach, the leader defines a complete unit of work and assigns responsibility for that unit to a group, who share responsibility for determining what each of them will do, for deciding how they will accomplish it, and for scheduling and completing the work. The group itself assumes the responsibility for supervising its work.

In addition, Cyncar (2007) advocated four approaches: employee involvement in decision making, with work–life balance resulting from flexible scheduling that allows the employees to manage demands in their personal lives as well as on the job; providing clearly defined opportunities for financially supported continuing education and training; providing health and safety benefits such as stress management, weight loss, and smoking cessation programs; and clearly defined opportunities for employee recognition, both monetary and nonmonetary.

Informal Organizations

The Significance of Informal Organizations

One of the most significant and far-reaching conclusions of the Hawthorne studies concerns the importance of the informal organization and its relation to the total work situation. The informal organization is a network of personal and social relations not established or required by formal authority but arising spontaneously as people associate with one another. In the formal organization, authority and power coincide with a position in the structure. Power in the informal organization resides with the person. Since informal organizations exist within formal organizations, the behavior of people in organizations is influenced by the informal as well as formal organization.

Informal worker networks emerge spontaneously in organizations from the needs of the worker. They are not planned but occur as individual social interactions within the formal organization. These informal networks have their own leaders, unwritten policy, hidden agendas, communication channels, and even their own goals. Informal networks can play a significant part in organizational life. Informal organizations arise and persist as a means of compensating for the inadequacy of formal organizations in providing individual need satisfactions and/or as a means of adding to the need satisfaction provided by membership in formal organizations (Davis, 1977; Kossen, 1987; Roethlisberger & Dickson, 1939). Workers enter into

organizations with individually shaped expectations and bring with them differing values, interests, and abilities. Informal activities emerge when some particular need is not being fulfilled by the formal organization. Informal organizations help members of formal organizations satisfy needs by performing three important functions: social interaction, social control, and communication.

One of the most important functions provided by informal organizations is the provision of social interaction. Individuals have social needs that they attempt to satisfy at work in formal organizations; however, the social satisfaction provided by the formal organizations is limited. The second major function provided by informal organizations is social control. This function helps preserve and maintain the existence, identity, and values of the informal organizations. Informal organizations also attempt to exert control over people outside their group but within the formal organization (e.g., by influencing the leadership or staff personnel). Much of this external control is exerted indirectly by regulating the behavior of members of the informal organizations. A third informal organization function is communication. To keep its members informed of what is taking place and how it may affect them, the informal organization develops a system of communication, the grapevine, to supplement the information provided by the formal organization. Grapevines are inevitable, as it is practically impossible for formal organizations to keep everyone well informed. They have a tremendous capacity for carrying and disseminating important information quickly.

Informal Leaders

The leaders of informal organizations arise for various reasons and under slightly different circumstances. Typically, several informal leaders of varying importance exist in an informal organization, but one primary leader usually has the most influence. In return for their services, informal leaders usually enjoy certain rewards and privileges, such as esteem and power (Davis, 1977; Wolman, 1956). As a result, these people's informal roles may take on more importance than their formal work roles. The informal organization may be a desirable source of potential leaders for the formal organization. However, caution is necessary here, as the agendas of informal leaders often may not coincide with organizational agendas.

The Effects of Informal Organizations

The existence of informal organizations always affects the operation of formal organizations. In most cases, informal organizations have both detrimental and beneficial effects (Davis, 1977; Kossen, 1987; Ruben, 1988; Sanford, 1977; Scott, 1981). Four potential disadvantages exist in informal organizations. They may transmit false information, resist changes, cause excessive conformity to group norms, and develop goals that conflict with formal organizational goals.

The existence of informal organizations can also benefit the formal organization. Informal organizations satisfy employees' social needs, provide a useful employee communication network, provide employees with emotional escape valves, and complement the formal organization.

Overall, the existence of informal organizations tends to facilitate the functioning of a formal organization in certain important respects. They fill gaps in the formal organization's management, can promote more efficiency in the formal system, often supplement authority and responsibility mechanisms within the formal organization, and provide additional channels of communication.

The Inevitability of Informal Organizations

Informal organizations are inevitable for at least two reasons: they supplement satisfaction provided by formal organizations, and membership in formal organizations tends to stimulate people's needs for more information than formal organizations can provide. Informal organizations therefore will always be present and cannot be eliminated.

Realizing the inevitability of the informal organization, leaders must consider the possible effects their actions have on informal systems in order to integrate as far as possible the interests of informal organizations with those of the formal organizations and to keep formal activities from unnecessarily threatening informal organizations in general. The most desirable informal/formal organization relationship seems to be one in which the two systems maintain unity toward goals. Leaders of the formal organization would be wise to consider the value of the informal organization and work to maintain and enhance overall group cohesiveness and teamwork through it (Davis, 1977; Scott, 1981).

Not only should leaders understand the effects of informal organization structures, noted Goldsmith and Katzenbach (2007), but that information can be very helpful to employees as well. Those persons who can use the informal network by learning who can help get things done and those midlevel managers who can balance the formal structure with the informal structure will find their effectiveness on the job enhanced.

ACTIVITY 5.2

Community Relationships

Addresses ISLLC Standards 1, 2, 3, and 4

You are the superintendent of schools. At recent school board meetings, you and the board have been confronted on several occasions by irate parents and a highly vocal special interest group who identify themselves as budget watchdogs. Somehow these groups have gained access to privileged state budget documents. The new budget has granted a sizable pay increase to teachers. However, the community is not satisfied with recent student achievement scores. In addition, the student scores have been poor for several years running.

In light of these circumstances, consider the following:

1. What might you and the board do to improve relations with the community and, most particularly, with the informal network that seems to have access to privileged information?
2. What steps can you as the superintendent take to try and support the morale of your teachers under these difficult circumstances?

Human Relations Theory in Educational Administration

The Application of Human Relations Concepts

Human relations management does not imply simply liking people. It is not a belief that workers adversely affect productivity or that participation leads to job satisfaction and greater productivity. Its major emphasis is on ways to make workers feel like contributors to worthwhile task accomplishment and that they are doing something constructive and meaningful about working relationships within the organization. Human relations theorists work to reduce discrepancies between individuals and their organizations and to channel the remaining discrepancies into constructive results (Argyris, 1957; Davis, 1967; Sanford, 1977).

The human relations view of educational administration incorporates two distinctive bodies of thought. The first school is democratic administration, a philosophy originating shortly after 1900 in John Dewey's work. The second arose after 1945, when notions about democratizing school organizations were combined with humanistic studies drawn from behavioral science and the industrial studies discussed earlier. The fusion of these two bodies of thought in the 1940s was described first as democratic human relations and later as simply the human relations approach to educational administration (Campbell, Fleming, Newell, & Bennion, 1987).

Democratic Educational Administration

Unlike the human relations approach that originated in industrial and social science research, the democratic view of educational administration first evolved among educators in the early years of the 20th century in response to several factors. These included new social changes in the character of school organizations and reactions on the part of some to autocratic and authoritarian supervisory practices in schools. One of the earliest promoters of democratic administration in education, John Dewey (1946), argued against the increasing popularity of scientific management techniques among school leaders and emphasized the need for educational managers to

secure the consent of those they governed. Scientific management's preoccupation with efficiency did little to foster what he described as a well-balanced social interest. Dewey argued that this was contrary to the proper ends of education. He felt that giving teachers opportunities for greater participation changes both the character of the school organization and the quality and kind of relationships between teachers and administrators. For the educational leader, a cooperative approach to school management would necessitate that leadership provide intellectual stimulation and direction through give-and-take with others. A cooperative approach would not produce an aloof, official, imposing, or authoritarian environment. Others who supported democratic leadership include educational scholars, social reconstructionists, and social and philosophical scholars.

The democratic administration that originated in educational settings and the human relations movement of the industrial era bear close resemblances. On the surface, both approaches react against autocratic administrative practices associated with scientific management. More important, human relations research seems to confirm empirically what supporters of democratic administration have believed for some time: that organizational morale and productivity could be enhanced by humanistic leadership practices.

The Human Relations Movement in Education

Interest in applying human relations ideas to problems of school administration has been spurred by several developments. The growing urban character as well as improvements in transportation have narrowed the distance between home and school. Also, schools are being located in suburban areas to accommodate the educational needs of the nation's middle class, who are increasingly abandoning the cities (Link & Catton, 1967). This trend facilitates community involvement in educational affairs. Parent–teacher associations and interactions between school staff and the public have increased. The changing environment around the schools and the need for better public relations provide sound reasons for educators to adopt a view of management that promises to enhance their social and interpersonal skills. Conditions inside school organizations also cause administrators to look to human relations. Staffing difficulties, which began after 1941 when teachers left the classroom to join the armed forces or work in wartime industry, became an acute administrative problem by the end of the war (Link & Catton, 1967). At that time, teacher shortages and the general high rate of attrition within the profession were aggravated by economic factors that made teaching an unattractive occupation (Hill, 1947). To address such problems, school managers needed to gain public understanding and support and improve morale among school staff.

The changing character of school populations in the late 1940s and early 1950s was another factor that encouraged educators to develop human relations skills. More students from varied backgrounds were enrolled in public schools than ever before (Moehlman, 1940). In addition, the increasing mobility of postwar society, the quickening pace of events, and the loosening of long-held values and traditions posed new and different problems, especially in the decades after the Supreme Court's landmark *Brown v. Board of Education* decision. Others condemned public schooling for its alleged anti-intellectual tone, its dominance by professional educators, and its undemocratic methods in preparing and selecting pupils for careers. In light of such criticisms, it is not surprising that professors of education recommended a form of management that suggested strategies for cooperation borrowed from industrial research.

Ralph Tyler was one of the first educators to appreciate the changing view of administration that human relations research espoused. Tyler (1941) noted the relevance of recent human relations research to school administrators and suggested that future research in educational management be guided by the Hawthorne studies. Wilbur Yauch's and Daniel Griffiths's studies were two other important milestones that applied concepts of human relations to education. Yauch (1949) provided one of the first complete educational studies that combined ethical generalizations from democratic administration with human relations research drawn from industry. He

brought together the prescriptive approach to school management advanced by educators throughout the 1920s and 1930s with a more objective appreciation of administrative problems. He advocated teacher involvement in all areas of administration, including staff participation in decisions concerning supervision, budget allocation, curriculum, general policymaking, and clerical duties associated with operating a school.

Griffiths's (1956) study synthesized more than a quarter of a century of educational and social science thought about administration. Griffiths believed that staff morale was related to the kind of leadership operating within schools. He saw the school leader as someone whose chief responsibility is to facilitate the actions of others: an initiator, a coordinator, a helper, and a resource person. The school leader should be a social person, sensitive to the human needs of all concerned. Griffiths's study was not intended as a handbook containing lists of human relations rules and techniques that can be applied to various situations; rather, it sought to provide an intellectual basis for the study of schools drawn from research in other social sciences and other fields of professional study. It signaled the beginning of a shift in educational interest from a practical application of human relations research to a concern with theoretically grounded understanding of human behavior derived from the social sciences, a change later characterized as one in which educators begin to conceive administration as a domain of study rather than a domain of action.

The Effects of the Human Relations Movement on Educational Administration

The human relations movement had relatively little impact on school district administrators compared to its substantial impact on supervisors (Owens, 1987). Superintendents today continue to emphasize organization, while supervisors emphasize such human relations concepts as morale, group cohesiveness, collaboration, and the dynamics of informal organizations.

Those who see their roles as educational administrators tend to emphasize budgets, politics, control, and asymmetrical exercise of power from the top down, whereas those concerned with instruction and curriculum place much more emphasis on participation and communication. Status–power relationships have been deemphasized. This difference in emphasis has persisted. Additionally, motivation, the core concept of the human relations movement, was not implemented well in schools or the school environment. A good fit did not exist between teachers who tried to achieve excellence and at the same time demanded more entitlement.

A New Frame of Leadership

In ordinary times, people look to managers for predictable, smooth-running, and cost-effective operations. Managers help supply the clarity, certainty, and efficiency required to get the job done right. In times of crisis, however, good management is not enough. People facing uncertainty turn to leaders for direction, confidence, and hope. Leaders encourage long-range planning, spirit, and cohesion when doubts about the future of the organization occur. Leadership must consistently sense its history and, at the same time, look ahead to discover or rediscover why the organization exists, what it stands for, and where it might be headed. As external circumstances shift, organizations waver between their need for management and their need for leadership. The issue is not which is better but what balance is best in view of contemporary challenges.

Studies of administrators in business, higher education, and schools suggest that most administrators operate primarily from either a human resource or a structural orientation (Bolman & Deal, 1991). Both orientations are linked significantly to their administrator's effectiveness as a manager and their effectiveness as perceived by subordinates. Today, however, political and symbolic orientations play much more dominant roles. Attention to symbols appears to be a very significant factor in effective leadership. Leaders operate more as negotiators and poets than as servants, catalysts, or social architects. In terms of crisis, effective leaders barter and build coalitions and shape and reshape symbolic forms that influence organizational purpose and meaning.

The frame of reference of a leader becomes particularly significant when viewed in the context of the actions that a leader may take. A leader seeking to develop strategic planning within the human resources framework may gather groups together to promote participation as opposed to working in isolation. Decision making in the human resources frame of reference implies an open process involving others and intended to secure the commitment of others to the decisions to be made. Evaluation of organizational activities in the human resources framework is a process for helping people grow rather than an opportunity for the leader to confirm and exercise power. Conflict management in the human resources context is preventive rather than remedial. It involves developing relationships that will minimize future conflicts. Communication in the human relations frame of reference is informal as well as formal; up, down, and lateral rather than one way. Its function is exchanging information, needs, and feelings rather than simply influencing and manipulating others (Bolman & Deal, 1997).

A New Paradigm for Educational Leadership

The leadership role in education is assuming new dimensions. The public expects educational leaders to improve the quality of schooling significantly. These expectations require leaders first to clarify educational outcomes and assessment strategies. They also require leaders to be proficient in staff development practices and experiments in labor relations. School leaders are expected to develop new political, social, and business connections within the broader community (Wallace, 1992).

Student achievement in the United States compares unfavorably with achievement outcomes in Asia and Europe (Ornstein & Levine, 2008; Stevenson & Stigler, 1992). These results raise questions about the economic model and the human resources models used so pervasively in educational systems throughout the nation. Unless future generations are more effectively educated, serious deficiencies will continue to mount as achievement continues to wane further. For example, changing demographics suggest that schools must be more effective in educating an expanding population of poor and minority students. Reports today indicate that these pupils are under-served by the public schools. It is likely that in the future, these students will form a major portion of the workforce (Edmonds, 1979; Little, 1981). With these realizations, school leaders will be required to exhibit a higher level of educational, civic, and political leadership. Citizens must be better prepared to participate effectively in societies of the 21st century.

Perhaps the most significant recent change in educational administration is the demand for aggressive and effective leadership at the building and district levels. More than ever, the general public expects school administrators to be active leaders of the instructional program. Educational leaders must envision strengthened schools and be able to bring about conditions that will ensure a high-quality education. They must also be capable of conveying symbolic meaning to nourish aspirations and achieve these goals. They must articulate a coherent vision as well as define the components of quality education for students. More important, they must motivate professionals at the school and district levels to implement these new visions. In a word, schools need to become more collegial and less bureaucratic.

A Motivational Model for Educational Leadership

Research indicates that recognition, achievement, advancement, and responsibility are major forces in motivating educators to lift their performances to their maximum potentials (Savage, 1967; Schmidt, 1976; Wickstrom, 1971). Sergiovanni and Carver (1973) also found that routine housekeeping, such as taking attendance, paperwork, lunch duty, insensitive or inappropriate supervision, irritating administrative policies, and poor relationships with colleagues and/or parents, are major sources of job dissatisfaction among educators. Sergiovanni and Carver argued that teaching offers little opportunity for advancement. These general dissatisfactions cause teachers to consider other, more satisfying professions in the educational realm.

In the past, there were two focal points in educational leadership. The first emphasized such things as planning, organizing, coordinating, commanding, and controlling. This approach long defined leadership as task structure and initiating structure. On the job, this means attending to scheduling, organizing, supervising, and monitoring, all of which are absolutely essential to running schools well. The second focal point of educational leadership is consideration based and develops concern for subordinates, morale, motivation, group process, conflict management, and decision making, in essence a participative and human resource orientation.

Educational leadership entails more than this. Exemplary educational leaders are adept at diagnosing educational problems, counseling teachers, developing curriculum, developing staff, evaluating, and remediating the educational work of teachers. However, to move to excellence in schools, two other forms of leadership, symbolic leadership and culture-building leadership, are also necessary.

Symbolic leadership signals and demonstrates to others what is important, what is valued, what is wanted, and what goals override others. Symbolic leaders create and communicate a vision for followers; they describe a desired state of affairs to which followers commit themselves.

Symbolic leadership alone is incapable of achieving excellence in schools (Sergiovanni, 1984). Excellent schools are characterized by a distinctive organizational character and must be managed so that teachers feel that they belong to effective work groups, feel good about the work they do, and believe that their achievements are worthwhile. Leaders of excellent schools must take care not only to preserve inherited traditions but also to set about building new higher-order traditions. Development of an organizational culture means building behavioral norms that exemplify the best that a school stands for. It means building an institution in which people believe strongly, with which they identify personally, and to which they gladly render their loyalty. All this gives meaning to the work that they do and additionally builds greater significance into the school environment.

Leaders who attempt to build strong organizational cultures in schools spend time articulating the mission of the school. They bring others together to accept these values as the uniqueness of the school is constantly redefined. These schools are characterized by the bonding that occurs between people and organizations in which they have faith and toward which they have commitment. Under such leadership, students and teachers alike come to understand that they are part of an important and worthwhile larger mission.

Burns (1978) and Bass (1985) conceptualized leadership as transactional and transformational. *Transactional leadership* is an exchange process or problem intervention relationship and correlates with the traditional command-and-control styles of management. In *transformational leadership*, leaders attribute their own power to better interpersonal skills, hard work, networking, and inspiration. In this view, leadership is individual consideration and intellectual stimulation and inspires followers to raise their own levels of self-awareness.

Sergiovanni (1992) proposed that transformative leadership is capable of enhancing the ability of members in social organizations to realize their visions and achieve goals. He added a moral dimension to leadership that allows for the creation of a covenant of shared values, commitment, and vision that can move members to develop an effective, successful organization. However, he also asserted that transactional leadership has a role to fill within organizations. This can be seen in the expanded needs for instructional and interpersonal leadership. Burns (1978) and Greenfield (1987) also called for a moral aspect to leadership. Burns translated this as the ability to raise followers to higher levels of motivation and morality. Greenfield referred to the leader's ability to see things as they are and as they might be within a moral context.

Bass (1981) identified transactional leadership with first-order change based on expected performance. Transactional leaders provide rewards when merited, encourage individual self-interests, and attempt to align self-interests with organizational goals. He identified transformational leadership as second-order changes in attitudes, beliefs, and values, based on performance beyond expectations. Both Bass and Sergiovanni asserted that the practice of transformational leadership can result in organizational members achieving beyond expectations because of the intrinsic self-motivation. Organizational members become committed to a shared set of values and beliefs that become a professional covenant embodied in their thoughts and actions.

Sergiovanni's leadership concept is illustrated in Figure 5.5. Each circle is enveloped by a shared vision that drives all beliefs and actions within the district. This vision originates from the chief supervisor and is developed through meanings attached to that supervisor's actions, decisions, and behaviors. Congruent with this vision are the shared values, beliefs, and understandings that are developed by other organizational partners. The chief supervisor works with this constituency to develop means for shared planning and decision making.

From these actions a compact forms that fuels the activities of each school or department. Shared actions result in the school or departments as a culture forms to build shared commitment to action and enhance student success as outlined in the vision. In this budding environment, leaders must be adept at communication, team building, and instructional management. Equally important, a third arena represents the tactical leadership skills needed by the chief supervisor of the district. Members of newly formed teams will need to learn to rely on each other's expertise, develop collaboration mechanisms, become reflective, and, together, formulate plans, make decisions, and act. Supervisors must be adept at instituting an environment that builds the capabilities for all concerned.

Rosner (1990) studied this transactional–transformational continuum in relation to women's leadership roles and developed a style of leadership she termed *interactive*. Women, she said, tend to encourage participation, share power and information, enhance other people's self-worth, and inspire excitement about work and the work environment. Rosner's views supported a new view of the way that women lead and contribute an added level of knowledge and understanding for human resource authors, theorists, and users.

In large part, human relations thinkers have adopted McGregor's theory Y viewpoint, in which human beings are viewed as full of potential. This potential can be tapped by holding and encouraging high expectations. To develop human potential in organizations, leaders need to provide workers with a supportive climate, more feedback, training

FIGURE 5.5

Conceptualization of transformative leadership

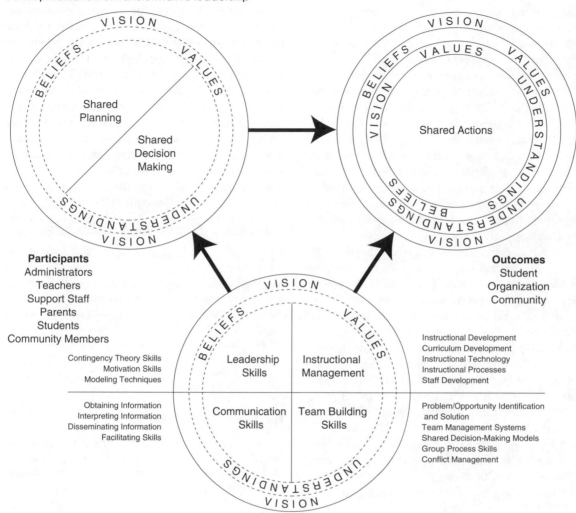

Participants
Administrators
Teachers
Support Staff
Parents
Students
Community Members

Contingency Theory Skills
Motivation Skills
Modeling Techniques

Obtaining Information
Interpreting Information
Disseminating Information
Facilitating Skills

Leadership Skills   Instructional Management

Communication Skills   Team Building Skills

Outcomes
Student
Organization
Community

Instructional Development
Curriculum Development
Instructional Technology
Instructional Processes
Staff Development

Problem/Opportunity Identification
 and Solution
Team Management Systems
Shared Decision-Making Models
Group Process Skills
Conflict Management

programs for professional growth, and challenging opportunities.

Contemporary Issues in Human Relations

Discrimination is a continuing problem in all organizational environments. It may be particularly critical in the educational environment as educators become more accountable for developmental responsibilities that once were largely family centered. Although much progress has been made in recent decades, prejudicial and discriminatory practices remain. Too often, these are directed at ethnic minorities and other special employment groups. Prejudice stems from internal judgments based on insufficient evidence. A prejudiced person often tends to think in stereotypical terms without considering individual differences. That becomes a serious human relations problem when actions become discriminatory.

In our attempts to build a just working environment, we must somehow learn to create a fair and equal working climate. Leaders and managers alike must balance objectivity and sensitivity. Kossen (1987) identified some typical problems that contribute to discrimination in the workplace. For example, some managers stereotype ethnic minorities and other special employment groups as being less capable than white males. As a result, managers tend to expect less from these groups, and poor work results. These managers may be eliciting the exact poor behavior they expect. Their insensitivity to their own prejudices causes discrimination as they view these groups from an inappropriate perspective. In other cases, in attempts to avoid prejudice managers may assign more difficult projects to these special groups to create an appearance of equal treatment.

Racial discrimination is an emotional issue. Research demonstrates that society is moving slowly to overcome racial discrimination (Wildstrom, 1986). Many events in the recent past have aroused greater public interest and protest. African Americans were the first to recognize that protests and demonstrations play a significant part in forcing public recognition of racial injustice (Coulmad, 1992; Kossen, 1987). Their demands for new laws, better education, and government action have brought change. Strong self-pride has helped the African American cause in the search for equal job opportunity and a better place in society. Discrimination against Hispanics, Native Americans, and Asian Americans are as problematic for our society and educational institutions.

Women's rights has made progress in recent decades. One of the major concerns of women in the workplace has been equal pay for equal work. This issue asserts that women should be paid equally for performing tasks requiring the same skills, training, responsibility, and effort as men. Other issues are equally significant: calls for more and better-quality child care, better promotion potential, better legal protection against sexual harassment, broader maternity benefits, and equal political power. Although much improvement in these areas is evident, more needs to be done.

Much still needs to be accomplished in the human resource realm, as noted by the numerous commissions exploring reform and restructuring in the educational environment. Most problematic will be how to ensure that educational leadership pinpoints action strategies that deal effectively with broad human resource activities. Most important, practitioners today must become adept at understanding human relations and devising visionary practices that elicit the best of human potential. The best outcomes generally occur in an environment where concern for the individual worker or administrator is present in a team atmosphere, where individual need achievement transcends entitlement, and where people strive for and have the opportunity to achieve excellence in their own terms.

SUMMARY AND FUNDAMENTAL CONCEPTS

The public demand for excellence in the schools is increasing. That excellence cannot be achieved and maintained without strong, effective leadership in the schools. Effective school leaders must demonstrate skills in the managerial, instructional, and interpersonal arenas. Developing interpersonal skills in the work environment can be aided by a thoughtful study of human relations.

Looking ahead, in chapter 6 we explore communication as an element in educational systems and as a vital tool for the effective leader of an educational enterprise.

Fundamental Concepts

The fundamental concepts that follow have been discussed in this chapter. The citations that conclude each concept indicate the Interstate School Leaders Licensure Consortium (ISLLC) standards and functions related to the concept. The Arabic numeral refers to the ISLLC standards, and the letters refer to the functions as presented in the table found inside the front cover.

- Development of the main concepts of the study of human relations occurred in six stages: classical thinking (pre-1930s), systematic development (1930–1950), training and practice (1950–1960), refinement (1960–1970), decline (1970–1980), and evolving (1980–present). (2A, 2C; 3B, 3D; 4B, 4C; 5B, 5C, 5E)
- Human relations is generally defined as the interactions of people in all types of endeavor. (2A, 2C; 3B, 3D; 4B, 4C; 5B, 5C, 5E)
- Researchers define human relations based on four concepts: optimistic assumptions about human

nature, clinical and ethical dimensions, human needs, and human motivation. (2A, 2C; 3B, 3D; 4B, 4C; 5B, 5C, 5E)

- Studies of human relations fall into four categories:

  Human nature:

  Theories X and Y and Pygmalion leadership

  Human motivation:

  Process models, including expectancy models, behaviorist models, and social learning models

  Content models, including common human needs and human motivation at work

  Morale in organizations, including morale, job satisfaction, and productivity informal organizations (2A, 2C; 3B, 3D; 4B, 4C; 5B, 5C, 5E)

- The human relations view of educational administration has evolved two bodies of thought: democratic administration beginning in 1900 and democratic administration combined with humanistic studies beginning in 1945, commonly called human relations management. (2A, 2C; 3B, 3D; 4B, 4C; 5B, 5C, 5E)

- Human relations has had greater impact on supervisors, who emphasize morale, group cohesiveness, collaboration, communications, and the dynamics of informal organizations, than on administrators, who emphasize formal organization, budget, and top-down management. (2A, 2C; 3B, 3D; 4B, 4C; 5B, 5C, 5E)

- Past educational leadership has had two focal points: one emphasizing planning, organization, coordination, and command and control and the other emphasizing morale, motivation, group process, conflict management, and a participative orientation. The second is a human resources orientation. (2A, 2C; 3B, 3D; 4B, 4C; 5B, 5C, 5E)

- Educational leadership may also be seen as transactional or transformational. Transactional leaders focus on rewarding performance, encouraging self-interest, and aligning self-interest with organizational goals. Tranformational leaders focus on performance beyond expectations, shared sets of values, and beliefs that become a shared vision and shared action. Contemporary issues in human relations in educational organizations include ethnic discrimination and women's rights. (1A; 2A, 2C; 3B, 3D; 4B, 4C; 5B, 5C, 5E)

- Contemporary human relations issues in educational organizations include ethnic bias and women's rights. (2A, 2C; 3B, 3D; 4B, 4C; 5B, 5C, 5E)

Case Study

The Case of the New Hire

Addresses ISLLC Standards 1, 2, 3, 4, 5, and 6

Valerie Rizzo has just been appointed the new principal of the East Ruxton Middle School. East Ruxton is a city of approximately 20,000 persons serving as a marketing and light manufacturing center for the two adjacent rural counties. The city school district at one time had been one of the outstanding programs in the state for a community of its size. However, over the past decade, that reputation began to slip as changes in the economy caused reductions in the tax base and thus cutbacks in the schools' budgets and services. The superintendent and current administration have all held their positions for a number of years, with the junior administrator having 7 years of service. The teaching staff also have tended to stay in place. In the middle school, only two of the teaching faculty have less than 5 years of tenure.

When she was hired, Valerie was told by the superintendent that the most recent school board election had brought in three new persons and that the balance of voting power on the new board lies with them. The new members ran on a platform of reform and upgrading for the schools, and they are looking to Valerie as the new administrator to spearhead change in her school. The new members are hoping that changes in the middle school will provide an example that will influence the rest of the district.

Questions

1. If you were Valerie Rizzo, what steps would you take in the first 30 days of your incumbency as the middle school principal to introduce the previously mentioned change-related issues while establishing effective human relations with your building staff?

2. How will you approach the previously mentioned issues with your administrative peers across the district?

3. What model(s) of human needs and leadership discussed in this chapter will you use to guide you in your new role? Why?

4. Prepare an action plan for yourself for the first half year that will allow you to begin the job, operate your school, and initiate appropriate changes. Be prepared to discuss the means by which you will motivate your staff to meet the challenges to come and explain why you are selecting those particular means.

References

Aldag, R. J., & Brief, A. P. (1979). *Task design and employee motivation*. Glenview IL: Scott, Foresman.

Alderfer, C. P. (1969). An empirical test of a new theory of needs. *Organizational Behavior and Human Performance, 4*, 143–175.

Alderfer, C. (1972). *Existence, relatedness, and growth: Human needs in organizational settings*. New York: Free Press.

Ardrey, R. (1966). *The territorial imperative*. New York: Atheneum.

Argyris, C. (1957). *Personality and organization*. New York: Harper & Row.

Argyris, C. (1964). *Integrating the individual and the organization*. New York: Wiley.

Bandura, A. (1968). A social learning of interpretation of psychological dysfunctions. In P. London & D. Rosenhan (Eds.), *Foundations of abnormal psychology* (pp. 293–344). New York: Holt, Rinehart and Winston.

Bandura, A. (1969). *Principles of behavior modification*. New York: Holt, Rinehart and Winston.

Bandura, A. (1976). Social learning theory. In J. T. Spence, R. C. Carson, & J. W. Thibait (Eds.), *Behavioral approaches to therapy* (pp. 1–46). Morristown, NJ: General Learning.

Bandura, A. (1977). *Social learning theory*. Upper Saddle River, NJ: Prentice Hall.

Bandura, A., & Walters, R. H. (1963). *Social learning and personality development*. New York: Holt, Rinehart and Winston.

Bass, B. M. (1981). *Stogdill's handbook of leadership: A survey of theory and research* (Rev. and exp. ed.). New York: Free Press.

Bass, B. M. (1985). *Leadership and performance beyond expectation*. New York: Free Press.

Benge, E., & Hickley, J. (1984). *Morale and motivation: How to measure morale and increase productivity*. New York: Franklin Watts.

Berlew, D. E., & Hall, D. T. (1966). The socialization of managers: Effects of expectations on performance. *Administrative Science Quarterly, 11*(11), 207–223.

Blake, R. R., & Mouton, J. S. (1964). *The managerial grid*. Houston: Gulf.

Bolman, L. G., & Deal, T. E. (1991). *Reframing organizations: Artistry and choice in management*. San Francisco: Jossey-Bass.

Bolman, L. G., & Deal, T. E. (1997). *Reframing organizations: Artistry, choice and leadership* (2nd ed.). San Francisco: Jossey-Bass.

Brophy, J. E. (1985). Teacher–student interaction. In J. B. Dusek, V. C. Hall, & W. J. Meyer (Eds.), *Teacher expectancies* (pp. 303–328). Hillsdale, NJ: Lawrence Erlbaum Associates.

Burns, J. M. (1978). *Leadership*. New York: Harper & Row.

Campbell, J. D., & Pritchard, R. D. (1983). Motivation theory in industrial and organizational psychology. In M. D. Dunnette (Ed.), *Handbook of industrial and organizational psychology* (pp. 63–130). New York: Wiley.

Campbell, R. F., Fleming, T., Newell, L. J., & Bennion, J. W. (1987). *A history of thought and practice in educational administration*. New York: Teachers College, Columbia University.

Champagne, P. J., & McAfee, R. B. (1989). *Motivating strategies for performance and productivity: A guide to human resources development*. New York: Quorum Books.

Coulmad, F. (Ed.). (1992). *Attitudes and accommodation in multilingual societies*. New York: Mouton de Gruyter.

Cyncar, A. (2007). Whole workplace health: Psychologist are taking a more comprehensive approach to wellness at work. *Monitor on Psychology, 38*(32). Retrieved September 30, 2007, from http://www.apa.org/monitor/mar07/whole.html

Dachler, H. P., & Mobley, W. (1973). Construct validation of an instrumentality–expectancy–task–goal model of work motivation: Some theoretical boundary conditions. *Journal of Applied Psychology, 58*, 397–418.

Davis, K. (1967). *Human relations at work* (3rd ed.). New York: McGraw-Hill.

Davis, K. D. (1977). *Human behavior at work: Organizational behavior* (5th ed.). New York: McGraw-Hill.

Dennison, H. (1931). *Organizational engineering*. New York: Macmillan.

Dewey, J. (1946). *Problems of men*. New York: Philosophical Library.

Duchon, D., Green, S. G., & Taber, T. D. (1986). Vertical dyad linkage: A longitudinal assessment of antecedents and gender label. *Journal of Personality and Social Psychology, 46*, 991–1004.

Eden, D. (1990a). Pygmalion without interpersonal contrast effect: Whole groups gain from training manager expectations. *Journal of Applied Psychology, 75*, 394–398.

Eden, D. (1990b). *Pygmalion in management: Production as a self-fulfilling prophecy*. Lexington, MA: Lexington Books.

Edmonds, R. (1979). Effective schools for the urban poor. *Educational Leadership, 37*, 15–24.

Etzioni, A. (1961). *The moral dimension: Toward a new economics*. New York: Free Press.

Feldman, J. M., Reitz, H. J., & Hiterman, R. J. (1976). Alternatives to optimization in expectancy theory. *Journal of Applied Psychology, 61*, 712–720.

Fiedler, F. E. (1967). *A theory of leadership effectiveness*. New York: McGraw-Hill.

Fitability Systems. (2000). *Organizational diagnostics*. Retrieved September 20, 2007, from http://www.od-online.com/orgmsrs.asp

Flanders, J. P. (1968). A review of research on imitative behavior. *Psychological Bulletin, 69*, 316–337.

Follett, M. P. (1930). *Creative experience*. London: Longmans, Green.

Frankel, L. K., & Fleisher, A. (1920). *The human factor in industry*. New York: Macmillan.

Gantt, H. L. (1916). *Industrial leadership*. New Haven, CT: Yale University Press.

Goldsmith, M., & Katzenbach, J. (2007, February 14). Navigating the "informal" organization. *BusinessWeek*. Retrieved September 30, 2007, from http://www.businessweek.com/careers/content/feb2007/ca20070214

Greenberg, P. D., & Glaser, E. M. (1983). Viewpoints of labor leaders regarding quality of worklife improvement programs. In R. M. Steers & L. W. Porter (Eds.), *Motivation and work behavior* (3rd ed., pp. 547–561). New York: McGraw-Hill.

Greenfield, W. (1987). *Instructional leadership: Concepts, issues, and controversies*. Newton, MA: Allyn & Bacon.

Griffiths, D. E. (1956). Human relations in school administration. In *63rd yearbook of the National Society for the Study of Education* (Pt. II). Chicago: University of Chicago Press.

Hackman, J. R. (1983). Work design. In R. M. Steers & L. W. Porter (Eds.), *Motivation and work behavior* (3rd ed., pp. 490–516). New York: McGraw-Hill.

Hall, J. (1980). The managerial lens: What you see is what you get! In J. A. Shtogren (Ed.), *Models for management: The structure of competence* (pp. 4–10). The Woodlands, TX: Teleometrics International.

Halloran, J. (1978). *Applied human relations: An organizational approach*. Upper Saddle River, NJ: Prentice Hall.

Hammond, K. R. (1966). *The psychology of Egon Brunswick*. New York: Holt, Rinehart and Winston.

Hamner, W. C., & Hamner, E. P. (1976). Behavior modification on the bottom line. *Organizational Dynamics, 4*(4), 3–21.

Hellriegel, D., & Slocum, J. W., Jr. (1976). *Organizational behavior: Contingency views*. St. Paul, MN: West.

Herzberg, F. (1966). *Working and the nature of man*. New York: Crowell.

Herzberg, F. (1968). One more time: How do you motivate employees? *Harvard Business Review, 46*, 56–57.

Herzberg, F. (1981). Motivating people. In P. Mali (Ed.), *Management handbook*. New York: Wiley.

Herzberg, F., Mausner, B., & Snyderman, B. B. (1959). *The motivation to work*. New York: Wiley.

Hill, H. (1947). Personal problems in American education. In *American Association of School Administration official report (1946)*. Washington, DC: National Educational Association.

Knezevich, S. (1984). *Administration of public education: A sourcebook for the leadership and management of educational institutions*. New York: Harper & Row.

Komaki, J. I. (1986). Toward effective supervision. *Journal of Applied Psychology, 71*, 270–279.

Kossen, S. (1987). *The human side of organization* (4th ed.). New York: Harper & Row.

Lawler, E. E., III. (1992). *Ultimate advantage: Creating the high involvement organization*. San Francisco: Jossey-Bass.

Lewin, K. (1951). *Field theory in social science: Selected theoretical papers*. D. Cartwright (Ed.). New York: Harper & Row.

Likert, R. (1961). *New patterns of management*. New York: McGraw-Hill.

Likert, R. (1967). *The human organization*. New York: McGraw-Hill.

Link, A. S., & Catton, W. B. (1967). *American epoch: A history of the United States since the 1890s*. New York: Knopf.

Little, J. W. (1981). *School success and staff development in desegregation schools*. Boulder, CO: Center for Action Research.

Mahoney, M. J. (1974). *Cognition and behavior modification*. Cambridge, MA: Ballinger.

Maslow, A. H. (1954). *Motivation and personality*. New York: Harper & Row.

Maslow, A. H. (1962). *Toward a psychology of being*. New York: Van Nostrand.

Mayo, E. (1933). *The human problems of an industrial civilization*. Cambridge, MA: Harvard University Press.

McClelland, D. C. (1955). *Power: The inner experience*. New York: Irvington.

McClelland, D. C. (1961). *The achieving society*. Princeton, NJ: Van Nostrand.

McClelland, D. C. (1975). *Power: The inner experience*. New York: Irvington.

McClelland, D. C. (1976). Power is the great motivation. *Harvard Business Review, 54*(2), 100–110.

McClelland, D. C. (1987). Characteristics of successful entrepreneurs. *Journal of Creative Behavior, 3*, 219–233.

McGregor, D. (1960). *The human side of enterprise*. New York: McGraw-Hill.

Merton, R. K. (1948). The self-fulfilling prophecy. *Antioch Review, 8*, 193–210.

Miles, R. E. (1975). *Theories of management*. New York: McGraw-Hill.

Mischell, W. (1973). Toward a cognitive reconceptualization of personality. *Psychological Review, 80*, 284–302.

Moehlman, A. B. (1940). *School administration*. Boston: Houghton Mifflin.

Ornstein, A. C., & Levine, D. U. (2008). *Foundations of education* (10th ed.). Boston: Houghton Mifflin.

O'Toole, J. (1981). *Making America work*. New York: Continuum.

Ouchi, W. G. (1981). *Theory Z: How American business can meet the Japanese challenge*. Reading, MA: Addison-Wesley.

Owens, R. G. (1987). *Organizational behavior in education* (3rd ed.). Upper Saddle River, NJ: Prentice Hall.

Pinder, C. C. (1984). *Work motivation: Theory, issues, and applications*. Glenview, IL: Scott, Foresman.

Plous, F. K. (1987, March). Redesigning work. *Personnel Administrator*, 99.

Porter, L. W. (1961). A study of perceived need satisfaction in bottom and middle-management jobs. *Journal of Applied Psychology, 45*, 1–10.

Porter, L. W., & Lawler, E. E. (1968). *Managerial attitudes and performance*. Homewood, IL: Irwin.

Reitz, H. J. (1987). *Behavior in organizations* (3rd ed.). Homewood, IL: Irwin.

Roethlisberger, F. J., & Dickson, W. J. (1939). *Management and the worker.* Cambridge, MA: Harvard University Press.

Rosenthal, R. (1974). *On the social psychology of the self-fulfilling prophecy.* New York: MSS Modular.

Rosenthal, R., & Jacobson, L. (1968). *Pygmalion in the classroom.* New York: Holt, Rinehart and Winston.

Rosner, M. (1990). *The second generation: Continuity and change in the kibbutz.* New York: Greenwood Press.

Ruben, B. D. (1988). *Communication and human behavior* (2nd ed.). New York: Macmillan.

Saltonstall, R. (1959). *Human relations in administration: Text and cases.* New York: McGraw-Hill.

Sanford, A. C. (1977). *Human relations: The theory and practice of organizational behavior* (2nd ed.). New York: Macmillan.

Savage, P. M. (1967). *A study of teacher satisfaction and attitudes: Causes and effects.* Unpublished doctoral dissertation, Auburn University, Auburn, AL.

Scandura, T. A., Graen, G. B., & Novak, M. A. (1986). When managers decide not to decide autocratically: An investigation of leader–member exchange and decision influence. *Journal of Applied Psychology, 71,* 579–584.

Schmidt, G. L. (1976). Job satisfaction and secondary school administrators. *Educational Administration Quarterly, 12,* 81.

Schuler, A. J. (2004). *Turning around low morale.* Retrieved September 20, 2007, from http://www.schulersolutions.com/html/turning_around_low_morale.htm

Scott, W. G. (1962). *Human relations in management: A behavioral approach.* Upper Saddle River, NJ: Prentice Hall.

Scott, W. R. (1981). *Organizations: Rational, natural and open systems.* Upper Saddle River, NJ: Prentice Hall.

Sergiovanni, T. J. (1984). Leadership and excellence in schooling. *Educational Leadership, 41*(5), 4–13.

Sergiovanni, T. J. (1991). *The principalship: A reflective practice* (2nd ed.). Boston: Allyn & Bacon.

Sergiovanni, T. J. (1992). *Moral leadership: Getting to the heart of school improvement.* San Francisco: Jossey-Bass.

Sergiovanni, T. J., & Carver, F. D. (1973). *The new school executives: A theory of administration.* New York: Dodd, Mead.

Shamir, B. (1990). Calculations, values, and identities: The sources of collectivistic work motivation. *Human Relations, 43,* 313–332.

Skinner, B. F. (1953). *Science and human behavior.* New York: Macmillan.

Skinner, B. F. (1971). *Beyond freedom and dignity.* New York: Knopf.

Skinner, B. F. (1974). *About behaviorism.* New York: Knopf.

Smith, B. (2000). Well chosen words of praise can keep staff from straying. *New Orleans City Business, 20*(28), 19.

Staats, A. W. (1975). *Social behaviorism.* Homewood, IL: Dorsey Press.

Steers, R. M., & Spencer, D. G. (1977). The role of achievement motivation in job design. *Journal of Applied Psychology, 4,* 472–479.

Stevenson, H. W., & Stigler, J. W. (1992). *The learning job.* New York: Summit Books.

Tannebaum, R., & Schmidt, W. H. (1958). How to choose a leadership pattern. *Harvard Business Review, 36,* 95–101.

Taylor, F. W. (1911). *The principles of scientific management.* New York: Harper & Brothers.

Tolman, E. C. (1932). *Purposive behavior in animals and men.* New York: Century.

Tosi, H. L., & Hamner, W. C. (1974). *Organizational behavior: A contingency approach.* Chicago: St. Clair.

Tyler, R. T. (1941). Educational adjustments necessitated by changing ideological concepts. In W. C. Reavis (Ed.), *Administrative adjustments required by socioeconomic change: Proceedings of the 10th annual conference of administrative officers of public and private schools.* Chicago: University of Chicago Press.

Ure, A. (1835). *The philosophy of manufacturers.* London: Knight.

Vroom, V. H. (1964). *Work and motivation.* New York: Wiley.

Wallace, R. C., Jr. (1992). Leadership in school. In S. D. Thomson (Ed.), *School leadership: A blueprint for change* (pp. 8–9). Newbury Park, CA: Corwin Press.

Watson, J. B. (1930). *Behaviorism.* Chicago: University of Chicago Press.

Wickstrom, R. A. (1971). *An investigation into job satisfaction among teachers.* Unpublished doctoral dissertation, University of Oregon, Eugene, OR.

Wildstrom, S. H. (1986, January 27). Affirmative action: A deal to patch up the Brock–Meese feud. *BusinessWeek,* 51.

Wolman, B. (1956). Leadership and group dynamics. *Journal of Social Psychology, 43,* 11–25.

Yauch, W. (1949). *Improving human relations in school administration.* New York: Harper & Brothers.

Communication: The Breath of Organizational Life

Many definitions of communication exist in the literature, but certain elements recur. These elements include the sender of the message, the message, the channel by which the message is sent, the receiver of the message, interference with accurate transmission of the message, and feedback from receiver to sender that allows judgment of the accuracy of the transmission (Allen, 1994). This traditional understanding of linear communication fails to model the webs of communication in which school administration, instruction, and leadership function. To view communication systemically is to see communication as relating to and affecting the organizational body. A metaphor for this is to refer to communication as the "breath of organizational life."

At root, communication beliefs and strategies depend on the administrator's personal view of the world and his or her participation in that worldview. If an administrator's view of the world is narrow or static, bounded by narrow past experience and biases of a limited, old paradigm, one type of communication environment will emerge in the school system. This administrator will seek to design and control and even inhibit the process of communication in the organization. If, on the other hand, an administrator's worldview takes into account the diversity of evolving systems in the world and the evolution of schooling within those systems, a different communications environment will exist. This administrator will recognize that communication is embodied in a variety and dynamic set of system properties distributed across every part of the school and its environment.

The shift in emphasis from the administrator who values control of communication to the administrator who values the dynamics of communication is a shift from a fixed and proprietary perception of "knowledge" as something gained and owned to a dynamic and open perception of "knowing." Knowing becomes a requisite for the entire system. Clearly, the communication processes in such a dynamic environment will often have to be "made up" to meet a need. There is no one communication formula that may be taught or unilaterally applied.

In chapter 5, we considered the development of the human resources movement and its growing relationship with educational leadership. In this chapter, the reader will continue to develop insights into what leading means in highly informed organizations, what effective communication requires, how data are gathered and used, and how to ensure that the entire organization is communicating systemically.

Communications Theories

Communications theories are based on several assumptions. Cragan and Shields (1995) identify these as human beings possess a natural theory-making and theory-using ability; communications theories focus on the discovery of one or more types of social science facts: material, social, or symbolic; communications theories flow primarily from one of three paradigms: rational, relational, or symbolic; and a theory's true value flows from its utility. According to Kovacic (1997), bases for evaluating the effectiveness of a theory consist of the existence of explicitly developed theoretical components that contain both philosophical elements and empirical or practical elements. Such a theory would contain three structures: mechanisms that would produce observable communications patterns in a number of circumstances, simple or complex models that would specify a precisely verifiable set of relationships among the observed patterns, and important empirical findings that explain the nature of a large number of communications patterns over time.

Rapid, complex societal changes create the need for new communication theory. Most researchers agree that communication involves senders, receivers, information transmissions between senders and receivers, and interferences or enablers acting on those transmissions. Message meaning, provision of feedback, and implications for human action are also attached to most definitions of communication as evidence of the social nature and function of the process. Some theorists and researchers include extrasensory information, intuition, and unconscious phenomena as part of the communication event. Others are more interested in the overlapping of discontinuous messages from different systems and how that overlap becomes congruent and integrated in the human mind. Nearly everything else about human communication is left to be defined in the situation-specific operational definition of a particular researcher. Dance (1970) found 95 different and sometimes contradictory definitions of communication in use.

Berlo (1960) reported that the meaning of any communication is in the minds of the communicators. Individual experience confirms that communications are often misunderstood. A message may never mean to the receivers exactly what the sender intended it to mean. Why, then, do people continue to struggle so determinedly to share meanings, find common ground, and act in concert? The answer may be simply that humans are social beings. Research seems to show through discourse analysis that groups of people who eventually act in concert are doing so not on the basis of full agreement on motivations or rationale but rather because they have agreed on certain mechanisms of communication that allow them to retain their autonomous values and points of view (Donnellon, Gray, & Bougon, 1986). If what these researchers found can be generalized, participants in an activity do not need to agree on their reasons for taking action or on their perceptions of how they will benefit. They do need to agree on taking collective action.

Theory Genres in Communication

Littlejohn (1989) described four basic genres of communication theory, each having characteristics that provide unique ways to understand communication. These are identified as structuralist and functionalist, cognitive and behavioral, interactional and conventional, and interpretive and critical.

Structuralist–functionalist theories are identified by their emphasis on a series of communication exchanges that occur and function almost simultaneously rather than over time, a curiosity about unintended consequences of actions at least as often as about purposeful outcomes, a shared belief in independent and objective reality, and insistence on the separation of symbols and language from the objects and thoughts being symbolized in communication. The genre borrows from general systems theory as well as from structuralist and functionalist philosophies.

Cognitive–behavioral theories of communication arise from the disciplines of the psychological sciences, employing many of the same assumptions about human knowledge and behavior that one finds in the structuralist–functionalist genre. The difference is that in the cognitive–behavioral paradigm, knowledge is generated through the discovery of psychological "mechanisms." Cognitive–behavioral theories address communication as a manifestation of individual behavior and thought processes, including the neural basis for these manifestations. According to this genre, major variables having an impact on one's cognitive functioning and its appearances in behavior, including language behavior, are outside the person's control. Still, there are interactional components of the person's behavior that contribute to the particular psychological manifestations studied in this genre.

Interactional–conventional theories of communication are derived largely from sociology, anthropology, and the philosophy of language. The cornerstone concept in this theory is symbolic interaction. Social existence is viewed as a process of continuous interaction that establishes, maintains, and sometimes alters certain social conventions, such as language and symbols. It is interactions, then, that create rules and norms, establish traditions, and on occasion overturn these traditions. Communication is a process of creating social reality and its corresponding culture, norms, and values.

Interpretive–critical theories arise from a variety of investigative traditions, including interpretive sociology, phenomenology and hermeneutics, Marxism and the Frankfurt school, and various text analysis and literary traditions. Common character- istics of interpretive–critical theories include a pre- eminence of subjectivity and a high value associated with individual experience. In the constructs of the interpretive–critical genre, meaning has great signifi- cance. This genre also borrows concepts from gen- eral systems theory.

Each of the genres that Littlejohn described tends to cluster around specific communication con- texts. These clusters and contexts provide a hierarchy defined by the size of the groups involved in the com- munication acts. From lowest population numbers to highest, these groups include interpersonal, group, organizational, and mass communication.

Interpersonal theories address communication between individuals, attending primarily to personal and discourse processes and relationships. Group communication theories focus on the interpersonal behaviors and influences that occur in small groups. Therefore, group communication researchers are interested in issues associated with group dynamics, interaction within the group, effectiveness, decision making, and stages of change in both personal and group development. Organizational communication researchers are mindful of interpersonal and group theories, but their primary concern is the role of com- munication in the achievement of organizational goals (Shockley-Zalabak, 1988). Mass communication car- ries interpersonal, group, and organizational commu- nication theories into the public realm, concerned generally about the impact of various media on public understanding and resulting public actions.

Although interpersonal, group, and mass commu- nication are of interest to the school administrator, orga- nizational communication constitutes the "breath" of educational organizational life. Without effective com- munication, an organization is forced to languish in a state of suspended animation, without the energy to pur- sue its collective goals. Understanding what constitutes communication in the organizations in which we

live is of vital concern—most of our life is spent in or interacting with organizations (Etzioni, 1964).

Metaphors and Assumptions in Organizational Communication

The assumptions that everyday communicators make about humans and human organizations inevitably create differences in the way that organizational communication phenomena are conceptualized, researched, adjusted, and used. Explicit assumptions are associated with differing metaphors. For example, a theory essentially conceptualized as mechanistic in approach and terminology may be based on the metaphor of the organization-as-machine. In these theories the instrumentality of good communication for getting work done is a constant theme. Theories that emphasize growth and change in organizations may be fundamentally conceptualized in the notion of the organization-as-organism. Here organizational communication is viewed as a crucial element in the organization's survival, akin to a life force that in part drives the entire organization. For the past sev- eral decades, the prevalent metaphor that repre- sents the anthropological perspective is the metaphor of organization-as-culture. Communication from this perspective takes on cultural–historical charac- teristics. Other theorists think of the organization as a complex psychological entity. Organization- as-psychoentity uses metaphors of the mind or psyche to describe organizational communication.

Three emerging metaphors of considerable inter- est to organization specialists are the metaphor of organization-as-art, implying a continual shaping and reshaping by inner and outer forces or personal agents (e.g., Peters, 1992; Schein, 1989); the metaphor of organization-as-brain (Marsick, 1990; Morgan, 1986), envisioning the organization primarily as an intelligent information-processing center; and the metaphor of the organization-as-learner (Argyris & Schön, 1978), suggesting that organizational learning flow may be critical for success. In these newer per- spectives, the systemic properties of organizations and organizational communication are dynamic and qualitative.

The first four of these ruling metaphors—organization-as-machine, organization-as-organism, organization-as-culture, and organization-as-psychoentity—roughly parallel Littlejohn's theory genres. However, the metaphors of organization-as-art, organization-as-brain, and organization-as-learner are not as clear-cut. These metaphors may be the forerunners of the search for more holistic views of and metaphors for organizational communication. Similarly, the literature about school management and supervision, human resource development (HRD), and organizational theory are filled with competing metaphors as writers search for new ways to represent and think about old problems in human organizations. Many attempt to utilize general systems theory as the foundational thinking system.

Watkins's (1989) discussion of alternative theories for HRD based on five metaphors of practice serves as a prominent example. HRD professionals, including staff developers for educational institutions, typically are concerned with organizational communication. In HRD, skill-building workshops, new-rule communication events, and other instructional leadership efforts are not exempt from inquiry and often use metaphors for their explanatory power. As an example, Watkins names these alternative metaphors for the HRD role: organizational problem solver; organizational change agent, interventionist, or helper; organizational designer; organizational empowerer or meaning maker; and developer of human capital. If school administrators are performing or guiding the performance of others in light of any one role or any combination of these roles, they are engaged in metaphor-based activity.

Watkins (1989) linked field and intervention theory with the metaphor of the HRD practitioner as organizational change agent, partly on the strength of Kurt Lewin's (1951) field theory contribution to organizational development principles and practices. In using these new metaphors for organizations, Watkins developed new metaphors for leaders in organizations. The organizational empowerer is a metaphor for the believer in critical theory. The developer of human capital uses human capital theory. The point of making these metaphors and their theoretical origins explicit, Watkins believes, is to enrich and enlarge the understanding of the field of practice.

Other images are Morgan's (1986) pictures of organizations as political systems, psychic prisons, flux and transformation, and/or instruments of domination. Hall (1991) preferred a realistic notion of organizations as actors, and Helgeson (1990) noted that women in charge of organizations often think of them as intricate webs of relationships.

An image that provides a particular insight into the nature of organizations is Pegals's (1998) description of a *learning organization*. This he defined as an organization where there is a climate in which people are encouraged to learn and develop to their full potential, development of the human resources within the organization is a central organizational policy, and continuous organizational transformation takes place. Communication is central to achievement of all three of these characteristics. These examples do not exhaust the metaphoric possibilities. However, they do verify the fact that single-notioned models of organizations are prevalent and that these differ drastically from the current life of modern organizations.

It is a practical necessity for educators to examine whatever is said about organizational communication with a healthy skepticism and an eye to discovering what metaphors and theories are actually in use in each exchange. For example, although educators in school settings may prefer to think of themselves as the developers of human beings, they often find that role obscured by "control" functions that seem contradictory in purpose or emphasis. What views of the world and what theories are associated with control, what views and theories are associated with development, and what part does communication play as we continue investigating schooling through these metaphors? Such questions should guide school administrators' and teachers' critical reflection about goals, purposes, processes, outcomes, and shareholders in organizational communication.

Distinguishing Features of Organizational Communication

Communication occurs in differing contexts in organizations. Berelson and Steiner (1964) defined four properties of organizations that affect these contexts. First, a typical organization is characterized by formality. Specifically, it has goals, regulations, policies, and procedures that give rise to its form and determine how it will communicate officially. Second, organizations are structured in a hierarchical manner. This structure patterns multidirectional communications. Third, the size of organizations tends to prohibit the development of close personal relationships with all other members and limits the scope of informal organizational communications. Finally, organizations most often exist beyond the time frame of a given member's life. Those who work in schools will surely recognize these features as pertaining to educational organizations.

If the feature of organizational communication that separates it from other kinds of communication is its deliberate focus on the achievement of a common or collective goal, then the specific form of any organization can be expected to be mirrored in its forms of organizational communication. According to Berelson and Steiner's premise that form follows goals, communicating organizational goals becomes a "first cause" and shaper of all organizational communication. This is perhaps one impulse behind the first school assembly of each academic year and the traditional goal setting that some school leaders undertake in that forum. Goals are useless if they are not communicated in ways that enlist the cooperative effort of members of the organization. It is not surprising that those who write about organization see goal attainment and communication systemically intertwined (Hoy & Miskel, 1987). They believe there can be no organization without communication. This places a clear responsibility on school leaders not only to establish and maintain communication but also to be sure that it is both effective and efficient for goal attainment.

Many studies support the importance of communication in organizational leadership. Hoy and Miskel (1987) stated that "superintendents and principals spend 70% or more of their time communicating" (p. 356). Sigband and Bell (1989) reported that chief executive officers in corporations spend 78% of their time in oral communication, with lower-level managers spending more than 80% of their time similarly. Murphy and Peck (1980) cited the ability to communicate as the critical factor in manager promotability. It

would appear that competent communication is regarded more highly than such skills as motivating employees, decision making, delegating, flexibility, and developing educational background. In educational institutions, Striplin (1987) found that the ability of school principals to perform effectively as instructional leaders is contingent on their degree of competence in communication.

Communication's potential contribution to organizational success is present in virtually all organizational activities: envisioning, planning, problem solving and decision making, and coordinating, controlling, accomplishing, evaluating, and reporting organizational results. It is tempting to conclude that effective organizational communication is therefore a panacea for all organizational stresses and difficulties. To the contrary, Hoy and Miskel (1987) pointed out that the diffusion of communication processes throughout an organization makes organizational communication difficult to examine as a separate process. Difficulties in organizational communication are often reflected in other problems in the school. Although communication can help resolve problems, it can also obscure other problems not directly under consideration. Finally, communication evokes action even though the quality of the action is questionable and there is no general commitment to the action. Poor leaders can unknowingly use communication to expedite inadequate or irrelevant plans.

To ensure effectiveness, the school leader must be fully aware of the intricacy of the school unit or district communication channels on both the formal and the informal level. The school leader needs to be aware of the power of all communication as a potential force for maintaining or destroying some aspects of the organizational life. Theoretically, this calls for the school administrator to borrow from Yukl's (1989) theory about the role of a "leader" versus that of a "manager" in a school. Yukl suggested that the effective administrator may know when to communicate as a manager and when to communicate as a leader. In the former case the administrator chooses to minimize noise by sending messages, developing channels, and monitoring feedback in settings that are clearly role defined. For example, a school administrator might give his staff a written questionnaire regarding supply requisitions. The staff writes a written response that the administrator subsequently responds to in the format of existing policy. On the other hand, as an administrator seeks staff support on an issue, he is best advised to use a variety of communication skills in an effort to gain commitment to an issue. This is a function of leadership and, according to Yukl, requires administrative understanding of communication and a varied repertoire of communication skills. In examining communication processes, the school administrator in a continuous process shifts from the role of manager to that of leader.

Factors Affecting Clarity, Credibility, and Directionality of Organizational Messages

Khandwalla (1977) stated that the primary objectives of communication are to gain attention and to gain understanding and acceptance of a message. Sigband and Bell (1989) contended that the purposes of communication are to be understood exactly as intended, to secure the desired response, and to maintain favorable relations with those with whom one communicates. Reitz (1987) believed that the primary functions of communication are to provide information that makes an organization adaptable to change, to command and instruct employees, and to influence and persuade the organization's members. The processes involved in accomplishing these purposes

are recognized as contributing to the success or failure of a given end. A leader may subscribe to any of these communication objectives either as an expression of commitment to the organization and its goals or as an expression of a personal desire for power and self-aggrandizement. The communicator's worldview and personal motivations therefore affect clarity, credibility, directionality, and even the process of communication itself. Modeling communication as a quasi-mechanical process, a means to an end, leaves out important psychological data. Nevertheless, the linear, mechanical model of information processing, sender–message channel–receiver–feedback, is the usual starting point for talking about communication (see Figure 6.1).

Using a quasi-mechanical model of communication allows the researcher to examine discrete elements of the communication process without the burden of holistic analysis. Thus, in speaking of the elements sender and receiver, the linear model makes it possible to conceptualize communication as a sharing of messages, ideas, or attitudes that produces a degree of understanding between those elements. The idea of shared meaning permits the study of how well a particular meaning is shared. Shared meaning can be problematic, however, as the receiver's intention may differ from that imagined or meant by the sender.

The linear model provides a starting point not unlike the starting point of behavioral psychology. A sender or stimulus source exists somewhere in the environment that acts on and elicits a response from the receiver. Communication models insert a channel between the sender and the receiver to locate and account for response variations. Recognition of intrapsychic processes within the senders and receivers helps account for human barriers to communication and for discrepancies in message meaning. The feedback loop overcomes the essential linearity of the early models, looping to revisit any element in the process.

A basic assumption about organizational communication is that if messages are sent and if the clarity, frequency, and completeness of those messages are increased, the probability that organization members will be working toward a common or shared goal is also increased. This leads organizational communication specialists to place considerable emphasis on

FIGURE 6.1

Model of communication: input–throughput–output

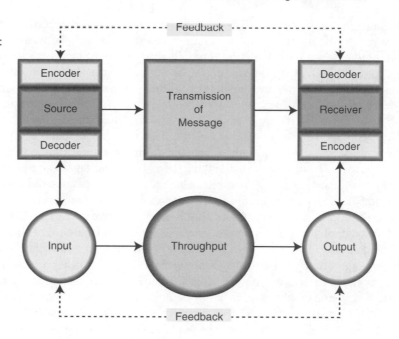

message form and on channels that carry the messages. Their intention is to avoid channels that produce static or distortion or, if those channels must be used, to reduce occurrence of noise, static, or distortion within them. Channels include oral, written, and mediated routing of messages.

Sigband and Bell (1989) identified two types of communication channels: formal and informal. *Formal channels* of communication include the organizationally sanctioned flows of information, such as electronic mail, scheduled meetings, and other functional necessities. *Informal* ("grapevine") *channels* provide access to information not normally obtained through formal channels. Khandwalla (1987) cited telephone and face-to-face conversations as the primary means of informal communication. Administrators can monitor the organizational climate by paying attention to messages in the grapevine. They may even intentionally "leak" off-the-record statements to informal channels to monitor communication flow. The advantage of using informal communication is that it transfers information very rapidly. The informal communication network prevents a communication vacuum. If the formal channels do not work, the informal ones will take over. The problem with informal channels is their potential

inaccuracy. The lack of official sanction leaves informally conveyed messages at the mercy of unchecked distortions as they travel through the grapevine.

Sigband and Bell (1989) classified the major barriers to communication under two headings: nonverbal and verbal. *Nonverbal barriers* include differences in perception; lack of interest (particularly on the part of the receiver); lack of fundamental knowledge or specific cognitive basis for understanding a message; personal characteristics such as personality, emotions, and prejudices; reactions to the appearance of the communicator; distractions or actual interference; poor organization of the message; poor listening; and competition for attention. Common *verbal barriers* include language, which may result in semantics problems, or inadequate vocabulary, both of which affect comprehension.

Another large category of barriers to communication results from cultural differences. This is particularly evident in the United States, where educators constantly must address the cultural differences of diverse populations in both the student body and the community. Hentges, Yaney, and Shields (1990) noted that because "no two groups ever experience the same cultural history, messages become more dissonant and ambiguous in a more heterogeneous population. To reduce the possibility of misunderstanding or dissonance potential, messages must be repeated many times" (pp. 39–40). Misunderstandings arise out of biases regarding accents and language, culturally defined signs and body language, acceptable degrees of physical proximity, the meanings of a handshake and eye contact, preferences for or against strong authority figures, and class systems brought from other countries. The diversity of cultural references to adversity or joy may seem inexplicable or bizarre to those outside that particular culture. A cultural or privation-induced orientation toward the "here and now" instead of toward the future may be misconstrued as lack of ambition or ability to plan. The roles and significance of particular minority family members may seem unusual to the dominant culture. An Asian student, for example, may not be able to answer a direct question until many older family members are consulted. Choices between being indirect or direct may be culturally determined, and symbolic messages are often unique to the country of origin. Surmounting these communication barriers calls for providing for shared experiences—regularly, often, and in great variety—with an emphasis on valuing rather than judging differences. Future school administrators in the United States cannot ignore demographic information that mandates multicultural awareness.

Communications problems may spring from a variety of other sources as well as those that have a basis in the individual personality. Some of these as identified by Fredrickson (1991) include personal bias, anxiety and defensiveness, hidden agendas, and participating in groupthink. The sender's credibility is always at stake in organizational communication. Khandwalla (1977) noted that to be credible, the source of information must be perceived as knowledgeable. Thus, a memo about the financial status of a school district needs to come from the district's financial officer rather than the curriculum specialist if it is to carry maximum credibility. However, credibility does not hinge on position alone. Both advance reputation and ongoing experience with a communicator create a track record of credibility or noncredibility. Once credibility is lost, it is difficult, if not impossible, to regain within the organization where the loss occurred.

Read (2007) noted that an effective communicator must be aware not only of the individual's culture but of the organization's culture as well. Language structure and word choice should be consistent with organizational culture to be most effective.

Message originators can assess the extent to which successful transmission has occurred by encouraging feedback from receivers. This is especially critical in school settings. The concept of feedback is often attributed to Wiener (1954) in his early discussions of cybernetics. In cybernetics, *feedback* refers to the ability of a person and of some machines to detect an error or deviation from that desired in an operation. Feedback identifies deviation and communicates that deviation to a control mechanism that makes a subsequent correction. Expert systems may even suggest alternative new actions. In popular communication practice, feedback refers to the verbal or nonverbal response received from the individual or groups to whom the message is directed. Feedback implies at least a two-way communication. With feedback, the message originator can at least make a rough assessment of whether a message was received as intended (i.e., decoded to yield the same basic meaning as was encoded by the sender). Misunderstandings are detected when feedback is accurate and timely. If delayed or distorted by interpersonal or organizational "noise," feedback may be useless. Feedback is most effective when it is obtained as close to the time of message transmission as possible (Shockley-Zalabak, 1988; Sigband & Bell, 1989).

Recognizing organizational features that affect the clarity, credibility, and directionality of messages is a function of the school administrator in the role of a leader. Discovering barriers to effective communication requires the leader to examine an organization's channels through multidimensional lenses. This examination might occur through the school leader's reflection on critical incidents in the communication process. Just as clarity, credibility, and directionality are influenced by organizational changes, an administrator's clear perception of the organization and the power of communication as a shaping agent must constantly sharpen. No set formula for monitoring the quality of communication exists for application in a complex school organization. In this context the school administrator bases communication processes on the situational needs that create the communication event. As Smith and Piele (1989) believe, communication choices made by school leaders, like other aspects of their practice, must reflect three abilities: situational sensitivity that enables them to diagnose problems, style flexibility that allows them to match certain practices appropriately to situations, and situational management skills that enable them to alter aspects of a situation to fit work styles. Leadership in schools is context bound. Nowhere is this more evident than in communication events, where administrators must act on a constantly changing climate and culture that influences the accuracy and diffusion of messages.

Types of Message Directionality

In hierarchical organizations, communications are directed downward, upward, and horizontally. An example in education would be an elementary school, where communication could take place faculty to faculty, faculty/staff to and from parents, administration to and from faculty/staff, certificated to and from classified staff, administration to and from district, and administrator to and from administrator (Badal, 2003).

In most organizations (and certainly in most traditionally designed American schools), vertical, top-down communication dominates (Khandwalla, 1977) and filters through successive layers of an organization until it reaches schoolchildren and nonsupervisory personnel. Channels are typically of the formal variety. They direct, instruct, indoctrinate, inspire, or evaluate. Common forms of downward communication include policies and procedures, orders and memoranda, handbooks and reports for various stakeholders, and announcements considered to be of general public interest.

A problem with vertical, top-down communication is that it is premised on the "need to know." The stakeholders farthest away from the executive offices are presumed to need only that amount of information that enables them to perform the tasks assigned to them. Messages become more narrow as they move through the organization, often leaving those members of the lowest levels without a sense of connectedness to the organization and its purpose. School administrators, business managers, and supervisors decide how much to communicate in original form and how much to edit, add, interpret, or eliminate at each successive level. In one study, Reitz (1987) demonstrated that by the time a message from top management in business reaches individual workers, 80% of the original message has been filtered out.

To overcome message erosion, school organizations need to formulate specific methods for communicating messages. Planning should minimally address basic issues such as informing all concerned groups of ongoing activities and/or problems; announcing future plans, directions, and goals; encouraging two-way communication; ensuring timeliness of messages; and allocating funds for communication purposes. Sigband and Bell (1989) noted that administrative sponsorship of downward communication can forestall the fabrication in the grapevine of "facts." Establishing good communications from the onset is least costly.

Lateral or horizontal communication occurs between individuals at the same authority level in the hierarchy. Organizational peers spend a significant amount of time communicating with each other, more time than they spend communicating with their superiors (Reitz, 1987). Sigband and Bell (1989) questioned the value of lateral communication, considering how little pressure there is in organizations to use it productively. Problem solving and coordination are clearly enhanced by lateral communication, and duplication of effort is often avoided by means of this fast, direct exchange of messages apart from the chain of command. However, potential disadvantages of lateral communication might include overuse, a burying of peers in inconsequential memos, or an increase in "activity" that carries with it a false impression of productivity. An unequal exchange may also occur, with some peers withholding information as an exercise of power. Usually no system of accountability is involved in lateral communication, so the arbitrary bartering for power that occurs in these settings can be dangerous to an organization.

The efficacy and volume of upward communication depends on the degree of trust that lower-level stakeholders have in their superiors. Upward communication serves to alert upper levels of school management to the climate, activities, and performance declines or improvements that are of concern at the grassroots level of the organization. As is the case with downward communication, selective filtering occurs. Filtering occurs because lower-level employees often tell their superiors what they think those supervisors want to hear, thus introducing a positive bias toward themselves through the information they pass upward (Krivonos, 1982). Personnel at the bottom of the organizational pyramid rarely take the risk of initiating upward communication of their own accord. Mechanisms are often put into place to encourage such communication, including the use of employee suggestion boxes, the creation of quality circles, employee (or student) councils, and the use of various employee and client–customer survey techniques. Anonymity is always an issue in data gathering at all levels of an organization.

Educational organizations are generally alert to the need to communicate with the community at large as well as the need to enlist participation from that external environment. It is incumbent on school administrations to maintain open-system perspectives so that information coming in and going out is useful to all concerned. Kefalas (1977) considered careful monitoring and response to incoming communication an identifying characteristic of an effective organization. Reitz (1987) underscored the importance of external communication by citing a study of small businesses that showed a direct positive relationship between time spent in outward communications and business financial success. Communication with the community at large requires a definite leadership role for a school administrator. The possibility for organizational noise increases as the size of the receiver group increases because of cultural and psychological interference.

Schools must learn to rely on the support of local communities. The administrator should use communication to influence that support. In this sense the administrator, like his or her counterparts in other organizations, must project a vision and seek to implement that vision through partnerships with the community. However, vision is not enough. Schools must utilize the "human agency," whether it be school board meetings, newsletters, or public appearances, to mobilize community members to share the values of the vision. This requires selective and direct communication. The creation of new communication channels can operationalize shared values with the community. The community and school become active partners in the larger system, society.

Communication networks are a special case of directionality, involving vertical and horizontal (or lateral) communication. Much of the early research on communication networks was conducted in a laboratory setting and focused on the comparative effects of centralized and decentralized networks on the quality of communication. Although variations and elaborations exist, two basic patterns can be used to represent centralized and decentralized networks: the wheel and the circle. In the *centralized network*, or *wheel pattern*, persons at the periphery of the wheel send their communications to the hub person, who has control over the distribution of information. The structure of this network imposes its own brand of hierarchy, with the hub person becoming the executive figure. In the *decentralized network*, or *circle pattern*, all members communicate with those on either side of them, and the network avoids the hierarchical structure. Helgeson's (1990) *web* image of organizations combined wheel and circle networks, with communication nodes at each intersection of the web.

Using success in problem solving as the criterion of efficiency, Hall (1991) contended that repeated investigations have found the wheel pattern to be superior to the circle pattern. Khandwalla (1977) qualified that position and suggested that the effectiveness of the differing patterns depends on the nature of the task. He found that centralized patterns are faster and more error free for simple tasks, whereas decentralized networks perform better if the problems are complex and unexpected. Fisher (1978) noted that although the wheel can be an effective form of network, its effectiveness is largely contingent on the encoding and decoding skills of the person occupying the "hub" position.

Other Factors Affecting Organizational Communication

Reitz (1987) listed other major variables that affect direction, frequency, and participant satisfaction with communication. These include the availability of opportunities to interact, the degree of coherence of groups, the status of individuals or groups, and two-direction communication flow. Each is of considerable importance in school environments.

To maintain cohesion, groups require communication, which needs to reflect the value that individuals have in the group and the value that the individuals set on the group. Leaders bear responsibility for encouraging this communication and serve as models for the rest of the group (Abbott, 2007b). Communication among individuals and groups can be fostered by arranging physical and psychological distance so that common facilities are shared and interaction is a natural occurrence. Campbell and Campbell (1988) showed in a study of physical environment and interaction that the location of lounges is a strong predictor of lounge use and that an effect on informal types of communication can therefore be inferred. A variety of business studies have shown that managers interact most often with subordinates who are located in offices closest to them. The resulting inequities in organizational communications are obvious. Altering spatial relationships can occur through the leadership of a school administrator. Modeling new spatial arrangements may improve communication and shape relationships.

Cohesiveness and communication are mutually reinforcing. As the level of one rises, so does the level of the other. Status affects both the frequency and the direction of communication because people tend to direct their communication to those of similar or higher status. Reitz (1987) attributed this to perceptions of common interests, to shared experiences, or to mutual reinforcement. The desired outcome of interaction with a person of higher status may be to move closer to the person who controls the organizational reward structures.

Two-step communication flow refers to a process that depends on personal contacts with "opinion leaders," who in turn are influenced by mediated information from inside and outside the organization. Information transmitted to opinion leaders is disseminated to large numbers of people, who turn to the opinion leaders for "news" and for "reality testing" of their own points of view. This is an important process for educational administrators, who depend on such contacts for successful interface with the local community. Aside from effects that are triggered by status or distance, preference and perception also affect comprehension and overall effectiveness of a communication environment.

Reitz (1987) reported that face-to-face communication tends to be more effective than written communication (if the verbal and nonverbal cues are compatible) but admitted that written communication tends to yield greater comprehension. In general, nonverbal cues can influence communication effectiveness either by corroborating or contradicting a given verbal message or by conveying a message that is independent of verbal material, such as wearing a business suit or engaging in impatient pencil tapping.

Approaches to Organizational Communication

Structural and Functional Approaches

Productivity and task accomplishment are outputs (goals) of major concern to proponents of structural–functional approaches to communication. Shockley-Zalabak (1988) asserted that this results from adopting the principles of scientific management, following the lead of such writers as Max Weber, Henry Fayol, and Frederick Taylor. This approach stems from a bureaucratic management theoretical basis and results in communication style that is top-down, formal, of moderate load, and subject to minimal distortion. This utilitarian model underpins most public schools in the United States today.

Structural–functional theories of organizational communication have been dominated by the systems approach (Kefalas, 1977; Littlejohn, 1989; Shockley-Zalabak, 1988). These researchers view information processing as the primary function of organizational communication systems. The organization is defined as a system made up of interrelated units or subsystems. The system as a whole can be distinguished from other systems or organizations because it maintains organizational boundaries. If, however, the system is open (i.e., accepting and using environmental information and also communicating outward to the environment), its chances of success are greater than if it maintains closed boundaries and subsists only on internally generated, more bounded information. Because schools are so sensitive to their environments, the systems approach appeals to school administrators as a model for studying internal and external communication.

In the open communication system, incoming information is called *input*. The process by which input is transformed into a form usable by the system is known as *throughput*. Information transmitted from the system outward to its environment, whether intentionally or unintentionally, is referred to as *output*. Figure 6.1 demonstrates an input–output model of communication. Many general systems theorists warn that the model is too simplistic; it lacks the ability to model the complex elements and dynamics of the actual communication process. System theorists find such a figure too linear and much more systematic than systemic since the models obscure the richness and holistic orientation of the systems paradigm.

Farace, Monge, and Russell (1977) defined an organization as a system composed of members who are characteristically interdependent; who process input, throughput, and output; and who treat information as a critical resource for reducing uncertainty. Within this framework, communication depends on the use of common symbolic forms that have widely understood referents. Here information is subdivided into two types: *absolute information*, which refers collectively to all the information within the system, and *distributed information*, which resides in different places throughout the system. Distributed information is often neglected by school administrators and other managers.

Farace et al. (1977) indicated that conceptualization promotes discussion of communication at three levels: the system, the functional, and the structural levels. At the system level, three hierarchical interchanges

occur: individuals communicate in dyads, the dyads cluster into groups, and the interconnected groups form the organization or macronetwork. At the functional level, there is evidence of three organizational operations: production, innovation, and maintenance. At the structural level, communication elements of the frequency, regularity, and patterns of communication are plotted.

At the individual communication level, load is an important concept. *Load* refers to the quantity, volume, rate, and complexity of messages (Shockley-Zalabak, 1988). Major problems related to load include the extremes of underload, which is evident when the flow of messages falls below a person's capacity to process them, and overload, which represents a flow of messages that exceeds the person's information-processing capacity. Technological advances enabling the transmission of vast quantities of messages at extremely high rates have been the source of chronic overload for many people, resulting in impaired decision making. *Chronic overload* is a term that resonates with teachers and administrators alike. It is imperative that an administrator understand technology and its impact on communication.

At the dyad level of organizational communication, the key concept is *rules*, explicit and implicit norms or axioms for communications within an organization. Generally, rules are either thematic or tactical. *Thematic rules* are behavioral norms that reflect organizational values and beliefs, and *tactical rules* prescribe behaviors relevant to more general themes, such as referring analogically to the organization as a "family." A person who is socialized into an organization and who learns to identify with it will generally comply with both thematic and tactical rules.

Littlejohn (1989) considered three structures within the group setting: the micronetwork, the pattern of group interactions; the power structure; and the leadership structure, including interpersonal influence roles of group members. The various members and their links constitute the communication network. Links have five properties: symmetry, the extent to which linked members interact on an equal basis; strength, the frequency of interaction; reciprocity, the extent to which people concur about the links; the content of the interactions; and mode, the vehicle that carries the interaction (e.g., verbal or written communication). Within the micronetwork, people have distinct roles: acting as liaisons with other groups, becoming isolated and in essence "unlinked," or performing as gatekeepers who control information coming into or released by the group. Using the systems approach to organizational communication, large numbers of variables can be addressed. Littlejohn (1989) contended, however, that such approaches do not adequately account for situational variables that are not systemlike.

No single approach can serve to explain or identify all the variables in the communication process; therefore, no single method of communication will suffice for all situations that a school administrator encounters. Again, the concern for situational leadership (Yukl, 1989) emerges. The more complex an organization is, the more complex communication will be.

Behavioral Approaches

As management theories change to accommodate a more humanistic view, complementary changes occur in the way that organizational communication is viewed. The *Hawthorne effect* demonstrates that giving management attention to human relations factors has a favorable impact on organizational success. This is an early example of many subsequent studies that reached the same conclusion. When communication theorists felt that the complexity of human behavior was misrepresented in the structuralist–functionalist approach, they sought other approaches.

Human relations theorists believe that messages move in all directions, through both formal and informal networks. They emphasize oral over written channels and suggest a moderate communication load with predictable levels of distortion. One theoretical model representing this position is Likert's four systems. Likert (1967) suggests that organizations operate along a continuum of high- to low-control leadership styles, which have correlates in organizational communication styles.

The first style, *exploitative–authoritative*, is associated with top-down management. This style rarely accommodates feedback and therefore limits both the direction and the frequency of communication.

The second style, *benevolent–authoritative*, is also identified with top-down management, but the communication patterns here tend to give at least the appearance of management sensitivity to employee needs. The third style, *consultative*, accommodates vertical communication interchanges both upward and downward in the organization. The fourth style, *participative management*, accommodates the greatest amount of multidirectional communication, with employees expected to participate fully in organizational decision making. Critics of Likert's model suspect that participative management is also constrained by hierarchical assumptions and suggest that there may be yet another, structurally different power-sharing style (Schein, 1989). Leadership styles are discussed in more detail in chapter 4.

Human relations approaches are often criticized because of the implied notion that high morale leads without exception to high productivity, which is not necessarily true. Other critics see a failure to address important structural and functional variables. In this regard the human relations perspective may be suffering from the same misapprehensions and "turf wars" that system thinkers experience. Regardless of this academic criticism, in reality organizations function on the basis of morale and missions of productivity at some echelons. How organizations are modeled for an understanding of the shaping and life-giving effects of communication may not be determined solely by viewing the organization through one of the less structured approaches. Nevertheless, these approaches provide important elements for consideration by school administrators, whose very job it is to promote the delivery of a human service and to enable teachers, students, and staff to achieve. The school administrator cannot ignore the inevitable "humanness" of the school's character, especially in attempting to understand communication needs and responses.

Approaches Related to the Process of Organizing

Weick (1969) believed that organizational environments do not preexist but are enacted. Organizational members continually enact and reenact the environment as warranted by attitudes, values, and experience.

Organizing is therefore evolutionary and is contingent not only on enactment but also on information selection and retention processes. Enactment incorporates an acknowledgment of equivocality, but selection enables a group to admit certain relevant information and reject other data as irrelevant to the enactment. Retention entails decisions about which information should be saved for future use. In Weick's theory, assembly rules and interlocking behavior cycles are viewed as the basic mechanisms for organizing. Assembly rules guide the choice of routines that are used for enactment, selection, and retention. Interlocking behavior cycles are sets of interrelated behaviors that enable a group to agree on which meanings should be included and which rejected. After retention occurs, organizational members must decide whether to reenact the environment in some manner or to modify their behavior to achieve consistency with the information they hold. The flexibility implied by these evolving decisions may be of particular interest to school administrators.

Poole and McPhee (1983) extended the principle of structuration (organizing) into the realm of organizational communication. Interactions create norms and rules relative to the achievement of organizational goals and markedly affect both structure and climate. Poole and McPhee believed that organizational structure is a product of organizational communication. Structure is also an indirect way of informing employees and others about an organization.

Structuration can occur at three sites: the site of conception, any site where individual or group decisions are made about what will happen in an organization; the site of implementation, locations from which formal codification and dissemination of decisions about what will happen in the organization are proceeding; and the site of reception, those points at which organizational members act in accordance with the decisions made. Although anyone in the organization can participate in communication at any of the three sites, structuration tends to be specialized. For example, administrators are involved primarily at the site of conception. At this site administrators have the most opportunities to serve as leaders by establishing the means to influence the commitment of staff and students. Through the deliberate creation of channels (i.e., committees, forums, jobs, and so on), administrators may lead their organizations to build efficient communication systems. These systems can promote the general health of an organization.

Equally important, Poole and McPhee (1983) defined the organizational members' collective attitude as *climate*, an attitude that is constantly affected by organizational interactions. Climate is viewed as both a medium and an outcome of interactions, influenced not only by the structure but also by such climate-modifying strategies as publication of newsletters or holding contests. Climate is also affected by the composite of individual attributes, such as the possession or lack of knowledge and skills.

In contrast to organizational climate, the term *organizational culture* commonly refers to the shared realities that are played out in "performances" displayed during interchanges (Pacanowsky & O'Donnell-Trujillo, 1982). These performances can be classified as personal, task, or social rituals, performances that are regularly repeated; passions, including storytelling or passionate repartee exchanged in dramatic and lively interactions; sociality, including social performances dedicated to the creation of a group sense of identity, such as joking, talking shop, or sharing personal experiences; organizational politics, which create and reinforce notions of power and influence and perhaps involve activities such as bargaining; and enculturation, including performances aimed at initiating new members into the accepted organizational culture. Most school-based educators easily accept the notion that schools are cultural entities.

Organizational reputation is in part a reflection of organizational culture. It is a result of organizational communication, both conscious and subconscious (Nelissen, 2007), and it is often a focus of resources and energy as the organization works to create a positive reputation that will help the organization meet its goals.

As cultural entities, schools present myriad communication opportunities. The administrator must choose how to emphasize positive school-cultural traits at each opportunity. In an increasingly multicultural context, the role of the school administrator must be defined by communication that is reflective of school values and a school culture that is open to all stakeholders.

Sociopsychological Perspective on Individual Communication in Organizations

Elements of other theories and approaches to organizational communication are incorporated in sociopsychological theories. Paramount in this genre of communications theory are the effects created by individual communication acts. Here we revisit elements and processes associated with basic, quasi-mechanistic communication models in order to add psychological perspectives.

Psychological perspectives conceptualize organizational communication as a loop in which a sender initiates a message and a receiver obtains it and then considers possible courses of action. If the receiver responds or provides feedback, the roles of sender and receiver reverse. This looping behavior occurs in an organization's bureaucratic structure, which is subject to noise from the informal structure. This extraneous noise often interferes with message understanding. The meaning of a message depends not only on the content but also on the organizational context. O'Reilly and Pondy (1979) utilized the following formula to depict this process: meaning = information + context.

The message source may be a person or an intermediary medium, such as a newspaper, a memorandum, or a visual image. Credibility of the sender is critical in sociopsychological theory. Receivers may ignore noncredible messengers at will, regardless of message content. Not only are there psychological interpretations of the right of the sender to comment, but there are also psychological demands regarding a particular sender's choice of media. The encoding and decoding processes both allow "mental sets" to detract from or enhance message communication. According to psychological theorists, personality variables, values, gender or cultural differences, and personal interest ensure that a filtering process occurs at all points in the flow of communication.

Because the message form is often contingent on the channel or medium selected for message transmission, individual preferences can either override a communication system or be overridden by it. The channels or media selected determine, in large part, the routing pattern the message will follow (i.e., whether the message will be conveyed vertically or horizontally, formally or informally). Formatting the message also has psychological implications because people do not perceive or process information in identical ways. Business executives have been increasingly concerned that the medium selected may determine the richness and the impact of the information processed by receivers (Daft & Lengel, 1984; Lengel & Daft, 1988). Richness of medium is determined by the overall reception of a message. School administrators are also selective about the medium they use. Face-to-face verbal communication is preferred, with telephone communications and "written personal" next in order. "Written formal" and "numeric formal" complete the low end of the richness continuum. Face-to-face, filmed, or televised speech is considered "primary oral" communication.

Communicators in educational settings place some reliance on the relationships between the message chosen and the medium selected. Message comprehension tends to be higher when it is in written form, but opinion change is greater when face-to-face communication is employed. Media redundancy (i.e., a combination of written and oral) increases both message richness and accuracy of reception. Written communication tends to be effective when the message contains general information or requires future action. Oral communication tends to be effective in situations demanding immediate feedback. Examples of such situations are offering praise, giving procedural directions, settling disputes, issuing reprimands, and even saying "good morning" to other organizational members.

Nonverbal as well as verbal signals have meaning, and this meaning may conflict with or reinforce verbal message sending. Even nonword sound expressions, such as grunts or laughter, complicate the problem of message accuracy. Sociopsychological theorists seem to believe that the best to hope for is that the message received will be functionally comparable to the message sent.

Because both the range of message-sending options and the range of responses are subject to individual differences, feedback itself becomes a psychosocial phenomenon. Feedback varies even in its degrees of purposefulness, especially in its nonverbal aspects. For example, an unintended yawn can convey entirely the wrong feedback message. The concept of feedback implies that constant adjustments in the communication process can and should be made on the basis of clues the communicators get from feedback. Feedback can improve task performance and positively influence organizational climate.

On the other hand, feedback can either reflect or create situational noise. If physical, social, or psychological barriers are in place, feedback can either strengthen or reduce those barriers. Telling a partner that your boss is in the office helps the partner understand a reluctance to stay on the phone, and telling a partner that a particular phrase or mannerism is upsetting helps that person either adjust or decide not to adjust behavior according to his or her intent. Feedback is a powerful tool for educational administrators who can set the tone and examples for the entire school system. Feedback can be verbal or nonverbal; however, in any form, it must be situationally appropriate.

Nonverbal communication has been researched extensively in a variety of settings. For educators, two nonverbal modes are of particular interest: the impact of facial expressions and the use of spatial cues. Lipham and Francke (1966) studied nonverbal behavior of school principals as influencing promotability or nonpromotability. The variables they examined were the structuring of self (i.e., self-maintenance, clothing, physical movement, and posture); the structuring of interaction, including interaction initiation, interaction distance, and interaction termination behaviors; and the structuring of environment, including such matters as office decor, spatial arrangements, neatness, and status symbols. Researchers found significant differences in interaction and environmental structuring. Promotable principals tended to keep less distance in their interpersonal encounters. They also tended to use status symbols more casually, such as using a desk nameplate as a paperweight rather than using it as a psychological fence.

Communication satisfaction suggests that a real or perceived lack of two-way communication is a critical variable in educational institutions. Situational noise also poses a considerable threat to the success of organizational communication. Interpersonal communication seems always to be more effective than organizational communication because face-to-face situations rule out many sources of distortion, permit immediate feedback, and encourage message reframing.

Bureaucratic models of organization described by Barnard (1938) require that the channels of communication reach every organizational member, take the most direct route, remain available for constant use, and be authenticated by position power that tells receivers that the sender has the required authority to be a sender. The model assumes that such formality ensures message accuracy because it is "in writing," is from competent superiors, and is contextually the same for everyone. Although context may change to coordinating activities, providing information, influencing or directing, or simply telling organizational stories, formality is prominent. School bureaucracies display these dimensions to the extent that they are centralized, hierarchically shaped, and either more or less dependent on information technology.

Formal communication channels can carry both instrumental and expressive content to help the organization reach its goals and to affect attitudes, norms, and values. Informal channels are complementary in the sense that they typically reflect the impact of content carried in the formal channels. Informal communication also serves to gratify social needs of busy people by helping them express themselves personally and socially.

To understand formal and informal communication, researchers have used content analysis, sociometry, interaction analysis, participant observation, continuous observation, communication sampling, and general survey or network survey techniques. In educational institutions, general and network survey techniques are widely used. Surveys are designed to assess communication accuracy, openness, and frequency. Surveys provide useful representations of informal communication patterns and structures and often identify attractions, resistance, or lack of opportunity to communicate. Communication problems identified sociometrically can be adjusted so that information and social meanings are not lost.

Pathways to the Future

People in leadership positions spend the majority of their working days communicating. However, communication skills are an acknowledged weakness of many leaders (Baeshen, 1987). In the United States, millions of dollars are spent every year on efforts to develop the leadership, communication, and interpersonal skills of business, industry, and government leaders (Carnevale & Gainer, 1989). Middle managers are especially targeted for such training, with close to one-fourth of Fortune 500 training and development budgets allocated for these purposes. School administrators do not have access to comparable developmental resources and, after professional education, are expected to attend to their own development.

Although school personnel may already be alert to interpersonal and organizational communication issues, business organizations more clearly understand the impact of communication processes on the organizational "bottom line." Schools do not have the same clear, generally agreed-on standards of productivity, although the current efforts for national achievement standards and the high emphasis placed on test scores suggest that some stakeholders want more identifiable, unilateral outcomes. In the new millennium, the public, especially political and business/industry leaders, are indicating that schools should be producing literate, law-abiding citizens who are well prepared to enter the workforce. At the same time, school-based administrators and staff struggle to maintain safe, effective, future-oriented environments. With varied perceptions of productivity and varied goals of stakeholders, communication in school systems becomes even more important as diverse actors seek to agree on reform and restructuring efforts.

Effective communication contributes to employee performance. It enhances job satisfaction, a sense of personal accomplishment, and increased productivity. The working environment, quality of work, performance appraisals, and clarity of information provided by managers all are factors that contribute to employee job satisfaction (Javed, Manzil-e-Maqsood, & Qaiser, 2004).

Able administrators need to analyze and interpret their personal frames of reference—their metaphors, beliefs, and biases about organizations and organizational communication. Are they finite, firmly bounded scientific management systems using finite control mechanisms? Are they open, dynamic, holographic, reenacting systems using multiple variety stimulation/regulation strategies? Whatever the case, both administrators and teachers must be able to understand their own preferences and how their beliefs affect practice.

The challenge for school administrators is to examine all organizational arrangements for their critical effect on communication processes and for their ultimate effect on schoolchildren, communities, and the future labor force. School administrators are called on to imagine the unimaginable: new forms of schooling, new visions, new plans, new procedures, and new assessments to measure success.

Synthesizing Known Principles of Organizational Communication

General agreement exists that communication is purposive, sociopsychological, carried in both formal and informal channels, and incomplete without feedback. However, disagreement exists about the importance of information theory in sociopsychological approaches. In essence, all the approaches to organizational communication can make valid claims to definitions of communication because multiple perspectives and frames of reference are inevitable. By the same token, all the approaches described can be challenged because they do not incorporate all possible perspectives or account for all possible communication variables. A more comprehensive understanding and use of general systems theory may help integrate multiple perspectives and accommodate richer mixes of variables. This integrative theory building seems to be a task for the future.

Message-sending and message-receiving skills are so important (Haugland, 1987) that procedural models have been devised to help the communicator. Khandwalla (1977) suggested a front-end analysis to include determining the objective of the message and analyzing the situational variables, including available channels, best media, time constraints, and the nature of recipients. In this model the communicator seeks to anticipate potential communication difficulties and devise strategies for overcoming them. At a minimum, words and phrases that are likely to be emotional triggers are avoided, and calls to action are crafted and understood as a collective enterprise rather than military-style commands. The message sender thinks about potential miscommunication effects, even though there is no guarantee that negative effects will not occur. The school administrator will find that messages encouraging participation are generally well received but that, by tradition, some organization members will expect and even welcome the military command. Steering through the minefields of individual differences is never easy and is always a judgment call.

Employees and client groups want straight answers, straight information, and candid talk from their leaders (Ragan, 1990), even though there is often no agreement about what exactly should be communicated. Constituents reflect both a fear of communication and a fear of candor, but a fear of the unknown is far more unsettling (Wartenberg, 1990). The atmosphere of "waiting to find out" is an atmosphere of skepticism, insecurity, and cynicism. This leads lower-level stakeholders to engage in counterproductive speculations or self-preservation tactics. On such occasions, messages in informal communication channels can be organizationally destabilizing.

The old adage that some news, however unpleasant, is better than no news remains true in organizational communication. Using "leaks," opinion leaders, and increased face-to-face communication can help educational administrators relieve the tension in such a situation. By openly accepting feedback from all parts of the organization, the administrator can build the unity and health of the organization.

The amount of redundancy and feedback, along with the amount of face-to-face communication needed, is situationally dependent. Giving short, concise messages or addressing problems of organizational climate are occasions for face-to-face communication, whereas delivering messages that require an understanding of background or context may best be accomplished in writing. Considerable value may exist in communicating in both ways at the same time.

Personal skill and planning are essential for giving and receiving useful feedback. For positive effect, feedback should be helpful. It should be very specific and descriptive, accompanied by examples if possible. It should be given by someone who is perceived as trustworthy, should be timely, and should be presented in such a way that the receiver feels confident to do something about the situation. However, it should be noted that feedback is not automatic and often not voluntary; it may need to be pursued. Feedback consists of verbal and nonverbal messages that may or may not be congruent. It may even consist of misleading information that is meant to be tactful. Misleading information may also be used as a manipulative strategy by a person who fears for survival in a given organization.

The filtering of messages in all directions remains a serious problem in the communication process. If open and complete honesty is a threatening condition for either school leaders or followers, the filtering process can close down cooperation and yield erroneous messages. If open communication can prevail, subordinates can use it to get their work done with satisfaction, and leaders will have reliable sources of information to enable them to avert organizational problems. A positive organizational climate is the outcome of open communication. Miller (1978) cautioned, however, that even in the preferred channel-and-network arrangement of organizational communication, the relay nodes are also potential bottlenecks. He also noted the obvious: the longer the channels, the slower the flow of information.

Educational administrators serve organizational and personal interests well if they can devise a number of different ways to encourage upward and horizontal communication. One successful method has been the use of "linchpin" or liaison structures, where a person who communicates in two or more separate communication networks is deliberately charged with transferring information upward, downward, and horizontally across groups. Such linchpins can transcend a number of hierarchical levels. Another linking method is the formation of communications matrices where each educational staff member participates in at least two formal subsystems (e.g., instructional and schoolwide). One should be warned, however, that these communication strategies are effective only as long as trusting relationships are maintained. Any serious breach of trust can take years to repair since many layers of the communication network are damaged simultaneously when trust is breached in one area of the network.

Boundary spanning roles, either formal or informal, can be established to help individuals or groups form communication links with their environments. The triangulation principle applies here. Multiple and independent sources of information provide data about matters that may not be researchable in any direct fashion. Creating overlapping and redundant information systems can be a means to overcome the possibility that some gatekeepers, liaisons, or isolates may misuse the power inherent in their position. Even isolates have power, for either by their withdrawal or by their job demands they may block projects on which they are genuinely needed. Assigning isolates to task groups and altering job assignments to allow them to participate may enable the organization to draw on their skills and experience effectively.

Combining the Metaphors

Returning to the sets of metaphors and assumptions cited earlier in this chapter, it becomes clear that some metaphors are more helpful than others for exploring new forms of organization and new

requirements for organizational communication. The machine metaphor has already been labeled problematic. The heavy burden for productivity moves from the shoulders of humankind to the electronic databases that support human thinking and information processing. The organization possesses machine-based components of organizational communication but is not itself a machine.

The organization-as-organism model is still feasible and supports the idea that human beings and their interactions are microcosms of the organizations that they create around themselves. The holographic metaphor extends this idea. "Common cultural assumptions in an organization could be thought of as genetic codes that permit reconstruction of the whole from any part" (Schein, 1989, p. 12). The reference to genes as cellular reproductive microcosms of whole organizations is both biological in functioning and holographic in image. Organizational communication can be depicted similarly, as shown in Figure 6.2.

The organic model overlaps with the cultural–anthropological model but moves the focus from individual organism or organization to the organization as a culture embedded in a larger culture. The communication emphasis shifts accordingly, with cultural transmission becoming its primary rationale. This perspective supports the mores of particular organizations and may even legitimize leaders as organizational gurus even though a culture may be expected to change over time (see Figure 6.3).

Psychological metaphors remind organizational communication specialists that no two human beings send, receive, perceive, or interpret data—even sensory data—in exactly the same way. Human psychological uniqueness intrudes on every formulation of organizational communication. These claims cannot be denied and must be taken into account in modeling (see Figure 6.4).

The metaphor of the organization as brain permits analogies of computer-like information processing, much less dependent on structures and organizational layering for productive activity. It also allows for continuous research and action. The difficulty some have with this metaphor is that it is easily confused with leader as brain of the organization. No such idea is intended. Rather, the brain metaphor is meant to

FIGURE 6.2

Organic migration and enlargement of microcosmic interactions in organizational communication

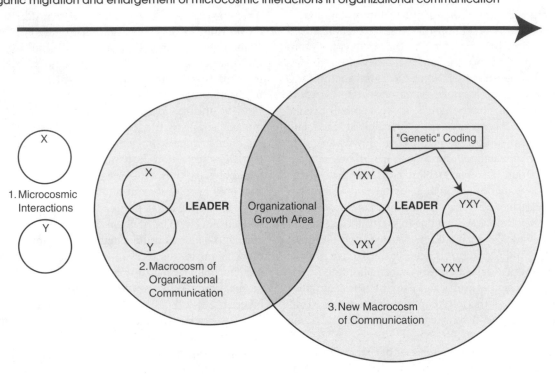

FIGURE 6.3

Culture-coded (YXY) organizational parts in systemic relationship, with organizational communication overlay

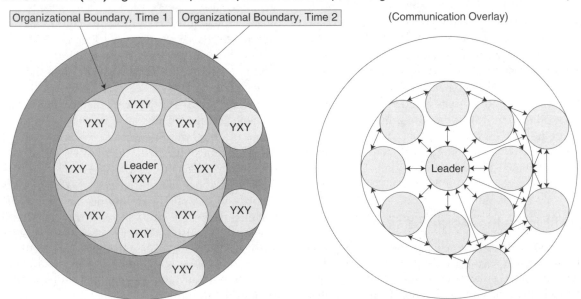

FIGURE 6.4

Psychological impacts of organizational communication

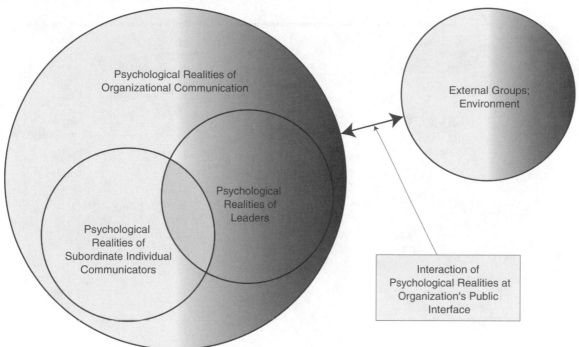

convey a broader, more holistic, more versatile picture of organizational thought and activity.

Organization as art easily allows the interpretation of organizational communication as a selective repertoire of plastic arts and media. Communication then becomes drama, painting and drawing, sculpting, prose or poetry, oration, conversation, or any other art form that conveys meaning throughout the organization. Art that is hung throughout corporate and other executive offices may be a minor acknowledgment of this point of view.

The metaphor of organization as learner shares many elements with the metaphor of organization as organism, brain, or art form. This metaphor optimistically represents a human organization acting as a cooperative learning community that thinks, feels, performs, values, and adjudicates its own work and its relation to human life at every level of the organization. In many ways, it requires that informed systems erase the image of people as production machines and insist on a restored

image of people as perpetually learning, growing, exchanging, and caring about those exchanges in both the personal and the organizational sense. Communication modeling for such holographic, artistic, learning–growing models can be only rudimentary at this time (see Figure 6.5).

People need to breathe to live, as do organizations composed of living human beings. Metaphorically, communication becomes the "breath" of the organization, enabling its electronic and human systems to work in concert, to reach outside the organization, and, perhaps, to work with a new sense of craftsmanship. In an ailing organization, an administrator with a clear understanding of the stakeholders' mission can provide the life-support system to sustain the breath of the organization. That life support needs attentive monitoring, constant updating, and vision changing. This life-support role may be the opportunity for an administrator to exercise a leadership role.

FIGURE 6.5

Informed atmosphere of organizational communication: the breath of organizational life

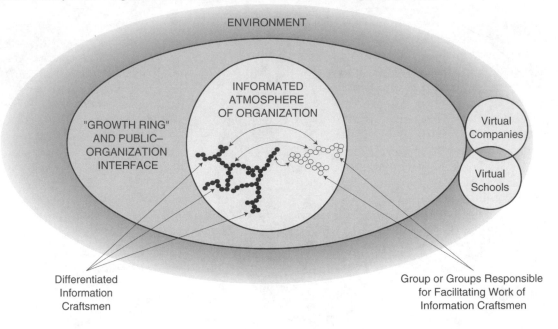

Moving Forward: Potential New Directions

Greenfield (1987) stated that the top-down leadership style is characteristic of educational institutions. This style reduces distortion but also strangles organizational communication in the participative sense and drains creative energy away from the system. Educational administrators have the opportunity to set a cooperative tone for the entire organization and can deliberately model the behaviors that they want to see in others. Instructor involvement in the organization itself—and not just in the classrooms—is crucial to organizational success.

To be an instructional leader means to be concerned at least as much about instruction and learning as about organizational policies, rules, and regulations. If instructors do not see evidence of this concern, whatever else an administrator may say or do will be received skeptically. The administrator is immediately relegated to the role of a mundane manager. A powerful and probably unintended message has been communicated.

Zuboff (1988) noted that organizational emphasis on wholeness causes leaders and many employees to feel disoriented initially. Changes in the distribution of authority are frightening. The level of involvement and commitment required in a new, flexible organization is daunting. Implications exist for social integration that many fear are a precursor to the loss of individual rights. The fact is that while top-down regimes allow for little creativity, they also protect members from ambiguity. Different people have different thresholds for enjoying, tolerating, or breaking apart under conditions of ambiguity. This is a real concern for new organization planners.

New divisions of learning based on the premise that learning is the new work of organizations are at the heart of the posthierarchical organization. In such organizations, the new leadership role that Zuboff (1988) described is facilitative, teacherlike, and very vulnerable. For leaders the new risk is needing constantly to admit that one does not have all the answers and that the answers where they exist at all may be found only by cooperative action. The new leaders in schools, as in other organizations, will need to be concerned about intellectual skill development, technology development, strategy formulation, and social system development. However, they cannot actually control any of these in the old sense of giving orders and being sure of specific action. The new leaders can only orchestrate opportunities to promote community and to develop communication skills throughout the organization.

Playing this different role imposes new communication imperatives. Optimal communication in the formal bureaucracies have been regarded as two way, but in an informated organization, two ways are not enough. In the informated organization an explosion of information is available to everyone. The communication questions become how to share, interpret, and feed back information at specific points and times to specific places in the organization when it is needed. Communication in this sense becomes interdependent and fluid. An implication is that a higher baseline of entry-level communication skills may be required of the leader. Communication in the informated organization changes the internal functioning of the organization itself and so changes the environmental expectations of the organization and of its leaders.

Educational administrators may wish to ignore the possibilities and challenges of inviting new forms of organization and new requirements for communication, but many are already thinking and writing seriously about such organizational changes and can scarcely be ignored. At present school leaders are already trying to manage complexity, perhaps with old ideas and tools and quite possibly with less-than-perfect success. Life has changed dramatically in the past few decades; schools have not. The lack of change has trapped administrators in structures that were designed to be successful in another age. The popular image of a successful "little red schoolhouse" is inadequate today considering emerging circumstances. Only risk takers who are willing to envision and create new school structures have an opportunity to develop a successful model appropriate for the future.

Creating Effective Communication in an Organization

In great part the nature of formal communication within an organization is the responsibility of the leader. Unless management takes responsibility for working toward better communication, little change is likely to take place.

Creating an atmosphere that is conducive to effective communication calls for the leaders to set an example by communicating openly with each other and with those who report to them. Rewards should be available for open communication that provides useful information. The rewards need not be monetary but should involve recognition of the value of the contribution. And the communication should produce some concrete, visible results so that the contributor and others can see the positive effect of making such an effort (Abbott, 2007a).

A wide variety of tools can be used for organizational communication. Traditional methods have included meetings, direct interaction between managers and employees, internal newsletters, and suggestion boxes and employee surveys, among others. Newly come onto the scene are individually controlled electronic communications tools, such as instant messaging and e-mail, which are showing a positive effect on the sense of open communication and improvement of productivity (Shaw, Scheufele, & Catalano, 2006; Turner, 2006).

Ten key principles for developing a successful communications program, according to Weatherly (2003), include the following:

1. The leader should serve as a role model.
2. Senior management should serve as an extension of the leader in modeling the desired communications behavior.
3. A plan for improving communications should be developed, and all members of the organization need to understand the purpose and functions of the plan.
4. Multiple means of communication should be planned for and employed over time.

5. Training in the fundamentals of communication should be provided that includes the organization's communications philosophy, the cultural language used, and clarification of the roles of responsibilities of the members of the organization for communication.

6. Credibility should be guarded carefully. "Do as I say, not as I do" is not productive of an effective program.

7. Leaders and organization members must be listeners as well as speakers.

8. Leaders need to actively seek input about the performance of the organization.

9. Leaders need to actively provide feedback to communications that they receive.

10. The communications plan needs to be reviewed periodically and adjusted to meet changing conditions.

SUMMARY AND FUNDAMENTAL CONCEPTS

Theories concerning the nature and functions of communication are numerous. They highlight communication in personal, social, and organizational settings. Effective communication is significant to the success of schools and school districts. Such communication is not singular but multiple, not linear but systemic and complex. Effective educational leaders need to be aware of and able to work with both the formal communications processes deliberately built into their systems and the informal communications processes that develop to meet particular needs of members of the systems.

In chapter 7, we discuss ethical aspects of decision making by leaders. Following discussion of philosophic views of the world and related ethical perspectives, we consider the impact of those views and perspectives on decision making, particularly in educational settings.

Fundamental Concepts

The fundamental concepts that follow have been discussed in this chapter. The citations that conclude each concept indicate the Interstate School Leaders Licensure Consortium (ISLLC) standards and functions related to the concept. The Arabic numeral refers to the ISLLC standards, and the letters refer to the functions as presented in the table found inside the front cover.

- The basic elements of a communication are the sender, the receiver, the message, interference, and feedback. (1; 2A, 2C, 2E, 2I; 3A, 3B; 4; 5A; 6A, 6B)
- Communication is a requisite for any system, living or nonliving. (1; 2A, 2C, 2E, 2I; 3A, 3B; 4; 5A; 6A, 6B)
- Four basic types of communication theories are structuralist/functional, cognitive/behavioral, interactional/conventional, and interpretive/critical. (1; 2A, 2C, 2E, 2I; 3A, 3B; 4; 5A; 6A, 6B)

ACTIVITY 6.3

Creating Communication Systems

Addresses ISLLC Standards 1, 2, 3, 4, 5, and 6

You have been hired by the Riverbend Central School District to serve as principal for their new middle school. You have had 10 years of very successful experience in two previous principalships, one an elementary school and one a junior high school.

During your interviews for the job, you found that the school district has a history of difficult relations with some segments of the community and that negotiations between the school board and the various unions serving the district have historically been protracted and sometimes intense. In your discussions with the superintendent, she made it clear that she and the school board were looking for someone who can work toward reducing some of these problems.

The new school is to be opened for instruction as of the first week in January. You have been hired as of the first of September and charged with supervising the preparations for opening the school.

What formal communication systems do you plan to establish for your new school? What informal communications systems can you anticipate being developed? What can you do to help reduce the long-standing problems in the Riverbend district that you know exist? Prepare an action plan for dealing with these questions and be ready to review it with the superintendent by October 1.

- Some metaphors for organizational communication include organization as machine, organism, culture, learner, political system, prison, instrument of domination. Each metaphor carries a particular view of the nature and function of communication. (1; 2A, 2C, 2E, 2I; 3A, 3B; 4; 5A; 6A, 6B)
- The metaphor of the learning organization is particularly significant to educational systems. (1; 2A, 2C, 2E, 2I; 3A, 3B; 4; 5A; 6A, 6B)
- Organizational communication is distinguished from other types of communication by its deliberate focus on achievement of a collective goal. (1; 2A, 2C, 2E, 2I; 3A, 3B; 4; 5A; 6A, 6B)
- Organizational communication is prevalent throughout a system and so is of great importance to a leader. (1; 2A, 2C, 2E, 2I; 3A, 3B; 4; 5A; 6A, 6B)
- Factors affecting the clarity, credibility, and directionality of organizational communication include formal/informal, verbal/nonverbal, cultural differences, bias, anxiety/defensiveness, hidden agendas, and groupthink. (1; 2A, 2C, 2E, 2I; 3A, 3B; 4; 5A; 6A, 6B)
- Other factors affecting the direction, frequency, and participant satisfaction with communication include the opportunities to interact, the degree of coherence of groups, the status of individuals or groups, and two-stage communication flow. (1; 2A, 2C, 2E, 2I; 3A, 3B; 4; 5A; 6A, 6B)
- Communication is purposeful, sociopsychological, carried on both formal and informal channels, and incomplete without feedback. (1; 2A, 2C, 2E, 2I; 3A, 3B; 4; 5A; 6A, 6B)
- Effective leaders of organizations need to be aware of the ubiquitous nature of communication within the system and ways in which communication can be used to move the system toward desired goals. (1; 2A, 2C, 2E, 2I; 3A, 3B; 4; 5A; 6A, 6B)
- Development of effective communications within an organization calls for deliberate action by the leader, widespread participation thoughout the organization, and continuous monitoring over time. (1; 2A, 2C, 2E, 2I; 3A, 3B; 4; 5A; 6A, 6B)

Case Study

Communication for Accountability

Addresses ISLLC Standards 1, 2, 3, 4, 5, and 6

You are the chairperson of a school board. You and the majority of the board are new in office, having won an election recently on a reform platform. Part of the reform platform called for increased accountability to the community by the school system.

In your professional life, you are supervisor of a division of employees in a corporate environment, and you have learned to respect a system in which responsibilities are clearly defined, goals and objectives are clear, results are measurable, and accountability is clearly assignable for those results.

With that in mind, you have been looking at ways in which your district is accountable for its results. You have found that students receive report cards once a quarter during the school year, and parents are required to sign and return those cards. Students in grades 3, 6, 9, and 11 take state examinations based on the state curriculum guidelines. Satisfactory scores on the exams are significant in determining whether a student progresses to the next grade. The results of the scores are released by grade to the public through the local press.

The district participates in the regional Association of Colleges and Secondary Schools, a national self-monitoring accreditation program that holds a major review once every 10 years, with a midcycle report submitted during the fifth year. The results of those activities are reported to the public through the local press.

You also know that the state exam scores and regional accreditation processes are discussed in open board meetings that are held at published times and places, as required by state law, and often covered by the local press. Budget hearings are held in open meetings. The board's meetings are closed to the public for executive session only under circumstances prescribed by law, such as discussion of personnel issues and union negotiation. In such cases the results of the discussion must be voted on in an open public session.

Questions

1. Decide if the previously discussed information and the existing means of communicating that information constitute sufficient communication and accountability toward the community.
2. If you feel that it is sufficient, develop a presentation to make to the board in an open session explaining in what ways the present situation meets your expectations when you were a candidate for election. Be prepared to respond to questions both from the other board members and from the public and press present at the meeting.
3. If you feel that it is not sufficient, develop a plan for improving communication and accountability toward the community. Prepare a presentation to make to the

board in open session that will explain what you feel should be done, how, and why. Be prepared to respond to questions both from the other board members and from the public and press present at the meeting.

REFERENCES

Abbott, R. F. (2007a). *A climate for communication*. Retrieved October 5, 2007, from http://www.communicate-with-confidence.com/climate-for-communication

Abbott, R. F. (2007b). *How to build a cohesive team*. Retrieved October 5, 2007, from http://www.communicate-with-confidence.com/how-to-build-a-cohesive-team

Allen, D. (1994). *Training directors in communication for the rehearsal process: A pilot study*. Unpublished doctoral dissertation, Texas Tech University, Lubbock.

Argyris, C., & Schön, D. A. (1978). *Organizational learning: A theory of action perspective*. Reading, MA: Addison-Wesley.

Badal, A. (2003). *Organizational communication strategies in elementary education*. East Lansing, MI: National Center for Research on Teacher Learning. (ERIC Document Reproduction Service No. ED481541)

Baeshen, N. (1987). *The effect of organizational communication on the middle and lower-level managers' participation in the decision-making process in Saudi Arabia*. Unpublished doctoral dissertation, University of Arizona, Tucson.

Barnard, C. (1938). *The function of the executive*. Cambridge, MA: Harvard University Press.

Berelson, B., & Steiner, G. (1964). *Human behavior: An inventory of scientific findings*. New York: Harcourt Brace.

Berlo, D. K. (1960). *The process of communications*. New York: Holt, Rinehart and Winston.

Campbell, D. E., & Campbell, T. A. (1988, March). A new look at informal communication: The role of the physical environment. *Environment and Behavior, 20*(2), 211.

Carnevale, A. P., & Gainer, L. J. (1989). *The learning enterprise*. Alexandria, VA: American Society for Training and Development and U.S. Department of Labor.

Cragan, J. F., & Shields, D. C. (1995). *Symbolic theories in applied communication research*. Cresskill, NJ: Hampton Press.

Daft, R. L., & Lengel, R. H. (1984). Information richness: A new approach to managerial behavior and organizational design. *Research in Organizational Behavior, 6*, 195–198.

Dance, F. E. X. (1970). The "concept" of communication. *Journal of Communication, 20*, 201–210.

Donellon, A. G., Gray, B., & Bougon, M. G. (1986). Communication, meaning, and organized action. *Administrative Science Quarterly, 31*(1), 43–55.

Etzioni, A. (1964). *Modern organizations*. Upper Saddle River, NJ: Prentice Hall.

Farace, R. V., Monge, P. R., & Russell, H. (1977). *Communicating and organizing*. Reading, MA: Addison-Wesley.

Fisher, A. (1978). *Perspectives of human communication*. New York: Macmillan.

Fredrickson, M. P. (1991). *Design juries: A study in lines of communication*. Unpublished doctoral dissertation, University of California, Los Angeles.

Greenfield, W. (1987). *Instructional leadership: Concepts, issues, and controversies*. Newton, MA: Allyn and Bacon.

Hall, R. H. (1991). *Organizations: Structure, processes and outcomes* (5th ed.). Upper Saddle River, NJ: Prentice Hall.

Haugland, M. (1987). Professional competencies needed by school superintendents, as perceived by school board members in South Dakota. *Spectrum, 5*(4), 40–42.

Helgeson, S. (1990). *The female advantage: Women's ways of leadership*. New York: Doubleday/Currency.

Hentges, K., Yaney, J., & Shields, C. (1990). Training and motivating the new labor force: The impact of ethnicity. *Performance Improvement Quarterly, 3*(3), 36–44.

Hoy, W., & Miskel, C. (1987). Communication. In *Educational administration: Theory, research, and practice* (3rd ed., pp. 356–381). New York: Random House.

Javed, T., Manzil-e-Maqsood, & Qaiser, D. S. (2004). A survey to examine the effect of team communication on job satisfaction in software development. *ACM SIGSOFT Software Engineering Notes 29*(2), p. 6.

Kefalas, A. (1977). Organizational communications: A systems viewpoint. In R. Huseman, C. Logue, & D. Freshley (Eds.), *Readings in interpersonal and organizational communication* (3rd ed., pp. 25–43). Boston: Allyn & Bacon.

Khandwalla, P. (1977). *The design of organizations*. New York: Harcourt Brace.

Kovacic, B. (Ed.). (1997). *Emerging theories of human communication*. Albany: State University of New York Press.

Krivonos, P. (1982). Distortion of subordinate to superior communication in organizational settings. *Central States Speech Journal, 33*(1), 335–352.

Lengel, R. H., & Daft, R. L. (1988). The selection of communication media as an executive skill. *Academy of Management Executive, 2*(3), 225–232.

Lewin, K. (1951). *Field theory in social science*. New York: Harper.

Likert, R. (1967). *The human organization*. New York: McGraw-Hill.

Lipham, J. M., & Francke, D. C. (1966). Nonverbal behavior of administrators. *Educational Administration Quarterly, 2*, 101–109.

Littlejohn, S. W. (1989). *Theories of human communication* (3rd ed.). Belmont, CA: Wadsworth.

Marsick, V. J. (1990). Altering the paradigm for theory building and research. *Human Resource Development Quarterly, 1*(1), 5–23, 29–34.

Miller, J. G. (1978). *Living systems*. New York, McGraw-Hill.

Morgan, G. (1986). *Images of organization*. Beverly Hills, CA: Sage.

Murphy, H., & Peck, C. (1980). *Effective business communication*. New York: McGraw-Hill.

Nelissen, P. (2007, May 24). *Dialogue in organizational communication*. Presented at Non-Divisional Working Symposium on "Making communication studies matter:

Field relevance/irrelevance in media, library, electronic, communication systems designs, policies, and practices," San Francisco, CA. Retrieved September 20, 2007, from http://communication.sbs.ohio-state.edu/sense-making/meet/2007/meet07_nelissen.pdf

O'Reilly, C. A., & Pondy, L. R. (1979). Organizational communication. In S. Kerr (Ed.), *Organizational behavior*. Columbus, OH: Grid, pp. 137–144.

Pegals, C. C. (1998). *Handbook of strategies and tools for the learning company*. Portland, OR: Productivity Press.

Pacanowsky, M., & O'Donnell-Trujillo, N. (1982). Organizational communication as cultural performance. *Communication Monographs, 50,* 126–147.

Peters, T. (1992). *Liberation management: Necessary disorganization for the nanosecond nineties*. New York: Knopf.

Poole, M. S., & McPhee, R. D. (1983). A structuratural theory of organizational climate. In L. Putnam & M. Pacanowsky (Eds.), *Organizational communication: An interpretive approach*. Beverly Hills, CA: Sage.

Ragan, L. (1990). The great debate. *Communication World*, 7(6), 85–87.

Read, S. L. (2007, September 13). *Communicating with clarity and confidence*. Retrieved October 5, 2007, from http://ezinearticles.com/?Communicating-with-Clarity-and-Confidence

Reitz, H. J. (1987). Communications. In *Behavior in organizations* (3rd ed., pp. 301–330). Homewood, IL: Irwin.

Shaw, B., Scheufele, D, & Catalano, S. (2006, October 5). *The role of instant messaging as a tool for organizational communication: An exploratory field experiment*. Paper presented at the annual meeting of the International Communication Association, New York. Retrieved October 5, 2007, from http://www.allacademic.com/ meta/p14438_index.html

Schein, E. (1989, May). Corporate teams and totems. *Across the Board, 26,* 12–17. (Reprinted from *Sloan Management Review*, Winter 1989).

Shockley-Zalabak, P. (1988). *Fundamentals of organizational communication*. New York: Longman.

Sigband, N., & Bell, A. (1989). Communication in organizations. In *Communication for management and business* (5th ed., pp. 23–51). Glenview, IL: Scott, Foresman.

Smith, S. C., & Piele, P. K. (Eds.). (1989). *School leadership: Handbook for excellence*. Eugene: ERIC Clearinghouse on Educational Management, University of Oregon.

Striplin, P. (1987). An exploratory study of teachers' opinions to important competencies needed by principals to perform effectively as instructional leaders (Doctoral dissertation, Florida State University, 1987). *Dissertation Abstracts International, 48,* 12A.

Turner, J. W. (2006). Exploring the dominant media. *Journal of Business Communication, 43*(3), 220–250.

Wartenberg, M. R. (1990). How to merge—and survive. *Management Review, 79*(6), 64.

Watkins, K. (1989). Five metaphors: Alternative theories for human resource development. In D. Gradous (Ed.), *Systems theory applied to human resource development* (Theory to Practice Monograph). Minneapolis: University of Minnesota Training and Development Research Center and American Society for Training and Development Research Committee, pp. 167–184.

Weatherly, L. A. (2003, May). *Ten key principles required for a successful communications program*. Society for Human Resources Management Research. Retrieved October 4, 2007, from http://www.shrm.org/hrresources

Weick, K. (1969). *The social psychology of organizing*. Reading, MA: Addison-Wesley.

Wiener, N. (1954). *The human use of human beings: Cybernetics and society*. Garden City, NY: Doubleday/Anchor.

Yukl, G. A. (1989). *Leadership in organizations* (2nd ed.). Upper Saddle River, NJ: Prentice Hall.

Zuboff, S. (1988). *In the age of the smart machine*. New York: Basic Books.

Values, Analysis, and Information

Part III focuses on values and philosophies and their influence on behavior, decisions, and research and how we interpret information. Chapter 7 examines the impact of personal values on organizational decision outcomes, chapter 8 the impact on evaluation and research, and chapter 9 the impact of information technology on decisions and the decision-making process.

Chapter 7: The Impact of Personal Values on Decision Outcomes. Ethical aspects of decision making is the focus of chapter 7. Drawing from social science perspectives, we focus on values and value hierarchies as they are found in individuals and organizations. How leaders analyze the world in the context of value systems is described. We show how values in the form of metavalues shape the perception of reality in organizations and challenge administrative leaders to accept those value parameters or transform them to make change possible. In the final section, the influence of values and beliefs is shown on the structuring of formal inquiries into educational issues and their effects on the outcomes of those inquiries.

Chapter 8: Evaluation. Judgments of the effective functioning of an organization are based on monitoring outcomes and measuring them against established goals and objectives. The standards movement and its relation to program evaluation, student achievement, and staff evaluation are examined, including standards-based assessment activities at both national and state levels.

Chapter 9: The Role of Information and Technology. The nature and importance of information systems is the central theme of chapter 9. Good information is critical for making good decisions and developing wise strategies, effective plans, and efficient allocation of human and economic resources within educational organizations. Note is taken of the astounding advances in information and communication technologies and the relevance of these changes to the organization of schools, a major segment of the information industry. Particular attention is paid to the changing nature of leadership and organizational structure due to these developments.

The Impact of Personal Values on an Organization's Decision Outcomes

Practically all our activities occur within the context of decisions made about good and bad, right and wrong, or better and worse. Behavior is therefore a constant reflection of beliefs about how the world is structured and decisions are made, and actions taken are based, implicitly or explicitly, on those philosophical considerations (Foster, 1986). Everyone has a philosophical view of life even though it may not have been thoroughly thought through and articulated. To be an effective guide to administrative behavior, however, it is best if this philosophy is understood and intellectualized. Such an understanding permits a leader to act consistently on pertinent issues and to reflect critically on those actions. For this reason, it is important that persons in leadership roles learn "to do" philosophy for themselves rather than leave it by default to be done by others.

Chapter 6 examined communications concepts as applied to social systems. A key ingredient of effective leadership, communications is the conduit for inquiry that develops understanding within and across environments. In this chapter, we investigate ethical aspects of leadership. Drawing from social science perspectives, we focus on values and value hierarchies as they are found in individuals and organizations. How leaders analyze the world in the context of value systems is described. We show how values in the form of metavalues shape the perception of reality in organizations and challenge administrative leaders to accept those value parameters or transform them to make change possible. In the final section, the influence of philosophic views, values, and beliefs is shown on the structuring of formal inquiries into educational issues and their effects on the outcomes of those inquiries.

Philosophical Guides to Leadership

Philosophical Foundations

Philosophy, in its broadest meaning, is a systematic attempt to make sense out of our individual and collective human experience (De George, 1999). The philosopher's primary intellectual tool is reason. Ethics is that part of philosophy concerned with morality, a complex of ideals showing how people *should* relate to one another in particular situations. The study of ethics yields principles of conduct guiding those human interactions and suggests the kind of reasoning that one engages in when thinking about such ideals and principles (L. M. Smith, 1990).

In the second of his four seminal treatises on the philosophy of administration and leadership, Hodgkinson (1983) observed that the essence of the art of administration is the manipulation of people by people about goals. He saw the most persuasive reason for doing philosophy in the field of executive action as being derived from the fact that administrators possess power and make decisions that affect other people. "If morality is interpreted as a concern for others, then it follows that administration is a peculiarly moral activity" (p. 29):

> The field of executive action and the administrative endeavor which embraces it make philosophical demands. It is the highest function of the executive to develop a deep understanding of himself and his fellows, a knowledge of human nature which includes motivation but reaches beyond into the domain of value possibilities. . . . At its lowest level, organizational life is sort of a daily combat. Even here, however, the deadliest weapons in the administrative armory are philosophical: the skills of logical and

critical analysis, conceptual synthesis, value analysis and commitment, rhetoric and most fundamentally, the depth understanding of human nature. So in the end philosophy becomes intrinsically practical. (Hodgkinson, 1983, p. 53)

Prior to the turn of the 21st century, preparation programs for school administrators typically emphasized organizational, behavioral, and managerial theories while neglecting contextual considerations of culture, politics, morals, and ethics. Criticism of this omission began as early as 1964 and continues today (Beck, Murphy, & Associates, 1997; Bolman & Deal, 2003; Culbertson, 1964; Erickson, 1977; Farquhar, 1968; Foster, 1986; Goldhammer, 1983; Greenfield, 1975; Griffiths, 1979; Harlow, 1962; Osterman & Kottkamp, 1993, 2004). Others whose scholarship confirms the importance of ethics, morals, and values in educational administration include Begley and Stefkovich (2004), Fullan (2003), Greenfield (2004), Sergiovanni (2001), and Shapiro and Stefkovich (2001).

While many preparation programs have corrected or are correcting the omissions independently, the critics' arguments were first acknowledged nationally with the establishment of the National Commission on Excellence in Educational Administration (NCEEA) by the University Council on Educational Administration (Forsyth, 1999). The NCEEA published *Leaders for America's Schools* in 1987. Subsequently, the National Policy Board for Educational Administration (NPBEA) came into being as a loose-knit association of 10 national professional and higher-education organizations with major interests in school administration (Thomson, 1999). The NPBEA in turn created the Interstate School Leaders Licensure Consortium (ISLLC) in 1994 to craft model standards for school leaders (Murphy, Yff, & Shipman, 2000). The ISLLC operated under the aegis of the Council of Chief State School Officers and the standards it developed (highlighted on the flyleaf and throughout this book) were published in 1996 under the title *Standards for School Leaders* (ISLLC, 1996) and subsequently updated in 2007 (Council of Chief State School Officers, 2008).

The publication of the ISLLC standards initiated a period of dissemination, discussion, and debate. By 2003, however, the education community was

beginning to coalesce around the standards (Murphy, 2003). They were being used by approximately 40 states as the platform for thinking about school administration, and several of those states were requiring universities to align their preparation programs with the standards. Most states adopting ISLLC standards have also revised their licensure regulations to conform to the standards. Further, the National Council for the Accreditation of Teacher Education (NCATE) adopted the ISLLC standards for the accreditation of preparatory programs in school administration, causing all such programs in NCATE institutions in approximately 45 states to fall under the professional and state-policy umbrella of the standards. Finally, ISLLC contracted with the Educational Testing Service to develop an examination for principals (School Leaders Licensure Assessment [SLLA]) and one for superintendents (School Superintendent Assessment [SSA]). The SLLA is required by 14 state licensing boards to measure the knowledge and skills needed to perform competently on the job of entry-level school professionals aspiring for certification as principals and other school leadership positions. Only Missouri requires the SSA for superintendent certification (http://www.ets.org, July 6, 2007).

All six of the ISLLC standards involve philosophical and ethical issues and have implications for leaders' values and beliefs, but they are the core concern of Standard 5: An educational leader promotes the success of every student by acting with integrity, fairness, and in an ethical manner. Figure 7.1 relates the five functions associated with Standard 5 as revised.

In studying trends in the reform of school administrator preparation programs, Joseph Murphy (1993), chair of the ISLLC when the standards were issued and their subsequent revision, observed that there was a new and general concern for including ethics in the curriculum. He reasoned that sound professional judgment and conduct are contingent on sound ethical judgment and conduct and that, in on-the-job contexts, routine practical decisions and ethical decisions are often indistinguishable. More specifically, administrators are representatives of values, and the responsibility of principals to their students, teachers, and communities is to provide leadership based on an informed ethical reflection about education and public life. Murphy believes

FIGURE 7.1

ISLLC Standard 5

An educational leader promotes the success of every student by acting with integrity, fairness, and in an ethical manner.

Functions

A. Ensure a system of accountability for every student's academic and social success
B. Model principles of self-awareness, reflective practice, transparency, and ethical behavior
C. Safeguard the values of democracy, equity, and diversity
D. Consider and evaluate the potential moral and legal consequences of decision making
E. Promote social justice and ensure that individual student needs inform all aspects of schooling

Source: National Policy Board for Educational Administration, *Educational leadership policy standards: ISLLC 2008.* Washington, DC: Council of Chief State School Officers, 2008.

that unless leaders develop a moral and ethical conscience, they will find it difficult to make decisions and will lose a sense of purpose.

To be effective, administrative behavior must rest on certain philosophical assumptions about such fundamental considerations as human nature, the nature of reality, conditions of knowledge, and the nature of value. Further, such behavior must be in harmony with great cultural movements and the ideas that impel them—ideas that are inevitably philosophical in character (Fullan, 2003; Furman, 2004; Graff, Street, Kimbrough, & Dykes, 1966; Sergiovanni, 2001). Today's leaders must develop a holistic perspective that enables them to comprehend the myriad forces and conditions affecting important social, economic, scientific, and governmental institutions.

School administrators today are faced with pressures from all sides. Bewildering expectations are placed on the schools and the people who staff them. Bitter conflict exists over what the purposes of education should be and how educational services should be delivered. The function of administration in relation to educational leadership is not clearly understood. In such a fluid and uncertain environment, school administrators desiring to provide effective leadership need a philosophical reference point from which to evaluate and base their actions. Without such a reference point, the administrator drifts like a rudderless ship on a stormy sea, battered about by one special interest group after another.

Some of the major philosophical systems that have been or that are particularly influential in shaping Western culture and the lives of individuals include idealism, liberalism, realism/positivism/postpositivism, pragmatism, existentialism, critical theory, and interpretivistic theory/constructivism. One system is not necessarily better than another, but the orientation to life and the resulting behavior of a person subscribing to one system will be different from that of a person subscribing to another. Concurrently, one's philosophical orientation shapes the way one approaches formal inquiry into social dilemmas, the interpretation of data, and, ultimately, conclusions arrived at and decisions made (the focus of the second major section of this chapter). Personal philosophies tend to be eclectic, having elements of several of the basic systems.

ACTIVITY 7.1

Articulating Your Personal Philosophy

Addresses ISLLC Standard 5

Everyone has a philosophical view of life even though it may not have been thoroughly articulated.

a. Reflect on your philosophical view of life and summarize it in a few paragraphs.
b. How does your philosophy of life affect your professional behavior?

Implications for Inquiry and Practice

Nyberg (1993) divided philosophers (and other people) into two broad orientations toward formulating moral judgments: moral principle and personal value. The *moral-principle orientation* favors "ideas that are extensive, inclusive, universal and elegant in their simplicity" (p. 206). These would tend to include idealists and positivists. The *personal-value orientation* prefers to see "individuals with perfect clarity, in all their literal, particular, factual fullness . . . no matter how fragmented the world may then seem" (p. 206). These would include existentialists and constructivists.

The moral-principal orientation tends to view rationality as the striving for economy of means of thought by holding allegiance to a single conception or idea that can be applied broadly. The personal-value orientation's view of rationality is that "people can think and act in ways they themselves can understand and alter, that individuals are not merely victims of structural causes, and that justifications and explanations of human conduct must be in terms of personal, subjective motives and reasons, however idiosyncratic they may seem" (Nyberg, 1993, p. 198).

Gage (1989) labeled the continuing conflict among educational researchers who adhere to one or another of the competing philosophies as "The Paradigm Wars." He admonished our educational intellectual leaders—philosophers, scientists, scholars, and research workers—not to become bogged down in an intellectual no-man's-land and reminded them that "even as we debate whether any objectivity at all is possible, whether 'technical' research is merely trivial, whether your paradigm or mine should get more money, I feel that I should remember that the payoff inheres in what happens to the children, the students. This is our end concern" (p. 10). Our tasks carry with them moral obligations.

In this vein, Sergiovanni (1984a) called for a multiple-perspective approach to the analysis of administration and organizations:

> Theories of administration . . . should not be viewed as competing, with the thought that one best view might emerge. Instead, the alternative and overlapping metaphor is offered. When viewed this way, each theory of administration is better able to illuminate

and explain certain aspects of the problems administrators face but not others. Increased understanding depends upon the use of several theories, preferably in an integrated fashion. (p. 1)

Foster (1986) proposed a three-tier model for the study of administration. The first tier involves the empirical study of organization and administration through descriptions of perceived reality and economic and political structures. The second tier consists of the development of individual constructions and interpretations of reality. The third tier is critical inquiry, a reflective process that includes dialogue intended to achieve true democratic participation by all members of the community.

A great divide seems to exist between those who view the world in terms of a single paradigm and those who accept none as absolute but are willing to be guided by insights provided by many. The authors of this book fall into the latter category. We recognize that educational administration is a moral pursuit and that the effective administrator must act with an understanding of the relevance of value structures to his or her executive actions. We also appreciate, however, the contributions of the social sciences to the enlightenment of the practice of educational leadership. These "scientific" aspects are highlighted later in this chapter.

Values and Value Systems

Values Defined

Values are conceptions of the desirable (Hodgkinson, 1996). A value is an enduring belief that a specific mode of conduct or state of existence is personally or socially preferable to an opposite or converse mode of conduct or state of existence (Hoy & Miskel, 2005; Parsons, 1951; Willower & Licata, 1997). Values are synonymous with personal beliefs about the "good," the "just," and the "beautiful"; they propel us to a particular kind of behavior and lifestyle (Lewis, 1990). Values reflect the worldview (philosophy) of an individual or organization (Hall, Kalven, Rosen, & Taylor, 1990). They are consciously or unconsciously held priorities that are expressed in all human activity. A value system is an enduring

ACTIVITY 7.2

Seeking Additional Information and Opinion about Administrative Philosophy and Ethics

Addresses ISLLC Standard 5

- Visit the Web site of the Center for the Study of Leadership and Ethics of the University Council on Educational Administration at Pennsylvania State University at http://www.ed.psu.edu/UCESACSLE. Note details about the annual conference on values and leadership. Explore the archives of the electronic journal *Values and Ethics in Educational Administration* for articles of interest. Get a sense of the current "hot" issues in leadership ethics by scanning the site's "Resource Lists."

- Concern over organizational ethics is not limited to educational organizations. Visit the Web page of the Ethics Resource Center, http://www.ethics.org, which has been in business since 1922 to promote the advancement of high ethical standards in public and private institutions. Explore the site and note similarities and differences in the topics posted on this site compared with those on the Pennsylvania State University site.

organization of values along a continuum of relative importance (Rokeach, 1973).

"Values are subjective because they are concepts. They have to do with the phenomenology of desire" (Hodgkinson, 1996, p. 114). We value things or states because we choose to attribute worth to them, not because of any innate worth. In so doing, we superimpose onto a thing a subjective element to indicate its level of importance for us (Beare, Caldwell, & Millikan, 1989). To be functional collectively, others must assign similar degrees of value to the same thing or state. "The essential point to grasp in thinking about value is that values do not exist in the real world. They are utterly phenomenological, subjective facts of the inner and personal experience" (Hodgkinson, 1983, p. 31).

In his seminal work on values, Rokeach (1973) made five assumptions about the nature of human values: the total number of values that a person possesses is relatively small; all people possess the same values to different degrees; values are organized into value systems; the antecedents of human values can be traced to culture, society and its institutions, and personality; and the consequences of values will be manifested in virtually all phenomena that social scientists might consider worth investigating and understanding. A person holds countless beliefs that are organized into thousands of attitudes, several

dozens of hierarchically arranged instrumental values, and several hierarchically arranged terminal values. Taken together, they form a belief system in which terminal values are more central than instrumental values and instrumental values are more central than attitudes. *Terminal values* refer to desired end states of existence; they can be either self-centered or society centered. *Instrumental values* refer to morality (having an interpersonal focus) and competence (having a personal focus without interpersonal implications) aspects of modes of conduct. Terminal values are motivational in that they represent supergoals beyond immediate, biologically urgent goals. Since the total belief system is functionally interconnected, a change in any part of it should affect other parts and should ultimately affect behavior. To make a lasting change on human perception and behavior, the most central part of the system—terminal values—must be changed according to Rokeach (1973).

Christopher Hodgkinson's four books on the philosophy of administration and leadership (1978, 1983, 1991, 1996) represent the most sustained treatment of values in administrative action, theory, and philosophy that are currently available (Allison, 2002). He offers the tools by which the problems of valuation, education, and administration may be approached, addressed, and resolved (Greenfield,

1991). In his 1996 treatise, Hodgkinson organized values into a hierarchy according to the approach implied in determining what is good, defined as "desired" or right "defined as "desirable," the latter being the higher order in the hierarchy. His four grounds or justifications for valuing are principles (type I), consequences (type IIA), consensus (type IIB), and preference (type III). The hierarchy is illustrated in Table 7.1.

Type I values are transrational; they go beyond reason, implying an act of faith or will as it is manifested in the acceptance of a principle. "Though such principles may often be defended by rational discourse they are essentially metaphysical in origin or location" (Hodgkinson, 1996, p. 118). Their philosophical orientations are found in religion and intuition. They are the universal ideas of the idealists and the natural law of libertarians.

Type III, preference, justifies a value solely on the grounds that the object or action is liked or preferred by the individual holding the value; these values may be innate or learned. All animals possess such values, and such values are self-justifying. Type III values originate from affect, emotion, and feeling.

Their philosophical orientations are found in postmodernism, behaviorism, positivism, and hedonism.

Type II values are divided into two subsets, A and B, both justified on the ground of rationality. The lower level (IIB) is established by consensus, while the higher level (IIA) is established on an analysis of the consequences of holding it. The philosophical orientations of type II values lie in utilitarianism, pragmatism, humanism, democracy, and liberalism.

Type II values represent a middle ground between the commitments of ideology (type I) and the turbulence of affectivity (type III). At one extreme is immediate experience (type III) and at the other ideology (type I); in between is the realm of pragmatics and common sense:

> This is fortunate for human nerve and tissue. Even at best the demands of ideology are rooted in abstraction and men do not live in intellectual abstractions, however much they may subscribe to them or be governed by them. As for affect, men cannot constantly be engaged in the internecine warfare of the ego. Between Type III realities and the Type I blueprints there lies the vast region of normality—the everyday, workaday world of organizational life. A banal world

TABLE 7.1

The Value Paradigm

Value Type	Grounds of Value	Psychological Faculty	Philiosophical Orientations	Value Level	
I	Principles	Conation Willing	Religion Existentialism Intuition	I	Right
IIA	Consequence (A)	Cognition Reason	Utilitarianism Pragmatism Humanism Democratic	II	
IIB	Consensus (B)	Thinking	Liberalism		
III	Preference	Affect Emotion Feeling	Postmodemism Behaviorism Positivism Hedonism	III	Good

Source: C. Hodgkinson, *Administrative philosophy: Values and motivations in administrative life* (p. 115). Tarrytown, NY: Elsevier Science, Inc., 1996.

perhaps, but one in which man is at relative ease: habituated, conditioned, programmed, modest and content. (Hodgkinson, 1983, p. 121)

If values were completely stable, individual and social change would be impossible. If values were completely unstable, continuity of human personality and society would be impossible. The hierarchical conception of values enables us to define change as a reordering of priorities and, simultaneously, to see the total value system as relatively stable over time. Consensus is easier where type III values are involved and most difficult where type I values are present; indeed, in the latter case, conflicting type I commitments may be irreconcilable. Because of this, the practical person seeks to avoid engagement on matters of principles and searches instead for the politically possible (Hodgkinson, 1983, 1996; Lindblom, 1959).

Value analysis neither implies nor entails any demands for logical closure where values are in contention. According to Hodgkinson (1983), true value conflict is always intrapersonal; the essential subjectivity of values dictates that any conflicts between values must occur within the individual consciousness. Hodgkinson views what is usually thought of as inter-value conflict as really a conflict of interests; ultimately, it is, in fact, a power struggle between value actors. Overt value actions of value actors tell us nothing of the value conflict within the individual actors. For example, does the loser of a war or a civil suit thereby change his or her conception of the desirable?

Nyberg (1993) holds a somewhat different position from Hodgkinson on the clash of values. Both agree on the intrapersonal conflict of values, but Nyberg also sees interpersonal and intergroup value conflicts that are not merely conflicts of interests. Nyberg contends that the pluralism of competing values is as much a part of society as it is of each individual consciousness because it is human nature to see things differently. "This collision of values is the moral core of what it is to be human" (p. 198).

Values and Archetypes of Leadership

Hodgkinson (1983) used several archetypes to describe leaders as they act within his value hierarchy (Table 7.1). The lowest archetype from the

standpoint of moral or ethical regard is that of "careerist," which is characterized by the values of the ego, self-interest, primary affect, and motivation. Self-preservation and enhancement, self-centeredness, and self-concern are the dominant value traits. The careerist functions at the type III level in the values hierarchy. The basal form of the careerist archetype is predator, and the higher form is opportunist. Such persons may subscribe to the philosophical orientations of behaviorism or hedonism.

The second level of the value paradigm is the modal level for administration. According to Hodgkinson (1996), most administrators tend to either the politician (type IIB) or the technician (type IIA) archetype. He classifies both types as rational, humanistic, and pragmatic but discriminates between them by the grounding of their value logic. The former (IIB) relies on the politics of consensus and the ideology of the day, while the latter (IIA) is utilitarian, consistently relying on the rational analysis of the consequences of value judgments (policy) in action.

The *politician archetype* is associated with the administrator whose interests have extended beyond those of self to the point where they embrace a collectivity or group (Hodgkinson, 1983). This group, typically the organization for which he or she is responsible, is then allowed to have some degree of influence over the establishment of organizational values to the point of affecting the leader's own value structure and behavior. It thus refers to a value complex that takes into account the values of others, individually and corporately.

The politician is both moral and rational. The archetype is moral because his or her concern goes beyond that of self. The basic claim to rationality is that group preferences, if actualized, will advance the potential for individual realization of preference more than if laissez-faire pursuit of private desires is permitted. In all this, the politician has a relatively short-term orientation; it is the immediate problem that is pressing. "True politicians practicing the true art of the possible make the organizational world work. . . . But one can go beyond it" (Hodgkinson, 1983, p. 167). The politician, at worst, is a demagogue and, at best, a democrat.

The *technician archetype* is primarily rational–cognitive and rational–legal. The values of Weberian bureaucracy, including dispassion, impartiality, logical analysis and problem solving, efficiency, effectiveness, goal accomplishment, planning, and maximization of the good, fit with this archetype. Justice is interpreted as fairness—economic distribution found in equality of opportunity and a seeming reconciliation of elitism and egalitarianism. The greatest good of the greatest number is an underlying tenet. Implicit too is a faith that if human problems can be stated, then they can, in principle (ultimately) be resolved (Hodgkinson, 1996). In contrast to the politician, the technician stresses institutional concerns over individual concerns. Utilitarian doctrines best reflect the philosophical orientation of the technician.

The technician "represents the highest of the archetypes that it is ordinarily possible for the administrator to aspire to and attain. This sets the safe limit to the moral ambitions and aspirations of administration" (Hodgkinson, 1983, p. 177).

Using a values hierarchy based on a growth process, Hall et al. (1990) have developed a contrasting leadership hierarchy. In their hierarchy, Hall et al. recognize the reciprocal relationship between leadership and followership. Their seven leadership cycles are reported in column II of Table 7.2. Operative values for each cycle are reported in column I. Since value development is seen as a growth process, the leader experiences a tension between contiguous values as he or she shifts priority from the lower to the higher. The leadership mode is reported in column III. Leadership and followership characteristics are summarized in columns IV and V, respectively.

The lowest level of leadership in Hall et al.'s (1990) hierarchy, *primal*, operates from values of self-preservation and security. Such a leader functions in an autocratic mode, controlling the organization closely and making all major decisions. The primal leader maintains a discrete distance from subordinates and demands loyalty to him- or herself and to the organization. Followers respond with passivity and docility, exhibiting immature behavior. They view the leader as being unapproachable and as having an aura of infallibility. This type of leadership is preferred only at times of imminent danger.

In the *familial* cycle, the leader is a benevolent despot, assuming a parent–child relationship with subordinates. Such a leader operates from values of security and self-worth. While listening to subordinates, the familial leader still reserves all decisions to him- or herself. A personal loyalty to superiors and compliance with the rules of the organization are demanded. Followers develop a feeling of dependency. They view the leader as approachable but recognize that he or she is clearly in charge. Leadership of this type is most appropriate when the leader is highly skilled and the followers are not. Relationships are based on fairness and mutual respect.

Managerial efficiency becomes a primary concern in the *institutional* cycle of leadership. This type of leader works from values of self-worth and self-competence. The institutional leader functions in a bureaucratic mode, managing by objectives and stressing the need for order and clear policies. Loyalty to the institution is demanded. Some delegation of authority exists, but only to the skilled and to the loyal. Interpersonal, social, and technical skills are required at this level. This type of leader is likely to be rigid and resistant to change. Followers adhere to the clearly stated policies. They accept the delegation of authority and view the leader as being approachable and a good listener.

The *intrapersonal* cycle of leadership represents a transition from a self-oriented to a socially oriented philosophy. As a result, it is characterized by confusion and inconsistency in decision making and by conflict between values of organizational efficiency and human needs. The leader acts as a listener and clarifier and operates from the values of self-competence and independence. Followers exhibit confusion derived from the mixed signals given by the leadership. A general willingness exists to express feelings, and there is a need among followers to display good interpersonal skills.

The *communal* or *collaborative* cycle works from the values of independence and new order. Its mode is charismatic. Hall et al. (1990) view this as being the ideal level of leadership for educational institutions, especially for secondary and postsecondary schools. "Individuals have passed successfully through the often paralyzing laissez-faire period and now have a new sense of personal creative energy and renewed vision of an institution that can be efficient, as well as dignifying, for its members" (p. 61).

TABLE 7.2

Summary of Hall, Klaven, Rosen, and Taylor's cycles and educational leadership

I Value Stage	II Leadership Cycle	III Leadership Mode	IV Leadership Characteristics	V Follower Characteristics
Self-preservation, security	Primal	Autocratic	Makes all major decisions; seeks absolute control; demands loyalty; maintains distance from followers	Docility, blind obedience, passivity; infantile; views leaders as distant and infallible
Self-worth	Familial	Benevolent authority	Listens, but makes all major decisions; demands loyalty; seeks adherence to rules	Feels cared for; dependency, views leaders as approachable, but in control
Self-competence	Institutional	Bureaucratic	Management by objectives; stresses order, clear policies, goals, and rules; demands loyalty to institution; delegates only to highly skilled and loyal employees	Exercises delegated authority; views leader as approachable and good listener
Independence	Intrapersonal	Enabling	Attempts to reconcile institutional demands and personal values; acts as listener/clarifier uncertain in making decisions	Confusion; willingness to express feelings; needs good interpersonal skills
New order	Collaborative	Charismatic	Democratic; clear vision about how to make institutions humane; modifies rules to personal conscience	Small group interactions; participation as peers in some decision making; group dynamic skills; conflict resolution skills
Interdependence	Mystical or integrative	Servant	Concern over impact on society and productivity; maximizes individual development; seeks agreement of values	Willing to assume responsibility; works at high levels of trust and intimacy; well-developed imaginal skills
Rights/world order	Prophetic	Interdependent	Leadership and followership are merged; collaborative efforts to improve balance between material and personal needs; seeks reconciliation among conflicting groups and the creative and humane use of technology	

Source: Adapted from B. P. Hall, J. Kalvin, L. S. Rosen, & B. Taylor, *Developing human values.* Fond du Lac, WI: International Values Institute of Marian College, 1990.

Leaders operating at this level are democratic in their style and able to modify rules according to their personal consciences. Followers are characterized by small-group interactions; they need well-developed skills in group dynamics and conflict resolution. Followers regularly participate as peers in some decision making. This level bears some resemblance to Hodgkinson's (1996) technician.

At the *mystical* or *integrative* cycle, values of new order and interdependence dominate. Leadership is interactive and collaborative, with the leader functioning as servant. In addition to organizational productivity, there is concern for the quality of organizational interactions and the organization's impact on society. Group decision making is the norm, with mutual responsibility and collegiality assumed by all members of the organization. Followers are willing to assume responsibility, and they have well-developed inventive skills. All members work at high levels of trust and intimacy. The values of new order and interdependence are dominant.

Although rarely found, Hall et al.'s (1990) highest level of leadership is *prophetic*, where the concepts of leadership and followership are merged. The mode of operation is interdependent or transformational. All persons are engaged in the task of improving the balance between material goods and human needs and dedicated to reconciling conflicts among groups and using technology in creative and humane ways. The values of interdependence and rights/world order dominate at this level (Bolman & Deal, 2001).

Values as Part of Organizational Cultures

Values are motivating determinants of behaviors (Hodgkinson, 1996). Persons joined together in an organization by a similar set of values, beliefs, priorities, experiences, and traditions are said to form a common culture (Deal & Kennedy, 1982; Hoy & Miskel, 2005; Ouchi, 1981; Peters, 1988; Peters & Waterman, 1982; Wheatley, 2006; Wheatley & Kellner-Rogers, 1996). The values involved in this common culture according to Hodgkinson's (1996) hierarchy (Table 7.1), however, are of the socially generated type II, leaving the individually seated type III values to vary among members of the organization, a source of tension within the organization. This is illustrated in Figure 7.2, showing the basic organizational dichotomy between the organizational nomothetic dimension motivated by type II values and the personal idiographic dimension motivated by type III values.

From a sociological standpoint, as illustrated by Figure 7.2, organizations can be viewed nomothetically as systems of roles as defined by job descriptions accompanied by stated or unstated sets of expectations; monitoring this dimension is the domain of administrators. Both administrative and nonadministrative roles are filled by individuals with distinct personalities and needs dispositions, the idiographic dimension. The resulting observed behaviors by all role incumbents are compromises

FIGURE 7.2

The basic organizational dichotomy model

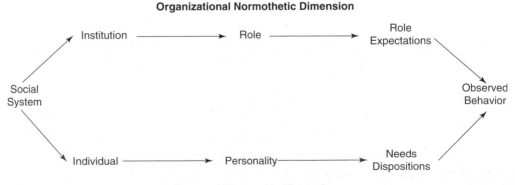

between the organization's role expectations and the needs dispositions of individuals. Since no role incumbent perfectly fits the formal role expectations of the organization and always embodies uniqueness and peculiarities, an important function of the administrator is to observe and evaluate the behavior of the members of the organization and of those external to the organization but interacting with the organization in some manner. The administrator must decipher their ego defense mechanisms of language and expression used to self-justify their roles and rationalize their behaviors so that the administrator can accurately understand the significance of their nonconforming behavior. "Crudely put, to lead is to know what makes people tick and use this knowledge for the common ends" (Hodgkinson, 1996, p. 152).

The institutional dimension (nomothetic), for nonadministrative members, is viewed as constraints that limit their satisfactions while providing the rational–legal foundation for their contracts with the organization. The task of the executive is one of reconciliation: reconciliation of the organization to society and of organization members toward organizational goals. The executive prevents the disintegration of the organization by continuously keeping its members focused on the collective interest (Hodgkinson, 1996).

In Figure 7.3, Hodgkinson (1996) extends the basic organizational dichotomy model (Figure 7.2) to include groups that monitor and evaluate the administrator and the cultural ethos. Level V_1 represents the value structure of the individual within the organization, the ideographic dimension of the basic model, and level V_3 represents the organizational or nomothetic dimension as in the basic model. Since the individual does not normally encounter the nomothetic dimension directly but rather through formal groups such as the union or through informal groups, level V_2 has been inserted to represent the shared value structures of such groups that modulate individual belief structures within the organization. Similarly, the overarching cultural ethos (level V_5) does not impact the organization directly but rather through level V_4, which represents the value structures of subcultures external to the organization that influence the organization's operations, such as professional organizations and other special interest groups and government.

FIGURE 7.3

The administrative value field

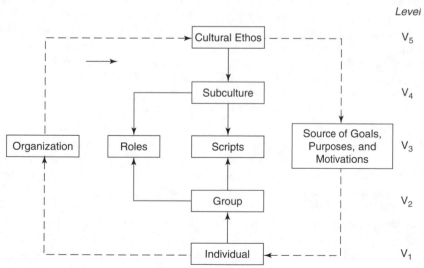

Source: C. Hodgkinson, *Administrative philosophy: Values and motivations in administrative life* (p. 45). Tarrytown, NY: Elsevier Science, Inc. 1996.

The field of administrative philosophy is comprised of five levels of value orientation and value action. These levels (V_1–V_5) overlap, intertwine, and interact in complex dynamic and contingent relationships. Any synthetic view of administrative reality must therefore take into account the modulating, buffering, and filtering effects of subcultures (V_4 and V_2) as major determining influences that have to be considered ultimately for their bearing on V_3 the nomothetic dimension, the dimension of value for which the administrator is formally, ethically, and morally responsible (Hodgkinson, 1996).

Organizational Leadership: Values and Vision

Greenfield (1984) postulated that "organizations are built on the unification of people around values. The business of being a leader is therefore the business of being an entrepreneur for values" (p. 166). Greenfield referred to organizations as cultural artifacts that are founded in meanings, in human intentions, actions, and experience. They are systems of meaning that can be understood only through interpretation. The task of leaders is to act as interpreters, creating a moral order that binds them and the people around them.

Of the five leadership forces identified by Sergiovanni (1984c)—technical (management), human, educational, symbolic, and cultural—the last two are the most relevant in studying values. "The object of symbolic leadership is the setting of human consciousness, the articulation of key cultural strands that identify the substance of a school, and the linking of persons involved in the school's activities to them" (pp. 7–8). The symbolic leader signals to others what is of importance in the organization. In so doing, the leader gives to the organization purpose and direction. Vision becomes the substance of what is communicated through symbolic aspects of leadership. It provides a source of clarity, consensus, and commitment for students and teachers alike (Vaill, 1984).

The cultural leader seeks to define, strengthen, and articulate those enduring values, beliefs, and cultural strands that give a school its unique identity:

The net effect of the cultural force of leadership is to bond together students, teachers, and others as believers in the work of the school. Indeed, the school and its purposes are somewhat revered as if they resembled an ideological system dedicated to a sacred mission. As persons become members of this strong and binding culture, they are provided with opportunities for enjoying a special sense of personal importance. (Sergiovanni, 1984a, p. 9)

Sergiovanni (1992) noted that two important things happen when purpose, social contract, and school autonomy provide the foundation on which to build the structure of schooling: the school is transformed from a mere organization to a covenantal community, and the basis of authority changes from an emphasis on bureaucratic and psychological authority to moral authority. In other words, the school changes from a secular to a sacred organization—changing from an instrument designed to achieve specific ends to a virtuous enterprise.

The mission of the cultural leader is to focus sharply the minds of the membership of a school organization on collectively held values, symbols, and beliefs. The more that these are understood and accepted, the better able the school is to move in concert toward the ideals it holds and the goals it wishes to pursue. A strong culture is characteristic of excellent schools. A tight value structure permits an otherwise loosely structured organization to allow wide discretion among the professionals working within the organization. Shared values and beliefs become the glue holding the organization together, not close managerial supervision (Wheatley, 2006; Wheatley & Kellner-Rogers, 1996).

Organizations need leaders who can provide a persuasive and durable sense of purpose and direction, rooted deeply in human values and spirit. Leaders need to be deeply reflective, actively thoughtful, and dramatically explicit about their core values and beliefs. The best managers and leaders create and sustain a tension-filled balance between core values and elastic strategies. They know what they stand for and what they want, and they communicate that vision clearly and forcefully. They also know that they must understand and respond to the complex array of forces that push and pull organizations in many different directions (Bolman & Deal, 2003).

Bennis (1984) aptly summarized the function of leadership within the context of organizational culture:

> In sum, the transformative power of leadership stems less from ingeniously crafted organizational structures, carefully constructed management designs and controls, elegantly rationalized planning formats, or skillfully articulated leadership tactics. Rather, it is the ability of the leader to reach the souls of others in a fashion which raises human consciousness, builds meanings, and inspires human intent that is the source of power. Within transformative leadership, therefore, it is vision, purposes, beliefs, and other aspects of organizational culture that are of prime importance. (p. 70)

Values, Democracy, and Followership

Maxcy (1991) proposed a pragmatic theory of value that stresses the importance of democratic cultural consensus in arriving at plans and policies that affect the school community. He argued that the quality of life is enhanced and pedagogical responsibility fulfilled when the deliberative process is enlarged to include all those involved in or affected by schooling. He observed that leadership is always truncated and narrow when power is invested in the few.

With democratic cultural consensus, leadership needs the capacity to interact with self or others in terms of moving a discourse/practice toward an end based on criteria that are at once rational and moral. "Leading is not so much telling others what is true or false, but rather helping them to come to know for themselves the merits and demerits of a case" (Maxcy, 1991, p. 195). Maxcy called for a reconstruction and reconceptualization of leadership as enlightened, critical, and pragmatic action—a notion of leadership that looks to everyone who participates in the teaching–learning process for the kinds of thought and effort that will result in a reformed education.

In a similar vein, Cambron-McCabe (1993) argued that moral principles guiding groups or organizations are not a matter of personal preference or intuition but must be subjected to a democratic deliberative process. She asserted that values must be determined in a democratic context for democratic ends.

Sergiovanni (1992) pointed out that leadership and followership are reciprocal in an empowered organization. He believes that in many ways, professionalism and leadership are antithetical insofar as, beyond a certain point, the more professionalism is emphasized, the less leadership is needed. Professionalism has a way of encouraging principals to be self-managers. Conversely, providing too much leadership, at least of the traditional type, discourages professionalism. Self-management and professionalism are complementary concepts. "If self-management is our goal, then leadership will have to be reinvented in a fashion that places 'followership' first" (p. 68).

Subordinates need external motivation. They do what they are supposed to do but little else; they want to know exactly what is expected of them— they work to the rule. Followers, on the other hand, are self-motivated and work well without close supervision, assessing what needs to be done, when and how, and taking effective action on their own:

> Followers are people committed to purposes, a cause, a vision of what the school is and can become, beliefs about teaching and learning, values and standards to which they adhere, and convictions. . . . When followership and leadership are joined, the traditional hierarchy of the school is upset. It changes from a fixed form, with superintendents and principals at the top and teachers and students at the bottom, to one that is in flux. The only constant is that neither superintendents and principals nor teachers and students are at the apex; that position is reserved for ideas, values, and commitments at the heart of followership. Further, a transformation takes place, and emphasis shifts from bureaucratic, psychological, and technical rational authority to professional and moral authority. As a result, hierarchical position and personality are not enough to earn one the mantle of leader. Instead, it comes through one's demonstrated devotion and success as a follower. The true leader is the one who follows first. (Sergiovanni, 1992, pp. 71–72)

The interaction between leadership and followership was noted earlier in the presentation of the work of Hall et al. (1990) on developing human values (see Table 7.2). In their leadership hierarchy, the highest level was placed at the point where the concept of leadership and followership merge and the distinctions between them become meaningless.

Greenleaf (1977) wrote of the servant-leader. He referred to two polar types of leadership: that provided by persons naturally inclined to lead first and that provided by persons naturally inclined to serve first but through service are endowed with leadership authority. Between the poles are many shadings. Leadership is bestowed on the servant-leader; it is sought by the leader-leader. Greenleaf noted a reassessment of the issues of power and authority whereby people are learning to relate to one another in less coercive and more creatively supporting ways. "A new moral principle is emerging which holds that the only authority deserving one's allegiance is that which is freely and knowingly granted by the led to the leader in response to, and in proportion to, the clearly evident servant stature of the leader" (p. 10). Servant-leaders differ from other persons of goodwill because they act on what they believe. Greenleaf stressed the importance to the functioning leader of listening carefully and understanding. He expressed a strong bias that only a true natural servant responds automatically to any problem by listening first. Greenleaf saw the only viable institutions of the future as being mainly servant led.

These concepts of leadership, democracy, and followership were first developed by Burns (1978) and were summarized in the discussion of transformational leadership in chapter 4. His foundational thoughts on leadership, particularly the moral implications of transforming leadership, are fundamental to this discussion. They place the reciprocal nature of transforming leadership in perspective in terms of followers transforming leaders.

Metavalues

Nyberg (1993) contended that "the moral universe is the same for everyone in that it is based on concern for human dignity, decency, voluntary relations that are not oppressive, and some kind of spiritual fulfillment" (p. 196). The specifics differ from person to person, group to group, place to place, and time to time, but the basis of concern remains consistent. We are all similar, but each is unique.

Hodgkinson (1996) defined the term *metavalue* as "a concept of the desirable so vested and entrenched that it seems to be beyond dispute or contention. It may thus pass unnoticed as an unspoken or unexamined assumption into the value calculus of individual

or collective life" (p. 125). In administration and organizational life, he identified the dominant metavalues as maintenance, growth, efficiency, and effectiveness.

Rokeach (1973) sought to identify ideals or values that are singled out for special consideration by all political ideologies. He hypothesized that the major variations in political ideology are fundamentally reducible to opposing value orientations concerning the political desirability or undesirability of freedom and equality in all their ramifications.

Getzels (1957, 1978) referred to national core values as "sacred." He identified four sacred values as being at the core of the American ethos: democracy, individualism, equality, and human perfectibility.

The literature on educational policy makes frequent explicit or implicit reference to these and similar values. Guthrie, Garms, and Pierce (1988) referred to equality, efficiency, and liberty as values of particular societal concern. Wirt (1987) referred to general agreement among nations that the major values in education are quality (excellence or human perfectibility), equity, efficiency, and choice (liberty or freedom). Boyd (1984) focused on liberty, equality, and efficiency as "three competing values" in educational policy and school governance in Western democracies (p. 4). King, Swanson, and Sweetland (2003) identified five values that have been historically prominent in shaping Western societies and that are also particularly relevant to provision and consumption of educational services: liberty, equality, fraternity, efficiency, and economic growth. A good deal of overlap exists among the various lists, with freedom and equality appearing on most.

The name of a metavalue may continue to be the same, but definitions may vary from place to place and over time. Nyberg (1981), for example, cautioned that *freedom* (or liberty) derives its meaning at least in part from the times in which it is used. He pointed out that the United States saw a transformation between 1787 and 1947, as "freedom as natural rights (rights *against* the government, rights of independence)" became "civil rights (rights to *participate* in civil government)" and later became "human freedoms (rights to the *help* of government in achieving protection from fear and want)" (pp. 97–98).

Parallel transformations took place in the meaning of equality (or equity). Initially, equality consisted only of rights and not conditions; that is, people were to be treated the same by law, custom, and tradition, with equality the instrument for guaranteeing liberty as originally defined. In recent times, the operational definition of equality has expanded to include factors of condition. For example, some persons are handicapped in enjoying liberty because of circumstances beyond their control, such as minority status, gender, poverty, and physical and psychological impediments. Although liberty and equality complemented one another as defined in 1787, the broader contemporary definition of equality brings it into direct conflict with the value of liberty (as originally defined) because the policies of remediation involve not only the disadvantaged person but all others. Liberty requires an opportunity for expression through individual freedom, whereas equality of condition requires some curbing of individual freedom.

Because of the conceptual inconsistencies among values, it is not possible to emphasize all of them at the same time in public policy—or in individual lives—desirable though each may be. Individuals and societies must establish priorities. This is a dynamic process. Priorities of individuals change with circumstances, and where there has been a sufficient change among individuals, shifts in public priorities follow (Ravitch, 1985). Agreement on priorities is not necessary for private- or market-sector decisions beyond the family level. In the public sector, however, a singular decision is required involving negotiations and compromises among interested partisans (subcultures and groups), generating significant social stress in the process. The higher the level of aggregation, the more difficult agreement becomes because of the greater amount of heterogeneity introduced.

Spindler (1955) explained the attacks on public education in the 1950s by citing major societal value shifts following World War II. (Reference to Spindler's analysis reminds us that this is not the first generation of educators to be the recipients of hostile public criticism.) Spindler saw the criticism of that day as products of an American culture that was experiencing a real shift in values. Populations going through cultural transition are characterized by conflict and, in its most severe form, demoralization and disorganization. The conflict goes beyond groups

and institutions because individuals in a transformational society are likely to hold elements of both the dominant and the emerging value systems concomitantly. Such situations are confused not only by groups battling each other but also by individuals fighting themselves.

Spindler (1955) described traditional values as Puritan morality, work-success ethic, individualism, achievement orientation, and future orientation. These values were being threatened by emergent values: sociability, relativistic moral attitudes, consideration for others, hedonistic present-time orientation, and conformity to the group. He concluded that there is staunchness and virility in the traditional value set that many viewed with nostalgia. But in his view, rugged individualism (in its expedient, ego-centered form) and rigid moralism (with its capacity for displaced hate) had become nonfunctional in a society where people are rubbing shoulders in polyglot masses and playing with technology that may destroy—or save—with the push of buttons.

More recently, Nyberg (1993) similarly concluded that a moral-principle or positivist orientation thrives in a supportive environment but finds it difficult to adapt to new conditions when the environment changes. On the other hand, the personal-value or constructivist orientation has a better chance of long-term survival in this moral world of constant changes because of its flexible adaptiveness and its willingness to live with uncertainty.

The shifting of values identified by Spindler and referred to by Nyberg is likely to continue. In addition, the geopolitical situation in the world has become fluid. These, coupled with unparalleled technological advancements, seem to have accelerated the rate of major shifts in value priorities and in expressed dissatisfaction with the status quo. As a ripple effect, demands for educational reform have materialized. The old paradigms do not seem to fit anymore.

Major contemporary issues revolve around the competing social objectives of equality, personal liberty, and productive efficiency, among others. The question of whether each can be furthered jointly through public policy is being hotly debated. The most likely scenario is that one or two values will be given priority, as in the past, to the jeopardy of the others. The ferment that we

ACTIVITY 7.3
Metavalues and Educational Reform

Addresses ISLLC Standards and Functions 5C, 5E, and 6

Numerous proposals have been presented for reforming education. Identify the metavalues associated with each of the proposed reforms listed here and show how each marks a departure from metavalues inherent in the status quo.

a. Family choice of public schools
b. Unconstrained educational vouchers
c. Tax credits for private school tuition
d. School-based decision making
e. Full state funding of schooling
f. Mandated state curriculum

are experiencing today is a function of the dynamic political struggle to achieve the best balance among legitimate interests. The best balance has varied and will continue to vary from society to society and over time within a society as contexts and value definitions and priorities change (Wirt, 1986).

Values Analysis

Values analysis is complicated by the fact that values are very difficult to measure. Determining the espoused values (or theories [Argyris & Schön, 1978]) is relatively simple; you just ask. *Espoused theories* exist at the conscious level and can be changed relatively easily with new information. They describe what we believe we believe, but they do not necessarily guide our actions. *Theories-in-use* (Argyris & Schön, 1978), however, are much more formidable to identify. These theories reside deeply within our subconscious and are difficult for us to articulate; they are tacit. As such, they are hard to change, yet they are the values and beliefs that truly guide our actions. "Theories-in-use build up and solidify over a long period of time through acculturation and are reinforced by ongoing experience in the culture. They become such an integrated part of

our beings that they are difficult to isolate. They disappear from our conscious foreground and become background" (Osterman & Kottkamp, 1993, p. 10).

To change a theory-in-use, it is necessary to bring it into consciousness. We are usually unaware of differences between our espoused beliefs and our actions, and we are usually also unaware of discrepancies between our intended outcomes and the actual outcomes, especially when the outcomes deal with immeasurable attributes such as attitudes. "Without this awareness, the individual may not personalize the new information or ideas to make the connection between the criticism and his or her own behavior" (Osterman & Kottkamp, 1993, p. 12).

Despite these difficulties, methods for analyzing and addressing the practical impact of values have been developed (with severe limitations) for application at three levels: the problem, the organization, and the individual. In this section we describe approaches that have been used at each level.

Reflection in Practice. At the personal level, Sergiovanni (1984b) identifies several dimensions of leadership. One of these is *platform*, an articulation of one's principles into an operational framework. "Platforms are governing in the sense that they represent a set of criteria and an implicit standard from which decisions are made" (p. 109). The platform enables the determining of worth and separation of the trivial from the important. "More colloquially, it is one's philosophy of education or administration, a concise statement of what one intends to do, to accomplish, and how" (Osterman & Kottkamp, 1993, p. 67).

Osterman and Kottkamp (1993, 2004) have advocated a form of professional development that attempts to align implicit values and beliefs of individual professional educators with desired outcomes of school reform initiatives. Their process focuses on bringing beliefs and values into the conscious mind and comparing them with the beliefs and values implicit in a person's behavior. They begin the process by having people develop a written professional platform.

The platform describes a person's beliefs about teaching, learning and its context, and views about the orientations and means that are required to facilitate and support the learning process. More specifically, the platform may address aims of education, image of the learner, value of the curriculum, image of the teacher, preferred student–teacher relationship, purpose of supervision, and the preferred process of supervision, as suggested by Sergiovanni and Starratt (1983, 2007).

The written platform is espoused theory, but writing it sets into motion a powerful reflective process. The writing process can be extremely difficult and emotionally intense. The platform could be developed in isolation, but Osterman and Kottkamp recommend that it be done with the assistance of at least one other person in whom the writer has complete trust. The colleague can react to the writings in a nonjudgmental way and analyze it for implicit beliefs and values.

Once the espoused theory has been documented, the next step is to gather information about theories-in-use by the individual. This can best be done through observing behavior and reflecting on it to detect the assumptions that might have prompted it. The observations may be made by another, or they may be done by the individual through such means as keeping a journal or developing case records. Having carefully established the espoused theories and the theories-in-action, the stage is set for reflection and perhaps realignment of theories-in-use and behavior/actions.

Similarly, Hodgkinson (1996) proposes a "value audit." The attendant demands are for "ruthless honesty, the courage to remember, and not to look away" (pp. 241–242). One's value audit may be done hypothetically, but he recommends that it be done with a specific focus on a problem being faced in a real situation. Closure of the audit should be deferred until a threshold of inner certainty is achieved. Among the issues to be addressed in a praxis-based value audit are the following: What are the values in conflict? What fields of values are most affected? Who are the value actors? How is the conflict distributed, interpersonally or intrapersonally? Is the conflict interhierarchial or intrahierarchial? What are the metavalues involved in the case? Is there a principle (type I value) raised or avoided? Can the tension of nonresolution be accommodated? What rational and pragmatic consequences attach to the possible and probable scenarios? What bodies of value consensus

ACTIVITY 7.4
Building a Professional Platform

Addresses ISLLC Standards and Functions
1A, 2, 3C, 3D, 3E, 5, and 6

Beginning with the philosophical view of life you prepared in activity 7.1, develop for yourself a "professional platform" that can serve you as an operational framework for decision making. Use as a guide the discussion in the section "Reflection in Practice" in this chapter. Include the following:

a. A description of your own system of beliefs
b. A statement of your opinion as to the mission of schooling as a social process
c. A statement as to the reasons you want to be a school administrator
d. A statement of your views on the role of administrators in schools, their ideal relationships with other members of the school and system, and how they should implement their role.

and political interest, if relevant, are affected within and without the organization? To what extent does the leader have control over the informative and affective media in the case (press, radio, television, lines of communication, informal organization, and so on)? What is the extent of affect control among the parties in the case? What is the extent of commitment among the parties in the case to their respective positions? What is my true will in the case before me?

Identifying Theories-in-Practice of Organizations. Hall et al. (1990) saw the collection of reliable data about the values expressed implicitly or explicitly by an institution as critical to the process of organizational development. Comparisons and discrepancies can then be analyzed and compared using a consistent methodology. In their analytical scheme, organizational diagnosis consists of three parts: document analysis, personal values inventories, and group values analysis.

Documents examined include mission statements and statements of philosophy that express the intent and purpose of the organization and policies and procedures focusing on stated behavioral expectations and sanctions. Using content analysis and looking for value clusters, a value profile of the organization can be developed. Values being reinforced, intentionally or unintentionally, can be identified through this process, enabling a school to develop strategies to help it become more consistent and more focused in what it does and says.

A number of instruments are available for assessing personal values such as the Rokeach Value Survey (Rokeach, 1973), the Hall–Tonna Inventory (Hall et al., 1990), and the Schwartz Values Inventory (Schwartz, 1992, 1994). Such instruments generate personal values profiles that are useful for self-analysis and therapy or for aggregation by unit or organization permitting group analysis. Aggregated profiles can be compared with the intended values of the organization as revealed by the document analysis. Inconsistencies may reveal a need to restate the organizational values, to bring personal values in line with intended organizational values through staff development programs, or a combination of the two:

> Taken altogether, document analysis, individual and group analyses can provide insight into a number of critical aspects of the school's organizational culture. The information collected will reveal the possible stress areas between teachers and administrators as well as between administrators and board members. It will identify and measure current priority issues and values which can then be examined in an objective manner. The process will reveal operative leadership styles among teachers, administrators and school board members. It will identify, describe and analyze underlying value patterns in mission, philosophy and procedures, and will suggest ways in which these value patterns impact on a school's day-to-day culture. Finally, the data generated will indicate needed skills training for individuals and groups of teachers, administrators, or board members. (Hall et al., 1990, pp. 64–65)

Value Analysis of Problems. Willower and Licata (1997) have developed a similar approach called *moral valuation*. They justify the need for values and valuation in educational administration decision making by pointing out that the work of administrators is political and frequently rife with conflict. Administrators are generally engaged in a variety of brief, fragmented, and often interrupted activities, and they face an array of individuals and groups with special interests. The intense pressure for action, often to conflicting ends, represents a continuing threat to distract the administrator from the guiding principles of the school.

Willower and Licata (1997) define *valuation* as "the process of choosing from and implementing conceptions of the desirable with an awareness of and sensitivity to their potential consequences for a variety of individuals and groups, as well as the multiplicity of values typically affected by implementation" (p. 26). The steps that they employ in valuation are those of ordinary scientific method applied to decision situations: a problem is formulated, alternative solutions are identified, the probable consequences of each alternative are elaborated conceptually, and a course of action is selected that seems most likely to attain the outcomes sought. In the analysis, they attempt to make the ethical considerations concrete and particular. They emphasize mitigating negative consequences as part of larger ethical decisions. Finally, they emphasize the utility of social science concepts and explanations in assisting administrators and others in their search for probable consequences and likely desirable outcomes.

Inquiry into Educational Issues

Earlier in this chapter, we showed how personal philosophies and values influence decisions made by individuals; we also showed how the value priorities of members of an organization and the mission of that organization are blended together to form an organizational culture that may work to further or impair the effectiveness of that organization. Consequently, we have stressed that leadership of organizations must understand its ethical dimentions and include ethical considerations in any attempt at problem solving—or formal inquiry, the focus of this section. Willower and Licata's (1997) moral evaluation approach to problem solving discribed previously provides a good transition from a focus on philosophy and values to a focus on their relationship with inquiry in support of decision making, problem solving, policy development, and research.

Inquiry has been described as the process of knowing, of solving puzzles, probing, and finding truth (Eisner, 1981; Guba, 1990; Kuhn, 1996). With varying degrees of success, scholars have attempted to characterize the nature of inquiry to answer the question, What is going on here? Dewey (1938) defined inquiry as "the controlled or directed transformation of an indeterminate situation into one that is so determinate in its constituent distinctions and relations as to convert the elements of the original situation into a unified whole" (p. 104). Kuhn (1996) referred to normal science as puzzle solving. Babbie (1989) simply defined inquiry as a search for regularity. Littlejohn (1992) defines inquiry as the "systematic, disciplined ordering of experience that leads to the development of understanding and knowledge" (p. 8). Inquiry as a process implies a system with component parts, outcomes, methods to change, and a philosophical base around which the process itself is built.

In a cyclical process of questioning, observation, and generalization, investigators stage the continued development of knowledge creation and discovery. The process is structured and ordered by a community of professionals who ensure that the data are "true" or adequate to meet the demands of a culture, time, or person. Thus, the normative force of logic is applied in an ever-unfolding process termed *inquiry* (Dewey, 1938). Dewey maintained that the logic of theory is subservient to the metaphysical and epistemological preconceptions of the inquirer. The process of inquiry, then, arises from an historical and cultural environment and can be understood only within the context of that environment.

Although many inquiry paradigms are derived from established philosophies, knowledge creation is generally thought to evolve from three distinctive approaches. Littlejohn (1992) labeled them knowledge of discovery, knowledge of interpretation, and knowledge of criticism. In Littlejohn's view, the discovery approach seeks to achieve objective observations that, when refined, produce instances of structural reality. In contrast, the interpretive approach seeks to construct a picture of reality through the eyes of both the participant and the observer. Knowledge is then reconstructed as the next instance(s) of reality. The critical approach seeks to define knowledge through

critical judgments, which then lead to social improvement and change.

From another vantage point, Eisner (1991) clarified building and defining the origins of inquiry further. Objectivity is surely among the world's most cherished beliefs. Objectivity seeks to see things the way they are. To see is to know. In this context, then, the aim of inquiry is to achieve truth and certain knowledge. In addition, understanding is derived from the community of believers. What inquirers say, therefore, is of equal importance. Just as important is the understanding that knowledge is used and developed via certain methodology. In part, knowledge is freed from personal judgment as a result of choice of method.

Representation, too, is problematic. Any account that furthers knowledge is offered via a symbol system (Eisner, 1991). Representations of knowledge are revealing and at the same time concealing, depending on the constraints of the symbol system. In this respect we can begin to sense how the subjective view gains its stature. Subjective knowledge becomes an important distinctive view. But similarly, as we have developed the objective view in this chapter, so can we erode the premier stations that comprise subjectivity. Eisner (1991) summarized the disparities herein as he explained that ontological subjectivity is possible if we accept the idea that truth exceeds belief. That is a belief in itself. Active minds in commerce with the world are the product of an active mind. To seek more than what ultimately is referenced in our own beliefs after using appropriate criteria for holding them is to retreat to a higher authority or to seek a dominant view that bypasses the mind's observation of nature.

Eisner concluded that a different belief structure is needed to avoid the dichotomy between objectivity and subjectivity. What is needed is a process by which we can enlist the strength of objectivity and subjectivity from their separate consequences and move to a unification of understanding and principle. Since what we know of the world is a product of the arbitration of our subjective life and an axiomatic objective world, life and worlds cannot be separated. To separate them would require that we engage the mind, and since the mind would need to be employed to make the separation, anything separated as a result of its use would reflect a mind as well as what was separated from it (Eisner, 1991). Inquiry in the absence of reality is simply a picture. We can already sense that inquiry has become a difficult and controversial subject.

Paradigms of Inquiry

Currently, methods of scientific inquiry can be described as suffering an identity crisis. Each of the three methods described earlier have avid disciples and equally avid critics. The general patterns of inquiry, or *paradigms*, have received special attention over the past 30 years. Kuhn, in *The Structure of Scientific Revolutions* (1962), challenged the traditional view of science as developing knowledge by accumulation or the knowledge of piecemeal facts. He suggested that the growth of knowledge also occurs through scientific revolution and enables thinkers to move from current assumptions to new paradigms of understanding. Normal science, according to Kuhn, was the building of existing knowledge in a developmental fashion. The growth of knowledge, he surmised, is bounded, restricted by the worldview of scholars and educators in the community. Within a paradigm, then, science accumulates knowledge related to that particular worldview, using its own paradigm symbols, tools, and values learned from its own narrow existing scientific community. However, for progress or change to occur, science must undergo a revolution. Science (normal science in Kuhn's view) proceeds from anomaly in a current context, to preparadigm struggles, to crisis, and finally to revolution. During the crisis period, existing paradigm symbols, tools, and values are discarded in exchange for new ones. The revolution frees the community from the restrictiveness of the old paradigm to allow new questions to be asked within the restrictions of the new paradigm.

Inquiry paradigms form the basis of how theorists and practitioners see the world. As we internalize our paradigms, they take on great power and determine how we interact with the world. Like inquiry in general, educational inquiry revolves around numerous paradigms. Our inquiry paradigms become so powerful that more concern is often given to methods of inquiry than to determining what has

really happened. Practitioners of the positivistic paradigm, Littlejohn's (1992) first approach to inquiry, often refer to it as scientific, experimental, or behavioral or, very loosely, as simply quantitative. The second mode of inquiry, interpretivistic, is dominated by ethnographic research and is often termed qualitative or constructivistic inquiry. Finally, the critical theorist inquiry paradigm, sometimes termed conflict theory, explores power, dominance, and conflict in society.

Inquiry and Educational Administration

Evers and Lakomski (1991) provide a vehicle for relating the philosophical underpinnings described earlier to educational practice. They also identify three major approaches to inquiry that correspond to those previously discussed: the theory movement, the paradigm approach, and coherence. The theory movement in educational administration flourished during the third quarter of the 20th century. During these years educational researchers looked to the "hypothetical-deductive structure with laws at the top and facts at the bottom" (Evers & Lakomski, 1991, p. 3). The purpose of research was to provide educational administrators with findings that would allow them to predict events more accurately and to control those events better. Organizational elements were identified, operationalized, and measured in an attempt to increase efficiency and effectiveness within the educational environment.

In this classical paradigm, educational organizations were viewed as simple, hierarchical, and mechanical. Predictions of events were considered and research faithfully followed foundational scientific practice. Inquiry's goal was unchanged: break down the object of inquiry into discrete parts, examine them, and arrive at generalizations to extend to other domains. While this approach produced important new understandings about teaching, learning, and educational organizations, experience with this approach also revealed serious limitations (Cziko, 1989; Howe & Eisenhart, 1990).

The subsequent generation of researchers began to utilize other methods to increase the value of their scholarly activity. Descriptions of programs, material, teaching strategies, and organizational patterns attempted to broaden the scope of inquiry results but retained much reliance on quantification. This approach brought beneficial change as more broad-based curricula resulted, deeper understanding of students occurred, and testing revealed whether students learned what teachers had intended. However, more changes were still needed and the next generation of inquirers broadened the scope of inquiry to include value determination.

In this new period, researchers became seasoned adjudicators of differing research methods in addition to masters of measurement and description. Not only performance but also goals and objectives were matters of concern to inquirers. Researchers now were required to deal with merit, both inside and outside the school's educational research perspective, and politics became an issue.

Quandaries of Inquiry

Understanding the series of practical problems that emerge in research approaches is now necessary. Agger (1991), Eisner (1981), and Guba and Lincoln (1989) each have provided thoughtful discussions of the limitations of research in general and in educational research more specifically.

Eisner (1981) postulated several points of concern. Given the reliance on interpretivistic inquiry found today, exploitations of the inquirer's own unique strengths are paramount. Whereas some see this as a singular political problem, others point to broader ethical concerns. Researchers in classrooms or schools or from universities must address the privilege of both the agent and the client. In this light, thoroughness of research training, an individual researcher's attributes, and contractual arrangements each reflect a necessary concern that inquiry be more thorough. Another consideration involves the timeliness of research outcomes. Thorough research in the interpretivistic frame is very time consuming (Argyris, 1985), taking many months and even years before a study is completed. Thus, the research often gravitates to procedural preoccupations, losing focus on the original objective. In light of this, Eisner submits that qualitative research is frequently viewed as less deterministic than older methodologies. Clients may become discouraged, as results cannot generate immediate and effective change as assumed for postpositivistic research.

From another frame of reference, Guba and Lincoln (1989) contended that three major defects have dominated administrative inquiry in education: a tendency toward managerialism, the failure to accommodate value pluralism, and overcommitment to scientific inquiry. In the first case, they argue that managerialism yields a number of faults, in effect disempowering the participant stakeholders, disenfranchising evaluators' findings, and lacking the ability to assert accountability. In the aggregate, managerialism combines several distasteful features that can compromise an entire research scenario. Also important is the realization that value pluralism is paramount in all research efforts. Research that disregards value tenets sets aside differing heritages of students in schools and differing learning rates and disassociates researcher bias. Finally, Guba and Lincoln contend that educational inquiry is still overly committed to the scientific approach. This reliance often strips evaluations from their context and renders research results of questionable value.

Agger (1991), a critical theorist, contends that applications of postmodernism and critical theory are resolved by commodifying popular culture. Although it may be important to transform society's structures, this cannot be accomplished simply by remembering the collective experience of events. It must develop by identifying the meaning and identity of events— both their text and texture. Concentration on the events of popular experience creates the possibility that, as events become more common, they will tend to be idealized and be considered the norm of behavior. Investigation, in a sense, then stops and does not critically examine those events further except from superficial points of view. All seem intent on defining their own unique versions of needed change. Replacing substance with style can be seen in numerous instances of reform initiatives—quick-fix adjustments such as teacher empowerment, school choice, or school-based management.

Guba and Lincoln (1985) outlined the parallel movement of inquiry paradigms as a result of ongoing change in organizations. Seven contrasting concepts provide the basis for an in-depth exploration of the impact of ongoing change in the way we construct knowledge: simple to complex, hierarchical to heterarchical, mechanical to holographic, determinacy to indeterminacy, linear causality to mutual causality, assembly to morphogenesis, and objective to perspectival. Understanding this parallelism can further substantively help to counteract some of the problem areas previously cited.

Simple to Complex. This change implies and is largely a result of an organization's inability to change and its tendency to continue to view the world simplistically. In previous eras our ability to identify, comprehend, and quantify the entirety of a problem was assumed. For example, it is unlikely that we would fully comprehend the impact of high dropout rates only by surveying those who left or by including a sequence of other variables in search of correspondence. A more complex question demands a more complex approach to science, one that includes, in this case, a systemic panorama of the school, the family, the teaching environment, and more. Even more important, this situation demands an exploration of the relationships among other variables. Most important may be the realization that there is no objectivity. Identifying poor teaching or any other single or multiple conditions as being causal excludes relationships and conceals more appropriate findings.

Hierarchical to Heterarchical. In looking at organizations today, we find many examples of unusual organizational structures. Clusters, networks, upside-down pyramids, interlocking links, and more are representations of changes in organizational structure necessitated by other forces. Similarly, in educational circles, further revision of organizational structure has emerged in such examples as school-based management, team-based structures and combinations, and more decision-making interaction between learner and teacher. Pluralism or multiplism is replacing "pecking order" in organizations. In the new worldview, any set of factors can become a controlling phenomenon, depending on the context.

The literature in educational administration is laden with organizational charts reflecting a top-down organization, full of sequential–linear–systematic curriculum development charts and saturated with stepwise models of instructional practice. In times past, inquiry validated the hierarchical nature of school organizations and schooling.

The newer paradigms view educational organizations as heterarchical, oriented to pluralism and a heteracity of guiding principles (Guba & Lincoln, 1985). For example, the realization that language is descriptive or that visual arts depict opens new knowledge, creating venues that cannot be subsumed as singular, top down, or stepwise. Latitude must be available that allows a variety of approaches to reconstitute our understanding.

Mechanical to Holographic. Metaphors connect mental images with reality. Elementary and secondary schools have been described as "machinelike" and as "iron cages:" classes are 45 to 50 minutes long, five or six classes per day is common, the school year is 180-plus days long, and it takes 12 years to complete schooling. Even teachers are like robots. The agenda of inquiry in this environment reflect the metaphors.

Holograms are dimensional images from reflected light, but, more important, they possess unique properties. Conceptualizing the school organization as a hologram is difficult and attempts to visualize a holographic school often result in chaos and confusion. In a hologram, every part contains enough information to reconstitute the whole. "The part is in the whole and the whole is in the part. . . . Parts have access to the whole" (Wilbur, 1982, p. 2). When light is shown on the holographic image, the image can be reconstituted from any portion or part. Consider then, the holographic school organization, an organization in which compartmentalization is absent, where teachers share information broadly, or where students are colleagues. Learning is the issue in this school, as the whole school is built to facilitate learning. In the holographic sense, as you walk into a school, can you sense the learning going on, or did you sense those iron cages? Educational inquiry needs to consider the relevance of alternative organizing features that inspire holistic knowledge creation.

Determinacy to Indeterminacy. Is it possible to predict and control, or is everything relative? These disparate views evolve from distinctly different organizational theories, and the choice of paradigm has far-reaching implications for the conclusions of inquiries. If, as the traditionalists believe, there is one right way to organize and administer education, hypothetic-deductive inquiry will result in a body of knowledge about that "right way." Weber (1947) thought that the bureaucratic system was "superior in precision, in stability, in the stringency of its discipline, and its reliability" (p. 337). Time studies and efficiency models served to validate a determinate approach to administration.

Emerging research paradigms, however, provide a critique of logical empiricism and assumes an indeterminate universe where prediction is not possible. The goal of organizational inquiry would have to be to "realize an interpretive understanding of the meanings people give to their own situations and their interactions with others" (Smith & Blase, 1991, p. 11). Lawlike generalizations are not possible because the social world is not determinate. Therefore, the best an inquirer can hope for is to describe the complexity of organizations in the context of their history, people, and environment. Matters of human significance will render interpretive understanding possible (Smith & Blase, 1991).

Linear Causality to Mutual Causality. Instances of singular cause-and-effect scenarios in real life are hard to imagine. But traditional research establishes just such causality as foundational. Assuredly, if our purpose is to reduce the origin of events to finite causal variables, we may find them, perhaps even proper ones. But generalizing from these finite circumstances back to issues more complex must be done with extreme care. If–then relationships are established in normative inquiry and represent a specific set of variables for the relationship to hold true. Stepping outside the confidence of the relationship leads to error.

Naturalistic inquiry, on the other hand, assumes mutual causality, nonlinear, and growth-oriented relationships between variables. As an inquiry methodology, case studies are built purposely as a historical–cultural sketch of, for example, a school or classroom environment. In this sense, the case study is a living example from which actions are connected to their total environment. Once actions are

understood to occur within, an interpretive discourse can reconstitute the school or classroom environment from the view of the inquirer and a deeper understanding of the total environment can result.

Assembly to Morphogenesis. In the inquiry paradigms, assembly implies construction from simple to complex. In the reductionist view, wholes are separated into smaller and smaller segments as a method to control/manipulate experimental parameters and arrive at truth. Experimental findings then generalized are attached to larger and larger wholes. An aggregate of findings must not, however, substitute for license to apply across greater and greater ranges. Poor mathematics scores in New York inner-city schools may not be related to poor mathematics scores in Los Angeles or anywhere else. Generalizations can transfer only when we can confidently relate across those environments.

Morphogenesis is a mutual change that occurs across parts and the whole of a structure. It can be considered the combined use of objectivity and subjectivity, a balance of rigor and relevance, or other paradoxical features of inquiry. Although a rigorous school-based experiment may serve to address a local issue, relevance of broader issues to the whole issue is then lacking. Proper balance of these two validity concerns creates a different whole. Thus, disparate measures combine to re-create a greater whole.

School organization was long thought to revolve around building the proper functions into the environment and operationalizing them; when needed, additional functions were added, not taking into account their impact on existing functions and the organization. In this sense the school was never truly able to adapt itself and create those new organizing relationships necessary as a result of growth or any other measure. Without a process–relationship orientation, the large school becomes cumbersome, inflexible, procedural, and bureaucratic. If our previous decision making and problem solving had included concern for form as well as function, perhaps flexibility mechanisms could have codeveloped or procedures could have been adapted to encompass newer relationships. In this sense, schooling could become self-organizing and self-renewing.

Objective to Perspectival. As a corollary to the change discussed previously, newer inquiry paradigms seek to expose multiple perspectives through inquiry and enable multiple findings. If we continually reduce the variety of issues that can affect a research effort, we also reduce the ability of the inquirer to pursue the most informed effort. Inquiry needs requisite variety to function effectively.

These axioms, as Guba and Lincoln (1985) describe them, allow the possibility for developing a new view of knowledge creation in educational organizations. Traditional methodologies continue to have a strong impact on administrative inquiry. However, there has been a steadily growing body of research based on the interpretivistic perspective and the previously mentioned "new" axioms. We must be familiar with both the traditional and the newer views of organizational inquiry. As Gage (1989) pointed out, we are still in the midst of a battle for paradigm supremacy or, alternatively, cooperation. Educators need to heed these multiple approaches to research into aspects of educational administration in order to achieve the most comprehensive understanding of the "reality" in which they work and strive to improve.

Summary and Fundamental Concepts

A person's philosophy determines how he or she interprets what is experienced. To be an effective tool of administrative action, however, it is preferable for this philosophy to be understood and intellectualized by each administrator and for the values and beliefs that it implies be made explicit. To facilitate this process for the aspiring school administrator, we surveyed various perspectives on values. Further, we examined how a person's values and beliefs are integrated into the visions, missions, and goals of an organization. The role of megavalues held by society as a whole in shaping an organization's policymaking process was explored.

The chapter concluded with an examination of the interrelations between philosophies, values, and modes of inquiry. Inquiry was defined as the close examination of a phenomenon in order to understand it. It is the process of knowing, of puzzle solving, of finding truth.

In chapter 8, the impact of philosophies, values, and beliefs on "evaluation" is demonstrated. The focus of the chapter is the means by which leaders pursue the process of mobilizing resources to enable organizations through evaluation to function effectively. Judgments of effective functioning are based on monitoring outcomes and measuring them against established goals and objectives. The standards movement and its relation to program evaluation, student achievement, and staff evaluation are considered.

Fundamental Concepts

The fundamental concepts that follow have been discussed in this chapter. The citations that conclude each concept indicate the Interstate School Leaders Licensure Consortium (ISLLC) standards and functions related to the concept. The Arabic numeral refers to the ISLLC standard, and the letters refer to the related function as presented in the table found inside the front cover.

- Philosophy, in its broadest meaning, is a systematic attempt to make sense out of our individual and collective human experience. (5; 6)
- Leadership is a peculiarly moral activity. (5; 6)
- To be effective, leadership behavior must rest on certain philosophical assumptions about such fundamental considerations as human nature, the nature of reality, conditions of knowledge, and the nature of value. (1D; 2F; 3D; 5; 6)
- Leaders need to be deeply reflective, actively thoughtful, and dramatically explicit about their core values and beliefs. (1D; 2F; 3D; 5; 6)
- Values are conceptions of the desirable; a value is an enduring belief that a specific mode of conduct or state of existence is personally or socially preferable to an opposite or converse mode or state of existence. (1D; 2F; 3D; 5; 6)
- If values were completely stable, individual and social change would be impossible; if values were completely unstable, continuity of human personality and society would be impossible. (1D; 2F; 3D; 5; 6)
- Persons joined together by a similar set of values, beliefs, priorities, experiences, and traditions are said to form a common culture, whether it be in a small organization such as a school, a large nation such as the United States, or a group of nations such as the "West" or the "Western world." (1A, 1D; 2F; 3D; 5; 6)
- Shared values define the basic character of an organization and give it meaning. (1A, 1D; 2F; 3D; 5; 6)
- Metavalue is a concept of the desirable so vested and entrenched that it seems to be beyond dispute or contention—one that usually enters the ordinary value calculus of individual and collective life in the form of an unexpressed or unexamined assumption. (1A, 1D; 2F; 3D; 5; 6)
- Inquiry is the process of knowing, solving puzzles, probing, and finding truth. (1B, 1E; 2E, 2I; 3A; 4A; 5A, 5D; 6)

- Inquiry paradigms form the basis of how theorists and practitioners see the world. (1B, 1E; 2E, 2I; 3A; 4A; 5A, 5D; 6)
- The process of inquiry is intended to answer specific questions and thereby results in specific knowledge. (1B, 1E; 2E, 2I; 3A; 4A; 5A, 5D; 6)
- Researchers need to realize that no one paradigm can fulfill all the needs of educational research. (1B, 1E; 2E, 2I; 3A; 4A; 5A, 5D; 6)
- If researchers do not look to the real world more often, they may end up researching the least educationally significant aspects of that reality. (1B, 1E; 2E, 2I; 3A; 4A; 5A, 5D; 6)

Case Study

Standardized Test Scores: A Potential Scandal[1]

Addressing ISLLC Standards 2, 4 and 5

Analyze this case from the perspective of the director of pupil personnel services.

Part 1: Artificial Success

For the past several years, the results of the standardized tests for St. Stephen Elementary School have been considerably higher than the test results for the other elementary schools in the district. You are the district's test coordinator and have always found that fact curious. The students from St. Stephen do not seem to do any better than the students from the other schools in the district when they get to high school. This year you decide to investigate the matter more closely.

You begin by speaking to St. Stephen's principal, Dana Winters. You are told that the scores went up after the school started taking a week to prepare the students for the exam. The teachers know that the tests cover specific areas, and they simply review the areas included on the tests. They also review the testing format and have the students take sample tests similar to the ones they will be given. The principal says that tests should measure students' academic achievement, not their level of test anxiety or test-taking ability.

Dana proudly shows you the test preparation materials the teachers use. For each grade there are thick compilations of questions in the same categories as those on the exam: math computation, vocabulary, spelling, math concepts, and so on. There are also answer sheets that correspond to

the ones used on the actual exam. You ask if you can borrow the materials to look them over more closely in your office. Dana hesitates, but she agrees.

When you get back to your office, you read through the questions in the test preparation materials. They seem very reasonable. Then you get out a copy of the actual test corresponding to the preparation materials you are reviewing. About every third question in the preparation materials corresponds exactly to a question on the test. Your district owns the testing materials, and you have two sets of question booklets, Form A and Form B. You used Form B this year, but you find a copy of the Form A test. About a third of the questions on the test preparation materials come directly from the alternative form.

Questions

1. What will you do?
2. What will you say to the superintendent?
3. What additional information, if any, do you need?
4. What are the legal, moral, and ethical issues here?
5. Do you believe that the teachers at St. Stephen are involved in a conspiracy to cheat on the tests?
6. For years the local press and the community have commended St. Stephen for its test results. What will happen if this matter is discovered?
7. The test results are used to place students in the proper tracks when they get to seventh grade. A disproportionate number of students from St. Stephen are in the higher tracks. What, if anything, will you do about that matter?

Part 2: The Story Is Leaked

It has taken hours, but you have gone through all levels of the test preparation materials Dana gave you and all levels of both forms of the actual tests, highlighting all the questions on the preparation materials that duplicate actual test questions. The ratio has remained the same: one-third of the questions come from each form of the test, and the remaining one-third come from neither.

You take the fifth-grade materials in to show the superintendent, leaving the remainder on your desk. The superintendent knew about the week of test preparation and had even commended Dana for it. The superintendent did not know about the duplication of the actual test questions. The disclosure obviously would have many ramifications, and the two of you discuss how to handle the situation for some time. Before you come to any conclusions, the superintendent realizes that it is time to eat a quick supper and go to a school board meeting at Eastwick. You agree to consider the matter and decide on an approach the next day.

---

[1]*Source:* R. E. Kirschmann, *Educational administration: A collection of case studies* (pp. 127–129). Upper Saddle River, NJ: Merrill/ Prentice Hall, 1996.

When you get home, you discuss the matter with your spouse, giving all details of the discussion between the superintendent and you. The next day is Friday, and the superintendent is out with a stomach virus. The question of the test preparation must wait. No pressing need for immediate action seems to exist. The tests for this year have already been completed and the results distributed. Your discussion will have to wait until Monday.

On Monday morning you are greeted by headlines in the local newspaper that read, "Standardized Tests Rigged at St. Stephen Elementary School." You have not even finished reading the article when the superintendent calls to ask who you told about the test situation. During the course of the conversation, it becomes apparent that neither of you said anything about this situation to anyone except your spouses. The highlighted test preparation materials and the tests themselves are still on top of the worktable in your office, except for the fifth-grade materials, which are on the superintendent's desk.

You search your memory to make sure that you did not mention the matter to anyone except your spouse. The superintendent does the same. Both of you also question your spouses. All four of you conclude that you have told no one or even made hints about the matter. The other people who might have known about the tests were the business manager, the assistant superintendent, the secretaries, and the custodian. The custodian comes in at night for a few hours and is an unlikely suspect.

The information in the newspaper is accurate and fairly detailed. It strongly suggests the possibility of a leak in the central office.

Questions

1. What moral and ethical questions do you now face?
2. What criteria are you going to use to place St. Stephen's sixth-graders in the junior–senior high school next year?
3. What measures will you take to deal with the faculty and principal of St. Stephen?
4. How will you protect your own reputation?
5. What will you say to the press?
6. How will you investigate the question of who leaked the information to the newspaper?
7. Who had anything to gain by disclosing the information at this time?
8. If you find out who told the press, what will you do?
9. What do you imagine is likely to happen now?
10. Now that the news is public, how will you handle the question of St. Stephen's test preparation? How can you carry on your internal investigation?

References

Agger, B. (1991). *A critical theory of public life: Knowledge, discourse, and politics in an age of decline.* New York: Falmer.

Allison, D. J. (2002). Hodgkinson's paradoxical paradigm. *Values and Ethics in Educational Administration, 1*(1), 1–8.

Argyris, C. (1985). *Action science.* San Francisco: Jossey-Bass.

Argyris, C., & Schön, D. A. (1978). *Organizational learning: A theory of action perspective.* Reading, MA: Addison-Wesley.

Babbie, E. (1989). *The practice of social research* (5th ed.). Belmont, CA: Wadsworth.

Beare, H., Caldwell, B. J., & Millikan, R. H. (1989). *Creating an excellent school: Some new management techniques.* London: Routledge.

Beck, L. G., Murphy, J., & Associates. (1997). *Ethics in educational administration programs: Emerging models.* University Park, PA: University Council for Educational Administration.

Begley, P. T., & Stefkovich, J. A. (2004). Education, ethics, and the cult of efficiency: implications for values and leadership. *Journal of Educational Administration, 42*(2), 132–136.

Bennis, W. (1984). Transformative power and leadership. In T. J. Sergiovanni & J. E. Corbally (Eds.), *Leadership and organizational culture* (pp. 64–71). Urbana: University of Illinois Press.

Bolman, L. G., & Deal, T. E. (2001). *Leading with soul: An uncommon journey of the spirit.* San Francisco: Jossey-Bass.

Bolman, L. G., & Deal, T. E. (2003). *Reframing organizations: Artistry, choice, and leadership.* San Francisco: Jossey-Bass.

Boyd, W. L. (1984). Competing values in educational policy and governance: Australian and American developments. *Educational Administration Review, 2*(2), 4–24.

Burns, J. M. (1978). *Leadership.* New York: Harper & Row.

Cambron-McCabe, N. H. (1993). Leadership for democratic authority. In J. Murphy (Ed.), *Preparing tomorrow's school leaders: Alternative designs* (pp. 157–175). University Park, PA: University Council for Educational Administration.

Council of Chief State School Officers (CCSSO). (2008). *Educational Leadership Policy Standards: ISLLC 2008 as adopted by the National Policy Board for Educational Administration on December 12, 2007.* Washington, DC: CCSSO.

Culbertson, J. A. (1964). The preparation of administrators. In D. E. Griffiths (Ed.), *Behavioral science in educational administration* (63rd NSSE Yearbook, Pt. II, pp. 303–330). Chicago: University of Chicago Press.

Cziko, G. (1989). Unpredictability and indeterminism in human behavior: Arguments and implications for educational research. *Educational Researcher, 18*(3), 17–25.

Deal, T. E., & Kennedy, A. A. (1982). *Corporate cultures: The rites and rituals of corporate life.* Reading, MA: Addison-Wesley.

De George, R. T. (1999). *Business ethics* (5th ed.). Upper Saddle River, NJ: Prentice Hall.

Dewey, J. (1938). *Logic: The theory of inquiry.* New York: Holt, Rinehart and Winston.

Eisner, E. W. (1981, April). On the differences between scientific and artistic approaches to qualitative research. *Educational Researcher,* 5–7.

Eisner, E. W. (1991). *The enlightened eye: Qualitative inquiry and the enhancement of educational practice.* New York: Macmillan.

Erickson, D. A. (1977). An overdue paradigm shift in educational administration, or how can we get that idiot off the freeway. In L. L. Cunningham, W. G. Hack, & R. O. Nystrand (Eds.), *Educational administration: The developing decades* (pp. 114–143). Berkeley, CA: McCutchan.

Evers, C. W., & Lakomski, G. (1991). *Knowing educational administration: Contemporary methodological controversies in educational administration research.* Oxford: Pergamon Press.

Farquhar, R. H. (1968). The humanities and educational administration: Rationales and recommendations. *Journal of Educational Administration, 6*(2), 97–115.

Forsyth, P. B. (1999). The work of UCEA. In J. Murphy & P. B. Forsyth (Eds.), *Educational administration: A decade of reform* (pp. 71–92). Newbury Park, CA: Corwin Press.

Foster, W. P. (1986). *Paradigms and promises: New approaches to educational administration.* Buffalo, NY: Prometheus.

Fullan, M. (2003). *The moral imperative of school leadership.* Thousand Oaks, CA: Corwin Press.

Furman, G. C. (2004). The ethic of community. *Journal of Educational Administration, 42*(2), 215–235.

Gage, N. L. (1989). The paradigm wars and their aftermath: A historical sketch of the research on teaching since 1987. *Educational Researcher, 18*(7), 4–10.

Getzels, J. W. (1957). Changing values challenge the schools. *School Review, 65,* 91–102.

Getzels, J. W. (1978). The school and the acquisition of values. In R. W. Tyler (Ed.), *From youth to constructive adult life: The role of the school* (pp. 43–66). Berkeley, CA: McCutchan.

Goldhammer, K. (1983). Evolution in the profession. *Educational Administration Quarterly, 19*(3), 249–272.

Graff, O. B., Street, C. M., Kimbrough, R. B., & Dykes, A. R. (1966). *Philosophic theory and practice in educational administration.* Belmont, CA: Wadsworth.

Greenfield, T. B. (1975). Theory about organization: A new perspective and its implication for schools. In M. G. Hughes (Ed.), *Administering education: International challenge* (pp. 71–99). London: Athlone.

Greenfield, T. B. (1984). Leaders and schools: Willfulness and nonnatural order in organizations. In T. J. Sergiovanni & J. E. Corbally (Eds.), *Leadership and organizational culture* (pp. 142–169). Urbana: University of Illinois Press.

Greenfield, T. B. (1991). Foreword. In C. Hodgkinson, *Educational leadership: The moral art* (pp. 3–9). Albany: State University of New York Press.

Greenfield, W. D. (2004). Moral leadership in schools. *Journal of Educational Administration, 42*(2), 174–196.

Greenleaf, R. K. (1977). *Servant leadership: A journey into the nature of legitimate power and greatness.* New York: Paulist Press.

Griffiths, D. E. (1979). Intellectual turnout in educational administration. *Educational Administration Quarterly, 15*(3), 43–65.

Guba, E. G. (1990). The alternative paradigm dialog. In E. G. Guba (Ed.), *The paradigm dialog* (pp. 17–27). Newbury Park, CA: Sage.

Guba, E. G., & Lincoln, Y. S. (1985). *Types of inquiry.* Unpublished paper, Indiana University, Bloomington.

Guba, E. G., & Lincoln, Y. S. (1989). *Fourth generation evaluation.* Newbury Park, CA: Sage.

Guthrie, J. W., Garms, W. I., & Pierce, L. C. (1988). *School finance and education policy: Enhancing educational efficiency, equality and choice.* Upper Saddle River, NJ: Prentice Hall.

Hall, B. P., Kalven, J., Rosen, L. S., & Taylor, B. (1990). *Developing human values.* Fond du Lac, WI: International Values Institute of Marian College.

Harlow, J. G. (1962). Purpose-defining: The central function of the school administrator. In J. A. Culbertson & S. P. Henchley (Eds.), *Preparing administrators: New perspectives* (pp. 61–71). Columbus, OH: University Council for Educational Administration.

Hodgkinson, C. (1978). *Towards a philosophy of administration.* Oxford: Basil Blackwell.

Hodgkinson, C. (1983). *The philosophy of leadership.* Oxford: Basil Blackwell.

Hodgkinson, C. (1991). *Educational leadership: The moral art.* Albany: State University of New York Press.

Hodgkinson, C. (1996). *Administrative philosophy: Values and motivations in administrative life.* Tarrytown, NY: Elsevier Science.

Howe, K, & Eisenhart, M. (1990). Standards for qualitative (and quantitative) research: A prolegomenon. *Educational Researcher, 16*(1), 5–13.

Hoy, W. K., & Miskel, C. G. (2005). *Educational administration: Theory, research and practice* (7th ed.). New York: McGraw-Hill.

Interstate School Leaders Licensure Consortium. (1996). *Standards for school leaders.* Washington, DC: Council of Chief State School Officers.

King, R. A., Swanson, A. D., & Sweetland, S. R. (2003). *School finance: Achieving high standards with equity and efficiency.* Boston: Allyn & Bacon.

Kirschmann, R. E. (1996). *Educational administration: A collection of case studies.* Upper Saddle River, NJ: Merrill/Prentice Hall.

Kuhn, T. S. (1962). *The structure of scientific revolutions.* Chicago: University of Chicago Press.

Kuhn, T. S. (1996). *The structure of scientific revolutions* (3rd ed.). Chicago: University of Chicago Press.

Lewis, H. (1990). *A question of values: Six ways we make the personal choices that shape our lives.* New York: Harper & Row.

Lindblom, C. E. (1959). The science of muddling through. *Public Administration Review, 19,* 79–88.

Littlejohn, S. W. (1992). *Theories of human communication* (4th ed.). Belmont, CA: Wadsworth.

Maxcy, S. J. (1991). *Educational leadership: A critical pragmatic perspective.* New York: Bergin & Garvey.

Murphy, J. (Ed.). (1993). *Preparing tomorrow's school leaders: Alternative designs.* University Park, PA: University Council for Educational Administration.

Murphy, J. (2003). *Reculturing educational leadership: The ISLLC Standards ten years out.* Fairfax, VA: National Policy Board for Educational Administration.

Murphy, J., Yff, J., & Shipman, N. (2000). Implementation of the Interstate School Leaders Licensure Consortium Standards. *International Journal of Leadership in Education, 3*(1), 17–37.

National Commission on Excellence in Educational Administration. (1987). *Leaders for America's schools.* Tempe, AZ: University Council on Educational Administration.

Nyberg, D. (1981). *Power over power: What power means in ordinary life, how it is related to acting freely, and what it can contribute to a renovated ethics of education.* Ithaca, NY: Cornell University Press.

Nyberg, D. (1993). *The varnished truth: Truth telling and deceiving in ordinary life.* Chicago: University of Chicago Press.

Osterman, K. F., & Kottkamp, R. B. (1993). *Reflective practice for educators: Improving schooling through professional development.* Newbury Park, CA: Corwin Press.

Osterman, K. F., & Kottkamp, R. B. (2004). *Reflective practice for educators: Professional development to improve student learning* (2nd ed.). Thousand Oaks, CA: Corwin Press.

Ouchi, W. G. (1981). *Theory Z: How American business can meet the Japanese challenge.* Reading, MA: Addison-Wesley.

Parsons, T. (1951). *The social system.* Glencoe, IL: Free Press.

Peters, T. J. (1988). *Thriving on chaos: Handbook for a management revolution.* New York: Knopf.

Peters, T. J., & Waterman, R. H., Jr. (1982). *In search of excellence: Lessons from America's best-run companies.* New York: Warner Books.

Ravitch, D. (1985). *The schools we deserve: Reflections on the educational crises of our times.* New York: Basic Books.

Rokeach, M. (1973). *The nature of human values.* New York: Free Press.

Schwartz, S. H. (1992). Universals in the content and structure of values: Theoretical advances and empirical tests in 20 countries. *Advances in Experimental Social Psychology, 25,* 1–65.

Schwartz, S. H. (1994). Studying human values. In A. Bouvy, F. van de Vijver, P. Boski, & P. Schmitz (Eds.), *Journeys into cross cultural psychology* (pp. 239–254). Lisse: Swets & Zeitlinger.

Sergiovanni, T. J. (1984a). Cultural and competing perspectives in administrative theory and practice. In T. J. Sergiovanni & J. E. Corbally (Eds.), *Leadership and organizational culture* (pp. 1–17). Urbana: University of Illinois Press.

Sergiovanni, T. J. (1984b). Leadership as cultural expression. In T. J. Sergiovanni & J. E. Corbally (Eds.), *Leadership and organizational culture* (pp. 105–114). Urbana: University of Illinois Press.

Sergiovanni, T. J. (1984c). Leadership and excellence in schooling. *Educational Leadership, 41*(5), 4–13.

Sergiovanni, T. J. (1992). *Moral leadership: Getting to the heart of school improvement.* San Francisco: Jossey-Bass.

Sergiovanni, T. J. (2001). *The principalship: A reflective practice perspective* (4th ed.). Needham Heights, MA: Allyn & Bacon.

Sergiovanni, T. J., & Starratt, R. J. (1983). *Supervision: A definition* (3rd ed.). New York: McGraw-Hill.

Sergiovanni, T. J., & Starratt, R. J. (2007). *Supervision: A definition* (8th ed.). New York: McGraw-Hill.

Shapiro, J. P., & Stefkovich, J. A. (2001). *Ethical leadership and decision making in education: Applying theoretical perspectives to complex dilemmas.* Mahwah, NJ: Lawrence Erlbaum Associates.

Smith, J. K., & Blase, J. (1991). From empiricism to hermeneutics: Educational leadership as a practical and moral activity. *Journal of Educational Administration, 29*(1), 6–21.

Smith, L. M. (1990). Ethics, field studies, and the paradigm crisis. In E. G. Guba (Ed.), *The paradigm dialog* (pp. 139–157). Newbury Park, CA: Sage.

Spindler, G. D. (1955). Education in a transforming American culture. *Harvard Education Review, 25*(3), 145–156.

Thomson, S. D. (1999). Causing change: The National Policy Board for Educational Administration. In J. Murphy & P. B. Forsyth (Eds.), *Educational administration: A decade of reform* (pp. 93–114). Newbury Park, CA: Corwin Press.

Vaill, P. B. (1984). The purposing of high-performance systems. In T. J. Sergiovanni & J. E. Corbally (Eds.), *Leadership and organizational culture* (pp. 85–104). Urbana: University of Illinois Press.

Weber, M. (1947). *The theory of social and economic organization* (A. Henderson & T. Parsons, Trans.). New York: Oxford University Press.

Wheatley, M. J. (2006). *Leadership and the new science: Discovering order in a chaotic world* (3rd ed.). San Francisco: Berrett-Koehler.

Wheatley, M. J., & Kellner-Rogers, M. (1996). *A simpler way.* San Francisco: Berrett-Koehler.

Wilbur, K. (1982). *The holographic paradigm and other paradoxes.* Boulder, CO: Shambhala Publications.

Willower, D. J., & Licata, J. W. (1997). *Values and valuation in the practice of educational administration.* Thousand Oaks, CA: Corwin Press.

Wirt, F. M. (April, 1986). *Multiple paths for understanding the role of values in state policy.* Paper presented at the annual meeting of the American Educational Research Association, San Francisco, CA (ERIC Document Reproduction Service No. ED278086).

Wirt, F. M. (1987). National Australia–United States education: A commentary. In W. L. Boyd & D. Smart (Eds.), *Educational policy in Australia and America: Comparative perspectives* (pp. 129–137). New York: Falmer.

Evaluation in Education

In chapter 7, decision making by leaders was discussed in the light of philosophic views of the world, values, and beliefs as they affect those decisions. The impact of those perspectives on educational decision making was a particular focus.

The performance of educational systems has become an issue of public concern over the past half century. Concern for the overall effectiveness of the educational system has increased. Various methods of assessment and evaluation have been applied in attempting to determine if schools were performing effectively and, if not, to try to determine areas where they were performing less than adequately, why, and how to reform the system.

This chapter considers the history of educational assessment and evaluation, their various components and functions, and various models that have been recommended and applied to student learning, the performance of teachers and administrators, and the effectiveness of schools and the educational system overall. Standards and requirements for valid assessment and evaluation are considered. Particular attention is paid to the federal No Child Left Behind Act, an effort to improve the performance of public elementary and secondary schools overall.

Educational Evaluation: A Brief History

The Beginnings of Evaluation

The concept and practice of evaluation are hardly new. Equivalent terms for *evaluation* can be found in ancient languages and texts, and the use of evaluation for educational purposes, to assess learning, knowledge, and skill, was also known in early times.

Teachers in ancient Greece, such as Socrates, engaged in verbally mediated evaluations as part of the dialogic learning process, and emperors in China as early as 200 b.c. made use of regular exams and proficiency tests to evaluate candidates for government service positions (Tyler, 1970; Worthen, 1973). Despite its ancient roots, educational evaluation did not begin to take shape as a distinct field until the advent of the industrial revolution. Evaluation issues emerged with the development of modern education systems in Europe and North America.

The Modern Development Stages of Evaluation

A helpful outline of the modern history of educational evaluation is provided by Madaus, Scriven, and Stufflebeam (1983). They trace the development of educational evaluation in the United States through six periods from 1800 to the present:

1. The *Age of Reform* (1800–1900) was characterized by the development of the first mental tests, application of psychological and behavioral measurements to educational problems, the rise of experimental pedagogy, and the use of external school inspectors to evaluate and promote schooling standards.

2. The *Age of Efficiency and Testing* (1900–1930) saw evaluation efforts that were largely dedicated to the development and use of standardized achievement tests and test batteries. Publication of *The Principles of Scientific Management* by Frederick Taylor in 1911 marked the influence of the ideas of systematization, standardization,

and scientific method on industry and provided a methodology for the administration of education along progressive lines (Taylor, 1911).

3. The *Tylerian Age* (1930–1945) is associated with the work and thinking of Ralph W. Tyler, who is often considered the founder of modern educational evaluation. Tyler was initially concerned with educational measurement, but he also stressed the importance of considering the goals and objectives of educational programs when evaluating student learning and program outcomes. Tyler's emphasis on goal identification and goal achievement had the effect of widening the field of educational evaluation, both theoretically and practically, and allowed learning evaluation measurements to be criterion referenced as opposed to being norm referenced.

4. The *Age of Innocence* (1946–1957) saw the proliferation of Tylerian-style evaluation, especially its application in local school programs. Educational evaluation and measurement courses became common at teachers' colleges. Refinements of tests and testing methodologies were developed throughout this period. Leading educators praised evaluation as a major foundation element for building new systems of schooling, curriculum, and program delivery. Evaluation also became a major issue in teacher employment and in-school supervision.

5. The *Age of Expansion* (1958–1972) is most notable for an increased emphasis on personnel evaluation and the development of improved, multifactor evaluation models. During this period in the United States, the federal role in education greatly expanded with enactment of the Elementary and Secondary Education Act (ESEA) in 1965. Numerous programs under Title I of ESEA were established that required the development of evaluation programs for continuation of funding. These requirements led to the acceptance and use of new qualitative evaluation models and systems models by expert practitioners.

6. During the current *Age of Professionalism* (from 1973 to the present), educational evaluation has emerged as a distinct realm of professional specialization. This period is marked by a recognition that useful evaluation must draw on a number of different models and methods, both quantitative and qualitative, and a more general acceptance of the fundamental philosophical positions that tend to divide the profession (Cronbach, 1982). In addition, frustration over lack of success of educational reforms initiated during the latter part of the 20th century led to enactment of "accountability" legislation in the 21st century, such as the No Child Left Behind Act at the federal level, similar acts at the state level, and programs at the district level.

Basic Aspects of Educational Evaluation

Commonality within Diversity

Although much accountability legislation of the 21st century has treated it as a science, evaluation is more an applied art than a science. Evaluation approaches and designs are influenced by a variety of theories and models; evaluation practices can vary to suit different purposes (Shadish, Cook, & Leviton, 1991). Educational evaluation lacks any single overriding theory or "best" method. A consensus is growing that the existence of multiple evaluation approaches and methods presents no great problem for evaluation specialists and professionals. Rather, problems seem to arise only when evaluation models are used inconclusively or inappropriately for purposes that are inconsistent with their inherent properties (Meier & Wood, 2004; Peterson & West, 2003).

Diversity within the field of educational evaluation need not prevent recognition of several major principles and conceptual features that give shape to the field as a whole. This awareness of commonalities has stimulated attempts to develop integrated theoretical frameworks for the field (Shadish et al., 1991).

Formal definitions of *educational evaluation* emphasize three prevalent viewpoints. Some definitions emphasize a mode of evaluation that is concerned primarily with the achievement of specified norms or goals (e.g., Tyler, 1970). Other definitions emphasize a type of evaluation that is qualitative, open ended, or goal free and dedicated primarily to insightful descriptions and judgments of educational realities (e.g., Guba & Lincoln, 1989; Patton, 1984; Scriven, 1980a). Some definitions emphasize the pragmatic aspects of the evaluation process: information gathering, followed by analysis and judgmental assessment, followed by decision making and action. The pragmatic, process-based definitions of educational evaluation appear to be the most serviceable ones for administrators. These methods also reflect current thinking in the field.

Within this frame of reference, evaluation may be defined as a systematic collection and interpretation of evidence leading to a judgment of value with a view to action. This definition does not limit the evaluation process to any prescribed target or methodological approach but does serve to emphasize the essential, purposeful connections among information, evaluation (i.e., judgment), and action. Evaluation forms the rational center of a wider educational management process.

Evaluation sometimes becomes confused with two other terms, measurement (or assessment) and research. *Measurement* or *assessment* simply identifies the act of measuring, which is essentially a value-free technical exercise for collecting and arraying data. *Research* is a process that attempts to generate new knowledge for the sake of theory testing and theory building. The results of research are often compared and generalized. But evaluation, by definition, is more valuative than measurement or assessment and more decision and action oriented than research (Kowalski, 1988).

Evaluation Modes and Purposes

Educational evaluation is generally understood to fall into two primary categories: summative evaluation and formative evaluation. People typically think about *summative evaluation*, evaluation that occurs at (or near) some identifiable end point of a project, program, or course. Comprehensive final exams and course grades for students, annual performance and merit reviews for teachers, and program assessments are different forms of summative evaluation applied to education.

Summative evaluation is usually conducted with the intent of making summary judgments about the overall worth of educational endeavors, activities, and programs. These value judgments become the basis for

making decisions. Examples are decisions regarding the continuation or noncontinuation of programs, school activities, teacher assignments, student placement, and grade promotion. (Scriven, 1980a, 1980b).

The term *formative evaluation*, on the other hand, refers to evaluation that occurs while processes or products are being designed or processes are ongoing. Formative evaluation is used principally to foster improvement, and it can be thought of as evaluation that accompanies some larger development effort or change process.

Formative evaluation is highly desirable, for instance, when implementing new programs or instructional delivery systems. These measures provide the means to detect and solve problems before they become unwieldy. Formative evaluation methods are also very useful in conjunction with programs aimed at staff development and organizational change. Formative evaluations also nurture effective teaching and educational testing, the normal concerns related to "student development."

In addition to summative and formative evaluation, Tuckman (1985) suggested a third mode of evaluation: *ex post facto evaluation*. These after-the-fact reviews study events and data in a longitudinal manner to determine the factors that contributed to educational success or failure. This form of evaluation is usually done to obtain information and review assessments needed for educational planning and to note outcomes, trends, and problem factors. However, summative and formative modes of evaluation still command the most attention among evaluation researchers and school practitioners.

Summative and formative evaluations can be regarded as complementary. Often the same evaluation study can be viewed by one client as summative and by another client as formative (Borich, 1974; Lewy, 1990; Scriven, 1980b). Much depends on when and where the mechanisms are utilized and by whom. Indeed, many experts suggest that evaluation designs ought to include related plans for summative and formative evaluation (e.g., Edwards, Guttentag, & Snapper, 1975; Lewy, 1990; Mark & Cook, 1984).

It is possible to identify other purposes for educational evaluation. These purposes for evaluation reveal the basic reasons for conducting evaluations in the first place. Educational evaluation may be undertaken for sociopolitical and psychological purposes, such as gaining public support and professional commitments. Evaluation may also be carried out for authoritative and administrative purposes, such as demonstrating administrative control and authority over educational systems and processes.

Programs of instruction are commonly measured in terms of student performance. Miller, Imrie, and Cox (1998) categorized these measures of performance as measures of student potential (most commonly diagnostic tests used to place students appropriately) and measures of achievement (most commonly used to measure student mastery of concepts or skills that have been taught). Measures of achievement may be criterion referenced (performance matched to an absolute standard) or norm referenced (performance matched to the performance of others in a specified group). Evaluation of school improvement (and, by extension, evaluation of programs) may be used to improve the quality of the school and its programs, to determine the success of attempted improvements, and/or to provide ongoing feedback and improvement of performance.

Evaluation Targets and Processes

Whether formative or summative in nature, evaluation can be carried out for motivational purposes on the one hand or for corrective purposes on the other. It may focus on a variety of targets or objects of interest. In general, evaluation targets tend to fall into five main categories or areas of visible concern:

1. *Evaluations of learning:* Measurements, assessments, and inquiries regarding student learning gains, learning rates, and performance

2. *Evaluations of instruction:* Measurements, assessments, and appraisals of instructional quality, competence, and success in relation to instructional standards, goals, and norms

3. *Evaluations of courses:* Evaluations of course design and content, of instructional support, and of testing and remediation systems

4. *Evaluations of programs:* Evaluations of program curricula and course combinations and evaluation of program design, efficiency, and effectiveness, including assessments of administration, institutional fit, social impact, and cost benefits

5. *Evaluations of institutions and wider education systems:* Evaluations of multiprogram or multisite education systems, including institutional and sectoral evaluations of national (or even international) education systems

These target categories are interlinked, and when taken together they represent an integrated continuum of evaluation targets. Evaluation of targets in any one category of primary concern can easily lead to consideration of targets in other categories. Evaluations of learning (target level 1), for example, are not simply restricted to a consideration of student behaviors or test scores; learning evaluations can include related assessments of instruction and course content. Similarly, course evaluations (at target level 3) can include assessments of instructional methods and materials (target level 2) in one direction and of program design and institutional support (at target levels 4 and 5) in the other direction.

In practice, educational evaluation may focus on as few or as many targets as the specific evaluation situation dictates and allows. In this regard evaluation becomes *situational*, as targets of any given evaluation will depend on the immediate concerns of the evaluators, participants, and audiences involved in the process and the commitment of resources and time.

A composite list of the core processes of educational evaluation from the viewpoint of educational administrators and leaders would include the following elements. (a) Problem setting: determining the situation to be evaluated, the objects and people involved in the situation of interest, and the purpose(s) of the evaluation. (b) Problem specification: determining relevant elements for examination in the evaluation problem, selecting the appropriate evaluation mode and method(s) of inquiry, selecting participants and sample groups, and identifying likely data sources, informants, and so on. (c) Data collection and analysis. (d) Communication of findings and recommendations. (e) Decision making. (f) Action derived from decision making. (g) Assessment of the evaluation in relation to the initial purpose, the process used, and the expected results.

Throughout these evaluation stages, interaction among participants, evaluators, evaluation subjects, and evaluation audiences is necessary and especially advantageous. Interaction can occur at any stage of the evaluation process, but it is especially beneficial in the problem-setting, communication, and evaluation review stages (Cronbach, 1982; Glasman & Nevo, 1988; Holloway, 1988).

The last stage of the prototype evaluation process, overall assessment, has an impact apart from the evaluation reviewed. Assessments of any given evaluation ought to serve a corrective function. Problems and inadequacies noticed in the evaluation process are addressed to improve *future* evaluation efforts. Unless problems encountered in evaluation projects are thoroughly aired and examined, improvements in the process probably will not occur. Without corrective mechanisms in place, participants may come to regard evaluations as frustrating exercises devoid of worth.

Evaluation Perspectives and Models

Educational evaluation encompasses a wide range of theoretical perspectives and approaches. Models include both descriptive and prescriptive approaches in various categories: research models, quantitative versus qualitative models, goal-attainment versus goal-free models, specialized limited-purpose models (such as cost-effectiveness) versus comprehensive systems models, and more. Some models are highly theoretical, while others are more pragmatic and oriented toward field use by nonspecialists.

A number of different classification schemes have been developed for educational evaluation. One classification, presented by Popham (1988), grouped evaluation models into five basic categories. Table 8.1 includes Popham's five model categories:

TABLE 8.1

Categories of Educational Evaluation Models

Category/Model Type	Method/Terms	Proponents
Goal-attainment models: The degree to which predetermined goals are reached is the sole criterion for evaluation.	• Goal sources and goal screens • Five-step model • Eight-step model	Tyler Hammond Metfessel and Michael
Judgmental models: Major attention is given to the evaluator's professional judgment. The evaluator concentrates on inputs or outputs of the system being evaluated and determines their value.	• Accreditation model • Comparative evaluation • Countenance model • Payoff evaluation • Goal-free evaluation	School associations Cronbach Stake Scriven Scriven
Decision-facilitation models: Evaluation is viewed as the recollection of data to service decision makers. Models center on obtaining relevant information.	• CIPP model • "Evaluator as teacher" • Discrepancy model	Stufflebeam Cronbach Provus
Naturalistic models: The main instrument for data collection is the human being, and constraints imposed on the evaluation situation and evaluation activities are held to a minimum.	• Human instruments • Responsive evaluation • Connoisseurship mode • Ethnographic evaluation	Guba and Lincoln Stake Eisner LeCompte and Goetz
Self-evaluation models: The main source of data collection *and* analysis are the subjects being evaluated. The evaluator is more a facilitator who helps the group evaluate itself.	• LEA schemes • Curriculum reviews • School-initiated and/or teacher-initiated evaluation • GRIDS	Turner McCormick and James Elliot McMahon

Source: Adapted from Popham, (1988, p. 23).

goal attainment, judgmental, decision-facilitation, naturalistic, and self-evaluation. The fifth category, self-evaluation models, was added to make the table reflect other methods in use, including approaches suggested by Clift, Nutall, and McCormick (1988), Holt (1981), and Wilson (1988).

Given the numerous models, some experts have suggested that an eclectic approach is both possible and desirable in coming to grips with the multifaceted evaluation problems facing educators (Glasman & Nevo, 1988; Popham, 1988; Wilson, 1988). Brandt (1981) showed how different methods and techniques can be used by professionals to address identical evaluation problems. However, an eclectic blend of approaches and methods can be effective only to the degree that practitioners know about different approaches and feel confident about their worth. This implies that educators need to be more knowledgeable, competent, and experienced with respect to educational evaluation.

Applications of Educational Evaluation

Scriven (1980a, 1980b) introduced the term *evaluand* to refer to the entity or set of targets being evaluated. He noted that virtually anything can serve as an evaluand. Judgment of student learning is the universally practiced form of evaluation in education. Walberg and Haertel (1990) have suggested that outside the popular realm of assessing student learning, the most common foci of educational evaluations are program and teacher evaluations. These do seem to be the most prominent. Evaluation of educational administrators has also become an issue.

Evaluation: Teachers

Teacher evaluation is receiving increasing attention. Both the theory and the practice of teacher evaluation reflect disagreements as to whether instructor evaluations should detect incompetencies, prevent incompetence, or correct deficiencies, all of which suggest different methodologies and approaches. Additionally, different characterizations of the act of teaching mandate a variety of ways for collecting information and making evaluative judgments about the worth of instructional abilities and quality.

Teacher evaluation may be accomplished for a variety of reasons, none of which are or can be explicitly measured in isolation. In this sense, teacher evaluation, in fact all evaluation, remains problematic.

Perspectives on Teaching and Teacher Evaluation. Darling-Hammond, Wise, and Pease (1983) contended that the work of teaching is variously perceived as a labor, a craft, a profession, or an art. Each viewpoint suggests a theoretical framework for teacher evaluation. When teaching is viewed as labor, teaching activities are characterized by standard operating procedures, and evaluation involves direct inspection of the teacher's work (e.g., monitoring lesson plans and classroom performance). If teaching is conceptualized as a craft, it requires a repertoire of specialized techniques, and the corresponding evaluation is indirect in ascertaining whether a teacher has the requisite skills to practice the craft. As a profession, teaching requires a repertoire of specialized techniques similar to the craft perspective. But evaluation here calls for judgment about when those techniques should be applied. Thus, some evaluation standards are developed by peers, and evaluation focuses on the degree to which teachers are competent at professional problem solving. When teaching is perceived as an art, it calls primarily for intuition, creativity, and expressiveness. Corresponding evaluation methods that address holistic qualities and involve both self-assessment and critical assessment by others are applicable.

In practice, these four perspectives on teaching will not be found in their pure form. People will have mixed or overlapping opinions about what teaching entails or ought to emphasize. Such overlapping of teaching perspectives is natural given the fact that instructional behaviors that are effective in moderation can produce negative effects when they are overutilized or applied in inappropriate circumstances. The very nature of teaching makes it impossible to define a single perspective or set of behaviors that are globally successful (Coker, Medley, & Soar, 1980). In addition, as noted by numerous authors (e.g., Darling-Hammond et al., 1983; Millman, 1981; Shavelson & Stern, 1981), these perspectives on teaching determine varying definitions of success as well as corresponding values that are evident in different teacher evaluation systems.

Purposes of Teacher Evaluation. Teacher evaluation generally addresses four purposes: individual improvement, school improvement, individual accountability, and organizational accountability (Darling-Hammond et al., 1983). Individual and organizational improvement needs are addressed primarily via formative evaluation. Accountability needs are typically satisfied by summative evaluation, with evaluation results subsequently used for personnel decisions and school status decisions (Darling-Hammond et al., 1983). However, some purposes, such as teacher promotion or tenure, are most frequently served by focusing the assessment on teacher competence, performance, or effectiveness (Millman, 1981).

Teacher Evaluation Methods. Teacher evaluations utilize quantitative or qualitative methodologies depending on whether the evaluation is used to determine competence, performance, or effectiveness. Darling-Hammond et al. (1983) reported that eight evaluation methods are most common: teacher interviews, competency tests, indirect measures, classroom observation, student ratings, peer review, student achievement, and faculty self-evaluations.

Darling-Hammond et al. (1983) also noted that in the past, teacher appraisal interviews and classroom observation constituted the instructor evaluation process. Currently, the interview is used as just one element of the broader evaluation procedure. The two common uses of the teacher interview are to facilitate employment or promotion decisions and to communicate performance appraisals to practicing instructors. Moreover, the interview process has evolved from a primarily unstructured activity into a more formal one that employs standardized methodologies, such as teacher–perceiver interviews (Haefele, 1981). Teacher–perceiver interviews are designed to identify teachers who stimulate students' learning.

Teacher competency tests represent a growing trend in response to the public's demand for institutional and professional accountability. Although there are also numerous state and locally developed examinations, the most widely used professional test is the National Teacher Examination (NTE). Competency tests are most commonly used for initial certification and hiring. These instruments offer the advantages of eliminating interviewer bias and

verifying minimum standards of knowledge. The tests are usually legally defensible as screening mechanisms (Darling-Hammond et al., 1983). However, critics contend that the tests cannot assess actual performance or higher levels of knowledge and that success on the tests does not necessarily guarantee effective teaching. This is reflected in data showing that only 11% of teachers believe that NTE scores are valid measures of effectiveness (Haefele, 1981). In practice, teacher competency as measured by the NTE may be a minimal necessity and should be combined with other evaluation mechanisms.

An effort toward evaluating teachers' skills and motivation that is growing rapidly is certification by the National Board for Professional Teaching Standards. The certification is intended to identify those teachers who will demonstrate that they can meet a set of national standards for good teaching and so demonstrate professional competence (National Board for Professional Teaching Standards, 2007). While the program is showing success in terms of teacher involvement, there is still debate about the relationship between national certification and improved teacher performance over an extended period of time (Keller, 2007).

Traditionally, indirect measures such as work experience and educational level have been linked to teacher promotion opportunities. However, no single set of skills, attitudes, interests or abilities has been identified as capable of distinguishing between ineffective and effective instructors, although some research suggests a correlation between flexibility and effectiveness (King, 1981). Less indirect measures connected to career and job performance, such as indications of professional advancement and commitment, seem appropriate as supplementary sources of evaluation data.

Classroom observation is a central aspect of most instructor evaluations. It is typically used as a formative technique to address performance improvement (Mitzel, Best, and Rabinowitz, 1982). Classroom observations may include a preliminary interview. Observation protocols reflect a range of structures and methodologies, from observations that entail standardized observation forms to those that address items agreed on by both the instructor and the evaluator (Darling-Hammond et al., 1983). Observations are often conducted by an administrator. This offers the advantage of including information as to the instructional climate and performance that is not available to outsiders. However, the numerous limitations of this method include observer bias, insufficient sampling of performance to provide reliable data, and measurement instruments that frequently lack appropriate focus (Darling-Hammond et al., 1983; Mitzel et al., 1982).

In actuality, student ratings are simply another form of classroom observation. These ratings provide a different perspective from that of an independent evaluator or administrator. Although this form of evaluation is most typically utilized at the higher education level, several authors (e.g. Haefele, 1981; Peterson & Kauchak, 1982) contend that student ratings could be effectively applied at the secondary level or, in some cases, even at the elementary level. Student evaluations have several inherent advantages, including the proven correlation between student ratings and student academic achievement (i.e., minimally 0.8). Even so, some authors have debated the validity and utility of this form of evaluation (Darling-Hammond et al., 1983).

Research has indicated that the connection between student test scores and teacher effectiveness is quite low, so the connection between appropriate teaching behaviors and resultant learning appears to be situational (Darling-Hammond et al., 1983). In addition, the use of student test results to measure teacher effectiveness often leads to putting instructors' teaching to the test (Centra & Potter, 1980). Cochran and Mills (1984) have argued that efforts to link student achievement to the performance of individual teachers has been ineffective because the measurement does not take the teaching context into account, time on task is not considered, and the measures are generally not congruent with best practices in modern education. However, when student scores are used as a formative evaluation methodology as part of a larger evaluation system, students' scores provide a mechanism of addressing the overall goal of the teaching endeavor: student outcomes (Darling-Hammond et al., 1983).

Examples of programs that have used student achievement as a component of teacher evaluation with some level of success include the ProComp program in the Denver, Colorado, public schools (Denver Public Schools, 2007); the Cincinnati, Ohio, public schools; the Vaughn Charter School in Los Angeles, California; and the Coventry, Rhode Island, public schools (Heneman, Milanowski, Kimball, & Odden, 2006; White, 2004).

Mitzel et al. (1982) noted that despite the potential benefits of teachers evaluating their colleagues, peer review is rarely used and is not desired by teachers themselves. This form of evaluation usually entails peer examination of lesson plans, examinations, and other instructor-designed materials and documents, plus classroom observation. Peer review is based on the assumption that peers are in the best position to assess competence and performance because of their familiarity with classroom conditions and subject matter. In addition, peers are in a position to render specific practical suggestions for improvement. However, many authors (Darling-Hammond et al., 1983; Haefele, 1981; Mitzel et al., 1982) concur that this form of evaluation should serve a formative function and not be used for personnel decisions or summative purposes.

Faculty self-evaluations are an important source of information and evaluation in a broader evaluation program. Two of the most widely discussed teacher evaluation models, Manatt's mutual benefit evaluation model and Redfern's management by objectives evaluation model, include faculty self-evaluation components. Self-evaluation allows an instructor to use data derived from any technique (such as peer ratings, student ratings, or student achievement) to assess his or her own strengths and weaknesses. Although this approach should not be considered an evaluation method in itself, self-evaluation is becoming a more popular technique in teacher evaluation systems. When combined with goal setting, self-evaluation may lead to self-reflection and motivation promoting professional change and growth (Darling-Hammond et al., 1983).

Problems with teacher evaluation include the facts that many evaluation systems are developed for reasons of accountability external to teachers and are not used to improve teaching practice, that the multiplicity of relevant factors to be evaluated can make results difficult to interpret, and that it is difficult to find consistent factors that work in most situations

(House, 1996). Overall, the low levels of reliability, generalizability, and validity attributed to teacher evaluation methods suggest that one-dimensional approaches to assessing effectiveness, competence, or performance are unlikely to capture adequate data about teaching attributes to completely satisfy any of the purposes of the evaluation process. Additional research is needed in this area to determine and develop instructor evaluation systems that rise above the limitations already noted.

Teacher Evaluation Models. The methodologies and processes used for teaching evaluation are often classified as models. Borich (1977) contended that teaching models generally can be divided into two major categories: planning models and quantitative models. One basic planning model that serves as a basis for many others is Knezevich's systems evaluation model. This model, which is formative in nature and addresses personnel and organizational improvement, includes four phases: determination of the purpose and effectiveness of the system, development of monitoring procedures, data collection, and decision making and actions (Borich, 1977). Although Knezevich's model is not specific, precise, and verifiable, it does include all the steps necessary to develop an appraisal system.

The planning model by Coleman (cited in Borich, 1977) offers advantages over Knezevich's model in that it is more precise. Coleman's model specifies a number of teacher behaviors (i.e., warmth, indirectness, cognitive organization, and enthusiasm) and suggests corresponding measurement methods. This model is intended to address both formative and summative data. However, a limitation of the model is that research fails to support the assumption that Coleman's four teaching behaviors have wide application as effective instructional behaviors; rather, the behaviors may have only relative, situational merit (Darling-Hammond et al., 1983).

Two common quantitative models that have served as the basis for other models of this genre are Klein and Aikin's model and Dyer's model. Klein and Aikin's model uses an objective-based approach that excludes all subjective judgments of teachers. This model uses a regression analysis to measure the performances of one teacher's pupils against those of all teachers being appraised, to weigh only those variables under a teacher's control, and to adjust for variables considered as contaminating influences, such as differing pretest score levels (Borich, 1977). Dyer's model is also quantitative in nature, addressing four groups of variables: input variables of the students, output of the students, educational process variables of the school, and surrounding conditions. However, Dyer's model has diagnostic advantages not inherent in Klein and Aikin's model. Using Dyer's model, it is possible to adjust pupil outcome measures and those variables beyond the teacher's control and to focus on teacher behaviors that are "easy to change" (Borich, 1977).

While quantitative models tend to be underrepresented in teacher evaluation systems, the planning approach is strongly reflected in two of the most widely discussed evaluation models: Manatt's mutual benefit evaluation model and Redfern's management-by-objectives evaluation model (Darling-Hammond et al., 1983). Both models have been implemented in numerous schools and are characterized by centralized teaching standards and criteria and by goal setting and teacher involvement in the evaluation process. Both models are designed to address teacher improvement by promoting professional growth and by integrating individual performance objectives with school policies. Both models straddle the competency- and outcomes-based evaluation philosophies and are results oriented while they accommodate the numerous perspectives of "results."

Manatt's model includes four major steps: the administrative establishment of minimum teaching standards, diagnostic evaluation to determine instructors' status as compared to standards via a multimethod approach, cooperative establishment of measurable objectives for teacher improvement, and reevaluation leading to the establishment of new job targets. The steps in this model are basically similar to those included in Redfern's model. They are based on the management-by-objectives approach borrowed from the field of business. However, in Redfern's model, the teacher is involved in the development of mutually established objectives and standards prior to any evaluation. In this model, self-evaluation is more integral to the process (Darling-Hammond et al., 1983).

The models for teacher evaluation discussed previously are the seminal models on which most other models are based (Mitzel et al., 1982). These key models assume that teacher effectiveness should be evaluated in an environment in which teaching occurs in order to address stable consensual programmatic and instructional goals. However, Knapp (1982) contended that in practice, most teacher evaluation systems are based on other (often multiple) organizational demands. Evaluations must simultaneously strive to be legally "defensible" and address the needs to rate teachers, maintain staff morale and collegiality, and maintain organizational distance from environmental demands. Moreover, despite idealistic claims, most teacher evaluation schemes tend to call for improvements that require only modest, incremental change.

As part of the accountability reform movement in education, state legislatures and state school boards are mandating standards for curriculum, school accreditation, and student learning. These mandates are increasing the expectation for formal accountability at all levels of school personnel, from teachers to superintendents (DiPaola & Stronge, 2001).

An example of state-directed teacher evaluation is the process put in place by the Tennessee legislature in 1997 and revised in 2004 (Tennessee Department of Education, 2004). The goals and processes of evaluation of teachers are spelled out in detail at the state level.

The Tennessee model for teacher evaluation specified six domains for review: planning of instruction, teaching strategies, assessment and evaluation of student performance, creating and maintaining learning environment, professional growth, and communication with students, parents, and others. In each case the state guidelines specify detailed indicators, performances, and performance levels for the evaluating school administrator to use when reviewing the performance of the teacher (Tennessee Department of Education, 2004).

ACTIVITY 8.1

Teacher Evaluation

Addresses ISLLC Standards 1, 2, 3, and 4

You have been a teacher at Hamilton Consolidated High School for 8 years. You have a bachelor's degree in your discipline and a master's degree in secondary administration with a concentration in your discipline. Approximately 6 months ago, you were appointed as chair of your department, which consists of eight teachers besides yourself. Three of the faculty have less teaching experience than you do and are not tenured, and five of the faculty are tenured and have more experience than you do, including two persons who have taught for more than 20 years at the school.

Over the past 3 years, there has been increasing community interest in more accountability in the school system. Last month, the school board and the faculty union negotiated a new system of annual evaluations for all faculty in return for pay increases and substantial fringe benefit increases, including support for medical costs. The previous system called for annual evaluations for teachers for the first 3 years and then evaluations every 3 years thereafter once a tenure appointment was achieved.

The format for the first 3 years of faculty evaluations remains the same: classroom visits by a supervisor, a written self-evaluation by the faculty member, and a meeting with the supervisor where goals and objectives for the next year are worked out. The school board has agreed to leave the format of the evaluations for the tenured faculty to be developed by the teachers and the administration, with the stipulation that it must demonstrate effectiveness in improving teaching and learning in the classroom.

Your Task

Drawing on the information provided in this chapter and your experience as an employee and/or supervisor, design a proposed evaluation system to be presented to the faculty in your department for discussion. Prepare a presentation for your department members that will explain your proposed model and its rationale. Since you will need to develop agreement between the principal and the faculty for this model, what issues do you expect to have to negotiate between them before the model is accepted and implemented?

Evaluation: Administrators

Informally, administrators are evaluated continuously. The real issue is to determine why, when, and how formal evaluation should take place.

Arguments against formal evaluation include program diversity, role diversity, and evaluation participant diversity, all of which make it difficult to get a consistent evaluation system for persons with similar titles; lack of technique, which argues that no valid, reliable means of evaluating administrators has been devised; and politics, which argues that evaluation is used simply to bolster subjective impressions and political agendas when dealing with educational administrators.

Supporting arguments for formal evaluation of administrators include that diversity is a fact of academic life and must be coped with by devising a flexible system and attending to the problem of inappropriate data, that there are techniques that have been tested and validated over time, and that establishing clear criteria for evaluation and developing good descriptive data can minimize the impact of politics on the process.

The basis of effective administrative evaluation is to define clearly the role of the person being evaluated. Then the procedure, including appropriate instruments, should be designed to match the circumstances.

A national-level approach to the evaluation of administrators in education has been the development of standards for administrative performance by the Interstate School Leaders Licensure Consortium (ISLLC), which is discussed in the preface and elsewhere in this volume. Initiated in 1994, they have become a strong influence nationally, particularly since their adoption by the National Council for Accreditation of Teacher Education (NCATE) in 2003.

Purposes of Administrative Evaluation. Given the time-consuming and complex nature of administrator evaluation, the single most important step for any institution is to make sure that there are compelling reasons for starting a formal program of administrator evaluation. Reasons for an evaluation include establishing and attaining institutional goals; helping individual administrators improve their performance; making decisions on retention, salary, or promotion; increasing the effectiveness and efficiency of the administration as a team; keeping an inventory of personnel resources for reassignment or retraining; informing the governing body of the degree of congruence between institutional policy and institutional action; sharing governance; informing internal and external audiences on administrative effectiveness and worth; and conducting research on factors related to administrative effectiveness.

As with teacher evaluation, there are three major functions of administrative evaluation: formative, summative, and institutional. Formative functions are to serve as a basis for administrative development; help administrators compare their perceptions of performance with those of superiors, peers, and faculty; provide a vehicle for team building; and determine factors that influence effectiveness by analyzing evaluation data. Summative functions are to determine retention, promotion, and salary decisions and formulate and measure an administrator's specific program objectives. Institutional functions are to explicitly define desired administrative roles and relationships, assess strengths and weaknesses of administrative staff in order to assign them to appropriate tasks, determine the congruence between instructional policy and administrative action, extend participation in decision making by permitting staff input in the personnel process, serve as a model and inducement for other evaluative processes, and increase awareness of administrative efforts and achievements with external audiences, such as legislators and funding agencies.

Principles of Administrative Evaluation. Two basic principles underlie all effective evaluation: uniqueness, in that there needs to be mutual understanding of the unique set of job expectations under which the administrator works, and contextual interpretation, in that evaluation should be done within the context of the resources available to work with, the personal and situational obstacles encountered, and other factors beyond the administrator's control. Further criteria for effective evaluation are the principles of credibility, validity, and fairness.

Credibility. Concerned parties must have confidence that the procedures are appropriate and will yield meaningful results. To be credible, an evaluation needs to be developed with input from all parties affected. In addition, there needs to be a clear understanding that the evaluation has potential for producing positive results.

Validity. Validity of evaluations is based on their comprehensiveness and accuracy. To accomplish this, a description of relevant outcomes for each major activity of the evaluated person needs to be developed. Based on these criteria, the evaluation should measure meaningful change in persons that resulted from the administrator's efforts. Further, any evidence used in the evaluation must have a direct relationship to the criteria identified. Face value of the evidence is vital. Finally, there should be a representative sampling of respondents to the evaluation from as wide a variety of sources as is feasible.

Fairness. The evaluation must be open, even though it may create some problems in validity. Participants in the evaluation, both the evaluee and the respondents, should know what they are doing, why they are doing it, and how the results will be used. Further, the person being evaluated should not be held responsible for events or conditions beyond his or her control. If this person does not establish salary scales or assign levels of pay, that is not a reasonable area to include in the evaluation.

Administrative Evaluation Models. Evaluation of an administrator must be tied to the context of the person's work. Lists of the tasks and responsibilities of an administrator abound in the literature. A representative example would include accomplishment of goals and objectives, implementation of policy, organizing skills, position knowledge, quality of work, quantity of work, innovating or taking the initiative, professional development, judgment, facilities management, planning, budgeting, delegating, staffing, communications, decision making, evaluating, supervising, professionalism/integrity, reliability/dependability, personal qualities, attitude, fairness, human relations, public/internal relations, (conflict management, recognition of performance, and producing

reports. Not all these items are of equal value or even relevant for all administrative personnel, nor is their relative value fixed. It is the breadth of this list and its fluidity that make definition of the role in the specific case such a vital initial step.

Once the role is defined and the areas to be evaluated are selected, the standards against which the person is to be measured must be identified. Among these are the person's past performance, stated performance goals, and the performance expectations of others as workable standards. The performance of predecessors, the performance of others in similar positions, and the ideal standard should not be used since conditions may have changed.

Participants in the evaluation process should include as broad a representation as possible of those directly affected by the administrator's performance. These might include faculty, peers, supervisors (both upper-level administrators and boards), students, alumni, clerical staff, and members of the public, depending on the situation.

With these elements determined, the means of evaluation must be determined, including rating scales, growth contracting, ad hoc committee, and management by objectives.

Rating Scales. Rating instruments include forms, scales, and questionnaires. They may be a closed form with a limited number of preset answers or an open form. Although seemingly the least complicated of the models to use, rating scales are considered the most abused because of the skill needed for valid construction and proper interpretation of the results. Rating scales allow the user to classify information from various sources rapidly and efficiently. They are relatively easy to make confidential, allow for the classification of responses, and allow for longitudinal study when the same questions are used from year to year. However, professionally produced rating scales do not generally include institutional expectations for specific administrators, nor do they match the administrator's performance to institutional goals. Rating scales are often low in validity, subject to the biases of the respondents, and may relate only to the simplest and most quantifiable aspects of the evaluee's performance. Because they tend to fragment responses, they do not generally give an effective overall picture of the person being evaluated. To be effective, rating scales need to be developed for each person in his or her specific situation, with the attendant difficulty of producing a valid and reliable instrument.

Growth Contracting. Growth contracts are evaluation plans that allow the evaluee to think through and write out goals and objectives for the future. These goals and objectives are generally job related but often will include personal as well as professional development issues. Growth contracts are generally considered an acceptable means of demonstrating professional competence. They can lead to improved personal and professional growth. They have the advantage of specificity in setting goals when they are done properly.

Growth contracts generally contain four elements: self-evaluation, including a statement of past performance and a perception of strengths and weaknesses; areas for improvement, selected from those areas of difficulty discussed in the self-evaluation; plans for improvement, based on the areas selected for improvement and phrased as clearly defined objectives; and long-range goals, which allow the person to place the improvement plan into a larger context.

Ad Hoc Committee. The ad hoc committee is an extension of the screening committee concept. Ad hoc committees are appointed for a specific evaluation. They should be broadly representative of the constituency served by the administrator but should not be so large as to be ungainly. They should operate within stated rules and guidelines that are recorded in writing and open to all. Parameters for effective ad hoc committee evaluations include assurance of confidentiality and dignity, understanding that criticism as well as recognition is inherent in evaluation, open disclosure of the evaluative processes and criteria, understanding of the complexity of a valid evaluation, and understanding of the specifics of time and place, expectations at the time of appointment, and issues at the time the administrator was hired as they impinge on the administrator's work and evaluation.

Management by Objectives. Management by objectives (MBO) is a systems planning and management process that includes evaluation as a component. Evaluation (as performance review) follows naturally on the process steps of goal clarification, establishment of measurable objectives, unit and individual self-analysis, action planning, and implementation. Following implementation, evaluation, feedback, and renewed planning and implementation complete the system.

The premise of MBO is that one person cannot direct all the activities of the complex organization. Under the MBO model various administrators assume responsibility for a defined set of institutional outcomes for a defined period of time. At the end of that period the results are matched to previously stated measurable objectives and performance evaluation results.

For the purposes of this discussion, we simply note that its strengths and weakness stem from the same source: the people involved. If the participants are committed, clearly definable and measurable progress can be made toward specific individual and organizational goals. If the participants are not committed, MBO deteriorates to ineffectiveness.

As with teachers, many of the states have been taking a more direct role in evaluation of school administrators. New Jersey's Professional Standards for School Leaders are a direct adoption of the ISLLC standards discussed throughout this volume, with the addition of a seventh standard: "A school administrator is an educational leader who promotes the effective use of technology to maximize student learning and efficiently manage school operations" (New Jersey Association of School Administrators, 2002).

The Massachusetts State Department of Education operating under legislation CMR 35.00, Evaluation of Teachers and Administrators, has issued "Principles of Effective Administrative Leadership and Examples of Descriptors." This document spells out in detail expectations for school administrators. It contains six areas for consideration, each with a series of descriptors detailing the behavior of an effective leader. These include effective instructional leadership: working with others to create learning environments that address the needs of students; effective organizational leadership: creating a self-renewing organizational environment that consistently focuses on enabling all students to achieve high levels; effective administration and management: acting within legal and ethical guidelines to accomplish educational purposes and improve student learning; promotion of equity and appreciation of diversity: striving to ensure equity for all students and valuing diversity in the school environment; effective relationships within the community: interacting with the community responsibly to address the needs of students; and fulfillment of professional responsibilities: modeling professional behaviors that contribute to addressing the needs of students (Massachusetts Department of Education, n.d.).

In Connecticut, the state department of education has established standards of accountability through their School Leader Evaluation and Professional Development Guidelines of 2002. Using the Best Practice Model for School Leader Evaluation and Professional Development, the Connecticut approach calls for use of multiple sources of data concerning the school(s) that are systematically collected by teachers and administrators. The school leader analyzes these data and uses them as the basis of his or her own evaluation and professional development plan. The Best Practice Model incorporates four steps: a needs assessment identifying significant student learning needs, a school improvement plan based on the identified student learning needs, evaluation of the student learning results once the school improvement plan has been acted on, and identification of the next steps required to continue the process of student learning. (Connecticut State Department of Education, 2006).

Evaluation: Programs

Fink (1995) defined program evaluation as a "diligent investigation of a program's characteristics and merits [intended to] optimize outcomes, efficiency, and quality" (p. 2). Cronbach (1982) justified the need for eclectic methods in program evaluation. He explained that varied educational situations, epistemological perspectives, methodologies, and political concerns each demand unique consideration. Given this, no single model or methodology for educational program evaluation can hope to prevail. Cronbach's eclectic view also focuses the evaluation process distinctly in the political realm, as it is considered natural for people involved to structure the evaluation in ways that coincide with their own priorities, preferences, and abilities. The content and dynamics of any program evaluation will be determined by evaluators and other participants according to their motivation, intellectual outlooks, and expectations.

Perspectives on Program Evaluation. Theoretical and philosophical assumptions help shape any program evaluation. The scientific method of inquiry, which is based on hypothetic and deductive principles, has had a strong influence on education. Educational program evaluations in earlier eras demonstrated a distinctive slant toward hypothesis testing via the collection and analysis of "hard" or quantitative data, preferably obtained via experimental or quasi-experimental studies. However, with the proliferation of education programs during the 1960s and 1970s, it became obvious that rigorous study designs and strict insistence on quantitative methods was insufficient to meet the needs of educators, administrators, and policymakers. This led to an expanded use of qualitative methods and of less rigid, more interpretive evaluation models using qualitative techniques.

Ultimately, program evaluation involves a judgment of the value of a given endeavor. However, the issues to be addressed by evaluation must be clarified prior to selection an appropriate strategy and methodology. Mitzel et al. (1982) cited five questions that help clarify the issues inherent in a given program evaluation: is this thing any good? (an intrinsic value question), what is it good for? (an instrumental value question), is it better than something else? (a comparative value question), can I make it better? (an idealization value question), and is this the right thing to do? (a decision question).

Many purposes exist for conducting a program evaluation within a school or school district. Commonly identified purposes include understanding how students are doing in the educational system, identifying problems within the system, reviewing cost-effectiveness, and assessing the impact of attempts to improve the system.

Identification of purpose helps clarify selection of models and methods. For example, addressing an idealization value would be best served by both formative

ACTIVITY 8.2

Administrator Evaluation

Addresses ISLLC Standards 1, 2, 3, and 4

You are the superintendent of schools in the Hamilton Consolidated School District. Your district includes five elementary schools, two middle schools, and a senior high school that provides college preparation, general, and vocational academic programs. You have held the superintendency for 6 years and have enjoyed general support from the school board and the community.

Your administrative staff consists of an assistant superintendent for curriculum, a business manager, a personnel director, a principal and assistant principal in each secondary school, and a principal in each elementary school. Their experience on the job ranges from one building principal who is in her first year to the business manager who is in his fifth year to one junior high principal and the high school principal who have been in their positions for more than 10 years. Department chairs, the director of vocational programs, the director of special education, and the director of the evening school are all faculty appointments and so remain within the faculty union.

Six months ago, the school board elections brought in a new majority, including a new chairman, that promised the community improved accountability from the school system. In the 6 months since election, they have negotiated an increase in formal evaluations for tenured teachers with the faculty union and directed you to develop a formal system of evaluation for the administrative staff of the district, who are appointed annually by the board on your recommendation. Historically, administrative evaluations in your district have been relatively informal, generally leading to recommendations for reappointment. In your 6 years as superintendent, you have not felt it necessary to refuse any administrator reappointment.

Your Task

Prior to starting to work on this activity, interview a member of the school administration or school board in your local school district to determine what is being done about evaluation of school administrators in your district. Also do a cursory search of the literature. Then complete this activity as directed.

1. Describe how you would go about establishing a working committee from among your administrative staff to develop an evaluation model that would be appropriate for the various roles that your administrators play. Assuming equal competence among the staff for this task, who should serve on the committee? Why?

2. Develop a charge for this committee that will produce an evaluation model that will provide you and the school board with evidence of effective leadership on the part of the evaluated persons. Your goal is to demonstrate to the board that your district is working toward becoming an effective learning organization.

3. Describe a likely evaluation model that might emerge from the committee and develop a presentation for you and the committee chair to make to the school board and separately to the administrative staff that will gain each group's support. Since you will need to develop agreement with the school board and acceptance from the administrators for this model, what issues do you expect to have to negotiate between them before the model is accepted and implemented?

and summative methodologies and would usually require a comparison against a standard. However, a decision question, such as developing a new program, may not entail any existing standard. In that case, no comparative judgment could be made.

Value assumptions are often determined by external perspectives. In many cases, programs that have federal or private funding bases may require some form of strict accountability to demonstrate effective utilization of funding. In such cases the

political-economic and cost-benefit perspectives are most commonly used to determine the worth of a given program.

The political-economic perspective focuses on the principle of utilitarianism and implies that program value can be determined by the benefits, the greatest worth or utility. However, social interventionists have questioned the utilitarian perspective by noting that occasionally concern should be focused on subgroups within the population. Therefore, the principle of utility has been expanded using five criteria that address the distribution of benefits: *equity*, emphasis on the equalization of outcomes or the minimization of individual differences; *Pareto optimality*, achieving outcomes for all, regardless of individual gains; *majority*, majority distribution of gain, even if those gains are minimal; *minimax*, addressing those at the bottom or in the most need, regardless of the status of the majority; and *dominance*, making comparisons across competing groups in terms of outcome measures and implying that those evidencing better concluding measures experience better programs.

Another common method to determine the worth of a given program is a cost-benefit approach, or cost-effectiveness analysis as applied to educational issues. This approach transcends the outcomes for a given group and explores the consequences of such distributions. The field of economics has derived a variety of methods that accommodate the conversion of values to costs and benefits. But given the diverse thinking of multiple parties typically involved in most programs, consensus on the costs and benefits corresponding to a specific value can be problematic (Levin & McEwan, 2001, 2002). Debate over the worth of a program occasionally results in examination of intrinsic versus pragmatic values, as shown through classical, organizational, or bureaucratic decisions.

Program Evaluation Approaches and Models.

Mitzel et al. (1982) contended that the field of educational program evaluation is dominated by four major evaluation viewpoints: experimental, eclectic, descriptive, and cost-benefit. Table 8.2 compares the characteristics of these four orientations along 10 dimensions noted in the left-hand column. Distinctive features of these four orientations may help us understand program evaluation more thoroughly.

An experimentalist attempts to discover causal links between a program and its outcomes. The eclectics draw on experimental or quasi-experimental designs that accommodate intervening variables, such as contextual constraints, and search for multiple causality to generate probable explanations of reality. The describers reject experimental designs, contending that meaningful data can be obtained only through in-depth, contextual descriptions of the program and through personal testimony. The cost-benefit analyzer attempts to gauge a program's economic worth. However, rather than adopt any single generic approach and attempt to adapt it to the needs of specific applications, evaluators may want to utilize a mixed evaluation approach, one that is suitable for the program environment and its sociopolitical context. While there is no single generalizable model for conducting program evaluations and there is debate over what can be classified as a model, constructing a model gives direction to evaluation design and provides a mechanism for explicitly or implicitly conveying the evaluation assumptions and evaluand relationships. For this reason, model building for program evaluation is extensive, and most evaluations are planned with one model or another in mind.

Like the educational evaluation models discussed earlier, models for program evaluation take various forms. A comprehensive classification scheme for program evaluation models was provided by House (1978) in a taxonomy. This taxonomy, shown in Table 8.3, includes eight basic model types that are applicable to program assessment and evaluations.

The limitations and complications regarding general evaluation discussed earlier exist for program evaluation models. Program evaluations must therefore be designed with reference to certain external factors and constraints in addition to the primary evaluands. In education, program evaluations include instructional effectiveness information gained through teacher evaluation. As noted by Stufflebeam (1990), it is "fundamentally impossible to remove personnel evaluation from sound program evaluation" (p. 104). In the educational environment, that directs attention to teacher evaluation.

Examples of Program Evaluation Models.

Without attempting an expansive presentation of program evaluation models, it is at least possible to consider briefly a few of the more prominent all-purpose models that educational administrators might find most useful and that have had an extensive history of use.

TABLE 8.2

Four Methodological Approaches to Program Evaluation

	Approaches			
Dimensions	**Experimentalists**	**Eclectics**	**Describers**	**Benefit-Cost Analyzers**
Proponents	Cook and Campbell	Bryk	Parlett and Hamilton	Haller
	Riecken and Borich	Cronbach and Associates	Patton	Levin
	Rivlin and Timpane	R. S. Weiss and Rein	Stake	Thompson
Philosophical base	Positivist	Modified positivist to pragmatic	Phenomenological	Logical/analytical
Disciplinary base	Psychology	Psychology; sociology; political science	Sociology; anthropology	Economics; accounting
Focus of methodology	Identify causal links	Augment search for causal links with process and contextual data	Describe program holistically and from perspective of participants	Judge worth of program in terms of costs and benefits
Methodology	Experimental and quasi-experimental designs	Quasi-experimental designs; case studies; descriptions	Ethnography; case studies; participant observation; triangulation	Benefit-cost analysis
Variables	Predetermined as input–output	Predetermined plus emerging	Emerging in course of evaluation	Predetermined
Control or comparison group	Yes	Where possible	Not necessary	Yes
Participants' role in carrying out evaluation	None	None to interactive	Varies (may react to field notes)	None
Evaluator's role	Independent of	Cooperative	Interactive	Independent of program
Political pressures (internal–external)	Controlled in design; or ignored	Accommodated	Describe	Ignore
Focus of evaluation report	Render "go/no-go" decision	Interpret and recommend for program improvement	Present holistic portrayal program in process	Render judgment

Adapted from Mitzel et al., 1982, p. 600.

TABLE 8.3
Taxonomy of Major Program Evaluation Models

Model	Proponents	Major Audiences	Assumes Consensus on:	Methodology	Outcome	Typical Questions
Systems analysis	Rivlin	Economists, managers	Goals; known cause and effect; quantified variables	PPBS: linear programming; planned variation; cost–benefit analysis	Efficiency	Are the expected effects achieved? Can the effects be achieved more economically? What are the most efficient programs?
Behavioral objectives	Tyler, Popham	Managers, psychologists	Prespecified; objectives; quantified outcome variables	Behavioral objectives; achievements tests	Productivity; accountability	Are the students achieving the objectives? Is the teacher producing?
Decision making	Stufflebeam, Alkin	Decision makers, especially administrators	General goals: criteria	Surveys, questionnaires, interviews; natural variation	Effectiveness; quality control	Is the program effective? What parts are effective?
Goal free	Scriven	Consumers	Consequences: criteria	Bias control; logical analysis; modus operandi	Consumer choice, social utility	What are all the effects?
Art criticism	Eisner, Kelly	Connoisseurs, consumers	Critics, standards	Critical review	Improved standards	Would a critic approve this program?
Accreditation	North Central Association	Teacher, public	Criteria, panel, procedures	Review by panel; self study	Professional acceptance	How would professionals rate this program?
Adversary	Owens, Levine, Wolf	Jury	Procedures and judges	Quasilegal procedures	Resolution	What are the arguments for and against the program?
Transaction	Stake, Smith, MacDonald, Parlett-Hamilton	Client, practitioners	Negotiation; activities	Case studies, interviews, observations	Understanding, diversity	What does the program look like to different people?

Source: Adapted from House (1978).

One type of total evaluation model is the *CIPP model*, developed by Daniel Stufflebeam and others (Stufflebeam, 1990; Worthen, 1973). The CIPP model for educational program evaluation is billed as a total model for several reasons. First, it compels evaluators to consider four integral areas of concern, indicated by the letters C-I-P-P: context evaluation, focused on the program context and evaluation situation; input evaluation, focused on the resources and human energies pertaining to the evaluation problem(s); process evaluation, focused on the internal program dynamics and interactions related to the evaluation problem; and product evaluation, focused on program products and accomplishments. The main conceptual aspects of the CIPP model include the relationships among program decisions, program activities, and program evaluation influences. The CIPP model and its nearest cousins can be used for both formative and summative evaluations. It is best regarded as a decision-making model, strongest when used in a formative mode to plan and implement change.

The CIPP model is multifaceted, applicable to evaluations of programs, projects, personnel, products, institutions, and systems, according to Stufflebeam (2002). It has undergone five revisions, starting with the first publication in 1966, which focused on the need for process as well as product. The second version in 1967 included context, input, process, product, and needs evaluations and emphasized goal setting guided by context evaluation. The third version came out in 1971 and placed the evaluation in a systems framework. The fourth version came out in 1972 and developed summative as well as formative applications. The fifth version is illustrated by the CIPP evaluation model checklist discussed here (Stufflebeam, 2002).

The checklist is intended to drive an assessment of long-term projects. It contains the following elements. (a) Contractual agreements: establish explicit advance agreements between the client and the evaluator, and updated these during the evaluation. (b) Context evaluation: review the context in which the program and the evaluation take place and determine the impact of the context on the evaluation both. (c) Input evaluation: assess competing strategies for meeting the needs of the client and the costs

in financial and other resources of the alternatives and select an alternative. (d) Process evaluation: monitor, document, and assess program activities. (e) Impact evaluation: assess the program's ability to reach the target audience and delivering the results desired. (f) Effectiveness evaluation: assess the quality and significance of the program's outcomes. (g) Sustainability evaluation: assess the extent to which the program's contributions are successfully built into the institution and continue over time. (h) Transportability evaluation: assess the extent to which the program has been (or could be) successfully adapted and applied elsewhere. (i) Metaevaluation: assess the evaluation's adherence to pertinent standards of sound evaluation. (j) Final synthesis report: report findings to client, including what was attempted and accomplished, what was learned, and the overall assessment of the program (Stufflebeam, 2002).

A similar type of model to CIPP is the Provus model (Saylor & Alexander, 1981). This model is developed in five stages. At each stage input, process, and output are considered: Stage 1, design: is the design adequate at the input, process, and output levels? Stage 2, installation: is the installation true to its purpose at the input, process, and output levels? Stage 3, process: what process adjustments are (or need to be) made at the input, process, and output levels? Stage 4, product: is the product appropriate at the input, process, and output levels? Stage 5, program comparison: what is the cost-benefit analysis at the input, process, and output levels? (Saylor & Alexander, 1981).

Critical features of Provus as an example of the discrepancy evaluation model include comparison of a standard to performance with recognition and resolution of discrepancies; recognition of planning, implementing, monitoring, and assessment functions; the concept of stage recycling; and development of a design and evaluation plan for each stage (Morra, 1978).

Like the CIPP model, the Provus model can be regarded as a planning and decision-making model, useful for monitoring program innovations. Evaluation is both formative and summative in the Provus model so that it can be viewed as an ongoing event that produces information needed for decision

You are a teacher of foreign languages in a large urban high school. The district has received a significant federal grant to strengthen its academic programs, and one element of the grant supports establishment of a computer laboratory. You have been named as director of the lab.

As part of the responsibilities of your new position, you are required to develop an evaluation system that will demonstrate to the federal funding agency and to the local district that the laboratory is an effective instructional tool for a variety of clients.

Your Task

Develop an evaluation model for the computer lab that will demonstrate what services the lab is providing and how effective they are for each type of client served. Prepare a presentation for the school board that will demonstrate that effectiveness.

---

making from the beginning to the end of a project or change attempt.

Stake's (1969) congruence-contingency model, like the CIPP and Provus models, seeks to provide as complete an understanding of program contexts and problems as possible. It gathers information from as many sources as are available. These include antecedents or conditions existing before the evaluation begins such as student and teacher characteristics, curricular context, instructional materials, physical plant, school organization, and community context; transactions or interactions among students, teachers, materials, and the environment, such as communication flow, time allocation, sequence of events, reinforcement schedules, and social climate; and outcomes, such as student achievement, student attitudes, student motor skills, effects on teachers, and institutional effects. This information is then considered in the light of what was intended, what was observed, applicable standards, and judgments of what is found. Data collection using the Stake model tends to be naturalistic because it relies on in-depth interviews and status reviews.

The analytic framework of Stake's (1969) model seeks to compare intended program conditions or logical contingencies to program conditions that are actually found to exist (empirical contingencies). If congruence is lacking between what is intended and what actually exists within a program, the "gap" or problem indicated can become the focus of corrective action.

Kirkpatrick's four levels of learning evaluation model was first published in 1959. It is considered a standard in the human resources and training fields and was updated in 1998 by Kirkpatrick (Chapman, n.d.). The model incorporates four levels of training evaluation: the reaction of the student to the training, the student learning resulting from the training, the change in student behavior resulting from the training, and the effects on the business or environment resulting from the trainee's posttreatment behavior (Naugle, Naugle, & Naugle, 2000).

The program evaluation models discussed in this section are intended to help educational administrators appreciate the theoretical and practical implications of model building that have taken place in the evaluation field.

Standards and Requirements for Educational Evaluation

During the past 40 years, there have been substantial efforts in the United States to control and ensure the quality of evaluation endeavors, a trend that has accompanied the emergence and growth of educational evaluation as a distinct discipline. In 1974, representatives of the American Psychological Association, the American Education Research Association, and the National Council of Measurement in Education created a task force to consider how tests might be used in program evaluation. The task force became known as the Joint

Committee on Standards for Educational Evaluation (JCSEE) (Sanders, 1999). One result of these efforts was the document produced by the JCSEE titled "Standards for Evaluations of Educational Programs, Projects and Materials" issued in 1981. The document sets forth program evaluation standards in four major areas: utility standards, feasibility standards, propriety standards, and accuracy standards. Moreover, the document promotes the view that evaluation itself should be subject to quality assurance efforts (Stufflebeam, 1990).

Revised in 1994, the *utility standards* are intended to guide the evaluation process so that it will be timely, informative, and influential and address the needs of the audiences to be served by the process. The utility standards focus on seven areas: stakeholder identification, or specifying the group to be served so that their needs can be addressed; evaluator credibility, which requires that the person conducting the evaluation be both trustworthy and ethical; information scope and selection, which suggests that the evaluation information gathered should sufficiently address pertinent questions about the program being evaluated and be responsive to the needs of the audiences served; values identification, which requires careful description of the perspectives, procedures, and rationale used for interpretation of findings so that the reasons for corresponding judgments are clear; report clarity, which specifies that the evaluation report should clearly describe the program being evaluated and its context and the evaluation's purposes, procedures, and findings; report dissemination, which specifies that interim findings and reports should be given to intended users so that they can be used in a timely fashion; and evaluation impact, which suggests that evaluations should be planned and conducted in a manner that fosters appropriate follow-through by the audiences served by the process (JCSEE, 1994). These utility standards require that evaluators give priority to the interests of clients and stakeholders and that evaluators satisfy the intended purposes of evaluations, even if it requires that they supersede their own interests or methodologies.

The *feasibility standards* are designed to ensure that program evaluations are realistic, prudent, diplomatic, and cost effective, particularly since such assessment efforts occur in a political environment. The feasibility standards advocate practical procedures to ensure that the evaluation process is minimally disruptive, political viability to ensure that the process is planned and conducted in a manner that promotes cooperation among the various constituencies while inhibiting the misuse of the results, and cost-effectiveness to ensure that resource expenditures are justified, given the value and adequacy of the information generated by the process (JCSEE, 1994).

Propriety standards reflect the American value system. They are intended to ensure that an evaluation will be conducted legally, ethically, and with regard to the welfare of those involved in evaluation and those affected by the results. The propriety standards advocate service orientation so that the evaluation will address and effectively serve the needs of all targeted participants; formal agreements, done in writing and specifying what is to be done, how, by whom, and when, so that all parties are obligated to abide by the agreement or formally renegotiate it; rights of human subjects so that evaluations will be designed and conducted in a manner respectful and protective of the rights and welfare of human subjects; human interactions that respect the dignity and worth of all persons associated with an evaluation and no participant feels threatened or harmed; complete and fair assessment, recording the strengths and weaknesses of the program being evaluated so that strengths can be built on and problems addressed; disclosure of a full set of findings and pertinent limitations to persons affected by the evaluations and any others with legal rights to the results; open and honest approach to conflict of interest issues so that they do not compromise the evaluation and its results; and fiscal responsibility so that the evaluator's allocation and expenditure of resources reflects sound accountability, prudence, appropriateness, and ethical responsibility (JCSEE, 1994).

Worthen, Worthen, and Sanders (1987) also suggested that one of the most useful means of addressing evaluation propriety is through an evaluation contract that can protect the evaluator against arbitrary or unethical actions by a client while protecting the client from an unscrupulous evaluator.

Accuracy standards address whether an evaluation has produced sound information that determines the merit of the program being evaluated. Stufflebeam (1990) contended that the rating of an evaluation against these accuracy standards provides a good indication of the evaluation's overall "truth value." The 1994 accuracy standards advocate clear and accurate program documentation; context analysis in sufficient detail to show likely influences on the program; detailed monitoring and description of the evaluation's purposes and procedures; defensible information sources described in sufficient detail to allow assessment of their adequacy; information-gathering procedures producing information valid and reliable for the purposes of the study; systematic review of information that is collected, processed, and reported for the evaluation so that errors may be found and corrected; analysis of quantitative and qualitative information so that evaluation questions are answered effectively; justifiable conclusions so that stakeholders can assess them; impartial reporting, with distortion caused by personal feelings and/or biases of any party guarded against; and metaevaluation, formative and summative evaluations using these standards of the program evaluation itself so that stakeholders can closely examine the strengths and weaknesses of the evaluation (JCSEE, 1994).

In 1981, when *Standards for Evaluations of Educational Programs, Projects and Materials*, was first released, the JCSEE realized that standards for personnel evaluation were also needed, as these could not be logically separated from other forms of evaluation (Stufflebeam, 1990). Responding to the sensitivity of personnel evaluations because of concerns over support from teachers' organizations, the *Personnel Evaluation Standards* document was not initially released until 1988 (JCSEE, 1988). The personnel evaluation standards are classified into similar categories used for presentation of the program evaluation standards (i.e., utility, feasibility, propriety, and accuracy). However, some of the topics out of necessity differ between the two sets of standards. For example, the program evaluation propriety standard of full and frank disclosure is not included in the personnel standards because of confidentiality requirements; similarly, service orientation (i.e., requiring that evaluators show concern for the rights of students to be taught well), a key entry in personnel evaluation standards, is not included in the program standards.

In 1989, the JCSEE became an accredited committee of the American National Standards Institute (ANSI). ANSI approval of standards proposed by the JCSEE means that those standards become American national standards internationally as well as in the United States (Sanders, 1999). Under this arrangement, the 1994 Program Evaluation Standards became the first American National Standards published by the JCSEE.

In 2003, the JCSEE released a third set of standards focused on student evaluation (JCSEE, 2003). These standards follow the same overall design as the two previous sets, with focus on propriety, utility, feasibility, and accuracy as they apply to student evaluations.

It is noteworthy that none of these evaluation standards promote or endorse any single approach to evaluation. They encourage the use of a variety of methods and approaches to meet the needs of the evaluation project and client. The overall message in these important documents on standards is that all evaluators should strive to make their evaluations useful, feasible, ethical, and accurate, regardless of the evaluation situation or targets. These standards may be most beneficial when examined a priori and used as guidelines for designing evaluations.

Evaluation and Accountability

From the point of view of the general public, educational accountability has become an increasing issue as educational costs have risen and as there has been growing concern about the competency of graduates of the K–12 system. The issue of equity exists as well. Closing the achievement gap among ethnic groups is a major social policy concern and a major motivation for the passage of the No Child Left Behind Act of 2001. While formal educational evaluation is a growing profession as noted previously, informal evaluation of the educational system by the general public takes place on an ongoing basis. The term *accountability* implies someone or something to be accountable for performance. From the public point of view, in the case of the publicly supported education system that someone or something is the taxpaying public.

In its broadest sense, accountability incorporates many of the elements discussed previously. Accountability implies existence of a known standard against which performance is to be measured, research to determine what performance is taking place, assessment/measurement to determine the level of that performance, and evaluation or judgment of the nature or level of the performance when matched against the standard expected.

In the public arena, accountability is not generally held to the careful standards of validity and reliability that are sought in the work of the professional educator or educational evaluator. However, the public's sense of accountability can carry great political weight and can be highly influential in decision making both in educational systems and in government.

Two major national concerns have been the achievement gap between American minority and nonminority students and the performance of American students when compared to students of other nations. The achievement gap between the performance of African American and Latino students and that of nonminority students has been a long-standing problem in American education. It had decreased during the 1970s and 1980s, but in the 1990s those improvements ceased. Increasing gaps in reading achievement among 17-year-olds and math achievement among 13-year-olds were identified, for example. By the end of the 1990s there were significant differences in the rates of high school completion and movement to further education. In the 18–24-year-old group, about 90% of whites and 94% of Asians either completed high school or earned a general equivalency diploma. For African Americans the rate was 81%, for Latinos 63%. African Americans are only about half as likely to complete a bachelor's degree as white graduates; Latinos are only about one-third as likely. (Haycock, 2001).

The International Association for the Evaluation of Educational Achievement began assessing international student achievement in the 1960s. Assessment included performance in civic education, foreign languages, literature, reading comprehension, and the sciences. In most areas of assessment, American students ranked near the middle among nations included in the studies. Later studies, such as the Program for International Student Assessment, the Progress in International Reading Literacy Study, and the Third International Mathematics and Science Study, confirmed these general findings (Ornstein & Levine, 2006). From public discussion about these conditions and findings a range of educational reform efforts have arisen at the state and local levels, including standards-based education and the back-to-basics movement.

These concerns and efforts gave rise to federal Public Law 107-110, the No Child Left Behind Act of 2001 (NCLB), which authorized a group of federal programs intended to improve the nation's elementary and secondary educational systems and increased accountability standards for the various states, school districts, and schools. The theory underlying the act is standards-based educational reform, a set of beliefs that establishing high expectations and goals within the educational system will lead to success for all students. In this case the public sense of accountability was expressed through governmental action.

The NCLB contains several major provisions of relevance to this chapter's focus on evaluation:

1. *Adequate yearly progress:* The various states are required to create an accountability system of assessments, graduation rates, and other measures. Schools are required to make adequate yearly progress as determined by the state in raising the achievement levels of target subgroups, such as African Americans, low-income students, and special education students. All students must meet proficiency requirements by the 2013–2014 academic year. Assistance is provided to students who are in schools that do not improve in these efforts. Schools receiving Title 1 federal funds to supplement their budgets that do not meet these standards are identified as "in need of improvement." In such a case the school is required to offer parents the option to send their children to another school, to develop an approved plan for improvement, and to make changes necessary to implement the plan, which may include tutorial programs in the private sector.

2. *Teacher quality:* The NCLB required that by the end of the 2005–2006 school year, all teachers be "highly qualified." A highly qualified teacher is defined in the act as one who has met the state's certification and licensure requirements. Both new and experienced teachers must hold at least a bachelor's degree and pass relevant state competency exams. The mandated 2005–2006 deadline was not met. As of May 2006, no state had met the requirement, and nine states (Alaska, Delaware, Idaho, Iowa, Minnesota, Montana, Nebraska, North Carolina, and Washington) and Washington, D.C., and Puerto Rico were in danger of losing federal aid for failing to make a sufficient effort to comply with the provision (Safier, 2007).

3. *Student testing:* Student progress is measured annually in reading and math in grades 3 through 8 and at least once in high school. Student progress in science will have been tested once during grades 3 to 5, 6 to 9, and 10 to 12 starting in the 2007–2008 school year. Selection and/or development of the tests is left to state discretion.

4. *Parent involvement:* States are required to publicly issue report cards detailing the status of schools and districts. Parents must be informed if their children are being taught by a teacher who does not meet the "highly qualified" standard. Schools are required to involve parents in their school improvement processes.

5. *Scientifically based research:* Schools must use "scientifically based research" strategies in the classroom and in professional development programs for staff. Scientifically based research is defined as large quantitative studies using control groups as opposed to partially or entirely qualitative or ethnographic studies.

The NCLB has been controversial. While it was initially passed in Congress almost unanimously with strong bipartisan support, controversy developed later, not over the intent but what many have seen as heavy-handed administration of the program.

Central to the education standards movement, the testing process has also been central to the debate over the NCLB. On the one hand, there is a call for uniformity of testing (i.e., national development of tests) because the rigor among states varies greatly (Kahlenberg, 2007). On the other hand, there is a call for testing controlled at the state rather than the federal level on the grounds that a single national testing process would be too narrowly focused and not responsive to state and local level issues and concerns (Au, 2007; Klein, 2007).

Proponents of the legislation have claimed that the act encourages accountability in the public schools, provides better educational options for parents, and helps reduce the achievement gap between minority and white students. Federally mandated standardized testing is claimed to be the means for achieving these ends. Some of the statements of general support for NCLB, however, do call for specific changes in the act (Lecker, 2005; "Poll Shows Broad Support for NCLB," 2007; McKeon, 2007).

Opponents of the legislation (or its implementation as currently seen) have argued that it is not effective because it has not been adequately funded on the federal level; encourages schools, districts, and states to manipulate test results to their advantage; is excessively based on standardized testing; encourages setting low educational targets by schools, districts, and states because of the implications for not meeting those targets; defines evaluation too narrowly; and establishes greater federal control over education rather than reducing federal impact (Guilfoyle, 2006; Houston, 2007; Meier, 2002; Safier, 2007; Weaver, 2006).

Based on four years of monitoring the NCLB and its emphasis on test-driven accountability, the Center on Educational Policy, a national advocacy group for effectiveness in the public schools, has identified a series of effects resulting from the effort. These include state and local officials report that student achievement on state tests is rising; schools are spending more time on reading and math but sometimes at the expense of subjects not tested; schools are paying more attention to the alignment of curriculum and instruction and analyzing test date more closely; low-performing schools are undergoing makeovers rather than radical restructuring; schools and teachers have made progress in demonstrating that teachers meet NCLB qualifications, but there is question whether this will improve the quality of teaching; students are being tested more frequently; schools are paying more attention to achievement gaps and the learning needs of particular groups of students; the percentage of schools on state "needs improvement" lists has been steady; the federal government is playing a bigger role in education nationally; and NCLB requirements have meant that state governments and school districts have expanded their roles in school operations but often without adequate federal funding to discharge their duties (Jennings & Rentner, 2006).

Beyond the NCLB, efforts at establishing standards intended to improve the performance of the educational system also have been directed at specific elements of the system, including teachers, administrators, programs, and secondary schools and colleges. Some of these include the following.

For teachers, state certification and licensure standards have existed, but they are specific to the individual states and vary from state to state. In addition to the NCLB demand for highly qualified teachers, for the first time there is a national certification for teachers. Sponsored by the National Board for Professional Teaching Standards, which was formed in 1987, the National Board certification is a voluntary advanced teaching credential that goes beyond state certification and licensure. Offered to teachers with at least three years experience, it is intended to supplement rather than replace state certification. Candidates take part in a yearlong assessment of their teaching practices. National Board certification requires demonstration of effective teaching and development of an extensive professional portfolio, among other activities (Harman, 2002).

While some districts have recognized nationally certified teachers with salary adjustments, the effectiveness of national certification in improving student performance is currently a matter of discussion. The results of recent studies are mixed (Viadero, 2007), with some finding improvement in student performance (South Carolina State Department of Education, 2005) and others not finding improvement (McColskey & Stronge, 2006). It is early in the history of the national certification process, so it is reasonable to expect that this picture will be clarified in the future.

Two examples of establishing accountability standards for school administrators are the ISLLC, which is referenced in this book, and the Educational Leadership Constituent Council (ELCC).

ISLLC is a program of the Council of Chief State School Officers. The program was established in 1996 and was intended to provide "a common core of knowledge, dispositions, and performances that would help link leadership more forcefully to productive schools and enhanced educational outcomes" (Murphy & Shipman, 1996). The program defines six standards for school leaders that have been further discussed in the preface to this volume. Those standards are intended to be compatible with the National Council for the Accreditation of Teacher Education (NCATE) Curriculum Guidelines for school administration and a variety of reports on the future of school leadership (Murphy & Shipman, 1996).

Approved in their final form in 1996, the ISLLC standards have exerted a good deal of influence on the profession of school administration (Murphy, 2005). In fact, the standards have been accepted by a majority of the states as guides in developing their certification standards for administrators.

The ELCC is a set of standards for preparation and development of school principals created jointly by NCATE and ISLLC. These standards address the process of developing a school within its political, social, economic, legal, and cultural context (Wilmore, 2002).

In both of these cases (the ISLLC and ELCC standards), an attempt has been made to provide a set of known standards for the performance of school leaders that are qualitative in nature but could be supported with quantitative data.

The NCLB is an example of establishing public accountability for the public schools. As can be seen from the discussion in this chapter, the major emphasis in that effort is on the elementary schools in an attempt to establish a base of academic success for students to build on in their further education. In addition, most secondary schools and colleges participate in multistate (regional) accreditation associations. Eight regional associations exist in the United States. These schools and colleges participate in a self-assessment process designed to provide accountability for their programs. The process involves an extensive self-evaluation based on an established set of institutional goals and objectives. This evaluation normally takes a full year. The self-evaluation is followed by a validation review conducted by representatives of peer institutions in states other than the school or college being reviewed. The results of the self-evaluation and the peer review are then considered by the regional association's governing body, and action is taken to provide full or partial accreditation or to request further action toward accreditation for the institution under review. Accreditation is the means by which schools and colleges use self-regulation to ensure quality and improvement. Using the Middle States Association of College and Secondary Schools Policy Statement as an example, the purpose of the evaluation is to help an institution "analyze its functions, appraise its educational effectiveness, and discover means by which its work can be strengthened" (Middle States Association on Higher Education, 1998).

Gross and Goertz (2005) looked at the impact of state accountability policies on a sample of 48 American high schools drawn from 36 school districts in six states. The conclusions that came from this study were that accountability can be effective in bringing change in high schools. The district was the most powerful influence on how the high school responded to external demands for accountability in states with both strong and weak accountability perspectives. Building the capacity of districts and schools to instigate, manage, and monitor the changes resulting from responding to external accountability demands is key to success.

The Future

Predicting the future of educational evaluation is as risky as predicting the future of the educational effort in general. However, some things seem reasonably clear. As long as education remains a human process, it will remain imperfect and open to improvement. As long as education remains a broad public concern, it will continue to be subject to scrutiny from multiple constituencies. As long as education remains a complex system, it will need to consider evaluation and feedback as legitimate components of that system.

The assessment of the performance of educational institutions has been increasing. This has taken clear form in the student outcomes assessment provisions of the NCLB. Developed in part as an extension of management by objectives, outcomes assessment has drawn widespread public and professional attention. In one form or another, its emphasis on defining prospective outcomes and then looking closely at the results can be expected to figure strongly in the future design of the overall educational enterprise.

If we use earlier discussions as a reference point, we must realize that, to date, evaluation mechanisms have been highly systematic. They lack the critical systemic emphasis and action orientation that ties evaluation to its other subsystems. Evaluation systems need to be rethought as the era of the knowledge worker unfolds (Drucker, 1993), as society becomes more global (Friedman, 2006), and as we recognize the interdependence of seemingly disconnected systems and subsystems.

With increasing emphasis on accountability, Worthen et al. (1987) foresaw a series of trends that they anticipated would have an impact on the future of program evaluation, including increasing emphasis on internal evaluation, expanded use of combined quantitative and qualitative methods, preference for multiple-method models, introduction and development of theory-based models, and increasing concern over ethical issues in conducting program evaluations.

Evaluation is and will continue to be pervasive in the field of education. Evaluation aids in improving the overall enterprise (i.e., personnel performance, student and program outcomes, and school- and systemwide success). Even so, the benefits of evaluation must be balanced against corresponding limitations. As a general rule, evaluations do not yield generalizable results. They are time dependent since most objects of the evaluation are not static. Although they may be useful in diagnosing problems, they may not be help in identifying and developing appropriate solutions. In addition, both evaluators and their clients must be sensitive to relevant ethical issues, such as informed participation, and be able to weigh and make use of evaluation results in arriving at educational judgments and decisions.

Problems are inherent in both program and personnel evaluation applications. For example, program evaluations often do not involve curricula appraisal; there is little empirical evidence regarding the efficacy of alternative evaluation plans, techniques, or components common in most models; evaluators rarely call in outside expertise, even when warranted; and discipline-prone evaluators sometimes tend to cluster around their respective evaluation banners like "vassals in a form of provincial bondage" (Worthen, 1990, p. 47). Many of these faults apply to teacher and administrative evaluations, but major problems in these areas occur for other reasons as well. No definitive agreement exists regarding effective teaching competencies, behaviors, and skills, and administrative tasks and responsibilities vary greatly, even under the same job titles. In addition, most personnel evaluations are conducted by administrators or supervisors who have little or no training in evaluation, and they may lack the knowledge needed to make informed, eclectic decisions in planning and carrying out the evaluation process (Walberg & Haertel, 1990).

In view of the problems that exist in the realm of applied evaluation, there is a significant need for empirical research, particularly with regard to instructor applications. This need is supported by an observation by Worthen et al. (1987) that the literature regarding educational systems shows large deficits on topics concerning effective educational evaluation.

In the future, as evaluation of the educational system and its various components continue to be a significant issue for all, professional educators and public alike, these issues will need to be addressed.

Summary and Fundamental Concepts

Interest has been increasing in educational evaluation because of rising costs and increasing taxpayer/community expectations for competence in all persons regardless of ethnic group or economic status completing educational programs and going on to higher education or the job market. The NCLB requires school districts to participate in complex evaluation programs, resulting in a greater use of a variety of evaluative techniques and the development of educational evaluation as a professional field.

Evaluation is defined as the systematic collection of evidence leading to judgment of value with a view to action. Formative evaluation takes place during the process being evaluated and focuses on improvement. Summative evaluation takes place after the process being evaluated and focuses on accountability. Evaluation may be targeted toward several areas of interest: learning, instruction, courses, personnel, programs, institutions, and wider educational systems.

A variety of evaluative models were discussed, including goal-attainment models, judgmental models, decision-facilitation models, naturalistic models, and self-evaluation models. Each has its particular applications, and each has its particular strengths and weaknesses.

Applications of educational evaluation to student learning, personnel including teachers and administrators, and programs were discussed. Standards for valid evaluations were seen to include utility, feasibility, proprietariness, and accuracy.

It is clearly in the national mood to utilize the results of educational evaluation in judging the quality of schools nationally, as seen by the widespread interest in regional accreditation of colleges and secondary schools and in the NCLB.

In chapter 9, information systems and their significance to educational organizations are discussed. The impact of major advances in information and communication technologies on leadership is a central issue that is considered.

Fundamental Concepts

The fundamental concepts that follow have been discussed in this chapter. The citations that conclude each concept indicate the Interstate School Leaders Licensure Consortium (ISLLC) standards and functions related to the concept. The Arabic numeral refers to the ISLLC standards, and the letter refers to the functions as presented in the table found inside the front cover.

- Evaluation is a critical component of educational leadership. (1B, 1D, 1E; 2E, 2I; 3A, 3E; 4A; 5A)
- Educational evaluation has broad applicability for improving performance by educational programs, faculty and staff, and students. (1B, 1D, 1E; 2E, 2I; 3A, 3E; 4A; 5A)
- Evaluation is parallel to but different from research. (1B, 1D, 1E; 2E, 2I; 3A, 3E; 4A; 5A)
- Evaluation is a "systematic collection and interpretation of evidence leading to judgment of value with a view toward action." (1B, 1D, 1E; 2E, 2I; 3A, 3E; 4A; 5A)
- A wide variety of models of educational evaluation has been developed, particularly within the past century. (1B, 1D, 1E; 2E, 2I; 3A, 3E; 4A; 5A)

- Evaluation of teachers is intended to produce improvement by the individual and by the school and accountability by the individual and by the organization. (1B, 1D, 1E; 2E, 2I; 3A, 3E; 4A; 5A)
- Evaluation of administrators is intended to form a basis for establishing and attaining institutional goals. (1B, 1D, 1E; 2E, 2I; 3A, 3E; 4A; 5A)
- Evaluation of programs is intended to maximize program outcomes, efficiency, and quality. (1B, 1D, 1E; 2E, 2I; 3A, 3E; 4A; 5A)
- Each level of application (teachers, administrators, and programs) employs a variety of models and methods, depending on the circumstances and intent. (1B, 1D, 1E; 2E, 2I; 3A, 3E; 4A; 5A)
- Standards for evaluation of programs, personnel, and students have been articulated by the Joint Committee on Standards for Educational Evaluation. (1B, 1D, 1E; 2E, 2I; 3A, 3E; 4A; 5A)
- A national movement toward educational accountability is increasing. (1B, 1D, 1E; 2E, 2I; 3A, 3E; 4A; 5A; 6B, 6C)
- The No Child Left Behind Act of 2001 is a national effort at increasing educational accountability; it contains elements of evaluation focused on performance of school districts, individual schools, teachers, and students. (1B, 1D, 1E; 2E, 2I; 3A, 3E; 4A; 5A; 6B, 6C)
- Given the national concern with educational accountability, there is a growing need for credible and effective evaluation models and techniques. (1B, 1D, 1E; 2E, 2I; 3A, 3E; 4A; 5A; 6B, 6C)

Case Study

Assessment and Evaluation: The Case of Washington High School

Addresses ISLLC Standards 1, 2, 3, 4, 5, and 6

You have just completed your second year as assistant principal at Washington High School. As a teacher in this building for 5 years prior to your current assignment, you noticed a number of problem areas. Some teachers appeared to be growing more complacent, others more frustrated; student achievement and progress had steadily declined as demonstrated by scores on state examinations; course work often had little to do with job skills needed for the community workforce; low overall performance has led to concerns about the school's not receiving full accreditation by the regional Association of Colleges and Secondary Schools at the next accreditation review, which

is coming in 2 years; the district seemed to lack the resources to combat even the simplest of these problems; and school administrators seemed to lack the know-how to effect change.

This morning you were called in to meet with the building principal, who was appointed 3 months ago. During the discussion it was clear that the principal shared your view of the school. The principal is developing a long-range plan to attack the problems described here. The principal expects to present the plan to the faculty and staff and to the superintendent of schools in 60 days. As part of that plan, you have been asked to develop an evaluation model for the school.

Your Task

Design an evaluation model for Washington High School. Draw on the information provided in this and other chapters; on your own experience as a student, teacher, administrator, parent, and/or taxpayer; and on other relevant reading and experience. Your overall model should include subsystems that evaluate programs, teaching, and administration. Be sure to consider issues of responsibility for follow-up and continued assessment of results. When you have completed designing the model, be prepared to discuss the implications of putting the plan into effect in a real school in the real world.

References

Au, W. (2007). High stakes testing and curricular control: A qualitative metasynthesis. *Educational Researcher, 36*(5), 258–267.

Borich, G. D. (Ed.). (1974). *Evaluating educational programs and products.* Upper Saddle River, NJ: Educational Technology.

Borich, G. D. (1977). *The appraisal of teaching: Concepts and process.* Reading, MA: Addison-Wesley.

Brandt, R. S. (Ed.). (1981). *Applied strategies for curriculum evaluation.* Washington, DC: Association for Supervision and Curriculum Development.

Centra, J. A., & Potter, D. A. (1980). School and teacher effects: An interrelational model. *Review of Educational Research, 50*(2), 273–291.

Chapman, A. (n.d.). *Kirkpatrick's learning and training evaluation theory.* Retrieved September 15, 2007, from http://www.businessballs.com/kirkpatricklearningevaluationmodel.html

Clift, P., Nutall, D., & McCormick, R. (Eds.). (1988). *Studies in school self-evaluation.* New York: Falmer.

Cochran, J. & Mills, C. (1984). *Teacher competency as determined by student achievement.* Retrieved September 9, 2007, from http://education.statuniversity.com/pages/2481/Teacher-Evaluation.html

Coker, H., Medley, D., & Soar, R. (1980). How valid are expert opinions about effective teaching? *Phi Delta Kappan, 62*(2), 141–144, 149.

Connecticut State Department of Education. (2006). *Best practice model for school leader evaluation and professional development*. Hartford: Author.

Cronbach, L. J. (1982). *Designing evaluations of educational and social programs*. San Francisco: Jossey-Bass.

Darling-Hammond, L., Wise, A. E., & Pease, S. R. (1983). Teacher evaluation in the organizational context: A review of the literature. *Review of Educational Research, 53*(3), 285–328.

Denver Public Schools. (2007). *Professional compensation system for teachers*. Retrieved September 9, 2007, from http://denverprocomp.org/stories/storyReader#33

DiPaola, N. F., & Stronge, J. H. (2001). Credible evaluation: Not yet state-of-the-art. *The School Administrator*. Arlington, VA: American Association of School Administrators.

Drucker, P. (1993). *Post capitalist society*. New York: HarperBusiness.

Edwards, W., Guttentag, M., & Snapper, K. (1975). A decision-theoretic approach to evaluation research. In E. L. Strevening & M. Guttentag (Eds.), *Handbook of evaluation research* (Vol. 1, pp. 139–181). Beverly Hills, CA: Sage.

Fink, A. (1995). *Evaluation for education and psychology*. London: Sage.

Friedman, T. L. (2006). *The world is flat: A brief history of the twenty-first century*. New York: Farrar, Straus and Giroux.

Glasman, N. S., & Nevo, D. (1988). Evaluation in education. In *Evaluation in decision making: The case of school administration* (pp. 31–45). Boston: Kluwer Academic.

Gross, B., & Goertz, M. E. (2005). *Holding high hopes: How high schools respond to state accountability policies* (CPR Research Report Series RR-056). Philadelphia: Consortium for Policy Research in Education, University of Pennsylvania Graduate School of Education.

Guba, E. G., & Lincoln, Y. S. (1989). *Fourth generation evaluation*. Newbury Park, CA: Sage.

Guilfoyle, C. (2006). Is there life beyond testing? *Education Leadership, 64*(3), 8–13.

Haefele, D. L. (1981). Teacher interviews. In J. Millman (Ed.), *Handbook of teacher evaluations*. Beverly Hills, CA: Sage, pp. 21–31.

Harman, A. E. (2002). *National Board for Professional Teaching Standards' National Teacher Certification*. East Lansing, MI: National Center for Research on Teacher Learning. (ERIC Document Reproduction Service No. ED460126)

Haycock, J. (2001, March). Closing the achievement gap. *Educational Leadership*, pp. 6–11.

Heneman, H. G., III, Milanowski, A., Kimball, S. M., & Odden, A. (2006, May 26). *Standards-based teacher evaluation as a foundation for knowledge- and skill-based pay*. (CPRE Policy Briefs, RB-45). Philadelphia: University of Pennsylvania.

Holloway, M. L. (1988). Performance appraisal. In R. Middler & E. Holzapel Jr. (Eds.), *Issues in personnel management*. San Francisco: Jossey-Bass.

Holt, M. (1981). *Evaluating the evaluators*. London: Hodder & Stoughton.

House, E. R. (1978). Assumptions underlying evaluation models. *Educational Researcher, 7*(3), 4–12.

House, E. R. (1996). A framework for appraising educational reforms. *Educational Researcher*, 6–14.

Houston, P. D. (2007, May 17). The seven deadly sins of No Child Left Behind. *Phi Delta Kappan*. Retrieved September 9, 2007, from http://www.pdkintl.org/kappan/k_v88/k0706hou.html

Jennings, J., & Rentner, D. S. (2006, September 26). Ten big effects of the No Child Left Behind Act on public schools. *Phi Delta Kappan*. Retrieved September 9, 2007, from http://www.pdkintl.org/ kappan/k_v88/k0601jen.html

Joint Committee on Standards for Educational Evaluation. (1988). *The personnel evaluation standards*. Thousand Oaks, CA: Corwin Press.

Joint Committee on Standards for Educational Evaluation. (1994). *The program evaluation standards*. Thousand Oaks, CA: Corwin Press.

Joint Committee on Standards for Educational Evaluation. (2003). *The student evaluation standards*. Thousand Oaks, CA: Corwin Press.

Kahlenberg, R. D. (2007, September 4). No Child Left Behind: What would Al say? *Education Week*. Retrieved September 9, 2007, from http://www.edweek.org/ew/articles/2007/09/05/02haklenberg.h27.html

Keller, B. (2007, August 10). The national board: Challenged by success? *Education Week*. Retrieved September 9, 2007, from http://www.edweek.org/ew/articles/2007/08/15/45nbpt.h26.html

King, J. A. (1981). Beyond classroom walls: Indirect measures of teacher competence. In J. Millman (Ed.), *Handbook of teacher evaluation*. Beverly Hills, CA: Sage, pp. 167–179.

Klein, A. (2007, August 30). Host of lawmakers offer bills to revise NCLB. *Education Week*. Retrieved September 9, 2007, from http://www.edweek.org/ew/articles/2007/09/05/02nclb.h27.html

Knapp, M. S. (1982). *Toward the study of teacher evaluation as an organizational process: A review of current research and practice*. Menlo Park, CA: SRI International.

Kowalski, T. T. (1988). Program evaluation. In *The organization and planning of adult education*. Albany: State University of New York Press, pp. 87-107.

Lecker, W. (2005, March 24). Public speaks out on No Child Left Behind. *Access*. Retrieved July 30, 2007, from http://www.schoolfunding.info/news/federal

Levin, H. M., & McEwan, P. J. (2001). *Cost-effectiveness analysis* (2nd ed.). Thousand Oaks, CA: Sage.

Levin, H. M., & McEwan, P. J. (2002). *Cost-effectiveness and educational policy: 2002 yearbook of the American Educational Financial Association*. Larchmont, NY: Eye on Education.

Lewy, A. (1990). Formative and summative evaluation. In H. J. Walberg & G. D. Haertel (Eds.), *The international encyclopedia of educational evaluation* (pp. 26–27). New York: Pergamon Press.

Madaus, G. F., Scriven, M. S., & Stufflebeam, D. L. (1983). *Evaluation models: Viewpoints on educational and human services evaluation.* Boston: Kluwer-Nijhoff.

Mark, M. M., & Cook, T. D. (1984). Design of randomized experiments and quasi-experiments. In L. Rutman (Ed.), *Evaluation research methods: A basic guide* (2nd ed., pp. 65–120). Beverly Hills, CA: Sage.

Massachusetts Department of Education. (n.d.). *Principles of effective administrative leadership and examples of descriptors.* Retrieved September 15, 2007, from http://www.doe .mass.edu/lawsregs/603cmr35.html?section=aled

McColskey, W., & Stronge, J. H. (2006). *Teacher effectiveness, student achievement, and national board certified teachers.* Washington, DC: National Board for Professional Teaching Standards.

McKeon, H. P. (2007, June 19). *Strong support for NCLB reauthorization in national, bipartisan survey.* Retrieved July 30, 2007, from http://republicans.edlabor.house.gov/ PRArticle.aspx?NewsID=84

Meier, D. (2002). *In schools we trust: Creating communities of learning in an era of standardization and testing.* Boston: Beacon Press.

Meier, D. & Wood, G. (Eds.). (2004). *Many children left behind: How the No Child Left Behind Act is damaging our children and our schools.* Boston: Beacon Press.

Middle States Commission on Higher Education. (1998). The evaluation and accreditation process. In *Policies and procedures* (5th ed.). Philadelphia: Commission on Higher Education, (n.p.).

Miller, A. H., Imrie, B. W., & Cox, K. (1998). *Student assessment in higher education: A handbook for assessing performance.* London: Kogan Page.

Millman, J. (Ed.). (1981). *Handbook of teacher evaluation.* Beverly Hills, CA: Sage.

Mitzel, H. E., Best, J. H., & Rabinowitz, W. (1982). *Encyclopedia of educational research* (5th ed., Vol. 2). New York: Free Press.

Morra, L. G. (1978). The discrepancy evaluation model: A strategy for improving a simulation and determining effectiveness (ERIC ED161880). Retrieved September 17, 2007, from http://eric.ed.gov/ERICWebPortal/custom/ portlets

Murphy, J. (2005, February). Unpacking the foundations of ISLLC standards and addressing concerns in the academic community. *Educational Administration Quarterly, 41*(1), 154–191.

Murphy, J., & Shipman, N. (1996). Introductory letter. In *Interstate school leaders licensure consortium: Standards for school leaders.* Washington, D.C., Council of Chief State School Officers, p. iii.

National Board for Professional Teaching Standards. (2007). *Every child deserves a great teacher.* Retrieved September

9, 2007, from http://www.nbpts.org/the_standards/the_ five_core_propositions.html

Naugle, K. A, Naugle, L. B., & Naugle, R. J. (2000, Fall). Kirkpatrick's evaluation model as a means of evaluating teacher performance. *Education.* Retrieved September 15, 2007, from http://findarticles.com/p/articles/mi_qa3673/ is_200010/ai_n8926146

New Jersey Association of School Administrators. (2002). *New Jersey professional standards for school leaders.* Retrieved September 15, 2007, from http://www.njasa.net/ 701792313223425/blank/browse.asp?A=38

Ornstein, A. C., & Levine, D. U. (2006). *Foundations of education* (9th ed.). Boston: Houghton Mifflin.

Patton, M. Q. (1984). Data collection: Options, strategies, and cautions. In L. Rutman (Ed.), *Evaluation research methods: A basic guide* (2nd ed., pp. 39–63). Beverly Hills, CA: Sage.

Peterson, K., & Kauchak, D. (1982). *Teacher evaluation: Perspectives, practices and promises.* Salt Lake City: Center for Educational Practice, University of Utah.

Peterson, P. E., & West, M. R. (2003). *No Child Left Behind: The political practice of school accountability.* Washington, DC: Brookings Institution Press.

Poll shows broad support for NCLB—with changes. (2007, June 22). *California school news.* Retrieved July 30, 2007, from http://www.csba.org/csn/csnStoryTemplate.cfm? app=csn&id=648

Popham, J. W. (1988). *Educational evaluation* (2nd ed.). Upper Saddle River, NJ: Prentice Hall.

Safier, K. L. (2007, January). Improving teacher quality in Ohio: The limitations of the highly qualified teacher provision of the No Child Left Behind Act of 2001. *Journal of Law and Education, 36*(1), 65–87.

Sanders, J. R. (1999, April). *General background on the Joint Committee on Standards for Educational Evaluation.* Retrieved April 12, 2007, from http://www.wmich.edu/ evalctr/jc/JC_Genl_Bckgrnd.html

Saylor, J. G., & Alexander, W. M. (1981). *Curriculum planning for better teaching and learning* (4th ed.) New York: Holt, Rinehart and Winston.

Scriven, M. (1980a). *Evaluation thesaurus* (2nd ed.). Inverness, CA: Edgepress.

Scriven, M. (1980b). *The logic of evaluation.* Inverness, CA: Edgepress.

Shadish, W. R., Cook, T. D., & Leviton, L. C. (1991). *Foundations of program evaluation: Theories of practice.* Newbury Park, CA: Sage.

Shavelson, R., & Stern, P. (1981). Research on teachers' pedagogical thoughts, judgments, decisions and behavior. *Review of Educational Research, 51*(4), 455–498.

South Carolina State Department of Education. (2005, December 20). *Study shows national board certification improves student academic performance.* Retrieved from http://ed.sc.gov/news/more.cfm?articleID=633

Stake, R. E. (1969). Language, rationality, and assessment. In W. H. Beatty (Ed.), *Improving educational assessment and an inventory of measures of affective behavior.* Washington, DC: Association of Curriculum Development, pp. 14–40.

Stufflebeam, D. L. (1990). Professional standards for educational evaluation. In H. J. Walberg & G. D. Haertel (Eds.), *The international encyclopedia of educational evaluation* (pp. 94–105). New York: Pergamon Press.

Stufflebeam, D. L. (2002, June). *CIPP evaluation model checklist.* Retrieved September 15, 2007, from http://www.wmich.edu/evalctr/checklists/cippchecklist.html

Taylor, F. W. (1911). *The principles of scientific management.* New York: Harper & Brothers.

Tennessee Department of Education. (2004, June). *Framework for evaluation and professional growth.* Retrieved September 17, 2007, from http://www.state.tn.us/education/frameval/index.shtml

Tuckman, B. (1985). *Evaluating instructional programs* (2nd ed.). Boston: Allyn & Bacon.

Tyler, R. W. (1970). *Educational evaluation: New roles, new means.* Chicago: University of Chicago Press.

Viadero, D. (2007, March 7). Studies mixed on national certification for teachers. *Education Week, 26,* 5–14.

Walberg, J. J., & Haertel, G. D. (Eds.). (1990). *The international encyclopedia of educational evaluation.* New York: Pergamon Press.

Weaver, R. (2006). A positive agenda for ESEA. *Educational Leadership, 64*(3), 32–36.

White, B. (2004, April). *The relationship between teacher evaluation scores and student achievement: Evidence from Coventry, R.I.* (CPRE-UW Working Paper Series). Madison: University of Wisconsin Center.

Wilmore, E. L. (2002). *Principal leadership: Applying the new Educational Leadership Constituent Council (ELLC) standards.* Thousand Oaks, CA: Corwin Press.

Wilson, J. D. (1988). *Appraising teacher quality.* London: Hodder & Stoughton.

Worthen, B. R. (1973). *Educational evaluation: Theory and practice.* Worthington, OH: Jones.

Worthen, B. R. (1990). Program evaluation. In H. J. Walberg & G. D. Haertel (Eds.), *The international encyclopedia of educational evaluation* (pp. 42–47). New York: Pergamon Press.

Worthen, B., Worthen, B. R., & Sanders, J. R. (1987). *Educational evaluation: Alternative approaches and practical guidelines.* New York: Longman.

The Role of Information Technology

Our age has been dubbed the *information age*, and educational institutions at all levels and of all types represent a major segment of the *information industry*. A primary function of schooling is to pass the information of past generations to the youngest generation. Schools, colleges, and universities go beyond the mere transmission of information, however, and provide students with skills and constructs for organizing data into useful knowledge and enable them to make new discoveries. At the same time, schools depend on information and information processing to carry out their missions effectively.

Managing information that is increasing at exponential rates has been possible only because of the corresponding growth in sophistication of information technology and software. Supercomputers, fiber-optic cable, communication satellites, and powerful software have fueled this information explosion, changing the way we live, work, do business—and even think. The fabric and meaning of culture, time, distance, and space are being changed (Westbrook, 1998).

The greater availability of information can assist in making better plans for the classroom, the school, the district, the state, and the nation and in monitoring the implementation of those plans; alternatively, teachers, administrators, and policymakers can be paralyzed into inaction with an overload of data and information or misled by faulty analyses. Good plans need to be built on good information, and good information is required to monitor implementation. Information systems can provide critical support in making decisions and in maintaining organizational memory from the classroom to the highest levels of government. Information technology, including

software, can be an important tool in reaching educational achievement objectives when intelligently integrated into instructional processes.

In chapter 7, we saw that a person's philosophy, beliefs, and values strongly influence how he or she interprets what is experienced and his or her orientation toward decision making. Similarly, we examined how they influence the selection, implementation, and interpretation of formal inquiries into issues and problems confronting an organization. In chapter 8, we extended the discussion to models of evaluation including goal-attainment, judgmental, decision-facilitation, naturalistic, and self-evaluation models applied to student learning, personnel including teachers and administrators, and instructional programs.

Chapter 8 concluded that the nature of educational evaluation in the future is uncertain; however, it is clearly in the national mood to utilize the results of educational evaluation in judging the quality of schools nationally, as seen by widespread interest in regional accreditation of colleges and secondary schools and in the federal No Child Left Behind Act, to cite only two examples.

The primary focus of this chapter is on the actual and potential roles of information technology for improving the quality of decisions made and the quality of instruction in schools in the quest for preparing students to meet the intellectual and vocational demands of the 21st century. We begin with a discussion of the nature of information and the importance of informal information systems. Following the discussion of the structure of formal information systems, we examine the issue of the interfaces between information technology, learning/instructional processes, and the structure of schooling. We conclude with a discussion of proposed and actual integrated information systems that focus on the learning progress of individual students with links to the supporting instructional, business, personnel, and community resource systems.

Types of Information Systems and Their Uses

Informal Information Systems

A learning or self-renewing organization can maintain its fluidity (and stability) only if it has continuing access to new information about external factors and internal resources. The information available to us affects the way we form our organizations—and reform them as necessary (Wheatley, 2006):

> A system needs to access itself. It needs to understand who it is, where it is, what it believes, what it knows. These needs are nourished by information. Information is one of the primary conditions that spawns the organization we see. If it moves through a system freely, individuals learn and change and their discoveries can be integrated by the system. The system becomes both resilient and flexible. But if information is restricted, held tightly in certain regions, the system can neither learn nor respond. (Wheatley & Kellner-Rogers, 1996, p. 82)

When we speak of information sources, we are usually thinking in terms of formal information systems. Although such systems are important and useful, they have a bias of treating information as linear and inert, devoid of the vitality that Wheatley and Kellner-Rogers describe. In truth, much important information is tacit or gained from structured and casual exchanges among individuals and not recorded in any formal system. This type of information is usually referred to as *soft information,* while the quantified facts usually found in formal information systems are referred to as *hard information* or data. Unfortunately, there is a general tendency to discount the value of soft information.

Much of the information used in strategy formulation, to be discussed in chapter 11, and by managers of day-to-day operations is of the soft type. Whereas hard information may be available to every

trusted party, soft information cannot be captured by formal systems and is available only to those exposed to it directly. "The decisions so quickly available from intuition must sometimes be checked for accuracy by formal analysis, while those produced by careful analysis must generally be confirmed intuitively for face validity" (Mintzberg, 1994, p. 328). Thus, while structuring formal information systems, it is also important to design organizations and nurture organizational cultures that allow for and encourage the informal sharing of information among members and provide them discretionary freedom to exercise their tacit understandings.

Formal Information Systems

With respect to formal information systems, school districts routinely collect all kinds of data—from birth dates and achievement test results to records of measles vaccinations. But data are not information. Data consist of raw facts, such as an employee's name, Social Security number, address, salary, and number of dependents. Such data must be retained by the employer as a routine business procedure in order to make payrolls and to comply with governmental regulations concerning withholding income and payroll taxes. When facts or data are organized in a meaningful manner, they become information. *Information* is a collection of facts organized in such a way that they have additional value beyond the value of the facts themselves (Stair, 1992).

For example, in collective negotiations, the superintendent and union negotiators need to know the total cost of salaries, their distribution, their average cost, and how all relate to salaries paid in similar districts. The raw data, except for the comparative information, are available in the payroll office but organized for a different purpose. To serve the negotiators' purposes, it is not necessary to collect the data again, only to organize the existing data differently.

Similarly, teachers need to know by name and date what students in their classes are absent so that the students can make up missed instructional opportunities. As the administrator of compulsory attendance laws, however, the superintendent (or attendance officer) needs to know only who the individual truants are but does not need to know about those who are legally absent. The superintendent may also wish to monitor trends in absence behavior as part of an evaluation of district attendance policies. Thus, the same data can be organized in numerous ways to meet the information needs of a variety of decision makers.

Information management has been achieved successfully for thousands of years without the availability of computers, telecommunications, and networks. *Information systems*, however, as they are emerging today, are a product of the past 40 years (Rowley, 1996). An information system is a set of interrelated elements or components that collect (input), manipulate and store (process), and disseminate to targeted persons data and information (output). An information system also typically has a feedback process whereby adjustments can be made to input and processing activities to enhance the efficiency of the system.

Rowley (1996) identifies six types of information systems: transaction processing systems, management information systems, decision support systems, executive information systems, expert systems, and office information systems.

Transaction processing systems are dominated by accounting applications, recording data about events or transactions. Most district financial transactions, for example, would be of this nature, as are inventories, attendance, report cards, and library management systems (checking out and in of books). Data are captured as events occur. The data entered update master files and are validated and checked for errors through master files. Input can take many forms, from card swipes to teacher grade sheets or direct teacher entry to voice, video, and touch activation devices. An efficient information system will collect each data element only once for the entire system and eliminate the redundancy of having each department and office collect similar data from the same people over and over again. Outputs are usually in the form of documents and reports but can take a variety of other forms, including that of paychecks, report cards, tuition billing, letters, or computer display screens.

Management information systems (MISs) provide information on computer screen or hard copy to managers in support of decisions they have to make. MISs are used when the information requirements can be determined in advance and where the need for information occurs on a regular basis. Data used in MISs may be drawn from many parts of the organization and are usually collected through the transaction-processing system. School districts typically use MISs to manage their business functions. MISs could be equally effective for teachers in managing, monitoring, and recording student learning experiences and their accomplishments, although currently such use is not widespread.

Decision support systems (DSSs) are designed to address those special situations where an MIS does not provide all the information required. Analyses are produced that assist managers with unique, nonrecurring, and relatively unstructured decisions. DSSs build mathematical, statistical, or financial models that permit what-if, sensitivity, optimization, and simulation analyses (Taylor, 1995; Wholeben, 1995). These models provide managers with great flexibility in evaluating alternative solutions to problems. DSSs are relied on in strategic and tactical situations where the risk associated with error is high and the consequences of a mistake are serious.

Executive information systems are similar to MISs but are tailored to provide top management (superintendent) and policymakers (board of education) with the broad picture of the district's operations without overloading them with unnecessary detail. Executive systems provide access to all databases within an organization for those occasions when detail is needed and to external databases for comparison purposes. "Typically, EISs seek to combine the power and data storage capacity of organizational information systems, with ease of use and graphics capability" (Rowley, 1996, p. 14).

Expert systems fall within the field of artificial intelligence and are likely to draw on computerized knowledge bases from outside the organization through networks. Expert systems do not make decisions but offer decision support in situations where data are incomplete and where it is necessary to take into account the effects of uncertainty and judgment.

Rowley's (1996) last category is *office information systems*. These support the daily functioning of an office; some of the information captured may be entered into master files, but much is maintained only for the convenience of specific persons to assist them in carrying out job-related activities. Components include word processing, scanners, voice mail, facsimile transmission, e-mail, Internet access, electronic filing, and diaries.

Integrated Information Systems

Data abound in schools and school districts. Information systems are legion, but they tend not to be compatible to one another in structure; thus, data cannot readily be transferred from one system to another. This means that data collection is unnecessarily duplicated and the scope of analyses limited.

The demand for an integration of existing information systems in schools and school districts and even state systems is growing. School districts, state education departments, and the federal education department tend to archive information to meet legal requirements rather than to place it in databases to facilitate analysis and support decision making. Data pertinent to employee salaries are collected and maintained by the payroll office. Other financial data are maintained in the business office. Teacher-assigned grades may be found only in a student's file, while his or her scores on state required tests may be recorded in an electronic file in a state format and transmitted to the state education department. Records concerning student disabilities may be in a file held by the committee for special education, and attendance information may be maintained by the attendance officer independently of any other file. To understand a school or district thoroughly and to monitor its operations effectively, all information sources need to be linked so that information may flow freely from one to another and so that analysts may draw data from any combination of sources in undertaking new analyses (Fullan, Hill, & Crevola, 2006; Fulmer, 1995; Leithwood, Aitken, & Jantzi, 2006).

An integrated system would facilitate analysis and support decision making by teachers and administrators alike. Such a system would have multiple input ports, allowing teachers, administrators, and clerks to record transactions (attendance, disciplinary actions, grades and other accomplishments, lesson plans, student assignments, and so on) at the point where the action originates. The system needs to be designed to accommodate multiple types and forms of data, including normative, ordinal, interval, ratio, qualitative, feedback, self-evaluation, samples of writing, student journals, parent feedback, and other forms of student attitude, performance, and behavior. Teachers and administrators should be able to access the total database when faced with a decision to be made about an individual student (Rowley's MIS) or collectively in the development of school policy. The system needs to be designed so that data may be aggregated into alternative units of analysis (Rowley's DSSs). Prototypes of integrated systems are presented in a later section of this chapter.

Using Information Systems

A district's information systems come into play throughout the processes of strategy formation and planning (discussed in chapter 11). They are particularly important in providing information for the internal analysis of assessing strengths and weaknesses of the organization. It comes into play again in designing action plans and in building and administering the budget. The information system plays a critical role in contrasting actual accomplishments against expectations, that is, evaluations. Most important, a good information system enables all members of an organization to monitor the effect of their actions and decisions. Without good information, an organization is blind to its past achievements and failures and to its future potential.

That which cannot be measured cannot be controlled or understood. This understanding is driving the current standards movement. In the past it has been common for educators to claim success on very little tangible evidence other than the intuitive feeling of those professionals involved in designing and implementing a program. Now the states through their respective standards and accountability systems and the federal government through its No Child Left Behind Act as well as the public in general are asking, "How do you know? What evidence do you have that supports your perceptions and opinions?"

One of the most articulate champions of management (and decision making) by fact was W. Edwards Deming (1986). The Deming principles were originally applied to the management of business organizations, first in Japan and subsequently in the United States. Now they are being applied to the organization and management of schools, school districts, and other educational organizations (Frazier, 1997; Schmoker & Wilson, 1993). Deming contended that collecting and analyzing data around an organization's priority objectives is essential for improvement, for validating efforts, and for refining strategies. What is more important to schools, parents, and the public in general than the quality of student outcomes? Equally important to the taxpayers who pay for the personnel, facilities, equipment, and supplies used in developing those outcomes is the assurance that those resources are being applied as efficiently as is humanly possible.

The information system can be critically important in monitoring, evaluating, and adjusting the implementation and effectiveness of action plans and programs. The proper use of statistics, for example, is central to Deming's (1986) philosophy of *total quality management.* According to him, management in any form is prediction. Statistical data are essential to improvement; facts, reasoning, and evidence should drive operational decisions, not power or authority or personality (Fullan et al., 2006; Leithwood et al., 2006).

We need to look to data continually in checking our progress. Research, experimentation, and data gathering are built into the daily routine of learning organizations. Such organizations are able to anticipate and to accept new knowledge and to modify old organizational premises in order to optimize processes and achieve excellence in schooling (Schmoker & Wilson, 1993).

Deming (1986) identified the individual worker as key to program quality. The only proper use of data, according to him, is to help employees perform better and to provide them with a basis for taking pride in their workmanship. The workers (e.g., principals, teachers, secretaries, bus drivers, and cleaners) are the experts in what they do and are fully capable of improving their own performance when given feedback that enables them to monitor their own work. Deming placed much importance on the gathering of numerical data, but he emphasized that it must never be used to place blame on any employee or group of employees. Data are to be used to isolate problem areas, design corrective action, and identify staff training

needs. Data do not have to be of the standard statistical variety, however; the most useful kinds of data are frequently those generated by the employees themselves.

The Role of Information Technology in Instruction and Learning

To this point, the discussion in this chapter has focused mostly on administrative and managerial aspects of information technology and information systems in schools and school districts, but their potential for strengthening instructional systems and revolutionizing schooling is equally powerful. To date, however, that potential is largely unrealized (Dede, 1998; Fullan et al., 2006; Fullerton, 1998; Leithwood et al., 2006; Trotter, 1997), but growing external pressures for change cannot be delayed much longer by a largely reluctant profession.

Technological Change and Education

Instructional technology is the application of scientific knowledge, including learning theory, to the solution of problems in education. Education and technology are concurrently cause and effect in relation to the other. Technological developments place continuing pressure on educators to keep curriculum and instructional methods up to date. At the same time, educational institutions are essential to the generation and assimilation of new technology.

Although society in general has tended toward enhanced technological sophistication and increased capital intensity, the education sector has retained a traditional, labor-intensive, craft-oriented technology (Bolton, 1994; Butzin, 1992; Cuban, 1988; Goodlad, 1984; Murphy, 1993). This "standing still" creates both sociological and economic problems. From an economic standpoint, labor-intensive education is unnecessarily expensive and in general does not produce a workforce with prerequisite attitudes and skills needed for a rapidly changing workplace. From a sociological standpoint, technologically unsophisticated schools are losing their credibility and thereby their effectiveness with pupils because they are no longer congruent with the larger societal context (Gewertz, 2007; Prensky, 2006).

Nonservice industries (e.g., manufacturing) generally understand that technological structure is not inalterably fixed, especially under competitive market conditions. Instead, there is an ongoing search for alternative, more efficient production methods that require different mixes of human and nonhuman resources. These alternatives are judged by their potential costs and effectiveness. Education, however, which is largely a state monopoly with weak market incentives for efficiency, appears to be locked into one labor-intensive mode of production. (See related discussions in chapters 7 and 12.) Even when parents enter the educational marketplace, they exercise choice among public and private schools that differ in size and philosophies but are remarkably similar in the teaching technologies employed. Glennan and Melmed (1996) note,

> Compared with the private sector, [social service providers in general and educational agencies in particular] lack an investment mentality. School districts do not regularly set aside a specified portion of their revenues for investing in activities to improve school performance. The reasons for this are found in the *political* nature of resource allocation in public education. (p. 2, emphasis added)

It has long been argued that "inherent in the technological structure" of such service industries as education "are forces working almost unavoidably for progressive and cumulative increases in the real costs incurred in supplying them" (Baumol, 1967, p. 415). If productivity is to be enhanced in education (and other service industries), there must be a willingness to develop alternative means of providing services, including modifications in their technological structures. The purpose of technology is to make labor go further by replacing it, to the extent possible, with less expensive nonhuman devices and more efficient organization in order to produce better products and services and/or to reduce the costs of providing them (Benson, 1961).

It is not that schools have neglected new technologies; the concern expressed is over the way in which schools have chosen to use them. Technological devices have been used as add-ons to assist or supplement teacher efforts rather than as integral parts of new learning systems that combine the capabilities and energy of students and teachers with those devices to achieve results superior to that which could be achieved without them or to achieve equal results at a lower cost (Dede, 1998; Trotter, 2007; Willett, Swanson, & Nelson, 1979). When technology is used as an add-on or as an enrichment, costs are increased and efficiency is decreased unless there is evidence of greatly improved outcomes (Butzin, 1992).

Using technology in school as an add-on is not a recent phenomenon. Vaizey, Norris, and Sheehan (1972) noted that teacher costs accounted for at least half of all school costs and that unless increases in pupil/teacher ratios took place as a result of the use of new technologies, new technologies would necessarily add to total costs. The authors accurately predicted that increases in pupil/teacher ratios would not happen: "It seems unlikely that any teacher substitution will occur—certainly none has yet taken place [and still hasn't 35 years after this was written]. Thus for new methods to be used on a wider scale, the decision will have to be taken that the educational benefits are worth the resulting increases in costs" (p. 234).

Because educators have used technology almost exclusively as an add-on to traditional instructional procedures, there is a tendency for them to think of instructional technology as being very expensive, but this is the case only when technology is not used for labor substitution. One of the most telling shortcomings of current leadership in the public schools is its failure to understand the role of technology. Employing new technologies has only one purpose: to increase productivity (i.e., improving quality or reducing costs). This is the reason that most of the rest of the economy spends billions of dollars annually on new technological devices in order to remain competitive by keeping unit production costs low. Public schools need to learn from the practice of other organizations (mostly in the private sector) and squarely address the issue of productivity (Doyle, 1994). (See the discussion of the concepts of efficiency and educational production functions in chapter 12.)

Another explanation for the generic failure of educational technologies is due "to a misplaced obsession with hardware and neglect of software, other resources, and instructional setting [including teacher readiness] that are necessary to successful implementation" (H. Levin & Meister, 1985, p. 9). Levin and Meister (1985) provide a rule of thumb that the purchase of equipment should represent only about 10% of the total cost of an innovation if that innovation is to be effective. A substantial proportion of the remaining 90% needs to be invested in the involvement of the persons who must design and operate the systems and in staff development (Zehr, 1997).

Bromley (1998) points out that one of the most significant mistakes made by designers and implementers of new instructional technologies is the assumption that the issues are only technical and can be solved by technicians. Rather than being technological, he argues, the dominating issues deterring effective use of educational technology are social and cultural.

The growth of the availability of information technology in schools over the past decade has been phenomenal, but, as with other reforms, the results in terms of improved academic achievement, while significant, are small and much less than advocates promised (Viadero, 2007). As recently as 1997, only 14% of the schools in the United States had access to the Internet. A decade later, nearly all schools have the capability to get online, 95% of them with high-speed access. Digital cameras and video recorders are giving students and teachers new and vivid ways of expressing themselves. Blogs, podcasts, and social networking sites provide new arenas for communicating, sharing ideas and creations, and posting assignments and lectures. Digital whiteboards and liquid-crystal-display projectors are gracing many classrooms with a high-tech feel. "Yet, few experts would argue that America's schools are making optimal use of the new digital tools they have received. Likewise, few can point to evidence that all the new technology has translated into great leaps forward in student learning" (Trotter, 2007, p. 10).

Emerging Information-Age Schools

In chapter 1, we addressed the urgent need to make fundamental changes to formal schooling as it is currently organized. The conclusion of the New Commission on Skills of the American Workforce (2007), that "we have no choice but to set a goal of getting all of our students ready to the level of literacy to do college-level work" (p. 44), was cited. Data from the National Assessment of Educational Progress were reported showing that less than one-third of American students have reached such a level of proficiency by high school graduation. Fullan et al. (2006) set the new mission for schools to reach the 90% to 95% range of success.

We also quoted in chapter 1 long-term students and strategists of the public schools, such as Theodore Sizer (2004), who concludes,

> Americans have run out the string on "school" as it has evolved over the past century. Tinkering with it, testing it, belittling it, pouring money into it as it is makes even less sense. The painful work of reconstituting what we mean by "school" . . . is no longer avoidable. (p. 115)

The very limited success of four decades of efforts intended to raise the academic and other forms of student achievement may be because those reforms have failed to focus on classroom instruction itself. Another likely contributor is the failure to recognize the pervasive impact of digital technology on the minds and lives of students from pre-K through college and to integrate that technology into the instructional process. With respect to the latter, Prensky (2006) has noted that today's students have spent their entire lives surrounded by and using computers and the Internet, video games, DVD players, video cameras, cell phones, iPods, and all the other digital tools and toys of the era. He notes that today's college graduates have spent less than 5,000 hours of their lives reading but more than 10,000 hours each playing video games and on their cell phones and 20,000 hours watching television. Further, collectively, they download 2 billion ring tones per year and 2 billion songs per month and exchange 6 billion text messages every day.

Prensky (2006) has dubbed this student generation "digital natives" and older generations "digital immigrants," marking the emergence of all generations into a new digital world. The current student generation has known no other world and is fluent in the digital language, but the older generations retain to varying degrees accents from their linear pasts. This intense digital exposure by the student generation has led to new thinking patterns on their part that are quite different from those assumed in the 20th-century curricula still dominating most schools during the first decade of the 21st century. This disparity is irritating to many digital natives and reduces their enjoyment of school and may slow their rate of learning in such a school environment. It is still unusual to find blogs, MP3 players, podcasting, video games, or cell phones used as instructional tools in today's classrooms (Borja, 2007).

Thinking skills that have been shown to be enhanced by repeated exposure to digital media include representational competence (reading visual images as representations of three-dimensional space), multidimensional visual–spatial skills (the ability to create mental maps and picturing the results of various origami-like folds in your mind without actually doing them), inductive discovery (applying the steps of the scientific method in figuring out the rules governing the behavior of a dynamic representation), and attentional deployment (the ability to focus on several things at the same time and to respond faster to unexpected stimuli) (Prensky, 2006, pp. 35–36). He identifies only one skill that may have been reduced in digital natives: reflection. He suggests that building skills in reflection

---

ACTIVITY 9.1

Identifying Types of Information Systems

Addresses ISLLC Standards and Functions 1B, 1E; 2E, 2H; 3A, 3B, 3D; 4A; 5A; and 6

Study the information systems in your school and district.

1. How many of the types identified by Rowley (1996) are used? Are they integrated?
2. What kinds of digital information technology are used in your school? Is the technology an integral part of the instructional system, or does it stand apart?
3. Develop a set of recommendations with rationale for the school board for improving the effectiveness of the district's information support systems.
4. Develop a set of recommendations with rationale for the school principal for improving the instructional use of digital technology.

---

and critical thinking still needs to be a function of instructor-led questioning and debriefing.

With respect to the first likely reason for limited reform success—lack of focus on classroom practice—Fullan et al. (2006) point to the culprit as reform emphasis on external accountability, such as by the No Child Left Behind Act and the absence of internal accountability, that is, agreement and coherence around expectations for student learning and the means to influence instructional practice in classrooms that result in student learning. In support of their argument, they quote Elmore's (2007) contention that reform strategies "are often not explicitly connected to fundamental changes in the way knowledge is constructed, nor to the division of responsibility between teacher and student, the way students and teachers interact with each other around knowledge, or any of a variety of other stable conditions in the core" (p. 10). Later, Elmore (2007) laments that "there is no well worked out theory of how you get from performance-based accountability to improvements in teaching and learning. Performance-based accountability may have a powerful political logic behind it, but it has no causal theory that would explain how applying increased scrutiny to performance will in fact lead people in schools to do their work more effectively" (pp. 220–221). Fullan et al. (2006) conclude, "If the school does not have its internal act together, it simply does not have the capacity to improve. In fact, it doesn't know how to improve, and no amount of external browbeating will produce capacity where it doesn't exist" (p. 8).

Leithwood et al. (2006), however, point to the limitation of reforms that focus only on classroom curriculum and instruction. Without also considering the interdependence between classroom practice and the organization's structure and culture, such initiatives are unlikely to become institutionalized and will dissipate within a few years. To consider reform of classroom curriculum and instruction within the context of the school and district organizational structures and cultures requires a systems approach to designing the reform and in developing implementation strategies. Thus, it is a matter not of either/or but of both. In implementing school reforms, the interaction of classroom and organizational factors must be considered systemically.

There is hope on the horizon, however. In an increasingly literate and sophisticated society, ways are being found to meet the unique needs of individual students at affordable costs. No longer need cost be a prohibiting factor in delivering quality instruction when the traditional practices of the classroom are redesigned to take full advantage of digital technology and software now available. Such is happening in a few new schools designed specifically for the information age. These schools place the learner in a role of active participant, restructure the ratio of human and capital inputs in the schooling process, and take advantage of existing information and communication technologies. To make them cost effective, these schools are designed systemically (Dede, 1998), making the use of instructional technology an integral part of the teaching–learning process. Innovations in pedagogy, curriculum, assessment, and school organization are developed simultaneously with innovations in instructional technology.

Personalization/Individualization of Instruction.

Our system of schooling began to develop 150 years ago to make "book learning" available to every person. Most of the schools we have today are remnants of the industrial age, when we lived in communities that were nearly self-contained, served by local newspapers, local merchants, and locally owned factories (Mecklenburger, 1994). Ideas of that period about how the industrial world worked were adapted to schooling, and those industrial concepts of standardization and economies of scale continue to dominate thinking about the organization and administration of schools today, even though modern technology has rendered them virtually irrelevant. Large schools are still believed necessary for enabling variety in course offerings and specializations except in a few major cities (e.g., New York, Philadelphia, and Chicago) that are experimenting with small schools, especially at the secondary level. This industrial-age thinking has made today's schools so rigid that they cannot adequately respond to individual differences of students or changing conditions in the environment.

In our current school organization, too little recognition is given to the fact that learning is primarily a function of the interest, motivation, and hard work of the student (Fullan et al., 2006; B. Levin, 1994). We usually assume that learning takes place best in the physical presence of a teacher to guide and supervise learning activities from moment to moment and discount the value of informal learning and self-directed learning by students. The practical effect of this assumption has been to claim that for a child to learn, a course has to be established. More critically, the course requires a certified teacher, and cost considerations require approximately 20 or more pupils per class. Under these assumptions, individualization (or "personalization" as used by Fullan et al., 2006) requires many courses, many teachers, and many students.

Contemporary schooling is too often rigidified and standardized in ways that actually thwart learning and fail to educate young people for productive lives in a society now facing accelerating technological change (Prensky, 2006) and diversity. Rather than create self-directed learners who can function independently and interpret change, the school has continued to create teacher-dependent role players. The industrial-age school assumes that students are raw materials to be "processed" by teachers according to specifications dictated by schedules, programs, courses, and exit tests (Darling-Hammond, 1993). It further assumes that children are passive instead of active, incapable instead of capable, in need of direction instead of self-directed, acquiescent instead of assertive, and dependent rather than independent (Des Dixon, 1994).

Only a handful of entirely new schooling efforts are actually in operation. Darling-Hammond (1993) described emerging information-age schools as assuming that students are not standardized and that teaching is not routine:

> This view acknowledges that effective teaching techniques will vary for students with different learning styles, with differently developed intelligences, or at different stages of cognitive and psychological development; for different subject areas; and for different instructional goals. Far from following standardized instructional packages, teachers must base their judgments on knowledge of learning theory and pedagogy, of child development and cognition, and of curriculum and assessment. They must then connect this knowledge to the understandings, dispositions, and

conceptions that individual students bring with them to the classroom. (p. 758)

The emerging schools provide regimens and instructional methods that are flexible enough to provide students with programs and content that are personalized according to their learning abilities and interests. A constructivist view of learning has replaced a positivist view (Leithwood et al., 2006). Learning is no longer considered a linear process; rather, it is recognized that stimuli are received largely at random and that the role of the teacher is to help the learner develop procedures for processing the stimuli and for constructing meaning (Butzin, 1992; Leithwood et al., 2006; Mecklenburger, 1994; Trotter, 2007). School curricula are becoming interrelated across subject boundaries in order to permit integration of ideas and to emphasize the interrelatedness of problems. Students learn how to prioritize and manage the enormous array of data impacting them, how to think critically about what they find, and how to communicate well using multiple media (Viadero, 2007).

New Roles for Teachers and Other Staff. In an information-rich society, the teacher's role as purveyor of information is rapidly becoming obsolete. Communication and digital technologies provide the means whereby any student knowing how to read well and to use these resources can obtain most information needed in a manner of presentation that is at least as effective as today's typical teaching (Butzin, 1992). This portends new roles for educational professionals. In the information-age schools, teachers—if we continue to call them that (Prensky [2006] refers to them as "learning counselors")—become experts in managing information resources and in designing learning experiences for individual students relevant to their needs, growth, and development. They are involved primarily in diagnosing individual learning needs, prescribing personalized learning experiences (i.e., curriculum design), motivating each student, and evaluating the results (B. Levin, 1994). In carrying out these functions, the primary interaction with students is, of necessity, on a one-to-one or small-group basis, in essence eliminating the classroom as we have known it.

The emerging schools focus on learning rather than teaching. With the nearly unlimited accounting capabilities of computer networks, emphasis is placed on *continuous* rather than discontinuous learning that is *individualized* (or personalized) to capitalize on student strengths and interests and to remedy student weaknesses as these are diagnosed. For four decades, it has been the law of the land that children with learning disabilities and other disabling conditions receive individual diagnoses and education prescriptions; all children are so treated in information-age schools.

A multimedia approach to learning does not eliminate traditional teaching, but traditional teaching becomes only one of many methods. Other media include books, drill, computer-assisted instruction, Internet access, lecture (large group), discussion (small group), drama, chorus, band, athletic teams, tutors (teacher, aide, volunteer, or other student), collaborative learning, laboratory, field experiences, and so on (Halal & Liebowitz, 1994). In these schools, student-to-teacher ratios are relevant only where particular group sizes can be shown to contribute to greater efficiency, including effectiveness, in the *learning* process.

The learning experience is viewed as a function of all life experiences, not just those in school. A school building is viewed as a *place* of learning but not the *center* of learning, which is the student. Kozma and Schank (1998) argue that technology can be the instrument for breaking the relative isolation of schools and firmly linking them with the outside world:

Schools, homes, and workplaces today function separately—connected always by geography and circumstance, but only infrequently by common purpose and collaborative action. In our vision of communities of understanding, digital technologies are used to interweave schools, home, workplaces, libraries, museums, and social services to integrate education into the fabric of the community. Learning is no longer encapsulated by time, place, and age, but has become a pervasive activity and attitude that continues throughout life and is supported by all segments of society. Teaching is no longer defined as the transfer of information; learning is no longer defined as the retention of facts. Rather, teachers challenge students to achieve deeper levels of understanding and guide students in collaborative construction and application of knowledge in the context of real-world problems, situations, and tasks. Education is no longer the exclusive responsibility of teachers; it benefits from the participation and collaboration of parents, business people, scientists, seniors, and students across age groups.

How can technology support this transformation? First, the Internet is connecting schools with one another and with homes, businesses, libraries, museums, and community resources. This connection between school and home will help students extend their academic day, allow teachers to draw on significant experiences from students' everyday lives, and enable parents to become more involved with the education of their children and find extended educational opportunities for themselves. Connections between school and work will allow students to learn in the context of real-life problems and will allow teachers to draw on the resources of other teachers, a range of professional development providers, and technical and business experts. Connections among schools, homes, and the rest of the community will enable students to relate what is happening in the world outside to what is happening in school, will allow teachers to coordinate formal education with informal learning, and will allow the community to reintegrate education into daily life. (p. 5)

Until Kozma and Schank's (1998) vision is realized, Prensky (2006) urges today's parents to pursue aggressively an "at-home" curriculum, overcoming the current reticence of schools to embrace fully the digital technology imbruing the 21st-century youth culture and taking instructional advantage of the digital tools (or toys) and software (or games), already standard accruements of that culture:

> Even if you are not already one of the over one million U.S. parents who home-school their children totally or partially, your kids are already on the road to a new "at home" curriculum. The curriculum at home is not generally thought of as such, but, in fact, it surpasses, in its breadth (and often depth) the one taught in our schools. It has the potential to launch our kids, far beyond their teacher's capabilities and knowledge, into the twenty-first century—*their* century. (p. 213)

To take full advantage of available technology, information-age schools rely on computers for their complete range of capabilities, but these machines are subject to human direction, planning, and control.

ACTIVITY 9.2

"Don't Bother Me Mom—I'm Learning!"

Addresses ISLLC Standards and Functions 2; 3D; 4A; 5A; and 6C

Visit Marc Prensky's Web site that accompanies his book *Don't Bother Me Mom—I'm Learning* (http://www.games parentsteachers.com) and find out what computer/video games have strong educational content and how they can be used at home or in the classroom. Check out the other resources, including one link to "Teachers Using Games." Write a short position paper on the potential of "serious" games for instructional purposes.

Teachers are still absolutely essential, but their role is changed from one of director, leader, and final authority to one of diagnostician, prescriber, motivator, facilitator, and evaluator. Teachers, students, and aides are seen as multidimensional human resources leading to specialization and division of labor, breaking the self-contained classroom mold of today's schools. Tasks requiring professional judgment are separated from those that are routine. High-cost, professionally trained persons are assigned to the former, and lower-cost paraprofessionals are assigned to the latter. The pupil-to-teacher ratio is likely to increase over time, but the pupil-to-adult ratio is likely to remain the same or even decline from current levels as more paraprofessionals assume routine tasks.

Intelligent direction for these emerging schools depends on the professional educators associated with them, and school-based decision making is the norm for them. Their teachers have become experts in learning theory, curriculum design, motivational techniques, and developmental procedures. They have highly specialized skills in diagnosing the strengths and weaknesses of individual students with various intellectual skills and backgrounds and in prescribing best combinations of available learning experiences and resources (Darling-Hammond, 1993; Des Dixon, 1994).

The use of teaching teams results in distinct advantages for professional personnel. Each professional can specialize in the areas of expertise to

ACTIVITY 9.3
Internet Resources on Digital Instructional Technology

Addresses ISLLC Standards and Functions 1B; 2B, 2C, 2H; 4A; and 6C

Explore the following three Web sites and keep them in mind for future reference.

- http://www.schooltechleadership.org: This site, of the University Council for Educational Administration (UCEA) Center for the Advanced Study of Technology Leadership in Education at Iowa State University at Ames, is geared to the technology-related needs of school administrators. It offers several services, including a graduate-certificate program in school technology leadership, links to research and best practices, and a blog titled *Dangerously Irrelevant*.
- http://www.schooldatatutorials.org: *School Data Tutorials* is another online project of UCEA. Even when principals and teachers have access to data, they often are not sure what to do with it. This site

is intended to help K–12 educators work with raw student and school data. The tutorials highlight many of the Excel skills that are helpful when working with building- and district-level data.
- http://www.k12one2one.org: *The One-to-One Information Resource* provides a one-to-one teaching and learning environment in which each participating student is provided access to a personal computing device on a direct and continuous basis throughout the school day and, if possible, beyond. This site is useful for educators interested in knowing where other school districts/states are undertaking one-to-one initiatives as well as background information, news, announcements, and research about one-to-one teaching and learning programs for K–12 schools and organizations across the United States.

---

which that person is best suited by personality and training. The required "omniscience in the classroom," assumed under the present system as necessary for the professional, is relaxed.

Student assistants (Johnson & Johnson, 1987; Lippitt, 1975) and paraprofessional adults have become valuable staff members in these schools. The roles of both are arranged to complement and supplement that of the highly trained professionals who have the prime responsibility for guiding student instruction. For a long time, teacher supply was so abundant and teacher salaries were so low that little attention was given to maximizing teacher time available for making decisions that required professional discretion. As a result, teachers have been expected to assume assignments such as collecting lunch money, preparing worksheets and other instructional aids, and monitoring buses, cafeterias, lavatories, and hallways, all of which could be accomplished as well or better by persons without full professional teacher training. With a growing shortage of well-qualified teachers and salaries that are reaching professional levels in some districts, it becomes imperative that teachers' time be concentrated on tasks requiring

professional discretion. Less expensive persons can be employed to carry out clerical and routine tasks.

Prototype and Implemented Integrated Information Systems to Manage Individualized Instruction

The Information-Age System

Figure 9.1 illustrates an integrated information system designed to be used within the context of a learning environment committed to individualized instruction in support of information-age schools described in the preceding sections. Each of the subcomponents of the system parallels the essential functions that the teacher must perform as an instructional manager. At the center of the model is depicted the interaction between a teacher and a student meeting together (individually or in a small group) on a regular basis to develop, monitor, and update an instructional plan for the student.

The first tasks are needs assessment and accounting for the progress of the student. Both are supported by one subsystem, the *student information*

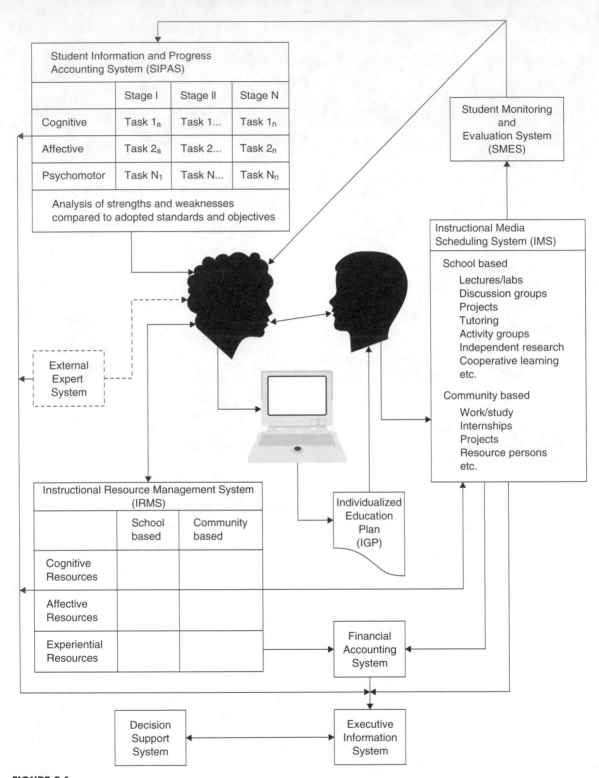

FIGURE 9.1

Information age school prototype integrated information system in support of individualized instruction *and progress accounting system* (SIPAS), for they deal with portrayal of student growth before and after specific instructional activities. Whether one emphasizes this portrayal as a process of needs assessment or evaluation is relatively unimportant. The important concept is that instructional planning requires a comprehensive picture of the student's "growth status," with sufficient information regarding his or her strengths and weaknesses. The SIPAS also contains descriptive information about the student and his or her background as well as the student's achievement over the years in all experiences within the school or district compared to expected standards and objectives as determined by the school, district, and state and augmented by the student, teacher, and family. The descriptive information about the student includes the student's physical, psychological, and emotional needs, capabilities, attitudes, perceptions, inclinations, likes, and dislikes.

With this information, possibly in consultation with an expert system in particularly troublesome situations, the teacher makes a diagnosis of the types of instructional resources and/or learning experiences needed for the student to reach the next developmental level and enters the diagnosis into the *instructional resource management system* (IRMS). The IRMS contains an inventory of all available instructional tools and strategies classified according to content, pedagogical approach, and instructional objectives (Osin, 1995). IRMS responds to the teacher's entry by listing all the available experiences that meet the teacher's criteria. The teacher then selects the experience(s) he or she feels is most appropriate for the student, and the request is forwarded to the *instructional media scheduling system* (IMSS). Again, the concept of IRMS is a simple one although very laborious to implement.

The IMSS is a master schedule of sorts, including all learning experiences available to students, such as projects, lectures, discussion groups, books, independent research, cooperative learning, tutoring, activity groups (e.g., athletics, music, drama, and debate), and so on. The important trend toward using community resources outside the school can be accommodated. Employers willing to participate in cooperative work experience can be listed, as can available internships and opportunities for youth participation in community projects. Instructional programs offered by museums, art galleries, and other cultural institutions would be included.

Once the IMSS has ensured that needed personnel, space, supplies and equipment, software, and so on are available at appropriate times and places for the event or activity ordered by the teacher for the student, the student is scheduled for the experience, and it is recorded in the IMSS; the *financial accounting system* (FAS) is notified of resources committed and, simultaneously, the experience is entered into the student's *individualized education plan* (IEP), reporting the learning goals and objectives, time and place of activities, and the nature of the assessment.

Combining input from the needs assessment and resource management systems makes possible the development of an IEP for each student; however, individualization of instruction increases the problems of scheduling and control. In existing high school systems, it is typically the task of the guidance counselor to assist students in the selection and scheduling of courses to be taken over the course of a semester. When the student's coordinating teacher assumes the role of instructional manager, as has been more typical of primary and intermediate teachers, the function of counseling is assumed as well. Because scheduling will be on an individual and objective-by-objective basis, a capability must be built into the system for handling far greater complexities of scheduling than are currently experienced by schools; many prototypes are currently in operation although not necessarily in education.

An important aspect of control is to know that activities are being pursued according to plan. In this sense, the planning capability provided by the needs assessment and resource management systems contribute to the school's control capability. Nevertheless, even greater control is desirable; the model provides a means to ensure that students actually engage in the learning activities prescribed and according to schedule. Whether the unit of study is an individualized learning packet that can be completed in 1 hour or a full-semester internship, controls are provided through the SMES. Attendance at each session of an activity is monitored. End-of-unit test results or other performance measures are implicit in every unit of instruction and are entered as evidence when an activity is completed satisfactorily. A computerized system for comparing projected completion dates with end-of-unit notifications alert teachers to difficulties and the need for modifications in a student's IEP. Linking this system with systems containing information on district finances and school and community demographic information opens the possibility to types of analyses to inform policy formulation that are impossible for virtually all schools and districts to do with the information systems typically available today (Bernhardt, 1998).

Similar prototype integrated instructional information systems have been proposed by Fullan et al. (2006) and Leithwood et al. (2006).

The Breakthrough System

Fullan et al.'s (2006) "Breakthrough" model moves away from what has always been done in classrooms "toward a new reality in which diagnostic practitioners, who have a solid core of beliefs and understandings, develop highly personalized programs that match the needs of individual students" (p. xv). The key to their system is the smart use of data to drive instruction. The core components of the Breakthrough system are personalization, precision, and professional learning. Personalization places the focus on the learner and provides an education that is designed to meet the student's learning and motivational needs.

Fullan et al. (2006) differentiate between "precision" and "prescription," which they associate with laying down rigid rules, the hallmark of current state and federal accountability programs. They link "precision" with "being uniquely accurate," as when data are used as tools for improving teaching and learning. "The problem that we tackle in Breakthrough is not only to make data more manageable but also precisely *how to link data to instruction on a daily basis.* . . . And we must do so without falling into the precision trap of fostering student dependency" (p. 20).

The third element of Breakthrough is professional learning, that is, focused, ongoing learning for each teacher. The authors are critical of typical professional development programs because they reach only a small proportion of teachers (10%–20%), they are not focused, and they are ineffective in transforming instructional strategies and content in classrooms. "You can't have personalization and precision without

daily learning on the part of teachers, both individually and collectively" (Fullan et al., 2006, p. 21).

The heart of the Breakthrough system is development of a computerized expert instructional system as a daily support to teachers providing personalized instruction to students. The massive undertaking is intended to be an ongoing research and development process with constant refinement and improvement. Design and evaluation of the expert system would involve the most experienced and competent teachers among other coresearchers and codesigners.

A key design feature of the expert instructional system is the critical learning instruction path (CLIP), an adaptation to education of critical care paths that have been critical to reforming the provision of health care. A critical care path in medicine involves mapping the typical path taken by a patient with a specific ailment from diagnosis to discharge. The map includes timing and the sequence of actions and interventions involved. The map also anticipates variations to the typical path and specifies appropriate actions to take in case of a variation. Multidisciplinary teams of specialists are involved in mapping critical care paths. The next step in developing a critical care path is to develop a system for collecting data and monitoring each patient progressing through a path. The rationale for adapting this procedure to education is "to give schools and teachers access to validated knowledge and to provide them with powerful tools to manage instruction in the most expert way possible" (Fullan et al., 2006, p. 55).

The *knowledge base* of the Breakthrough system would include the critical paths of the expert instructional system, teaching strategies, available resources, supporting research, and other relevant information. The knowledge base is joined with a *database* containing updated information on students, their progress and classroom, and school and systems characteristics. Primarily through a series of if-then algorithms, an *inference system*, using data stored in the database and knowledge base, provides professional staff with information and expert advice they seek in the form of preformatted or user-generated reports. For the classroom teacher the inference system would generate a report in the form of a focus sheet for the next lesson. The Breakthrough system provides for a *project design editor* to input information specifying how CLIP is to be implemented in different classrooms, building alternative paths, and designing experiments. The *data capture system* collects and enters into the system pre- and posttest data and other data on a daily basis and makes them available immediately to teachers and other decision makers. The *user interface* delivers the output from the system, tailored to the user's requests and position.

Fullan et al. (2006) acknowledge that

> building such a system is a major task. Indeed, it could only be done through a rigorously planned and conducted, large-scale, and adequately resourced research and development effort. It would require high levels of investment and a partnership between publicly funded university research centers, school systems, and private companies with expertise in online testing and publishing. We are convinced, however, that only through such a concerted effort and partnership will the Breakthrough occur. (p. 84)

The Making Schools Smarter System

The primary target of the information-age and Breakthrough systems previously presented is for use by classroom teachers for the purpose of improving instruction by shifting the focus of attention from interactions between teacher and class to teacher and individual learners. Making Schools Smarter (Leithwood et al., 2006) is a "monitoring system" intended primarily for district and school leaders. In the reform process to improve learning among students, the monitoring system provides school leaders with a knowledge base that enables them to make more informed decisions, thereby "leading with evidence," the subtitle of their book.

In designing the Making Schools Smarter monitoring system, the authors had to make certain assumptions about the schools and districts it would serve. They point out that all monitoring systems collect information, evaluate it, and initiate action on the basis of the evaluation; but the nature of the action taken will vary according to the nature of the organization. In a bureaucratic organization (Weber, 1947), the information generated by the evaluations will be used to diagnose deviations from policy, to determine the organization's strengths and weaknesses with respect to realizing specific goals, and

then to launch remedial action. If it is assumed that an organization is a community (Sergiovanni, 1994), the immediate impact of information derived from evaluations of the monitoring system is the enlightenment of individuals in the organization with the expectation that this will lead eventually to positive change in the actions of at least some members of the organization. The authors prefer the perception of schools and districts as *professional learning communities* (PLC), "an organization with the collective dispositions and structural characteristics enabling it to learn, through its own and others' experiences, how to continuously 'get better,' to behave more 'intelligently.' When conceived of in such terms, a monitoring system ought to serve as a powerful stimulus for raising the organization's collective capacities" (Leithwood et al., 2006, p. 6). The authors characterize the fundamental assumptions of a PLC as the staff and students being motivated by both intrinsic sources (affiliation, esteem, and self-actualization needs) and extrinsic sources (security needs) as defined in Maslow's (1954) needs hierarchy (see chapter 5). The PLC also assumes a constructivist learning process where the learner is actively involved in developing personally and socially based understandings.

The information-age and Breakthrough systems, previously discussed, are based on the conclusion that educational reform strategies currently being pursued are inadequate for realizing their intended learning objectives and that the information systems they embrace represent, in and of themselves, "radical" instructional reforms centered on the learner. The authors of the Making Schools Smarter system, on the other hand,

> believe that the curriculum frameworks and other aspects of many reform efforts will prove to be essentially correct: correct in their image of the educated person and the goals of education that need to be pursued for that image to be realized, and certainly on the right track with respect to the basic principles guiding the development of curriculum and instruction. . . . The "first order" changes called for by many of these initiatives (the goals for students and the direct services provided to help accomplish those goals) are justified by current and professional and research-based knowledge about such matters. (pp. 17–18)

Thus, the purpose of the Making Schools Smarter monitoring system is to identify the reasons for accomplishing or not accomplishing important instructional outcomes within the framework of the organization's strategic plan (see chapter 11), which may include implementation of externally generated school reform packages. In responding to failures to realize intended outcomes, the authors urge policymakers to look beyond first-order changes to second-order changes (i.e., changes in the organization of the school or district, including policies, resource allocation, structure, and/or culture).

The monitoring system organizes data into five dimensions: human, social, cultural, and economic inputs; characteristics, conditions, and processes of the school district, such as leadership and management, decision making, planning and instructional services, structure and organization, policies and procedures, and community partnerships; characteristics, conditions, and processes of the schools paralleling those of the district; immediate outcomes, such as achievement, engagement, equality, and equity; and long-term outcomes, including individual welfare and the public good. The assumption of a simple one-way causal flow of the characteristics within the first dimension through those in the fifth is not appropriate; however, there may be circumstances when causality can be assumed among the dimensions.

Districts and schools routinely collect significant amounts of data for dimension 1—human, social, cultural, and economic inputs, usually of a quantitative nature—although the data are not usually organized systemically into a database that can be easily accessed and analyzed. Dimensions 2 and 3 relating to district and school characteristics and conditions do not lend themselves as easily to quantification, but qualitative data abound. Supplementing existing data, Leithwood et al. (2006) have developed nine surveys each for the two dimensions. Achievement and other standardized test scores for students are typically available at the district and school levels, but information on student attitudes and perceptions about their schools is not usually available; the authors provide a five-part survey instrument for capturing such information. The author's assume that relevant data on dimension 5—long-term outcomes—can be easily obtained or is already available.

Student@Centre Ultranet and CASES21

The department of education in the state of Victoria, Australia (of which Melbourne is the capital city), is operationalizing an integration of several specialized information systems in support of its program of school-based decision making within the context of state standards and assessment instruments. The resulting integration is similar to that conceived in the prototype models, information-age schools and Breakthrough, presented previously. Victoria's schools are administered directly out of the Ministry of Education; that is, there are no intervening school districts. The Victoria school-based governance structure is modeled after the Edmonton, Alberta, Canada, model.

Student@Centre Ultranet is a student-centered information system that supports teaching and learning, curriculum delivery, and the management of knowledge in Victorian schools. Students and parents are provided with access to school information, class work, and school reports. Teachers are able to create and share class work, mark attendance, and conduct assessments and reporting. It was developed under contract with Oracle Australia, based on its L360 system. Development began in 2004; in 2005, Ultranet was piloted in 12 government schools in the Melbourne metropolitan area. The pilot involved approximately 630 teachers, 10,000 students, and 300 parents. General deployment commenced in 2008 and is to be completed by the end of 2010. When fully deployed, the user group will include approximately 1.5 million persons as follows:

- 1,600 government schools
- 2,850 principals and department of education and regional office staff
- 44,000 registered teachers
- 14,000 school service officers
- 300 school technical staff
- 540,000 students
- 900,000 parents
  (http://www.education.vic.gov.au/management/ultranet/ tender.htm, September 7, 2007)

Victoria has been a world leader in the provision of technology to government schools, building schools' and teachers' capacity to engage with information communication technology (ICT). Development of the Ultranet marks a change in focus from peripheral engagement and supply to holistic intent and demand. The primary purpose of the Ultranet is to provide an ICT framework that allows the whole school community to engage with learning in ways not previously possible by doing the following:

- Enabling better communication between all key stakeholders, including students, teachers, parents, support staff, principals, school administrators, and regional and departmental administrators

- Simplifying many of the administrative requirements of schools and teachers—less time on gathering data, more time acting on it

- Facilitating greater collaboration between individual teachers and teams of teachers within and across learning areas and schools

- Supporting teaching and learning through the sharing of ideas and resources

- Extending the scope of what can be achieved by circumventing many of the physical and organizational constraints placed on the classroom teacher

- Enabling unprecedented transparency of the classroom

- Providing continuous feedback to parents, students, and student managers

- Creating knowledge about every student's learning and progress as well as knowledge about the process of teaching and learning

Functions of the Ultranet that teachers found to be particularly useful by the evaluation of its pilot implementation (Griffin & Woods, 2006) are reported in Table 9.1. Ultranet brings together seamlessly various aspects of the classroom (teaching and learning plus associated administrative functions) into a single, central, logical environment. It has had a profound effect on the way teachers, students, parents, and other staff share information and cooperate where knowledge builds on knowledge within the organization itself rather than remaining with individuals that make up the organization. It brings together the key processes involved in the day-to-day running of a school and a classroom, pervading the very culture of the school.

The Computerized Administrative System Environment in Schools (CASES) is the platform that has provided a standard administrative system for the state's school-based decision-making structure since the 1980s. CASES stores and processes a range of school-generated data, including student records and financial, physical, and human resource data. CASES is designed for principal use and provides a direct link to the department of education in support of policy analyses at the state level.

The current integrated school administration and finance software system is known as CASES21. It is a customized version of the MAZE school software system marketed commercially by RM Asia-Pacific. It provides school staff with secure access to data entry and reporting modules that support the broad range of school administration and finance functions. It also helps schools provide key data required for central accountability reporting. The software is regularly modified and enhanced to meet evolving school business needs and accountability requirements. School use of CASES21 is supported by a centrally provided standard operating environment, including hardware and communications infrastructure, an extensive training program, support documentation, a service desk, and regional support staff (http://www.sofweb.vic.edu.au/ict/cases21/index.htm, September 5, 2007).

SUMMARY AND FUNDAMENTAL CONCEPTS

According to Wheatley (2006), information forms us as individuals and our organizations. For an organization to be true to its mission, information must flow freely within that organization and between it and its environment. For most of recorded history, information developed slowly and linearly, making the task of assimilation relatively simple. Today, information is expanding at exponential rates, and individuals and organizations are bombarded with overwhelming amounts of data at random. Separating the relevant from the nonrelevant and making sense of it all has become an essential task of individuals and of organizations. Information systems have been developed to assist the process, supported by a burgeoning information and communications technology.

Educational institutions were precursors of the information age. Ironically, however, schools, with few exceptions, have not kept pace with the rest of society in

TABLE 9.1

Functions of the Ultranet that Teachers Perceived as Particularly Useful in Different School Contexts

Primary Schools	Secondary Schools	Special Education Schools
Curriculum planning that is shared and agreed across the school.	Vehicle for delivery of a unified and equitable curriculum so that all students have similar access to quality teaching and resources.	Being able to share resources, ideas, and materials with other special education teachers within the school, in other special schools, and in mainstream schools. Teachers hope that the information they post will be useful to teachers working with integrated students in mainstream classrooms.
Easy access to VELS and learning materials when planning tasks and activities: "It's particularly useful for teachers to look into the Ultranet, find what they need, when planning a new unit of work." "There's a really good buzz about the Learning Federation materials."	Shift away from end of semester reporting toward a constant and ongoing feedback model. Teachers are pleased about the possibility of allowing parents to get a clear indication of student progress and track whether students are handing work in on time and to a satisfactory standard.	Teachers would like to have a facility to upload each student's individual learning plan (ILP) and be able to asses, record, and report against that ILP.
Opportunities to share resources, information, and ideas with other schools and other teachers. "One of the best things is building communities of like-minded schools and teachers regardless of geographic area."	Attendance marking to monitor absenteeism and habitual lateness but preferably linked to a timetabling package.	Potential for the future in terms of cutting down paperwork, reducing time spent checking back over resources, and modifying existing resources. Teachers appreciate that everything is stored together and that comments and feedback can flow through to reporting.
Students having access to high-quality resources anywhere and anytime, especially for older primary students.	Access to VELS for students to monitor their progress and to gain a clear understanding of what is expected of them.	The Learning Federation resources are attractive for students in special education schools.
Maintenance of consistency, of teaching across grades, through mutual support and sharing resources.	Supporting communication and collaboration between teachers, minimizing "reinvention of the wheel," duplication of teaching materials.	
Being able to look more closely at grouping students when setting project work and using a buddy system to support students.	Teachers expect to be able to decrease the amount of photocopying and build up a resource bank.	
Students being able to chat with students at other schools.	Ensuring equity in assessment (all students being assessed against similar tasks and the severity of marking being open to comment).	
	Helping students manage their own workload and keep up to date.	
	Building education partnerships between teachers, parents and students. The ability to support communication with the parents is widely welcomed in secondary schools.	

Source: Adapted from Griffin and Woods (2006, pp. 37–38).

adapting to that age. This is a source of the widespread public dissatisfaction with schools. Most of today's schools were designed for conditions existing in the industrial era, a simpler and slower time. To accommodate the educational needs of an information age, schools themselves must be reinvented.

In this chapter, we discussed the role of information in organizations and how data are collected, processed into information, and used to make policy or to design curricula through information systems. We described a new breed of schools that are designed to meet the challenges of the information age. Finally, we presented prototypes of information systems in support of information-age schools.

Chapter 10 begins a three-chapter discussion of the decision-making process in and about schools. We describe the functioning of the economic and political sectors in which those decisions are made and implemented. We also address issues of when and how governments should become involved in the decision-making and implementation processes. The chapter closes with detailed descriptions of the decision processes that led to major reform of several districts.

Fundamental Concepts

The fundamental concepts that follow have been discussed in this chapter. The citations that conclude each concept indicate the Interstate School Leaders Licensure Consortium (ISLLC) standards and functions related to the concept. The Arabic numeral refers to the ISLLC standard, and the letters refer to the function as presented in the table found inside the front cover.

- A learning or self-renewing organization can only maintain its fluidity (and stability) if it has continuing access to new information about external factors and internal resources. (1B; 1D; 2E, 2H, 2I; 3A, 3B; 4A, 4B; 5A, 5D; 6)
- It is important to design organizations and nurture organizational cultures that allow for and encourage the informal sharing of information among members and provide them discretionary freedom to exercise their tacit understandings. (1A; 2A, 2F; 3D)
- Data consist of raw facts, whereas information is a collection of facts organized in such a way that they have additional value beyond the value of the facts themselves. (1B; 2E, 2I; 3A; 4A; 5A; 6C)
- An information system is a set of interrelated elements or components that collect (input), manipulate and store (process), and disseminate to targeted

persons data and information (output). (1B; 2E, 2I; 3A; 4A; 5A; 6C)
- To understand a school or district thoroughly and to monitor its operations effectively, all information sources need to be linked so that information may flow freely from one to another and so that analysts may draw data from any combination of sources in undertaking new analyses. (1B; 2E, 2I; 3A; 4A; 5A; 6C)
- That which cannot be measured cannot be controlled or understood. (1B; 2E, 2I; 3A; 4A; 5A; 6C)
- Collecting and analyzing data around an organization's priority objectives is essential for improvement, for validating efforts, and for refining strategies. (1; 2E, 2I; 3A; 4A; 5A; 6C)
- Management in any form is prediction, statistical data are essential to improvement, and facts, reasoning, and evidence should drive operational decisions, not power or authority or personality. (3)
- Research, experimentation, and data gathering are built into the daily routine of learning organizations. (1B; 2E, 2I; 3A; 4A; 5A; 6C)
- The workers of the school—principals, teachers, secretaries, bus drivers, cleaners, and so on—are the experts in what they do and are fully capable of improving their own performance when given feedback that enables them to monitor their own work. (1A, 1B; 2E, 2F, 2I; 3A, 3D; 4A; 5A; 6C)
- From an economic standpoint, labor-intensive education is unnecessarily expensive, and in general it does not produce a workforce with prerequisite attitudes and skills needed for a rapidly changing workplace. (2H; 3B)
- From a sociological standpoint, technologically unsophisticated schools are losing their credibility and thereby their effectiveness with pupils because they are no longer congruent with the larger societal context. (2C, 2H; 6C)
- The purpose of technology is to make labor go further by replacing it, to the extent possible, with less expensive nonhuman devices and more efficient organization in order to produce better products and services and/or to reduce the costs of providing them. (2H; 3B)
- Technological devices should be integral parts of new learning systems that combine the capabilities and energy of students and teachers with those devices to achieve results superior to that which could be achieved without them or to achieve equal results at a lower cost. (2C, 2H; 6C)
- The purchase of equipment should represent only about 10% of the total cost of an innovation if that innovation is to be effective. (3A, 3B)

- The very limited success of four decades of efforts intended to raise the academic and other forms of student achievement may be because those reforms have failed to focus on classroom instruction, itself. (2; 3E)
- Another likely contributor to the lack of success of reform efforts is the failure to recognize the pervasive impact of digital technology on the minds and lives of students from pre-K through college and failure to integrate that technology into schools' instructional processes. (2H; 6C)
- Intense digital exposure by the student generation has led to new thinking patterns on their part that are quite different from those assumed in the 20th-century curricula. (2; 6C)
- In implementing school reforms, the interaction of classroom and organizational factors must be considered systemically. (3B)
- No longer need cost be a prohibiting factor in delivering quality instruction when the traditional practices of the classroom are redesigned to take full advantage of digital technology and software now available. (2H; 3B)
- Learning is primarily a function of the interest, motivation, and hard work of the student. (2C)

References

Baumol, W. J. (1967). Macroeconomics of unbalanced growth: The anatomy of urban crisis. *American Economic Review, 57*(3), 415–426.

Benson, C. (1961). *The economics of public education.* Boston: Houghton Mifflin.

Bernhardt, V. L. (1998). *Data analysis for comprehensive school-wide improvement.* Larchmont, NY: Eye on Education.

Bolton, W. R. (1994). *Factors that may influence the use of computer technology in the teaching and learning process.* Unpublished doctoral dissertation, State University of New York at Buffalo.

Borja, R. R. (2007). Teaching assistants. *Education Week, 26*(30), 18–22.

Bromley, H. (1998). Introduction: Data-driven democracy? Social assessment of educational computing. In H. Bromley & M. W. Apple (Eds.), *Education/technology/power: Educational computing as a social practice* (pp. 1–25). Albany: State University of New York Press.

Butzin, S. M. (1992). Integrating technology into the classroom: Lessons from the Project CHILD experience. *Phi Delta Kappan, 74,* 330–333.

Cuban, L. (1988). *The managerial imperative and the practice of leadership in schools.* Albany: State University of New York Press.

Darling-Hammond, L. (1993). Reframing the school reform agenda: Developing capacity for school transformation. *Phi Delta Kappan, 74,* 752–761.

Dede, C. (1998). The scaling-up process for technology-based educational innovations. In C. Dede (Ed.), *Learning with technology: Association for Supervision and Curriculum Development Yearbook* (pp. 199–215). Alexandria, VA: Association for Supervision and Curriculum Development.

Deming, W. E. (1986). *Out of the crisis.* Cambridge, MA: MIT Press.

Des Dixon, R. G. (1994). Future schools: How to get there from here. *Phi Delta Kappan, 75,* 360–365.

Doyle, D. P. (1994). The role of private sector management in public education. *Phi Delta Kappan, 76,* 128–132.

Elmore, R. F. (2007). *School reform from the inside out: Policy, practice, and performance.* Cambridge, MA: Harvard Education Press.

Frazier, A. (1997). *A roadmap for quality transformation in education.* Boca Raton, FL: St. Lucie Press.

Fullan, M., Hill, P., & Crevola, C. (2006). *Breakthrough.* Thousand Oaks, CA: Corwin Press.

Fullerton, K. (1998). Common "mythstakes" in technology planning. In K. C. Westbrook (Ed.), *Technology and the educational workplace: Understanding fiscal impacts* (pp. 63–76). Thousand Oaks, CA: Corwin Press.

Fulmer, C. L. (1995). Maximizing the potential of information technology for management. In B. Z. Barta, M. Telem, & Y. Gev (Eds.), *Information technology in educational management* (pp. 3–8). Padstow, England: TJ Press.

Gewertz, C. (2007). Outside interests. *Education Week, 26*(30), 24–27.

Glennan, T. K., & Melmed, A. (1996). *Fostering the use of educational technology: Elements of a national strategy.* Santa Monica, CA: RAND Corporation. Available: http://www.rand.org/publications/MR/MR682/contents.html

Goodlad, J. I. (1984). *A place called school: Prospects for the future.* New York: McGraw-Hill.

Griffin, P., & Woods, K. (2006). *Evaluation of the pilot implementation of the Student@Centre Ultranet in Victorian schools.* Melbourne: University of Melbourne, Assessment Research Centre.

Halal, W. E., & Liebowitz, J. (1994). Telelearning: The multimedia revolution in education. *Futurist, 28*(6), 21–26.

Johnson, D. W., & Johnson, R. (1987). *Learning together and alone: Cooperative, competitive, and individualistic learning* (2nd ed.). Upper Saddle River, NJ: Prentice Hall.

Kozma, R., & Schank, P. (1998). Connecting with the 21st century: Technology in support of educational reform. In C. Dede (Ed.), *Learning with technology: Association for Supervision and Curriculum Development Yearbook* (pp. 3–21). Alexandria, VA: Association for Supervision and Curriculum Development.

Leithwood, K., Aitken, R., & Jantzi, D. (2006). *Making schools smarter: Leading with evidence* (3rd ed.). Thousand Oaks, CA: Corwin Press.

Levin, B. (1994). Improving educational productivity: Putting students at the center. *Phi Delta Kappan, 75,* 758–760.

Levin, H., & Meister, G. (1985). *Educational technology and computers: Promises, promises, always promises* (Project Report 85-A13). Stanford, CA: Stanford Education Policy Institute, Stanford University.

Lippitt, P. (1975). *Students teach students.* Bloomington, IN: Phi Delta Kappa Educational Foundation.

Maslow, A. H. (1954). *Motivation and personality.* New York: Harper & Row.

Mecklenburger, J. A. (1994). Thinking about schooling in the Global Village: We can see into the future of schooling, now. And its name is not just "reform." *Inventing Tomorrow's Schools, 4*(2), 2–9.

Mintzberg, H. (1994). *The rise and fall of strategic planning.* New York: Free Press.

Murphy, J. (1993). What's in? What's out? American education in the nineties. *Phi Delta Kappan, 74,* 641–646.

New Commission on the Skills of the American Workforce. (2007). *Tough choices or tough times.* San Francisco: Wiley/Jossey-Bass.

Osin, L. (1995). Educational management in Israeli elementary schools. In B.-Z. Barta, M. Telem, & Y. Gev (Eds.), *Information technology in educational management* (pp. 209–214). Pasdstow, England: TJ Press.

Prensky, M. (2006). *"Don't bother me mom—I'm learning!"* St. Paul, MN: Paragon House.

Rowley, J. (1996). *The basics of information systems* (2nd ed.). London: Library Association Publishing.

Schmoker, M. J., & Wilson, R. B. (1993). *Total quality education: Profiles of schools that demonstrate the power of Deming's management principles.* Bloomington, IN: Phi Delta Kappa Educational Foundation.

Sergiovanni, T. (1994). *Building community in schools.* San Francisco: Jossey-Bass.

Sizer, T. R. (2004). *The red pencil: Convictions from experience in education.* New Haven, CT: Yale University Press.

Stair, R. M. (1992). *Principles of information systems: A managerial approach.* Boston: Boyd & Frazier.

Taylor, R. G. (1995). Graphic information and school facility planning. In B.-Z. Barta, M. Telem, & Y. Gev (Eds.), *Information technology in educational management* (pp. 153–161). Padstow, England: TJ Press.

Trotter, A. (1997). Taking technology's measure. *Education Week, 17*(11), 12–18.

Trotter, A. (2007). Getting up to speed. *Education Week, 26*(30), 10–16.

Vaizey, J., Norris, K., & Sheehan, J. (1972). *The political economy of education.* New York: Wiley.

Viadero, D. (2007). Collecting evidence. *Education Week, 26*(30), 30–33.

Weber, M. (1947). *The theory of social and economic organization.* New York: Free Press.

Westbrook, K. C. (1998). *Technology and the educational workplace: Understanding fiscal impacts.* Thousand Oaks, CA: Corwin Press.

Wheatley, M. J. (2006). *Leadership and the new science: Discovering order in a chaotic world* (3rd ed.). San Francisco: Berrett-Koehler.

Wheatley, M. J., & Kellner-Rogers, M. (1996). *A simpler way.* San Francisco: Berrett-Koehler.

Wholeben, B. E. (1995). Interactive simulation for planning, coordination, and control: Mathematical decision support systems in education. In B.-Z. Barta, M. Telem, & Y. Gev (Eds.), *Information technology in educational management* (pp. 162–169). Padstow, England: TJ Press.

Willett, E., Swanson, A., & Nelson, E. (1979). *Modernizing the little red schoolhouse: The economics of improved schooling.* Englewood Cliffs, NJ: Educational Technology.

Zehr, M. A. (1997). Teaching the teachers. *Education Week, 17*(11), 24–29.

Decision Making

All that has gone before—understanding education as a complex network of systems, grasping the nature of leadership, and developing the skills of observation, inquiry, evaluation, human relations, and communication—is a prelude to the ultimate tasks of the educational leader: decision making and implementation. Unless decisions are made and implemented, all the other activities and understandings are only intellectual exercises; it is when they are translated into action that their potential for good becomes reality.

Educational decision making assumes many forms. Formally, it is practiced in the political context of educational policy development at the school, district, regional, state, and national levels. The resulting policies affect the daily operation of all educational enterprises: public and private schools, colleges, universities, and vocational/technical training programs.

The central theme of part IV is decision making as it takes place at four levels (school, district, state, and national). Chapter 10 centers on policy development at the three higher levels, while chapter 11 centers on decision making at the district and school levels and by individuals. Chapter 12 is devoted specifically to human and economic resource allocation decisions made at all four levels.

Chapter 10: Educational Policy Formulation in a Mixed Economy.

Policy formulation as collective decision making through the market (economics) and through governments (politics) is the focus of chapter 10. We begin by examining the basic arguments for providing elementary and secondary education through the public sector (i.e., government) and the social tensions this creates in attempting to accommodate both societal and personal preferences. Then we turn our attention to describing the political and economic processes that determine how many and what kind of resources will be used for educational purposes, how those resources will be used, and who the beneficiaries will be. Special attention is given to the role of the courts in policy formulation and to collective bargaining with unions. The chapter includes descriptions of the reform processes of three major cities and the governance revolution being brought about by charter schools.

Chapter 11: District and School-Based Decision Making: Strategy Formation and Planning.

Decision making as done by individuals and within relatively small organizations as schools and school districts is examined in chapter 11. The first section of the chapter discusses decision theory. The second section presents a structure for making decisions within educational organizations at the district and school levels. Factors that should be considered in distributing authority between districts and schools are examined.

Chapter 12: The Allocation of Resources to and within Educational Organizations: Adequacy, Equity, and Efficiency.

Issues concerning the allocation of human and economic resources to the education sector and within educational enterprises are addressed in chapter 12. This represents an essential part of planning and strategy implementation. Demands for resources always exceed their availability; therefore, it is incumbent on educators to use available resources to maximize productivity within the context of organizational priorities. Throughout the chapter, special attention is given to the values of adequacy, equity, and efficiency.

Educational Policy Formulation in a Mixed Economy

Any organization, whether it is the U.S. government, a state government, a business or an industry, a voluntary or a charitable association, a local school district, or a school, needs to agree on a set of rules under which it will operate. These rules are called *policies*— or *laws* in the case of government when formally adopted through a prescribed legislative procedure. Rules and regulations generated by a government bureau or agency under authorization of a law are also considered policy.

Policies establish the parameters within which an organization will function. They specify the activities that the organization will or will not carry out. Policies act to guide coherent action by channeling the thinking of employees and other members of the organization. They set constraints within which discretion can be exercised. They are necessary so that all partners in an endeavor have the same "marching orders," visions, and intentions (Kaufman & Herman, 1991).

The state and federal constitutions specify the formal procedures to be followed in adopting laws. But laws are usually written in quite broad terms and must be interpreted in order to be implemented. The interpretation begins with the bureau within the executive branch of government given the responsibility for administering the law (e.g., state education departments and the U.S. Department of Education). Decisions made by bureaucrats to guide actions at lower levels of authority and written in the form of regulations are as much policy as the laws themselves. Sometimes policies by bureaucrats and laws by legislatures are contested in courts; the decisions of jurists then become incorporated into operating policy.

State law specifies general procedures to be followed by local school districts in formulating policy, although variation is permitted in specific practices. School districts may specify procedures to be followed by schools in setting policy, or they may let schools establish their own procedures subject to district review and approval, as with some charter schools. Private organizations may go through formal incorporation that specifies a corporate procedure to be followed in making decisions, or they may informally agree on a constitution or a set of bylaws to guide corporate decision making. In the public sector, policies are usually (and preferably) written. Policies may, however, be informal, unwritten, and unstated agreements by which members of an organization bind their actions.

Although constitutions, laws, charters, bylaws, and so on spell out the formal steps to be followed in arriving at group decisions (i.e., policy), the human interactions in carrying out those steps are not specified. Often these interactions involve elaborate strategies, power plays, and intrigue employed by individuals and groups bonded by common interests to shape an organization's (or government's) decisions. These interactions, whether simple or elaborate, can be referred to as *politics*. Indeed, Hodgkinson (1983) referred to politics as "administration by another name." The nature of both the structure of the policy-making process and the politics employed within the structure are believed to influence policy outcomes (Dye, 1987). Major structural reform strategies, such as charter schools, education vouchers, and parental choice of schools, are based on this belief.

In the United States, 89% of the boys and girls enrolled in elementary and secondary schools are in schools operated by government (i.e., public schools, including public charter schools). The other 11% are in home schooling or schools operated independently or by religious or other not-for-profit organizations (National Center for Education Statistics [NCES], 2006), but even these schools are monitored to varying degrees by governmental agencies and are formally chartered or incorporated by a governmental unit. Public schools, on the other hand, are strongly influenced by what goes on in the nongovernment sector through their dealings in "the market" and through formal and informal pressures placed on governmental decision-making processes by individuals and private interest groups.

It is not possible to understand why public schools have acquired the nature they possess or how to change that nature without understanding how decisions about schooling are made and how public and private resources are transformed into the realization of societal and individual aspirations for education. In this chapter we describe the functioning of the economic and political arenas in which those decisions are made and implemented.

We begin this chapter by examining the basic arguments for providing elementary and secondary education through the public sector (i.e., government) and the social tensions this creates when attempting to accommodate personal preferences. Then we turn our attention to describing the political and economic processes that determine how many and what kind of resources will be used for educational purposes, how those resources will be used, and who the beneficiaries will be. Special attention is given to the role of the courts in policy formulation and to collective bargaining with unions.

Education: A Public and Private Good

Education brings important benefits to both individuals and society. If public benefits were simply the sum of individual benefits, there would be no conflict, but this is not the case. Frequently, there are substantial differences between societal and individual interests (Labaree, 1997). Full public interest would not be realized if provision of education were left solely to private vendors and to people's ability to pay for education. Conversely, it is unlikely that the full private or individual interest would be satisfied if education were left solely to public provision. Thus, education is considered to be both a public and a private *good*.

Private goods are divisible, and their benefits are left primarily to their owners. If a person desires a particular item or service, he or she can legally obtain the item by negotiating an agreed-on price with the current owner. The new owner can enjoy the item or service, whereas those unable or unwilling to pay the price cannot. A good is private if someone who does not pay for it can be excluded from its use and enjoyment. This is known as the *exclusion principle*. Such goods are readily provided through the market system (i.e., the private sector).

The private (or individual) benefits of education, whether gained through public or private institutions, include the ability to earn more money and to enjoy a higher standard of living and a better quality of life. As part of this, educated persons are likely to be employed at more interesting jobs than are less educated persons. Schooling opens up the possibility of more schooling, which in turn leads to even better employment possibilities; long-term unemployment is much less likely. Similarly, educated persons, through knowledge and understanding of the arts and other manifestations of culture and with greater resources at their disposal, are likely to have more options for the use of leisure time and are likely to use such time in more interesting ways. As informed consumers, they are likely to get more mileage out of their resources. Finally, better educated persons are likely to enjoy a better diet and have better health practices; this results in less sickness and a longer productive life.

Educational opportunities can be excluded from those unwilling or unable to pay for them; thus, schooling could be provided exclusively through the private sector as it was prior to the organization of public schools during the 19th century. But if this were the case, there would be a number of socially undesirable external effects because the public (or societal) benefits of publicly provided education would be lost or at least severely diminished. These benefits include enlightened citizenship among the general population, which is particularly important to a democratic form of government. In addition, in projecting a common set of values and knowledge, schools can foster a sense of community and national identity and loyalty among a diverse population. A public school system can provide an effective network for talent identification and development, spurring the creation of both cultural and technological innovations and providing the skilled workforce required for the efficient functioning of society. This is believed to contribute to economic growth and to a generally more vital and pleasant quality of life for everyone.

These benefits are considered to be of such social importance that public funds are used to provide for the schooling of 89% of the school-age population in the United States. At the same time, parents of at least 11% of the school-age population hold private preferences so compelling that they are willing to pay for the private instruction of their children as well as taxes in support of the public schools (NCES, 2006). Pure private provision would probably mean that education services would be less available than is socially desirable. Public provision by taxation is called for when social benefits exceed private benefits. When private benefits dominate, user fees or full-cost tuition becomes appropriate.

Structuring the decision-making process for education is particularly complex because education provides both social and private benefits. Procuring educational services incurs costs and produces benefits that accrue to individuals independently while incurring social costs and producing benefits that accrue to society collectively. Levin (1987) concluded that there is a potential dilemma when schools are expected to provide both public and private benefits:

> Public education stands at the intersection of two legitimate rights: the right of a democratic society to assure its reproduction and continuous democratic functioning through providing a common set of values and knowledge and the right of families to decide the ways in which their children will be molded and the types of influences to which their children will be exposed. To the degree that families have different political, social, and religious beliefs and values, there may be a basic incompatibility between their private concerns and the public functions of schooling. (p. 629)

To ensure that both individual and societal demands of schooling are met, decisions about the provision of education are made in both the public and the private domains. Decisions in the public sector are made through political processes by governments, whereas decisions in the private sector are made by individuals using market mechanisms. Easton (1965) described politics as the process by which *values* are allocated within society. Economics, on the other hand, is the study of the allocation of *scarce resources* within society. Economics is concerned with production, distribution, and consumption of commodities and services. Efficiency in the use of resources is the objective of economics. Politics is powered by collective (societal) concerns, whereas economics is powered by individual or private concerns.

Obviously, one's value priorities strongly influence one's judgment as to what are efficient and equitable allocations of material resources. Thus, there is continuing interaction between economics and politics. Decisions about the nature of education for a society's youth, how it will be provided, and how it will be financed are prime points of interaction. Decisions about public involvement in education are made in political arenas, but the decisions made in those arenas will have strong economic implications for individuals and for private businesses as well as for communities, states, and the nation. Individuals and businesses will respond independently to political decisions by deciding whether to participate in government programs or to supplement or substitute for government programs by purchasing services provided through the private sector.

The Influence of the Marketplace on Public Policy

The Free Market

Any society has to make certain fundamental economic decisions: *What* shall be produced? *How* shall it be produced? *For whom* shall it be produced? (Samuelson, 1980).

In a capitalistic economy, people prefer to make such decisions for private goods through unrestrained or self-regulating markets. Figure 10.1 illustrates the circular flow of a monetary economy between two sets of actors: households and producers. It is assumed

FIGURE 10.1

Circular flow of resources in a monetary economy

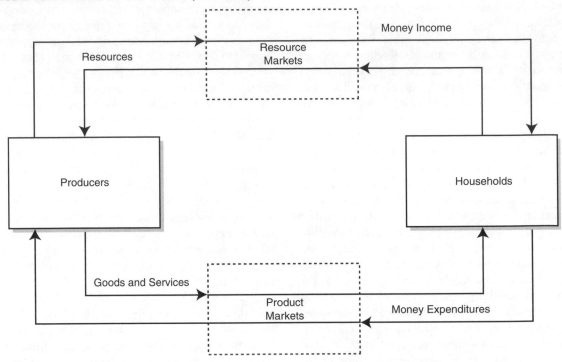

that households own all resources (capital) and that producers (or enterprises) have the capacity of converting resources into finished goods and services desired by members of the households.

Resources are traditionally grouped into three categories called *factors of production:* land, labor, and physical capital. *Land* refers not only to the dry surface area of the earth but also to its vegetation, wildlife, and mineral content. *Labor* represents the human resources that go into production. Originally, economic analysts defined labor in quantitative terms only as the number of workers and the time they worked. With the advent of human capital theory (T. W. Schultz, 1963), the quality of labor has also been considered to be an important economic characteristic of labor. Formal education is, of course, an important means of improving the quality of the workforce. A primary motivating force of the current school reform movement is the fear that the United States is not improving the quality of its workforce as rapidly as its international competitors and as more sophisticated technologies demand.

Physical capital refers to the produced means of production, such as infrastructure, buildings, machinery, and computers. Households may own land and capital outright or as shareholders in a corporation, and they also control the availability of their individual labor. The education level of the workforce correlates directly with the level of sophistication of capital that may reasonably be used in the production process.

The households (e.g., teachers and their families) and the producers (e.g., schools and school districts, colleges, and universities) each have something the other wants and needs. Producers need the resources controlled by households in order to produce finished goods and services. Households need the goods and services provided by the producers: for survival in the case of food and shelter and for improved quality of life in the case of many other goods. To facilitate the exchange, markets provide a means of communication. Producers acquire the resources they need through resource markets by making money income available to households in the form of wages, rents, interest, and profits. Households in turn use the money acquired through the sale of resources to purchase finished goods and services in product markets (e.g., private schooling). It is these sales that provide producers with money to purchase resources from the households. And so the cycle continues.

Through markets, households and producers negotiate prices to be paid for resources and finished goods and services. The outcomes of these negotiations ultimately determine the answers to the three economic questions raised previously. Resources are scarce and unevenly distributed among households, while household wants are unlimited. This means that each household must prioritize its wants and satisfy as many of them as possible within the constraints of the resources it controls and the cost of those resources. The value, or price, of resources depends on supply and demand.

Figure 10.2 illustrates the interaction between supply and demand as related to the number of teachers that schools employ and the amount they pay for their services. The demand curve shows that there is an inverse relationship between the level of teacher salaries and the number of teachers that school districts are willing to employ. Conversely, the supply curve shows that the number of persons willing to take jobs as teachers is high when salaries are high and low when salaries are low. Thus, if salaries

are at P_1 as illustrated in Figure 10.2, there is a gap (Q_1 to Q_3) between the number of persons willing to work at that wage and the number of teachers desired to be employed by school districts. To close the gap, school districts must raise salaries to P_3 in order to attract the desired number of teachers (Q_3) or strike a compromise whereby the number of teachers to be employed is reduced to Q_2, for example, and raising salaries it is willing to pay to P_2. With fewer teachers than the number originally desired, a shift in strategy is required for organizing schools in the district. One strategy is to substitute technology for teachers. As teacher salaries increase, technological substitutes become relatively less expensive. Thus, fewer teachers being responsible for larger numbers of students using sophisticated instructional technology may be able to achieve academic results comparable to more teachers responsible for smaller numbers of students using little instructional technology. Alternatively, rather than purchasing instructional technology, a district may provide low-cost teacher aides to assist teachers in managing the instruction of larger numbers of students.

Producers in the private sector will produce only that which will incur reasonable profits. Profit depends on the amount of a good or a service that is sold, the price, and the cost of production. If the demand for a product is not sufficient to sell all units produced at a price above the cost of production, no profit can be made. Under such circumstances, the producer has three options: reduce the cost of production by adopting more efficient means of production, shift production to another product that can be sold for a profit, or go out of business. When conditions permit an above-average profit for producing a given good or service, more producers are attracted into the field. The number of units produced increases and the price drops to the point at which supply equals demand and the rate of profit returns to a normal range.

Each dollar controlled by each consuming household is a potential vote to be cast in favor of the production of one good or service over another or the product of one producer over the product of a competitor. The influence of a household over producers is approximately proportional to the value of the resources controlled by the household. This

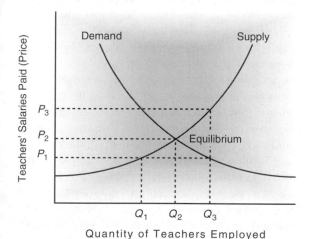

FIGURE 10.2

Supply and demand curves

poses ethical dilemmas. The rich make expenditures for improving the quality of life, while the poor lack basic necessities. In addition, development of highly efficient low-cost technologies leads to a reduction in the demand for labor, causing reductions in wages and/or widespread unemployment. The design and operation of highly sophisticated instruments and techniques is usually done by well-educated persons; thus, the burden of unemployment and low wages is likely to fall disproportionately on those with little formal education. The issue of equity with respect to allocation of resources for education is discussed in chapter 12.

Government and the Market

We do not rely solely on market mechanisms to make economic decisions, however, because society has many needs that cannot be met through the market. More than 40% of our gross domestic product is distributed according to political decisions made by governments (e.g., municipalities and school districts). Important differences distinguish governmental units from households and producers in the ways they answer economic questions and the criteria they use. Downs (1957) identified government as that agency in the division of labor that has as its *proper* function the maximization of social welfare. When results generated by free markets are ethically or economically unsatisfactory from a societal perspective, government can be used as a tool of intervention to set things right. Governments have the unique power to extract involuntary payments, called *taxes*, from households and producers alike, and the federal government controls the money supply, on which both public and private sectors depend. Governmental programs and agencies are not profit oriented, and they rarely "go out of business." When they do, it is the result of political decisions and not market forces, although conditions in the market may influence political decisions. Efficiency has not traditionally been an overriding objective of the public sector, but growing numbers of persons think that it should be as evidenced by the emergence of school and teacher accountability for student achievement as an educational reform option. Thus, efficiency of educational operations

has become an important criterion in evaluating the progress of school reform.

Figure 10.3 inserts government (the public sector) into the center of the circular flow of a monetary economy. As noted, government obtains money for its operations through taxes on producers and households. With this money, government acquires resources through resource markets and goods and services through product markets the same as do households and producers. No separate markets exist for the private and public sectors; government demands are factored into the resource and product markets in establishing prices. Thus, there is not a unique market for school personnel, for example; school districts compete with businesses, professions, and other governmental units for desired human services. When governments borrow heavily from the financial market, interest rates go up for everyone alike—for the school district borrowing to build a schoolhouse as well as for a person borrowing to buy an automobile or a house.

Governments produce many goods and services that are desired by households and producers. These include public schooling, national defense, fire and police protection, airports, harbor facilities, parks, and roads. Typically, such services are neither distributed through the market nor priced through the market. Decisions concerning supply and efficiency of production become political decisions; thus, the "price" of such goods and services is equivalent to their "cost." Efficiency of public schools, for example, becomes an issue only when the electorate makes it an issue since public schools do not go out of business due to market forces because of high costs or poor performance. By serving 89% of the potential clientele and having access to the power of taxation to meet their revenue needs, public schools take on many of the characteristics of a monopoly.

Because public-sector decisions are political and, ideally, political power is distributed evenly among the electorate (i.e., one person, one vote), there are marked differences in the answers given to the three economic questions cited earlier than if the decisions were made through the private sector (market), where influence is distributed in proportion to the amount of resources controlled (i.e., the rich have much influence and the poor have little).

FIGURE 10.3

Circular flow of resources, including government (the public sector)

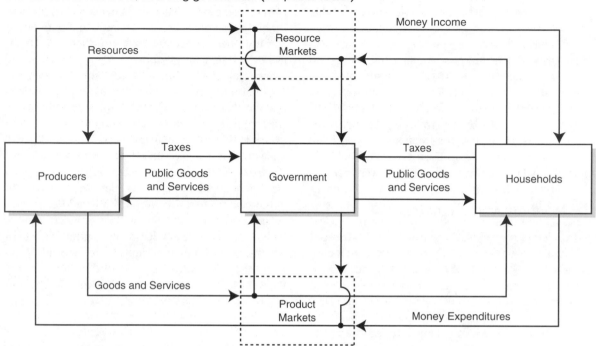

The greater relative power of the poor in the public sector compared with the private sector leads to an equalitarian bias in decisions made in the public sector. The private sector has a bias toward efficient use of resources as well as a libertarian bias to permit the exercise of individual preferences within the limits of resources available to each person.

Thus, in making decisions about education, natural tensions exist among households, members of the teaching profession, and society at large. To the extent that decisions are made in the private sector, individuals and families can maximize their personal aspirations within the limits of their economic resources and according to individual value preferences. Professionals are free to provide or to withhold services and to determine the nature of those services. But when decisions are made through the political process, individuals and groups of varying value orientations must negotiate a single solution, and their value preferences may be compromised in the process.

Proponents of decentralizing and privatizing the public educational bureaucracy, school-based decision making, and family choice of schooling share the view that too many educational decisions are being made by government. Some proponents believe that this has led to an unwarranted emphasis on social values, such as equity, making difficult the realization of a variety of privately held values through public education. Others believe that governmental operation of public schools has resulted in the inefficient use of resources, resulting in high costs and poor performance. In contrast, supporters of governmental operation of schools fear that educational services will be even more inequitably distributed than they are now if schooling enterprises are privatized and that the sense of community that binds us together as a people would be weakened.

Alternative Methods of Government Intervention. Government can intervene in the natural functioning of the market in many ways. Public schools are currently owned and operated by government. So are police and fire departments and the U.S. armed forces. Ownership is not the typical type of governmental intervention, however. Governments may also oversee the public interest through regulation, licensure, taxation, subsidies, transfer payments, and contracts or charters (as in charter schools discussed later in this chapter).

Most communication systems, utilities, and inter-city transportation enterprises in the United States are privately owned, yet they are carefully monitored and regulated by government. Restaurants are regularly inspected for health code violations. The licensing of professionals is done by governments, although most professionals (an important exception being teachers) work in the private sector. Even private schools and home schooling are regulated by state government.

Governments can attempt to influence human behavior by changing the price paid for specific items through subsidies or taxation. Consumption of cigarettes, alcoholic beverages, and gasoline is discouraged through excise taxes that increase the cost to consumers with the intent of reducing demand. On the other hand, the government may pay subsidies to farmers to encourage them to increase (or decrease) production of specific products or to businesses to enable them to remain in operation in the face of foreign competition. Similarly, subsidies and scholarships that reduce the cost of higher education encourage families and individuals to pursue education beyond high school. Complete subsidization makes universal elementary and secondary education possible.

Governments also contract for services from private companies. Federal, state, and local governments rely on contractors to build their buildings, highways, and parks. While the federal government coordinates space exploration, privately contracted vendors conduct research and development and manufacture space vehicles. During periods of rapid enrollment increases, school districts may rent or lease space from private vendors. Instead of providing their own services, many school districts contract with private vendors for transportation, cleaning, and cafeteria operations. Contracting for the operation of individual schools, that is, for specific administrative services or the administration of the entire business of a school district, is becoming increasingly common.

Many governmental responsibilities are met through transfer payments to individuals. Social Security, Aid for Dependent Children (i.e., welfare), unemployment insurance, food stamps, and educational vouchers

are examples. Through transfer payments the government can equalize the distribution of resources while permitting the individual maximum discretion as to how the payments are used. For example, prior to Social Security, elderly indigents were institutionalized in facilities owned and operated by local government as are schools. Now, with monthly payments through the Social Security system, recipients have many options open to them, such as living in their own homes, in smaller apartments, in retirement communities, in residences for the elderly, or in nursing homes as well as living with relatives. The public policy of providing senior citizens with at least a subsistence living standard is realized without prescribing their lifestyles. The GI Bill, which paid the tuition of World War II and Korean War veterans to public and private postsecondary institutions, is an example of education vouchers. The use of education vouchers at the elementary and secondary levels is an option increasingly exercised by states and by the federal government, as in the No Child Left Behind legislation for children in consistently failing public schools.

Allocation of Authority among Levels of Government and Individuals. Within any given context, significantly different patterns of allocation of authority among levels of government and potential individual decision makers can be structured depending on the relative priorities given to policy objectives (Kirst, 1988). For elementary and secondary schooling, extreme centralization of authority means making all decisions collectively and by administering them through public institutions; extreme decentralization of authority means making all decisions individually through markets with no governmental intervention. Extreme decentralization would result in no public schools and no subsidies to individuals, leaving the production and distribution of educational services to be determined solely by market forces. Extreme decentralization enhances the potential for realizing values of efficiency and personal freedom, but it has severe negative implications for the realization of other societal values, such as equity.

Increasing centralization of authority has been used in the post–World War II years as a vehicle for promoting equity considerations, but the efficiency of the education system may have suffered. To promote values of efficiency and liberty while retaining considerable control over equity, some school districts have taken steps to decentralize some decision making by adopting policies that create magnet and charter schools and/or permit open enrollment among schools and sometimes granting subsidies for private school tuition through the use of education vouchers. Most states have allowed the chartering of publicly financed schools to be operated by other than school districts (e.g., see the cases of Chicago and Houston described later in this chapter). Other districts have devolved substantial policymaking authority to schools and teachers. (For examples of school-based decision making, school-based budgeting, and teacher empowerment, see the cases of Houston and Seattle later in this chapter.) Such reforms also include enhancing family discretion by allowing them to choose among publicly operated schools and among private schools through vouchers, creating quasi-market conditions. Centralizing policies aimed at improving efficiency and effectiveness of the educational system include setting state and national standards for student academic performance and raising state standards for entering the teaching profession.

It appears that some decisions about education may best be made by central authorities, particularly those involving equity, but others are best left to those with professional expertise at the school level or to those having a personal stake in the happiness and welfare of a specific child—the family (Coleman & Hoffer, 1987; Coons & Sugarman, 1978; Cremin, 1976; McNeil, 1986; Wise, 1979, 1988). Determining the optimal allocation of authority in education is a complex and unending process.

Thus, centralization and decentralization of authority should be viewed as means toward desired ends, not as ends in themselves (Hanson, 1986). The same is true of state power, teacher power, and people power. Legitimate concerns exist about education at all levels of the sociopolitical hierarchy; the critical issue is determining the best balance in the distribution of authority among decision makers with legitimate interests. This requires approaching the issue systemically. The best balance will vary from society to society and over time within a society as contexts, value definitions, and priorities change (Wirt, 1986).

Models of Political Decision Making

For more than two decades, the American people have focused their collective attention on improving the effectiveness of the public schools of the nation. The grave condition of public schools was well articulated by *A Nation at Risk* (National Commission on Excellence in Education, 1984) in 1983, and improving them has been high on the national agenda ever since. On the occasion of the 25th anniversary of that report, however, the Forum for Education and Democracy (2008) issued a reanalysis and found that "we continue to fall short of this most basic democratic commitment" (p. i).

Through a quarter of a century of rigorous debate and experimentation, as noted in chapter 1, a pattern of consensus has emerged as to what needs to be done and the means for doing it, and these patterns are remarkably similar to those evolving in other Western democracies that face similar challenges. The current wave of reforms in the United States, beginning in the 1990s, include the No Child Left Behind legislation at the federal level preceded by pioneering reforms undertaken by several states. This wave is a systemic amalgamation of earlier reforms (Cuban & Usdan, 2003). It calls for the establishment and monitoring of standards by central authorities at the state and national levels and the design and implementation of instructional delivery systems by school authorities. The optimal placement of authority among the levels of school governance remains under dispute:

> This systemic strategy . . . emphasizes state (and to a lesser degree federal) actions to complement school and district restructuring by creating a more coherent environment within which successful schools can thrive and by creating external pressure for change when it does not emerge spontaneously. The linchpin in the system is the development of content standards expressing shared understandings about what students need to know and be able to do, with which other elements of the educational system (school curricula, assessments, teacher education and professional development, and accountability) can be aligned. (Ladd & Hansen, 1999, p. 156)

Thus, a core issue in school reform today is governance, the place where special interest politics intersects with direct democratic control (Cuban & Usdan, 2003; McAdams, 2000). While there is considerable agreement as to the general pattern for reform, there is little agreement on the details. Achieving agreement is a political process taking place in school districts, state legislatures, Congress, and state and federal courts. The ultimate resolution will vary from place to place, tailored to varying local conditions.

No overarching general theory of political decision making exists, but there is a "grab bag" of heuristic theories and contrasting methods (Wirt & Kirst, 1982). *Heuristic theory* is a method of analytically separating and categorizing items in experience. Among the most useful for understanding public policy relating to schools are institutionalism, incrementalism, group theory, elite theory, systems theory, and rationalism. These theories and models complement one another. Each emphasizes a particular aspect of the policymaking process. Taken together, they provide a rather complete picture of the total process. Although these theories were developed primarily to describe policy formulation at the national level, they are fully applicable at the state level and can provide much insight to understanding the policymaking process at the school district and school levels as well.

In the sections that follow, we describe each of the models and illustrate them with the development of charter schools and synopses of the reform histories of Chicago, Houston, and Seattle.

Institutionalism

Institutionalism focuses on the structure of the policymaking process (Elazar, 1972; Grodzins, 1966; Walker, 1981). Unlike most of the rest of the world, where education is a function of the national government, educational governance in the United States has been historically characterized by the primacy of state governments, with power delegated within states to school districts. This is not to say that the federal government does not have influence on education policy out of proportion to the relatively small amount of financial support it provides (less than 10% of the total [NCES, 2006]). On the positive side, this arrangement has produced educational systems that are quite diverse, dynamic, and responsive to local conditions. On the negative side, the structure has resulted in gross financial and curricular inequities. Some school districts spend several times as much per pupil as do other districts. Some districts operate schools that are unequaled in quality throughout the world, whereas others operate schools that are an embarrassment to the profession and to the nation. The devolved nature of school governance has impeded state and federal efforts to equalize educational opportunities in terms of finance, curricular provision, and the integration of students and staff with respect to socioeconomic status and ethnicity.

But the structure of educational governance has changed over the years, and it continues to change. The change is reflected in Table 10.1, which shows the trends in school revenue provided by each level of government in the United States since 1920. During the early part of the 20th century, state governments on average paid less than 20% of the cost of elementary and secondary education; the rest was provided by school districts and/or local governments. The state share grew steadily after 1930. By 1980, total aggregate state aid of the 50 states exceeded revenue raised from local sources for the first time. Federal participation grew from virtually nothing at the beginning of the 20th century to nearly 10% in 1980. Federal aid then declined to 6.1% of all revenues for public schools in 1990 but increased to 8.5% in 2003 (NCES, 2005b, Table 44.2).

While small districts have consolidated, large districts have embraced small school policies. Table 10.1 also charts the number of schools and school districts. It shows that the number districts steadily declined from 117,108 in 1940 to 14,383 in 2003. The number of schools declined correspondingly through 1990 but increased from 87,004 to 95,726 in 2003.

The growing participation by state and federal governments in the financing of schools parallels their growing interest in and influence over educational policy in general. While state education departments and the U.S. Department of Education have increased in size and influence, state governments have become particularly active in the prescription of basic curricula, monitoring student progress through mandatory testing programs, and the certification of teachers.

TABLE 10.1

Revenue Sources for Public Elementary and Secondary Schools, 1920–2003, and Number of Schools and Districts

Year	Total Revenue (Millions)[a]	Sources (Percentage of Total)			Number of Districts	Number of Schools
		Local	State	Federal		
1920	$ 970	83.2	16.5	0.3	—	271,319
1930	2,089	82.7	16.9	0.4	—	248,117
1940	2,261	68.0	30.3	1.8	117,108	226,762
1950	5,437	57.3	39.8	2.9	83,718	—
1960	14,747	56.5	39.1	4.4	40,520	—
1970	40,267	52.1	39.9	8.0	17,995	—
1980	96,881	43.4	46.8	9.8	15,929	87,004
1990	207,753	46.8	47.1	6.1	15,367	83,425
2000	372,944	43.2	49.5	7.3	14,928	92,012
2003	449,600	42.8	48.7	8.5	14,383	95,726

[a] Current dollars.

Source: National Center for Education Statistics (2005b).

According to Wirt and Kirst (1982), "The 1970s will be remembered as an era when the previous hallmark of American education—local control—became fully a myth" (p. v). The local superintendent has lost his or her once preeminent position in setting the school district agenda and controlling decision outcomes. The discretionary range of superintendents and school boards has been narrowed at the top by federal and state action and at the bottom through collective bargaining with employee unions. The more recent trend toward school-based management is narrowing the range even further. Nevertheless, local school districts continue to exert a considerable though declining amount of influence on educational policy (Odden & Marsh, 1989).

Other structural changes of educational institutions are also taking place that have impacted the decision-making process and the ultimate nature of decisions made. The practice of letting parents choose the schools their children attend is gaining in popularity, as are mayoral control of large urban school districts, educational vouchers, and tax credits, which have changed the face of educational governance. The recent changes in school governance structures in Chicago, Houston, and Seattle (all described in following sections) are dramatic examples of the contemporary belief that the nature of the decision-making structure of educational institutions influences the quality of the decisions they make, the efficiency of their operations, and, ultimately, how well their students learn. Another example is charter schools, which we highlight next as an example of institutionalism.

Charter Schools as an Illustration of Institutionalism. Charter schools are one of the fastest-growing innovations in public policy today. They enjoy broad bipartisan support from presidents, governors, and state legislators. Although the late Albert Shanker, longtime president of the American Federation of Teachers, was one of the early proponents of charter schools, opposition to them comes largely from teachers unions and local school boards. Forty states and the District of Columbia have enacted charter legislation since 1991, when Minnesota was the first state to do so. As of April 2006, approximately 3,613 charter schools were operating, serving over 1 million children—or about 2% of the public school enrollment (National Alliance for Public Charter Schools, 2006). The numbers would be much larger except for caps placed on charter school growth by 27 states. As examples, caps have been placed on the absolute number of charter schools, on the number of new charters permitted each year, and on a percent of a school district's spending directed toward charters. Thirty-nine percent of charter schools reported having waiting lists of applicants in 2003 averaging 135 students (Center for Education Reform, 2004).

Charter schools are intended to inject marketlike competition into the public provision of elementary and secondary schooling. They provide parents with more schooling options within the public sector and free operators from many of the constraints imposed on other publicly financed schools in order to stimulate innovation. They are funded under the resources-follow-the-child principle in that the school district of residence must pay to the charter school in which a child is enrolled a prescribed amount in support of the child's education. The school is held accountable to meet the terms of its charter by its authorizer and is subject to closure if it fails to do so.

Charter schools are public schools that come into existence by a contract between a sponsoring party and a state agency, a local school board, or other authorizer designated by state enabling legislation. The charter, or contract, defines the framework within which the school operates and how public support for the school will be provided. Charters are for a specific period of time, usually 3 to 5 years, at the end of which they may be renewed. A school's charter gives it autonomy over its operation and frees it from many regulations that other public schools must follow. In exchange for the flexibility afforded by the charter, a school is held accountable by the authorizer for achieving the goals set out in the charter, including improving student performance (U.S. Department of Education, 2000).

School charter laws vary widely from state to state but usually contain the following provisions:

- Who may propose a charter, how they are granted, and the number to be granted
- How the school is legally defined and related to governance, operations, and liability issues
- The levels and type of funding provided and the amount of fiscal independence and autonomy
- How schools are to address admissions, nondiscrimination, racial/ethnic balance, discipline, and special education

- Whether the school may act as an employer, which labor relations laws apply, and staff rights and privileges
- The degree of control the school has over the development of its instructional goals and practices
- Whether the charter serves as a performance-based contract, how assessments are made, and charter revocation and renewal issues (http://www.uscharterschools.org, accessed January 9, 2002)

Charter School Authorizers. A charter school is empowered by its charter, which is a legal contract between the school operator and a state-designated authorizer. For the charter school movement to succeed, both operators and authorizers must do their jobs effectively. An operator must run a successful school that delivers the results it promised. An authorizer must see that this happens by providing various forms of oversight and assistance and by renewing the charter if all goes well—or closing if it does not. The role of the authorizer, therefore, is pivotal to the overall success of the charter movement (Palmer & Gau, 2005).

About 600 charter school authorizers exist nationwide (Vanourek, 2005). Palmer and Gau (2005) and Palmer, Gau, and Gau (2003) categorize them into seven types: local school board; county, regional, and intermediate district; state school board; state chartering board; university or community college; city or mayor's office; and nonprofit organization. Of these, 90% of the authorizers are local school boards, 3% are state agencies, and 2% are higher-education institutions. About a quarter of the states in 2002–2003 had established only a state agency as a charter school authorizer, and another quarter established only local school boards; the remaining half established more than one type of authorizer (U.S. Government Accountability Office, 2005). Although 90% of the potential authorizers are local school boards, they have issued only half the charters. On the other hand, the 3% of authorizers who are state agencies have issued 39% of the charters, and the 2% of authorizers who are higher-education institutions have issued 10% of the charters.

Charter school authorizing has three distinct phases. The first is the approval phase, when the authorizer reviews the application and holds formal hearings. If it is determined that the proposed school meets the authorizer's criteria and has a good chance of being successful, the application is approved and the school authorized. The authorizer can reject proposals it finds unsatisfactory and may permit a revision of an application that addresses its concerns. A rigorous approval process is a key factor in charter school accountability (Vanourek, 2005).

Once a school becomes operative, the oversight phase begins. During this phase, the authorizer monitors the school for compliance with the charter, student achievement results, financial management, and other applicable regulations. A study of 24 states found that most authorizers were doing an adequate job of oversight, but there was concern that some were not being rigorous enough about performance results and overemphasized ability by compliance (Palmer et al., 2003).

The final phase is a decision made by the authorizer near the end of the charter period whether to renew the charter, impose sanctions, or close the school. In making this decision, such factors are considered as students' academic performance, charter and regulation compliance, audit results, student attrition, quality of school leadership and staff, and governance. As of January 2004, more than 300 charter schools had been closed, about 9% of those ever opened. A U.S. Government Accountability Office (2005) survey in 2003 indicated that of the 93 closures that year, 61 were voluntary; 28 charters were revoked or terminated, seven for financial reasons and none for academic reasons. Four charters were not renewed, one for academic reasons.

In their evaluation of charter school authorizers in 24 states (including the District of Columbia), Palmer and Gau (2005) and Palmer et al. (2003) concluded that local school boards (with some notable exceptions like Chicago and Houston) do not make good authorizers. They are often hampered by the influence of charter-adverse interest groups, such as teachers unions and local politics. In addition, they usually do not have the necessary infrastructure to conduct the task effectively. State agencies generally do a better job. The researchers identified two key factors for effective authorizers: the ability to make rational data-driven decisions rather than politically driven ones and having sufficient staff members dedicated to the tasks of authorizing and who are not driven by traditional forms of compliance-based accountability. They recommend that there be one or more nonlocal authorizers, such as separate chartering boards or universities that can distance themselves from local politics and traditional compliance-driven accountability. As for how many authorizers are needed for each state, they suggest at least one, but not dozens.

Charter School Impact. Berman, Nelson, Ericson, Perry, and Silverman (1998) found that parents and students choose charter schools in part because of dissatisfaction with their former public schools, expressing concerns about low academic standards, a dehumanizing culture, student safety, and unresponsiveness to parental involvement. Chief characteristics attracting them to their charter school are a nurturing and safe environment, its value system, quality of academic program, high standards for achievement, small school and class size, clear goals for each student, and a central role for parents. Gill, Timpane, Ross, and Brewer (2001) found strong evidence that parents are satisfied with their choices.

Newly created charter schools (77% of the total) tend to be established to realize an alternative vision for public education or to serve a special target population of students. Public schools that convert to charter status (16% of the total) also seek to realize better an educational vision but often start from an established and, frequently, highly regarded educational program. The primary motivating factor to convert is to gain autonomy from their districts or to bypass various regulations. Private schools that convert to charter status (7% of the total) seek public funds so that they can stabilize their finances and often to attract students whose families can not afford private school tuition (U.S. Department of Education, 1998).

Most charter schools are small with a median size of 250 in 2003–2004 compared with 475 for other public schools (Vanourek, 2005). Fifty-seven percent of charter schools enroll fewer than 200 pupils. At least 10% of charter schools are operated by education management organizations. Seventy percent of charter schools have a racial/ethnic composition similar to their surrounding districts; about 17% enroll a higher percentage of students of color, and about 14% enroll a lower percentage of students of color (U.S. Department of Education, 2000).

The National Assessment of Educational Progress conducted its first study focusing on charter schools as part of its 2003 national assessment of fourth-graders in reading and mathematics (NCES, 2005a). The pilot study found that charter school fourth-grade enrollment is made up of 45% white students compared to about 58% for other public schools. Black students made up 31% of charter school enrollments and Hispanics 20%; comparable figures for public schools are 17% and 19%, respectively. Charter schools enroll a slightly lower percentage of students eligible for free or reduced-price lunch (42%) than do other public schools (44%). Students with limited English proficiency represent 9% of enrollments for both classifications. Enrollment of students with disabilities in charter schools (8%) is lower than for other public schools (11%). Charter schools are evenly split between central city and noncentral city locations, while only 29% of other public schools are located in central cities.

Charters often enrich the schooling options available to parents in a given area. The evidence is clear that charters have produced innovations in organizational activities, but there is little evidence of unique teaching and learning practices in charter classrooms (Lubienski, 2003).

Charter schools do, however, offer parents diversifying alternatives with respect to class sizes, use of technology, and programmatic options; they also provide innovations in governance, management, and other organizational practices (U.S. Department of Education, 2000).

Financing Charter Schools. Per pupil–based funding is at the heart of charter school financing. In some cases this is based on state average per pupil expenditure, in others it is based on average district revenue or expenditures, and in still others it is negotiated between the charter schools and the chartering agency (Nelson, Muir, & Drown, 2000). Typically,

funding flows from school districts to charter schools. About half the states fund elementary and secondary students in charter schools at the same rate. Most states provide supplementary funding for at-risk children either directly or through negotiations. Special education is a contentious issue with six states funding it on a school-district-average cost rather than according to the specific needs of the students, which may explain, in part, the underrepresentation of special education children in charter schools. Other states link special education funding to actual cost through pupil weighting formulas or negotiations.

Charter schools are eligible for federal and state categorical program funding, such as Title I and special education, and for specific programs, such as technology literacy. Transportation is provided by the district or aided by the state. Some funding is provided for facilities in a few states and the District of Columbia, but such assistance is not available in most states. Charter schools may acquire debt in most states. About half the states provide some accelerated funding for charter schools to help address cash flow difficulties, especially during the opening months; this represents a serious problem for schools in the other states. Twelve states require charter schools to participate in the state teacher retirement system, but participation level is high in most states. All states require charter schools to conduct an independent financial audit.

Speakman and Hassel (2005) concluded that charter schools typically receive much less funding per child for instructional services from state and local taxes than do other public schools except in Minnesota and New Mexico. Further, they receive few if any central office services or separate funds for facilities, and they are unlikely to share fully in federal funding for disadvantaged students. Little state or district funding is available for start-up and planning costs; this is usually provided by the sponsoring organization, supplemented by philanthropy and federal grants. Given that studies to date have found little difference in student achievement between charter schools as a group and other public schools, charters appear to be economically more "efficient" or "productive" in that they achieve comparable results to other public schools at a lower cost per pupil.

Incrementalism, Group Theory, and Elite Theory

In this section, we describe Lindblom's perception of the policymaking process in the United States and two complementary perceptions: group theory and elite theory. They are nicely illustrated with the history of reform in Chicago.

Incrementalism. Lindblom (1959) described the public policy process in the United States as a continuation of past government activities, with only incremental modifications. He insightfully labeled the process as "muddling through." Although some deplore his exaltation of the process, one of his most ardent critics credits him with presenting "a well considered theory fully geared to the actual experience of practicing administrators" (Dror, 1964, p. 153).

   Lindblom (1968) took issue with the popular view that politics is a process of conflict resolution. He argued that "governments are instruments for vast tasks of social cooperation" and that "conflicts are largely those that spring from the opportunities for cooperation that have evolved once political life becomes orderly" (p. 32). Within this context, he described the play of power as a process of cooperation among specialists. It is like a game, normally proceeding according to implicitly accepted rules. "Policy analysis is incorporated as an instrument or weapon into the play of power, changing the character of analysis as a result" (p. 30).

   The focus of the play of power is on means (policy), not ends (goals or objectives). This, according to Lindblom, is what permits the political system to work. Because of the overlap in value systems among interested groups and the uncertainty of the outcomes of any course of action, partisans across the value spectrum are able to come to agreement on means where agreement on ends would be impossible.

   Since, according to Lindblom (1968), agreement on goal priorities is impossible in a pluralistic society, the type of analysis appropriate to the political process is termed *partisan analysis*. It is analysis conducted by advocates (organized interest groups) of a relatively limited set of values and/or ends, such as teacher associations, taxpayer groups, and religious and patriotic organizations. Comprehensiveness is provided by the variety of partisans participating in the political process. The responsibility for promoting specific values thus lies in the hands of advocates of those values (pressure groups and lobbyists) and not in the hands of an "impartial" analyst (as is the case with rationalism, discussed later).

   The net result of this advocacy process is incremental rather than revolutionary policy change. In light of our grand state of ignorance about the relationships between public policy and human behavior, Lindblom viewed incremental policy decisions as being well justified. Incrementalism permits the expansion of policies that prove successful while limiting the harm caused by unsuccessful policies. Within the context of strategic planning, incrementalism can ensure that each increment leads toward desired goals while minimizing organizational disruption. Incrementalism preserves the system while changing it.

Group Theory. Truman (1951), a leading proponent of group theory, saw politics as the interaction among groups (as opposed to individuals) in the formulation of public policy. Individuals band together into formal or informal groups, similar to Lindblom's partisans, to confront government with their demands. The group is the vehicle through which individuals can influence government action. Even political parties are viewed as coalitions of interest groups. Elected and appointed officials are seen as being involved continually in bargaining and negotiating with relevant groups to work out compromises that balance interests.

Group theory, as portrayed by Dye (1987), is illustrated in Figure 10.4. Public policy at any point in time represents the equilibrium of the balance of power among groups. Because the power alignment is continually shifting (e.g., in Figure 10.4, toward group B as it gains supporters or partners in coalition on a particular issue), the fulcrum of equilibrium also shifts, leading to incremental changes in policy (in the direction desired by group B, as illustrated).

Stability in the system is attributed to a number of factors. First, most members of the electorate are latent supporters of the political system and share in its inherent values. This latent group is generally inactive but can be aroused to defend the system against any group that attacks it. Second, there is a great deal of overlap in the membership of groups; a given person is likely to be a member of several groups. This tends to have a dampening effect with respect to any group taking extreme positions because, although the group may be focused on a single issue, its membership is much more broadly oriented. The third factor promoting system stability results from group competition. No single group constitutes a majority in American society. Coalitions are easily formed to counter the influence of any group appearing to gain undue influence. As a result, the political process is characterized by evolution as in incrementalism rather than revolution.

Elite Theory. Elite theory focuses on actions by a select group of influential citizens. Elite theory (Dye & Zeigler, 1981) characterizes the general public as apathetic, ill informed, and uninterested where public policy is concerned, not unlike the characterization of the latent group in group theory. This leaves a power vacuum that is readily filled by an elite group. Elites do more to shape the opinion of the masses on public issues than the general public does to shape the opinions of elites, although influence is reciprocal (e.g., civil rights legislation [Dye, 1987]). According to this theory, policy is developed by elites within the trappings of democratic government.

Elites tend to be drawn from upper socioeconomic levels. They are not necessarily against the general welfare of the masses, as shown by their support of civil rights legislation, for example, but approach their welfare through a sense of noblesse oblige. Although not agreeing on all issues, the elite share a

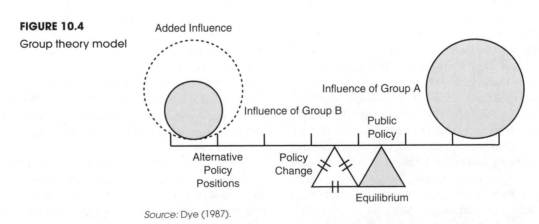

FIGURE 10.4
Group theory model

Source: Dye (1987).

consensus as to basic social values and the importance of preserving the system. The masses give superficial support to this consensus, which provides a basis for elite rule. When events occur that threaten the system, elites move to take corrective action. According to elite theory, changes in public policy come about as the result of elites redefining their own positions, although this redefinition may be a function of external pressures. Because of the elites' conservative posture with respect to preserving the system, policy changes tend to be incremental.

The Chicago School District as an Illustration of "Muddling Through". One of the most ambitious attempts at restructuring public school governance in the United States is taking place in Chicago. It has undergone two phases in an incremental process beginning in 1988 and is entering a third phase. The first phase focused on decentralization, featuring the creation of a locally elected council for each school with the power to hire and fire principals and to make limited budgetary decisions. The second phase, beginning in 1995, focused on recentralization with the state legislature granting newly reelected Mayor Richard Daley sweeping authority over the schools and making the schools accountable for the academic progress of their pupils. The third phase began in June 2004, when Mayor Daley unveiled the Renaissance 2010 plan to create 100 new performance-focused charterlike schools (Lake & Rainey, 2005).

The Illinois legislature adopted the 1988 decentralization plan in a desperate attempt to reform a school system that had been characterized the previous year as the "worst in America" by then U.S. Secretary of Education William Bennett. The primary strategy was to realign district incentives and power structure by creating school councils controlled by parents and authorizing them to make decisions that had been made previously by the district's education bureaucracy (Hess, 1990). These decisions included the power to hire and fire principals, approve the school's annual improvement plans, and allocate chapter 1 Elementary and Secondary Education Act funds from the federal government. Complementing school-based decision making was an open enrollment plan that allowed parents to enroll their children in any school in the district with available space. The

reforms, phased in over a 5-year period, had 10 goals, but priority was given to the goals to raise student achievement, attendance rates, and graduation rates to national norms for *all* schools. The decentralization strategy did not meet the public's expectations, however. Even supporters of the plan acknowledged that only about one-third of the elementary schools had developed the organizational capacity to address educational needs. Progress was no better at the secondary level (Wong, 2003).

This led to the second phase in 1995, when the plan was amended, reorganizing the district level structure by reducing the size of the school board from 15 to 5 members and empowering the mayor to appoint the board members, its president, the district's superintendent of schools, and all other high-level central office administrators. The new board was charged with establishing systemwide curriculum objectives and standards that reflected the multicultural diversity of the city. School councils were continued, but the central board's power of oversight was enhanced, and the school councils' authority has gradually eroded (Lipman, 2002). The 1995 legislation also authorized a new position to improve the financial efficiency of the district and to oversee privatization of district services (Wong, 2001).

The mayor's appointments to the school board were chosen from his business and city hall allies. His appointments to the top administrative posts in the district, including the superintendent of schools, were nearly all noneducators. An analysis of 111 top administrative appointments in the central office between 1995 and 1998 showed that 40% came from outside the school system; in areas not directly related to instruction, 60% of those appointed were from outside the system (Wong, 2003). Within months of the implementation of the new law, an existing $150 million deficit was erased; a significant capital improvement program was undertaken; a program for monitoring school accountability was established; and, ensuring labor peace in the midst of reform, a 4-year contract was negotiated with the teachers union (Shipps, 2003).

The accountability structure permitted by the 1995 reform act was a business management model, and administrators acted quickly to demonstrate a commitment to efficient management (Wong, 2001).

The board adopted curricular frameworks and achievement standards. In 1996, 109 of the district's 550 schools (38 high schools and 71 elementary schools) were placed on academic probation because 15% or less of their students scored at grade level on nationally norm-referenced tests. Seven high schools were reconstituted. Of these reconstituted schools, five principals were replaced. All teacher and staff positions were vacated, but former staff members were permitted to apply to be retained. Seventy percent were retained. Of those not retained, about 30% were unable to find employment elsewhere in the district and faced dismissal (Hess, 1999).

In 1998, the minimum achievement benchmark for schools to avoid being placed on probation was raised from 15% to 20% of students scoring at or above the national average and is expected to be raised further in subsequent years. Another seven high schools were reconstituted, and 108 schools remained on probation.

The 1995 reform legislation gave the system direction and coordination that was lacking in the 1988 reform legislation and created a tension for excellence that failed to be provided by most local school councils, principals, and staff, as was the intent of the 1988 legislation. Bryk (1999) summed up the combined effect of these two pieces of reform legislation this way:

> The division of responsibilities under decentralization gives local schools the authority to act and the resources and assistance to use that authority productively in advancing children's learning. Schools in turn are held accountable to assure that serious efforts are advanced in this regard. The educational work of the system center focuses on policy-making to support decentralization, maintaining an external assistance capacity for local schools, engaging rigorous external accountability for improvement, and stimulating innovation. (p. 89)

Shipps (2003) credits the Chicago experience with showing that "giving school leaders the fiscal flexibility to allocate funding where needed and the legal authority to set priorities free from layers of regulation may be as important as who is in charge" (p. 31). She is critical of the lack of educational expertise in top decision-making posts, however.

The third wave of reform in Chicago began in June 2004, when Mayor Daley unveiled the Renaissance 2010 (Ren 10) plan to create 100 performance-focused schools. The plan incorporates much of Chicago's experience with authorizing and monitoring charter schools that began in 1996, when Illinois lawmakers enacted a charter school law. The law allowed Chicago to create up to 15 charter schools. Lake and Rainey (2005) suggest that the district turned to charters out of necessity because decentralization and accountability failed to improve student academic performance fast enough, especially in the high schools.

Chicago embraced the opportunity to create charter schools, now numbering 20 on 27 campuses (some schools have more than one campus). A national study of charter school authorizing by the Thomas B. Fordham Institute (Palmer et al., 2003) had praised Chicago for its positive attitude toward charters, clear application process, and technical assistance given. The experience gained informed the structuring of the Ren 10.

Ren 10 will close about 70 low-performing schools and open 100 replacements. Some of the replacement schools will be charter schools, and the others (contract and performance schools) will resemble them. The schools will be located in areas of the city identified as having the worst schools in a study by the Illinois Facility Fund commissioned by Chicago Public Schools (CPS) (Kneebone, Logue, Cahn, & McDunnah, 2004). They will have a high level of autonomy but will be accountable for performance. They will be schools of choice within a specific neighborhood, although some may be designated to serve the entire city.

The "charter school" designation is given to those organized under the state charter school law and approved by CPS. They will operate under a charter or contract with CPS, renewable every 5 years. The policymaking bodies of these schools are governing boards exempt from some local and state regulations, but they must meet the same educational standards as other Chicago schools. At least half the teachers must hold state certification. A charter school governing board is the employer and sets compensation. The curriculum must meet state standards as set forth in the charter school agreement.

"Contract schools" are run by outside organizations as are charter schools, but they must follow all state education laws. They differ from charters in that they may be unionized and all teachers must be certified. Their authority is granted and specified through a contract between CPS and the sponsoring organization. The policymaking bodies are either governing boards or local school councils. Unionization of teachers is optional, as is affiliation with the Chicago Teachers Union. The governing boards are the employers and determine compensation. Curricula must meet CPS and state learning standards as specified in the performance agreement.

"Performance schools" are run by CPS and may be granted specific autonomies regarding budgeting, hiring, scheduling, and curriculum. They are bound by collective bargaining agreements, and all teachers must be certified and members of the Chicago Teachers Union. The policymaking bodies are local school councils. The employer is CPS, and compensation is provided in accordance with CPS salary schedules. The curricula must meet CPS and state learning standards as specified in the performance plan.

It took external pressure from the state in 1988 to get school reform moving in Chicago. Decentralization of much authority to local school councils was in keeping with national thinking about educational reform at the time. But by 1995, it was clear that decentralization was improving the school experience of children in only about one-third of the schools, and the state moved to recentralize some functions, entrusting school governance into the hands of the city's mayor. The influence of the Chicago business community in bringing about both reforms is an example of elite theory. Curricular frameworks and achievement standards were developed at the district level. School-level professionals are held responsible for the performance of students in their charge, but they were given increased authority and resources to accomplish the task of increasing student achievement. Schools with unacceptable achievement levels are reconstituted with about one-third of the principals being removed along with about 30% of the teachers. Greater pressure is also placed on students by eliminating social promotion and requiring summer school for those who fail to make the grade. Quasi-market forces are being injected through Ren 10 with the creation of more than 100 new schools of choice. Mayor Daley's Ren 10 plan resembles reform models developing elsewhere in the United States. The net result of this incremental process is a revolutionary restructuring of the institution itself.

Prior to 1988, the electorate in Chicago appear to have been inert (group theory) and apathetic (elite theory) with respect to the condition of the public schools. This had left the field open to the teachers unions and the school board. The academic performance of the district's students deteriorated, as did the state of its finances. In 1988, the Illinois legislature moved to mobilize elements of the electorate through the creation of school councils with real power. The move was successful in stirring the district out of its lethargy but only partially successful in improving academic achievement among students and the financial crisis grew worse.

In 1995, Mayor Daley sought and the state legislature granted control of the school district. He appointed his political and business allies to the school board and key administrative posts, reshaping the thinking at the center. Both groups were elites of sorts. The financial crisis was quickly resolved.

The previous school board had alienated the teachers unions, and they were without contract. The mayor moved quickly to make peace with them, knowing that they would play a key role in implementation of the reforms he had in mind. While they might not be ardent supporters of those reforms, he wanted to neutralize their outright opposition as much as possible. In addition, through tough negotiations, greater flexibility was gained for the school board and central administration.

Many of the constraints for innovation had been relaxed, but progress in improving student achievement was still unsatisfactory. This led to the more radical proposals of Ren 10. By actively involving community groups through school councils, the business leaders of the city, and the politically elite in the policymaking process, the policy fulcrum with respect to education was moved dramatically in support of greater and greater school reform.

ACTIVITY 10.2
Reform Chicago Style

Addresses ISLLC Standard 6

Chicago is not presented as an ideal model of how to approach school reform. Rather, it demonstrates the complexity of bringing about positive school reforms in large urban core districts and the obstacles that stand in the way. In a way, it represents Lindblom's theory of incrementalism, or "muddling through."

Not too long ago, Chicago had the reputation of being the worst public school system in the country. It was forced into reform mode by the Illinois legislature; now, the mayor and many Chicago-based groups, notably business leaders, are backing the reform efforts. See the Chicago Public Schools Web site to learn about the latest developments and consult the citations for a historical perspective. (http://www.cps.K12.il.us).

Systems Theory

The most comprehensive of the models represents an application of systems theory to the political process. As explained in chapter 2, a system is made up of a number of interrelated elements. An open system, which is characteristic of political systems, draws resources from its environment, processes them in some fashion, and returns the processed resources to the environment. All systems tend toward entropy or disorganization, and they must consciously combat this tendency in order to maintain equilibrium. A key function for combating entropy is feedback (i.e., continual monitoring of a system's internal operations and its relationship with its environment). Accurate feedback is particularly critical to a system's health in that the system depends on the environment for resources without which the system would atrophy. Equilibrium is maintained by modifying or adapting system structures and processes based on analysis of feedback (cybernetics). Maintaining equilibrium is a dynamic process leading to growth and evolution of a system in harmony with its environment.

Easton (1965) adapted general systems theory to political systems. His model, illustrated in Figure 10.5, conceptualizes public policy as a response by a political system to forces from the environment. Environmental pressures or inputs come in the form of demands for public action through interest groups and support of government by individuals and groups through obeying laws, paying taxes, and accepting outcomes of elections. The inputs are processed through the political system and transformed into policy outputs. Political systems consist of sets of identifiable and interrelated institutions and activities at all levels, such as those associated with the U.S. Congress, state and county legislatures, common councils, town councils, village boards, school boards, commissions, authorities, and courts. Feedback in a political system is both formal and informal. Formal feedback is provided through elections, referenda, hearings, and policy analyses. Informal feedback occurs through personal interactions with constituents and others.

FIGURE 10.5

Simplified model of a political system

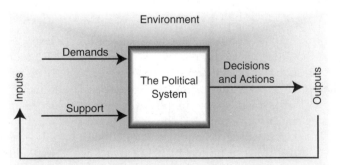

Source: D. Easton. *A systems analysis of political life* (p. 32). Chicago: University of Chicago Press, 1965. Copyright 1965 by University of Chicago Press. Reprinted by permission of the author.

The Houston Independent School District as an Illustration of Systems Theory. Unlike Chicago's reform history, starting with the Illinois legislature and later championed by the city's mayor, reform of the Houston Independent School District (HISD) was initiated by a reform school board and implemented by a nontraditional superintendent, Rod Paige, who later was appointed to head the U.S. Department of Education during the first term of the presidency of George W. Bush, former governor of Texas. The district enrolls 210,000 students, making it the largest school district in Texas and the seventh largest in the United States. Fifty-eight percent of its students are Hispanic, and 30% are African American. Two-thirds are considered "educationally at risk," and 82% are economically disadvantaged. More than half are English-language learners or bilingual (http://www.hisd.org, accessed February 7, 2007).

The reform began in 1989 with the election of a reform-minded school board that adopted the *Beliefs and Vision* statement in 1990 that provided direction by describing the characteristics of the education system the board sought to achieve. The statement put forth four major propositions: HISD exists to support the relationship between the teacher and the student; HISD must decentralize; HISD must focus on performance, not compliance; and HISD must require a common core of academic subjects for all students. The *Belief and Visions* statement was reaffirmed by school boards in 2001 and again in 2004 and continues to be district policy. The statement is accompanied by statements of purpose for the district, strategic intent, goals, and an expression of core values. In 2003, the school board adopted a monitoring system designed to allow it to monitor progress made toward realizing these guiding principles. The monitoring system was expanded in 2005 (http://www.hisd.org, accessed February 7, 2007).

When the incumbent superintendent procrastinated in developing an implementation plan for the vision statement, the reform majority on the school board engineered a buyout of her contract in 1990. A new superintendent was hired (from Dade County, Florida), and 1 year later he had implemented shared decision-making committees in 235 schools that developed school improvement plans for each school financed through school-based budgets. At this early stage, however, many schools had gone through the motions of school empowerment without changing anything behaviorally (McAdams, 2000).

A school accountability system was much more difficult to design and to put in place, but it was accomplished in May 1994. The state already had enacted an accountability system that focused on performance level. Against this criterion alone, however, most of Houston's schools and school children would fare poorly. (Houston students passed only 50% of all the state tests they took in 2005 compared with a state average of 62%.) What the district needed to improve the functioning of its many low-performing schools was an accountability system that highlighted school improvement en route to reaching the goal of acceptable performance levels for all. Three principles guided development of the HISD accountability system: all students would be expected to reach the same standard, progress would be measured by comparing grade performance in the current year with the performance of the same cohort of students the previous year (e.g., the pass percentage of fifth-graders in a school would be compared with their pass rate the previous year when they were fourth-graders), and schools with lower performance records would be expected to make larger gains than schools with higher performance (McAdams, 2000).

Student achievement was measured using the same test as the state in its accountability system, the Texas Assessment of Academic Skills (TAAS), a criterion-referenced test built around the Texas state curriculum. (The TAAS was replaced by the Texas Assessment of Knowledge and Skills [TAKS)] in 2003.) The TAAS (as does the TAKS) measures whether a student has mastered the curriculum's essential elements in reading, writing, and mathematics; a student either passes or fails.

The Houston accountability rating procedure set an expected rate of growth in percent of students passing the TAAS for each grade cohort. Schools with fewer than 20% passing the TAAS were expected to increase their passing percentage by 8% the next year; *unacceptable* (21% through 39%), 6%; *acceptable* (40% through 64%), 4%; and *recognized* (65% through 89%), 2%. Schools in the *exemplary* category (90% and above) *were expected to maintain a pass rate above 90%* (McAdams, 2000).

Schools in the *clearly unacceptable* category were subject to intervention. Intervention included close supervision by the superintendent of schools, appointing a school intervention team containing a mentor principal, recruiting parent and community leader volunteers to work with the school, and analyzing available data on school performance to inform reform, along with other external support. A more elaborate system of rewards, sanctions, responses, and consequences was subsequently developed for all schools.

Reflecting on the HISD accountability system, one of the reform school board members wrote,

> No other reform during my years on the board did more to improve school performance. School accountability drove accountability upward and downward through the system. Accountable schools need authority. HISD would have to decentralize management authority by moving significant resources, numerous professional staff, and responsibility for decisions from central office to area offices and schools. Accountable schools needed timely, effective support from administrative service providers: HISD would have to examine, evaluate, and review every process that delivered services to schools. And accountable schools would require accountable principals and teachers. HISD would need to develop effective personnel management policies. (McAdams, 2000, p. 83)

The struggle for student and employee accountability bridged the terms of two superintendents. Early in 1994, the first superintendent appointed by the reform board returned to Florida to head the Broward County school district. The reform majority on the board wanted to avoid a national search for a new superintendent and the ethnic conflict that could easily result. Further, they wanted a person who was committed to the *Beliefs and Visions* statement, who would protect the reform progress that had been made and move aggressively to advance the vision further. They also wanted a person who understood the complexity of HISD, who was trusted by the administrators and teachers of the district and respected by business, political, and civic leaders in recognition of the concepts of group theory. They turned to one of their own, Rod Paige (McAdams, 2000).

Paige was dean of the Texas Southern School of Education and had been active for years as a teacher and scholar. Paige was not involved in the behind-the-scene maneuvering that led to his appointment, and there were possible complications. He would have to agree to accept the position, he did not hold Texas certification as school superintendent, and he would have to resign from the school board before he could officially be considered for the position. What proved to be the most formidable complication, however, was his race. He was African American, and the majority of students in the district were Hispanic. When confronted in executive session, Paige was willing to accept the position. Subsequently, he resigned from the board, obtained temporary certification, and was hired as superintendent by a six-to-two vote of the board. The negative votes came from the Hispanic members of the board who had been excluded from the behind-the-scene maneuvering.

The Hispanic community was furious over the appointment. The appointment process was challenged as being illegal. A lawsuit was brought. The Texas Education Agency investigated. Political pressure was brought on elected officials and their appointed bureaucrats by the Hispanic community and countered by the African American community. After months of investigations and hearings, it was determined that no laws had been broken in the appointment and that there was no discrimination (McAdams, 2000).

School district decentralization was one of the priorities set forth in the *Beliefs and Values* statement, and some progress had been made. Shared decision making was beginning to work, and school-based budgeting was popular with the principals, but "the central office was still trying to manage schools with a highly centralized, unitary management structure. All significant decisions and many insignificant ones were made by the superintendent" (McAdams, 2000, p. 123). In public session, prior to the executive session in which the board decided to seek to appoint Paige as the new superintendent, a decentralization strategy was presented by a task force previously appointed by the board consisting of HISD administrators and others and supported by full-time consultants and loaned executives from the Houston business community. The board adopted the plan at the same meeting. Implementing the plan became one of the first responsibilities of the new superintendent, Rod Paige.

The school board reduced its role in management, including relinquishing to the superintendent its authority to approve personnel appointments, promotions, and transfers. It reduced its number of meetings per month from two to one, improving the quality of staff preparation for the meetings and freeing up staff time for other purposes.

A public school choice program was established whereby any HISD student could attend any HISD school if space was available. Charter, magnet, and out-of-district transfers were made available also.

A curriculum audit was launched to determine the degree to which the district's written, taught, and tested curricula were aligned and the extent to which the district's resources were organized to support the development, implementation, and monitoring of the curricula. The district spent 3 years and more than $10 million to create its new curriculum called CLEAR.

Employee incentives and accountability monitoring procedures were strengthened. HISD adopted the state-developed Professional Development and Appraisal System (PDAS) as its official teacher evaluation system. Teachers were no longer offered continuing contracts. After a 3-year probationary period, only 2-year term contracts are offered. In January 2006, HISD adopted a new teacher-performance-pay system designed in consultation with teachers and administrators. A year later, $14 million in bonuses were distributed to nearly 8,000 teachers (out of about 13,000 instructional employees). The bonuses ranged up to $7,175 and averaged $1,847, or about 4% of the average teachers annual salary (http://www.hisd.org, accessed February 7, 2007). The program contains three different levels of performance pay based on state school accountability ratings or yearly improvement of individual student scores on Stanford or Aprenda normed reference tests or the state TAKS tests.

Supported by grants from Houston businesses, HISD overhauled its management infrastructure by installing four new operating systems: a directive and information system, a desk manual program, an approval control program, and a systems control program. All district managers (including principals and assistant principals) receive training in basic management techniques and in the use of the new programs. Building repairs, maintenance, and food service are outsourced. The information system of the human resources department was reengineered, introducing modern information technology and permitting it to be fully integrated with the payroll process.

D. R. McAdams, a reform member of the Houston school board from 1990 through 2001, believes that the Houston experience in school reform has relevance for reformers in other large urban districts. He concludes,

> Urban school reformers everywhere must deal with public opinion, the media, state education agencies, business interests, teacher unions, organized labor, political parties, tax payer groups, neighborhood interests, discrimination and ethnic conflict, and the core educational issues of curriculum, teaching, learning, assessment, accountability, and management effectiveness. (McAdams, 2000, p. 248)

The incremental implementation of reform practices by HISD, from 1989 through the present, is an excellent demonstration of incrementalism. The building of coalitions demonstrates the workings of group theory. The adoption of *A Declaration of Beliefs and Visions* acknowledged the interaction of elements in a system and laid the basis for a rationalistic approach to reform. The role of the business community and other civic and political organizations illustrates elite theory. The net result of this incremental process is a revolutionary and systemic restructuring of the institution itself.

Rationalism

Adherents of rationalism seek to shape the policy-making process in such a fashion as to ensure the enactment of policies that maximize social gain. According to Dror (1964), the assumptions of pure rationality are deeply rooted in modern civilization and culture and are the basis of certain economic theories of the free market and political theories of democracy. Rationalism is derived from the postpositivist philosophy described in chapter 7. Dror characterized the pure rationality model as having six phases: establishing a complete set of operational goals, with relative weights allocated to the various degrees to which each may be achieved; establishing

ACTIVITY 10.3

Houston Functions within the Texas Model

Addresses ISLLC Standards 6 and Most of the Others

The Houston story dramatically illustrates the politics of reform in a large urban center (standard 6), but because of its enlightened approach to reforming the system, it also positively illustrates the implementation of most of the other standards and functions.

Houston faces most of the same problems and opportunities that Chicago does, but that did not stop its school board from initiating a massive reform effort under extrordinary lay leadership. Much of the early opposition to reform came from central office administrators, but they can be replaced, and they were. Further, the school board took a systems approach to reform, which is unusual even in small, homogeneous districts where agreement is much easier to achieve.

1. The federal No Child Left Behind Act was based largely on the Texas standards-based accountability model. Houston had to make a number of adjustments to the Texas model to accommodate its urban population and environment. See the Houston Independent School District Web site to learn more about its governance process and how it has evolved (http://www.hisd.org).

2. The politics of reform in Houston is brilliantly captured in McAdams (2000). We highly recommend that you read this book to gain insight into the politics of reform, especially as it applies to large urban school districts. As a member and two-time president of the Houston School Board during the early reform years, McAdams provides a detailed insider's perspective of the maneuvering that took place. He concludes, "Urban school reform must be broad and deep. And everything must be done with strategic intent and with a focus on the organization as a whole" (p. xiii).

---

a complete inventory of other values and resources, with relative weights; preparing a complete set of alternative policies open to the policymaker; preparing a complete set of valid predictions of the costs and benefits of each alternative, including the extent to which each will achieve the various operational goals, consume resources, and realize or impair other values; calculating the net expectation of each alternative by multiplying the probability of each benefit and cost for each alternative by the utility of each and calculating the net benefit (or cost) in utility units; and comparing the net expectations and identifying the alternative (or alternatives, if two or more are equally good) with the highest net expectation. These phases are organized sequentially in Figure 10.6.

In theory, rationalism involves all individual, social, political, and economic values, not just those that can be converted to dollars and cents. In reality, the measurement difficulties make inclusion of other than economic values unlikely. Thus, this model elevates economic efficiency above other

potential societal objectives, such as equity and liberty.

To "know" all that would be required to select a policy "rationally" (i.e., all of society's value preferences and relative weights, all available policy alternatives, and the consequences of each alternative) is what Lindblom (1959) termed *superhuman comprehensiveness* and Wise (1979) termed *hyperrationality*. In essence, rationalism attempts the impossible by quantifying all elements of the political process and human behavior and expressing the decision-making function in mathematical terms (Lavoie, 1985). Although imperfect, the representative legislature (e.g., school boards and Congress) is a political mechanism for approximating "all of society's value preferences and relative weights."

Rational techniques that are based on economic principles and procedures should be an important factor in budget development. However, Cibulka (1987) acknowledged that even budgetary decisions are not actually made on the basis of rationality. Wildavsky (1964) also argued that pure rationality is

FIGURE 10.6

Phases of pure-rationality policymaking

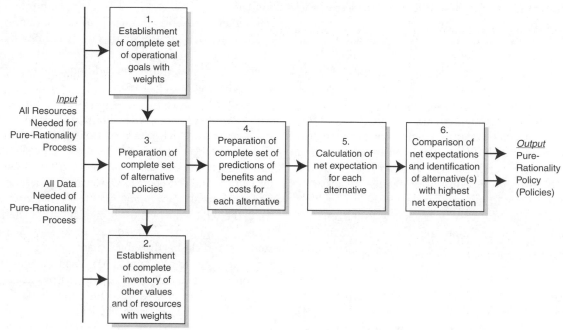

an illusion. Political realists argue that decisions in the public sector, including public education, are made on the basis of political rationality rather than economic rationality. To them, rationalism is at best irrelevant and can be downright dysfunctional to the political process (C. L. Schultz, 1968).

Rationalism was a key principle behind the comprehensive centralized planning schemes of socialist and communist countries. With the collapse of many of the latter and with the routine failure of 5-year plans in socialist—mostly developing—countries, rationalism has lost much of its credibility (Agarawala, 1984; Weiler, 1980).

Nevertheless, rationalistic philosophy has had an important impact on policy analysis and an indirect effect on policy decision making. Its bias of economic efficiency is a value that is all too frequently neglected in the traditional political process. The rational model has fostered such management devices as planning, programming, and budgeting systems; zero-based budgeting; management by objectives; and operations research as well as cost-benefit and cost-effectiveness analysis. The terms *accountability* and *assessment* are now a part of the schooling vernacular, and teacher, pupil, and program evaluations are accepted procedures. Local school boards and state and federal governments are adding to their long-standing concerns over the quantity and quality of school inputs; there is a similar concern over school outputs through mandatory evaluation and testing programs and achievement standards.

Whereas tools of rational analysis have had some effect on the educational decision-making process, rationalistic approaches have fallen short of the expectations of their supporters and have met with strong opposition from some segments of the traditional educational decision-making process. A major source of resistance to the use of analysis in schools is the teaching profession itself. In addition to their vested interests as employees, teachers are acutely aware of the almost impossible task of quantitatively measuring the complex variables associated with educational inputs and outputs and with the learning process.

The most ardent supporters of rational analysis are economic purists who seek economic efficiency in the public sector. Within the private sector, the market provides powerful mechanisms to weed out inefficiencies. Indeed, one of the roles of government is to police the marketplace, keeping in check those forces that would impede the functioning of these mechanisms. Few, if any, mechanisms to weed out inefficiencies operate in the public sector.

Unlike incrementalism, which focuses on means, rationalism requires agreement on outcomes, which is unlikely in pluralistic organizations (e.g., state and federal governments and large urban school districts). Because of the reduced number of conflicting interest groups at the school level (which may also be the case with small, homogeneous school districts), such agreement is frequently obtained, and rationalism can become functional at that level.

Seattle School District as an Illustration of Rationalism. Like Houston, Seattle's reform is strictly a local matter; it was initiated by the school board and engineered by two nontraditional superintendents. Seattle is not your typical urban core city. Its 500,000 population has a white middle-class majority and a reputation as being prosperous, cultured, and liberal. Its largest minority group is Asian American followed by African Americans and Latinos. It has relatively low rates of poverty and unemployment and a booming city center. Seattle's students average at or above the 50th percentile on nationally standardized tests in core content areas. But there are significant gaps in achievement between ethnic groups with whites averaging at the 70th percentile and African Americans at the 30th (Yee & McCloud, 2003).

Closing this ethnic achievement gap is one of three priority issues the district has been struggling with for the past half century. Related issues are compensating for the negative effects of de facto segregation along racial lines caused by the city's housing patterns, closing under utilized schools (mostly in the northern section of the city populated by white residents), and upgrading aged and overcrowded schools (mostly in the southern section of the city populated by minority groups). A primary strategy for addressing these issues was mandatory busing of students within the district. However, the burden of this strategy was borne primarily by ethnic minority children residing on the south side of the city by a ratio of about 10 to 1; busing was ended with the appointment of the first nontraditional superintendent, John Stanford, in 1995.

General John Stanford was an African American who had been head of logistics for the U.S. Army prior to his retirement and chief executive officer of Fulton County, Georgia, subsequently. General Stanford's first appointment as Seattle's superintendent was Joseph Olchefske, who was charged with managing a serious budget shortfall; developing a systemic strategy for using the school district's fiscal, human, and material resources to improve the academic performance of all students; and closing the achievement gap among ethnic groups (Yee & McCloud, 2003). General Stanford had broken the mold of previous district practice and begun the reform process when his untimely death in 1998 led to the appointment of Olchefske as superintendent to carry on what the general had initiated. Olchefske, an investment banker, was an economist by training.

The systemic plan began with district personnel translating the Washington State Essential Learning Requirements into academic standards for each grade level in four content areas. Those standards are used as guides for designing staff development experiences, designing curriculum, and adopting curricular and assessment materials. The mandatory busing program was replaced with a neighborhood assignment policy that offers students the opportunity to express a preference for attending a school in the geographic area in which they reside but with options to attend schools outside that area. (It is estimated that more than 80% of students attend their first choice school [http://www.seattleschools.org, accessed February 7, 2007].) A school-based budgeting policy was implemented, and a weighted student formula modeled after the one used in Edmonton, Alberta, Canada is employed to allocate fiscal resources to schools based on the educational needs of students in attendance at each school.

School principals are considered chief executive officers, as in Edmonton, providing them with greater discretion than in most school districts over their budgets, selection of new teachers, and selecting and organizing school site professional development programs. The district provides a leadership institute for principals to care for their professional development. Principal appointment, evaluation, and replacement decisions are the prerogative of the superintendent.

A negotiated contract with the Seattle teachers union went into effect at the beginning of the 1996–1997 school year that included a "trust agreement" modeled after the one between General Motors Saturn Division and the United Auto Workers. The contract provided for: a shared decision-making role for teachers at the school level with respect to budget, strategic planning, curriculum, and professional development; hiring flexibility with teacher input through site hiring teams; seniority reduced to "a factor" considered in hiring, transfer, and separation decisions; and a teacher evaluation policy tied in part to student achievement with measures of achievement jointly determined by administration and staff (Yee & McCloud, 2003). Student achievement is measured using a "value-added model" developed by Sanders and Horne (1994) that tracks growth in student performance from year to year. Principal evaluation includes a component of this model that captures schoolwide improvements.

Seattle's reform is an example of charismatic leadership as demonstrated by General Stanford. Ironically, the top-down decision process resulted in a highly decentralized system, not for democratic

reasons but because it promised to be more effective and efficient in closing the achievement gap among ethnic groups. The systemic approach to reform was as close to the rational model of policymaking as one is likely to find. Ethnic politics were (are) a peripheral problem in that they have been a deterrent to closing underutilized schools in the northern section of the city dominated by the white middle class. Quasi-market forces were induced by making available parental choice of schools for their children and outsourcing of some district services.

Distinctions between Judicial and Legislative Influence on Educational Policy Formulation

Federal and state courts are having an increasing influence on the formulation of school policy. In this section we examine that influence and how judicial procedures and influence differ from those of the legislative branch of government.

Judicial and legislative branches of government perform different functions in the formation of policy. Education programs can be enacted only through the legislative process, but the judiciary may be asked to test whether these policies satisfy societal expectations as expressed in federal and state constitutions. This external review provides a check on legislative actions, and judicial reviews often stimulate (even force) legislatures to alter legislated policies. The courts do not, however, initiate the subjects of judicial review; they react to conflicts and problems posed to them by members of society (i.e., plaintiffs).

In chapter 9, we discussed in detail inherent conflicts among the metavalues of equality and liberty (or individual freedom). Suffice it to say at this point that equality is a value that can best be championed at the societal level (by state or federal governments, i.e., centralization of authority). The value of liberty, on the other hand, is best realized through an unregulated market (i.e., decentralization of authority) that is anathema to equality. Adherents of each value battle incessantly in both courts and legislatures. Federal courts made equality a national concern through numerous decisions affecting education, starting with the Supreme Court's decision in *Brown v. Board of Education* (347 U.S. 483 1954). In the mid-1960s, Congress responded with such legislation as Title VI of the Civil Rights Act and the Elementary and Secondary Education Act to ease inequities in children's educational opportunities.

Despite strong national pressures from a variety of sources to improve educational opportunities for poor and minority students, state legislatures were slow to respond. The nature of the legislative process, characterized by "give-and-take, negotiation, and compromise" (Fuhrman, 1978, p. 160), inhibited reform by the states. Even when states responded to pressure brought by impending and actual court reviews, the equality thrust raised at the national level and by both state and federal courts deferred to consensus-building processes that shape the actual content of reforms adopted through state legislatures.

Unlike judicial decision making, which is narrowly focused on constitutional principles, policy development in legislatures is broadly influenced by their representative nature, the distributive nature of education policy, and the ongoing nature of the decision-making process (Brown & Elmore, 1982). First, legislators, as representatives of school districts to be affected by proposed reforms, are frequently more concerned with protecting their school districts' interests (subdivisions of state government) than with equalizing opportunities for poor children. The distributive nature of educational policy requires at least a majority of the population to perceive that the reforms benefit them. In the process of finding solutions, equity goals are frequently bargained away.

Major consideration in the bargaining and compromise process is given to which districts gain and which lose. Finally, the resolution of issues is not isolated from other concerns placed before legislators. Rather than concentrating solely on the specific merits of the proposal at hand, lining up votes on an education issue may depend on positions taken by legislators on prior and subsequent policy issues that are likely to have no relation to education whatsoever.

While the legislative process gives attention to school districts' interests and to consensus building, challenges to states' educational policies heard in the courts are more likely to consider inequities in the treatment of pupils. The plan that results from negotiations through the legislative process may or may not reflect the equity concerns of the courts or the original proponents of reform. "The closer one gets to the process of reform in specific states, the more elusive equity seems and the more complex are the values and objectives operating on reform proposals" (Brown & Elmore, 1982, p. 113).

On the whole, the evidence leaves little room for optimism about substantial and long-term improvements in educational equity through either the legislative or judicial process (King, Swanson, & Sweetland, 2003). The conflict among values of equity, personal freedom, and efficiency is ongoing; the policy result is an ebb and flow of emphasis from one to the other.

Impact of Collective Bargaining on Policy Formation

Over half the states have enacted legislation allowing collective bargaining by public employees. In the remaining states, teachers (and other employees) can join unions and typically participate in some form of "good-faith bargaining" involving representatives of unions and school boards, usually over conditions of employment. In either case, the agreements arrived at are school district policies. The difference is that in states formally authorizing collective bargaining, the agreement or contract is enforceable through courts or other venue designated by the enabling legislation. Such recourse would not normally be available in the other states, and compliance would depend largely on the integrity of the parties to the agreement.

The National Labor Relations Act, passed by Congress in 1935, was the first legislation protecting private-sector employees' right to organize and to bargain collectively with their employers through representatives of their own choosing on matters pertaining to wages, job-related benefits, and conditions of employment. The act also created the National Labor Relations Board to halt unfair practices on the part of employers and authorized it to seek enforcement of its orders through the federal courts. Employees in the public sector were excluded from all provisions of the act. It was not until 1959 that Wisconsin became the first state to enact legislation permitting unionization and collective bargaining by employees in the public sector. A state board was established to oversee the administration of the provisions of the law and to assist in the resolution of disputes. An executive order (number 10988) was issued by President John F. Kennedy in 1962 allowing collective bargaining for federal employees. The order provided federal workers with the right to join organizations of their own choosing and required federal agencies to recognize such employee organizations for the purpose of negotiations and to meet with representatives of employee designated organizations to confer about personnel policies and conditions of work. The order also established the procedure of advisory arbitration to resolve grievances with respect to the administration of agreements reached. The issuance of this order encouraged state and local government employees, including school district employees, to seek similar negotiation rights (Webb & Norton, 1999).

As collective bargaining spread in the public sector, it tended to follow the pattern established by the National Labor Relations Act for industrial unions even though the conditions of employment were quite different in the two sectors. The industrial approach to bargaining is prone to be adversarial in order to realize maximum gain through the use of authority, power, or withdrawal of services (i.e., strikes, which are generally illegal by public employees) (Webb & Norton, 1999). This approach is at odds with the types of labor–management relations encouraged by third-wave reforms, such as teacher involvement in school-based decision making.

In an effort to reduce conflict and to reach mutually satisfying solutions to problems faced by school districts and of professional concern to teachers and administrators alike, new approaches to bargaining have been encouraged in the education sector. An assessment of the evolution of teachers unions by Kerschner and Mitchell (1988) argues that by the 1980s the idea of "collective bargaining" was shifting to "negotiated policy" in which the agenda was greatly expanded beyond traditional issues of salaries and working conditions to include almost anything that happens within a school district. Kerschner and Koppich's (1993) study of the evolving nature of teacher unionism identified two new characteristics of union concerns that had emerged, blurring the traditional distinction between labor and management in schools and school districts. One is a focus on professional education issues, such as learning, instruction, curriculum, assessment, and student achievement. The second is collaborative and collegial involvement by teachers in all aspects of school operations and school systems. In light of these trends, Odden (1995) proposed "less direct union involvement in core education issues and more direct involvement of site teachers in those issues, and more involvement of the union in ensuring that management creates, sustains, and over time improves a decentralized management structure that devolves major responsibility to teachers in schools and their important subunits." (p. 144).

In the next chapter, we provide examples of the policy results of more than two decades of reforms intended to make schooling more effective and more equitable.

ACTIVITY 10.5
Political Decision Making
Addresses ISLLC Standards 1, 3, and 6

Public policy is shaped to provide quality education for students.

1. Interview your superintendent of schools and/or members of your school board about how educational policy is developed in your school district.
2. On the basis of the information gathered from these interviews, describe situations that illustrate each policymaking model discussed in this chapter.

SUMMARY AND FUNDAMENTAL CONCEPTS

In this chapter we have described how formal educational policy decisions are made. Because education provides benefits that are highly valued by individuals and society, often in different ways, the process is particularly complex and involves both government and the market. Allocation of scarce resources through markets was described, and several models of political decision making were presented.

Education issues were identified that any society must answer either through the political process of government or through market transactions. Since the political process is biased toward the metavalue of equity and the market holds biases toward metavalues of personal freedom and efficiency, preferences for the resolution of education issues are quite different, depending on the sector. The range of ways for structuring governmental involvement and the implications for placement of authority with local, state, and federal authorities or individuals were presented. The differences between the roles of the legislative and judicial branches of government in developing and evaluating educational policy were described, as was the impact of collective bargaining on policy development.

The impact of charter schools on the functioning of all public schools was used to illustrate the political decision model of institutionalism. The Chicago reform process illustrated incrementalism; Houston, systemic reform; and Seattle, rationalism.

Fundamental Concepts

The fundamental concepts that follow have been discussed in this chapter. The citations following each concept indicate the Interstate School Leaders Licensure Consortium (ISLLC) standards and functions related to the concept. The Arabic numerals refer to the ISLLC standards, and the letters refer to the functions as presented in the table found inside the front cover. If no function is indicated, the concept pertains to standard generally.

- Policies establish the parameters within which an organization will function; they set constraints within which discretion can be exercised. (1A; 3B; 6B)
- The nature of both the structure of the policymaking process and the politics employed within the structure are believed to influence policy outcomes. (3A; 6)
- Education is considered to be both a public and private good because it yields both social and personal benefits. (2A; 3B; 4B; 6B)
- To ensure that both individual and societal demands of schooling are met, decisions about the provisions of education are made in both the public and the private sectors. (1A; 2A; 3B; 4A, 4B; 5E; 6)
- Decisions in the public sector are made collaboratively through political processes by governments, whereas decisions in the private sector are made by individuals using market mechanisms as described by economics. (6)
- Government is that agency in the division of labor that has as its proper function the maximization of social welfare. (6)
- Governments have the unique power to extract involuntary payments, called taxes, from households and producers alike. (6)
- Decisions made in the public sector have an equalitarian bias while decisions made in the private sector have biases toward efficient use of resources and the unfettered exercise of individual preferences. (1B; 2H; 3B; 5C, 5E; 6)
- Governments can oversee the public interest through a variety of interventions, including direct ownership and operation, regulation, licensure, taxation, subsidies, transfer payments, and contracts or charters. (6)
- Significantly different patterns of allocations of authority among levels of government and individuals can be structured depending on the relative priorities given to policy objectives. (1A; 2A, 2F; 3B, 3D; 4C, 4D; 5C, 5D, 5E; 6)
- No overarching general theory of political decision making exists, but there is a "grab bag" of heuristic theories and contrasting methods, including institutionalism, systems theory, incrementalism, group theory, elite theory, and rationalism. (6)
- The devolved nature of school governance in the United States has produced educational systems that are diverse, dynamic, and responsive to local conditions (creating some of the best schools in the world—and some of the worst) and has impeded state and federal efforts to equalize educational opportunities in terms of finance, curricular provision, and integration of students and staff with respect to socioeconomic status and ethnicity. (6)
- Education laws can only be enacted through the legislative process, but the judiciary may be asked to test whether laws (or resulting policy) satisfy societal expectations as expressed in federal and state constitutions. (6)
- Judicial decision making is narrowly focused on constitutional principles, while the legislative process is broadly influenced by its representative nature, the ongoing nature of the legislative process, and the distributive nature of educational policy. (6)

- Equity is a value that can best be championed at the societal level by state and federal governments; the values of liberty and efficiency are best realized through unregulated markets. (1A, 1D; 2; 3; 4; 5; 6)
- A consensus in the pattern of educational reform is emerging whereby achievement and behavioral standards are established and monitored by state and federal authorities with local authorities designing and implementing instructional delivery systems and parents choosing among the options provided. (1A, 1D; 2; 3; 4; 5; 6)
- Charter schools are public schools that come into existence by a contract between a sponsoring party and a state agency, a local school board, or other approved authorizer; the charter defines the framework within which the school operates and how public support for the school will be provided. (6)
- An education voucher is an entitlement extended to an individual by a government permitting that individual to receive educational services up to the maximum dollar amount specified; the voucher can normally be redeemed according to the preference of the holder at any institution or enterprise approved by the granting agency. (6)

REFERENCES

Agarawala, R. (1984). *Planning in developing countries: Lessons of experience* (World Bank Staff Working Papers No. 576). Washington, DC: World Bank.

Berman, P., Nelson, B., Ericson, J., Perry, R., & Silverman, D. (1998). *A national study of charter schools: Second year report.* Washington, DC: Office of Research and Improvement, U.S. Department of Education.

Brown, P. R., & Elmore, R. F. (1982). Analyzing the impact of school finance reform. In N. H. Cambron-McCabe & A. Odden (Eds.), *The changing politics of school finance* (pp. 107–138). Cambridge, MA: Ballinger.

Bryk, A. S. (1999). Policy lessons from Chicago's experience with decentralization. In D. Ravitch (Ed.), *Brookings papers on education policy, 1999* (pp. 67–127). Washington, DC: Brookings Institution Press.

Center for Education Reform. (2004). *Charter schools today: Changing the face of American education—Statistics, stories and insights.* Washington, DC: Author.

Cibulka, J. G. (1987). Theories of education budgeting: Lessons from the management of decline. *Educational Administration Quarterly, 23*, 7–40.

Coleman, J. S., & Hoffer, T. (1987). *Public and private high schools: The impact of communities.* New York: Basic Books.

Coons, J. E., & Sugarman, S. D. (1978). *Education by choice: The case for family control.* Berkeley: University of California Press.

Cremin, L. A. (1976). *Public education.* New York: Basic Books.

Cuban, L., & Usdan, M. (2003). What happened in the six cities? In L. Cuban & M. Usdan (Eds.), *Powerful reforms with shallow roots: Improving America's urban schools* (pp. 1–15). New York: Teachers College Press.

Downs, A. (1957). *An economic theory of democracy.* New York: Harper & Row.

Dror, Y. (1964). Muddling through—"Science" or inertia? *Public Administration Review, 24,* 153–157.

Dye, T. R. (1987). *Understanding public policy* (6th ed.). Upper Saddle River, NJ: Prentice Hall.

Dye, T. R., & Zeigler, H. (1981). *The irony of democracy.* Monterey, CA: Brooks/Cole.

Easton, D. A. (1965). *A systems analysis of political life.* New York: Wiley.

Elazar, D. J. (1972). *American federalism.* New York: Harper & Row.

Forum for Education and Democracy. (April 2008). *Democracy at risk: The need for a new federal policy in education.* Washington, DC: Author.

Fuhrman, S. (1978). The politics and process of school finance reform. *Journal of Education Finance, 4,* 158–178.

Gill, B. P., Timpane, P. M., Ross, K. E., & Brewer, D. J. (2001). *Rhetoric versus reality: What we know and what we need to know about vouchers and charter schools.* Santa Monica, CA: RAND Education.

Grodzins, M. (1966). *The American system.* Chicago: Rand McNally.

Hanson, E. M. (1986). *Educational reform and administrative development: The cases of Colombia and Venezuela.* Stanford, CA: Hoover Institution Press.

Hess, G. A., Jr. (1990). *Chicago school reform: What is it and how it came to be.* Chicago: Chicago Panel on Public School Policy and Finance.

Hess, G. A., Jr. (1999). Understanding achievement (and other) changes under Chicago school reform. *Educational Evaluation and Policy Analysis, 21*(1), 67–83.

Hodgkinson, C. (1983). *The philosophy of leadership.* Oxford: Blackwell.

Kaufman, R., & Herman, J. (1991). *Strategic planning in education: Rethinking, restructuring, revitalizing.* Lancaster, PA: Technomic.

Kerschner, C. T., & Koppich, J. E. (1993). *A union of professionals.* New York: Teachers College Press.

Kerschner, C. T., & Mitchell, D. E. (1988). *The changing idea of a teachers' union.* Philadelphia: Falmer.

King, R. A., Swanson, A. D., & Sweetland, S. R. (2003). *School finance: Achieving high standards with equity and efficiency* (3rd ed.). Boston: Allyn & Bacon.

Kirst, M. W. (1988). Recent educational reform in the United States: Looking backward and forward. *Educational Administration Quarterly, 24,* 319–328.

Kneebone, E., Logue, T., Cahn, S., & M. McDunnah. (2004, October). *Here and now: The need for performing schools in Chicago's neighborhoods.* Retrieved from www.iff.org/resources/content/1/1/documents/cpsfullreport.pdf, March 31, 2008.

Labaree, D. F. (1997). Public goods, private goods: The American struggle over educational goals. *American Educational Research Journal, 34*(1), 39–81.

Ladd, H. F., & Hansen, J. S. (Eds.). (1999). *Making money matter: Financing America's schools.* Washington, DC: National Academies Press.

Lake, R. J., & Rainey, L. (2005). *Chasing the blues away: Charter schools scale up in Chicago.* Washington, DC: Progressive Policy Institute.

Lavoie, D. (1985). *National economic planning: What is left?* Cambridge, MA: Ballinger.

Levin, H. M. (1987). Education as public and private good. *Journal of Policy Analysis and Management, 6,* 628–641.

Lindblom, C. E. (1959). The science of muddling through. *Public Administration Review, 19,* 79–88.

Lindblom, C. E. (1968). *The policymaking process.* Upper Saddle River, NJ: Prentice Hall.

Lipman, P. (2002). Making the global city, making inequality: The political economy and cultural politics of Chicago school policy. *American Educational Research Journal, 39,* 379–419.

Lubienski, C. (2003). Innovation in education markets: Theory and evidence on the impact of competition and choice in charter schools. *American Educational Research Journal, 40,* 395–443.

McAdams, D. R. (2000). *Fighting to save our urban schools . . . and winning! Lessons from Houston.* New York: Teachers College Press.

McNeil, L. M. (1986). *Contradictions of control: School structure and school knowledge.* New York: Routledge & Kegan Paul.

National Alliance for Public Charter Schools. (2006). *Number of charter schools and students in 2005–06 school year.* Washington, DC: Author.

National Center for Education Statistics. (2005a). *America's charter schools: Results from the NAEP 2003 pilot study* (NCES 2005-456). Washington, DC: U.S. Department of Education.

National Center for Education Statistics. (2005b). *Digest of education statistics.* Washington, DC: U.S. Department of Education.

National Center for Education Statistics. (2006). *The condition of education 2006.* Washington, DC: Institute of Education Science, U.S. Department of Education.

National Commission on Excellence in Education. (1984). *A nation at risk: The full account.* Portland, OR: USA Research.

Nelson, F. H., Muir, E., & Drown, R. (2000). *Venturesome capital: State charter school finance systems.* Washington, DC: Office of Educational Research and Improvement, U.S. Department of Education.

Odden, A. R. (1995). *Educational leadership for America's schools.* New York: McGraw-Hill.

Odden, A. R., & Marsh, D. (1989). State education reform implementation: A framework for analysis. In J. Hannaway & R. Crowson (Eds.), *The politics of reforming school administration* (pp. 41–59). New York: Falmer.

Palmer, L. B., & Gau, R. (2005) Charter school authorizing: Policy implications from a national study. *Phi Delta Kappan, 86,* 352–357.

Palmer, L. B., Gau, L., & Gau, R. (2003). *Charter school authorizing: Are states making the grade?* Washington, DC: Thomas B. Fordham Institute.

Samuelson, P. A. (1980). *Economics* (11th ed.). New York: McGraw-Hill.

Sanders, W., & Horne, S. (1994). The Tennessee value-added assessment system: Mixed model methodology in educational assessment. *Journal of Personnel Assessment in Education, 8*(3), 299–311.

Schultz, C. L. (1968). *The politics and economics of public spending.* Washington, DC: Brookings Institution.

Schultz, T. W. (1963). *The economic value of education.* Berkeley: University of California Press.

Shipps, D. (2003). The business man's educator: Mayoral takeover and nontraditional leadership in Chicago. In L. Cuban & M. Usdan (Eds.), *Powerful reforms with shallow roots: Improving America's urban schools* (pp. 16–37). New York: Teachers College Press.

Speakman, S., & Hassel, B. (2005). *Charter school funding: Inequity's next frontier.* Washington, DC: Thomas B. Fordham Institute.

Truman, D. B. (1951). *The governmental process.* New York: Knopf.

U.S. Department of Education, Office of Education Research and Improvement. (1998). *A national study of charter schools.* Washington, DC: U.S. Government Printing Office.

U.S. Department of Education, Office of the Under Secretary, Planning and Evaluation Service, Elementary and Secondary Division. (2000). *Evaluation of the public charter schools program: Year one evaluation report.* Washington, DC: Author.

U. S. Government Accountability Office. (January 2005). *Charter schools: To enhance education's monitoring and research, more charter school-level data are needed.* Washington, DC: Author.

Vanourek, G. (2005). *State of the charter movement 2005: Trends, issues, and indicators.* Washington, DC: National Alliance for Public Charter Schools.

Walker, D. B. (1981). *Toward a functioning federalism.* Cambridge, MA: Winthrop Press.

Webb, L. D., & Norton, M. S. (1999). *Human resources administration: Personnel issues and needs in education.* Columbus, OH: Merrill.

Weiler, H. N. (1980). *Educational planning and social change.* Paris: UNESCO.

Wildavsky, A. (1964). *The politics of the budgetary process.* Boston: Little, Brown.

Wirt, F. M. (April, 1986). *Multiple paths for understanding the role of values in state policy.* Paper presented at the annual meeting of the American Education Research Association, San Francisco, CA (ERIC Document Reproduction Service ED278086).

Wirt, F. M., & Kirst, M. W. (1982). *School in conflict: The politics of education.* Berkeley, CA: McCutchan.

Wise, A. E. (1979). *Legislated learning: The bureaucratization of the American classroom.* Berkeley: University of California Press.

Wise, A. E. (1988). Two conflicting trends in school reform: Legislated learning revisited. *Phi Delta Kappan, 69,* 328–332.

Wong, K. K. (2001). Integrated governance in Chicago and Birmingham (UK). In M. C. Wang & H. J. Walberg (Eds.), *School choice or best systems: What improves education?* (pp. 161–212). Mahwah, NJ: Lawrence Erlbaum Associates.

Wong, K. K. (2003). The big stick. *Education Next, 3,* 44–49.

Yee, G., & McCloud, B. (2003). A vision of hope: A case study of Seattle's two nontraditional superintendents. In *Powerful reforms with shallow roots: Improving America's urban schools* (pp. 54–76). New York: Teachers College Press.

District- and School-Based Decision Making: Strategy Formation and Planning

In chapter 10 we took a macroview of collective decision making as it transpires in governments and global and national economic systems. In this chapter we examine decision making more narrowly as done by individuals and within relatively small organizations, such as schools and school districts.

In the traditional view of organizations, power was thought to reside solely in a top-down structure. As a consequence, superintendents, principals, deans, and directors possessed wide latitudes of authority, while those lower in the hierarchy held very constrained authority. Decision making in this tradition was thought to be the domain of those "in charge." Today, these traditional views of organizations are changing, and shared power and worker empowerment are being widely advocated. Contemporary thinking is that power, decision making, and responsibilities in educational settings and other service organizations dominated by highly skilled professionals should be shared among all stakeholders, including principals, teachers, students, and parents (Forum for Education and Democracy, 2008; Scott, 1991).

Decision making is choosing among alternatives (Baron, 1985; Conway, 1984; White, 1969). Numerous authors (Cornell, 1980; Hoy & Miskel, 1978; Krepel, 1987; Steers, 1977) concur that the ability to guide an organization toward making sound decisions is among the most critical skills for effective school leadership. The decision process is at the core of all leadership tasks, and all administrative action is dependent on making decisions. Decision making within an organization is the process whereby it chooses among alternative courses of action with the goal of maximizing the outcomes resulting from the choices made (such as high academic achievement and moral and ethical behavior).

Herbert Simon (1977), an early contributor to decision theory, noted that decisions may be considered to lie on a continuum, with programmed decisions at one end and nonprogrammed decisions at the other. The former tend to be repetitive and routine related to tactics and implementation. The latter are often uncommon, unstructured, and of greater importance dealing with organizational direction and purpose. Because of their unstructured and unusual nature, nonprogrammed decisions are more difficult to handle and are often more complex than programmed decisions.

The first part of this chapter discusses decision theory in general terms. The second section presents a structure for making decisions within educational organizations at the district and school levels as well as factors that should be considered in distributing authority between the two levels.

Decision-Making Models

Two major classifications of decision-making models exist: normative and descriptive (Bell, Raiffa, & Tversky, 1988; Grandori, 1984). Normative models are primarily quantitative and suggest how decision making *should* be conducted to be consistent with rational behavior. See the rationalism model in chapter 10. Descriptive models address how the process *actually* occurs, accommodating cognitive limitations and idiographic influences inherent in the decision maker as in the incrementalism model in chapter 10. Normative models are based on the assumption that the decision maker recognizes all possible alternatives and their corresponding consequences, can evaluate the consequences against some value system, and can rank and ultimately select the best alternative. In the normative realm, the economic model reflects the essence of this approach, and determining expected utility is a fundamental step in rational decision making. Researchers have found, however, that it is difficult to use highly complex social organizations to test the normative model experientially (Kahn, 2005). Nevertheless, these normative models have yielded important insights.

Descriptive models accommodate the psychological proposition that it is highly unlikely that any person will function in a consistent and highly rational manner (Reitz, 1987; Watson & Buede, 1987). Such models continue to emerge as social scientists attempt to apply theoretical constructs as lenses to understand or predict individual human or organizational behavior. The models are built on the assumption that decisions in organizations are made via complex processes.

Normative Models

Elemental to normative decision-making models are the concepts of maximization and rationality (Einhorn & Hogarth, 1988). These models have reflected the assumptions that every possible outcome of implementing a decision (e.g., selecting a specific strategy or tactic) may be assigned a utility (a subjective value of its usefulness) as well as a subjective probability or expectation for each possible outcome being the actual result of the strategy/tactic selected (Neel, 1977). (See the discussion of rationalism in chapter 10 and Figure 10.7.) According to Neel, five principles serve as the bases for rational, normative decisions: transitivity, comparability, dominance, irrelevance, and independence. *Transitivity* refers to a phenomenon in which a person prefers A to B and B to C when in reality he or she could also prefer A to C. *Comparability* implies a willingness to compare options and determine a preferred outcome or a lack of preference, such as indifference. *Dominance*, or the sure-thing principle, suggests that the alternative that is not worse than the others on any attribute and is better on at least one should always be selected (Montgomery, 1983). *Irrelevance* refers to

a situation in which two choices may yield the same outcome. Under these circumstances the selection should not matter. *Independence* suggests that a person's wishes for a particular outcome should not influence his or her "expectation about the outcome" (Neel, 1977, p. 547). The model that is often used to exemplify the normative approach to decision making is the economic model.

The Economic Model. The economic person is assumed to be a maximizer; that is, he or she will make decisions that will provide the highest return. Although this model represents idealized, rational decision making, its application is questionable given its limited ability to indicate the best choice in some situations. Bell et al. (1988) provided the example of a person in a gambling scenario who bluffs more than is profitable to maximize his or her personal monetary gain and suggests that psychological baggage may make the notion of maximization subject to loose interpretation. Simon (1976), among many others, rejected the concept of the economic man as rationally directed on the grounds that he could not be fully informed when making a decision. Emotions played a significant part in making economically related decisions related to selecting a university for matriculation (Menon, Saiti, & Socratous, 2007), participating in the stock market (Cassidy, 2006), and experimental gaming designed to study decision making (Wagner, 2003).

As the economic model exhibits limitations in actual application because of its inability to accommodate violations because of psychological factors, so too does the fundamental normative model. The expected utility model attempts to overcome this weakness, but, while it is the most extensively applied normative model, it is also the most often maligned (Bell et al., 1988).

The Expected Utility Model. Although expected utility has been used as a descriptive model of economic behavior, it serves primarily as one form of idealized rational behavior and addresses well normative applications. With the development of probability theory came the concept that the best choice was the one that maximizes the expected value of the decision, a major premise of this model. As early as

1738, Bernoulli proposed the concept of expected utility rather than expected value to explain the decision maker's violation of expected profit maximization (e.g., the more money a person possesses, the less he or she values additional increments of the same amount of money). More recently, Atkinson, Herrnstein, Lindzey, and Luce (1988) developed axioms to accommodate the "simultaneous measurement of utility and subjective probability" (p. 692).

The current assumptions underlying expected utility assume that a decision maker is capable of assessing probability for the state of the world, designating a utility value for each consequence, determining the expected utility value associated with each "lottery" corresponding to each alternative, and comparing the alternatives based on their utilities (Bell et al., 1988). Baron (1985) provided a useful explanation of the quantitative substance of expected utility, stating that "the relative attractiveness of behavioral choices should be determined by the expected utility of each of the (objective) probabilities of each outcome times its (subjective) utility, given the decision maker's goals" (p. 9).

Four axioms (similar to Neel's [1977] five principles of rational decision making) serve as the foundation of expected utility: *cancellation*, the elimination of any state of the world that regardless of choice yields the same outcome, a property encompassed in other formal properties, such as Von Neumann and Morgenstern's (1947) substitution; *transitivity*, the assignment of an option value that does not depend on the value assigned to other options; *dominance*, which suggests that an option should be selected if it is better in one state of the world and at least as good in all other states; and *invariance*, which suggests that differing representations of the same option should yield the same choice (Tversky & Kahneman, 1988). However, empirical studies (e.g., McNeil, Pauker, & Tversky, 1988; Tversky & Kahneman, 1988) have demonstrated that many of the axioms of expected utility theory are "systematically and consciously violated" (Slovic, Lichtenstein, & Fischhoff, 1988, p. 697), leading to the development of models and theories that weaken or eliminate axioms. For example, the cancellation axiom has been eliminated by many authors to address the violations noted in the alias paradox (cited in Slovic & Lichtenstein, 1983). Others have maintained invariance and dominance but relinquished transitivity. Some have eliminated invariance and dominance (Tversky & Kahneman, 1988).

Violations of expected utility theory have led to modifications and new developments in both normative and descriptive theories of decision making (Fishburn, 1988). The limitations of utility theory do not suggest that the model is not valid in some situations, as it "still forms the basis for the analysis of many applied decision problems . . . and provides an excellent approximation to many judgments and decisions" (Slovic et al., 1988, p. 674). One reason for continuing to use this theory is that it provides good approximations, even though it may be wrong in principle, so it is going to be used until a more useful theory comes along (Slovic et al., 1988). Although noted violations of expected utility theory have led to questions regarding previously held tenets of rationality, the controversy has facilitated useful developments in descriptive decision making.

Descriptive Models

Unlike normative models, descriptive models recognize that people do not always make ideally rational decisions; their preferences for consequences "are often ill-formed, labile, shifting and endogenous to the problem" (Bell et al., 1988, p. 20). Like normative models, descriptive models also run the continuum as to the level of complexity of decisions they address, from single attribute to multiattribute choice. "Even the most elaborate descriptive theories . . . are viewed by their creators as useful approximations, but incomplete and not fully adequate" (Slovic et al., 1988, p. 710). Furthermore, some descriptive models are modifications of the expected utility model, although not all are necessarily intended as such (Neel, 1977). As the economic model is frequently used to embody the normative approach, the administrative model is frequently employed as the model that embodies the vistas of the descriptive approach in educational practice.

The administrative model holds that the decision-making process is guided by the principle of *bounded rationality*. Because of computational limitations, decision makers use simplified decision procedures, or "satisfice," accepting the first simplified decision procedure rather than pursuing an optimal or perfectly rational solution (Bell et al., 1988; Simon, 1955, 1956; Watson & Buede, 1987). In developing the model, Simon (1955) conceded that, although perfectly rational decisions are ideal, they are unlikely because of the time and cost involved in attempting to undertake the normative model. There are several subsets of the administrative model.

Affiliative Decision Rules. Janis (1989) noted that in a crisis, decision makers seek solutions that will not endanger their relationships with those to whom they are accountable and will not be opposed by subordinates expected to implement the decision. To cope with the demands of such affiliative constraints, decision makers use a corresponding set of rules. Tetlock (1985) referred to the *acceptability heuristic*, the central theme of which is to avoid blame. It is applied by finding out whether other powerful persons in the organization already favor a particular action, then supporting that action without consideration of alternative choices. Janis called attention to the subtle effects of *groupthink*, an affiliative rule whose underlying motivation is the strong desire to avoid spoiling the harmonious atmosphere of a group from which members are dependent for maintaining self-esteem and for coping with the stress of decision making. The rule calls for preserving group harmony by going along with whatever consensus seems to be emerging (Janis, 1989).

Emotive Rules (Conflict Theory). Simon (1976) noted that emotions interfere with cognitive processes in decision making. He postulated that anxiety and stress are aroused when decision makers realize that whichever course of action they choose could turn out badly and that they will be held accountable. Mann and Janis (1977) specified conditions that determine whether the stress of decisional conflict facilitates or interferes with decision making. According to their conflict theory, extremely low and extremely intense stress produce defective coping patterns, whereas intermediate levels are associated with analytic decision making. Whenever decision makers deal with unconflicted adherence or unconflicted change, they are so unaroused by the risks that they resort to "lazy" or routine ways of making judgments because of lack of motivation to engage in the analytic process.

Vigilant or Reflective Approach. When the stakes are high, Janis (1989) observed that many executives do not stick to the seat-of-the-pants approach they ordinarily use in daily decision making. They adopt what he refers to as a vigilant decision-making approach, in which they do not ignore the various constraints but take full account of them and go out of their way to obtain more information about them. The state of vigilant, or reflective, problem solving requires the decision maker to ask and answer a variety of questions that can be conceptualized as a complex set of decision rules that put heavy emphasis on eliciting and critically evaluating information feedback. In contrast to giving one of the constraints top priority and resorting to one or two simple decision rules to cope with it, decision makers treat the constraints of which they are aware as requirements to be met in their search for a solution.

Prospect Theory. Prospect theory includes two distinct steps in the choice process: a framing and editing phase and an evaluation phase (Kahneman & Tversky, 1979). A major contribution of this model is the concept of *framing*, a phenomenon by which the choice process is influenced by the manner in which the choice problem is viewed relative to an adopted negative or positive reference point. This poses an interesting dilemma since many decisions can be viewed as either gains or losses.

Prospect theory holds that people are averse to risk in the positive or gains domain and risk seeking in the area of losses. Kahneman and Tversky's (1979) version of prospect theory, an algebraic model, addresses people's tendency to violate the implications of utility theory, specifically the axioms of dominance and invariance. The development of this theory demonstrates three pervasive phenomena: the *certainty effect*, the tendency to overweigh outcomes considered certain and to underweigh those considered as merely probable; the *reflection effect*, which addresses people's tendency to demonstrate risk aversion in the positive domain as compared to losses and gains determined by the reference point adopted by the decision maker; and the *isolation effect*, which reflects a tendency to discount characteristics common to alternatives and focus on those that differentiate them and lead to inconsistent preferences if the same option is presented in another form (Slovic et al., 1988).

Numerous authors (Kahneman & Tversky, 1979; McNeil et al., 1988; Slovic, Fischhoff, & Lichtenstein, 1982) have noted that manipulation of the decision frames presented to a decision maker can influence his or her preferences for options and that these effects are sizable. The effects sometimes include preference reversals and violate the tenets of rationality.

Concern for framing effects has been noted in the medical and legal literature with respect to their influence on patients' preferences in informed consent (Eraker & Sox, 1981; Meisel & Roth, 1983) as well as in discussions of the presentation of information to the users of computer decision support systems (Holtzman, 1989). Other studies have noted differences in framing effects by gender, although gender differences in response consistency may be an artifact of other underlying characteristics. Slovic et al. (1988) discussed the example of an insurance policy that actually provides only partial coverage (e.g., one that provides insurance protection against fire and theft but not flood) appears more attractive if framed as offering unconditional protection against a set of risks. This provides an illusionary sense of certainty.

When given decision tasks, decision makers appear to utilize only displayed information in problem formulation, which places significant responsibility on those charged with presenting decision makers with information (Slovic et al., 1982). Ewell (1989) suggested that institutional researchers should know those for whom they provide data and either organize information to address their preferences or explain why various formats are used. He failed to elaborate on the associated framing effects if this approach is adopted. Some authors (Bell et al., 1988; McNeil et al., 1988) suggested that the potential to influence a decision maker by intentionally or unintentionally framing decision options warrants further exploration as an ethical issue, particularly in cases such as framing information presented on informed consent forms. However, framing is also influenced by the decision maker's inherent characteristics (Tversky

& Kahneman, 1988). The knowledge of framing effects can therefore help decision makers consciously examine the choices before them from different frames.

Decision-Making Heuristics and Biases

People often use heuristics to simplify the decision-making process. Although heuristic processes can be economical by reducing cognitive load as well as effective, they occasionally result in serious decision-making errors. Tversky and Kahneman (1982a) claim that people "rely on a limited number of heuristic principles which reduce complex tasks of assessing probabilities and predicting values to simpler judgmental operations" (p. 3). Five such heuristics are addressed next: availability, representativeness, anchoring and adjustment, confirmation, and hindsight.

Availability. Occasionally, people assess the probability or frequency of an event by other instances of the same event that can be recalled or are available in memory. Tversky and Kahneman (1973) refer to this heuristic as *availability* and note that it can be very useful in addressing complex tasks that involve assessing probability or frequency "because instances of large classes are usually reached better and faster than instances of less frequent classes" (Tversky & Kahneman, 1982a, p. 11).

Bazerman (1991) noted three biases commonly associated with the availability heuristic: the ease of recall, retrievability, and illusionary correlation. The ease of recall bias is evidenced when people assign higher probabilities to events than are warranted. Based on their ability to recall easily more recent or vivid occurrences, use of these probabilities often overestimates unlikely events. For example, because plane crashes are spectacular, some people assume that they should be associated with a higher mortality rate than car accidents, which are usually less spectacular. In fact, it is not so.

As decision makers recall information, retrievability may influence their perceptions. Instances that are readily available in memory will seem more numerous than those that are less retrievable, even if they occur with equal or lower frequency (Tversky

& Kahneman, 1982b). Presumed associations, or illusory connections, refer to a bias in which individuals assume higher probabilities of phenomena co-occurrence than actually exist. These paired associations take precedence, whether or not the pairing is warranted (Bazerman, 1991). Paired associations are commonly evidenced in stereotypes, such as the "smart kid with glasses," or folklore.

Another bias associated with the availability heuristic is imaginability (Tversky & Kahneman, 1974). They point out that this bias may be exemplified by the risks imagined to be associated with a trip, even though the imaginable risks may exaggerate or underestimate the actual situations that could be encountered.

Although the availability heuristic may be useful in assessing probabilities, it can lead to biases that are predictable and cause decision makers to estimate incorrectly the probability of event occurrence because of their experiences and learned associations (Tversky & Kahneman, 1974). When decision makers are provided with contradictory information that demonstrates their erroneous and inaccurate assumptions, they tend to resist changing their conclusions.

Representativeness. Both naive and sophisticated people often assess the probability of a relationship by evaluating the extent to which one item or phenomenon is representative of or similar to another. The representativeness heuristic (Kahneman & Tversky, 1972, 1982b) is often used in making intuitive predictions regarding outcomes. However, this approach to the judgment of probability may lead to serious errors because similarity, or representativeness, is not influenced by numerous factors that affect judgments of probability. Use of this heuristic leads to decision-making errors when people attend to "normatively irrelevant" characteristics or ignore those that are "normatively important" (Slovic et al., 1988).

Biases associated with the representativeness heuristic include a failure to recognize base rates, insensitivity to sample size, misconceptions of chance, insensitivity to predictability, the illusion of validity, and misconceptions of regression (Bazerman, 1991; Tversky & Kahneman, 1974). Although people can use base rates correctly, they tend to overlook them in

assessing probabilities when descriptive information is provided, even if it is irrelevant (Kahneman & Tversky, 1972, 1973).

People frequently demonstrate an insensitivity to sample size, a fundamental issue in statistical generalizability, by assigning probabilities based on a sample of limited representativeness. This bias is evidenced by a study of Tversky and Kahneman (1974) in which subjects, provided with information that approximately 50% of all babies are boys, projected that an instance in which the birth of male babies exceeded 60% was likely to be the same for two different-sized hospitals, one with 15 births per day and another with 45. In reality, this phenomenon is more likely in the smaller hospital, the one with 15 births per day, because a larger sample is less likely to deviate from the mean. This bias is occasionally used intentionally, as illustrated by Bazerman's (1991) example of the advertising slogan "Four out of five dentists surveyed recommended sugarless gum for their patients who chew gum" (p. 461). The advertiser benefits from the fact that most consumers do not question whether the data cited in this claim are representative of all dentists.

Insensitivity to predictability reflects a tendency to violate normative statistical theory by making predictions based on "representativeness," regardless of the reliability or accuracy of the observation on which the conjecture is made. The illusion of validity refers to the overconfidence often placed in the correlation between an input observation and data used to predict a corresponding outcome (Tversky & Kahneman, 1974). This bias has been documented in experts and nonexperts and may be particularly problematic when used by people entrusted as expert decision makers. Einhorn and Hogarth (1978) claimed that research suggests that "neither the extent of professional training and experience nor the amount of information available to clinicians necessarily increases accuracy" (p. 395). People may persist in their overconfidence because they fail to learn from experience and selectively forget their incorrect judgment. Overconfidence and conjecture, operating in conjunction, can lead to an erroneous prediction based on the representativeness of evidence and overconfidence in the accuracy of the conjecture.

People generally understand that observations regress toward the mean but are less likely to acknowledge its occurrence in unusual circumstances and may develop spurious explanations for the phenomenon when it is noted. For example, McKean (1985) reported that flight instructors claimed that pilots' performances diminished after positive feedback and improved after reprimand. This change in performance was spuriously attributed to the feedback, even though "by regression alone, behavior is most likely to improve after punishment and to deteriorate after reward" (p. 25).

Anchoring and Adjustment. *Anchoring* refers to a process in which people develop estimates. In the process, people with a specific value or reference point adjust the point up or down to yield a final value. However, adjustments are typically insufficient to negate the influence of the initial anchor, as final answers tend to be biased toward the anchor, even when it is irrelevant (Slovic & Lichtenstein, 1971). The biases emanating from anchoring and adjustment include insufficient anchor adjustment, biases in the evaluation of conjunctive and disjunctive events, and overconfidence in judgments (Bazerman, 1991; Kahneman, Slovic, & Tversky, 1982; Tversky & Kahneman, 1974).

Bias in evaluating conjunctive and disjunctive events is reflected in people's tendency to overestimate the probability of chainlike conjunctive events and underestimate the probability of chainlike disjunctive events. Tversky and Kahneman (1974) contended that occasionally the anchoring bias direction can be inferred from the event structure. They noted that overestimating the probability of conjunctive events leads to unwarranted optimism in expecting that a plan will proceed or that a project will be completed on time and that underestimating the probability of disjunctive events can lead to underexpectation of failure in complex activities composed of multiple components, each with its own associated error or probable failure rate.

Bazerman (1991) stated that most people tend to demonstrate overconfidence in their estimation abilities, fail to acknowledge the appropriate level of uncertainty associated with their assessments, and are likely to evidence a confidence level inversely correlated to their knowledge level in a given subject area. This bias affects not only laymen in their everyday decision making, but researchers have demonstrated that this bias is also evidenced by experts in decision-making tasks within their own specialty area. Some of the overconfidence people place in their judgments may be due to confirmation bias discussed in the next section.

Anchoring is a bias that is particularly resistant to change. This bias may be detrimental to efforts to improve individuals' decision-making skills. Nisbett and Ross (1980) contended that the anchoring bias impedes efforts to improve individuals' decision strategies because existing heuristics and biases serve as cognitive anchors and are inherent in the corresponding judgment process.

Confirmation Bias. Confirmation bias occurs in the process individuals adapt to seek confirmatory data in the searching, recollection, and assimilation of information and exclude or overlook disconfirming evidence in this process (Bazerman, 1991; Einhorn & Hogarth, 1978). As a consequence of the confirmation trap, evidence tends to bolster an initial hypothesis or belief and sustain it. This is true even in the face of empirical rejection or attacks on the original evidence, a phenomenon evidenced by numerous researchers (L. Ross, Lepper, Strack, & Steinmetz, 1977):

Shermer (2002) notes that persons rarely sit down before a set of facts, weigh them pro and con, and choose the most logical and rational explanation unbiased by strongly held beliefs. Rather, most come to their beliefs for a varity of reasons having little to do with empirical evidence and logical reasoning. Beliefs are strongly influenced by such variables as genetic predisposition, parental predeliction, sibling influence, peer pressure, educational experience, and life impressions that shape personality preferences in conjunction with numerous social and cultural influences. People then sort through bodies of data, selecting those that most confirm what they already believe, and ignore or rationalize away those that do not.

In educational forums this bias is demonstrated through the *Pygmalion studies* (L. Ross & Anderson, 1982). Although this bias may help circumvent cognitive dissonance, Einhorn and Hogarth (1978) suggested that it may impede individuals' abilities to learn from experience just as the failure to attempt to disconfirm initially held beliefs precludes gathering new insight.

Hindsight Bias. The common axiom that "hindsight is 20-20" inadvertently reflects a decision-making bias. Hindsight bias refers to people's tendency, once given the results of a decision, to overestimate the degree of accuracy to which they would have predicted the correct outcome (Bazerman, 1991; Feinberg, 2006). Once people are given information about an occurrence, this information is integrated into their existing knowledge about the subject and reinterpreted to seem logical. The result is a tendency to view reported outcomes as having been relatively inevitable, an inclination that has also been called *creeping determinism* (Fischhoff, 1982). Hindsight is a temporal bias, dependent on the passage of time to have its effect (Sanna, 2004). Hindsight bias is sufficiently prevalent to lead to the Subsequent Remedial Measures Rule of the United States Federal Rules of Evidence, which attempts to mitigate hindsight bias in negligence trials by providing specific rules governing evidence that may be considered. (Eberwine, 2005).

Summary of Common Errors in Administrative Decision Making. School district decision makers rarely have the opportunity to make perfectly objective, deliberate decisions because the environments in which those decisions are made are complex and volatile, the information that they work from is often incomplete, and their own personal perspectives may introduce bias. Davis (2005) has identified a number of "cognitive traps" affecting administrative decisions that provide a concise summary of the decision-making heuristics and biases discussed in this section.

1. *Presumed associations:* Overestimating the probability that two events will occur together.

2. *Insensitivity to base rates:* Ignoring the fact that the majority of student problems result from the behavior of a relatively small number of students.

3. *Insensitivity to sample size:* Generalizing inappropriately from a small set of examples.

4. *Misconceptions of chance:* Overestimating statistical significance and underestimating the potential for randomness. Inappropriately linking student achievement scores to a particular teaching style would be an example.

5. *Regression to the mean:* Not recognizing that extreme events tend to regress toward the mean and that swings in achievement test scores tend to average out in the long run.

6. *Confirmation trap:* Giving greater weight to evidence that confirms an already existing belief and not giving due weight to contrary evidence.

7. *Hindsight:* Overestimating the degree to which one could predict a past outcome if the opportunity had arisen.

8. *Overconfidence:* Overestimating the infallibility of one's judgments. This can occur when the administrator has an exaggerated view of the impact of his or her decisions.

9. *Incrementalism:* At a decision point, selecting only the option that differs minimally from the status quo or focusing on only one aspect of the problem to the detriment of other aspects. This can keep the administrator from overcommitting, but it can also preclude bold, decisive leadership.

10. *Anthropocentric attributions:* Attributing events to intentional behavior rather than to chance.

11. *Information imbalance:* Depending too heavily on information acquired early in the decision-making process to the detriment of later clarifications or depending too heavily on the "latest word" without considering it in the light of early knowledge.

12. *Wishful thinking:* The ability to accurately predict future events and circumstances amid the volatility of a school district is very difficult.

13. *Opportunity risk aversion:* School leaders tend to "play it safe" to try to avoid controversy and difficulty. However, this approach can lead one to miss opportunities for growth and greater success.

14. *Opinion intransigence:* Changing a formed opinion can be difficult. The sheer volume of decision making required of a school principal during the working day can make it hard to rescind a decision already made and revisit an issue already apparently resolved.

15. *Susceptibility to simple arguments:* The tendency of leaders to be swayed by simple, easily understood arguments is often a consequence of the volatility of the work environment. Heuristic thinking, which reduces problem complexity and works toward decision-making efficiency, is often the result. This approach may be useful or even necessary under some circumstances, but there is the risk of a "rush to judgment."

Group and Participative Decision Making

Vroom and Jago (1988) emphasized the increasing importance of development of participative decision-making styles, with need for managers to encourage involvement in the decision-making process. The decision-making stages employed by individuals and groups may essentially be the same. However, in decision-making tasks involving several people, the process used to reach consensus is influenced by other factors, such as leadership, group pressures, status differentials, intergroup competition, and group size (Reitz, 1987). MacPhail-Wilcox and Bryant (1988) suggest that participative decision making may balance out the idiographic traits inherent in an individual and, in this respect, yield better decisions.

Reitz (1987) claims that group decision making may not be more effective than individual choice when the "situation requires a sequence of multiple stages, when the problem is not easily divisible into separate parts, and when the correctness of the solution is not easily demonstrated" (p. 346). Group decisions can be more accurate, particularly when a member or members of a group have experience with the problem

being addressed; tend to be compatible with widely held beliefs; and can result in greater member understanding and commitment. However, Conway (1984) suggested that participative decision making does not necessarily yield heightened support or other benefits commonly associated with the process and labels several of these claims "myths."

Although group judgment and problem-solving skills tend to exceed those of the average group member, they are frequently inferior to those of the best group member, who in a group forum is influenced toward mediocrity (Reitz, 1987). No group technique is capable of enabling groups to yield more numerous or creative ideas than the same number of individuals working alone (Hill, 1982). Furthermore, group decision making promotes the likelihood of problems specific to a collective process, such as groupthink, which results in premature consensus and failure to examine realistic decision options (Janis, 1989). Decisions involving risk and uncertainty can polarize a group toward prevailing cautions or a risk-taking stance. Group polarization hampers examination of decision options (Myers & Lamm, 1976).

In reviewing the literature on decision making, Carroll and Johnson (1990) found that many authors failed to extend the elements of individual decision concepts to groups by noting a lack of ease in applying the same concepts to inherently more complex groups. However, "studies that have directly compared groups and individuals on the same problems find that groups fall prey to the same errors and biases as do individuals" (p. 28).

Carson (1965) studied teacher participation in decision making in education and other local community activities in three communities in Oregon. In this early study, Carson found that teacher involvement in decision making was limited to decisions related to their own classrooms and curriculum matters. The teachers felt that they should be involved in educational decision making to a greater extent than they had been in the past. In areas outside education, although elementary teachers consistently desired a lower level of involvement, secondary teachers tended to be interested in issues related to business or local government. Carson's research is one example of several studies over the decades that indicate the desire and need for participative and group decision making in educational institutions and also in other institutions and organizations unrelated to education.

Since then, decision making has moved beyond individual choice discussions to also include the analysis of participation in the decision-making process. With the advent of productivity increases readily apparent in Japanese education and management, renewed interest has stirred in a participative decision-making model.

Participative decision making has widespread applications. Inherent in participation are questions about how subordinates respond to shared decision making. Subordinates may have been motivated to participate for various reasons: to meet needs of achievement, for financial incentives, and to bring meaning to work. Management may see other advantages: improved quality, increased worker commitment, increased productivity, and peer pressure. But studies to replicate these beliefs have not demonstrated accurate understanding about participation and decision making. It is possible to point to ambiguities. Participation may be a result of stronger training or differences within groups, better goal setting may be a more effective rationale, and distribution of control may advance participative effects more readily than needs, incentives, or other issues.

The impact of diversity in council membership on decision making in school-based leadership councils has been researched by Robertson and Kwong (1994), who found that moving the decision-making authority from central administration to the local school level enhanced value-driven organizations that are more responsive to their local markets and environment. Scott (1991) conducted a case study of a school district that engaged in a change from a top-down to a participative model of decision making in their budgeting process. It was found that the education institution was politicized. This was consistent with other literature related to budgeting, which indicates a dichotomy between politicization and economic rationality. Scott noted that since budgets are political documents, their formulation may be explained through models of group processes and through an understanding of participative decision making.

Conway (1984) provided a summary of the literature on participation. According to him, participation does not demonstrate a higher level of quality decisions, but it may increase feelings of self-worth. Participation may influence decision making because of strong goal setting among participants, and although this does seem to increase satisfaction, the satisfaction varies largely by type of organization. Much concerning participative decision making is still not clear.

In the next section we direct our attention to a systemic approach for school districts and schools to use in making decisions about direction, purpose, and organizing their resources in order to realize their intended outcomes.

Strategy Formation and Planning at the District and School Levels

While rational decision making may represent the ideal, the discussion in the previous section and in chapter 10 strongly suggests that rationality by individuals is highly unlikely on a consistent basis. Further, evidence suggests that shared decision making has not produced substantially better results. Argyris (1985) encourages that a systemic approach to inquiry and decision making be used as a way to improve outcomes. Such an approach would incorporate a reflective component making the process dynamic and iterative. In this section, we propose a decision-making model for schools and school districts in harmony with Argyris's intent. The schema enables educational institutions to develop a sense of direction and purpose and to make decisions about organizing themselves and allocating their resources efficiently in order to realize those purposes. The systemic process involves continuous monitoring of progress made toward organizational goals and objectives, adjusting implementation strategies to correct for unsatisfactory organizational performance, and adjusting direction and purposes to accommodate changes in the sociopolitical environment.

Although the process is usually referred to as *strategic planning*, we accept Mintzberg's (1994) distinction between strategy formation and planning as two separate but important procedures. He describes *planning* as a convergent, logical process that attempts to formalize decision making, strategy making, and management through decomposition, articulation, and rationalization. He characterizes *strategy formation* as a spontaneous, creative, and divergent process that cannot happen in isolation or on schedule and cannot be programmed. Because planning is an analytical process and strategy formulation is a synthesizing process, Mintzberg argues that they must happen separately. Strategy is thus not the consequence of planning; rather, planning takes place within the framework formed by strategy. Planning is intended as the first step in translating intended strategies into realized ones.

This section begins by addressing issues of strategy formation, followed by issues of planning within the context of an existing strategy at the district level. Attention is then directed to these issues within the context of site-based management, which includes a discussion of site-based budgeting.

Strategy Formation

Strategy is a guide or course of action into the future that provides an organization with direction. It can be explicit, but it is more likely to be observed in consistency of behavior over time. It is the organization's perspective on how things should be done, its concept of the business. Strategy formation involves visioning, mission setting, and goal development. It is concerned with change and development.

A difference in opinion exists as to who should develop strategy and how it is shaped. The traditional view is that strategy formation is a function of leadership and must emanate from the top. Frazier (1997) identifies several reasons why this must be: leaders are the only ones who have the best perspective on the big picture, leaders have overall responsibility for management of the organization, leaders have the authority to mold and arrange its various functions for strategic purposes, and leaders have the power to make course corrections when needed (p. 105).

Wheatley and Kellner-Rogers (1996), on the other hand, stress the importance of interdependencies and interrelationships among members of an organization in establishing its identity and direction. They lament the impact of traditional institutional leadership on members of the organization and on the organization itself:

> It is strange to realize that most people have a desire to love their organization. . . . But then we take this vital passion and institutionalize it. We create an organization. The people who loved the purpose grow to disdain the institution that was created to fulfill it. Passion mutates into procedures, into rules and roles. Instead of purpose, we focus on policies. Instead of being free to create, we impose constraints that squeeze the life out of us. The organization no longer lives. We see its bloated form and resent it for what it stops us from doing. (p. 57)

Instead of a formal process, Wheatley and Kellner-Rogers (1996) advance the idea of an emergent process, one where a self gets organized, a world of shared meaning develops, networks of relationships take form, and information is noticed, interpreted, and transformed. "From these simple conditions emerge bodily different expressions of organizational forms" (p. 81).

Senge (1990) promotes the concept of the *learning organization*, "organizations where people continually expand their capacity to create the results they truly desire, where new and expansive patterns of thinking are nurtured, and where people are continually learning how to learn together" (p. 3). He characterizes a learning organization as a place where people are persistently discovering how they create their reality and how they can change it.

Mintzberg (1994) also notes that strategies need not originate from central management. He observes that big strategies can grow spontaneously from little ideas or initiatives. Anyone in the organization can prove to be a good strategist given a good idea and the freedom and resources to pursue it. This view is especially appropriate in professional organizations, such as schools, composed of well-educated members who are regularly required to apply discretionary judgment to solve problems within their areas of expertise. Mintzberg's (1989) grassroots model of strategy formation calls for letting patterns emerge rather than forcing an artificial consistency on an organization prematurely. Such strategies become organizational when the patterns proliferate and pervade the behavior of the organization at large. Proliferation may be promoted consciously but need not be, and they may or may not be managed. The management of such strategies is not to preconceive them but to recognize their emergence and to intervene as appropriate. Emergent strategies are more likely to happen during periods of change than during periods of stability.

In addition to emergent strategies, Mintzberg (1994) identifies four other types of strategies, as illustrated in Figure 11.1: intended, unrealized, deliberate, and realized. As the figure indicates, realized strategy takes on a different characteristic from that intended. This does not mean that the intended strategy is a failure. Quite the contrary, it served to launch the organization in what at the time was considered a desirable direction, but the organization was flexible in its implementation and took advantage of unforeseen opportunities (emergent strategy) and sloughed off unfruitful endeavors (unrealized strategy). In the end, a portion of the intended strategy was actually realized

(deliberate strategy), enhanced by the emergent strategy. Mintzberg points out that few, if any, strategies are purely deliberate and few purely emergent. "One suggests no learning, the other, no control. All real-world strategies need to mix these in some way—to attempt to control without stopping the learning process" (p. 25).

In this section we present strategy as an encompassing set of ideas and attitudes that permeate an organization's behavior and guides the decision-making process. In Figure 11.2 we have illustrated it as an umbrella under which all organizational activities take place. Strategy formation is discussed in four parts, although each is intermeshed with the others: visioning, mission statement, belief statements, and strategic policies. Implementation, depicted in the figure as intermediate and tactical planning, is shaped by strategy.

FIGURE 11.1

Mintzberg's forms of strategy

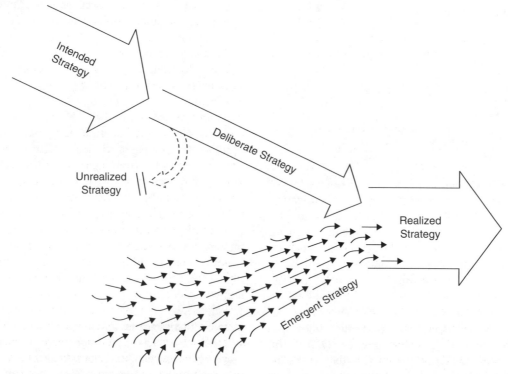

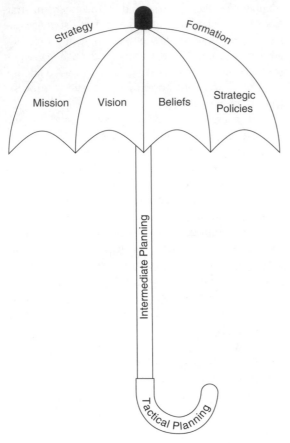

FIGURE 11.2

Relationship between strategy formation and intermediate and tactical planning

Visioning. A *vision* is a mental image of a possible and desirable future state for an organization (Bennis & Nanus, 1985). It can be as vague as a dream or as precise as a goal or mission statement. The vision, however developed, must permeate the organization, being embedded in its structures, processes, and behaviors so that it shapes its operation and every decision made (Caldwell & Spinks, 1988). It creates a "consistency of purpose" throughout the organization (Deming, 1986); it is controlled by concept (Wheatley, 1994). A vision sets the broad outlines of a strategy that leaves the specific details to be worked out later. Mintzberg (1994) argues that a visionary approach is a flexible way of dealing with an uncertain world so that

when the unexpected happens, the organization can learn and adapt.

Senge (1990) reminds us that shared visions must emerge from personal visions. "This is how they derive their energy and how they foster commitment" (p. 211). According to Senge, the first step in building shared visions is to give up the traditional notion that visions must originate from the top of the organizational hierarchy or from its institutionalized planning process. Visions that are truly shared take time to emerge:

> They grow as a by-product of interactions of individual visions. Experience suggests that visions that are genuinely shared require ongoing conversation where individuals not only feel free to express their dreams, but learn to listen to each others' dreams. Out of this listening, new insights into what is possible gradually emerge. (pp. 217–218)

To facilitate the process, organizational leaders must be fully involved in the conversations and be willing to share their personal visions as well. They must also solicit the membership's endorsement rather than assume it.

Fullan (1993) warns that visions can blind as well as enlighten. "Having a sense of moral purpose and vision can be a decided advantage, but clarity of purpose can also be a liability if the vision is rigid and/or wrong, and if the process of vision building does not result in a *shared* sense of purpose" (p. 67). Fullan cautions that vision formation not be rushed for two reasons. First, vision emerges from action more than precedes it; reflective practice is needed before a plausible vision can be formed. Second, the sharing of a vision must evolve through the dynamic interaction of organizational members and leaders, and this takes time. Vision seeking is an ongoing process. In avoiding premature formalization, visions may be pursued more authentically.

Mission Statements. A vision by its very nature is vague. In mobilizing the organization in pursuit of its vision, however, a time does come when it is useful to articulate the vision in more specific terms. This is commonly done through mission and belief statements.

The mission statement is a clear and concise expression of the district's purpose and function. It should be a bold declaration of what the organization aspires to be. The mission statement should address the specific, local situation and represent the uniqueness of the district (school). Mission statements do not have to be feasible, only desirable. Missions exist at the boundary between the organization and its environment; they represent expectations that constituents have for the organization (O'Brien, 1991). The mission is the focus toward which the planning process is directed. Every person in the organization should know and understand it; it frequently is the only formal statement of the organization's vision. Figure 11.3 presents the mission statement for the Clarence, New York, Central School District. Figure 11.4 presents the mission statement for the Maple West Elementary School.

Defining a district's mission is closely akin to what Drucker (1974) referred to as "knowing your business." According to Drucker, management must decide what its business is and what it should be. He argued that it is only on the foundation of the basic purposes and missions of the organization that more detailed objectives, strategies, and tactical plans can be worked out. Schools and school districts often labor under the mistaken assumptions that their missions are rigidly set by law. In actuality, they have considerable flexibility, and defining their missions enables them to become emancipated from common preconceptions and to focus on a common purpose.

Belief Statements. Common beliefs held by members of the organization represent one of its primary bonding forces. The statement of beliefs is a formal expression of those fundamental principles that guide all district (or other unit, such as a school) decisions and activities. It describes the organization's moral character—its ethical code. The statement provides the value basis on which subsequent portions of the planning process will develop and implementation will be evaluated; it is a public declaration of the moral essence of the district (Cook, 1990).

Developing a statement of beliefs begins with what Goodstein, Nolan, and Pfeiffer (1992) call a *value scan*. It examines the personal values of those assigned to do the scan, the current values of the organization, the organization's philosophy of operations, the assumptions that usually guide the organization's operations, the organization's preferred culture, and the values of the stakeholders in the organization's future. (See the related discussion

FIGURE 11.3

Mission statement of the Clarence, New York, Central School District

> ### Mission
> The mission of the Clarence Central School District is to produce independent, lifelong learners who are responsible, contributing members of a diverse society.

Source: Clarence Central School District. (n.d.). *Strategic Plan*, p. 5. Clarence, NY: The District.

FIGURE 11.4

Mission statement of the Maple West Elementary School

> ### Mission Statement
> ### Maple West Elementary
> Our mission at Maple West Elementary is to be responsible for the preparation of children for the future by providing an educational setting that has a nurturing environment where learning is valued, individual differences accepted, and potential maximized.

of values analysis in chapter 7.) In conducting the values scan, the scanners move from an individual focus to a broader examination of the organization and how it works as a social system. It focuses attention on the frequently unacknowledged underpinnings that guide the behaviors and decisions of organization members and, thereby, the organizational culture. Figure 11.5 illustrates a set of belief statements as developed by the Clarence, New York, Central School District.

Strategic Policies. Strategic policies establish the parameters within which the district will operate. They specify the postures that the district will either always take or never take. Strategies act to channel thinking and to serve as guides to action. They set

FIGURE 11.5

Belief statements of the Clarence, New York, Central School District

Beliefs

We believe that . . .

- Education and the development of learners is our highest priority.
- Education is the shared responsibility of parents, students, educators, and the community.
- Education is a process in which learning is applied to the solution of human problems.
- Education develops effective leadership among all participants.
- Education requires continuous improvement through staff and program development.
- The assessment of students, staff, and programs must take a variety of forms.
- Education must provide an adaptive environment that responds to the needs of a changing world.
- Education requires teaching to students' strengths and learning styles.
- A continuous examination and evaluation of the entire educational system is essential.
- Education must promote the development of self-esteem, health and wellness, intellectual growth, and social skills.
- Education must embrace differences, celebrate and reward success, encourage risk taking, and view failure as a learning experience.
- Education must provide nurturing, challenging, and exciting environments where all participants are successful learners.
- Education must develop the values of our participatory democracy while understanding local community values.
- Education requires a significant and continuing commitment of both human and financial resources.
- Education must develop a respect for and understanding of diverse cultures.
- Education must emphasize an appreciation for and an understanding of the accumulated knowledge of civilizations.

Source: Clarence Central School District. (n.d.). *Strategic Plan,* pp. 6–7. Clarence, NY: The District.

constraints within which discretion can be exercised. By adding the modifier *strategic*, the bulk of district policy that deals with the routine of daily operations is eliminated from consideration. Cook (1990) asserted that strategic policies "establish 'ground rules'; set in place protective mechanisms, ratios, formulas, and the like; dictate codes of behavior; define expectations; assert priorities; and define various boundaries" (p. 96). Strategic policies focus the mission statement and prevent overzealous pursuit of them. Figure 11.6 illustrates strategic policies as developed by the West Seneca, New York, Central School District.

Planning

Strategy formation provides an organization with direction (vision and mission) and a set of governing principles (beliefs and strategic policies) that will guide the organization over the long term. Planning addresses the issues of mobilizing the resources of the organization to enable its mission.

Planning brings order to strategy by putting it into a form suitable for articulation to others. It makes specific the assumptions of strategy. It identifies the major hurdles that are likely to be realized in pursuing the strategy. It makes sure (or at least attempts) to take everything into account. Planning is alignment. Whereas strategy formation was characterized as a creative, spontaneous, intuitive, divergent process, planning is highly rational, logical, formal, and convergent.

Strategy synthesizes; planning analyzes. Strategy integrates; planning decomposes. Planning designs the logistics necessary to implement strategy.

A well-organized planning system can provide an extremely useful communications network that links together all members of the organization. As plans approach completion, common understandings are generated about opportunities and problems that are important to individuals and to the organization. The choices made in the planning process are discussed in a common language and the issues are understood (or should be) by all those participating in decision making. According to Mintzberg (1994), "Planning sits toward the formal end of the continuum of organizational behavior. . . . It must be seen, not as decision making, not as strategy making, and certainly not as management, or as the preferred way of doing any of these things, but simply as the effort to formalize parts of them—through decomposition, articulation, and rationalization" (p. 15).

Planning must be recognized as a social–political process for coordinating and integrating the goals of the organization with those of the individual. (See the discussion of values as part of organizational cultures in chapter 7.) As a political process, planning may become a dynamic interaction and exchange involving bargaining, negotiations, and the exercise of power. Alternatively, as a social-consensual process, planning may be seen as developing uncoerced understanding and agreement among those involved

FIGURE 11.6

Strategic policies of the West Seneca, New York, Central School District

Strategic Policies

No student will be automatically promoted.

No curriculum will be implemented or modified without the input of the staff who will be required to teach it.

We will never add or eliminate programs without careful analysis.

We will always provide programs which will assist all employees to perform more effectively.

Each employee will be evaluated and no employee will be granted permanent status unless he/she achieves an above-average rating.

No student will participate in any extracurricular activity who does not satisfy the eligibility requirements for that activity.

We will not compromise health and safety laws.

through the free exchange of ideas. The latter is preferred to the exercise of power and adversarial bargaining assumed by the political model.

Throughout the planning process, individuals within the organization are constantly balancing their interests with those of the group (Lotto & Clark, 1986). Through negotiations, the preferences and activities of the organizational stakeholders are ordered and reordered singularly and in groups. Underlying the process is a basic assumption that people who will be affected by a proposed plan will be extensively involved in its development because all members of the organization have relevant expertise that will be translated into a better plan; in addition, the plan is more likely to be implemented successfully because of its enhanced pertinence and the sense of ownership on the part of stakeholders generated by involvement. The process strengthens the communal vision and understanding of the organization by its members.

Improved employee motivation and morale and community support are potential by-products of the planning process. Being involved in formulating organizational plans promotes a sense of satisfaction among participants gained from helping to shape—at least in part—their own destiny within the organization. Knowing what is expected of organizational members builds a sense of personal security and confidence. Taken together, these improved attitudes enable people to accept change more readily, a valuable attribute in any organization.

We divide the discussion of planning into two segments: intermediate and tactical. *Intermediate planning* has a time frame of 3 to 5 years, whereas *tactical planning* deals with the short term, usually 1 year. The process of intermediate planning asks and answers some key questions in a way that might otherwise be easily overlooked and establishes a scale of priority and urgency for dealing with the answers. Questions addressed include the following: What opportunities or threats exist in the years ahead that we should exploit or avoid? What are our strategic objectives? What major changes are taking place in the environment that will affect us? What resources will be available to us over the next several years?

Intermediate planning identifies and addresses only those areas where change is critical to the welfare of the organization. Tactical planning addresses all activities of the organization in the short term.

Intermediate Planning. We divide the discussion of intermediate planning into four segments: internal and external analyses, gap analysis and the identification of critical issues, the development of strategic objectives, and the formation of action plans to address the critical issues. The relation of the segments is illustrated in Figure 11.7.

Internal and External Analyses. The internal analysis consists of a thorough and unbiased examination of the current and projected strengths and weaknesses of the district or school. Strengths are internal qualities, circumstances, or conditions that contribute to the district's/school's ability to achieve its mission with respect to such attributes as financial, personnel, organizational, physical, and social characteristics. Strengths relative to similar organizations are not of particular interest here but, rather, strengths relative to the potential for accomplishing the district's or school's mission. Strengths signal areas in which success may be most easily realized. Weaknesses, conversely, are internal qualities, circumstances, or conditions that impede the realization of the district's or school's mission. Data for the internal analysis are drawn from the organization's information system discussed in chapter 9.

The external analysis emphasizes the importance of systemic assessment of environmental impacts. It looks beyond the district or school into its environment and into its possible futures, anticipating events and conditions likely to occur that will have a significant impact on the organization. The purpose of the external analysis is to reduce the likelihood of surprises that may negatively affect the organization's ability to accomplish its mission and to identify opportunities the district or school may wish to exploit. The analysis needs to deal with five categories of influence: social and demographic (e.g., family stability or instability, family structure, social structure, unemployment, general level of education, crime rate, and size and composition of the population); economic (e.g., economic trends, size of tax base, employment rate, and salary levels); political (e.g., agendas of special interest groups);

FIGURE 11.7

Components of intermediate planning

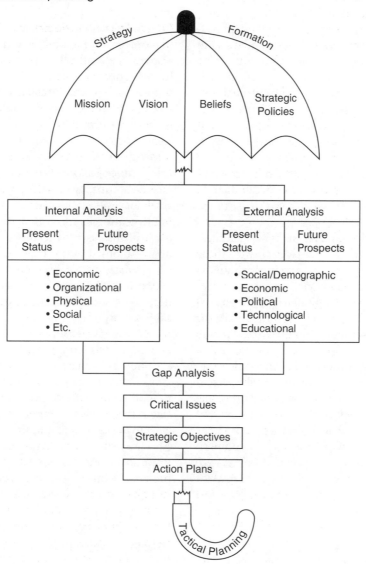

technological, scientific, and environmental (e.g., new inventions that may affect instruction or the life and employment of students and knowledge about human development and how people learn); and educational trends and influences (Cook, 1990).

Gap Analysis. The gap analysis determines "where we are" versus "where we want to be." It is an assessment by the school or district of its programs and

services; the strengths, weaknesses, and adequacies of its staff and facilities; resources available in the community; and challenges being made to the status quo by internal weaknesses and trends, external community conditions, pressures exerted by external community interest groups, and forces at the state and national levels. It is an analysis within the documented social, political, and economic environments of the district's or school's capabilities to meet challenges early when they are more easily managed with the resources available. Professional staff need to be proactive in looking for opportunities to serve its clients according to highest professional standards even when those standards are beyond the expectation or comprehension of its clients.

The gap analysis juxtaposes the internal and external analyses against the district's/school's mission. Data—past, present, and future—are analyzed in a fashion that provides a rationale for the formulation of strategic operating objectives and strategic commitment of resources. Organizations always represent states of inadequacy, the gap between the way things are and the way we want things to be (Hodgkinson, 1991).

Coming out of the gap analysis is an identification of critical issues that must be dealt with if the organization is to survive or re-create itself within the context of its stated mission. Identifying critical issues focuses attention on paramount threats and opportunities, thereby providing a compelling rationale for the deployment of resources (Cook, 1990).

Strategic Objectives. Strategic objectives are statements that commit the organization to achieve specific measurable end results intended to address the critical issues identified in the gap analysis. The strategic objectives are what the district/school must achieve in the next 3 to 5 years if it is to accomplish its mission and be true to its beliefs. Cook (1990) observes that most school districts experience difficulty in writing suitable objectives because most educators seem to be more process oriented than results oriented. True objectives create risks and impose accountability.

The strategic objectives list does not address all the outcomes for which a district or school is responsible. It includes only those that are to receive highest priority in the next 3 to 5 years. The list will change over time as strategic objectives are realized or as they are replaced by more urgent concerns. Strategic objectives for the West Seneca, New York, Central School District are illustrated in Figure 11.8.

Integrated Action Plans. Integrated action plans are the means by which a district or school will accomplish its strategic objectives in the process of implementing its mission. They specify the deployment of the district's resources in the quest of the organization's mission. They indicate its basic operational emphasis, its priorities, and the standards by which it will measure its own performance. They need to be stated conceptually and allow for practical flexibility as they are translated into action.

Action plans provide detailed descriptions of specific actions required in the short term to achieve specific results necessary for implementation of the strategic plan. They also address the ongoing business of the district or school in keeping with the statements of beliefs, mission, and strategic policies and giving special attention to strategic objectives. An effective action plan is conceived and written from an operations point of view. The content is predicated on progressive, direct cause-and-effect relationships and is immediately workable.

FIGURE 11.8

Strategic objectives of the West Seneca, New York, School District

---

Strategic Objectives

By June ... , increase by 50% the number of people who have a positive perception of the West Seneca Central School District.

By the year ... , 90% of our students will participate in at least one human service project annually.

By June ... , 100% of our students will perform at their expected achievement level.

By the year ... , to have 100% of our students, within six months after graduation, either gainfully employed or enrolled in an institution of higher learning.

Tactical Planning Including Budgeting. Entering into tactical (or operational) planning, the time frame shifts from several years to one year or less. Strategy formulation has provided the school or district with its long-term direction and guiding principles. Intermediate planning has ascertained where the organization is in relation to where it wants to be and has determined some key tactics intended to put the school or district on course to accomplish its mission. Tactical planning integrates these strategic initiatives into ongoing activities in the form of operational plans and budgets.

Tactical Planning. Tactical, or operational, planning is a process by which managers ensure that resources are obtained and used effectively and efficiently in the accomplishment of the organization's missions and strategic objectives (Cunningham, 1982). Because of their focus on operations, the instructional and service units initiate tactical planning. These include not only the expected instructional programs but also support services, such as administration, maintenance of building and grounds, food service, transportation, and new initiatives established in the intermediate plan.

Perhaps the best way to describe tactical planning is to contrast it with strategy formulation. Although principals, teachers, students, and members of the community may be involved in strategy formulation, the process is usually initiated and monitored by the policymakers of the district, the board of education, and the superintendent. Tactical planning, on the other hand, is a decentralized process that takes place under the umbrella of the governing strategy where principals, supervisors, department heads, and teachers are the primary participants; it is a bottom-up process functioning within the parameters of established strategy.

Tactical planning is bureaucratic in spirit; strategy formulation is entrepreneurial with intermediate planning serving as a transition between the two. Tactical planning focuses on current operating problems and realities in order to improve present performance, whereas strategy is directed toward long-term survival and development to ensure future school system success. Unlike strategy formulation and intermediate planning, tactical planning is constrained by present conditions and resources. Tactical planning seeks to maintain efficiency and stability in the organization, while strategy seeks to change the organization in order to develop future potential and flexibility. Tactical planning is based on information concerning teacher, parent, and student conditions. Strategy formulation uses such information as a baseline for making projections of future conditions, desires, and values.

The responsibility for tactical planning is placed with line administrators, who have intimate understandings of the intricacies of day-to-day operations. In splitting the planning responsibilities, the basis for a two-way discourse is established. The discussion is initiated at the center that establishes the framework and sets the parameters in which tactical planning takes place. The detailed plans are developed by line administrators and staff within the context provided by the center, which are, in turn, reviewed by the center to make sure that they are truly consistent with the established guidelines (Frazier, 1997).

Tactical planning addresses such issues as the following: What programs, procedures, and projects are required? What resources need to be committed? What is the schedule of events? Who will be responsible for implementing programs, procedures, and projects? What will be the impact on human resources? What progress has been made toward realizing strategic objectives and mission?

The logistics of addressing these tasks is illustrated in Figure 11.9. It is important to keep in mind that any general planning model—of which there are many—must be adapted to the specific circumstances under which it will be applied. A planning process for a school district must be different from that for a school. The process and format for a high school must be different from that for an elementary school, and the processes and formats will vary among elementary schools and high schools.

In response to the first and second questions, strategic policies and objectives are translated into operational objectives, programs, procedures, projects, and budgets for immediate implementation and added to or integrated with the continuing operations of the school or district. Performance objectives are set

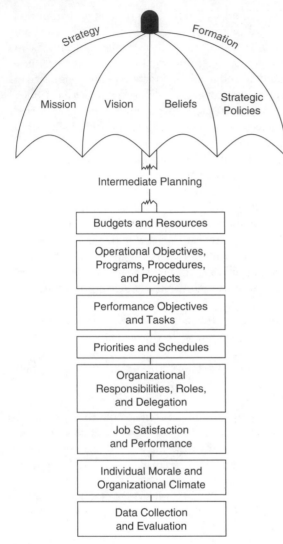

Mission   Vision   Beliefs   Strategic Policies

Intermediate Planning

Budgets and Resources

Operational Objectives, Programs, Procedures, and Projects

Performance Objectives and Tasks

Priorities and Schedules

Organizational Responsibilities, Roles, and Delegation

Job Satisfaction and Performance

Individual Morale and Organizational Climate

Data Collection and Evaluation

FIGURE 11.9

Components of tactical (or operational) planning

to deal with such changes, or serious problems may develop, damaging the ability to reach desired goals. Providing those implementing the plan with the necessary knowledge and skills may require new staff members and an extensive staff development program (responding to the question What will be the impact on human resources?).

Evaluation of the success of implementation comes at the end of a tactical cycle (What progress has been made toward realizing strategic objectives and mission?), but deciding what data need to be collected to monitor success and establish benchmarks need to be done before implementation begins. Measuring progress requires knowing the state of affairs before the plan was put into place; such information should have been part of the self-assessment made during the intermediate planning process. By comparing the state of affairs periodically after implementation with the state of affairs prior to implementation, progress made toward goals can be monitored. If progress is unsatisfactory, corrective measures need to be taken in future operational plans. The information collected can also contribute to evaluation of the overarching strategy that needs to be reviewed every few years to make sure that changing conditions have not rendered it obsolete.

Budgeting. Budgeting is an integral part of tactical planning, but, unfortunately, it is usually the only formal planning activity undertaken by many educational organizations. Typically, financial constraints are emphasized to the exclusion of educational plans and mission. Budgeting in the absence of a guiding strategy is directionless. Ideally, the budget should reflect the educational plan rather than vice versa.

The primary purpose of a budget is to translate a district's or school's educational priorities and programs into financial terms within the context of available resources and legal constraints (answering the question What resources need to be committed?). The important decisions as to who gets what, when, and how are made through this process, making it highly political (refer to chapter 10). Within the public sector, the budget is a legally adopted document that presents planned expenditures and anticipated revenues for a given fiscal year and is usually the legal basis for levying school taxes in

and tasks are assigned. Deadlines are established (What is the schedule of events?), and responsibilities for meeting those deadlines in the manner specified are placed with specific individuals (Who will be responsible for implementing programs, procedures, and projects?).

New programs, projects, and directions frequently require new skills, new organizational configurations, and, often, additional personnel. The members of the district/school must be well prepared fiscally independent school districts. For charter schools, it may be the basis for determining the amount of funding to be provided by the funding agency. It is this legal emphasis on financial aspects of the budget that largely explains the neglect of its programmatic aspects (Hartman, 1988).

The budget is one of the primary management tools of educational administrators and the major one in the fiscal area. In addition to its importance to the planning process, for public schools, the budget serves as a vehicle for public review and approval. Once approved, the budget becomes the legal basis for spending funds. During the course of the year, the budget serves as a management control document, providing specific spending limits that are not to be exceeded without prior authorization. Through careful monitoring, overexpenditures can be avoided, and compensation for possible revenue shortfall can be made at the earliest possible point, allowing maximum flexibility for dealing with it (Hartman, 1988).

School-Based Decision Making

The number of critics of public education who believe that it is the school governance structure itself that is the cause of inequities and inefficiencies in the education system is growing. This posture views the education policymaking process from the perspective of "institutionalism" as presented in chapter 10. Persons sharing this view include advocates of administrative decentralization (school-based decision making) and advocates of market solutions involving parental choice of schools, charter schools, and educational vouchers.

The concept of school-based decision making (SBDM) involves a *system* of schools within which a significant amount of authority to make decisions on curriculum and allocation of human and fiscal resources has been devolved to each school. This takes place within a centrally determined framework of goals, policies, standards, and accountabilities, that is, strategy formulation. In actuality, there is little

---

ACTIVITY 11.1

Planning, Budgeting, and Information Systems

Addresses ISLLC Standards 1 and 3

Select a school district (or a school if it has considerable autonomy over its budget) for the purpose of studying its planning, budgeting, and information systems.

1. Is a formal set of policies and procedures followed in establishing a planning process for the district?
   a. If such a policy exists, study it carefully and interview a number of key actors in the process to determine how closely the policy is adhered to; identify its perceived strengths and weaknesses.
   b. If no such policy is in place, interview a number of persons whom you would expect to be involved in the planning process, including the board of education, the central office, principals, teachers, parents, and students. Describe the de facto process and its perceived strengths and weaknesses.
2. Is a formal set of policies and procedures followed in establishing a budgeting process for the district?

   a. If such a policy exists, study it carefully and interview a number of key actors in the process to determine how closely the policy is adhered to; identify its perceived strengths and weaknesses.
   b. If no such policy is in place, interview a number of persons whom you would expect to be involved in the budgeting process, including the board of education, the central office, principals, and teachers. Describe the de facto process and its perceived strengths and weaknesses.
   c. Examine the complete budget, popularized versions of it, the budget calendar, and related forms.
3. Study the operating budget implementation process. How are purchases initiated, made, and paid for? How is payroll handled? How are expenditures monitored?
4. What is the nature of the information system(s) that supports the planning and budgeting processes? Are all systems integrated?

evidence that SBDM leads directly to improved pupil achievement (Conway, 1984; Malen, Ogawa, & Kranz, 1990; Smylie, 1994; Summers & Johnson, 1996; Wohlstetter, Smyer, & Mohrman, 1994). Therefore, SBDM must be viewed as an element of systemic reform if a connection with improved pupil achievement is to be made. Other elements need to involve higher performance expectations, more directed pedagogical demands, and clear accountability systems and may include such reforms as national and state curricula, performance standards and assessment, national teacher certification, and family choice of schools (Consortium on Renewing Education, 1998; Forum for Education and Democracy, 2008; Guthrie, 1998; Hannaway, 1996). Although not linked directly to improvement in student outcomes, SBDM is credited with being an efficacious means of addressing conflicts over the distribution of scarce resources and enhancing the legitimacy of institutions authorized to make those decisions.

The bottom line is that school-based management is not an end in itself, although research indicates that it can help foster an improved school culture and higher-quality decisions. School-based management is, however, a potentially valuable tool for engaging the talents and enthusiasm of many more of a school's stakeholders than traditional, top-down governance systems. Moreover, once in place, school-based management holds the promise of enabling schools to better address students' needs (Wohlstetter & Mohrman, 1994).

As a strategy of reform, SBDM is founded on the premise that the school is the fundamental decision-making unit within the education system. The school's administrators, teachers, and other professional staff, constituting the "technical core" of the educational system, make up a natural decision-making and management team. This core has knowledge about teaching methods and learning processes as well as information about the diverse learning styles and needs of the children for whom they are responsible. Thus, the school staff is equipped to make better decisions about appropriate educational programs than those removed from the specific teaching and learning process. Shifting decision-making responsibilities from central administrative

offices to schools means a redistribution of power and authority among principals, teachers, parents, and community that enables these key stakeholders to make schools more responsive to unique local conditions while effectively harnessing their knowledge, creativity, and energy to the task. Further, if the professional staff is to be held responsible for student progress, that staff should have flexibility in designing the learning environment.

Structures for making policy at the school level vary. Authority may be placed with the principal alone (i.e., administrative decentralization), or the responsibility may be shared in some combination among administrators, teachers, parents, community representatives, and upper-grade students. Some manifestations of SBDM place some authority with a school-based governing board as in Chicago. When power is placed with lay boards, specific provision is usually made for formal professional involvement in the decision-making process. In administrative decentralization, authority is devolved from the district to members of the professional staffs in the schools.

Under SBDM, school authorities *may* develop the budget, select staff, and refine the school's curriculum to meet specific needs of pupils within legal constraints set by the school district or higher levels of government (Cawelti, 1989; U.S. General Accounting Office, 1994). The school district, state, and federal government continue to set general priorities within which all schools within their respective jurisdictions must function and develop overarching educational objectives and the basic curriculum for meeting those objectives. School districts continue to allocate resources to schools based on student numbers and needs, negotiate labor contracts, and provide facilities and other support services such as transportation, payroll, and accounting.

School-Level Strategy Formation and Planning

Within a district planning scheme, the school is likely to be viewed as a program—one of the quasi independent units within the system. The growing practice of school based management has led to

ACTIVITY 11.2

Composition of School Policy Boards

Addresses ISLLC Standards 4 and 6

Imagine a policy board for each public school composed of the principal, serving as the chief executive officer, and representatives of teachers, parents, and students.

1. What are the advantages and disadvantages of such an arrangement?
2. Would you add representation from any other group?

3. Would you eliminate representation of any group?
4. Assuming each representative has one vote, how many representatives should there be from each group?
5. In what ways can the public interest be protected without bureaucratizing the school operations?
6. Provide your rationale for each response.

schools, themselves, becoming the primary planning unit. This is already true of charter schools.

The mere existence of decentralization mechanisms will not guarantee positive results, however. The nature of the culture, or attitudes/beliefs permeating the organization, is also influential. M. L. Ross (1997) concluded that schemes resulting in effective participation by teachers "require new forms of collaborative and collegial involvement that shift the traditional isolated decision-making environment to a team-based, power sharing one" (p. 317). A balanced approach of centralization–decentralization supports a combined top-down, bottom-up planning process to meet the competing needs of the organization. "A co-existing loose-tight coupling between horizontal and vertical levels of the organization underlies a framework focused on systemic, rather than piecemeal, reform" (p. 319).

M. L. Ross (1997) found the greatest SBDM success in schools where teachers were offered a high involvement form of participation, the power to influence decisions, and an enabling context for effective engagement of teachers. The pervading culture needs to be one of mutual respect and trust throughout all levels of the organization nurtured by effective leadership and top-down commitment and support. It is critical that principal–teacher relationships be based on mutual influence in the decision-making process and that professional learning and staff development be focused on creating an ongoing capacity for school improvement responsive to

student needs and meeting changes in the school community over time.

School-Based Budgeting

School personnel cannot make meaningful curricular decisions without the authority also to make the necessary resource commitment decisions that enable the implementation of those curricular decisions (Consortium on Renewing Education, 1998; Guthrie, 1998; Odden & Busch, 1998); SBDM must include school-based budgeting (SBB) as an integral component. The degree of empowerment of school staff is directly related to the proportion of the school budget under the control of school authorities. In this section we focus on issues related to SBB.

Wohlstetter and Buffett (1992) described the differences between traditional centralized budgeting at the district level and SBB. Regardless of the level at which it takes place, the budgeting process involves formulation, adoption, and monitoring. Under the traditional centralized mode, all three are accomplished at the district level with minimal involvement of school personnel. Human and physical resources are then assigned to schools for use in district specified areas. Schools are usually given discretionary control over a small allocation, primarily for the purchase of instructional supplies and the provision of student enrichment experiences.

Where budgetary authority has been decentralized, the district still forecasts the resources that will be available at the district level. But from that point on, the procedures become quite different. Decentralized districts must first determine the extent of budgetary authority to be extended to schools. The primary issue is the degree of control to be granted to schools over personnel expenditures that account for 60% to 80% of school and district budgets. Schools in Seattle and Edmonton, Alberta, Canada, are granted a lump-sum allocation, as described in chapter 10, covering virtually all costs encountered by schools with no specific amount designated for personnel—or any other expenditure category. Most school districts in the United States have been very cautious in delegating to schools budgetary authority (David, 1994; Dunn, James-Gross, & Trampe, 1998; Goertz & Stiefel, 1998; Odden, 1999).

The second district-level decision is how much to allocate to schools and according to what unit. Some districts make their allocations by pupil units and others by staff units. In either case, the number of students in a school, their characteristics, previous performance, and the nature of the school (e.g., grade levels served, and the presence of special programs) are primary determinants of the size of the school's allocation (Gurr, 1999; Wohlstetter & Van Kirk, 1996).

Once the district determines a school's allocation, action passes to school authorities to devise a detailed plan for using the funds in accordance with its curricular plan and within the constraints established by higher authority (Wohlstetter & Buffett, 1992). Whatever procedure is followed, budget building should be done within the context of a school's curricular plan.

With respect to budget adoption, the procedure between centralized and decentralized districts is similar. Final approval is by the board of education in either case. Wohlstetter and Buffett (1992) pointed out that the main difference is in the flow. While centralized districts may consult with school authorities, in the decentralized mode the school develops the budget and recommends its adoption to district officials. District review of school budgets should be in terms of compliance with district and other strategic and legal constraints and not in terms of educational substance, philosophy, and so on, which should be allowed to vary freely among schools.

Expenditures need to be monitored by both district and school personnel. The district role in the decentralized mode is primarily to provide information to the schools and to ensure that schools do not exceed their spending authorizations. In some school districts, the business office provides budgetary information to school personnel on a regular basis; increasingly, school-level officials have the option of being "online" to access financial information held in the district's computer memory at any time and the flexibility of establishing their own accounting codes within the constraints of the district code structure.

Before financial allocations can be made to schools, it is necessary to know what the total resource requirement of schools is, and most current school accounting procedures are incapable of providing such information. Except for minor portions of the budget such as instructional supplies, most accounting systems do not link expenditures to buildings, programs, or classrooms. Computer and accounting technology have the capacity to provide such linkages, and our ability to trace all expenditures to the school level will improve as the practice of SBB spreads.

Resource allocation and expenditure information is critical to the successful functioning of SBDM. Tracing resource demands to the school and classroom level is essential for informed decision making in SBDM and SBB environments and also holds the potential, with appropriate analysis, for advancing

---

ACTIVITY 11.3

Accounting for the Legal Expenditures of Funds

Addressing ISLLC Standard Functions 3A, 3B; and 5C

1. Under a school-based budgeting scheme, what factors should be taken into account in determining the amount of a school's lump-sum distribution?
2. To what extent, if any, should public control and regulation follow public finance? Give examples of alternative patterns for providing public financial support of the provision of educational services and the nature of public control and regulation appropriate to protect the public interest.

our understanding of the influences of inputs on educational outcomes and equity in the allocation of resources.

SUMMARY AND FUNDAMENTAL CONCEPTS

Unfortunately, many schools and districts are adrift on the social and political seas of this world, helplessly battered by the winds and currents of special interest groups and circumstances. It is little wonder that their impact on the academic and behavioral development of children falls short of national, state, and local expectations. It is also not surprising that their operations are judged to be less than efficient, one of the concerns of the next chapter. But this need not be the case. In this chapter, we focused on decision making, the fundamental process that determines the success or failure of any organization in fulfilling its mission. The chapter began by laying out the basic models and theories that have been developed to help understand the decision-making process, thereby enhancing the potential for arriving at better decisions when applied to practice. The second part of the chapter applied those concepts to educational institutions specifically and described a general scheme whereby they can develop a sense of direction and how they can mobilize the human and material resources at their disposal to move efficiently toward fulfilling their respective visions and missions. We provided examples of operational systems of strategy formulation and planning and budgeting at the school and district levels. Each must work out the particulars for itself. The way is not easy, but the rewards can be substantial.

In chapter 12, we focus on a particular type of decision, resource allocation, and examine the evidence available to inform such decisions. We begin the chapter by looking at the equity of the distribution of financial resources among schools and school districts and the adequacy of the amounts provided. We then review the evidence of relationships between inputs to the schooling process and desired outcomes. We look at these relationships at two levels: societal, where we are interested in the impact of resources used for education on desired social objectives such as economic growth, and the school or classroom, where we are interested in the impact of resources and their use on pupil behavior and pupil achievement. Such knowledge is necessary to improve the efficiency of educational institutions. The chapter concludes with a discussion of policy implications for improving the equity and efficiency of schooling.

Fundamental Concepts

The fundamental concepts that follow have been discussed in this chapter. The citations following each concept indicate the Interstate School Leaders Licensure Consortium (ISLLC) standards and functions related to the concept. The Arabic numerals refer to the ISLLC standards, and the letters refer to the functions as presented in the table found inside the front cover.

- Authority, decision making, and responsibilities should be shared among all stakeholders in educational settings. (1A; 2A, 2F; 3D; 4B, 4C, 4D; 5C)
- Decision making is the process of choosing among alternatives and is central to all leadership tasks. (1A; 3D)
- Normative models suggest how decision making should be conducted to be consistent with rational behavior. (2F; 3D)
- Descriptive models accommodate psychological constraints that establish as unlikely the possibility that a person will function in a consistent and highly rational manner. (2F; 3D)
- Various idiographic factors, such as personality and status, influence the decisions a person makes. (2F; 3D)
- People often use heuristics to simplify the decision-making process even though there is the danger that inherent biases can lead to serious decision errors. (2F; 3D)
- Strategy is a guide or course of action into the future that provides an organization with direction. (1C, 1D; 2B, 2F; 3D)
- Strategy in an organization includes a set of governing principles (beliefs and strategic policies) that will guide the organization over the long term. (1C; 2B, 2F;3D)
- Planning addresses short-term issues (of up to 3 years) of mobilizing the resources of an organization to accomplish its mission. (1C; 3B)
- Planning must be recognized as a sociopolitical process for coordinating and integrating the goals of the organization with those of the individual. (6C)
- Providing schools with authority to make critical decisions about their operations is based on the premise that the school is the fundamental decision-making unit within the education system. (1A; 2F; 3D)
- School personnel cannot make meaningful curricular decisions without the authority also to make the necessary resource commitment decisions that enable the implementation of those curricular decisions. (2H; 3B, 3D)

References

Argyris, C. (1985). *Action science.* New York: Jossey-Bass.

Atkinson, R. C., Herrnstein, R. J., Lindzey, G., & Luce, R. D. (Eds.). (1988). *Steven's handbook of experimental psychology* (Vol. 2). New York: Wiley.

Baron, J. (1985). *Rationality and intelligence.* Cambridge: Cambridge University Press.

Bazerman, M. H. (1991). Foundations of decision processes. In B. M. Staw (Ed.), *Psychological dimensions of organizational behavior* (pp. 451–478). New York: Macmillan.

Bell, D. E., Raiffa, H., & Tversky, A. (Eds.). (1988). *Decision making: Descriptive, normative and prescriptive interactions.* Cambridge: Cambridge University Press.

Bennis, W., & Nanus, B. (1985). *Leaders: The strategies for taking charge.* New York: Harper & Row.

Caldwell, B. J., & Spinks, J. M. (1988). *The self-managing school.* London: Falmer.

Carroll, J. S., & Johnson, E. J. (1990). *Decision research: A field guide.* Newbury Park, CA: Sage.

Carson, B. R. (1965). *Teacher participation in decision making and other local community activities in three Oregon communities.* Unpublished doctoral dissertation, University of Oregon, Eugene.

Cassidy, J. (2006, September 18). Mind games. *New Yorker, 82*(29). Retrieved October 28, 2008 from http://www.newyorker.com/archive/2006/09/18/060918fafact

Cawelti, G. (1989). Key elements of site-based management. *Educational Leadership, 46,* 46.

Consortium on Renewing Education. (1998). *20/20 vision: A strategy for doubling America's academic achievement by the year 2020.* Nashville, TN: Peabody Center for Education Policy, Vanderbilt University.

Conway, J. A. (1984). The myth, mystery, and mastery of participative decision making in education. *Educational Administration Quarterly, 20*(3), 11–40.

Cook, W. J., Jr. (1990). *Bill Cook's strategic planning for America's schools* (Rev. ed.). Arlington, VA: American Association of School Administrators.

Cornell, A. H. (1980). *The decision-makers handbook.* Upper Saddle River, NJ: Prentice Hall.

Cunningham, W. G. (1982). *Systematic planning for educational change.* Palo Alto, CA: Mayfield.

David, J. L. (1994). School-based decision making: Kentucky's test of decentralization. *Phi Delta Kappan, 75,* 706–712.

Davis, S. H. (2005). What was I thinking? *School Administrator, 62*(6), 36–41.

Deming, E. W. (1986). *Out of the crisis.* Cambridge, MA: MIT Press.

Drucker, P. (1974). *Management tasks, responsibilities, practices.* New York: Harper & Row.

Dunn, R. J., James-Gross, L., & Trampe, C. (1998). Decentralized budgeting: A study in implementation and implications. *Journal of School Business Management, 10*(1), 22–28.

Eberwine, K. (2005). Hindsight bias and the subsequent remedial measures rule: Fixing the feasibility exception. *Case Western Reserve Law Review, 55*(3), 663–666.

Einhorn, H. J., & Hogarth, R. M. (1978). Confidence in judgment: Persistence of the illusion of validity. *Psychological Review, 85*(5), 395–416.

Einhorn, H. J., & Hogarth, R. M. (1988). Behavioral decision theory: Processes of judgment and choice. In D. Bell, H. Raiffa, & A. Tversky (Eds.), *Decision making: Descriptive, normative, and prescriptive interactions* (pp. 113–151). Cambridge: Cambridge University Press.

Eraker, S. A., & Sox, H. C. (1981). Assessment of patients' preferences for therapeutic outcomes. *Medical Decision Making, 1*(1), 29–39.

Ewell, P. T. (1989). *Enhancing information use in decision making.* San Francisco: Jossey-Bass.

Feinberg, A. (2006, October). We're all market timers now. *Kiplinger's Personal Finance, 60*(10). Retrieved October 28, 2008 from http://www.kiplinger.com/magazine/archives/2006/10/feinberg.html

Fischhoff, B. (1982). For those condemned to study the past: Heuristics and biases in hindsight. In D. Kahneman, P. Slovic, & A. Tversky (Eds.), *Judgment under uncertainty: Heuristics and biases* (pp. 335–351). Cambridge: Cambridge University Press.

Fishburn, P. C. (1988). Normative theories of decision making under risk and under uncertainty. In D. Bell, H. Raiffa, & A. Tversky (Eds.), *Decision making: Descriptive, normative, and prescriptive interactions* (pp. 78–98). Cambridge: Cambridge University Press.

Forum for Education and Democracy. (2008). *Democracy at risk: The need for a new federal policy in education.* New York: Author.

Frazier, A. (1997). *A roadmap for quality transformation in education.* Boca Raton, FL: St. Lucie Press.

Fullan, M. (1993). *Change forces: Probing the depths of educational reform.* London: Falmer Press.

Goertz, M. E., & Stiefel, L. (1998). School-level resource allocation in urban schools. *Journal of Education Finance, 23*(4), 435–446.

Goodstein, L. D., Nolan, T. M., & Pfeiffer, J. (1992). *Applied strategic planning: A comprehensive guide.* San Diego, CA: Pfeiffer.

Grandori, A. (1984). A prescriptive contingency view of organizational decision making. *Administrative Science Quarterly, 29,* 192–209.

Gurr, D. (1999). *From supervision to quality assurance: The case of the State of Victoria (Australia).* Paris: International Institute for Educational Planning/UNESCO.

Guthrie, J. W. (1998). Reinventing education finance: Alternatives for allocating resources to individual schools. In W. J. Fowler Jr. (Ed.), *Selected papers in school finance, 1996* (NCES98-217) (pp. 85–107). Washington, DC: National Center for Education Statistics, U.S. Department of Education.

Hannaway, J. (1996). Management decentralization and performance-based incentives: Theoretical consideration for schools. In E. A. Hanushek & D. W. Jorgenson. *Improving America's schools: The role of incentives* (pp. 97–109). Washington, DC: National Academies Press.

Hartman, W. T. (1988). *School district budgeting.* Upper Saddle River, NJ: Prentice Hall.

Hill, G. W. (1982). Group versus individual performance: Are N + 1 heads better than one? *Psychological Bulletin, 91,* 517–539.

Hodgkinson, C. (1991). *Educational leadership: The moral art.* Albany: State University of New York Press.

Holtzman, S. (1989). *Intelligent decision systems.* Reading, MA: Addison-Wesley.

Hoy, W. K., & Miskel, C. G. (1978). *Educational administration: Theory, research, and practice.* New York: Random House.

Janis, I. L. (1989). *Crucial decisions: Leadership in policymaking and crisis management.* New York: Free Press.

Kahn, B. E. (2005). The power and limitations of social relational framing for understanding consumer decision processes. *Journal of Consumer Psychology, 15*(1), 28–34.

Kahneman, D., Slovic, P., & Tversky, A. (Eds.). (1982). *Judgment under uncertainty: Heuristics and biases.* Cambridge: Cambridge University Press.

Kahneman, D., & Tversky, A. (1972). Subjective probability: A judgment of representativeness. *Cognitive Psychology, 3,* 430–454.

Kahneman, D., & Tversky, A. (1973). On the psychology of prediction. *Psychological Review, 80,* 237–251.

Kahneman, D., & Tversky, A. (1979). Prospect theory: An analysis of decision under risk. *Econometrica, 4*(2), 263–291.

Krepel, T. L. (1987). Contemporary decision theory and educational leadership. *Educational Research Quarterly, 11*(4), 37–44.

Lotto, L. S., & Clark, D. L. (1986). Understanding planning in educational organizations. *Planning and Changing, 17*(1), 9–18.

MacPhail-Wilcox, B., & Bryant, H. D. (1988). A descriptive model of decision making: Review of idiographic influences. *Journal of Research and Development in Education, 22*(1), 7–22.

Malen, B., Ogawa, R., & Kranz, J. (1990). What do we know about school-based management? A case study of the literature—A call for research. In W. H. Clune & J. F. Witte (Eds.), *Choice and control in American education* (Vol. 2, pp. 289–342). Philadelphia: Falmer.

Mann, L., & Janis, I. (1977). *Decision making: A psychological analysis of conflict, choice, and commitment.* New York: Free Press.

McKean, K. (1985, June). Decisions, decisions. *Discover, 22–31.*

McNeil, B., Pauker, S., & Tversky, A. (1988). On the framing of medical decisions. In D. Bell, H. Raiffa, & A. Tversky (Eds.), *Decision making: Descriptive, normative, and prescriptive interactions* (pp. 562–568). Cambridge: Cambridge University Press.

Meisel, A., & Roth, L. H. (1983). Toward an informed discussion of informed consent: A review and critique of the empirical studies. *Arizona Law Review, 25,* 265–346.

Menon, M. E., Saiti, A., & Socratous, M. (2007, October). Rationality, information search, and choice in higher education: Evidence from Greece. *Higher Education, 54*(5), 705–722.

Mintzberg, H. (1989). *Mintzberg on management: Inside our strange world of organizations.* New York: Free Press.

Mintzberg, H. (1994). *The rise and fall of strategic planning.* New York: Free Press.

Montgomery, H. (1983). Decision rules and the search for a dominance structure: Towards a process model of decision making. In P. Humphreys, O. Svenson, & A. Vari (Eds.), *Analyzing and aiding decision making processes* (pp. 343–369). New York: Elsevier.

Myers, D. G., & Lamm, H. (1976). The group polarization phenomenon. *Psychological Bulletin, 83,* 602–627.

Neel, A. (1977). *Theories of psychology: A handbook.* New York: Schenkman.

Nisbett, R., & Ross, L. (1980). *Human inference: Strategies and shortcomings of social judgment.* Upper Saddle River, NJ: Prentice Hall.

O'Brien, P. W. (1991). Strategic planning and management for organizations. In R. V. Carlson & G. Awkerman (Eds.), *Educational planning: Concepts, strategies, and practices* (pp. 163–176). New York: Longman.

Odden, A. (1999). Formula funding of schools in the United States of America and Canada. In K. N. Ross & R. L. Levačić (Eds.), *Needs-based resource allocation in education via formula funding of schools* (pp. 198–227). Paris: UNESCO.

Odden, A., & Busch, C. (1998). *Financing schools for high performance: Strategies for improving the use of educational resources.* San Francisco: Jossey-Bass.

Reitz, H. J. (1987). *Behavior in organizations* (3rd ed.). Homewood, IL: Irwin.

Robertson, P. J., & Kwong, S. S. (1994). Decision making in school-based management leadership councils: The impact of council membership diversity. *Urban Review, 26*(1), 41–54.

Ross, L., & Anderson, C. A. (1982). Shortcomings in the attribution process: On the origins and maintenance of erroneous social assessments. In D. Kahneman, P. Slovic, & A. Tversky (Eds.), *Judgment under uncertainty: Heuristics and biases* (pp. 129–152). Cambridge: Cambridge University Press.

Ross, L., Lepper, M. R., Strack, F., & Steinmetz, J. L. (1977). Social explanation and social expectation: The effects of real and hypothetical explanations upon subjective likelihood. *Journal of Personality and Social Psychology, 35,* 817–829.

Ross, M. L. (1997). *A comparative case study of teacher participation in planning in three types of decentralized schools.* Unpublished doctoral dissertation, State University of New York at Buffalo.

Sanna, L. J. (2004, July). Integrating temporal biases. *Psychological Science, 15*(7), 474–481.

Scott, J. T. (1991). *Case study of a school district undergoing change from a top-down to a participative decision-making budget planning process.* Unpublished doctoral dissertation, State University of New York at Buffalo.

Senge, P. M. (1990). *The fifth discipline: The art and practice of the learning organization.* New York: Doubleday/Currency.

Shermer, M. (2002, September). Smart people believe weird things. *Scientific American, 287*(3). Retrieved October 28, 2008 from http://www.sciam.com/article.cfm?id=smart-people-believe-wei.

Simon, H. A. (1955). A behavioral model of rational choice. *Quarterly Journal of Economics, 69,* 99–118.

Simon, H. A. (1956). Rational choice and the structure of the environment. *Psychological Review, 63,* 129–138.

Simon, H. A. (1976). *Administrative behavior: A study of decision-making processes in administrative organizations* (3rd ed.). New York: Free Press.

Simon, H. A. (1977). *The new science of management decisions* (Rev. ed.) Upper Saddle River, NJ: Prentice Hall.

Slovic, P., Fischhoff, B., & Lichtenstein, S. (1982). Response mode framing and information-processing effects in risk assessment. In R. Hogarth (Ed.), *New directions for methodology of social and behavioral science: Question framing and response consistency* (pp. 21–36). San Francisco: Jossey-Bass.

Slovic, P., & Lichtenstein, S. (1971). Comparison of Bayesian and regression approaches in the study of information processing and judgment. *Organizational Behavior and Human Performance, 6,* 649–744.

Slovic, P., & Lichtenstein, S. (1983). Preference reversals: A broader perspective. *American Economic Review, 73,* 596–605.

Slovic, P., Lichtenstein, S., & Fischhoff, B. (1988). Decision making. In R. Atkinson, R. Herrnstein, G. Lindzey, & R. D. Luce (Eds.), *Stevens' handbook of experimental psychology* (Vol. 2, pp. 673–738). New York: Wiley.

Smylie, M. A. (1994). Redesigning teachers' work: Connections to the classroom. *Review of Research in Education, 20,* 129–177.

Staw, B. M., & Ross, J. (1991). Understanding behavior in escalation situations. In B. Staw (Ed.), *Psychological dimensions of organizational behavior.* New York: Macmillan.

Steers, R. M. (1977). *Organizational effectiveness: A behavioral view.* Santa Monica, CA: Goodyear.

Summers, A. A., & Johnson, A. W. (1996). The effects of school-based management plans. In E. A. Hanushek & D. W. Jorgenson (Eds.), *Improving America's schools: The role of incentives* (pp. 75–96). Washington, DC: National Academies Press.

Tetlock, P. (1985). Accountability: The neglected social context of judgment and choice. In B. M. Staco &

L. Cummings (Eds.), *Research in organizational behavior,* 311–314. New York: Oxford University Press.

Tversky, A., & Kahneman, D. (1973). Availability: A heuristic for judging frequency and probability. *Cognitive Psychology, 4,* 207–232.

Tversky, A., & Kahneman, D. (1974). Judgment under uncertainty: Heuristics and biases. *Science, 185,* 1124–1131.

Tversky, A., & Kahneman, D. (1982a). Evidential impact of base rates. In D. Kahneman, P. Slovic, & A. Tversky (Eds.), *Judgment under uncertainty: Heuristics and biases* (pp. 153–160). Cambridge: Cambridge University Press.

Tversky, A., & Kahneman, D. (1982b). Judgment under uncertainty: Heuristics and biases. In D. Kahneman, P. Slovic, & A. Tversky (Eds.), *Judgment under uncertainty: Heuristics and biases* (pp. 3–20). Cambridge: Cambridge University Press.

Tversky, A., & Kahneman, D. (1988). Rational choice and the framing of decisions. In D. Bell, H. Raiffa, & A. Tversky (Eds.), *Decision making: Descriptive, normative, and prescriptive interactions* (pp. 167–192). Cambridge: Cambridge University Press.

U. S. General Accounting Office. (1994). *Education reform: School-based management results in changes in instruction and budgeting.* Washington, DC: GAO.

Von Neumann, J., & Morgenstern, O. (1947). *Theory of games and economic behavior.* Princeton, NJ: Princeton University Press.

Vroom, V., & Jago, A. (1988). *The new leadership: managing participation in organizations.* Upper Saddle River, NJ: Prentice Hall.

Wagner, C. G. (2003). Money and brains. *Futurist, 37*(5), 12.

Watson, S. R., & Buede, D. M. (1987). *Decision synthesis: The principles and practice of decision analysis.* Cambridge: Cambridge University Press.

Wheatley, M. J. (1994). *Leadership and the new science: Learning about organizations from an orderly universe.* San Francisco: Berrett-Koehler.

Wheatley, M. J., & Kellner-Rogers, M. (1996). *A simpler way.* San Francisco: Berrett-Koehler.

White, D. J. (1969). *Decision theory.* Chicago: Aldine.

Wohlstetter, P., & Buffett, T. M. (1992). Promoting school based management: Are dollars decentralized too? In A. R. Odden (Ed.), *Rethinking school finance: An agenda for the 1990s* (pp. 128–165). San Francisco: Jossey-Bass.

Wohlstetter, P., & Mohrman, S. A. (1994, December). School-based management: Promise and process. *CPRE Finance Briefs.*

Wohlstetter, P., Smyer, R., & Mohrman, S. A. (1994). New boundaries for school-based management: The high involvement model. *Educational Evaluation and Policy Analysis, 16,* 268–286.

Wohlstetter, P., & Van Kirk, A. (1996). Redefining school-based budgeting for high-involvement. In L. O. Picus & J. L. Wattenbarger (Eds.), *Where does the money go? Resource allocation in elementary and secondary schools* (pp. 212–235). Thousand Oaks, CA: Corwin.

The Allocation of Resources for Education Adequacy, Equity, and Efficiency

Education is big business. More than $560 billion is spent annually on public elementary and secondary schools in the United States, making expenditures for education the largest single budgetary component of state and local governments (National Center for Education Statistics [NCES], 2006). These expenditures represent 4.5% of the nation's gross domestic product (GDP). More than 50 million children attend these schools, and they employ more than 6 million professional educators and support personnel. No matter how one looks at it, schooling involves a highly significant portion of the nation's human and economic resources.

But education is much more than big business. Education deals with matters that relate to the hearts and souls of individual citizens and, at the same time, is critical to the political and economic welfare of the nation and its security. The quality of the decisions made about how much is spent on schooling (adequacy), how that spending is distributed among children (equity), and how the economic resources are transformed into educational services (efficiency) are the focus of this chapter.

In chapter 10, we discussed the political structure and process for determining public policy including policies that affect issues of education. In chapter 11, we examined the process of organizational decision making, particularly as it relates to schools and school systems, the fundamental process that determines their success or failure in fulfilling its mission. The chapter began by laying out the basic models and theories that have been developed to help understand the decision-making process, thereby enhancing the potential for arriving at better decisions when applied to practice. The second part

of the chapter applied those concepts to educational institutions specifically and described a general scheme whereby they can develop a sense of direction and how they can mobilize the human and material resources at their disposal to move efficiently toward fulfilling their respective visions and missions. We provided examples of operational systems of strategy formulation and planning and budgeting at the school and district levels.

In this chapter, we focus on a particular type of decision, resource allocation, and examine the evidence available to inform such decisions. We begin the chapter by looking at the equity of the distribution of financial resources among schools and school districts and the adequacy of the amounts provided. We then review the evidence of relationships between inputs to the schooling process and desired outcomes. We look at these relationships at two levels: societal, where we are interested in the impact of resources used for education on desired social objectives such as economic growth, and the school or classroom, where we are interested in the impact of resources on pupil behavior and pupil achievement. Such knowledge is necessary to improve the efficiency of educational institutions. The chapter concludes with a discussion of policy implications for improving the equity and efficiency of schooling.

Equity in the Allocation of Resources to Schooling

Most nations have organized their school systems at the national level. In the United States, the responsibility for providing educational services has been placed with the states, and all states except Hawaii choose to assume only a limited supervisory role and created school districts (some 12,000 of them) to run and partially finance public elementary and secondary schools.

In a critical analysis of public education in the United States, Morrison (1943) referred to its structure disdainfully as "late New England colonial" (p. 258) and described the school district as "a little republic at every crossroads" (p. 75). Morrison was focusing on a characteristic of the system of U.S. public education that makes it unique among the school systems of the world—its extreme decentralization. Herein lay both its strengths and its weaknesses.

Decentralized systems seem to be more adept than highly centralized and bureaucratic ones at mobilizing the energies of their constituents and adapting curricula and instructional systems to the diversity of their constituents. Yet decentralized systems have a tendency to become inequitable, providing an uneven quality of services, especially when they are also responsible for providing a significant amount of their financial support. The good schools in a decentralized system tend to be very good, but such a system also generates—and tolerates—very poor schools. To bring about a greater degree of equity and set minimally accepted social standards requires intervention of higher levels of government (i.e., state and/or federal). This has been happening with increasing frequency over the decades since Morrison made his analysis.

Originally, "common" schools were financed primarily through locally levied property taxes, supplemented with voluntary contributions and some state subsidies. In 1920, 83% of elementary and secondary school expenditures were generated at the local level; less than 1% was provided by the federal government with the remaining 16.5% coming from state governments (NCES, 1999). State-generated revenues now account for 47% of all school expenditures, and the federal share is 9%, leaving about 44% to be generated at the local level, still primarily through the property tax (NCES, 2006). (See Table 10.1) Federal funds are provided mainly through categorical programs that direct monies and programs toward meeting the needs of children who are identified as being educationally at risk, including those qualifying for compensatory reading and mathematics instruction as well as those with disabilities. The states make some use of categorical type aids, but most monies are channeled to local school districts as *equalized* general aid (i.e., distributed inversely to the taxing capacities of districts to compensate in part for the great differences in taxable wealth among districts).

Equality is defined as the state, ideal, or quality of being equal, as in enjoying equal social, political, and economic rights. The operational definition of equality in the sociopolitical context also includes factors of condition, placing emphasis on the *appropriateness* of treatment. As such, *equality* has taken on the broader connotations of *equity*, defined as "the state, ideal, or quality of being just, impartial and fair" (*American Heritage Dictionary of the English Language*). We use the term *equity* instead of *equality* as reflecting more accurately modern usage in reference to public policy. For a more extensive explanation of the distinctions between equality and equity, refer to chapter 7.

In analyzing the impact of a policy on equity concerns, one must be fully aware of the level of equity the policy is intended to address and should consider horizontal as well as vertical dimensions of equity. Horizontal equity refers to the equal treatment of equals—the traditional meaning of *equality*. Vertical equity recognizes that equal treatment is not always fair and just for persons (or school districts) experiencing abnormal conditions such as poverty and physical, psychological, and mental disabilities (or high costs of living, dispersed populations, and municipal overburden in the case of school districts). Thus, *vertical equity* refers to the appropriate unequal treatment of "unequals." Some analysts add a third dimension, *equal opportunity*, defined in the negative as no differences in treatment according to characteristics (such as race or national origin) that are considered illegitimate (Berne & Stiefel, 1984). Other analysts treat equal opportunity as a condition of horizontal equity, the position taken here.

Virtually all studies of resource allocation equity deal only with the horizontal dimension (including equal opportunity). The lack of agreement on what appropriate treatment is for exceptional populations makes analysis of vertical equity very difficult if not impossible; nevertheless, recognition of the concept is very important in designing school finance policy. Indeed, the concept is recognized in public policy through such state programs as special and compensatory education and federal programs as Head Start and No Child Left Behind.

The Extent of Inequities in Resource Allocation

Despite the efforts to equalize resources available to school districts, great disparities remain. Table 12.1 shows the total per pupil current expenditures of school districts at the 5th-, median, and 95th-percentile reference points by state. Also included is the federal range ratio, number of districts, and number of students. The federal range ratio is a measure of the equity in the availability of revenue resources among the school districts within a state; if all the districts in a state had the same amount of revenue resources per pupil (i.e., perfect equity), the ratio would equal zero. The greater the revenue disparity among districts within a state, that is, the greater the inequity, the higher the ratio becomes.

West Virginia displays the greatest equity among the states (with the exception of Hawaii operating as a single unit) with a ratio of 0.3. North Dakota displays the greatest inequity with a ratio of 2.9. The difference in total revenue per pupil between the 5th- and 95th-percentile districts is $2,538 per pupil in West Virginia compared to $20,831 in North Dakota. The expenditure of the 5th-percentile district in New York State, with a ratio of 1.6, exceeds the expenditure of the median district in 39 of the states and the 95th-percentile district in 11 states. New York's median spending district exceeds the 95th-percentile district in 27 of the states, further illustrating the inequities among the states as well as within states with respect to the availability of financial resources. This is supported by the size of the federal range ratio for the United States as a whole, 1.8.

But equity is not the entire story; there is also the matter of adequacy. As shown previously, New York State does not score well with respect to equity, but it does much better with respect to adequacy. In an analysis of the school finance structures of four

provinces of Atlantic Canada, Lake (1983) came up with a similar finding that in the quest for equity, adequacy of support may suffer. A more recent analysis by Paquette (1999) of Ontario's move to full provincial funding of elementary and secondary education found that the reforms "promise more equal but lower funding for Ontario boards" (p. 24).

To further illustrate the disparities among school districts, Table 12.2 provides information on the student, financial, and teacher characteristics and student achievement measures of selected school districts in the metropolitan New York City area. The data, derived from a New York State Education Department (2006) report, show the inequity created by the proliferation of small school districts in one of the most densely populated regions in the United States. Enrollment in these districts ranged from more than 1 million pupils in New York City to 1,663 in Malverne.

Three items measure characteristics of the economic status of the districts: percentage of pupils receiving free or reduced lunches, Census Poverty Index, and the combined wealth ratio. With respect to the first measure, the percentage of pupils receiving free or reduced lunches, four districts have none, and three, including New York City, have more than 75%. The Census Poverty Index is the percentage of children ages 5 to 17 years living in families below the poverty level as determined by the 2000 federal

TABLE 12.1

Total Revenues per Pupil at the 5th, Median, and 95th Percentile Cutpoints, Federal Range Ratio, and Numbers of Districts and Students for Public Elementary and Secondary Regular School Districts, for Fiscal Year 2005

State and Independent Charter School Districts	Total Revenues per Pupil			Federal Range Ratio[1]	Number of Districts	Number of Students
	5th Percentile	Median	95th Percentile			
United States	**$7,021**	**$9,702**	**$19,680**	**1.8**	**13,830**	**47,861,248**
Alabama	6,756	7,649	9,902	0.5	130	729,342
Alaska	9,503	17,865	37,190	2.9	53	132,568
Arizona	6,519	9,341	18,882	1.9	215	920,235
Arkansas	7,213	8,021	10,433	0.4	254	461,667
California	7,118	8,801	16,181	1.3	966	6,233,136
Colorado	7,676	9,531	16,032	1.1	178	765,388
Connecticut	11,091	13,350	19,345	0.7	166	552,512
Delaware	10,126	11,544	14,373	0.4	16	106,734
District of Columbia	†	17,809	†	†	1	62,306
Florida	7,491	8,449	11,612	0.6	67	2,645,280
Georgia	7,656	8,948	11,746	0.5	179	1,552,483
Hawaii	†	12,415	†	†	1	183,185
Idaho	6,066	7,956	14,612	1.4	114	253,782
Illinois	7,136	8,985	15,252	1.1	876	2,072,437
Indiana	8,812	10,741	14,460	0.6	292	1,014,528
Iowa	8,099	9,295	14,153	0.7	367	478,319
Kansas	7,740	9,518	12,959	0.7	300	468,481
Kentucky	6,993	7,882	9,254	0.3	176	674,502
Louisiana	7,177	8,243	11,226	0.6	68	717,625
Maine	9,495	12,706	23,660	1.5	222	198,356
Maryland	9,344	10,504	14,269	0.5	24	865,561
Massachusetts	9,773	12,702	23,484	1.4	302	930,045
Michigan	7,864	9,012	12,920	0.6	552	1,647,296
Minnesota	8,197	9,763	13,246	0.6	345	814,546
Mississippi	6,382	7,464	9,191	0.4	152	494,382
Missouri	6,636	8,319	12,700	0.9	522	902,659
Montana	6,137	9,772	24,286	3.0	436	146,552
Nebraska	6,189	10,272	21,500	2.5	477	284,553
Nevada	8,010	9,353	27,941	2.5	17	400,083
New Hampshire	9,181	13,315	27,403	2.0	162	202,223
New Jersey	11,585	15,061	24,469	1.1	551	1,349,413
New Mexico	7,969	11,310	21,775	1.7	89	326,102
New York	11,886	15,115	30,609	1.6	695	2,818,858
North Carolina	7,054	8,464	10,430	0.5	115	1,347,177
North Dakota	7,102	10,263	27,933	2.9	206	100,413
Ohio	7,717	8,956	14,475	0.9	613	1,778,784
Oklahoma	6,046	7,554	11,992	1.0	540	629,145

TABLE 12.1 (Continued)

Total Revenues per Pupil at the 5th, Median, and 95th Percentile Cutpoints, Federal Range Ratio, and Numbers of Districts and Students for Public Elementary and Secondary Regular School Districts, for Fiscal Year 2005

State and Independent Charter School Districts	Total Revenues per Pupil			Federal Range Ratio[1]	Number of Districts	Number of Students
	5th Percentile	Median	95th Percentile			
Oregon	7,163	8,692	20,040	1.8	195	550,284
Pennsylvania	9,119	10,990	14,873	0.6	500	1,755,560
Rhode Island	10,111	12,202	20,837	1.1	36	153,596
South Carolina	7,453	8,716	11,543	0.5	85	701,176
South Dakota	7,021	8,860	14,512	1.1	165	124,862
Tennessee	6,134	6,832	8,750	0.4	135	940,769
Texas	7,421	9,064	17,732	1.4	1,039	4,336,944
Utah	5,908	7,401	14,082	1.4	40	488,055
Vermont	10,148	17,394	30,460	2.0	239	92,819
Virginia	8,011	9,347	13,042	0.6	132	1,203,697
Washington	7,560	9,186	20,086	1.7	296	1,019,925
West Virginia	8,490	9,640	11,028	0.3	55	279,456
Wisconsin	9,596	10,976	14,106	0.5	426	869,301
Wyoming	11,533	14,814	31,300	1.7	48	84,146

[1] The federal range ratio indicates the difference between the amount per pupil of the district at the 95th percentile and the district at the 5th percentile divided by the amount per pupil for the district at the 5th percentil.

Note: How to read this table: Using Alabama as an example, this table shows that 5 percent of school districts have total revenues per pupil of $6,756 or less. If all school districts were listed by size of total revenues per pupil, the district at the midpoint (median) would have total revenues per pupil of $7,649. Five percent of school districts have total revenues per pupil of $9,902 or more. The federal range ratio shows that the magnitude of the difference between total revenues per pupil at the 5th percentile of districts and the 95th percentile is 0.5, or approximately 50 percent. National figures do not include independent charter school districts. National and state figures include charter schools that are affiliated with regular school districts. Only regular school districts matching the Common Core of Data (CCD) "Local Education Agency Universe Survey" and with student membership greater than zero were used in creating the national and state figures; 92.1 percent of the school districts met this criterion. Independent charter school districts with revenues greater than zero and expenditures greater than zero were included in the charter school analysis; 96.8 percent of charter school districts met this criterion.

Source: U.S. Department of Education, National Center for Education Statistics, Common Core of Data (CCD), "School District Finance Survey (F-33)," fiscal year 2005, Version 1a.

census. Children living in poverty in New York City represent 28% of that age cohort, as do 27% in Yonkers and Hempstead. Three districts have fewer than 5% living in poverty: Chappaqua, Garden City, and Scarsdale. The combined wealth ratio is a statistic used by New York State in calculating the distribution of state equalization aid to school districts. It includes a measure of full market value of real property per pupil of a school district and its adjusted gross personal income per pupil. The ratio is formulated so that 1.0 represents average taxable wealth for the state; a ratio lower than 1.0 is below the state average and vice versa. New York City and Yonkers, the two largest districts in the table, are very close to the state average taxable wealth. Five districts in the table have ratios triple the state average: Chappaqua, 3.279; Cold Spring Harbor, 3.597; Garden City, 2.903; Great Neck, 3.815; and Scarsdale, 4.311.

Roosevelt, in Nassau County, Long Island, has an enrollment of less than 3,000 pupils, of which 99.4% are African American or of Hispanic origin. Nearby Garden City has more than 4,000 pupils that are 96% white and less than 2% African American or Hispanic. In the public schools of New York City,

TABLE 12.2

Pupil, Teacher, and District Characteristics for Selected School Districts in the New York City Metropolitan Area

Characteristics	New York City http://schools .nyc.gov	Chappaqua http://chappaqua .k2.ny.us	Cold Spring Harbor http://csh.k12 .ny.us	Garden City gardencity. http://.k12.ny.us	Great Neck greatneck. http://.k12.ny.us
Pupil characteristics Enrollment	1,017,951	4,169	2,132	4,212	6,189
% White	14.3	89.7	97.1	95.7	71.7
% Black	33.4	1.2	0.5	0.5	2.2
% Hispanic	38.9	1.8	0.7	1.4	7.5
% Other	13.3	7.2	1.7	2.4	18.6
% Limited English	13.8	1.3		0.6	5.8
% of School-age population with disabilities	11.5	9.3	10.2	9.3	11.3
Annual attendance rate	89.4	97.2	96	96.5	96.4
% Dropouts	8.2	0	0.1	0	0.2
District wealth and financial characteristics					
% Pupils receiving free or reduced lunches	76.4	0.8	0	0	12
Census Poverty Index	28	3	NA	4	7
Combined wealth ratio	0.998	3.279	3.597	2.903	3.815
Expenditure per pupil	$13,640	$18,346	$16,932	$17,325	$21,910
Median teachers salary	$52,947	$82,082	$78,599	$79,030	$87,444
Pupils per teacher	13.4	11.7	13.5	13.5	10.3
Pupils per support staff	176.2	112.7	120.5	150.4	109.8
Average class size: elementary	23	21	19	23	18
Average class size: 8th-grade English	28	23	23	19	19
Average class size: 10th-grade English	29	NA	19	22	25
Teacher characteristics					
% with Permanent certification	50	83	76	82	88
% with Provisional certification	31	16	23	18	10
% having master's degree plus 30 hours or doctorate		37			30
% Minority	40	4	2	2	5
% Annual turnover	20	10	14	11	6
Achievement					
Elementary: % meeting standards					
English	60	95	86	94	94
Mathematics	77	98	93	98	98
Science	65	99	92	99	100
Social Studies	60	98	97	98	99
Middle grades: % meeting standards					
English	33	88	81	85	81
Mathematics	41	91	93	84	92
Science	45	98	98	91	86
Social Studies	32	97	96	92	87
High School					
% Graduates receiving regents diploma	35	97	99	95	92
% Graduates going on to college	64	99	100	97	99

District and Web Page Address

Source: New York State Education Department (2006). *The state of learning: A report to the Governor and the Legislature on the educational status of the State's schools, Vol. 2. Statistical profiles of public school districts.* Albany (Author).

	Hempstead http://hempsteadschools.org	Malverne http://malverne.k12.ny.us	Mt. Vernon http://mtuernoncsd.org	Roosevelt http://rooseveltufsd.com	Scarsdale http://scarsdaleschools.k12.ny.us	Sewanhaka http://sewanhaka.k12.ny.us	Yonkers http://yonkerspublicschools.org
	6,913	1,663	10,249	2,945	4,593	8,630	25,546
	0.3	22.6	7.1	0.5	84.2	48.1	18.1
	53.2	62.6	78	77.8	1.9	25.3	28.9
	46.1	12	13.5	21.6	1.8	13	46.9
	0.4	2.8	1.4	0.1	12.1	13.6	6.1
	16.9	3.5	9.1	11.7	2.8	3.6	17.5
	10.4	15.3	9.2	10.8	7.5	11.5	11.4
	89.9	94.8	90.3	94.2	97.9	96.2	90.5
	7.1	3.7	4.6	34.6	0	0.4	3.9
	85.5	37.8	66.1	82.1	0	0	65.9
	27	6	19	19	4	6	27
	0.554	1.318	0.874	0.518	4.311	1.168	0.993
	$17,513	$17,916	$14,334	$18,020	$19,438	$12,881	$17,008
	$74,950	$69,449	$81,929	$63,298	$102,255	$68,216	NA
	14.5	11	14.7	11.8	12.6	16.6	15.4
	105	92.4	113.3	112.6	121.2	132	219.9
	23	20	21	19	20	0	22
	22	14	17	24	20	26	28
	20	20	24	20	21	26	26
	78	83	74	70	83	66	84
	17	17	18	26	14	33	15
	12	12	15	11	17	9	12
	53	36	29	33	57	33	48
	69	16	36	51	4	8	24
	12	9	12	11	8	10	14
	65	75	87	82	95	-	77
	80	92	91	82	98	-	87
	82	80	90	85	99	-	79
	71	92	88	75	98	-	83
	21	75	31	17	80	69	30
	33	88	32	26	92	64	39
	38	79	39	71	94	82	46
	39	78	40	45	91	77	36
	44	83	52	78	NA	91	63
	60	93	75	97	99	95	84

only 14% are classified as white, non-Hispanic; 33% are African American, 39% are Hispanic, and 13% are classified as other. Only Sewanhaka has an enrollment distribution that reflects the public school enrollment distribution of the region as a whole. Under these circumstances, the ideal of the common school as a socially integrated institution is difficult to realize.

School district differences in demographic characteristics are reflected in their financial provision for instruction. New York City's per pupil expenditure, $13,640, is among the lowest in the metropolitan area; Great Neck spends more than 50% more per pupil, $21,910. The median teacher salary in New York City ($52,947) is the lowest in the table and one of the lowest in the region. Scarsdale's median teacher salary is $102,255; four districts in the table have median salaries above $80,000.

The bottom line is pupil achievement, which again reflects the socioeconomic divide. Typically, for the affluent suburbs, 95% or more of their elementary students meet New York State standards in English language arts, mathematics, science, and social studies; of the middle-grade students, 90% or more usually meet the standards, but never less than 80% do. New York City's students meeting state standards at the elementary level range between 60% and 80%, while the other less affluent districts range between 70% and 90%. For the middle grades, however, there is a big dropoff for the less affluent districts, with those meeting the standards ranging between 20% and 40%. The dropout rates for the affluent suburbs are at or near zero; in New York City, it is more than 8%, the highest of the districts in the table.

Intradistrict Equity Studies

The focus of equity analyses has shifted in the 21st century from resource equity to output equity and equal opportunity. In addition, several studies examine the equity of the distribution of resources and outcomes to schools and pupils *within* districts.

Berne and Stiefel (1994) set the pattern for the study of equity within districts. Their analysis of equity among elementary and middle schools in New York City found that the glaring inequities in vertical

ACTIVITY 12.2

Qualitative Evidence of Inequities among Schools and School Districts

Addresses ISLLC Standards 1B; 3A; 4A; 5C, 5D; and 6C

Table 12.2 contains considerable quantitative data that are used in the related discussion in the text to describe some of the inequities that exist among schools in a major metropolitan area. The table also provides the Web site address under each district's name. Select several of the districts and study their Web sites in detail. Look for differences in philosophies, policies, style, programs, parent, student and staff access and involvement with the Web site, and other things that strike you as being significant. For example, the New York City Web site is available to readers in 10 languages; this is a powerful statement in and of itself. What is its significance? Using your "qualitative" observations as data, write a few paragraphs describing evidence of inequities among districts. In a small discussion group, share your thoughts. What are the implications, if any, for horizontal and vertical equity and adequacy? How well do these Web sites "market" their schools?

equity with respect to poverty that were common at the state level did not exist among schools within the city. Even though elementary schools budgeted and spent more resources per pupil of general education funds in lower- than in higher-poverty schools, categorical aids were sufficient to bring expenditures of high-poverty schools above those of low-poverty schools but not nearly to the level suggested by adequacy studies (e.g., Duncombe, Ruggiero, & Yinger, 1996; Duncombe & Yinger, 1997, 1999; Reschovsky & Imazeki, 2001). Greater amounts of general education funds per pupil were directed to higher-poverty schools in middle and junior high schools than was the practice to elementary schools. High-poverty schools, regardless of grade level, had greater access to most other resources (e.g., categorical aids) than did low-poverty schools.

Their analysis also found that an alarmingly low proportion of the general education budget was reaching the schools—$2,550 per pupil, compared to the almost $7,000 total per pupil budgeted for the district as a whole. They concluded that this finding was consistent with the claims of many school districts serving large numbers of poor children that nonclassroom management and oversight burdens associated with programs targeted at such children are substantial. They questioned whether this practice was productive.

Berne and Stiefel (1994) also found average teacher salaries in high-poverty schools to average $4,536 less than in low-poverty schools. This difference resulted from the seniority provisions in the district's contract with teachers unions. Teachers with greater longevity in the district had first choice in selecting school assignments, a common practice in large urban districts, and, overwhelmingly, they chose to teach in schools enrolling the more affluent children. As a result, low-socioeconomic-status students were taught by less experienced, less educated, and lower-salaried teachers. It should be noted that research on efficiency suggests that more experienced teachers with higher levels of academic preparation tend to be more successful in working with at-risk students than are less experienced teachers. These findings suggest that "measures of dollars alone are not sufficient in an equity analysis and that to some degree the education process must be examined" (p. 419). Equity studies of other large cities have produced similar findings (Hertert, 1996; Rubenstein, 1998; Stiefel, Rubenstein, & Berne, 1998).

Owens (1994) found that instructional expenditures in some elementary schools within Dade County, Florida, were much higher than in others. Unlike the New York City and California studies, he found that these differences were related to racial/ethnic and family income factors. High percentages of African American and low-income students and large schools had lower instructional expenditures per pupil than did schools without those characteristics for all methods of computing expenditures. As in the Chicago and New York City school-level studies, Owens attributed this inequity largely to the practice of permitting senior teachers to control where they will teach; less experienced teachers and teachers with less education were more likely to be found in traditionally minority and high-poverty schools.

Acknowledging the well-established differences in mathematical achievement according to ethnic membership, Raudenbush, Fotiu, and Cheong (1998), using a nationwide database, sought to discover if there were corresponding differences in the availability of instructional resources for students according to their ethnicity and SES as measured by parents' education. The four resources studied were school disciplinary climate, access to high school algebra, teacher with a major in mathematics, and an instructional emphasis on reasoning. In sum, they found evidence of ethnic and social inequity in access to the four resources across ethnic groups and education levels of parents. The authors concluded that

> just as high parental education predicts favorable outcomes, it also predicts access to schools with favorable climates, schools [middle school and junior high school] that offer algebra, teachers with training in mathematics, and classrooms that emphasize reasoning. Similarly, ethnic groups disadvantaged in outcomes (African Americans, Hispanic Americans, and Native Americans) also encounter less access to these resources for learning. (p. 261)

In still another nontraditional approach to looking at the equity of distribution patterns of resources, Wenglinsky (1998) found that instructional and capital expenditures were not related to mean achievement in mathematics but were related to *differences* in achievement among socioeconomic groups. Lower spending levels were associated with greater achievement gaps within schools among students of different socioeconomic levels. Higher levels of instructional and capital expenditures were strongly associated with reduced relationships between social background and achievement.

Doing equity studies at the school level allows researchers to move beyond district averages and brings the analysis closer to the classroom and student levels, where learning and teaching actually take place. Analyses at the school level also enable the examination of the distribution of resources, taking into account geographic location and characteristics of students. The major disadvantage is the lack of financial data at the school level, but this situation is improving as more districts budget and orient their accounting practices to schools.

Implementing Resource Allocation Policy

Addresses ISLLC Standards and Functions 1B; 3A, 3B; 4A; and 6

Interview your superintendent of schools, a member of your board of education, a principal, and a union official about how resource allocation decisions are made in your school district. Did you get similar perceptions from the people interviewed? Check the written school board policies and state and federal laws related to budget development and resource allocation. On the basis of your interview findings and policy analyses, write a description of the process and inaccuracies in perceptions you found, if any. Share and discuss your findings with other members of your class or discussion/study group.

Summary of Horizontal Equity Considerations

Horizontal equity of resource input is less among school districts nationally than it is among individual states. Horizontal equity within states is usually less than within districts. Within-district studies have shown a pattern of inequity in the distribution of general funds in favor of the more affluent. In part, this is compensated for by the inequity in the distribution of categorical aids in favor of the poor, but no satisfaction should be taken when categorical and general funds combined are distributed equitably among schools. This, in itself, is a violation of the intent of most categorical programs, especially at the federal level, that contain maintenance-of-effort provisions; in other words, categorical funding is to be *in addition* to equitably distributed general funds.

The concept of horizontal equity has become obsolete as public attention shifts to obtaining adequacy in resource allocation through vertical equity. Greater emphasis needs to be placed on equity analyses at the school, classroom, and even student levels because these levels are where teaching and learning take place.

In the next section, we examine the transition from older studies of horizontal equity to studies of vertical equity in search of its ideal: adequate educational funding.

Defining and Measuring Adequacy

Setting the national educational goal at educating *all* children to high standards has transformed the orientation of school finance policy. The challenge directly links finance to the purposes of education (Ladd & Hansen, 1999). Thus, while equity remains a primary goal of public policy, the object in analyzing equity has shifted from inputs to schooling outputs. Since public policy can affect these not directly but only indirectly through the amount of resources provided and specifying the practices of schools and related institutions, the *adequacy* of equitably distributed inputs has moved to the forefront of policy debates under the assumption that there are positive relationships between resource inputs and achievement and behavioral outcomes.

Although the assumption makes intuitive sense, the empirical evidence is weak, making the problem of achieving equity of outputs exceedingly difficult. While the evidence of positive relationships is growing, there is stronger evidence that an equal application of resources under similar conditions yields widely disparate results. Some schools are more adept (dare we say more efficient?) in transforming applied resources into the realization of desired educational objectives than are others. Efficiency in the use of resources is treated later in this chapter.

In the absence of full understanding of these relationships, the best that we can do at the moment from a policy standpoint is to identify resource levels that *can* produce the results we want to achieve with children of differing characteristics with a reasonable degree of probability. While providing resources at such levels of *sufficiency*, we must continue to study the mechanisms by which those resources are transformed into desirable changes in student behavior and accomplishments so that children in all schools can be successful.

Because of our meager understanding of the relationships between resource inputs and educational outputs and outcomes, it is important that adequacy be defined in the broadest of terms, such as operational expenditures per pupil, rather than by specific prescriptions, such as class size or particular curricula, sometimes called "opportunity-to-learn standards" (Clune, 1995; Guthrie & Rothstein, 2001). At some time in the future, our understanding may justify specific standards; nevertheless, we will always need to guard against bureaucratic inclinations toward policies of one size fits all.

Approaches used by contemporary analysts to study adequacy include statistical analysis of statewide databases that include schooling input measures, student achievement and other measures of output, and demographic information; analyzing costs of districts that seem to be achieving adequate outcomes; and costing out whole-school reform designs and other designs originating from professional judgment.

Econometric Approaches

In essence, *adequacy* is the cost of an instructional program that produces the range of results desired. When the adequacy criterion is met, costs are likely to vary among districts according to the characteristics of students served and to the characteristics of the districts themselves, but the results should be the same regardless of these considerations. The costs of adequacy under varying circumstances (vertical equity) can be estimated statistically when a sufficiently large database is available by estimating cost functions. A measure of the instructional cost per unit (pupil or classroom) serves as the dependent variable, with the independent variables consisting of measures of pupil performance, pupil characteristics, and district characteristics. Built on the set of basic relationships among variables in the sample, this treatment produces a regression equation that yields a unique cost for each district for producing the desired level of achievement given the districts' characteristics and those of its pupils. This approach carries with it the advantages that it bypasses the necessity to specify an instructional delivery system and eliminates the need to determine costs of instructional components.

Duncombe and Yinger (1997, 1999; Duncombe et al., 1996) used such an approach to estimate a cost function as described previously employing a sample of 631 school districts in New York State. These costs were then converted into cost indices showing the relative costs of providing comparable instruction among classifications of school districts. Their dependent variable was a measure of per pupil operating expenditures. Exogenous independent variables (over which the district has no policy control) consisted of enrollment, poverty indicators, percentage of students with severe handicaps, and percentage of students with limited English proficiency. Their endogenous independent variables (over which the district has some policy control) consisted of measures of pupil achievement, teacher salaries, percentage of nondropouts, and percentage of graduates receiving a state diploma (requiring the passing of a number of rigorous criterion-referenced subject matter examinations) rather than diplomas granted by school districts that have less challenging requirements. Duncombe and Yinger also included among their endogenous variables a measure of school district efficiency derived from a process known as data envelopment analysis. With this *best-practice* technique, a district is considered inefficient to the degree that it spends more than other districts realizing the same level of performance and with similar characteristics.

Duncombe and Yinger (1997, 1999) found great variation in the cost of producing comparable student achievement among types of districts. With 100 serving as average cost for New York State school districts obtaining average achievement, they found that bringing the achievement levels of New York City students to the state average would require resources costing nearly four times as much as the state average (an index of 396). The cost index for New York City suburbs was 108; large cities upstate, 190; rural areas, 99; upstate small cities, 109; and, upstate suburbs, 91.

Reschovsky and Imazeki (2001) produced similar results in a comparative study of Texas and Wisconsin. When adjustments were made for efficiency of school districts, the range in cost indices was 78 to 126 in Texas and 89 to 117 in Wisconsin.

Empirical Approaches

Through an empirical approach, those districts that have successfully achieved a defined level of acceptable student performance are identified and studied as to pedagogy and resource application under the assumption that such practice *can* yield the results desired.

In essence, this is the implicit theory supporting the New Jersey Supreme Court decision in *Abbott v. Burke* (1997). In a series of 11 decisions resulting from litigation beginning in 1970, the courts, responding to continuing pressure by tenacious plaintiffs and their attorneys, sought a practical definition of the state constitution's provision that the legislature shall provide for a "thorough and efficient" system of free and public schools. In responding to these court decisions, the legislature and the governor shaped legislation addressing the inequities in funding between affluent suburban districts and 28 poor urban communities (known as the Abbott districts) under the guidance of the court decisions. Early court decisions sought equity of inputs, but later decisions sought a level of inputs that would be adequate to enable the poor districts to narrow the achievement gap with the wealthy districts. This evolution signifies a shift in concern from horizontal to vertical equity.

In a 1990 decision, the court acknowledged that New Jersey had established general standards that could be used to test for conformity with the state constitution's requirement of a thorough and efficient system, but the court found that in practice this had not happened (Goertz & Edwards, 1999). Because of the absence of clear measures of substantive educational opportunity, the court adopted a default remedy: practices in the state's wealthiest districts. "Average spending on the regular education program in the states 108 wealthiest suburban districts thus became the presumptive standard of thorough and efficient for the states 28 poorest urban communities" (Goertz & Edwards, 1999, p. 16). This position was affirmed in the court's 1997 decision, and it ordered parity in regular education funding between the poorest and the wealthiest districts.

Attention was then directed to the scope and cost of supplemental programs for the poorest districts. These were defined in the 1998 decision, thereby confirming the shift in the court's purview from horizontal equity to vertical equity and adequacy:

> Spending on regular education programs in the state's 28 poorest urban districts, which educate 22 percent of the state's students and about 75 percent of its students

of color, is on par with the average expenditures of the states wealthiest communities. In addition, students in poor urban communities are guaranteed access to preschool programs, health and social services, and better educational facilities. All urban elementary schools must undertake some form of "whole school reform" as a way of delivering more effective educational services. (Goertz & Edwards, 1999, pp. 5–6)

That is the practical definition of adequacy as worked out by the powers that be in New Jersey.

A different approach to defining adequacy was taken by the Ohio Department of Education. Unlike New Jersey, where adequacy was defined on the basis of the experience of high-wealth and high-spending districts, Ohio followed a procedure whereby a representative pool of Ohio school districts included all school districts except those that were at the extremes (high and low) in property wealth and spending per pupil (Augenblick, 1997). A criterion-referenced measure of the percentage of students in a district meeting or exceeding state-defined minimum competency levels served as the measure of student performance in a district. The average practice of those districts served as a model of exemplary practice for districts whose students were not achieving at that level. An adequate program cost was also developed using the average per pupil expenditure of the reference districts.

From 607 Ohio school districts, 102 were identified for the reference pool that met the performance requirements and that were not outliers with respect to property wealth and per pupil spending. Based on 1996 spending levels in Ohio, Augenblick (1997) computed a weighted per pupil revenue amount of $3,930 that became the definition of cost adequacy. Additional resources would be added to this amount for students with special needs and other expense factors.

Using Whole-School Reform Models and Professional Expertise

A number of organizational strategies intended to make schools more effective have been developed. These "whole-school reform models" have been designed by practicing educators (or at least in consultation with them) and are in tune with national research. None of the models has been firmly established by research as being better than the rest, but several have been carefully evaluated with promising results. It could be argued that at least those that have a documented record of success can serve as models of adequacy. Costing out the implementation of such models (King, 1994) would provide a financial measure of adequacy. Odden and Picus (2000) have shown that by reallocating resources already committed, "the average elementary, middle and high school in America has sufficient resources to finance all these school designs, even after providing planning and preparation time" (p. 336). In New Jersey, while the court used the empirical approach to establish a level of adequacy for nonclassified students, it took the whole-school reform model approach in establishing an adequacy level for children at risk. Indeed, with the resources provided to New Jersey's Abbott schools, the most expensive of the whole-school reform models (Success for All/Roots and Wings) could be implemented with a substantial amount of discretionary money remaining (Odden & Picus, 2000).

Promoting High Student Achievement Efficiently

The term "efficiency" is not commonly used in the parlance of educators. They rarely concern themselves with the connections between the inputs supplied to them by the community, how those resources are used in the classroom, how students fare as a result of their instructional experiences in subsequent grades and in other classes, and the quality of life experienced by graduates as a result of their school preparation. This may explain, at least in part, the counterintuitive fact that statistical analyses find small or no relationships between and among these events. In other words, if we think of inputs in terms of dollars, there is, at best, only a weak connection between the amount of dollars spent on public schools and the quality of their impact on children. When confronted with evidence of failing schools, it is unusual for educators to look at their own behaviors and decisions as possible causes; rather, they are likely to respond that they have been given insufficient resources to do an adequate job.

Having increased expenditures on public schools at a rate of about 3% a year in inflation-adjusted dollars for more than four decades, this response no longer sits well with the public at large. A great deal of skepticism has developed as to how well resources are being used by school officials for the education of children. The question of productivity has been pushed to the forefront of the education policy agenda and has highlighted the importance of learning how to spend education dollars wisely (Ladd & Hansen, 1999).

External Efficiency

Investment in education in the United States for the period from 1959 through 2005 is reported in Table 12.3 along with the percentage of the total population enrolled in precollegiate and higher education. The percentage of GDP spent for all educational institutions rose steadily from 4.4% in 1959 to 7.0% in 1975. It then declined to 6.1% in 1985, rising to 7.4% in 2005. The 2005 peak allocation of GNP (7.4%) to education is for a smaller proportion of population than was the case in 1975.

For elementary and secondary school expenditures, the percentage of GDP rose from 3.3% in 1959 to 4.6% in 1970 and 1975. Although expenditure per pupil continued to increase in current and inflation-adjusted dollars, the percentage of GDP declined to 3.8% in 1985. It then increased to 4.5% in 2000 and has remained there. The increase in the percentage of GDP allocated to precollegiate education corresponded to increasing enrollments, which reached 25.1% in 1970, and a growing commitment to equalize educational opportunities through desegregation of schools, compensatory education (e.g., enactment of the Elementary and Secondary Education Act), and educating children with disabilities. The decline in the percentage can be attributed at least in part to the dramatic drop in the proportion of the total population attending elementary and secondary schools to 18.6% in 1990. Since then, it increased to 19.2% in 1995 but has since declined to 18.5% in 2005.

The percentage of GDP spent on colleges and universities rose steadily from 1.1% in 1959 to 2.9% in 2005. Actual enrollments in postsecondary education rose from 3,640,000 in 1959 to 8,581,000 in 1970 and continued to increase to more than

TABLE 12.3

Percentage of Gross Domestic Product (GDP) Spent on Education and Percentage of Total Population Enrolled in Educational Institutions by Level, 1959–2005

Year	Elementary and Secondary Schools		Higher Education		Total	
	Percentage of GDP	Percentage Enrollment of Population	Percentage of GDP	Percentage Enrollment of Population	Percentage of GDP	Percentage Enrollment of Population
1959	3.3	23.0	1.1	2.0	4.4	25.0
1965	3.9	24.9	1.7	3.0	5.6	28.0
1970	4.6	25.1	2.3	4.2	6.9	29.3
1975	4.6	23.1	2.4	5.2	7.0	28.3
1980	4.0	20.3	2.3	5.3	6.3	25.7
1985	3.8	18.9	2.3	5.1	6.1	24.1
1990	4.3	18.6	2.5	5.5	6.8	24.2
1995	4.3	19.2	2.6	5.4	6.9	24.7
2000	4.5	18.9	2.7	5.4	7.2	24.3
2005	4.5	18.5	2.9	5.9	7.4	24.4

Source: National Center for Education Statistics. (1999, 2006). *Digest of Education Statistics.* Washington, DC: U.S. Department of Education; U.S. Census Bureau. (2007). *The 2007 Statistical Abstract.* Washington, DC: Department of Commerce.

14,000,000. The percentage of the total population enrolled in higher education in 1959 was 2.0%. It has steadily increased to 5.9% in 2005 except for a slight dip in 1985.

In reviewing the amount spent on education at all levels and the proportion of GDP invested, Smith and Phelps (1995) concluded that the United States ranks among the highest in comparison with other large postindustrial countries. A smaller portion of U.S. investment in education is directed to the elementary and secondary sector, however, when compared with other advanced nations. For higher education, the United States spends more per student than does any other country (NCES, 2001). Its expenditure at the secondary level is exceeded only by Switzerland and Austria. At the primary level, its expenditure is exceeded only by Switzerland, Austria, Norway, and Denmark. It is only when U.S. expenditures are viewed as a percentage of GDP that it falls toward the middle of the pack of advanced nations. In assessing adequacy, though, the level of resources available per child is the critical indicator, and the United States ranks very well on this measure.

Recognition is growing that many schools are not effective in guiding children toward the goals society has set for them and that this is particularly true for schools serving primarily educationally at-risk children. It is not only the children who are being harmed by this ineffectiveness; when the schools are not doing their jobs properly, taxpayers are not receiving a just return on the investments they make through the taxes they pay. While the concepts of equity and efficiency are quite different, we concluded in the previous section that schooling cannot be truly equitable without also being efficient.

On average, the United States appears to be committing a responsible amount of resources to elementary and secondary education. As noted previously, however, the distribution of resources among children in the country is highly inequitable. In the next section on internal efficiency, we look at how wisely these resources are being distributed to the education of individual children and how well they are being used in the instructional process.

Internal Efficiency

The gradual increase in inflation-adjusted expenditures for elementary and secondary schooling since the mid-20th century, as documented previously, has sparked much interest and a number of investigations into where the money has gone. Rothstein and Miles (1995) reported that the bulk of the increase went into special education programs. The share of special education spending of all spending increased from 4% in 1967 to 17% by 1991. The share of expenditures for regular education actually declined from 80% in 1967 to 59% in 1991. Guthrie (1997) came to similar conclusions.

Odden, Monk, Nakib, and Picus (1995) concluded that increases in expenditures for schooling had been distributed unfairly and used ineffectively and that the public education system needed to be restructured so that new resources could be strategically linked to improving student achievement. They found that the largest portion of increased spending had been used to hire more teachers to reduce class size and to provide more out-of-classroom services, primarily "pullout" instruction for disabled and low-achieving students. Funds were also used to increase teacher salaries but not in a fashion that would enhance teacher expertise.

The focus on higher achievement standards has not necessarily been accompanied with a call for substantially more financial resources. A prevailing assumption exists among policy analysts (but not among educational practitioners) that current allocations for education are sufficient or nearly sufficient for reaching higher standards if existing resources are distributed more wisely and used more effectively. For example, the plan of the Consortium on Renewing Education (1998) to double the nation's academic achievement by 2020 calls for no additional resources to those currently provided beyond that which would be allocated for precollegiate education if the trend of previous financial increases continues. "Incremental dollars for increased student enrollments and cost of living increases should be sufficient to meet this goal, if the nation's systems of schools were concentrating intensively on academic achievement" (p. 12).

The approximate net cost (after savings) of the New Commission on the Skills of the American Workforce (2007) plan for preparing 95% of high school graduates for college entrance is $8 billion. This equals less than 1.5% of the current cost of elementary and secondary education.

Summarizing the deliberations of a panel of economists working in the field of education (the Panel on the Economics of Education Reform), Hanushek (1996), the panel's chair, wrote,

> Reform—in education as in other areas—is often thought of as the process of securing more resources. Here our panel breaks with tradition. Analysis of the history of schools in the twentieth century does not suggest that American society has been stingy in its support of schools. Quite the contrary, funding for schools has grown more or less continuously for 100 years. The fundamental problem is not a lack of resources but poor application of available resources. Indeed, there is a good case for holding overall spending constant in school reform. Not only is there considerable inefficiency in schools that, if eliminated, would release substantial funds for genuine improvements in the operation of schools, but there also is a case for holding down funding increases to force schools to adopt a more disciplined approach to decision making. Schools must evaluate their programs and make decisions with student performance in mind and with an awareness that trade-offs among different uses of resources are important. (p. 30)

Fuller and Clarke (1994) divided educators and researchers into two camps when it comes to defining and studying school effectiveness and efficiency: policy mechanics and classroom culturalists. Policy mechanics, working from a production function metaphor, attempt to identify instructional inputs and uniform teaching practices that yield higher achievement; that is, their focus is on economic efficiency. They search for universal determinants of effective schools that can be manipulated by central agencies (e.g., state education departments) and assume that the same instructional materials and practices will produce similar results across diverse settings. The classroom culturalists reject this orientation and "focus on the normative socialization that occurs within classrooms: the value children come to place on individualistic versus cooperative work, legitimated forms of adult authority and power, and acquired attitudes toward achievement and modern forms of status" (p. 120). The classroom culturalists tend to ignore narrower forms of cognitive achievement and have not been particularly interested in antecedent inputs and classroom rules that can be manipulated by central authority. Although they do not normally use the term, their focus is on what economists refer to as technical efficiency. Fuller and Clarke concluded,

> The classroom culturalists have advanced researchers' understanding of how motivated learning occurs within particular social contexts, like classrooms. The production function gurus continue to hold comparative advantage in empirically linking classroom tools to achievement. But this advantage will only be retained if these inputs and teaching practices are awarded real cultural meaning—within a particular context which is energized by variable forms of teacher authority, social participation, and classroom tasks. (p. 143)

Or, as Elmore (2004) observes, "improvement is a developmental process, not an act of compliance with policy" (p. 227).

In this section, we review the findings of both camps. We begin by examining production function and efficiency studies done by "policy mechanics" and then consider research and applications relating to technical efficiency as revealed by effective schools research, program evaluations, and evaluations of whole-school reform models. We continue by reviewing studies of economies of scale as they relate to schools and school districts. Finally, we consider policy implications for improving internal efficiency of schools among schools and students.

Education Production Functions. Studies that relate schooling outcomes to inputs have been classified by several terms, including education production functions, input–output analysis, and cost–quality studies. Such research has been pursued from a variety of disciplinary perspectives in an effort to understand and improve educational productivity. In this section, we refer to them by the economic classification, *production function*. We begin by providing a general explanation of the education production concept, followed by a synopsis of some of the more influential studies.

Production Functions Explained. A production function may be conceptualized as a set of relations among possible inputs and a corresponding set of outputs for a firm or industry—in this case, schools and education (Burkhead, 1967). According to Hanushek

(1987), "A firm's production possibilities are assumed to be governed by certain technical relationships, and the production function describes the maximum feasible output that can be obtained from a set of inputs" (p. 33). Monk (1989) states that a production function tells what is currently possible: "It provides a standard against which practice can be evaluated on productivity grounds" (p. 31). Monk goes on to identify two traditions with respect to the study of the production of education services. The first attempts to estimate the parameters of the education production function. The second uses the production function as a metaphor, allowing for application of broader economic theories and reasoning that can be used to guide inquiry.

An education production function may be expressed simply as output (O), being a function of inputs consisting of student characteristics (S), schooling inputs (I), and instructional processes (P):

$$O = f(S, I, P).$$

Outputs (O) include behavioral and attitudinal changes in pupils induced through school activities. Outputs are usually measured by standardized test scores but occasionally include other measures, such as high school graduation rate, attendance rate, and rate of graduates continuing on to postsecondary education. Student characteristics (S) range from SES of family and student IQ to previous achievement. Schooling inputs (I) include peer group characteristics, expenditures, teacher characteristics, class size, characteristics of buildings, and so on. Instructional processes (P) include student time on task, teaching methods, student–teacher interactions, and so on.

If there is an education production function, there must also be a common underlying technology of education, an assumption that may come as a surprise to many educators because instructional or teaching technologies in education are inexact. Nevertheless, the sameness of American schools (and schools around the world for that matter, both public and private) lends credibility to an assumption of an implicit technology. School buildings are typically arranged with classrooms and certain ancillary spaces such as libraries, auditoriums, and gymnasiums. Each classroom is usually presided over by one teacher only, and there is a large degree of similarity in the ways teachers organize and manage classrooms.

Illustrative Production Function Studies. The report by James Coleman (1966), *Equality of Educational Opportunity* (EEO), was one of the first production function types of studies ever attempted for education. It involved more than half a million students in 4,000 schools and thousands of teachers; the unit of analysis was the school. It is perhaps the best-known and most controversial of all the input–output studies. The controversy extended not only to its conclusion that schooling had little potential for closing the achievement gap between white and minority students but also to the methodology used.

A number of attempts have been made to overcome the weaknesses of early production function studies. Ferguson (1991) did a most promising study of a large and particularly rich data source that he assembled for the State of Texas. What set this study apart, besides the richness of the data, was the systematic preparation of data that preceded the final analysis. As a result of his refinements, Ferguson found a much larger school effect than had been found by similar studies. Between one-quarter and one-third of the variation among Texas school districts in students' scores on the Texas reading examination were explained by school effects, primarily teachers' verbal ability scores.

The power of teachers' verbal scores to predict student achievement is of particular interest and is in keeping with the findings of other studies beginning with the EEO study, which also found that attribute to be the strongest school effect on pupil achievement. Using threshold analysis, Ferguson also found that class size in the primary grades matters as well within a specific range, down to a district student/teacher ratio of 18 to 1 but not lower (equivalent to a class size of 23). Further, he found a threshold effect for teacher experience, up to 5 years at the primary level and up to 9 years at the secondary level; additional experience had no relationship with student performance. No upper limit was found for the positive effect of teachers' verbal scores, however. The major weakness of the Ferguson study is that data were aggregated at the district level.

Based on his findings, Ferguson makes the policy recommendation that, apart from the common focus by states on equalizing spending per pupil, a serious equalization policy should also equalize the most important of all schooling inputs: teacher quality. Similar recommendations have already been noted in the equity studies of New York City (Berne & Stiefel, 1994), Chicago (Stiefel et al., 1998) and Dade County, Florida (Owens, 1994).

Among those taking advantage of the new and rich data resource provided by the Texas accountability system are Hanushek, Kain, and Rivkin (1998). In their study, they found large differences in the quality of schooling in a way that ruled out the possibility that the differences were driven by nonschool factors, but the researchers concluded that "resource differences explain at most a small part of the difference in school quality, raising serious doubts that additional expenditures would substantially raise achievement under current institutional structure" (p. 31).

Ferguson and Ladd (1996) used a value-added model specification at two levels (school and district) in their production function study of Alabama schools and districts. For the school-level specification, students were treated as the units of observation. They found teachers' ACT test scores to have a positive and statistically significant relationship with reading achievement. The proportion of teachers holding master's degrees had little or no effect on reading scores but did have a slight positive effect on math scores. Teachers' experience exerted no effect on either reading or mathematics achievement. With respect to class size, average mathematics scores in classes with fewer than 19 students exceeded those with more than 29 by .14 standard deviations. The effect was greater for girls than for boys. For reading, the gains were smaller and leveled off at class sizes in the mid-20s.

The district-level analysis arrived at similar results and enabled Ferguson and Ladd (1996) to estimate the effect of expenditure increases on student test scores. They found that the effect of increased spending was concentrated among the districts whose spending levels were below the median. For these districts, a 10% increase in expenditures per pupil (about 1.5 standard deviations) was associated with a .881 standard deviation increase in student test scores. For districts above the median in expenditures, the effect of higher expenditures was not statistically different from zero.

Woessmann (2000) conducted a production function analysis using data gathered from the Third International Mathematics and Science Study (TIMSS). This is a particularly important study in that it is the first quantitative study that is able to investigate the impact of systemic structural reforms. Quantitative studies conducted within a single country or state cannot study systemic issues because all schools and districts are operating within the same framework. International studies afford such an opportunity, and the TIMSS database is particularly well suited for this purpose. The analysis uses data collected for middle grades for 260,000 students in 39 countries. Analyses were made at the student level and at the country level.

For the student-level investigation, an education production function was estimated of the influence of student background, resources, and institutions on students' educational performance. Achievement and background were measured at the student level, while resources and institutional characteristics were measured at the classroom, school, and country levels. After controlling for family background effects, measures of differences in the ways educational systems are structured added substantially to explaining differences in student performance in mathematics and science. Both centralized examinations and the size of the private schooling sector (i.e., providing competition to the public schools) had significantly positive effects on student performance. School autonomy with respect to the purchasing of supplies, the hiring and rewarding of teachers, and the organization of instruction were positively and significantly related to student performance. On the other hand, decisions about determining the curriculum syllabus, textbook lists, and the size of the school budget were found to be best left with central authority. While teachers acting independently in making decisions at the school level had a positive effect, when they acted collectively through teacher unions, the effect on student performance was negative.

The extent to which institutional differences can account for the cross-country differences in student performance was assessed by estimating country-level production functions. Analysis at this level indicated that structural differences matter a lot in explaining cross-country differences in pupil performance, but resource inputs do not. Three indicators of structural features had strong and statistically significant effects on explaining differences in cross-country student performance. Increased school autonomy in supply choice and increased central scrutiny of performance assessments were associated with superior performance levels. Large influence by teachers unions on the education process was associated with inferior performance levels. Together, the three factors explained three-quarters of the cross-country variation in mathematics test scores and 60% of the variation of science scores.

Woessmann (2000) concluded, "For education policy, this means that the crucial question is not one of more resources but one of improving the institutional environment of education to ensure an efficient use of resources" (p. 79).

The specific institutional features identified by Woessmann's research that affect student performance favorably are the following:

- Central examinations
- Centralized control of curricular and budgetary matters
- School autonomy in process and personnel decisions
- An intermediate level of administration performing administrative tasks and educational funding
- Competition from private educational institutions
- Individual teachers having both incentives and powers to select appropriate teaching methods
- Limited influence of teacher unions
- Scrutiny of students' educational performance
- Encouragement of parents to take interest in teaching matters

Technical Efficiency. "Technical efficiency" is a term used by economists, not educators, but most of the evaluation studies done by educators are of this nature.

Technical efficiency is concerned with discovering the most favorable combination of inputs on outcomes (pupil performance). Unlike economic efficiency studies, however, the cost of inputs is not a consideration. In this section, we have grouped technical efficiency like studies into three categories for discussion purposes: effective schools research, evaluation studies, and whole-school reform models.

Effective Schools Research. Effective schools research constituted another reaction to the conclusions of the EEO study and other production function types of studies that schools had little impact on closing the gap between minority and majority pupils in academic achievement. While education production function research takes a normative approach in studying school efficiency, effective schools research focuses on exceptions to the norm. It consists largely of case studies of schools and classrooms that have unusually positive effects on pupil achievement in order to identify practices that might cause or contribute to that effectiveness (Brookover & Lezotte, 1979; Edmonds, 1979; Jackson, Logsdon, & Taylor, 1983; Reed, 1985; Sammons, 1999; Venezsky & Winfield, 1980; Weber, 1971). Effective schools research usually ignores cost considerations; thus, its findings relate more to technical efficiency than to economic efficiency and to the philosophy of the classroom culturalists.

Effective schools have been found to be characterized by effective classroom teaching practices that include high teacher expectations, good classroom management techniques, and greater time on task than one would find in most schools. These schools are also characterized by strong leadership, usually in the person of the principal, who provides for the coordination of the instructional program at the building level in a manner that is tightly coupled but not bureaucratic. The principal appears to be a key factor in establishing a common school culture and sense of community consisting of "shared goals; high expectations for student performance; mechanisms to sustain motivation and commitment; collegiality among teachers, students, and the principal; and a school-wide focus on continuous improvement" (Odden & Webb, 1983, p. xiv). Given current assumptions about schooling, effective schools research has identified some ways for

schools to make more efficient use of the resources they already have.

Monk (1989) referred to effective schools research as "backwards-looking." He called effective schools "sites of excellence ... making exemplary use of traditional, labor intensive instructional technologies" (p. 38). According to him, effective schools accept all the parameters of the present system, and the methodology condemns them only to refine the current system's very labor-intensive and expensive organization and practice rather than to permit them to break through into the discovery and use of new technologies.

Evaluation Studies. Evaluation studies of schooling also have important implications for technical efficiency of schools. For the most part, like effective schools research, evaluation studies do not take into account the price of inputs. Evaluation studies have produced results that provide a basis for greater optimism about the impact of schools on pupil achievement than those conducted by economists and sociologists. Some examples follow.

• **Class size reduction** An excellent example of evaluation research is the Tennessee Project Star study of the relationship between class size and pupil achievement (Finn & Achilles, 1999). The study was a controlled scientific experiment involving more than 6,000 students in 329 classrooms in 79 schools in 46 districts the first year and nearly 12,000 students during the 4-year intervention. Students entering kindergarten within each participating school were assigned randomly to a small class (13–17 students), a regular class (22–26 students), or a regular class with a full-time teacher aide. Children were kept in the same experimental arrangement for four years. All pupils returned to regular classes in grade 4, but the researchers were able to follow the participants in ensuing years. Teachers were assigned to classrooms at random. A new teacher was assigned each year. No interventions other than class size and teacher aide were used. Students took both norm- and criterion-referenced examinations at the end of each school year. Teachers and aides completed questionnaires and time logs to document their perceptions and experiences. The study design permitted analysis of effects on groups of students by race, gender, and SES.

On average, students in small classes displayed higher academic achievement than students in other arrangements. Small class size advantaged boys and girls alike, but the positive impact was substantially greater for minority students and students attending inner-city schools. The small class achievement advantage in all subjects carried forward to grade 4 and beyond after all students had returned to a regular classroom environment. No statistical differences were found for most teacher activities, subject emphasis, classroom atmosphere, or quality measures. This led the researchers to conclude that "small classes are academically superior not because they encourage new approaches to instruction but because teachers can engage in more (perhaps even *enough*) of the basic strategies they have been using all along" (p. 103). A study by Stasz and Stecher (2000) suggests what these strategies might be; while teaching practices in reduced- and nonreduced-size classes were quite similar, teachers in reduced-size classes spent more individual time with students identified as poor readers and more time discussing students' personal concerns; they spent less time on student discipline.

In all cases in the Tennessee study, students in small classes outperformed those in regular classes with teacher aides (Gerber, Finn, Achilles, & Boyd-Zaharias, 2001). The researchers concluded that "teacher aides do not offer the academic benefits of small classes and would not constitute an effective alternative" (p. 133).

Levin and McEwan (2001) attribute much of the recent support for small class size in the primary grades to the Tennessee study. At least 19 states have considered class size reduction plans, and federal resources have been made available as well. Levin, Glass, and Meister (1987) compared the cost-effectiveness of four educational reforms including class size reduction. They concluded that class size reduction was one of the more costly options for obtaining a fixed gain in student achievement. Peer tutoring was found to be among the most cost-effective in terms of achievement gain per unit of cost.

One of the states adopting a class reduction policy is California. Picus (2001) notes that this policy made a severe teacher shortage even worse and threatened to dilute the quality of teaching staffs, especially in schools serving the greatest numbers of at-risk children. He pointed out that research also indicates that attention to teacher training and expertise may have a bigger payoff per dollar spent than class size reduction. The National Commission on Teaching and America's Future (NCTAF, 1996) proposed new designs for organizing schools that would enable specialized teachers to be used in ways that would permit class size reduction without hiring more teachers.

• **Extended school year** A study conducted on a randomly selected panel of 790 children in the Baltimore Public Schools provides impressive evidence rationalizing preschool and summer school programs (Alexander, Entwisle, & Olson, 2001). The students, selected at random, began first grade in 1982 in 20 Baltimore schools, selected through a stratified random process. Six schools were predominantly African American in enrollment, six were predominantly white, and eight were integrated. Fourteen of the schools were classified as serving a working-class clientele and six serving middle-class communities. Testing was done in the fall and spring each year beginning with the fall of 1982 and continuing through the spring of 1987, covering five school years and four summers. The achievement data were obtained from school records, as were demographic information and family socioeconomic standing. The latter was supplemented by parent interviews. Data were analyzed using descriptive procedures and hierarchical linear modeling.

Alexander et al. (2001) found that school-year gains in achievement were about the same across SES levels. The summer pattern was quite different, however. Lower-SES children stayed at about the same level in reading ability over the summer but lost in quantitative ability. Upper-SES children showed substantial gains in both reading and quantitative abilities over the summer, placing them well ahead of their lower-SES peers when they returned to school in the fall. The researchers concluded that schools do matter and that they matter most when support for academic learning outside the school is weak. Disadvantaged children "are capable learners. They keep up during the school year, but before they start first grade and in summers between grades the out-of-school resources available to them are not sufficient to support their achievement" (p. 183). Based on their findings, the researchers recommend preschool and full-day kindergarten experiences for all low-SES children as well as summer school or extended-year programs (see also Lynch, 2007).

International studies involving students from nearly 50 countries support the case for more time in school. Time spent on instruction in mathematics and science was found to be strongly linked to achievement test scores in those subjects (Schmidt et al., 2001). David and Cuban (2006) concluded, however, that just adding hours to the day and days to the year will not improve academic achievement without also improving the quality of time spent in the classroom with better-prepared lessons and a more engaging curriculum.

• **Special Education** Reynolds and Wolfe (1999) studied the effect on children's achievement from placement in special education during the elementary grades. They also examined the effects of grade retention and mobility from school to school. The sample, representative of children at risk in Chicago who participate in government-funded early childhood programs, included 1,234 children who were in sixth grade in 1992 and involved in the Chicago Longitudinal Study (Reynolds, Bezruczko, Mavrogenes, & Hagemann, 1996). Performance was measured by scores on standardized achievement tests, taken by each child in each grade from kindergarten through grade 6. The data base included extensive information on the 25 schools in which the children were enrolled and limited information on the children's families. Children in special education programs were divided into two categories: those with learning disabilities and all others.

Data were analyzed using multiple regression analysis for each grade level with achievement test scores for either reading or mathematics serving as the dependent variable. The core independent variable of interest was participation in special education. Achievement test scores for the previous year were included as a pretest control variable. Other control variables were included for demographic and

background factors, school characteristics, and school experiences.

Reynolds and Wolfe (1999) concluded that "only in the earlier grades, and only for children with disabilities other than learning disabilities (such as hearing, sight, or physical handicaps) does the [special education] program seem to add in a significant way to achievement in reading and math" (p. 263). Children with learning disabilities assigned to special education programs actually did worse than would be expected based on their scores from the previous year. Except for kindergarten retention, suggesting that some children enter school too immature to advance immediately, children who were retained tended to do worse after repeating a grade. Children who moved from school to school showed reduced achievement, and in schools where there was extensive mobility, the achievement of all children was negatively impacted. In discussing their findings, Reynolds and Wolfe noted the $10,000 per pupil (or more) additional cost of special education programs and suggested that the money might better be spent making improvements in the schools generally or for early childhood interventions, peer tutoring, or cooperative learning. Alternatively, special education programs could be integrated with or used in combination with other educational and family services.

School Reform Networks. A number of organizational strategies intended to make schools more effective have been developed over the past decade and a half. Eight of these were developed through the initiative of New American Schools (NAS), a private, nonprofit organization formed in 1991 by a group of corporate executives at the urging of President George H. W. Bush, who challenged them "to harness the nation's special genius for invention to create the next generation of American schools" (NAS, 2000, p. 15). Toward that end, in 1992, NAS awarded start-up grants to 11 design teams selected from 686 proposals. The teams developed eight model school designs, "a plan for reorganizing an entire school around a common vision of higher student achievement, replacing the traditional approach of piecemeal programs" (p. 15).

The RAND Corporation served as a third-party evaluator of the process from the beginning. In tracking 163 schools implementing one of the NAS designs over a 5-year period, RAND evaluators found that only about half had shown greater improvement in student achievement than other students in their districts (Kirby, Berends, & Nartel, 2001). They observed that programs were adopted more fully in smaller schools and in elementary schools. Schools where teachers tended to blame students and their families for poor achievement were less likely to embrace the models fully. Having a stable team of consultants who could provide staff development for the entire faculty rather than for a selected few greatly enhanced the possibility of success. Finally, active support from the principal was essential, as was district-level support. As noted previously, an analysis by Odden and Picus (2000) showed that by reallocating resources already committed, the average elementary, middle, and high school in the United States has sufficient resources to finance all these school designs, even after providing for planning and preparation time.

Subsequently, NAS evolved from a developer and supporter of specific whole-school improvement models to one that promoted their wider and more effective use. Beginning on January 1, 2005, NAS became a subsidiary of American Institutes for Research (AIR) (Olson, 2004). AIR, founded in 1946, is an independent, nonprofit research organization in the behavioral and social sciences. This acquisition, along with a subsequent acquisition of the McKenzie Group consulting firm, marks an expansion of AIR's mission from research to include the area of research to practice. AIR's role expansion has been attributed to the national need of school districts for expertise in designing and implementing whole-school reforms and for assessing their progress as required by the No Child Left Behind Act (Viadero, 2004).

Fashola and Slavin (1998) pointed out that classroom-level change cannot be dictated from above; however, not every school must reinvent the wheel. School staffs and community representatives can select among a variety of existing well-designed methods and materials that have been shown to be effective with children. Schools subscribing to a given set of organizing principles have formed net-

works, usually under the direction of the model designer.

Fashola and Slavin (1998) point out the advantages to schools and school districts in adopting these "off-the-shelf" instructional models:

> Organizations behind each of the school-wide models provide professional development, materials, and networks of fellow users. These reform organizations bring to a school broad experience working with high-poverty schools in many contexts. Unlike district or state staff development offices, external reform networks are invited in only if they are felt to meet a need, and they can be invited back out again if they fail to deliver. Their services can be expensive, but the costs are typically within the Title I resources available to high-poverty school-wide projects. (p. 371)

These reform models took on new importance with Congress' reauthorization of Title I of the Elementary and Secondary Education Act (ESEA) in 1994. This reauthorization made it easier for high-poverty schools to be designated a school-wide Title I Project. This designation, which can be obtained by any school with at least fifty percent of its students in poverty, allows a school to use Title I funds for school-wide change, not just for changes that serve individual students having difficulties. The Comprehensive School Reform Demonstration Program (CSRD), enacted by Congress in 1997, authorized $150 million in federal grants to schools to undertake "whole school" reform; seventeen models were listed in the bill as examples of the types of reforms that could be considered for funding.

Fashola and Slavin (1997, 1998) evaluated 13 schoolwide models for elementary and middle schools that they considered to be "promising, ambitious, comprehensive, and widely available." Subsequently, the AIR (1999) released *An Educators' Guide to Schoolwide Reform* rating 24 designs of whole-school reform. The development of the guide was commissioned by the National Education Association, the American Association of School Administrators, the American Federation of Teachers, the American Association of Elementary School Principals, and the American Association of Secondary School

Principals. The guide was intended to provide reliable information to school officials as they sought proven solutions to low-performing schools. The guide rated the reform models according to whether they improved achievement in such measurable ways as higher test scores and attendance rates. It also evaluated the level of assistance provided by model developers to schools that implemented the models and compared first-year costs of the programs.

As a consequence of federal funding through the Comprehensive School Reform Demonstration Program, the U.S. Department of Education contracted with Northwest Regional Educational Laboratory (NWREL, 1998) to develop a *Catalog of School Reform Models*, first published in 1998. The catalog is carried online at http://www.nwrel.org/scpd/catalog and is updated regularly as models are added and removed based on NWREL's formal review process.

The 2007 edition contained detailed descriptions of 29 whole-school reform and reading reform models. Each entry analyzes the model's general approach, results with students, implementation assistance, and costs, among other elements. Demographic data and contact information are also provided. Among the criteria for selecting models for inclusion are evidence of improving student academic achievement, extent of replication, implementation assistance provided to schools, and comprehensiveness.

Studies of technical efficiency provide clear evidence that some educational practices are better than others. This provides great hope for improving effectiveness of schooling. But public policy should not be built on the findings of these studies alone because they do not take into account cost, that is, the price of inputs. Effective practices need to be costed out, and studies of alternative policy options are needed that compare their costs and effectiveness. The next section looks at economies of scale, which is an area where we find both policy mechanics and classroom culturalists busily at work. Clearly, "economies of scale" is a term with strong economic implications; however, the recent triumphs of the "small-is-beautiful" advocates is due largely to the research of the classroom culturalists.

ACTIVITY 12.4

Selecting a Whole-School Reform Model

Addresses ISLLC Standards and Functions 1B; 2; and 5A

Visit the *Catalog of School Reform Models* on the Web at
http://www.nwrel.org/scpd/catalog

Investigate several whole-school reform models and identify the strengths and weakness of each for a particular school with which you are familiar. Check the catalog's user guide and develop a plan for selecting a model to be used for reforming the school.

Economies and Diseconomies of Scale. If we assume a universal educational production function, economies of scale are realized when average production costs decline as more units are produced or serviced. Conversely, there are diseconomies of scale when average production costs increase as more units are produced or serviced. Traditionally, the cost curve of educational institutions has been assumed to be continually falling, supporting policies of district consolidation and large schools. Now there is strong evidence that the cost curve for schools (and school districts), like most other enterprises, declines to a point and then rises. Finding the point of inflection is now an important target of scale research in education. These are key concepts that need to be taken into account in designing efficient educational enterprises.

Policies concerning school district consolidation are directed toward realizing economies of scale, whereas policies decentralizing large-city school districts are directed toward avoiding diseconomies of scale. Likewise, during periods of declining enrollments, closing underutilized buildings is a strategy for minimizing operating costs. Reorganizing very large schools into "houses" or "schools within schools" is a strategy for realizing the benefits of both large and small units while minimizing their disadvantages. Interest in scale economies derives from concern over both internal and technical efficiency.

Policy implications drawn from studies of relationships between school and district size, pupil achievement, and cost have taken a dramatic turn in the past two decades. From the beginning of the 20th century through the 1960s, the overwhelming evidence seemed to support large schools and school districts in terms of lower costs and the higher number, diversity, and caliber of professional and administrative personnel that they could attract. These early studies were concerned primarily with inputs (costs) and gave little, if any, attention to outputs and ratios of outputs to inputs. As researchers began to take into account total cost and the SES of pupils and to include measures of output such as achievement, pupil self-image, and success in college, economies of scale evaporated at relatively low numbers of pupils. The disadvantages of large size became readily apparent. A review of the literature on the impact of size on school effectiveness (Raywid, 1999) found consistent evidence that students learn more and better in small schools than in large ones, that they are more satisfied and drop out less often, and that they behave better. This is particularly true for at-risk students. Raywid concluded that these things have been confirmed with a degree of clarity and confidence that is rare in education research.

The new emphasis in research on the relationships between size and quality of schooling may have been a by-product of the disenchantment with large-city schools. City educational systems had served through the 1950s as the standard for measuring the quality of educational opportunities toward which rural and suburban schools aspired. Beginning in the 1960s and continuing through the present, evidence of low cognitive pupil achievement, low attendance rates, and high dropout rates surfaced in urban school systems. This, coupled with their inability to use substantial federal and state funds to raise significantly the achievement levels of most disadvantaged children, severely marred their image as exemplary educational institutions.

It now appears that, given present assumptions about how schools (and school districts) should be organized, the relationships between size and quality of schooling are curvilinear. The benefits brought by larger enrollments increase to an optimal point and then decline following an inverted U-shaped curve (Engert, 1995; Fox, 1981; Riew, 1981, 1986). Ballou

(1998) concluded that the evidence strongly suggests that urban districts exceed the size to realize scale economies: "It would appear that scale economies at the district level are exhausted somewhere between the typical suburban size (about 5,000 students) and the average urban enrollment of 15,000" (pp. 69–70).

Scale research has two foci: the district and the school. For very small districts, these are the same thing. Large districts have choices, however, as they may operate schools over a wide range of sizes. Thus, a large district may operate small schools as a matter of district policy, though most do not. Large districts may also formulate most policy centrally, or they may empower schools to make policy within general parameters established at the center. Large schools can operate as a single unit or organize "schools within schools" to secure the advantages inherent in both large and small schools.

What size should a school be? Barker and Gump (1964) presented a contrarian view for that period. Although they were not specific, they provided a guide that remains helpful today as they concluded their classical work with these words:

> The data of this research and our own educational values tell us that a school should be sufficiently small that all of its students are needed for its enterprises. A school should be small enough that students are not redundant. (p. 202)

Barker and Gump (1964) found that large school size has an undesirable influence on the development of certain personal attributes of students. Specifically, they found that, in most large schools, just a few students dominate the leadership roles, whereas in small schools, proportionally more students take an active part in school programs. The actual proportion of students who participated in extracurricular activities and the satisfaction of students with their schooling clearly supported small local schools over large centralized ones.

Although more varieties of subjects are available to students in large schools, Barker and Gump (1964) observed that a given pupil participates in proportionally fewer of these electives than do students in small schools. They concluded that "if versatility of experience is preferred over opportunity for specialization, a smaller school is better than a larger one; if specialization is sought, the larger school is the better" (p. 201).

Nearly two generations after Barker and Gump's defense of small schools, New York City discovered their value for educationally at-risk children when combined with parental choice and community involvement. More than 30 small schools of choice were created in its Central Park East Project in East Harlem, one of the poorest sections of the city (Bensman, 2000; Fliegel & MacGuire, 1993; Meier, 1995a, 1995b, 1998). Rather than try to fit all students into a standard school, a variety of schools have been designed so that there is a school to fit every student. The concept is now being replicated throughout the city (Bradley, 1995).

Meier (1995b) stressed the importance of smallness for the success of the pedagogical innovations implemented in the schools she founded in Central Park East. She recommended a maximum size for elementary schools of 300 pupils and for high schools of 400. She contended that small and focused educational communities enhance the climate of trust between families and schools and facilitate deep ongoing discussions in ways that produce change and involve the entire faculty. Small schools enable the faculty to know students and their work individually, and they permit adults to play a significant role in the development of a positive school culture. Small schools more easily provide for the physical safety of all and are more readily made accountable to parents and to the public. (For specific descriptions of successful small schools and how they developed, see Toch [2003].)

Apparently, no cost disadvantage exists in regard to smaller schools. Stiefel, Berne, Iatarola, and Fruchter (2000) studied the effect of size of high school on cost per graduate in New York City. Their sample included 121 high schools ranging in size from 185 to 4,957. When viewed on a cost-per-student-enrolled basis, small academic high schools (fewer than 600 students) were somewhat more expensive, but when viewed according to the number of students they graduate, because of their lower dropout rates, small high schools were less expensive than medium-sized ones (600–2,000) and about the same as large high schools (more than 2,000).

Through her work in Philadelphia, Fine (1993) saw large schools as promoting a general rather than a particularistic perspective on students: "They encourage passivity rather than participation, and they stress, by definition, the need to control students rather than to engage them critically" (p. 273). To address the concerns of Philadelphia school officials over low student achievement and high dropout rates, the city followed a strategy similar to that being pursued in New York. Big secondary schools are being broken up into charter schools of 200 to 400 students with 10 to 12 core faculty working with students from ninth grade through graduation. This restructuring aims to care for the emotional and social needs and wants of students and to engage the intellects and passions of educators and scholars. According to Fine, accomplishing these goals is much more difficult in large settings.

Research in Chicago also supports the value of small schools in the inner-city environment. Lee and Loeb (2000) studied 264 schools with a K–8 grade configuration. The schools ranged in size from 150 to nearly 2,000 students. They concluded that school size influences student achievement directly and indirectly through its effect on teacher attitudes. They found that teachers in smaller schools assumed more responsibility for student learning than did teachers in middle-sized and large schools. This resulted in more intimate and personal social relations among teachers and students. This atmosphere facilitated a wholesome learning environment and led to higher student achievement.

Citing supporting research, Darling-Hammond (1996) identified small size as one of the important characteristics of high-performing schools. All else being equal, small schools in the range of 300 to 500 students are associated with higher achievement, better attendance rates, fewer dropouts, and lower levels of misbehavior. Because they are less fragmented, are more personalized, and facilitate frequent and purposeful interaction among and between students and staff, "they are more effective in allowing students to become bonded to important adults in a learning community that can play the roles that families and communities find harder and harder to play" (p. 148).

A number of other studies have produced recommendations of optimal size. Chicago's Cross City

Campaign for Urban School Reform set the limits at 350 students for elementary schools and 500 students for high schools (Fine & Somerville, 1998). Williams (1990) recommended up to 800 students for high schools. Lee and Smith (1997) found the optimal range for high schools to be 600 to 900 students. Raywid (1999) concluded that studies emphasizing the importance of the school as a community tend to set lower limits than studies emphasizing academic effectiveness as measured by test scores. Nevertheless, most schools in urban and suburban areas (and even some rural schools) are larger than that supported by research conducted in the past 15 years.

Economist Ronald Coase (1988) developed a theory of "transaction costs" to explain such phenomena in organizations in general for which he received the Nobel Prize in economics in 1991. Transaction costs are costs of communication, coordination, and deciding. Eventually, expansion of an organization (e.g., school or district) can lead to diseconomies and higher unit costs because of managerial problems that are characteristic of large operations. Conventional estimates of economies of scale have vastly underestimated transactional costs.

Tainter (1988), an archaeologist, came to similar conclusions. He observed that sociopolitical organizations constantly encounter problems that require increased investment merely to preserve the status quo. This investment comes in such forms as increasing size of bureaucracies, increasing specialization of bureaucracies, cumulative organizational solutions, increasing costs of legitimizing activities, and increasing costs of internal control and external defense. The reason why complex organizations must allocate ever-larger portions of their personnel and other resources to administration is because increased complexity requires greater quantities of information processing and greater integration of disparate parts. All these increased costs are borne by the support population, often to no increased advantage. Educational organizations pose no exception; as complexity and specialization increase, so does the cost of education, while its marginal product declines.

For more than a decade, the Gates Foundation (n.d.) has invested many millions of dollars in the development of small high schools, especially in urban areas, as they strive toward the goal of enabling all students in the United States to graduate from high school with the skills necessary for college, work, and citizenship (http://www.gatesfoundation.org/UnitedStates/Education/TransformingHighSchools/default.htm). In their report *High Schools for the New Millennium: Imagine the Possibilities*, the foundation builds a case for small high schools:

> Smaller school size—generally no more than 400 students—can help to counteract many of the problems plaguing high schools today such as overburdened teachers who barely know the names of their students; low expectations for all except the highest performing students; inadequate support for students needing extra assistance completing their course work or planning for college; and curricula that fail to engage students in their own learning. Small schools are no panacea, but, done well, they offer environments that can make teaching and learning rewarding and successful.
>
> Strong small schools offer another benefit. Since several small schools replace one large comprehensive high school, students have a choice of schools that best meet their needs and interests. Aside from increasing the satisfaction of students and their families, choice provides a check on school quality. Few students will choose a school that offers a disruptive learning environment or an undesirable curriculum.
>
> Intuitively, it makes sense that smaller, more personalized schools are better positioned to serve students, and recent research confirms it. Small schools have been shown to increase graduation and college-going rates, improve attendance, bolster teacher morale and effectiveness, and reduce incidents of violence. Moreover, although small schools *may* be slightly more expensive on a *per-student* basis, new research suggests that they are actually more cost effective than large schools on a *per-graduate* basis, since they graduate significantly larger percentages of students. (pp. 6–7)

As with other organizations, large school districts and schools have experienced the dysfunctional forces of bureaucratization. But through restructuring, public school organizations appear to be able to at least partially compensate for these natural tendencies through practices such as those being tried in New York City, Philadelphia, and Chicago, among other places. In the past, providing

ACTIVITY 12.5
Small Is Beautiful

Addresses ISLLC Standards and Functions 2A, 2B, 2C; 3A, and 3B

Visit a large school and a small school serving the same grade levels and seek answers to the questions that follow. Alternatively, form a study group made up of persons with experience in different-size schools and compare those experiences as you discuss these questions.

1. Do you find any differences between schools that can be attributed to their variation in size?
2. What are the advantages and disadvantages of large schools? Of small schools?
3. What strategies might best neutralize the negative effects of school size for large schools? For small schools?

diversity in curriculum and support services at an affordable cost were the primary justifications for large urban schools and rural school consolidation. Now the disadvantages of bigness and the virtues of smallness have been well documented. Additionally, technological advances characteristic of the information age have made it possible for any individual in almost any place to access easily curricular diversity (see chapter 9). These developments combine to compel a reassessment of the large-school policies of central cities and state-school consolidation policies for rural areas. While there are disadvantages in being very small and in being very large, there is little agreement on optimal size. The challenge before us is to provide stimulating learning environments with broad educational programs characteristic of large schools along with the supportive social structure characteristic of small schools within the oversight of a responsive, coordinating centralized framework.

Aligning Economic and Technical Efficiency.

The analyses of economic and technical efficiency have presented us with conflicting results. Findings of economic efficiency studies suggest that schools

are using the resources allocated to them inefficiently and that there are, at best, tenuous links between financial inputs and student outcomes. Analyses of the technical efficiency of programs and even whole-school reform and small-school models, however, show that some approaches work much better than others and that students can experience significant educational gains from some program innovations. The disparity in findings of these two orientations suggests at least two possible explanations. Schools, in general, are not using what has been shown to be best practice. Or, since evaluation studies of technical efficiency do not consider the *cost* of resources as do studies of economic efficiency, the problem may lie with the pricing and distribution of resources commonly used in the instructional process. Both explanations are probably correct, but in this section we focus on the latter, paying for and distributing professional staff, since they represent over half of all school expenditures.

Current Practice. Teachers, with few exceptions, are paid according to a single salary schedule that has two dimensions: length of service and amount of formal education beyond the bachelor's degree. Thus, a teacher with 20 years of experience and 30 graduate credit hours beyond the master's degree is likely to earn about twice as much as a beginning teacher with a bachelor's degree. Yet research, some of which was cited previously on production functions, has shown that there is little evidence of any relationship between the number of graduate hours a teacher has accumulated and student achievement. Further, length of teaching service has been found to be generally unrelated to academic achievement of most students after the first 3 to 5 years, yet it is common practice for school districts to provide salary increments for length of service up to 15 years—and sometimes more. Some evidence exists, however, that experienced teachers are more effective in working with educationally at-risk children but not with advantaged children.

In assigning teaching duties, school districts recognize the weak relationships between student performance and teacher education level and longevity in that beginning teachers with a bachelor's degree are assigned nearly identical responsibilities as those assigned to teachers with long tenure and much graduate education. Thus, one first-grade teacher may be earning $30,000 per year, while the first-grade teacher in the adjoining classroom may be earning $60,000, even though their responsibilities are nearly identical. To make matters even more bizarre, it is not unusual for teachers to have gained the right through collective bargaining to transfer to open teaching positions on the basis of their seniority in service. This frequently results in the schools with the best working conditions (i.e., schools enrolling high-achieving and well-disciplined children) having the most senior and expensive staffs, while the schools with large portions of children "at risk" educationally have the least experienced and least expensive teachers. In effect, because of the higher salaries paid to teachers in the more attractive schools, proportionally more economic resources are placed in those schools than in schools with greater need, although physical resources (e.g., the numbers of teachers) in each school may be the same (Guthrie, 1997). Illustrations of this phenomenon were given in the earlier discussion of intradistrict equity for New York City, Chicago, and Dade County, Florida.

Another practice that contributes to the disparity in results between analyses of economic and technical efficiency is the growing use of specialists and support staff. While some research has indicated the importance of small class size and the continuity of relationship between teacher and student, school districts have added relatively fewer regular classroom teachers than they have professional specialists who supervise and consult with classroom teachers and operate "pullout" programs. This practice has been shown to weaken the relationships and influence of classroom teachers on their students while adding greatly to the cost of public schooling and doing little to enhance student achievement.

From 1980 to 2004, the number of pupils per classroom teacher dropped from 18.7 to 15.8 (down 16%). Over the same period, the number of pupils per certified instructional aides (not including librarians and guidance counselors) dropped from 125.5 to 69.0 (down 45%). The statistics clearly indicate that the professional specialist is increasing at a much faster rate than the classroom teacher (NCES, 2006).

Looking at the trends from a different perspective, the NCTAF (1996) reported that the proportion of professional staff classified as teachers declined from more than 70% in 1950 to 52% in 1993. Of the 52%, more than 10% were specialists not engaged in classroom teaching. For every four classroom teachers, there are nearly six other school employees. By contrast, the NCTAF reports that in other developed countries, teaching staffs represent from 60% to 80% of public education employees. One of the contributing factors influencing school districts to add specialists and support staff to their rosters is state and federal categorical aid program requirements and other mandates that only recently are being relaxed to allow greater discretion at the local level. The NCTAF has soundly criticized the resulting bureaucracy:

> Far too many people sit in offices at the sidelines of the core work, managing routines rather than promoting innovation aimed at improving quality. A bureaucratic school spends substantial resources on controlling its staff; a thoughtful school invests in knowledge and supports that liberate staff members to do their jobs well. A traditional school administers rules and procedures; a learning organization develops shared goals and talents. Our inherited school anticipates the worst from students and teachers; the school of the future expects and enables the best. (p. 101)

The NCTAF has expressed well the case for "whole-school" and, indeed, systemic reform.

Rethinking the Allocation of Teacher Resources. This situation has led a number of analysts to call for a reallocation of teaching resources. Miles and Darling-Hammond (1998) have observed six strategies of resource reallocation used by high-performing schools to improve achievement within general constraints of existing resources: reduction of specialized programs, more flexible student grouping by school-level professionals, structures that create more personalized environments, longer and varied blocks of instructional time, more common planning time for staff, and creative definition of staff roles and work schedules.

The NCTAF (1996) has developed a five-pronged strategy for ensuring that all school communities have teachers with the knowledge and skills they need so that all children can learn and that all school systems are organized to support teachers in this work. Two are particularly relevant to the concerns of this section: encourage and reward teacher knowledge and skill and create schools that are organized for student and teacher success.

Figure 12.1 illustrates how a typical elementary school of 600 pupils can be reorganized following the NCTAF's guidelines. The plan reduces average class sizes from 25 students to 16 or 17 and increases teachers' planning time from less than 4 hours per week to at least 10 hours. *All of this is accomplished using only the personnel normally assigned to such a school.* They do this by creating teams of teachers who share students. Almost all adults in these teaching teams are engaged in a way where they can share expertise directly with one another, reducing pullouts and nonteaching jobs requiring educator certification. "The school's resources are pushed into the core classroom structure where they can be used in the context of extended relationships with students rather than sitting around the periphery of the school to be applied in brief encounters with students or in coordinative rather than teaching roles" (NCTAF, 1996, p. 105).

The school is divided into two divisions: one for primary grades and one for intermediate grades. Each division has three instructional teams consisting of seven teachers, including one with counseling expertise, one with special education expertise, and one with arts expertise. Each team serves 100 students representative of all ages within a given division, permitting the team and students to remain together for at least a 3-year period (Osin & Lesgold, 1996; Veenman, 1995). The teams in each division share a media/computer specialist and a lead teacher who is released from teaching half time to facilitate planning and to cover classes while other teachers visit and observe one another. Support staff for the school consist of a principal, a secretary/bookkeeper, and a social worker. The

NCTAF also urges that the investment in teachers be accompanied with investments in technology that extends the capacity of every teacher and child to connect with an infinite variety of resources and tools for learning. (See related discussion in chapter 9.) The NCTAF proposes that principals come from the ranks of highly skilled teachers and that they continue to have some teaching responsibilities.

Odden (1996) notes that compensation theory counsels policymakers on the importance of matching pay practices to the strategic needs of organizations. The NCTAF does this through linking teacher salaries to a progressive demonstration of growing knowledge and skills that mark a career continuum. They start with the presumption that teachers will be hired only after completing a high-quality preparation program accredited by the National Council for Accreditation of Teacher Education (http://www.ncate.org)and passing tests of subject matter knowledge and teaching knowledge to receive an initial license.

Once hired, it is proposed that a new teacher go through a 1- or 2-year induction period during which the teacher receives mentoring and will be closely evaluated. After passing an assessment of teaching skills, recognition of *professional teacher* status is granted along with a substantial salary increment.

The NCTAF recommends that teachers should be encouraged through additional salary increments to become certified in more than one subject area. This would acknowledge the value to the school of being able to teach expertly in two or more subject areas or of bringing counseling or special education expertise to a teaching team. Having teachers certified in more than one area provides schools greater flexibility in organizing instructional teams.

For experienced teachers to gain the highest level of recognition, advanced certification from the National Board for Professional Teaching Standards (http://www.nbpts.org) would be recognized through additional salary increments. National Board certification would also be a prerequisite for qualification as lead teacher and principal.

There are numerous barriers to implementing reallocation of resources as proposed by the NCTAF and others. Most teacher–district labor agreements would have to be changed with respect to definitions

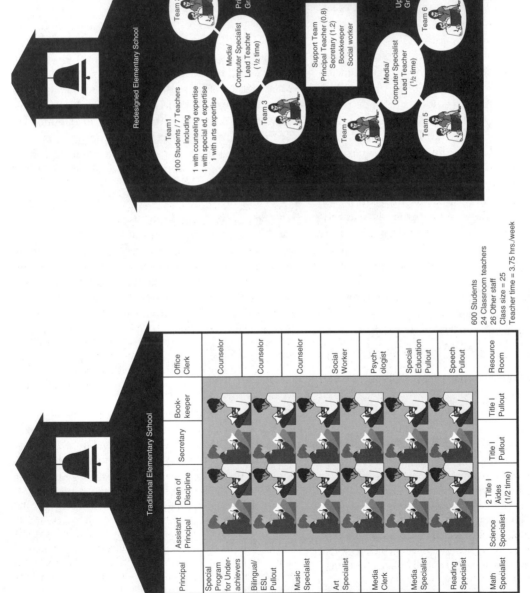

FIGURE 12.1

Traditional and redesigned elementary schools as developed by the National Commission on Teaching and America's Future

Source: National Commission on Teaching and America's Future. (1996). *What matters most: Teaching for America's future.* (p. 106) New York: NCTAF, 1996.

ACTIVITY 12.6

Paying Teachers

Addresses ISLLC Standards and Functions 2H; 3B; 5C; and 6B

This chapter challenges the efficacy of the single salary schedule by which most teachers are paid (i.e., salary being determined by education level and years of teaching experience) and seniority provisions in many teachers union contracts. Devise another remuneration policy for teachers that would link salary to responsibilities, teacher effectiveness, and market forces and that would ensure that the best-qualified teachers were available to the students in greatest academic need of them.

of teacher workday and seniority transfers. Some state and federal policies might need to be relaxed to enable breaking down barriers between programs, subjects, and age groupings. Teacher, parent, and student attitudes and expectations might also have to change (Miles, 1995; Miles and Darling-Hammond, 1998). Tradition dies hard, and it has many allies.

ACTIVITY 12.7

Making Schools Efficient in Terms of Student Learning and Teaching

Addresses ISLLC Standards and Functions 2H, 2I; 3A, and 3B

In this chapter, the authors conclude, along with many other analysts, that the United States is already devoting an adequate proportion of its resources to formal education and that any improvements in education will have to come from using those resources more wisely (i.e., more efficiently). Using the information provided in the section on internal efficiency, devise a configuration or configurations for using public school resources that are likely to achieve better results for students with economic resources already available than configurations typically employed at the present time.

SUMMARY AND FUNDAMENTAL CONCEPTS

In this chapter, we have looked at evidence concerning the equity and efficiency of elementary and secondary schools.

Equity and Adequacy

Equality was one of the fundamental principles on which Horace Mann's Common School was built, the guiding force in the spread of public schooling during the 19th century. Early in the 20th century, it was recognized that equal mediocrity was inadequate for providing the results (albeit not clearly defined) the nation desired from its public schools. Equity had to be provided at a level of resource allocation sufficient to enable public schools to produce the results the public expected of them. This resulted in states assuming a greater share of the financial burden for providing public elementary and secondary schools.

During the last two decades of the 20th century, a distinction was drawn between horizontal equity and vertical equity and it was only during the last decade of that century that any serious attempt was made to define the level of resources required to provide vertical equity. The results of these studies suggested that additional funds would be needed, especially in large urban school districts. At the same time, evidence mounted that resources entrusted to public schools were not being used effectively and efficiently. This circumstance led some analysts and policymakers to wonder if early vertical equity studies did not overstate the magnitude of the resource shortage because they did not treat the efficiency issue. Not all public schools are failing, however; indeed, most are not, and the level of support of schools that are succeeding is not too different from those that are failing—with many of the failing schools having access to more resources than the successful ones.

General agreement exists that the primary challenge to schools is closing the achievement gap between children from comfortable backgrounds and poor and non–English-speaking children. General agreement also exists, as shown by the billions of dollars allocated annually to disadvantaged children through categorical aids, that closing achievement gaps will cost more than to educate advantaged children. But how much more money is required? Given the current organization of urban schools and school districts, can society entrust to them significant new levels of resources in confidence that they will be used effectively and efficiently to produce the results desired?

Efficiency

Turning from equity considerations to efficiency, we concluded that, as a nation, the United States is spending more per pupil than are most other advanced nations. Most other nations, however, finance and administer their educational systems at the national level, and the resources committed are more evenly distributed throughout the school population than in the United States, where 50 states and thousands of school districts are involved. Strong evidence exists that the internal distribution of these resources to school districts and to schools within districts is seriously flawed.

Elmore (1994) argued that educators and those who influence them must think differently about resources and how they are applied to student learning:

> So at the core of the problem of adequacy, I would argue, is a problem of productivity and incentives. And behind the problem of productivity and incentives is a problem of knowledge and practice. There is virtually nothing in the background and preparation of educators that prepares them to confront the difficult and messy problems involved with using existing resources, or new resources, to cause dramatic shifts in student performance. Furthermore, there are many factors in the environment of schools that encourages educators not to think systematically about resources: categorical policies that "solve" the resource allocation problem for schools by mandating staffing patterns and ratios; collective bargaining contracts that set limits on the ability of schools to use resources flexibly; line-item budgeting practices; and the like. Most of the factors that limit the capacity of educators to pay attention to resource and output problems are either deeply ingrained in their background and prior experience or hard-wired in the organizational and policy context in which they work. (p. 457)

A most significant and consistent finding of the production function studies, beginning with the EEO study, is the very strong relationship between family background and pupil achievement. The relationship is so strong that findings of these studies have frequently been misinterpreted to mean that schools have relatively little impact on pupil achievement. It is well documented that schools have not been very effective in closing achievement gaps among racial and ethnic groups and among socioeconomic classes. Nevertheless, schools do have enormous impacts on the intellectual development of all children.

Even the most gifted of children learn—or at least develop—their basic academic skills in schools. Most children come into schools as nonreaders and leave with vary- ing levels of literacy skills. Similar statements could be made about mathematics, writing, and other academic skills as well as about knowledge and attitudinal development. Mayeski et al. (1972) stated it very well in a reanalysis of the EEO data: "Schools are indeed important. It is equally clear, however, that their influence is bound up with that of the student's background" (p. ix). Very little of the influence of schools can be separated from the social backgrounds of their students, and very little of the influence of social background on learning can be separated from the influence of the schools.

We are growing in our understanding of the relationships between educational inputs and outputs, but the causal relationships between school inputs and processes on pupil achievement remain largely unknown. This high degree of ignorance has serious policy implications for deploying strategies to improve student equity, and it places in serious question the efficacy of strategies, such as the never-implemented provision in the 1994 Educate America Act encouraging states to develop "opportunity- to-learn" standards. At this point, the posture of the classroom culturalists looks quite wise—focusing on the normative socialization that occurs within classrooms. Sufficient knowledge does not exist to specify a one best way for the organization, management, and operation of schools from the center, be it the state or the federal government.

Some production function studies, evaluation and scale studies, whole-school reform networks, and effective schools research have identified instructional and organizational interventions that do affect student achievement in cost-effective ways. Most if not all of these interventions require few new resources, but they do require a redirection of existing resources. We presented in some detail the recommendations of the NCTAF for restructuring the use of personnel in schools and their compensation as an example of the radical changes required to make schooling more effective and more efficient.

We do not know much about how to close the achievement gaps between children of varying ethnic and socioeconomic groups, but much of what we do know we are not using. The barriers to fundamental school reform relate more to politics and changing school structures and cultures than to economics. Political, structural, and sociological barriers are far more difficult to overcome than economic barriers. The nature of the task of educational reform must not be misdiagnosed, and the difficulty in bringing it about must not be underestimated. In the next chapter we direct attention to overcoming the political,

ACTIVITY 12.8

Who Should Lead School Reform Endeavors?

Addresses ISLLC Standards and Functions 1C; 2B; 3B, 3E; and 6

In this chapter, the authors concluded that the barriers to fundamental school reform are more closely related to politics and changing school structures and cultures than they are to economics. This thought was also reflected in Elmore's (1994) comments quoted in the "Efficiency" section. Elmore expresses doubt about professional educators' ablility of designing new methods of delivering instruction that would result in dramatic positive shifts in student performance in a cost-effective manner. He points out that the schooling bureaucracy is hamstrung with organizational limitations that make fundamental reform unlikely. These limiting factors include mandated staffing patterns and ratios, collective bargaining contracts that limit flexibility in the use of resources, incremental budgeting, and so on.

1. Do you agree with the authors' and Elmore's observations? Why or why not?
2. If education professionals are incapable of reforming the schools, then who are? What would be the role of professional educators in reform if they were not to lead it?

structural, and sociological barriers to meaningful educational reform. The focus is on resolving conflicts between change and tradition, self-fulfillment and participation, and decentralization and integration.

Fundamental Concepts

The fundamental concepts that follow have been discussed in this chapter. The citations that conclude each concept indicate the Interstate School Leaders Licensure Consortium (ISLLC) standards and functions related to the concept. The Arabic numeral refers to the ISLLC standard, and the letter refers to the function as presented in the table found inside the front cover.

- Decentralized systems are more adept than highly centralized and bureaucratic ones at mobilizing the energies of their constituents and adapting curricula and instructional systems to the diversity of their constituents, yet they have a tendency to become inequitable, providing an uneven quality of services, especially when they are also responsible for providing a significant amount of their financial support. (1D; 2B; 3B; 5A, 5C, 5E; 6)
- Equity is defined as the state, ideal, or quality of being just, impartial, and fair. (5; 6)
- Horizontal equity refers to the equal treatment of equals, the traditional meaning of equality; vertical equity refers to the appropriate unequal treatment of "unequals," the traditional meaning of equity. (5; 6)
- Apart from the common focus by states on equalizing spending per pupil, a serious equalization policy should also equalize the most important of all schooling inputs: teacher quality. (1C, 1D; 2; 3B,3D, 3E; 5A)
- Adequacy is the cost of an instructional program that produces the range of results desired. (5; 6)
- Efficiency, the ratio of outputs to inputs, is improved by increasing desired outputs produced from available resources or by maintaining a given level of output while using fewer resource inputs. (5; 6)
- When confronted with evidence of failing schools, it is unusual for educators to look at their own behaviors and decisions as possible causes; rather, they are likely to respond that they have not been given sufficient resources to do an adequate job. (1C, 1D; 2; 3; 5; 6)
- Schooling cannot be truly equitable without also being efficient. (1C, 1D; 2; 3; 5; 6)
- Relationships between inputs and student achievement are not robust across the board, but certain kinds of targeted expenditures can raise achievement, particularly for disadvantaged students; however, additional resources above current levels may not matter much for more advantaged students. (1C, 1D; 2; 3; 5; 6)
- The crucial question is not one of more resources but one of improving the institutional environment of education to ensure an efficient use of resources. (1C, 1D; 2; 3; 5; 6)
- Strong evidence exists that the cost curve for schools (and school districts), like most other enterprises, declines to a point and then rises; finding the point of inflection is now an important target of scale research in education. (1C, 1D; 2; 3; 5; 6)

- As with other organizations, large school districts and schools have experienced the dysfunctional forces of bureaucratization, but through restructuring, public school organizations appear to be able to at least partially compensate for these natural tendencies. (1C, 1D; 2; 3; 5; 6)
- Adequacy is the ultimate definition of vertical equity; in defining adequacy, however, we must be careful not to reward inefficiency. (1C, 1D; 2; 3; 5; 6)

REFERENCES

Alexander, K. L., Entwisle, D. R., & Olson, L. S. (2001). Schools, achievement, and inequality: A seasonal perspective. *Educational Evaluation and Policy Analysis, 23,* 171–191.

American Institutes for Research. (1999). *An educator's guide to schoolwide reform.* Arlington, VA: Educational Research Service.

Augenblick, J. (1997). *Recommendations for a base figure and pupil-weighted adjustments to the base figure for use in a new school finance system in Ohio.* Columbus: School Funding Task Force, Ohio Department of Education.

Ballou, D. (1998). The condition of urban school finance: Efficient research allocation in urban schools. In W. J. Fowler Jr. (Ed.), *Selected papers in school finance, 1996* (NCES 98-217) (pp. 65–83). Washington, DC: U.S. Department of Education, National Center for Education Statistics.

Barker, R. G., & Gump, P. V. (1964). *Big school, small school.* Stanford, CA: Stanford University Press.

Bensman, D. (2000). *Central Park East and its graduates: "Learning by heart."* New York: Teachers College Press.

Berne, R., & Stiefel, L. (1984). *The measurement of equity in school finance: Conceptual, methodological, and empirical dimensions.* Baltimore, MD: Johns Hopkins University Press.

Berne, R., & Stiefel, L. (1994). Measuring equity at the school level: The finance perspective. *Educational Evaluation and Policy Analysis, 16,* 405–421.

Bradley, A. (1995). Thinking small. *Education Week, 14,* 37–41.

Brookover, W., & Lezotte, L. (1979). *Changes in school characteristics coincident with changes in student achievement.* East Lansing: Michigan State University, College of Urban Development.

Burkhead, J. (1967). *Input and output in large-city high schools.* Syracuse, NY: Syracuse University Press.

Clune, W. H. (1995). Accelerated education as a remedy for high-poverty schools. *University of Michigan Journal of Law Reform, 28,* 655–680.

Coase, R. H. (1988). *The firm, the market, and the law.* Chicago: University of Chicago Press.

Coleman, J. S. (1966). *Equality of educational opportunity.* Washington, DC: U.S. Government Printing Office.

Consortium on Renewing Education. (1998). *20/20 vision: A strategy for doubling America's academic achievement by the year 2020.* Nashville, TN: Peabody Center for Education Policy, Vanderbilt University.

Darling-Hammond, L. (1996). Restructuring schools for high performance. In S. H. Fuhrman & J. A. O'Day (Eds.), *Rewards and reform: Creating educational incentives that work* (pp. 144–192). San Francisco: Jossey-Bass.

David, J., & Cuban, L. (2006). *Cutting through the hype: A taxpayer's guide to school reforms.* Mount Morris, IL: Education Week Press.

Duncombe, W., Ruggiero, J., & Yinger, J. (1996). Alternative approaches to measuring the cost of education. In H. F. Ladd (Ed.), *Holding schools accountable: Performance-based reform in education* (pp. 327–356). Washington, DC: Brookings Institution.

Duncombe, W. D., & Yinger, J. M. (1997). Why is it so hard to help central city schools? *Journal of Policy Analysis and Management, 16,* 85–113.

Duncombe, W. D., & Yinger, J. M. (1999). Performance standards and educational cost indexes: You can't have one without the other. In H. F. Ladd, R. Chalk, & J. S. Hansen (Eds.), *Equity and adequacy in education finance: Issues and perspectives* (pp. 260–297). Washington, DC: National Academies Press.

Edmonds, R. (1979). Effective schools for the urban poor. *Educational Leadership, 37,* 15–24.

Elmore, R. F. (1994). Thoughts on program equity: Productivity and incentives for performance in education. *Educational Policy, 8,* 453–459.

Engert, F. (1995). *Efficiency analysis of school districts using multiple inputs and outputs: An application of data envelopment analysis.* Unpublished doctoral dissertation, State University of New York at Buffalo.

Fashola, O. S., & Slavin, R. F. (1997). Promising programs for elementary and middle schools: Evidence of effectiveness and replicability. *Journal of Education for Students Placed at Risk, 2,* 251–307.

Fashola, O. S., & Slavin, R. F. (1998). Schoolwide reform models: What works? *Phi Delta Kappan, 79,* 370–379.

Ferguson, R. F. (1991). Paying for public education: New evidence on how and why money matters. *Harvard Journal on Legislation, 28,* 465–498.

Ferguson, R. F., & Ladd, H. F. (1996). How and why money matters: An analysis of Alabama schools. In H. F. Ladd (Ed.), *Holding schools accountable: Performance-based reform in education* (pp. 265–298). Washington, DC: Brookings Institution.

Fine, M. (1993). Democratizing choice: Reinventing, not retreating from, public education. In E. Rasell & R. Rothstein (Eds.), *School choice: Examining the evidence* (pp. 269–300). Washington, DC: Economic Policy Institute.

Fine, M., & Somerville, J. I. (1998). *Small schools, big imaginations: A creative look at urban public schools*. Chicago: Cross City Campaign for Urban School Reform.

Finn, J. D., & Achilles, C. M. (1999). Tennessee's class size study: Findings, implications, misconceptions. *Education Evaluation and Policy Analysis, 21*, 97–110.

Fliegel, S., & MacGuire, J. (1993). *Miracle in East Harlem: The fight for choice in public education*. New York: Random House.

Fox, W. F. (1981). Reviewing economies of size in education. *Journal of Education Finance, 6*, 273–296.

Fuller, B., & Clarke, P. (1994). Raising school effects while ignoring culture? Local conditions and the influence of classroom tools, rules, and pedagogy. *Review of Educational Research, 64*, 119–157.

Gates Foundation. (n.d.). *High schools for the new millennium: Imagine the possibilities*. Seattle: Author.

Gerber, S. B., Finn, J. D., Achilles, C. M., & Boyd-Zaharias, J. (2001). Teacher aides and students' academic achievement. *Educational Evaluation and Policy Analysis, 23*, 123–143.

Goertz, M., & Edwards, M. (1999). The search for excellence for all: the courts and New Jersey school finance reform. *Journal of Education Finance, 25*, 5–31.

Guthrie, J. W. (1997). School finance: Fifty years of expansion. *The Future of Children, 7*, 24–38.

Guthrie, J. W., & Rothstein, R. (2001). A new millennium and a likely new era of education finance. In S. Chaikind & W. J. Fowler Jr. (Eds.). *Education finance in the new millennium* (pp. 99–119), Larchmont, NY: Eye on Education.

Hanushek, E. A. (1987). Education production functions. In G. Psacharopoulos (Ed.), *Economics of education: Research and studies* (pp. 33–42). Oxford: Pergamon Press.

Hanushek, E. A. (1996). Outcomes, costs, and incentives in schools. In E. A. Hanushek & D. W. Jorgenson (Eds.), *Improving America's schools: The role of incentives* (pp. 29–52). Washington, DC: National Academies Press.

Hanushek, E. A., Kain, J. F., & Rivkin, S. G. (1998). *Teachers, schools, and academic achievement* (Working Paper 6691). Cambridge, MA: National Bureau of Economic Research.

Hertert, L. (1996). Does equal funding for districts mean equal funding for classroom students? Evidence from California. In L. O. Picus & J. L. Wattenbarger (Eds.), *Where does the money go? Resource allocation in elementary and secondary schools* (pp. 71–84). Thousand Oaks, CA: Corwin Press.

Jackson, S., Logsdon, D., & Taylor, N. (1983). Instructional leadership behaviors: Differentiating effective from ineffective low-income urban schools. *Urban Education, 18*, 59–70.

King, J. A. (1994). Meeting the educational needs of at-risk students: A cost analysis of three models. *Educational Evaluation and Policy Analysis, 16*, 1–19.

Kirby, S. N., Berends, M., & Nartel, S. (2001). *Implementation in a longitudinal sample of New American schools: Four years into scale-up*. Santa Monica, CA: RAND.

Ladd, H. F., & Hansen, J. S. (Eds.). (1999). *Making money matter: Financing Americas schools*. Washington, DC: National Academies Press.

Lake, P. (1983). Expenditure equity in the public schools of Atlantic Canada. *Journal of Education Finance, 8*, 449–460.

Lee, V. E., & Loeb, S. (2000). School size in Chicago elementary schools: Effects on teachers' attitudes and students' achievement. *American Educational Research Journal, 37*, 3–31.

Lee, V. E., & Smith, J. B. (1997). High school size: Which works best, and for whom? *Educational Evaluation and Policy Analysis, 19*, 205–227.

Levin, H. M., Glass, G. V., & Meister, G. R. (1987). Cost effectiveness of computer-assisted instruction. *Evaluation Review, 11*, 50–72.

Levin, H. M., & McEwan, P. J. (2001). *Cost-effectiveness analysis* (2nd ed.). Thousand Oaks, CA: Sage.

Lynch, R. G. (2007). *Enriching children, enriching the nation: Public investment in high-quality prekindergarten*. Washington, DC: Economic Policy Institute.

Mayeski, G. W., Wisler, C. E., Beaton, A. E., Jr.,Weinfeld, F. D., Cohen, W. M., Okada, T., et al. (1972). *A study of our nation's schools*. Washington, DC: U.S. Government Printing Office.

Meier, D. (1995a). How our schools could be. *Phi Delta Kappan, 76*, 369–373.

Meier, D. (1995b). *The power of their ideas: Lessons for America from a small school in Harlem*. Boston: Beacon Press.

Meier, D. H. (1998). Can the odds be changed? *Phi Delta Kappan, 79*, 358–362.

Miles, K. H. (1995). Freeing resources for improving schools: A case study of teacher allocation in Boston Public Schools. *Educational Evaluation and Policy Analysis, 17*, 476–493.

Miles, K. H., & Darling-Hammond, L. (1998). Rethinking the allocation of teaching resources: Some lessons from high performing schools. In W. J. Fowler Jr. (Ed.), *Developments in school finance, 1997* (pp. 31–57). Washington, DC: U.S. Department of Education, National Center for Education Statistics.

Monk, D. H. (1989). The education production function: Its evolving role in policy analysis. *Educational Evaluation and Policy Analysis, 11*, 31–45.

Morrison, H. C. (1943). *American schools: A critical study of our school system*. Chicago: University of Chicago Press.

National Center for Education Statistics. (1999). *Digest of education statistics*. Washington, DC: U.S. Government Printing Office.

National Center for Education Statistics. (2006). *Digest of education statistics*. Washington, DC: U.S. Government Printing Office.

National Commission on Teaching and America's Future. (1996). *What matters most: Teaching for America's future*. New York: Author.

New American Schools. (2000). *Every child a star*. Arlington, VA: Author.

New Commission on the Skills of the American Workforce. (2007). *Tough choices or tough times*. San Francisco: Jossey-Bass/Wiley.

New York State Education Department. (2006). *New York the state of learning: A report to the governor and the legislature on the educational status of the State's schools*. Albany: Author.

Northwest Regional Educational Laboratory. (1998). *Catalog of school reform models: First edition*. Portland, OR: Author.

Odden, A. (1996). Incentives, school organization, and teacher compensation. In S. H. Fuhrman & J. A. O'Day (Eds.), *Rewards and reform: Creating educational incentives that work* (pp. 226–256). San Francisco: Jossey-Bass.

Odden, A., Monk, D., Nakib, Y., & Picus, L. (1995). The story of the education dollar: No academy awards and no fiscal smoking guns. *Phi Delta Kappan, 77*, 161–168.

Odden A. R., & Picus, L. O. (2000). *School finance: A policy perspective* (2nd ed.). New York: McGraw-Hill.

Odden, A. & Webb, L. D. (1983). Introduction: The linkages between school finance and school improvement, In A. Odden & L. D. Webb (Eds.), *School finance and school improvement: Linkages for the 1980s* (pp. xiii-xxi). Cambridge, MA: Ballinger.

Olson, L. (2004). Research group, new American schools merge. *Education Week, 23*(34), 12.

Osin, L., & Lesgold, A. (1996). A proposal for re-engineering of the educational system. *Review of Educational Research, 66*, 621–656.

Owens, J. T., Jr. (1994). *Interdistrict resource allocation in Dade County Florida: An analysis of equity of educational opportunity*. Paper presented at the annual meeting of the American Educational Finance Association, Nashville, TN.

Paquette, J. (1999, March). *The Ontario approach to restraint: From burgeoning local share to full funding and central control*. Paper presented at the annual conference of the American Education Finance Association, Seattle, WA.

Picus, L. O. (2001). *In search of more productive schools: A guide to resource allocation in education*. Eugene, OR: ERIC Clearinghouse on Educational Management.

Raudenbush, S. W., Fotiu, R. P., & Cheong, Y. F. (1998). Inequality of access to educational resources: A national report card for eighth-grade math. *Educational Evaluation and Policy Analysis, 20*, 253–267.

Raywid, M. A. (1999). Current literature on small schools. In *ERIC Digest* (ED425049). Charleston, WV: ERIC Clearinghouse on Rural Education and Small Schools.

Reed, L. (1985). *An inquiry into the specific school-based practices involving principals that distinguish unusually effective elementary schools from effective elementary schools*. Unpublished doctoral dissertation, State University of New York at Buffalo.

Reschovsky, A., & Imazeki, J. (2001). Achieving educational adequacy through school finance reform. *Journal of Education Finance, 26*, 373–396.

Reynolds, A. J., Bezruczko, N., Mavrogenes, N. A., & Hagemann, M. (1996). *Chicago longitudinal study of children in Chicago Public Schools: User guide (version 4)*. Madison and Chicago: University of Wisconsin and Chicago Public Schools.

Reynolds, A. J., & Wolfe, B. (1999). Special education and school achievement: An exploratory analysis with a central-city sample. *Educational Evaluation and Policy Analysis, 21*, 249–269.

Riew, J. (1981). Enrollment decline and school reorganization: A cost efficiency analysis. *Economics of Education Review, 1*, 53–73.

Riew, J. (1986). Scale economies, capacity utilization, and school costs: A comparative analysis of secondary and elementary schools. *Journal of Education Finance, 11*, 433–446.

Rothstein, R., & Miles, K. H. (1995). *Where's the money gone? Changes in the level and composition of education spending, 1967–1991*. Washington, DC: Economic Policy Institute.

Rubenstein, R. (1998). Resource equity in the Chicago public schools: A school-level approach. *Journal of Education Finance, 23*, 468–489.

Sammons, P. (1999). *School effectiveness: Coming of age in the twenty-first century*. Lisse: Swets & Zeitlinger.

Schmidt, W., McKnight, C., Houang, R., Wang, H., Wiley, D. E., Cogan, L .S. (2001). *Why schools matter: A cross-national comparison of curriculum and learning*. San Francisco: Jossey-Bass.

Smith, T. M., & Phelps, R. P. (1995). Education finance indicators: What can we learn from comparing states and nations. In W. J. Fowler Jr. (Ed.), *Developments in school finance* (pp. 99–107). Washington, DC: National Center for Educational Statistics.

Stasz, C., & Stecher, B. M. (2000). Teaching mathematics and language arts in reduced size and non-reduced size classrooms. *Educational Evaluation and Policy Analysis, 22*, 313–329.

Stiefel, L., Berne, R., Iatarola, P., & Fruchter, N. (2000). High school size: Effects on budgets and performance in New York City. *Educational Evaluation and Policy Analysis, 22*, 27–39.

Stiefel, L., Rubenstein, R., & Berne, R. (1998). Intra-district equity in four large cities: Data, methods, and results. *Journal of Education Finance, 23*, 447–467.

Tainter, J. A. (1988). *The collapse of complex societies*. Cambridge: Cambridge University Press.

Toch, T. (2003). *High schools on a human scale: How small schools can transform American education*. Boston: Beacon Press.

Veenman, S. (1995). Cognitive and noncognitive effects of multigrade and multi-age classes: A best-evidence synthesis. *Review of Educational Research, 65*, 319–381.

Venezsky, R., & Winfield, L. (1980). *Schools that exceed beyond expectations in the teaching of reading: Studies on education, technical report #1*. Newark: University of Delaware.

Viadero, D. (2004). Acquisition of consulting firm signals new day at research group. *Education Week, 24*(9), 6.

Weber, G. (1971). *Inner city children can be taught to read: Four successful schools*. Washington, DC: Council for Basic Education.

Wenglinsky, H. (1998). Finance equalization and within-school equity: The relationship between education spending and the social distribution of achievement. *Educational Evaluation and Policy Analysis, 20,* 269–283.

Williams, D. T. (1990). *The dimensions of education: Recent research on school size* (Working Paper Series). Clemson, SC: Strom Thurmond Institute of Government and Public Affairs.

Woessmann, L. (2000). *Schooling resources, educational institutions, and student performance: The international evidence* (Kiel Working Paper No. 983). Kiel: Kiel Institute of World Economics.

Implementation of Systemic Change

The ultimate objective of educational organizations (or any organization for that matter) is to maintain internal stability.

Chapter 13: Systemic Change. Maintaining stability while existing within turbulent environments requires constant change. Educational leaders of the new millennium must be prepared to develop, articulate, and bring to fruition new educational systems and to do so in such a way that the new systems meet societal demands for flexibility and quality.

Chapter 14: Educational Leadership in a Flat World. This chapter builds a composite view of the complete work of the book by synthesizing the highlights of the previous chapters. It projects the emerging structure of education and concludes with a discussion of the implications of the projected structure for future school leaders.

CHAPTER 13

Systemic Change

Educational leaders have seen themselves as change masters, pathfinders, gamesmen, entrepreneurs, visionaries, and transformational leaders. Educational administrators everywhere have been called on to envision alternatives, to seek renewal, and to break the barriers of conventional practice. Although change is constant, change programs often fail as a result of their disruptiveness and from the confusion and threats they pose to participants who must change (Beer, Eisenstat, & Spector, 1990).

In chapter 12, we considered the allocation of human and economic resources to the educational system. Careful planning is the watchword in this situation because perceived need always exceeds the perceived availability of those resources. In this chapter, we explore how educational leaders can handle that system and those resources in unstable conditions, where change is the norm and stability is infrequent—and often suspect.

School systems are confronted with numerous pressures. The ideological, political, and economic environment, as viewed by the American public, is vastly different today from what it was. The public demands a more significant connection between effective schooling and national development in the light of dramatic changes in demographics and economic circumstances. A more learning-oriented literate workforce is in high demand. Continuous improvement is in high demand, while changes in schooling that have been judged as fundamentally inadequate will fade (Cetron & Gayle, 1991). Responding to these demands for change will necessitate an understanding of what change is, what change scenarios are available or can be developed, and how and why change is necessary. Leaders of change must learn to resolve several basic conflicts: change versus tradition, self-fulfillment versus participation, and decentralization versus integration (Hahn, 1991).

What Is Change?

Change in organizations is defined by Hanson (1985) as the altering of "behavior, structures, procedures, purposes, or outputs of some unit within an organization" (p. 286). Some describe change as innovation, others as adaptability, even novelty. Extensive organizational change was defined by Smith (2002) as any intentional shift in the way the organization does business as that organization relates to the strategic position of other competing organizations.

Change is a process rather than a single adjustment. Kanter, Stein, and Jick (1992) saw organizations as fluid entities that are constantly in motion. Managing change in this context is a matter of "grabbing hold of some aspect of the motion and steering it in a particular direction" (p. 10).

The literature of change process offers a number of step-based models. Typical are Caldwell's (1968) four-step model: identification and priority ranking of needs, development of broad strategies and specific plans, implementation of selected approaches, and assessment of outcomes; and Kohl's (1968) five-step model: awareness, interest, evaluation, trial, and adoption. Sheive (1981) described developmental organizational change, that is, periods in the life of an organization when it is significantly different. Basing her discussion on the work of Perrow (1961), and Pfeffer and Salancik (1978), among others, she proposed a recurring-cycle model of organizational life in which change takes place as a consequence of the influence of new situations and environmental factors encountered during the pursuit of organizational goals.

Change is the primary means by which any organization or system remains fit, healthy, and able to cope with new and differing demands. The adaptations produced by change in an organization constitute an evolution of the organization. Those organizations that are able to maintain flexibility and react appropriately to new environmental conditions survive and prosper. Those organizations that cannot become less and less able to serve society.

It is the responsibility of the school system to prepare our youth to function in an adult world. To do this, the school system must remain constantly aware of the nature and requirements of that environment. As the environment changes and as new technology, new social structures, and new values develop, school systems must be aware of those changes and be prepared to adjust curriculum, instruction, and organization to remain viable.

In addition, countervailing expectations exist that schools be conservators of culture, transmitting values and an understanding of the cultural history from one generation to the next. School systems must remain constantly aware of the nature and lessons of the past, constantly work to fit them into the current world, and seek to create their own new futures. The task is formidable, but any less may be insufficient.

These expectations, that schools continuously monitor the environment, initiate self-renewal, and adjust to change while remaining conservators of the past, mean that change in school systems will be complex. Educational systems are in a constant state of dynamic tension, drawn between the natural responsiveness to change necessary in a dynamic system and the natural stability of a conservator. Schools have therefore changed incrementally with too little consideration given to self-renewal or continuous improvement.

Types of Change

Lipham, Rankin, and Hoeh (1985) conceptualized change as enforced, expedient, or essential. *Enforced change* is the result of needs identified from external

forces. It would not have taken place if it were not for the external influence(s) involved. The task of leadership or management is to devise methods to cope with change, to act as a change master. In this sense the organization functions at the whims of those with more authority, influence, or political clout. Examples in the school environment could include state or federal mandates or the impact of community pressure groups.

Expedient change involves meeting immediate concerns and is generally short term or reactionary. Although it can also be internally driven, it is more likely that expedient change in the organization will result from meeting external demands. Examples in the school environment could include last-minute changes in the school budget or storm damage to a school building.

Essential change is derived from internal rather than external sources. It is driven by the ability of the system to monitor itself and work toward improved performance. It requires that persons within the system work cooperatively to transform behavior or system components. An example in the school environment could be updating the curriculum.

Change may also be seen as planned or unplanned. *Planned change*, as defined by Owens (1987), is a deliberate attempt to direct change within a set of predetermined goals and values. It is foreseen and managed. It is brought about by persons directly connected within the system that is changing. Strategic planning in the school district is an example of planned change. *Unplanned change* is often enforced change, unanticipated, and often forced on a school system or an organization. It generally meets the needs of an external agent rather than the needs of the organization being changed. An example would be a merger of two small but functional school districts that resulted from the budgetary needs of the state rather than any dysfunction in the local districts. Expedient change is generally also unplanned, meeting operational needs as they arise but not causing deep adjustments in the nature or overall activities of the organization.

Tucker (2007) addressed three different types of change, saying that each type requires a different approach to achieve successful implementation. The three types were developmental change, which occurs when an organization makes an improvement to current operations; transitional change, which occurs when new processes or procedures replace those that are current; and transformational change, which may involve both developmental and transitional change and results from shifts in the organization sufficiently major that the organization needs to transform itself.

Resistance to Change

Change efforts may be long awaited by some and strike fear in others. In any system, including educational systems, there is a built-in inertia that tends to maintain the stability of the organization. Kowalski and Reitzug (1993) noted that educational systems, as all social systems, resist change. A function of such organizations is to provide a framework for values, beliefs, and practices that allow people to function effectively. In schools, policy, regulation, and curricula provide a meaningful environment for the work of teachers, students, and staff. Change may threaten this framework of meaning and produce anxiety and resistance.

Change should be viewed as not only an intellectual process but a psychological process as well. Psychologically, change may be resisted because of interference with self-esteem needs, social status, and relationship fulfillment. The most obvious sources of personal resistance to change originate in the person's fear of the unknown. Organizational and individual routines have a high degree of certainty and are not easily altered without some opposition from an individual's or a group's concerns about the innovation's applicability, perceptions of their own abilities, concerns about other changes taking place at the same time, and the support that they are provided. People will resist change if they fear it will reduce their power and influence or make their knowledge and skills obsolete.

Much of the interest in the stages of the change process is related to the issue of resistance to change, according to Simek (1997). Resistance can be manifest in overt or covert behaviors. Stanislao and Stanislao (1983) outlined eight reasons for employee resistance:

1. *Surprise and fear of the unknown.* This emerges when radically innovative changes are introduced without warning or official announcement. The rumor mill creates its own informal sources of information.

2. *Climate of mistrust.* Mistrust can come from prechange organizational climates as well as from climates arising from the change process. The best-conceived changes can be doomed by mutual mistrust—mistrust perpetuates mistrust. Both leaders and followers suffer as the motivation necessary to change is absent.

3. *Fear of failure.* Self-doubt and lack of confidence drain growth and development when change participants are not allowed to prepare for change by participating in decision making or retraining.

4. *Loss of status and/or job security.* Resistance can quickly be triggered by real or perceived changes in power bases, loss of jobs, and loss of status due to administrative and technological changes.

5. *Peer pressure.* Resistance can arise not only in those directly affected by the proposed change but also in those who anticipate negative effects on peers, colleagues, or friends.

6. *Disruption of cultural traditions and/or group relationships.* If it is believed that the human element is the backbone of the organization, any modifications in work or personal relationships caused by transfers, promotions, or reassignments alter group dynamics and create disequilibrium.

7. *Personality conflicts.* The personality of the change agent can breed resistance if adversarial relationships develop between the change agent, the change-inducing system, and the target system.

8. *Lack of tact or poor planning.* The system's readiness is a key ingredient in successful change. A good idea may fall flat not on its own merits but because of poor timing or a poor manner of introduction.

Schuler (2003) expanded this discussion to a list of reasons for change resistance. They included the following: (a) The risk of change is seen as greater than the risk of the status quo. (b) People feel loyal to others who are identified with the old way. (c) Role models for the new way do not yet exist. (d) People perceive their own incompetence under the new way and fear it. (e) People feel overloaded and overwhelmed. (f) People are skeptical and want to be sure of the soundness of the new approach. (g) People fear hidden agendas on the part of the reformers. (h) People see the proposed change as threatening their self-images. (i) People anticipate loss of status or lessened quality of life. (j) People honestly see the proposed change as a bad idea—and they may be right.

The overall climate and culture of the educational system will also have a major impact on the ability to create lasting change. Climate can be defined as perceptions of expected work behavior based on existing patterns of behavior and existing organizational characteristics. Organizational culture can be defined as is knowledge of how things are and how things ought to be, including basic assumptions and beliefs shared by members of the organization. The shared assumptions and beliefs have often been developed over time as the organization produces resolutions to the problems of response to external demands and to the need for internal integration.

Climate and culture combine to provide a powerful matrix in which people function within the educational system. Because climate and culture are the organizational memory and an action context, they are also a powerfully conservative force within the organization. Therefore, during organizational change attempts that do not address culture and climate are at great risk of failure.

Change is resisted if it does not adhere to preestablished norms and values. Norms are products of culture in organizations and, according to Watson (1969), correspond to people's habits, making it possible for members of an organization to work together. Norms, as representations of an invisible framework of standard beliefs and values, are valuable to an organization if they have worked well in the past, helped participants interpret daily occurrences, and minimized confusion. Strong norms that project integrity and sensibility in an organization and are shared by the participants across organizational roles are especially difficult to change.

Additional obstacles that may impede change include resource limitations, or the inability to increase production, augment services, purchase new equipment, or hire staff. In contemporary school districts an additional barrier to change may be collective-bargaining agreements. These commonly stipulate that specific changes in job descriptions may be subject to negotiation, thus placing added constraints on an administrator's ability to implement a desired change. Additionally, it is often the case that management and administrative responsibilities carry more perceived importance than do leadership or change-agent roles. This barrier denigrates leadership and the ability of real change agents to act outside the normative–administrative functions of budgeting, scheduling, or even disciplining. Kowalski and Reitzug (1993) identified the structure of public schools as a quasi-monopoly, where bureaucratic structures with their division of responsibility and concentration of power create a sense of disenchantment and alienation on the part of many staff members.

Sarason (1971) observed that cohesiveness (or lack of it) is an issue in effecting change in schools. Teachers are relatively autonomous, with little to do with one another during the normal school day. "They may identify with each other in terms of role or place of work, and they may have a feeling of loyalty to each other and the school, but it is rare that they feel part of a working group that discusses, plans, and helps make educational decisions" (p. 113).

Connor and Lake (1988) grouped barriers to change into three general categories: barriers to understanding: not fully understanding what is proposed; barriers to acceptance: those affected will not accept the change; and barriers to acting: factors inhibiting implementation. Basom and Crandall (1991) identified seven common barriers that were specific to change in schools: discontinuity of leadership; managers' fears that change was unmanageable; lack of training in management regarding change; following a top-down model of decision making; socialization and conditioning of school staff, which leads to the belief that the system is not the problem; unresolved competing visions of what schools should be; and inadequate time and resources.

Research on barriers to change indicates that resistance can be reduced significantly when planning is cognizant of the barriers as described previously. Broad support from the change agent is also valuable. Additionally, Fullan (1982) found that four

ACTIVITY 13.1
Resistance to Change
Addresses ISLLC Standards 1, 2, 3, and 6

Consider an example of resistance to change in your place of work or school. Given the discussion on this issue, consider the following questions:

1. How would you describe the nature of that resistance?
2. Why did it arise?
3. How effective has it been in preventing change?
4. How might the resistance be (or was) the change overcome?
5. What insight does this situation give into effective leadership (or failure to be effective)?

other characteristics enhance the potential for success with regard to change: necessity; clarity of purpose with clear and consistent procedures and objectives; complexity, or whether change is worth the expanded effort; and practicality, or the ability to put the change into practice.

Theoretical Implications of Change

Social thinking about change takes two different approaches. The first emphasizes a historical–deterministic thread that often reduces change to inexorable laws. In a second perspective, the human component is given center stage. Recognizing that greater knowledge and greater self-awareness lead to progressive improvement, the latter approach appears to have spearheaded the "widespread acceptance of change as a natural process and the equally widespread desire to mold that change in one direction or another—to imbue social change with human purpose" (Warren, 1977, p. 3).

A sociologist often cited by those interested in broad social planning and social intervention is Mannheim (1940). He cited three stages in the development of human society. The first is change by chance, discovery, trial, and error. The second is that of intervention, where intermediate processes and tools devised by human beings enable them to pursue systematic social adjustment rather than merely accept society as it is. The third stage encompasses democratic planning. In this stage, most often observed in Western society, various individual efforts are coordinated toward democratically agreed-on ends. Both Mannheim and Ward, according to Warren (1977), were more interested in knowledge creation than in action or intervention strategies surrounding change.

Much of the action, intervention, and strategizing in social change literature focuses on three levels of social structure: across organizations, across communities, and across society. Literature related to organizational change falls into two camps. One focuses on the gradual change that formal organizations make over time and studies the complex processes that occur. The second focuses on planned or deliberate change and its outcomes. The intent is to learn how best to implement change objectives in organizations. Study of the formal organization, according to Warren (1977), then forms the basis for understanding change at other levels of social structure, in communities and society.

The second level of change literature is community development. Much of this literature evolves from the social action climate of the 1960s. Community organization and development projects emerged from attempts to bring about greater coordination among social service agencies. But this social action climate later broadened to include change in other parts of the community. Community change drives organizational change.

The social macrocosm, national society, was the third level for planned social change. Societal change has a long history and is more closely related to the *grand theory* of social change (Warren, 1977). According to Warren, "most major social change goals, whether or not this is recognized by their proponents, include or pre-suppose major changes in organizations, often in large numbers and types of them" (p. 6).

The contexts of change in organizations are viewed through several frameworks. The first and most prominent practice is through management. Change is seen through the eyes of the change agent since it is the change agents, most often leaders and managers, who dominate decision making in most organizations. In another view, organizational change is assumed to occur from within an organization. Forces within the organization, scanning and responding to the environment, set the change process into motion. In this view change may be merely an adaptation to environmental changes, or it may be a comprehensive and more innovative approach intended to capitalize on opportunities presented from the environment.

Literature related to informal organizational structures centers about two schools of thought. Summarizing that literature, Warren (1977) noted that the work of such people as Bernard, Simon, Cyert, and March challenged the bureaucratic–rational model first proposed by Weber. He stated that Bernard saw organizations not as always functioning as rational decision-making units but as organizational subsystems vying for different outcomes and making highly political decisions. More recently, he said, Argyris and Bennis emphasized the human relations aspects of change among people at and between all levels of the organization.

Change does not necessarily occur solely as a result of management manipulation of the formal structure. Organizational change can also be supported or resisted by the informal structure created by networks of people who may seek quite diverse ends. Minimizing the importance of informal structures on change efforts would create an inaccurate model for change. The significance of informal organizational structures was brought to light by the Hawthorne experiments of the 1930s. Informal structures came to be seen as fulfilling the function of making life more bearable while meeting the demands of the formal organization. The importance of informal structure in organizational change is widely recognized in the abstract, if not always in actual practice (Warren, 1977).

Strategies for Change

Change strategies developed by various authors emphasize a variety of aspects of the process. Some attempt to encompass the entire process, while others are restricted to a particular focus. Most tend to be very general or descriptive rather than prescriptive (Warren, 1977).

Lewin (1951) provided one of the earliest models of planned change. His model focuses on identifying and using sets of forces to bring about change. According to Lewin, states of equilibrium are maintained by two sets of forces: those maintaining the status quo and those that push for change. Both sets of forces must be present at relatively equal levels of tension for equilibrium to exist. To bring about change, it is necessary to shift tension toward change forces and away from state-maintaining forces. Various combinations can be seen; for example, by pushing for change and decreasing maintenance forces, change should occur more rapidly. Lewin felt that tension and resistance related to change could be minimized if the chosen approach involved modifying state-maintaining forces. This modification of state-maintaining forces can be encouraged by instituting three steps: unfreezing, changing, and refreezing. Lewin's model provides a general framework for understanding organizational change.

Chin and Benne (1969) traced change strategies to three basic roots: rational–empirical, normative–reeducative, and power–coercive. The *rational–empirical model* that underlies liberal education, scientific approaches to management, and expert or authoritarian views of what is right is clearly deterministic in nature. *Normative–reeducative strategies* are patterned after Lewin's (1951) work and emphasize intervention in a client system. Intervention strategies are devised based on the system's perception of its own problems and need for change. These strategies involve a change agent in collaboration with a client system working together to discover elements that may impede change. In essence, the change agent and the client search for a pathology and its remedy. The *power–coercive strategy* applies political, economic, and moral power in order to manipulate or reconstitute power elites. This model underlies many of community development and sociopolitical change strategies. Many consider them overly disruptive.

Change strategy can be seen as normative–reeducative. These models have been explored across a wide range of client systems: individual, small group, organizations, and large communities. In these models a client voluntarily engages a consultant as a change agent. In partnership, the client and consultant use a five-stage change model to invoke change. The steps of the model include definition of the need for change, establishment of the change–client relationship, implementation of change strategies, generalization and stabilization of change, and achievement of a terminal relationship. The model is premised, however, on the importance of information flow. Information must be shared freely and openly between the target system and the change agent. This information is useful only if it can be translated into action.

Considering the applicability of Chin and Benne's (1969) models, Nickols (2003) described the underlying assumptions and selection factors for each strategy as well as an additional strategy of his own devising. He established four categories:

1. *Empirical–rational.* The underlying assumptions are that people are rational beings and will follow their own best interests when they know them. Selection factors include casting doubt on the viability of the present state of affairs and targeting converts who will assist in supporting the proposed change.

2. *Normative–reeducative.* The underlying assumptions are that people are social beings and will adhere to cultural norms and values. Selection factors include that the fact that change focuses on culture, which is modified only slowly, and that informal as well as formal structures must be taken into account.

3. *Power–coercive.* The underlying assumptions are that people are compliant and will do what they are told or can be made to do. Authority is power. Selection factors include time and the seriousness of threat. If the threat is grave and time short, this choice is useful. In a benign culture, members will be likely to accept this approach to a clearly perceived threat. Members are less likely to accept this approach in a culture that is autonomous and entrepreneurial.

4. *Environmental–adaptive.* The underlying assumptions are that people oppose loss and disruption but can adapt. Change is based on building a new organization and gradually transferring people from the old to the new structure. Selection factors include the extent of the change. Another issue is the availability of appropriate personalities for seeding the new organization.

Bennis (1966) devised a parallel model to Chin and Benne (1969) that demonstrated additional consideration for a broader set of variables and resulted in a more lengthy topology. He outlined eight different types of change: planned, indoctrinary, coercive, technocratic, interactional, socialization, emulative, and natural.

Meyerson and Banfield's (1964) experience with the Chicago Housing Authority demonstrated a deterministic model. Their model involved analysis of the situation, end reduction and elaboration, designing courses of action, and comparative evaluation of consequences. During analysis, attention is devoted to identifying opportunities and limiting conditions such that differentiation is possible between incidental ends and principal ends. As elaboration of principal ends occurs, developmental action can ensue to more specific levels. consequences are then evaluated for effectiveness across cost-benefit criteria.

Walton (1965) proposed two strategies related to social change: a power strategy and an attitude-change strategy. The underlying assumption of the *power strategy* is that attainment of change is built on a power base involving strategic manipulation of this power. *Attitude change* can best be achieved by developing mechanisms that promote trust and goodwill. The change objective involves both a desired concession and a reduction of intergroup hostility. Although both strategies are useful, they may also demonstrate incompatibility. For example, hostile participants must learn to deal with power and trust, ambiguity and evasiveness, and bargaining through threat and, conversely, deal with openness and frankness and conciliatory gestures at the same time (Walton, 1965, cited in Warren, 1977).

Lauer's (1973) process incorporated targets of change, agents of change, and methods of change. Targets of change may be individuals, groups, societies, or a combination thereof. Differing strategies are undertaken depending on the chosen target of change. For example, if the change target is a group, change may be sought through recomposition of the group itself. Two forms of change agents may emerge: authoritative or participative. Lauer, like Walton, also found a distinction between power and attitude strategies. Lauer asserted that attitude strategies are best directed at changing individuals and gaining mass support for developmental programs, whereas power strategies are applied more within social movements and organizational and interorganizational change.

Koestler's (1973, cited in Lauer, 1973) process is one of social action rather than social change. This strategy addresses three causes of social change: helping, protest, and revolution. These self-explanatory causes are the objectives or goals that those undertaking the change believe will remedy an identified problem. This discussion also addressed the concept of change agency, identifying two types: leaders and supporters. Koestler's strategies for change include power, persuasion, and reeducative strategies. Targets of change can be classified as ultimate targets and intermediate targets. These targets are acted on through response or influence channels.

Nutt (1986) contributed a five-stage model of change he called the *transactional model*. In this strategy, management and a development team occupy a central role. The manager represents formal authority and maintains ultimate responsibility for the proposed change. Change development and implementation occur through the combined efforts of management and development committees or project teams. The manager and teams interact in each stage of the process: defining needs, clarifying premises and assumptions, weighing alternatives, and installing the change. Management ensures that needed structures and mechanisms are in place for the teams. The constituents of the developmental teams assist in problem identification, suggest objectives, recommend options and tentative plans, consider costs and benefits, and gather feedback information once the change has been installed.

The *action research model* of Huse and Cummings (1985) holds broad applicability and is adaptable to fit many different situations. This model focuses on planned change as a cyclic process involving collaboration between organization members and organizational development practitioners. It places strong emphasis on data collection and diagnosis as well as on careful evaluation of action results. The model involves seven steps:

1. *Problem identification*. Key organizational members who influence and hold power identify problems that might need attention.

2. *Consultation*. The change agent and the client begin developing a relationship wherein the change agent, mindful of the assumptions and values of both systems, shares his or her frame of reference with the client. This sharing establishes a beginning, essential atmosphere of openness and collaboration.

3. *Data gathering and preliminary diagnosis*. This stage takes place in collaboration with the change agent and members of the organization. Four basic data collection tools may be used: interviews, questionnaires, process observations, and organizational performance. Using different data collection tools ensures a more holistic set of data.

4. *Feedback*. Data gathered must be fed back to the client, usually in a group or work team meeting. The change agent provides the client with all relevant and useful data, which in turn help these groups to determine the strengths and weaknesses of the system or subsystem under study.

5. *Joint diagnosis of the problem*. To be useful, a diagnosis and recommendation must be understood and accepted. This occurs through an ongoing collaborative process by which data and diagnosis are shared with the group for validation and further diagnosis. Schein (1969) noted that the failure to establish a common frame of reference in the client–consultant relationship may lead to faulty diagnosis or a communication gap whereby the client is sometimes unwilling to accept the diagnosis and recommendations.

6. *Action*. A joint agreement is reached with regard to the action chosen. This is the beginning of the unfreezing process, as the organization moves toward a different state-maintaining equilibrium.

7. *Data gathering after action*. The cyclic process begins with the recollection of data as they relate to the actions taken. The action is monitored and measured to determine the effects of the action taken. Feedback of the results is communicated to the organization. This, in turn, leads to redefinition of the diagnosis and new action.

Models for Planned Change and Their Use

Beckhard and Harris (1977) presented a general model of change that encompasses a number of aspects of the planned change process. The general model had six facets: diagnosing the present condition, including the need for change; setting goals and defining the new state or condition after the change; defining the transition state between the present and the future; developing strategies and action plans for managing the transition; evaluating the change effort; and stabilizing the new conditions and establishing a balance between stability and flexibility.

Most models of change have steps similar to the general model of Beckhard and Harris (1977). A variety of other strategies for initiating and managing models of planned change exist. Lipham et al. (1985) identified four models: problem solving, research–development–diffusion–utilization, social interaction, and linkage.

Problem-Solving Models

According to Lippett, Langseth, and Mossop (1985), all organizational change is directed toward a specific end. Hersey and Blanchard (1988) noted that a problem exists "when there is a discrepancy between what is actually happening (the real) and what you or someone who hired you . . . would like to be happening (the ideal)" (p. 334). A problem situation in a school setting might involve a high level of absenteeism by students, a significant dropout rate, or poor achievement test scores.

Most problem-solving models involve the following elements: diagnosis: the problem is noticed, identified, and defined; alternative solutions: a variety of possible solutions are developed and the actions necessary to accomplish them outlined; selection and implementation: one possible solution is selected on the basis of its appropriateness and feasibility, and the solution is applied; and evaluation: the results of the actions taken are monitored. If the problem has been resolved, action ceases except to consider how to avoid the problem in the future. If the problem is not resolved, further alternative solutions are considered, and the model is recycled as appropriate.

According to Lipham et al. (1985), the most appropriate applications of the problem-solving model occur when problem solving is a norm within the system, when there is effective leadership to sustain the model, when problem solving is an agreed-on vehicle for accomplishing change, and when time, space, and finances allow solution of the problem.

Research–Development–Diffusion–Utilization Models

Like the problem-solving models, research–development–diffusion–utilization (RDDU) is a rational–empirical approach providing a systematic framework for managing planned change. The RDDU model involves the following elements: research: research leads to the discovery or invention of new knowledge, products, or techniques; development: the new knowledge, product, or technique is validated through pilot testing and experimentation and then modified as appropriate for practical use; diffusion: the new knowledge, product, or technique is packaged appropriately and marketed; and utilization: if it is supported, encouraged, and accepted, the new knowledge, product, or technique becomes a new element in the overall system. This model is most applicable when there are cooperative arrangements among developers, users, and distributors; when research products are perceived as legitimate solutions to real-world problems; and when there is political support and leadership that encourages the use of research.

According to Havelock (1973), RDDU models are based on a series of assumptions. First, there should be a rational sequence in the evolution and application of the change. Second, because the innovations under consideration are usually major, planning may take a long period of time. Third, the recipients of the changes are assumed to be passive but willing beneficiaries of the change.

Social Interaction Models

Social interaction models are also a rational approach to change. These models assess the need for change based on communication and information from outside the system and involve members of the change system in planning and implementation. Active participation in the process by the members of the system is the norm, unlike the passive role that members played in the RDDU models.

Social interaction models typically include four stages: knowledge: leaders and/or members of the system have information about a proposed innovation; persuasion: members of the system are provided with information leading to positive (or negative) attitudes about the innovation proposed; decision: members of the system can accept or reject the proposed innovation; and confirmation: there is confirmation from peers that the decision to adopt or reject was appropriate.

The most effective use of social interaction models occurs when there is support to establish external contacts; when opportunities to gather external information, such as journals and conferences, are available; when there are funds to purchase products; and when there is a desire to gain status or recognition. The social interaction model is widely used in educational systems.

Linkage Models

Linkage models encompass elements of the problem solving, RDDU, and social interaction models. An agent within the system has an interest both within and outside the system, thereby serving as a link.

Stages involved in linkage models include the following: identification: a problem is identified and defined; communication: communication channels linking the system to outside resources are established; research: external information and/or skills bearing on the problem defined are sought out and acquired; solution: with the assistance of the external resource, a solution to the problem is identified or designed; implementation: the solution is applied; and evaluation: the applied solution is monitored, often in collaboration with the external resource, and appropriate action follows if necessary. Linkage models offer the best of all worlds in that they encompass many of the parameters of other models.

ACTIVITY 13.2

Strategies for Change

Addresses ISLLC Standards 1, 2, 3, and 6

You have been engaged by the superintendent of the Alston Beach School District as a consultant to provide a series of workshops for the district's teachers. The superintendent has told you that the central issue of the series is to be professional development. He has asked that you design the series to include professional development for individual teachers, for grade sets of teachers at the elementary level, and for departments at the junior/senior high school level. You are to present a proposal for the series to him within 60 days.

Consider the preceding discussion of models for change. Which of these might be an appropriate base for developing one or more workshops for individual professional development? Which of these might be appropriate for workshops for grade sets of elementary teachers? For junior/senior high school departments? Why?

Leadership and Change

Throughout this book, *leadership* and management have been defined, and leadership has been contrasted with management. *Leadership* is a process whereby leaders and followers intend mutually agreed-on changes, whereas *management* involves an authority relationship between a manager and at least one subordinate that is intended to meet a specific goal. Leadership may be a requisite factor to create and spearhead change, whereas management is necessary to maintain the stability of that change.

London (1988) suggested that change agents are leaders and managers who see a need for change, visualize what can be, and seek those strategies that will produce the required effect. The classical rational vista of leadership focuses on two groups: those who are in charge and those who are not. The classical theorists define roles and delineate hierarchical structures and patterns of interaction. The classical rational view is impersonal, formal, and task centered. It focuses on optimizing organizational performance by optimizing organizational structure. It suggests a structural approach to change, with an emphasis on unilateral decision making, where people are assumed to be highly rational and where authoritative directions are considered the best motivator of results (Grenier, 1989). It is assumed that compliance will lead to more effective results. The classical approach often uses leadership and management interchangeably. Similarly, change strategies in this arena are rational.

Participative leadership models, in contrast, view the organization as a democratic network having as its goal establishment of an environment that addresses the needs of its members and those functionally related to it (Lorsch & Trooboff, 1989). Supportive leadership, group decision making, and open channels of communication and information flow contribute to the maintenance of a healthy organization. This model suggests that key people be made a part of the change process. "According to participative designers, change should start by altering the most influential causal variables affecting what needs to be changed. Then there should be systematic plans prepared to modify all other affected parts of the organization in carefully coordinated steps" (Lorsch & Trooboff, 1989, p. 74). Authority may be present, but there is a sharing of power. Both group decision making and group problem solving reflect the participative approach to change.

Closely allied to the participative leadership models are human resources leadership models. Vroom and Yetton (1973) provided an example. They advocated that leaders be open, sharers, listeners, coaches, and participants in working with others. Empowerment of others in producing change is a major goal for such a leader.

Organizations, particularly educational organizations, are essentially bureaucratic in design and highly rational. However, leadership within the bureaucratic structure is a decidedly social concept, "for it automatically presumes an interactive condition between leaders and followers" (Monahan & Hengst, 1982, p. 220). Leaders do not exist in a vacuum; leadership is a group phenomenon. Much of the literature on leadership focuses on how the leader views him- or herself in relation to followers or subordinates. The leader may assume an autocratic or democratic stance or employ an interactional or situational approach to leadership and change.

Contingency and situational approaches recognize that position is not enough to ensure commitment or compliance. However, compliance may be enhanced through interpersonal interactions. The situational approach suggests that leadership in organizations is more dependent on its members and the nature of the circumstances that confront the organization. "The leadership task within this context is to relate specific behaviors to effective group performance and satisfaction" (Monahan & Hengst, 1982, p. 248). Change in this environment tends toward a rational and reeducative stance.

Senge (1990) proposed that leadership in a learning organization involves three roles: designer, teacher, and steward. As designer, the leader creates a vision and establishes the core values and principles of the organization. As teacher, the leader helps others examine and restructure their views of organizational reality. As steward, the leader demonstrates commitment to the people being led and to the larger purposes of the organization. Through these roles, the leader functions as a change agent.

Change Agents

What Is a Change Agent or Change System?

A change agent is a person, group, or organization seeking to produce change in a system. The change agent may be external to the target system or may be an element in the target system. The change agent may initiate the change in question or may join a change process already under way and facilitate the activity. The change agent may be a chief executive officer, foreman, school superintendent, or principal.

Change agents, initiators of change, also may or may not hold formal leadership roles within the target system. In these instances it is vital to the success of the effort that significant elements of the formal leadership be incorporated into the change system. When that is not possible or when the leadership is in active opposition to the change effort, it may be necessary to supplement the existing leadership, change it, or force it into compliance with the effort.

A change system, according to Warren (1977), is the set of connections established between the change agent and the target system in which change is desired. This may be a system separate from the target system, or, in the case of self-change, the change system may be a subset of the target system.

Characteristics of Effective Change Agents

Effective change agents know about the task at hand, understand the cultural context in which the task must be performed, know their followers, and know themselves, according to Hodgkinson (1991). They are generally leaders who see a need for change, visualize what can be done, and move toward the strategies necessary to accomplish their ends. Effective leaders (change agents) possess high intellect, high initiative, strong orientation to both people and goal accomplishment, and a clear vision of what the organization can be (Lashway, Mazarella & Grundy, 1988; Stogdill, 1974; Yukl, 1981).

Functions of Effective Change Agents

Change agents perform three functions in establishing an effective change-inducing system. These are recruitment, development, and control. Since the change agent working alone is unlikely to be successful in seeking change, one necessary function is recruitment of like-minded persons or subsystems. Warren (1977) pointed out that the larger and more complex the system, the more likely it is that there will be others either actively seeking change or predisposed toward it.

Development of a change-inducing system may involve creating a coalition or mobilizing already existing change-minded individuals or groups to take control of assets they did not control previously. In either case, as the process develops three issues arise. One is to balance inclusion with coherence. That is, the more individuals or subgroups who are involved in the change effort the better, as long as the original purposes remain clear and coherent. The second is to balance the original goals with the interests and positions of new members of the change group and not to be diverted toward other and

sometimes private ends. Third, the change-inducing system should exist not for its own sake but in order to accomplish a clearly defined end. If resources are diverted to maintain the change-inducing system for its own sake rather than meeting the original goals, that perverts the process.

The change agent's ability to balance control of the change process and share control when appropriate is the third function to consider. Once the change system is established, the change agent will begin to lose sole control of the process. Sharing of control is necessary to broaden the base of the effort. Ideally, shared values among the members of the change system will lead to shared understandings and effective decisions made by consensus. Fombrun (1992) considered the ability of the leader to recognize the need for change and the ability to gain consensus in that vision to be fundamental to success.

Another concern for the change agent is the appropriate degree of change to be undertaken. This issue leads to incremental change, planning for change in stages with careful checks at intermediate points. This may lead to reducing the difficulty of the change objective while increasing the likelihood of success. Given these concerns, the change agent needs to be sensitive to what is possible as well as to what is desirable. Viewing the task in this way will lead the successful change agent to the development of allies, access to additional resources and sources of power when appropriate, and development of long-range multilevel plans that have an improved chance of success.

Even in the best of situations, the change agent may well run into either passive or active resistance. The change agent may use a variety of tactics to reduce that resistance. Lunenberg and Ornstein (1991) stated that change agents use six methods to reduce resistance to change: participation: involvement of those who will be affected by the change to participate in the planning, design, and implementation (participation establishes ownership, builds commitment, and reduces anxiety); communication: employees need to know the purpose of the change and how it will affect them; support: high-level support generates commitment; rewards: resistance will be less if some benefit, tangible or intangible, is seen; planning: well-thought-out infusion processes should be designed; and coercion: although coercion may ensure that change occurs, it may also produce anger and resentment.

Huse (1975) cited several factors that aid in reducing resistance to change. (a) Any change process needs to take into account the needs, attitudes, and beliefs of the people involved as well as the forces of organization. The individual must perceive some personal benefit to be gained from the change before willingness to participate in the change process will be forthcoming. (b) The greater the prestige of the supervisor, the greater the influence that he or she can exert for change. (c) Strong pressure for changes in behavior can be established by providing specific information desired by the group about itself and its behavior. The more central, relevant, and meaningful the information, the greater the possibility for change. (d) Facts developed by the individual or the group or the involvement and participation by the individual or the group in the planning, gathering, analysis, and interpretation of data highly influence the change process. (e) Change that originates from within is much less threatening and creates less opposition than change that is proposed from the outside. (f) Information relating to the need for change, plans for change, and consequences of change must be shared by all relevant people in the group.

London (1988) also identified several factors that can aid in minimizing resistance to change. (a) Evaluate the characteristics of the change. Consider complexity, psychological and financial cost, the extent to which the purpose and intended outcome are clear, and the amount of mutual agreement. (b) Consider who and what is affected by the change. Try to determine how the change affects the work that is done and the working and personal relationships of those affected. (c) Envision how the change will be implemented. Reduce uncertainty to a minimum. (d) Be prepared for multiple interventions. As an example, training staff for new tasks will not necessarily be effective unless the social system and the reward structure reinforce the desirability of implementing the new behavior.

The key point is that planned change is most effective when human systems are an integral part of the change process. Whether it focuses on the introduction of new personnel or new technologies, planned change must be based on knowledge and must incorporate strategies derived from such knowledge (Chin & Benne, 1969).

Effective change agents are systems thinkers prepared for and planning for the complexities of multisystem interactions and long-term ripple effects once a change is implemented. Indeed, they should be prepared for such complexities once a change is suggested since the anticipation of change will often produce an impact of its own.

Implementing this multisystem interactions perspective by the change agent involves development of clear answers to questions related to the situation, not only for the change agent but also for all involved in the process. Essential questions for condition are the following: What is to be changed? Why is it to be changed? How is it to be changed? When is it to be changed? Who will be involved in the change? What barriers to the change will need to be overcome? What impact can reasonably be expected on individuals, on subsystems, on the overall system, on the external environment? What support for the change can be expected? What will be the costs of the change? What will be the benefits of the change?

When contemplating making a change in an organization's behavior, Freeman (2006) recommended considering the personalities of staff members in terms of three constituencies: habit stakers, habit breakers, and habit makers. Habit stakers he defined as people who are preservers of the existing culture, the status quo. If the institutional habits—ways of doing things—are productive, that is all to the good. If they are dysfunctional habits, then they can interfere with the organization's performance. Habit breakers he defined as those people who want to see change in how things are done. The leader has the problem of separating the thoughtful from the unhelpful, but these people are source of the organization's change agents if their perspectives can be harnessed to the organization's goals. Habit makers are the people who institutionalize the new way of doing things. They need to be alert, aware, patient leaders by example at all levels of the organization if the new patterns are to be embedded in the organizational culture.

Managing Planned Change

Beckhard and Harris (1977) presented a general model that outlines six aspects of management of the change process: diagnose the present condition, including the need for change; set goals and define the new state or condition after the change; define the transition state between the present and the future; develop strategies and action plans for managing this transition; evaluate the change effort; and stabilize the new conditions and establish a balance between stability and flexibility.

Beckhard and Harris (1977) emphasized that there are two essential conditions for any change effort to be effectively managed. First, the organization leadership must be aware of the need for change and the consequences of their actions. Second, the desired end state must be relatively explicit. A clear differentiation between causes and symptoms is an essential component of the first aspect of the change process. What often occurs is poor system diagnosis that provides an inaccurate statement of the change problem. Change strategies can be effective if the symptom statement describes the fundamental condition needing change. Diagnosis must include probable causes of the problems as well as a goal statement. Such questions as "What would be different or better?" and "How much does it matter?" would provide clarity for the problem and goal statement. Problem definition and goal setting are interlinked, and both must be explicit. It is important to recognize that although the concern for change is often triggered by the existence of some need or set of problem symptoms, it is the goal set by the leadership that should be the determining factor in defining both the strategy and direction for change (Beckhard & Harris, 1977).

Detailed attention is required to define the present system and develop a description of what the system will appear to be when the desired change is achieved. Many organizations embark on a change process with erroneous assumptions about the current state of the organization. If action plans are developed on an inaccurate set of assumptions and then implemented, resistance, confusion, frustration, and general failure to achieve desired goals will result. Analyzing the present scenario involves analyzing what subsystems of the system are most significantly involved in the change process and what changes in their present attitudes or behavior or ways of work would have to occur if the desired goal is to be reached.

This requires a total organization perspective since change in one part of the system will affect the total system. It is best to anticipate the degree and direction of anticipated change within the total system. This allows a proactive rather than a reactive stance to changes in subsystems that were not direct targets of the change process.

An additional focus is on the processes that would need to be changed for the overall innovation to be effective. These could include required changes in attitude, practices, policy, and structure, including rewards. Once a diagnosis is complete, priorities need to be set, keeping in mind the potential domino effect inherent in the change process.

A clear understanding of each subsystem's readiness and capacity for change must exist. Motivation to change is directly related to readiness and capability. The state of readiness to change is closely connected to attitudes of the system. Attitudes of the subsystem toward anticipated change will be influenced by assumptions, reality based or perceived, about the effect of the change as it relates directly to this subsystem. The success of change efforts is influenced as much by the processes of change as it is by the actual tasks involved. Capacity for change is related to readiness and encompasses analysis of available resources to support the change and offset negative consequences. Resources include not only personnel and equipment but also technology, time, and funds.

Will the expected ends derived from the change offset the costs involved? This question can be answered accurately only if a whole system analysis is done. What may appear to have positive benefits for one part of the system may have immediate or long-term negative effects on other crucial elements.

Decision Making

Change in any part of a system will create impact on other parts of the system. Given that, the question becomes, Which change is the best approach for solving a particular problem? This is a particularly important concept in considering change in an educational system that operates with multiple layers of subsystems, each with its own goals and objectives that must be taken into consideration if the effort to change is not to be self-defeating.

Decision making has been described elsewhere in this book as a matter of choosing among alternatives. These choices involve assessment of the level of risk involved, the amount of information available, some level of rationality (although most recent students of decision making note that rationality is not the only base for making individual choices), evaluation of preferences, identification of probable consequences, and communication of the decision.

According to French and Bell (1973), decision making includes the processes of problem solving and action planning. Conducting these processes successfully involves getting necessary information, establishing priorities, evaluating alternatives, and choosing one alternative over others.

Training educational leaders and managers has traditionally included efforts to improve decision-making skills. This is seen as particularly important since the educational decision maker functioning in a public arena makes decisions and communicates them in a highly politicized environment. Decision making in this situation often calls for the ability to bargain and negotiate in the manner described by Lindbloom (1965) as well as for significant communications skills.

Decision making in education has a heightened level of risk because full information is rarely available. Therefore, the educational decision maker generally operates on the basis of Simon's bounded rationality: considering the real-world situation as he or she sees it, reviewing the choices, and then constructing a simplified model through which a decision can be made. While the behavior is rational within the frame of reference of the model, the rationality is bounded in the sense that the effective decision maker understands the model to be limited by such factors as time and available information and therefore is incomplete.

Once a choice has been made to initiate change, it remains to determine what needs changing and to increase the system's readiness and capacity for the change. Here the need for unfreezing and freezing

techniques may be considered as a means of increasing readiness and capability. This is particularly true if a system's norms, attitudes, and ways of work are entrenched. Goal-setting exercises may be helpful if the system's goals are not shared. Structural change would be called for if the organizational chart does not reflect the new tasks to be done. New information or technical knowledge or skills may be required to achieve the change conditions.

Following the decision to initiate change and identification of change targets, there must be a determination of where to begin. Potential targets could include the top of the system, subsystems known to be ready for and capable of change, the "hurting system," or new teams or systems that may be more open to change because of a lack of history and experience in the old ways.

Change needs to be initiated and moved forward. This is accomplished by selecting the appropriate intervention techniques and technologies. Beckhard and Harris (1977) made several points about these choices. One is to identify and think through the most likely possible early activities and their consequences. They also warned against falling into the "quick-fix" trap: the assumption that "we only need . . . [a management-by-objectives system, a planning exercise, new training programs]." What may be needed to initiate and move the change process forward is creation of a temporary system that can raise the possibility of novel solutions involving new approaches. It can be very difficult for a stable system to change itself.

Much can be accomplished through the use of planned change models, but there is no guarantee that these models will be appropriate. Problems may arise with the process: consultants can become wedded to one technique to the exclusion of others, organizations may not be willing to do what is necessary for success, or management may want to buy into only certain steps or may focus on validating their own or earlier positions. These and other problems may arise not from the change model but from its implementation.

Johansen (1967) investigated 59 school systems in Illinois to determine the relationship between teachers' perspective on the source of authoritative influence in local curriculum decision making and implementation of the resulting decisions. He noted that teacher participation in curriculum activities increased the chances of curriculum implementation. Perception on the part of teachers that they had been influential in decision making enhanced the chances of implementation, while perception that hierarchical authority was central to decisions decreased the chances of implementation.

Effecting Educational Change

Change is ever present in schools, as it is in any organization. Given the variety of challenges that educational systems face today, the ability to cope with change becomes even more of a necessity (Cetron & Gayle, 1991; Mauriel, 1989; Millard, 1991). The shift of school ownership, the advent of the information age, demographic shifts in funding, growing poverty among underclass children, demands of new market segments, and the quality of output of schools all have focused attention on reexamination of the efficiency and effectiveness of school systems.

Planned change in schools, however, is affected by the particular nature of educational systems. Schools tend to be loosely coupled with vague system boundaries, diffuse goals, relatively low technical capacity, a constrained decentralized structure, and a noncompetitive environment. These characteristics make effecting change in schools somewhat different from effecting change in other social organizations.

In the past, change in American education was viewed as an evolutionary process, a process of natural diffusion. As a result the systems changed quite slowly. Mort and Ross (1957) reported that the average school in the United States lagged a quarter of a century behind the best practice of the time. However, as the pace of change has increased in society, natural diffusion of educational change has given way to planned, managed diffusion (Owens, 1987). This shift has led to identification of a number of models for change that fit educational systems.

Models for Educational Change

"Educational change depends on what teachers do and think—it's as simple and as complex as that," said Fullan (1982, p. 107). He then went on to identify four categories of factors that affect implementation of educational change: characteristics of the change, characteristics at the school district level, characteristics at the school level, and characteristics external to the local system. The greater the number of factors in those four sets that supported the innovation, the greater the chances were that the change would be implemented.

Fullan's view was supported by Waugh and Punch (1987), who concluded that variables to be considered before implementing educational change involving teachers included the practicality of the new system in the classroom, alleviation of fears and uncertainties concerning the change, articulation of perceived expectations associated with the change, and support of the teachers' role changes in reference to the change.

Educational change can be considered in terms of the problem-solving, social interaction, RDDU, and linkage models discussed in this chapter. In recent years, these models have been refined to fit the specific nature of educational systems.

The problem-solving model is based on a rational approach to change. It is user centered, featuring user diagnosis of problems with emphasis on building the problem-solving capacity of users. The four basic stages are diagnosis of the problem, development of a number of alternatives, implementation of selected alternative(s), and evaluation of the outcomes. This model is useful when there is sufficient time and funding, there is little controversy, and the staff has an open mind. School systems have used this approach to change frequently in the past. But as complexity has grown, so has the ineffectiveness of these simplistic models.

The social interaction model emphasizes communication channels and messages for diffusing innovations, interpersonal influence, and the impact of external stimuli for adoption of changes. Four stages are involved: knowledge of the innovation, persuasion leading to the formation of attitudes about the innovation, a decision to adopt or reject the innovation, and confirmation by peers of the decision. This model can be effective when the organization provides sufficient information, when the information is accessible, and when sound organizational communication networks exist. As society continues to change rapidly, schools will need to use these models more frequently, as constituents will demand greater and greater say.

The RDDU model identifies four stages in the change process: research on a given topic; frameworks formed from the research findings; diffusion of the new knowledge, product, or techniques; and implementation of the change. This model can be effective when planning on a massive scale is desirable; when rational division of labor and coordination of tasks is essential; when a cooperative arrangement exists among developers, distributors, and users; and when there is sufficient time to discover and implement new products or processes. The model can be particularly useful considering the overwhelming magnitude of change needed in education today.

The linkage model involves reciprocal change. This model emphasizes establishing communications networks among the sources and users of an innovation. The user establishes a reciprocal relationship with outside sources who are experiencing events that correspond with the events experienced by the user. There are three basic elements to this model: identifying potential need for change, establishing effective communication channels, and transmitting new knowledge from researchers to potential users. This model is useful when the school administrator who must effect the change is able to connect with the larger educational community and serve as a change agent through all stages of the change process.

Phases of Educational Change

Effective educational change may come in a variety of sizes and shapes, depending on the system involved and the circumstances. However, the four models discussed previously suggest a general model comprised of a combination of several stages: awareness, initiation, implementation, routinization, renewal, and evaluation (Lipham et al., 1985).

The awareness stage of this general model involves the discovery of problems that indicate anomalies in the present goals or programs. Participation of staff is helpful in clarifying goals, identifying discrepancies, defining problems, and identifying tentative alternatives for improving existing conditions. The initiation stage involves evaluation of current conditions and practices in terms of existing goals and exploring both expanded and ultimate goals, along with various means for achieving them. At this point, decisions are made for further action. Implementation is the next stage of this general model. Activities to assist the full staff in understanding and initiating change are begun. Approval, commitment, and cooperation of others are important. The basic problems, goals, and roles of change are identified at this stage. Once the change is implemented, routinization is the next stage. Change agents assist implementers in their efforts. A facilitative, supportive environment must be established. Decision making moves from the group to the individual level. In the renewal stage, implementers develop their ability to maintain the change and continue appropriate use without external help. A supportive climate will encourage high morale. Continuous feedback on the ongoing change continues the change moving toward the desired goal. Evaluation is the feedback loop that reveals ways to improve the change. With utilization of this model, the change process and outcomes are continually monitored and evaluated. Both formative and summative approaches to evaluation are employed. Criteria for evaluation are developed very early in the change process and are used to guide the evaluation efforts. Positive results open the way to routinization and renewal. Negative results point in the direction of other alternatives for change.

The response of members of an organization to change is often conditioned by the fact that they typically will see the negative aspects of change before the positive aspects. Hathaway (2000) identified the four phases to the resulting reactions as ignoring the fact that the change is occurring and blaming others for what is happening to them, recognizing the change but perceiving it as worse than they initially thought and reminiscing about the "good old days," still focusing on the personal impact of the change but beginning to look ahead to the future and its challenges, and developing enough trust in the leadership to commit to the change and what it will bring.

Effective Change Agents in Schools

Moving an educational system through a desired change requires the efforts of a leader who functions as a change agent. In most cases the person will be either a formal organizational leader or brought in from the external environment. External consultants have proven useful in developing and guiding educational change, particularly when the educational administrators involved have limited experience in implementing change.

A change agent must be able to identify and analyze complex organizational problems; must have insight into the effects of culture and climate on employees; must be able to conceptualize and implement broad plans for change; must be able to share power and develop consensus for collaborative decisions; must be able to maintain the openness of the educational system while monitoring the quality of input, output, and change; and must be able to maintain the positive aspects of the system while working toward improvement through change. Ultimately, since a leader (either system administrator or consultant) by definition does not work in isolation, the change agent must be able to assist others to develop appropriate goals, motivations, and behaviors that will lead to the desired ends. Effective change agents recognize that implementing major change takes time. Enough time must be allowed for modifying existing roles or creating new roles and then internalizing the changes.

As a change agent, an educational administrator serves as catalyst, resources linker, solution giver, and process helper (Havelock, 1973; Lippett & Lippett, 1985). A change agent serves as a catalyst because of the built-in inertia of systems that leads to reluctance to change. The change agent can become a source of pressure, helping staff to see the need for change. As a resource linker, the change agent can bring human and nonhuman resources together, either external or internal to the system, and help to make the most effective use of those resources. During the process of change, the change agent can help set objectives, acquire resources, select solutions, adapt solutions, and evaluate the process and results.

Steeples (1990) elaborated on these tasks of the change agent in discussing management of change in higher education. He noted that the issue for leaders in higher education (and, by extension, in educational systems generally) is not whether to change but which changes will be required. A first consideration is to understand the necessity of identifying goals and means to accomplish change. Even when it is clear that external or internal developments dictate a change, it is not always obvious what changes are appropriate. Therefore, decisions about change must be based on a strategic concept. The educational leader must create a strategic vision that must precede and help structure plans for innovation so that the change meets more than short-term needs. Fullan (1991) held that change is a very personal experience, and the teachers who will be affected by change should be actively involved in the change experiences. They should be able to feel that the advantages of the change will exceed the disadvantages. Support for early efforts, which are often awkward, is vital.

The building principal is a key change agent in education. According to Goldring and Rallis (1993), such a person should be able to articulate a vision, provide direction, facilitate those working for change, coordinate the effort, and balance forces affecting the effort. Effective principals initiate change by using teacher leadership, Goldring and Rallis said. They do this through motivating teachers by creating a problem-solving climate, using participatory decision making, establishing collegial communication, providing for recognition and rewards, and obtaining the resources necessary to make and maintain the change.

In functioning as an effective change agent, the principal might well consider six questions posited by Fullan (1991): (a) Is the change appropriate to this specific situation? (b) Is the change understood, or do people just think that they understand? (c) Are both the goals and the implementation clear? (d) Will the status quo allow for change? (e) Does the change challenge a person's self-concept? (f) How do we know if the change is valuable?

Change in Your Local School/ School District

Addresses ISLLC Standards 1, 2, 3, 4, 5, and 6

Given the discussion of change in this chapter, consider the following questions:

1. What change or changes do you feel should take place in your school or local school district that would improve the effectiveness of the organization?
2. Why do you believe the change(s) would improve effectiveness?
3. Who should lead the effort for change? Why?
4. When should the change take place? Why?
5. How should the change be managed? Why?
6. What resistances to change can be anticipated, and how might they be overcome?

Planning for a Changing Future in Education

Cunningham (1982) proposed that school administrators or managers of educational systems must work to anticipate the future. As decision makers today, their roles as change agents are critical. "Those who cannot project themselves into the future can only respond to the immediacy of the present, unable to envision and assess possible futures," he warned. "The administrator cannot just decide whether or not to make decisions with futurity in mind; he or she must make them by the definition of the role" (pp. 246–247). He argued for the skill of anticipation as a key element in the success of any administrator or manager. Anticipation is the ability to foresee and evaluate the medium- and long-range consequences of current decisions. It is a key to effective planning and thus to effective management of long-range change.

Skillful participation in the work of leadership, inquiry-based use of data to shape decisions and practice, broad involvement and collective responsibility for student learning, and reflective practice that leads to innovation are major prerequisites for high leadership capacity in education, according to Lambert (2003).

The Fate of Educational Changes

Even with the best intent in the world, no change can be considered permanent. Some take hold, flourish, meet long-term needs, and become an integral part of the original system. Some meet relatively short-term needs and disappear when the need is gone. Research shows that organizations are now undergoing major changes about once every 3 years, while smaller changes are taking place almost continuously (Chartered Institute of Personnel and Development, 2006).

Hogen (1994) noted that although teachers attend many workshops and training programs, little or no change is evident in the classrooms. Lack of effective instruction in how to use the innovation and questions about the practicality of a new idea are among the factors that she identified that inhibit implementation.

Goodlad (1975), reviewing school reforms, noted that much good could be found in many new practices, but many suffered from unrealistic expectations on the part of practitioners, members of the school systems, and members of the general community.

Problematic Features of Change

As may be concluded from the brief comment by Goodlad (1975), major organizational change generates four types of issues, according to Bolman and Deal (1997): it affects a person's ability to feel effective, valued, and in control; it produces uncertainty by disrupting existing roles and working relationships; it creates winners and losers, which has the potential for conflict; and it can cause loss of meaning for people on the receiving end of the change.

A brief review of problematic features as discussed by Srivastva, Fry, and Associates (1992) is as follows:

1. Models of change frequently require practitioners to use a process that provides only brief glimpses of reality. Models are often too linear and forgo the dynamics of organizational life. Change may not be a phenomenon that begins, happens,

and ends. It may be drastically more disorderly than theorized. Change agents need to be more cognizant of the daily complexity found in organizational life and adapt action methodologies that observe what choices are framed with why choices are made.

2. Change scenarios may lack sufficient time horizons. Seldom are change intervention strategies concerned with lengths of time sufficient to display an alternative rationale for the events observed. In most studies of organizational culture, the broad history of basic assumptions is equally important to the constrained views that most models presume. Change must be immersed in the totality of organizational life: its old practices and its new ones. Both are necessary if cohesion is to be satisfied.

3. The study of change in organizations may lack true systemic understanding. More often than not the study of change excludes interrelationships, interdependencies, environmental contingencies, and relationship factors. The context of change may be as important as identifying common characteristics or factors. As is often the case, the best change programs may be employed without understanding their context and, more inappropriately, with purposeful disregard for important contextual parameters. Organizational change must be linked to its total environment, along with assurance of continuity with social, technical, and ecological consequences of organizational action. Understanding the systemic context of change is paramount to thorough change modeling.

4. Change often is paralyzed in existing, often limited paradigms. In organizational change, study frames are often bipolar. Theory X or theory Y exists, as do democratic or authoritarian styles. In reality, multiplicity is evident, as change strategies often encompass situational or contingency approaches. Even multiplicity can be a trap. It is possible to comprehend what applications are available but not why. A thorough understanding of change can seemingly be formative only if it is interpretive and interactive in its utilization of knowledge and conversion to praxis.

5. The deterministic–outcome orientations of change strategies may create problems. This may also result from a highly systematic approach to change. Although we view organizations as open systems, we also tend to worry more about the effects of remaining a closed system. In this regard, we rarely mobilize energy to change but more often draw attention to resistance factors. As a result, our models may be focused on reduction of barriers at the expense of equifinal methodologies.

This discussion of problematic features shows a need for a more systemic understanding of change. The organizational world is full of examples that demonstrate the systemic nature of organizational functioning. Schools often exhibit their systemic proclivities despite their traditional bureaucratic form. For example, teachers may ignore the mandates of curriculum with results equal to or better than prescribed by mandates, alternative organizational structures may increase teacher and administrator latitudes and work equally well, and new basics (critical thinking and creativity development) may create better-rounded graduates. Our attention needs to focus on why these work and where they work as much as on what they are and the processes involved. Just as important, our search for whys must include thinking about new methodologies. As Srivastva et al. (1992) believe, "Our cup is partly full (with useful models, guidelines, and experiences); it is also partly empty" (p. 9).

Challenge and Opportunity

The 21st century presents both challenge and opportunity for those interested in education. The challenges can be met and the opportunities for effective performance taken if we can understand and accept new ways of thinking about education as well as retaining useful aspects of current perspectives. Some things to consider are the following:

1. Education is and always will be a societal agency, a means of simultaneously preserving the culture as well as preparing for social change.

2. Because it is a societal agency, the educational system is and always will be accountable for the resources that it uses and for the results of using those resources.

3. Change is not an aberration. Disequilibrium and change are, as noted by Wheatley (1994), the basis for healthy growth in any system, including the educational system.

4. The educational system is dynamic, self-renewing, and evolutionary. Stasis is not its normal condition. Structures are temporary, responsive to current conditions in the larger societal system, and changing at need (Wheatley, 1994).

5. Effective leadership in such a changing environment is leadership that develops a vision that is flexible, forward thinking, and responsive to changing conditions.

6. Effective leadership sees the educational system as a set of nested systems, from the local to the regional to the state and national levels, and understands the need to approach change and reform at multiple levels simultaneously (Fullan, 2005, 2007).

7. Effective leadership understands that creating sustainable change means not creating a fixed condition but creating a condition that maintains a positive vision and that can be adjusted to changing conditions and circumstances without losing its core values (Fullan, 2005, 2007).

Summary and Fundamental Concepts

Change is universal in open systems. Economic, political, social, and ideological changes are pressing the educational system for change. Educational leaders of the 21st century must learn to function effectively in this unstable environment.

To function effectively in this environment, schools must fill the dual social roles of change agent and cultural conservator, existing in a state of dynamic tension.

Chapter 14 will draw together significant concepts discussed in the previous chapters, providing a view of the educational systems to come as the 21st century unfolds and considering implications of those developments for the educational leaders of the future.

Fundamental Concepts

The fundamental concepts that follow have been discussed in this chapter. The citations that conclude each concept indicate the Interstate School Leaders Licensure Consortium

(ISLLC) standards and functions related to the concept. The Arabic numeral refers to the ISLLC standards, and the letters refer to the functions as presented in the table found inside the front cover.

- Change is a process, not a single event. (1A, 1C, 1D, 1E; 2A, 2F; 3D; 6B, 6C)
- Types of change include enforced, expedient, essential, planned, and unplanned. (1A, 1C, 1D, 1E; 2A, 2F; 3D; 6B, 6C)
- Resistance arises as a common response to change if it does not adhere to established norms and values. (1A, 1C, 1D, 1E; 2A, 2F; 3D; 6B, 6C)
- Resistance to change can be reduced if planners are aware of barriers to understanding, to acceptance, and to action. (1A, 1C, 1D, 1E; 2A, 2F; 3D; 6B, 6C)
- Various strategies for change exist. They include rational–empirical, normative–reeducative, power–coercive, transactional, deterministic, social action, and action research. (1A, 1C, 1D, 1E; 2A, 2F; 3D; 6B, 6C)
- Four types of planned change models exist: problem solving, research–development–diffusion–utilization, social interaction, and linkage. (1A, 1C, 1D, 1E; 2A, 2F; 3D; 6B, 6C)
- Change agents are persons, groups, or organizations seeking to produce change in a system. (1A, 1C, 1D, 1E; 2A, 2F; 3D; 6B, 6C)
- Leaders who are change agents may use classical or participative styles. They perform three functions: recruitment, development, and control. (1A, 1C, 1D, 1E; 2A, 2F; 3D; 6B, 6C)
- Managing planned change involves six steps:
  1. Diagnosing the present condition
  2. Setting goals and defining the new condition
  3. Defining the transition state between conditions
  4. Developing plans for managing the transition
  5. Evaluating the change effort
  6. Stabilizing the new condition (1A, 1C, 1D, 1E; 2A, 2F; 3D; 6B, 6C)
- Planned change in the educational system involves several stages: awareness, initiation, implementation, routinization, renewal, and evaluation. (1A, 1C, 1D, 1E; 2A, 2F; 3D; 6B, 6C)
- Change agents in schools are usually an existing leader or an outside consultant. (1A, 1C, 1D, 1E; 2A, 2F; 3D; 6B, 6C)
- Problematic features of change in organizations include being too linear and not sufficiently complex, having insufficient time horizons, lacking understanding of the system to be changed, being blocked by existing conditions or views, and being too

systematic and not sufficiently attuned to open systems. (1A, 1C, 1D, 1E; 2A, 2F; 3D; 6B, 6C)

- Change is the norm in society. It is also the norm in educational systems. Effective leadership understands and works within that principle. (1A, 1C, 1D, 1E; 2A, 2F; 3D; 6B, 6C)

Case Study

The New Principal

Addresses ISLLC Standards 1, 2, 3, 4, and 6

When Dr. Jack Prince accepted the new post as principal of Norden Township Junior-Senior High School, he knew the tasks ahead of him were formidable. He had prior experience as a principal but in a smaller school. Jack knew that he would be replacing a principal who had stepped down after a vote of no confidence. It was also well known that some of the faculty of the business department would pose problems that Jack would have to face.

Jack's new management staff included an assistant principal at the junior high school and three department chairpersons. Two of the three department chairs had risen recently from within the faculty ranks, and the third chair, Dr. Bob Neuman, had held his position for more than 10 years.

After the announcement had been made concerning his acceptance as principal, Jack had met with the superintendent, Dr. Amy Kim. Dr. Kim was an old friend and colleague and had herself moved to the superintendency from a secondary principalship. At their first meeting, Dr. Kim warned about some issues Jack would have to work through during the term. She said that the faculty in the school were, for the most part, very effective educators, liked by the student body, and considered highly competent. This faculty would be a pleasure to work with. But Bob Neuman led a small group of faculty who had become complacent. Their material was outdated, their classes were avoided by students except when required, and their instruction was less than inspiring. Bob Neuman himself was probably the worst of them all. However, Neuman was influential with his own faculty and exerted methods to control much of the younger faculty. For the past several years, he had also been the president of the local teachers union.

Several days into the new fall semester, Jack contemplated how he would cope with his new challenge. It was too early to make any final judgments, but he was beginning to observe indications of exactly what Amy Kim had spoken about. After much thinking, Jack decided he would, in his words, "stir up the pot." He intended to call a faculty meeting and announce his intention to create quality teams. His intention was to give more power to faculty. He had been a strong advocate of the quality movement in his previous position as principal, and he would begin developing exactly that in the present situation.

Your Task

This case poses typical problems faced by a new administrator. Respond to the following questions:

1. What do you think about the "pot-stirring" approach that the new principal decided on? What are its advantages? What are its disadvantages?
2. Identify the following in the case: the change agent, potential supporters, and potential dissenters.
3. What would you have done in this situation? Why? Explain your proposal in terms of the material discussed in this chapter.
4. Identify a task that you as new principal might want to accomplish with your faculty. How would you go about this? What part might quality management play? How would you deal with potential supporters? Potential dissenters?

REFERENCES

Basom, R. E., & Crandall, D. P. (1991). Implementing a redesign strategy: Lessons from educational change. *Educational Horizons, 69*(2), 73–77.

Beckhard, R., & Harris, R. T. (1977). *Organizational transitions: Managing complex change.* Reading, MA: Addison-Wesley.

Beer, M., Eisenstat, R., & Spector, B. (1990). Why change programs don't produce change. *Harvard Business Review, 90*(6), 158–166.

Bennis, W. (1966). *Changing organizations: Essays on the development and evolution of human organization.* New York: McGraw-Hill.

Bolman, L. G., & Deal, T. E. (1997). *Reframing organizations: Artistry, choice, and leadership* (2nd ed.). San Francisco: Jossey-Bass.

Caldwell, M. S. (1968). An approach to the assessment of educational planning. *Educational Technology, 8*(19), 5–12.

Cetron, M., & Gayle, M. (1991). *Educational resistance: Our schools at the turn of the century.* New York: St. Martin's Press.

Chartered Institute of Personnel and Development. (2006, April). *Change management.* Retrieved September 29, 2007, from http://www.cipd.co.uk/subjects/corpstrtgy/changemmt/chngmgmt.html

Chin, R., & Benne, K. S. (1969). General strategies for effecting change in human systems. In W. G. Bennis, K. D. Benne, & R. Chin (Eds.), *The planning of change* (pp. 297–312). New York: Holt, Rinehart and Winston.

Connor, P. E., & Lake, K. L. (1988). *Managing organizational change*. New York: Praeger.

Cunningham, W. G. (1982). *Systematic planning for educational change*. Mountain View, CA: Mayfield.

Fombrun, C. J. (1992). *Turning points creating strategic change in corporations*. New York: McGraw-Hill.

Freeman, D. H. (2006, July). Making organizational changes stick. *Of Counsel 25*(7), 13, 14.

French, W. L., & Bell, C. H., Jr. (1973). *Organization development*. Upper Saddle River, NJ: Prentice Hall.

Fullan, M. (1982). *The meaning of educational change*. New York: Teachers College Press.

Fullan, M. (1991). *The new meaning of educational change*. New York: Teachers College Press.

Fullan, M. (2005). *Leadership and sustainability: System thinkers in action*. Thousand Oaks, CA: Corwin Press.

Fullan, M. (2007). *The new meaning of educational change* (4th ed). New York: Teachers College Press.

Goldring, E. B., & Rallis, S. F. (1993). *Principals of dynamic schools: Taking charge of change*. Newbury Park, CA: Corwin Press.

Goodlad, J.I. (1975). The dynamics of educational change. New York: McGraw-Hill.

Grenier, L. E. (1989). Common approaches to change. In R. McLennan (Ed.), *Managing organizational change* (pp. 138–140). Upper Saddle River, NJ: Prentice Hall.

Hahn, D. (1991). Strategic management: Tasks and challenges of the 1990s. *Long Range Planning, 24*(1), 26–39.

Hanson, E. M. (1985). *Educational administration and organizational behavior* (2nd ed.). Boston: Allyn & Bacon.

Hathaway, P. (2000, October). *Resistance to change* (Innovative leader 9[10] #495). Retrieved September 29, 2007, from http://winstonbrill.com/bril001/html/article_index/articles/451.

Havelock, R. G. (1973). *The change agent's guide to innovation in education*. Upper Saddle River, NJ: Educational Technology.

Hersey, P., & Blanchard, K. H. (1988). *Management of organizational behavior utilizing human resources* (5th ed.). Upper Saddle River, NJ: Prentice Hall.

Hodgkinson, C. (1991). *Educational leadership: The moral art*. New York: State University of New York Press.

Hogen, E. A. O. (1994). *Exploring teacher change: A study of five first grade teachers immersed in three major areas of change*. Unpublished doctoral dissertation, University of South Dakota, Vermillion.

Huse, E. F. (1975). *Organizational development and change*. St. Paul, MN: West.

Huse, E. F., & Cummings, T. G. (1985). *Organizational development and change* (3rd ed.). St. Paul, MN: West.

Johansen, J. H. (1967). The relationship between teachers' perceptions of influence in local curriculum decision-making and curriculum implementation. *Journal of Educational Research, 61*(2), 81–88.

Kanter, R. M., Stein, B. A., & Jick, T. D. (1992). *The challenge of organizational change*. New York: Free Press.

Kohl, J. W. (1968). A conceptual tool for implementing change. *Journal of Secondary Education, 43*(7), 324–325.

Koestler, P. (1973). The elements of social action. In R. H. Lauer (Ed.), *Perspective on social change*. Boston: Allyn & Bacon.

Kowalski, T. J., & Reitzug, U. C. (1993). *Contemporary school administration: An introduction*. New York: Longman.

Lashway, L., Mazarella, J., & Grundy, T. (1988). Portrait of a leader. In S. C. Smith & P. K. Piele (Eds.), *School leaders' handbook for excellence* (2nd ed.). Eugene: ERIC Clearinghouse on Educational Management, College of Education, University of Oregon, pp. 52–76.

Lambert, L. (2003, July). *Leadership capacity for lasting school improvement*. Alexandria, VA: Association for Supervision and Curriculum Development.

Lauer, R. H. (1973). *Perspective on social change*. Boston: Allyn & Bacon.

Lewin, K. (1951). *Field theory in social sciences*. New York: Harper & Row.

Lindbloom, C. E. (1965). *The intelligence of democracy decision making through mutual adjustments*. New York: Free Press.

Lipham, J. M., Rankin, R., & Hoeh, J. (1985). *The principalship: Concepts, competencies, and cases*. New York: Longman.

Lippett, G. L., Langseth, P., & Mossop, J. (1985). *Implementing organizational change: A practical guide to managing change efforts*. San Francisco: Jossey-Bass.

Lippett, G. L., & Lippett, R. (1985). The consulting function of the human resource development professional. In L. Nadler (Ed.), *The handbook of human resource development* (pp. 5.1–5.27). New York: Wiley.

London, M. (1988). *New roles and innovation strategies for human resource professionals*. San Francisco: Jossey-Bass.

Lorsch, J. W., & Trooboff, S. (1989). Two universal models. In R. McLennan (Ed.), *Managing organizational change* (pp. 68–75). Upper Saddle River, NJ: Prentice Hall.

Lunenberg, F. C., & Ornstein, A. C. (1991). *Educational administration: Concepts and practices*. Belmont, CA: Wadsworth.

Mannheim, K. (1940). *Man and society in an age of reconstruction: Studies in modern social structure*. New York: Harcourt & Brace.

Mauriel, J. J. (1989). *Strategic leadership for schools: Creating and sustaining productive change*. San Francisco: Jossey-Bass.

Meyerson, M., & Banfield, E. C. (1964). *Politics, planning, and the public interest: The case of public housing in Chicago*. New York: Free Press of Glencoe.

Millard, R. M. (1991). *Today's myths and tomorrow's realities: Overcoming obstacles to academic leadership in the 21st century*. San Francisco: Jossey-Bass.

Monahan, W. G., & Hengst, H. R. (1982). *Contemporary educational administration*. New York: Macmillan.

Mort, P. R., & Ross, D. H. (1957). *Principles of school administration*. New York: McGraw-Hill.

Nickols, F. (2003). *Four change management strategies*. Retrieved September 10, 2007, from http://www.nickols.us@att.net

Nutt, P. (1986). Tactics of implementation. *Academy of Management Journal. 29*(2), pp. 231–261.

Owens, R. G. (1987). *Organizational behavior in education* (3rd ed.). Upper Saddle River, NJ: Prentice Hall.

Perrow, C. (1961). An analysis of goals in complex organizations. *American Sociological Review, 26*, 854–866.

Pfeffer, J., & Salancik, G. R. (1978). *The external control of organizations*. New York: Harper & Row.

Sarason, S. B. (1971). *The culture of the school and the problem of change*. Boston: Allyn & Bacon.

Schein, E. (1969). *Process consultations: Its role in organization development*. Reading, MA: Addison-Wesley.

Schuler, A. J. (2003). *Overcoming resistance to change: Top ten reasons for change resistance*. Retrieved September 15, 2007, from http://www.schulersolutions.com/resistance_to_change.html

Senge, P. (1990). The leader's new work: Building learning organizations. *Sloan Management Review, 32*(1), 17–23.

Sheive, L. T. (1981). *A test and reformulation of three developmental models of organizational change in an organization of relative zero growth*. Unpublished doctoral dissertation, State University of New York at Buffalo.

Simek, R. (1997). *An investigation of the relationship between specific organizational variables and integration of emotionally disturbed and neurologically impaired students*. Unpublished dissertation, State University of New York at Buffalo.

Smith, M. E. (2002, January). Success rates for different types of organizational change. *Performance Improvement, 41*(1). Retrieved August 25, 2007, from http://www.ispi.org.

Srivastva, S., Fry, R. E., & Associates. (1992). *Executive and organizational continuity: Managing the paradoxes of stability and change*. San Francisco: Jossey-Bass.

Stanislao, J., & Stanislao, B. C. (1983, July–August). Dealing with resistance to change. *Business Horizons*, 74–78.

Steeples, D. W. (Ed.). (1990). *Managing change in higher education*. San Francisco: Jossey-Bass.

Stogdill, R. (1974). *Handbook of leadership*. New York: Free Press.

Tucker, J. (2007, August 12). *Types of change: Developmental, transitional, and transformational*. Retrieved September 29, 2007, from http://businessmanagement.suite101.com/article.cfm/types_of_change.

Vroom, V. H., & Yetton, P. W. (1973). *Leadership and decision making*. Pittsburgh, PA: University of Pittsburgh Press.

Walton, R. E. (Ed.). (1965). *A behavioral theory of labor negotiations: An analysis of a social interaction system*. New York: McGraw-Hill.

Warren, R. L. (1977). *Social change and human purpose: Toward understanding and action*. Chicago: Rand McNally College.

Watson, G. (1969). Resistance to change. In W. G. Bennis, K. D. Benne, & R. Chin (Eds.), *The planning of change* (2nd ed., pp. 488–498). New York: Holt, Rinehart and Winston.

Waugh, R. F., & Punch, K. F. (1987). Teacher receptivity to system-wide change in the implementation stage. *Review of Educational Research, 57*(3), 237–254.

Wheatley, M. J. (1994). *Leadership and the new science: Learning about organization from an orderly universe*. San Francisco, CA: Berrett-Koehler.

Yukl, G. A. (1981). *Leadership in organizations*. Upper Saddle River, NJ: Prentice Hall.

Educational Leadership in a Flat World

We are nearing the end of our treatise on the fundamental concepts of educational leadership and management. The review of scholarship and current thinking in a wide range of areas was intended to motivate the reader to consider critically the theoretical underpinnings of the subject within the context of current issues, problems, practice, and proposed solutions.

Our approach has been an analytical one of thinking between paradigms and mapping the theoretical and practical worlds in which leaders and managers function. An expanded version of systems theory and organizational theory were used as overarching vehicles for shaping the structure of the book and to connect the many concepts of educational leadership presented. Four dimensions of leadership were examined (inquiry and analysis, decision making, human interaction, and change) from several perspectives (leadership, philosophy, human relations, communication, information, planning, allocation of resources, evaluation, and policy formulation).

In this concluding chapter, we build a composite view of the complete work by synthesizing the discussions of previous chapters. In this final discussion we provide further illustrations of how education must contend with emerging issues and conditions and discuss scenarios that portray possible futures of education. The chapter begins with a synthesis of the challenge facing education leaders today followed by a summary of the response strategies to date. We then critique the fragmented approach that has characterized those responses and urge that a systemic approach be followed. We close with a summary of the role of persons in leadership positions during the transitional period that lies ahead and strategies that may be useful.

The Challenge

We are nearing the end of the third decade of the information age. When it was first described in book length detail by Alvin Toffler (1980), John Naisbitt (1982), and Peter Drucker (1989), we read them almost as science fiction, awed by the possibilities but never really believing that the futures described would ever become our reality. But they have, and in 2006, Thomas Friedman reported that beginning around 2000, the world had become "flattened." This time, we knew it was not fiction because he was describing what we were experiencing and put it into remarkable perspective for us.

For those who held university degrees and were in the upper income brackets, the quality of life was rapidly improving—not that it was that bad before. Communications were vastly improved, especially with colleagues overseas. Prices were unbelievably low as was the rate of inflation. And the selection of goods were remarkably varied—and, for the most part, of good quality.

For others, this flat world was not so great. Even before 2000, industrial jobs were beginning to move overseas, putting economic pressure on factory workers. In inflation-adjusted dollars from 1979 to the present, those with less than a high school education had actually lost about 20% of their purchasing power, and the earnings of those who have acquired a high school diploma or had some college have stagnated. Changes in the labor market in the 1980s included a shift from goods-producing industries (that had disproportionately provided high-wage opportunities for low-skilled workers) to technical service industries (that disproportionately employ college graduates) and low-wage industries, such as retail trade.

The within-industry shifts in labor demand away from less educated workers are, perhaps, a more important explanation of eroding wages than the shift out of manufacturing. Other factors related to the downward trend in wages of less educated workers include intensifying global competition and immigration, automation, the decline in the proportion of workers belonging to unions, the decline in the real value of the minimum wage, the increasing need for computer skills, and the increasing use of temporary workers (Jones & Weinberg, 2000).

Only persons holding bachelor's and graduate degrees have experienced significant increases in their real wages over the past 30 years. But since 2000, with the development of highly sophisticated collaborative work flow software, even these job holders are being challenged by lower-paid, well-educated workers overseas, many of whom were educated in American colleges and universities. The impact of this phenomenon is only beginning to play out; however, over the period since 1980 to the present, the net effect has been for the proportion of middle-income persons to shrink in comparison with the well paid and the poor.

The link between education level and earnings is well established. If the American workforce is to maintain its historic standard of living (to say nothing of increasing it), the United States must abandon low-skill work and concentrate on producing high value-added products and services. This means that the United States must maintain technological leadership in every field where it intends to be a major competitor (New Commission on the Skills of the American Workforce [NCSAW], 2007).

Friedman (2006) has concluded that wealth will increasingly gravitate to those countries that get three basic things right: the infrastructure to connect as efficiently and speedily as possible with the flat world platform, that is, from cheap Internet bandwidth and mobile phones to modem airports and roads; the right education program and knowledge to empower more of their people to innovate and to do value-added work on that platform; and the right governance to enhance and manage the flow to the flat world. Friedman points to American weaknesses

in all these areas, but we focus only on those related directly to education.

In Friedman's analysis, the existing educational system is the problem. It was designed during the late 19th and early 20th centuries, primarily to provide a low-skill labor force for the mass production industries of the time—only about 10% of the students were college bound. In essence, it provided basic literacy, mathematics, and citizenship skills that the system accomplished quite effectively. But those skills are no longer sufficient to qualify persons for jobs in the postmanufacturing era dominated by the information industry that pay at a level the average American worker enjoyed during the industrial era.

So what are the skills seen as basic for the higher-paying jobs in the labor force of the 21st century that would permit American workers to continue to enjoy their historic standard of living? Of course, some of the abilities honed by industrial-age schools will continue to be valued including linear, logical, and analytical skills that are characteristic of left-brain thinking; however, many of the jobs requiring those skills that can be reduced to a set of rules, routines, and instructions are being computerized or sent overseas to be done by well-qualified persons working at significantly lower wage rates. To flourish in this new era, "We'll have to supplement our well-developed high-tech abilities with aptitudes that are 'high concept' and 'high touch'" (Friedman, 2006, p. 308). This means that to maintain a competitive advantage in a flat world, it will become relatively more important to develop attributes of the right brain, such as artistry, empathy, seeing the big picture, and pursuing the transcendent, than it was to meet the requirements of the manufacturing labor market. The most important ability for continuing success, however, is to learn how to learn (Friedman, 2006).

The recommendations of the NCSAW (2007) echo Friedman's emphasis on honing right-brain abilities. The commission believes that the only way to justify higher wages in the United States relative to its international competitors is to focus on creativity and innovation:

> Creativity requires both deep knowledge and technical expertise with one area and very broad knowledge of many, apparently unrelated, areas. It depends on being able to combine disparate elements in new ways that

are appropriate for the task or challenge at hand. Thus, it relies heavily on synthesis, the ability to see patterns where others see only chaos. It will happen only in circumstances in which the creator is allowed to fail many times in order to succeed only once. (p. 30)

> This is a world in which a very high level of preparation in reading, writing, speaking, mathematics, science, literature, history, and the arts will be an indispensable foundation for everything that comes after for most members of the workforce. It is a world in which comfort with ideas and abstractions is the passport to a good job, in which creativity and innovation are the key to the good life, in which high levels of education—a different kind of education than most of us have had—are going to be the only security there is. (p. xviii)

With the exception of the best of our public and private schools, however, instruction in most schools currently emphasizes memory and analytical abilities almost to the exclusion of creative abilities, such as synthesis.

To meet these curricular and quality challenges, the NCSAW recommends that a very high proportion of high school graduates need to possess the skills typically required for college entrance. Currently, only about one-third of high school graduates have reached this level of proficiency according to National Assessment of Educational Progress (NAEP) testing results (National Center for Education Statistics, 2006). The implication is a single-track, college entrance high school curriculum for at least 90% of the students. The challenge is enormous.

The commission also agrees with Friedman that the source of the problem is the nature of the current school system and our fragmented approach to reform. The NCSAW (2007) criticized schools and districts for hopping from one unsuccessful partial reform solution to another rather than taking a systemic approach, that is, whole-school or whole-system reform. They speculate that most of the attempted partial solutions were not "wrong," just insufficient. "The worst of our schools are not short of initiatives and programs. They typically have too many of them in conflict with one another, a discordant symphony of barely controlled chaos" (p. 38).

The concept of a single high school curriculum is not new. In 1982, near the beginning of the current reform movement, *The Paideia Proposal: An Educational Manifesto* (Adler, 1982) was issued, proposing a single, rigorous curriculum for all high school students. It received a bit of attention at the time but was quickly dropped, perhaps because it was considered too radical and impractical. A quarter of a century later, it does not seem so radical. As for practicality, even though educators back in the 1980s professed to believe that all children could learn, their actions did not reflect their words. Lack of commitment to and belief in the concept that all children can learn by educators remains a challenge today and is among the factors causing some, as Elmore (2004), to wonder if the educating profession is capable of leading the reform of the educational system. Perhaps this is an opportune time to resurrect the *Paideia Proposal* and reassess its merits.

The Paideia Group was sharply critical of the lack of national progress in the United States in becoming a true democracy:

> Equality of educational opportunity is not, in fact, provided if it means no more than taking all the children into the public schools for the same number of hours, days, and years. If once there they are divided into the sheep and the goats, into those destined solely for toil and those destined for economic and political leadership and for a quality of life to which all should have access, then the democratic purpose has been undermined by an inadequate system of public schooling.
>
> . . .
>
> It fails because it has achieved only the same quantity of schooling, not the same quality. This failure is a downright violation of our democratic principles.
>
> . . .
>
> We are politically a classless society. Our citizenry as a whole is our ruling class. We should, therefore, be an educationally classless society.
>
> . . .
>
> We should have a one-track system of schooling, not a system with two or more tracks, only one of which goes straight ahead while the others shunt the young off onto sidetracks not headed toward the goals our society opens to all. (Adler, 1982, p. 5)
>
> . . .
>
> There are no unteachable children. There are only schools and teachers and parents who fail to teach them. (p. 8)

The Paideia Group's 12-year course of study is diagrammed in Figure 14.1. Each column represents a distinct mode of teaching and learning, increasing in successive gradations of complexity and difficulty. Column 1 is the acquisition of organized knowledge, column 2 the development of intellectual skills, and column 3 the enlargement of understanding, insight, and aesthetic appreciation. The curriculum would also include instruction in a second language of choice. Physical education and care of the body would run through all 12 years. There would also be instruction in the manual arts

FIGURE 14.1

The Paideia Group's same course of study for all

	1	2	3
Goals	Acquisition of organized knowledge	Development of intellectual skills—skills of learning	Enlarged understanding of ideas and values
	by means of	by means of	by means of
Means	didactic instruction, lectures, and responses textbooks and other aids	coaching, exercises, and supervised practice	maieutic or socratic questioning and active participation
	in three areas of subject matter	in the operations of	in the
Areas, Operations, and Activities	language, literature and the fine arts mathematics and natural science history, geography, and social studies	reading, writing, speaking, listening calculating, problem solving observing, measuring, estimating exercising critical judgment	discussion of books (not textbooks) and other works of art and involvement in artistic activities (e.g., music, drama, visual arts)

The three columns do not correspond to separate courses, nor is one kind of teaching and learning necessarily confined to any one class.

Source: Reprinted with the permission of Scribner, a Division of Simon & Schuster Adult Publishing Group, from THE PAIDEIA PROPOSAL by Mortimer J. Adler.

for an unspecified number of years. An introduction to the world of work and its range of occupations and careers would be given in the 11th and 12th years.

Adler (1982) refers to column 2 as the backbone of basic schooling and indispensable to the efficient teaching and learning of the subject matter in column 1 and indispensable to the teaching and learning in column 3. Column 3 supplements and reinforces the learning in the other two columns.

Responses to the Challenge

All three levels of school government have recognized that there is a serious problem and have been attempting to address it as they understand it—primarily as low academic achievement by minority and poor students.

The progress of the current school reform movement was described in chapter 1 as evolving in three waves. The first wave, beginning in the mid-1980s, focused on raising student performance and teacher quality by increasing high school graduation and teacher certification requirements, initiating longer school days and years, and introducing competency tests, standardized curricula, and more rigorous promotion criteria for students. A second wave formed in the late 1980s that called for a fundamental rethinking of the schooling process. This wave viewed schools as the basic unit of educational productivity and made them the focus for improvement. Change efforts at the school level emphasized capacity building, especially through professional development of teachers, and governance changes that brought teachers, parents, and other members of the immediate community into the decision process. The third and current wave is characterized by two themes: comprehensive change that focuses on many aspects of the system and policy integration and coordination around a clear set of outcomes by allowing greater professional discretion at the school site under the umbrella of centralized coordination. A listing and discription of specific reforms follows, organized into three divisions as structural reform, school reform, and curricular reform.

Structural Reform

Standards-Based Accountability. Forty-nine of the states have adopted academic standards in the core subjects. Iowa alone holds out as a matter of principle (i.e., local control of education). The state remains a relatively high-achieving state, but since 1992 it has been slipping relative to other states and the national average on reading and mathematics scores on the NAEP exams (Archer, 2006). Forty-four states have implemented tests custom designed to match state standards ("Standards and Accountability," 2006).

At the federal level, the No Child Left Behind Act (NCLB) was enacted in 2001 with near unanamous approval in both the House and the Senate. The centerpiece of the legislation is a requirement that states adopt a high-stakes accountablity scheme of the state's design with successful progress measured by an adequate yearly progress (AYP) statistic, defined by each state. Standards-based accountability and the NCLB were treated in chapter 8.

Parental Choice of Schooling. It has been only in the past 20 years that choice of public schools has been an option for most parents. Prior to that, parents could choose private schools, an option that few poor parents could afford—even low-tuition parochial schools or home schooling. Middle-class parents often used the reputation of the neighborhood school as a criterion when purchasing a house. Vehicles facilitating choice in public schools are open enrollment (elimination of school attendance boundries), charter schools, vouchers, and tax credits. References to parental choice and means for accommodating it arise throughout the book. Chapter 10 has a section specifically devoted to charter schools.

The argument behind parental choice is to inject marketlike discipline in the public school sector. With competition, poorly performing schools face the possibility of losing their clientele or at least a significant portion of it and ultimately being closed or at least reconstituted. Choice also permits parents to satisfy their preferences for philosophy and style.

School-Based Decision Making. The concept of school-based decision making (SBDM) involves a *system* of schools within which a significant amount of authority to make decisions on curriculum and allocation of human and fiscal resources has been devolved to each school. This takes place within a centrally determined framework of goals, policies, standards, and accountabilities (i.e., strategy formulation). In actuality, there is little evidence that SBDM leads directly to improved pupil achievement; therefore, SBDM must be viewed as an element of systemic reform if a connection with improved pupil achievement is to be made. With the advent of the accountability movement, teachers and administrators have argued that if they are to be held accountable for student outcomes, they need to be able to make decisions about how the school enterprise is to be organized, who works there, and how it deploys its assets. Chapter 11 discusses SBDM extensively.

School Reforms

Whole-School Reform. Classroom-level change cannot be dictated from above; however, not every school must reinvent the wheel. School staffs and community representatives can select among a variety of existing, well-designed methods and materials that have been shown to be effective with children. Support organizations behind each of the schoolwide models provide professional development, materials, and networks of fellow users. These reform organizations bring to a school broad experience working with high-poverty schools in many contexts. A section in chapter 12 called "School Reform Networks" is dedicated to the concept of whole-school reform. Whole-school reform is a strategy for a school (or group of schools) to systematically coordinate many state and federal programs as well as local initiatives into a well-integrated whole.

Small Schools. Policy implications drawn from studies of relationships between school and district size, pupil achievement, and cost have taken a dramatic turn in the past three decades. From the beginning of the 20th century through the 1960s, the overwhelming evidence seemed to support large schools and school districts in terms of lower costs and the higher number, diversity, and the caliber of professional and administrative personnel that they

could attract. These early studies were concerned primarily with inputs (costs) and gave little, if any, attention to outputs and ratios of outputs to inputs (efficiency). As researchers began to take into account total cost and socioeconomic status of pupils and to include measures of output such as achievement, pupil self-image, and success in college, economies of scale evaporated at relatively low numbers of pupils.

Small and focused educational communities enhance the climate of trust between families and schools and facilitate deep ongoing discussions in ways that produce change and involve the entire faculty. Small schools enable the faculty to know students and their work individually, and they permit adults to play a significant role in the development of a positive school culture. Small schools more easily provide for the physical safety of all and are more readily made accountable to parents and to the public.

Strong small high schools offer another benefit. Since several small schools replace one large comprehensive high school, students have a choice of schools that best meet their needs and interests. Aside from increasing the satisfaction of students and their families, choice provides a check on school quality. Few students will choose a school that offers a disruptive learning environment or an undesirable curriculum.

Chapter 12 offers an extensive discussion of small schools under the heading "Economies of Scale."

Extended School Day and Year. Research cited in chapter 12 concludes that schools do matter and that they matter most when support for academic learning outside the school is weak. Disadvantaged children have been shown to be capable learners. They keep up during the school year, but before they start first grade and in summers between grades, the out-of-school resources available to them are not sufficient to support their achievement. Preschool and full-day kindergarten experiences for all low-socioeconomic-status children (Lynch, 2007) as well as summer school or extended-year programs appear to be helpful in improving their achievement when coupled with improving the quality of time spent in the classroom through better-prepared lessons and a more engaging curriculum.

Curricular Reforms

Subject Matter. A number of researchers strongly believe that reform must start in the classroom and work out to the rest of the system (e.g., Elmore, 2007; Fullan, Hill, & Crevola, 2006). Curricular and instructional reforms leave their imprint directly on classroom practice and the interactions between students and teachers. Most attention has been given to reading and mathematics.

Many teachers recognize reading as the key to all academic learning. While there have been "reading wars" between phonics and whole-language proponents, a balanced approach seems to be preferred (David & Cuban, 2006). Phonics emphasizes the connection between letters or combination of letters and how they sound, enabling students to decode words through sound–letter relationships; understanding follows. Whole-language advocates stress reading for understanding, teaching spelling, and pronunciation along the way.

With respect to mathematics, NAEP scores have risen steadily for all groups since 1990 (http://nces. ed.gov/programs/coe/2005/section2/indicator10. asp). The basis for success is attributed to the publication of the standards developed by the National Council of Teachers of Mathematics in 1989 that spawned several new standards-based math programs. In addition, two camps exist among math teachers as to how best to teach the subject, but both agree over what students need to know: mastering the basic skills and the underlying concepts. Traditionalists favor memorizing facts and formulas, while reformers prefer allowing each child to develop his or her own understanding and procedures through experimentation. As with reading, most teachers favor a balanced approach (David & Cuban, 2006).

Individualized Instruction. In chapter 9, information-age schools are described that focus on students learning rather than teachers teaching. Teachers in such schools use the nearly unlimited accounting capabilities of computer networks to track student progress. Computerized information systems assist them in developing *individualized* (or personalized) curricula that take advantage of student strengths and interests to remedy their weaknesses as these are diagnosed.

Information-age schools rely on computers for their complete range of capabilities, but these machines are subject to human direction, planning, and control. Teachers are still absolutely essential, but their role is changed from one of director, leader, and final authority to one of diagnostician, prescriber, motivator, facilitator, and evaluator. Teachers, students, and aides are seen as multidimensional human resources leading to specialization and division of labor, breaking the self-contained classroom mold of today's schools. Tasks requiring professional judgment are separated from those that are routine. High-cost, professionally trained persons are assigned to the former, and lower-cost paraprofessionals are assigned to the latter. The pupil-to-teacher ratio is likely to be higher in these schools, but the pupil-to-adult ratio is likely to remain the same or even decline from current levels as paraprofessionals assume routine tasks.

Intelligent direction of information-age schools depends on the professional educators associated with them, and school-based decision making is the norm for them. Their teachers have become experts in learning theory, curriculum design, motivational techniques, and developmental procedures. They have highly specialized skills in diagnosing the strengths and weaknesses of individual students with various intellectual skills and backgrounds and in prescribing best combinations of available learning experiences and resources.

Professional Development. Reformers look to professional development as a sine qua non by which teachers can be equipped with the understandings and skills needed to increase student achievement, but professional development as currently provided has only tenuous links with classroom instruction for most teachers and little change in classroom practice ensues. Fullan et al. (2006) prefer the concept of professional learning communities where teachers have continuous opportunities to improve what they are doing by working and learning together. This involves having teachers who teach the same grades and subjects or the same students meet regularly to study data describing the progress of their students and researching and discussing how to provide better learning experiences for them in order to reach their achievement objectives. The reform view of professional development focuses the content on what teachers need to know and to do and locates the activities in the school where teachers can work together and get help to improve their teaching. "What is clear is that improvements in student learning must come from teacher learning. Without high-quality professional development, neither is likely to occur" (David & Cuban, 2006, p. 100).

Critique of the Reform Efforts

The previously listed reforms are only representative of the variety of strategies that have been embraced to improve student achievement. Schools and school districts typically have pursued a greater variety of reforms than have the state and federal governments, but some local reforms have required permissive legislation by the states, such as charter schools, and at no level of government has the process of reform regularly been approached strategically or systematically. Exceptions are Houston and Seattle.

The reform efforts of state and federal governments have focused on standards-based accountability as exemplified in the NCLB at the federal level. While NCLB has laudable goals, it is a patch on a school system that is no longer relevant to meeting many of the educational needs of the 21st century, and the rigidity of the enforcement of its accountability component may actually interfere with positive reform initiatives at state and local levels. As such, this strategy has the potential for becoming counterproductive.

While the NCLB is generally commended for its intentions of closing the achievement gaps among children of varying ethnic and economic groups, it is highly criticized for the means used in attempting to reach that goal. The remedies it imposes are driven by a single instrument, the standardized test, which can provide teachers with good data on students but does not provide the breadth and balance of information to assess accurately a child's mastery or a school's effectiveness, as urged in chapter 9. Further, its curricular focus is

on developing skills in two subject areas: reading and mathematics. Thus, the NCLB is inclined to narrow and distort the curriculum in ways that are antithetical to meeting the educational needs of the 21st century:

> The very definition of what constitutes an educated person is now dictated by federal legislation. A well-educated person is one who scores high on standardized math and reading tests. And ergo a good school is one that either has very high test scores or is moving toward them at a prescribed rate of improvement. Period. (Meier, 2004, p. 67)

To fix the NCLB, the law needs to be amended so that states are given the flexibility to use multiple measures in assessing student performance that are also diagnostically useful for informing curricular improvements. The emphasis of assessment should be identifying and improving the performance of failing students and schools rather than punishing them (Darling-Hammond, 2004). Success and failure should be measured using a "value-added" or "growth" model that takes into account the progress that has been made toward reaching a standard over a period of time instead of an arbitrarily determined absolute value. Struggling schools should receive intensive help to strengthen their staffs and instruction in support of their underachieving students.

The NCLB has also been criticized for leaving the definition and measurement of standards and AYP to the 50 states rather than being done at the national level (Cronin, Dahlin, Adkins, & Kingsbury, 2007). Support for this position is far from unanimous, but it is true that in 2005, only five states reported proficiency performance levels in reading and mathematics that corresponded closely to those of the NAEP. Other states varied widely from the NAEP statistics. Ravitch (2006, p. 54), a strong supporter of standards-based reform, observed, "With each state setting its own standards and measuring performance with its own tests, there are perverse incentives for the states to claim progress where it has not happened and to actually lower existing standards so as to demonstrate "proficiency" (p. 54). Ravitch is also critical of reducing testing solely to reading and mathematics. "If that is the only definition of success for schools today, then we veer dangerously close to the possibility that we are schooling our children, not educating them" (p. 58).

Certainly, setting standards, goals, and objectives are important aspects of leading an educational organization; we have devoted much attention to them throughout this text and especially in chapter 11. Assessment is another important aspect that we treated extensively in chapter 8. But the two, even together, are not the "be all and end all" of education. If the results are poor, teachers and administrators at the school level need detailed information on the performance of each child so that they can diagnose the problem that each child is having and develop a personalized curriculum to enable each child to overcome his or her difficulties. The purpose of the school is not to screen out the poorly performing students but to educate all of them—well. To this end, districtwide administrators are not only interested in identifying poorly performing schools to initiate remediation, but they are also concerned about what is going on in high-performing schools that might be helpful to those schools going through restructuring.

Reading and writing are very important subjects, and the skills involved are foundational to learning other subjects, but they are only part of a comprehensive curriculum and the role of the school goes far beyond teaching literacy and mathematics. As new curricula and new teaching methods are introduced, teachers must be prepared through professional development and parents must be apprised. The point is that everything of consequence is linked in some way to other aspects of the system. Every action has a reaction, that reaction generates another reaction, and the ripple effect broadens and moves outward.

A fundamental flaw of the reform initiatives collectively is that they have focused almost exclusively on schooling to the neglect of dealing with many root causes. We have known of the very strong linkages between school performance and family background at least since the release of Coleman's (1966) *Equality of Educational Opportunity*. Yet the campaign to eliminate achievement gaps among socioeconomic and ethnic groups has centered on schools and what they do and not on the students and the environment that shaped them in the years before they entered school and that continue to influence them during the years they are in school. A systems approach to attacking the achievement gap problem would have prevented the fragmented mélange we have today and permitted the fragments to be aligned into a network of reinforcement. A systems approach would have made policymakers more aware of environmental factors and that the problem does not begin and end at the school door. Granted, the authority to act by school people is limited to the confines of the schools, but this should not stop astute leadership from developing liaisons with those outside the school working with problems that affect what goes on inside the school.

We have used systems theory as an organizing concept of this book in the hope that it will engender in its readers a "disposition," to borrow a term used by the Interstate School Leaders Licensure Consortium, to anticipate the likely consequences of an action or strategy and to prepare for them. In the next section, we take a final look at how systems theory can be useful to educational leaders in analyzing problems and strategies for dealing with them.

Systems Theory as a Guide for Education Leaders

As used throughout this book, traditional systems theory has been expanded by accepting Flood's (1990) argument for a complementarist theoretical position that is open and conciliatory and that encompasses the emancipatory forces of critical self-reflection. Critical reflection views all theories and methodologies as complementary. Intellectual tension among competing theories and methodologies can lead to new understandings, whereas universality and convergence lead to complacency with what is known.

This approach allows researchers and practitioners to deal with such issues as employee empowerment, workplace diversity, cultural abnormalities, coercion, ideologies, and ownership of values in a deliberative, normative way. Subjectivity is openly acknowledged not as antithetical to system science but as part of its legitimate discourse. Postulating a role for critical systems theory immediately removes most two-value (either–or) constraints, thereby enabling machine images as metaphors for social systems complemented by contextual analysis. In this spirit, the aspects of leadership discussed previously can be viewed as subsystems, with the concept of leadership (chapter 4) serving as the system (chapter 2).

Each aspect of organizational leadership is related to every other aspect to some degree. The philosophy, values, and ethics of the leader (chapter 7) guide what is observed, his or her approach to inquiry, and the way the leader deals with other people (human relations; chapter 5). Leadership philosophy also has a strong influence on what decisions and policies (chapters 10 and 11) are made and how resources are allocated (chapter 12).

Inquiry (chapter 7), the process of finding and knowing, was discussed as a key component of leadership. It was viewed as a philosophical issue, beginning with a discussion of the various philosophical points of view that shape a person's interpretation of experience. The process of inquiry was considered directly, and the impact of the traditional scientific paradigm was balanced against the possibilities of different ways of gathering and interpreting data. A discussion was conducted of the possibility of taking an eclectic approach and drawing on several paradigms when working in the fields of education. This was considered further in the discussion of observation, which is a fundamental element in the ability of the school leader to detect and recognize relevant events and information.

Communication (chapter 6) was referred to as the breath of the organization. The means and networks of communication reflecting the value placed on human interactions and the extent to which leadership is open or closed to inputs from members of the organization and the community (environmental interactions) were considered. The function of communication as a significant element of school systems was explored, and communication was considered the binding agent in human interaction at the personal and group levels.

Analysis and planning as the prerequisites for rational decision making and management of change were considered (chapter 11). Strategic planning, a process that moves from development of a vision to

sharing the vision to implementation of the vision, was considered from the perspective of the educational leader who will have to implement that process. The relation of a variety of paradigms held by the leader and/or by the members of the organization was explored, and the effects of these paradigms and the related planning models on the allocation of resources were discussed (chapter 12). Planning grows out of the values held collectively by members of the organization and from the evaluation of the successes and failures of current efforts. Allocation of resources is a product of rational planning and political policy formulation. The problem of effective resource allocation and the concomitant need to monitor results was identified as a major concern for leaders at all levels of the educational enterprise (chapter 9).

Educational decision making—the raison d'être for all that has gone before—was considered with respect to collective policy formulation and with respect to individuals and groups (chapter 10). A variety of approaches to decision making that are applicable in a public setting were considered and evaluated. Decision making as the process of choosing among alternatives was identified as one of the most crucial skills needed by an effective educational leader. A circular model appropriate to the view of education as an open general system was proposed. Each activity of the organization requires innumerable decisions made informally by individuals with varying degrees of discretion and formally by the bureaucratic hierarchy. The impact of constant change within and outside educational systems on decision making and on the systems themselves was discussed. For the organization to adapt to ever-shifting environments (internally and externally), organizational change must take place (chapter 13). The success or failure of the change process depends to a large extent on the collective philosophy of the organization and the nature of its human relations and communication networks.

We have reviewed the scholarship on leadership in general terms (chapter 2). We found that there was little agreement on how leadership should be defined or how it works. For our purposes we have defined leadership quite broadly as influencing others' actions in achieving mutually desired ends. Leadership provides direction to an organization, concentrating on doing the right things. Leadership involves philosophy, values, and ethics. Leaders are people who influence the goals, motivations, and actions of others. Frequently, they encourage or initiate change to reach existing and new goals. Occasionally, they lead in order to preserve what is valuable, such as protecting core organizational functions. We have not viewed leadership as being role specific since the roles of leader and follower are interchangeable. Both roles are critical to an organization's success. Some roles, however, offer greater opportunities for exercising leadership, such as the role of principal or superintendent.

We do differentiate between the functions of leadership and management. Management is concerned with doing things right, focusing on the technology of administration. Although leadership and management are different, both are important, and, like leadership, management is not role specific, although its functions are more likely to be consentrated in some positions (e.g., school business administrator) than in others. The success of modern organizations requires both the objective perspective of the manager and the vision and commitment that wise leadership provides (Bolman & Deal, 1997). It may be possible to be an effective manager without strong leadership skills, but it is not possible to be an effective leader without good management skills. Seemingly superficial managerial tasks can be transformed by skilled leaders into opportunities for communicating organizational meaning and purpose in the context of the routine and the mundane (Sergiovanni, 1992).

Implications for Persons in Leadership Positions in Education

In this time of high educational expectations and professional accountability, today's educational leaders must possess a broad variety of skills that enable them to function comfortably and effectively in changing environments and highly politicized conditions. Under these circumstances, change is the only constant.

For better or for worse, this is a dynamic and exciting period in human history. Because of the fluidity of the situation, it is a period of unparalleled opportunity and of potential danger. To capitalize on the opportunities and to minimize the dangers demands extraordinarily wise leadership in all sectors and in all enterprises. While pervasive social change affects persons in every walk of life, there is bound to be greater impact on those in positions of great social visibility and concern—such as persons holding administrative and managerial responsibilities in educational organizations. Society has a right to expect proficient performance from people in those positions.

In a climate of change, expert leadership cannot be a matter of copying conventional behavior. To advance education, there is a clear need for educational leaders to have and exercise the ability to comprehend the dynamics of human affairs as a basis for relevant action under novel conditions, an understanding of issues and processes in educational institutions, and originality and collaboration in designing strategic policies. Their approach to the opportunities and problems confronting them must remain hypothetical and open ended so that more may be learned by what is done.

Past assumptions used by educators in designing schools and school curricula no longer hold across the board. Children are less likely to come from majority backgrounds, they are more likely to be members of nontraditional families, and they are more likely to be poor. Education through high school and beyond is essential if graduates are to be employed in other than menial jobs and to enjoy comfortable standards of living. Well-paying employment opportunities increasingly require sophisticated intellectual skills. Educational leadership is being challenged to design new curricula that recognize the multicultural nature of students, provide institutional support for those at risk, and link schooling to employment and citizenship. Solving our "educational" crises will also require coordination of schools' efforts with those of other social agencies in the community.

Not only will school leaders of the future be working with a student body markedly different from that of the past, but the organizational structures and professional and political relationships will also be quite different. These changes will produce a new climate for school organizations that demands transformational rather than hierarchical leadership.

Parents and community members are likely to have greater influence on the organization and operation of schools through membership on school councils or through parental choice of schooling. The relationships between teachers and administrators are likely to be collegial, not authoritarian. Principals and teachers are likely to have greater professional discretion as many decisions formerly made at the district, state, and federal levels are left to schools. Nevertheless, local, state, and federal authorities will increasingly set and monitor standards while progressively divesting themselves of operational detail. We can expect states, in particular, with the encouragement of the federal government, to set achievement standards, to design curricula to meet those standards, and to administer examinations to identify schools failing to meet those standards.

Coordinating a System of Schools

Because schools are affected continually by changes and pressures from their internal and external environments, educational leaders must be able to anticipate change, develop a broad knowledge base, and be cognizant of external and internal dynamics throughout the world, not just those of their local communities. Although state and federal government agencies have assumed a more active role in the regulation and policy formulation of schools, the local school board remains an important unit for forming policy and making decisions. The school remains the primary venue for implementing educational policy no matter where it is made.

The superintendent of schools, the school board's chief executive officer, possesses a position of high visibility within the community that is both practical and symbolic. However, less than a quarter of the superintendent's time is actually devoted to instructional or student matters; budgetary, financial, personnel, facilities, and public relations activities consume most of the superintendent's time. Nevertheless, school superintendents play a critical role in formulating district policy and programs to achieve educational excellence. Superintendents must be able to balance external political forces that call for change with the needs of pupils in district schools and with organizational needs.

History has demonstrated the ineffectiveness of mandated, top-down reform efforts imposed on local educational agencies by state and federal edict that weaken local control. Yet local control itself produces a dilemma: on the one hand, it provides vitality and a sense of school district ownership by parents and other residents that is lost in a monolithic organization; on the other hand, great inequalities are created. Because of the balkanization of our school governance, some districts, the ready and the able, are well in advance of state and federal leadership; other districts are neither ready nor able and fall far behind state and national aspirations. If governance is decentralized further, the possibility of even greater inequalities and disparities looms large. Issues of equality and coordination are best handled at state and federal levels of government. Developing a wholesome balance between central oversight and local enterprise continues to be a serious policy challenge in the 21st century.

At the district level, administrative control is zoned and can be loosely or tightly linked to constrain and shape principal behavior. These controls are designed to ensure principals' coordination, cooperation, goal achievement, and motivation. Administrative tasks tend to be more tightly controlled than instructional leadership tasks. A balance of control and autonomy is achieved when principals' administrative tasks or outcomes are strictly controlled while allowing autonomy in selecting methods to achieve ends. For significant instructional leadership and school improvement, principals have become the key agent for change.

Because of the loose coupling in school organizations, coordination of activities can be lost without district-level intervention. This can best be accomplished by midlevel central office administrators. They can provide linkages that facilitate change and promote improvement strategies among all schools. Hierarchical, top-down decision making can be replaced by an interactive top-down and bottom-up process.

The development of mission and goals statements for a school can help to achieve a school culture conducive to academic achievement; development of districtwide mission and goal statement is equally important. Such statements can be used to select administrators, to define administrative team composition, and to socialize administrators to share district goals. In addition, supervision, outcomes, and environment monitoring mechanisms can be used to disseminate district goals among schools.

Without strong internal motivation, principals may not become effective instructional leaders. Motivation increases commitment and persistence to achieve instructional goals and improve instructional programs. Limited motivation results in leaders who focus primarily on maintenance and stability behaviors. Directive controls used with management by objectives can lower principals' expectations of their effectiveness and lower their motivation. To ensure effective instructional leadership, district administrators should initially exercise close supervisory control to help shape values, provide feedback, and communicate high expectations. With increased experience, supervision should adopt less directive and more formative controls to reinforce district values and provide supportive feedback. As district administrators develop an optimal mix of controls for their districts, a balance between control and autonomy can result that enables principals to be effective instructional leaders working toward a shared vision and goals and focused on instruction and improvement of student performance.

Transformational Leadership

Effective schools are culturally tight (controlled by norms, group mores, patterns of beliefs, values, socialization, and socially constructed reality) and structurally loose (less emphasis on bureaucratic rules, management rules, contingency trade-offs, and rational reality). Transformational leadership is the norm that develops shared meanings and significance that leads to increased motivation and commitment among teachers and staff. It produces a broad value perspective that includes justice, community, excellence, democracy, and equality. Evidence of effective leadership is seen in long-range planning, attention to and manipulation of the external environment to achieve goals, attention to school vision and values, ability to cope with conflict and complexity, and desire to initiate change (Sergiovanni, 1989).

As a transformational leader, the school principal is the leader of a collegial team of administrators

and teachers, but the principal maintains the hierarchical position of accountability. Because of the loosely coupled nature of subsystems in schools, dispersed individuals within schools often perform leadership functions in a transformational environment. Understanding and acknowledging the gap between those who have the ability and those who have the authority to make decisions help to develop situations where leaders lend their authority to teachers in order to access teachers' abilities and expertise. Empowerment, coupled with purposing, promotes increased motivation and commitment among teachers and administrators.

While transformational leadership views as mandatory a commitment to a shared core of beliefs about the school by administrators, teachers, and students, it allows discretion in implementing these values in teaching, supervision, and administration. Transformative leaders shape school culture and protect school values, thus validating the importance and meaning of these cultural imperatives.

To succeed, leaders must be able to evaluate critically present social conditions and envision and forge an emancipatory community free of social, economic, and discriminatory constraints. Because leadership occurs within the school community, it resides in the community and is developed through communal relationships. Leadership is shared and exchanged among leaders and followers and does not reside consistently in a power position.

Moral Leadership

Moral leadership relies on the development of substitutes for leadership that are capable of initiating and sustaining changes in the school through the actions of and values held by the workers (e.g., the teachers and students). In addition to the traditional bases of authority that rely on bureaucracy, psychological knowledge, and technical rationality, professional and moral authority need to be added. Acting as a school community, the members of the school need to form a covenant based on their shared values that unite the members to act in morally responsive ways to satisfy the needs of the school. There remains a place for command leadership, instructional leadership, and interpersonal leadership, but the heart of one's leadership practice is to become the embodiment of one's ministerial role (Sergiovanni, 1992).

Authority based on bureaucratic, psychological, or technical–rational authority requires an external force to induce people to comply. However, professional authority (craft knowledge and personal expertise) and moral authority (obligations and duties resulting from shared values and ideas) derive from an inner responsibility, shared commitment, and communal interdependence. Thus, emphasis is placed on the teacher as being superordinate to the knowledge base. Teachers who are skilled and able to reflect and understand knowledge and experiences exercise professional authority by integrating these diverse inputs and applying this newly derived knowledge to practice.

Servant leadership is evidenced when professional competence and community values are the basis for defining the leader's actions rather than personal interests and commitments (Greenleaf, 1977). Moral leadership necessitates the replacement of the traditional hierarchical structure of schools where those in positions of authority reside at the apex with a structure in which leaders and followers have equal status and the apex is reserved for the values, commitments, vision, and covenants that guide community actions (Sergiovanni, 1992).

Visioning

Successful principals have a vision of what they want to accomplish, and that vision guides them in managing and leading activities. Situations and dilemmas addressed by principals require them to assign values to facts, evaluate alternative actions, and reach decisions. They need the ability to see the discrepancy between how things are and how they might be, not necessarily in terms of the ideal but in terms of what is possible.

The principal must be able to convey this vision and enlist the supportive actions of school community members. Through situational identity, the principal is able to influence others to a desired response. To achieve this, the principal must help develop a consensus among teachers in defining the situation and prescribing actions. To be successful in this endeavor, it is critical that principals be able to view and understand situations from other participants'

perspectives. Interpersonal competency thus requires sensitivity to others' views and work situations to elicit desired actions.

School Culture and Participatory Democracy

Participatory democracy in education requires an administration that deals with self-criticism, ethics, transformation, and education; appropriate use of participative and leader decision-making strategies where participants are educated to their democratic responsibilities; and an attitude of respecting the past while challenging the future. SBDM is one technique that can facilitate a participatory, or transformative, style of leadership. SBDM is a strategy of school governance that allows each school to act as a relatively autonomous unit, being responsible for budget, curricula, and personnel decisions. These decisions are made at the building level by building personnel and may include participation by parents, students, and community representatives. When SBDM is employed, the school board's role remains that of providing general goals and policies to guide decisions made throughout the district. Through SBDM, principals gain the authority and control necessary to lead and manage their buildings, and the opportunities for involving others in the decision-making process are greatly enhanced.

The dichotomy that exists between principals and teachers can erode as administrators and teachers collaboratively identify and meet the needs of diverse ethnic groups and student populations. Eliminating the isolation and hierarchical structuring of schools will require administrators who can deftly build an organizational culture that connects the varied members into a cohesive, collaborative network where expertise and leadership are shared willingly. The principal is often the only person who has access to all the varied systems operating more or less independently in the loosely coupled school.

In most cases, instructional leaders start with a preexisting program. They must be able to recognize the existing norms, culture, and resources of a school and apply strategies of persuasion and change to maintain and/or enhance the school culture and norms, thus having a positive impact on the instructional program. Principals can become a cultural expression of their schools through demonstrated modeling, daily routines, and commitment. For culture manipulation to be effective, principals must be able to weave both bureaucratic and cultural linkages to create an impact on curriculum and its delivery. Limits may be placed on the principal's authority, however, by external policies (district policies, judicial decisions, and legislated mandates) and the inclusion of others in the decision-making process. To ameliorate these influences, principals can capitalize on the ambiguity that exists in school organizations. Principals may interpret policies to influence favorably their instructional program and intercede on behalf of teachers to improve and/or protect the instructional climate (Firestone & Wilson, 1989).

ACTIVITY 14.1

Scoping the Future of Public Education

As a summary exercise, all ISLLC standards may be relevant

Develop your own scenario of public provision for the education of elementary and secondary students over the next decade and provide your rationale. What new demands will be placed on educational leadership? Refine your scenario in a discussion group of your colleagues. Give your scenario a reality check by discussing it with a local or state policymaker.

ACTIVITY 14.2

Agree or Disagree?

As a summary exercise, all ISLLC standards may be relevant

Identify those issues presented in this chapter on which you agree with the authors and those issues on which you disagree. Reflect on the areas of disagreement and reasons for them. Share your opinions with colleagues in a discussion group.

Parting Thoughts

So will the teaching profession go the way of the hotel dishwasher? Some believe that the current state of educational systems is part of a cycle of decline going on in many parts of the globe. It was apparent during the latter portions of the industrial age that populations were being created who would not be able to compete as the knowledge revolution and global markets continued to expand. Modernization of industrial and service organizations has been displacing human capital as broader educational needs have surfaced. A growing population of workers needs new or changed skills and abilities. The age of the knowledge worker has arrived and traditional school systems are not positioned to respond to these new needs. Similarly, traditionally minded education professionals may not be ready to meet the requirements of these new learners.

Our reality is dominated by pervasive social, economic, and technological change, and educational leaders have no choice but to reconstitute the ways in which we prepare our children and youth to be happy, productive citizens in the new environment of globalization and rapid change. Our current schooling structure was designed for an era long gone. It served that era well but is largely irrelevant for educating children to function effectively under the conditions of the information age. It is time to move on to build a new system sufficient to that task.

REFERENCES

Adler, M. J. (1982). *The paideia proposal: An educational manifesto.* New York: Macmillan.

Archer, J. (2006, January 5). The road less traveled. *Education Week, 25,* 34–37.

Bolman, L. G., & Deal, T. E. (1997). *Reframing organizations: Artistry, choice, and leadership* (2nd ed.). San Francisco: Jossey-Bass.

Coleman, J. S. (1966). *Equality of educational opportunity.* Washington, DC: Office of Education, U.S. Department of Health, Education, and Welfare.

Cronin, J., Dahlin, M., Adkins, D., & Kingsbury, G. (2007). *The proficiency illusion.* Washington, DC: Thomas B. Fordham Institute and the Northwest Evaluation Association.

Darling-Hammond, L. (2004). From "Separate but Equal" to "No Chld Left Behind": The collission of new standards and old inequalities. In D. Meier & G. Wood (Eds.), *Many children left behind: How the No Child Left Behind Act is damaging our children and our schools* (pp. 66–78). Boston: Beacon Press.

David, J. L., & Cuban, L. (2006). *Cutting through the hype: A taxpayer's guide to school reforms.* Mount Morris, IL: Education Week Press.

Drucker, P. F. (1989). *The new realities: In government and politics, in economics and business, in society and world view.* New York: Harper & Row.

Elmore, R. F. (2004). *School reform from the inside out: Policy, practice, performance.* Cambridge, MA: Harvard Education Press.

Firestone, I. J., & Wilson, B. L. (1989). Using bureaucratic and cultural linkages to improve instruction: The principal's contribution. In J. L. Burdin (Ed.), *School leadership: A contemporary reader* (pp. 275–296). Newbury Park, CA: Sage.

Flood, R. L. (1990). *Liberating systems theory.* New York: Plenum Press.

Friedman, T. L. (2006). *The world is flat: A brief history of the twenty-first century.* New York: Farrar, Straus and Giroux.

Fullan, M., Hill, P., & Crevola, C. (2006). *Breakthrough.* Thousand Oaks, CA: Corwin Press.

Greenleaf, R. K. (1977). *Servant leadership: A journey into the nature of legitimate power and greatness.* New York: Paulist Press.

Jones, A. F., Jr., & and Weinberg, D. H. (2000, June). The changing shape of the nation's income distribution: 1947–1998. *Current Population Reports.* Washington, DC: U.S. Census Bureau.

Lynch, R. G. (2007). *Enriching children, enriching the nation: Public investment in high-quality prekindergarten.* Washington, DC: Economic Policy Institute.

Meier, D. (2004). NCLB and democracy. In D. Meier & G. Wood (Eds.), *Many children left behind: How the No Child Left Behind Act is damaging our children and our schools* (pp. 66–78). Boston: Beacon Press.

Naisbitt, J. (1982). *Megatrends: Ten new directions transforming our lives.* New York: Warner Books.

National Center for Education Statistics. (2006). *The condition of education 2006.* Washington, DC: Institute of Education Science, U.S. Department of Education.

New Commission on the Skills of the American Workforce. (2007). *Tough choices or tough times.* San Francisco: Wiley/Jossey-Bass.

Ravitch, D. (2006, January 5). National standards: "50 standards for 50 states" is a formula for incoherence and obfuscation. *Education Week, 25,* 54–58.

Sergiovanni, T. J. (1989). The leadership needed for quality schooling. In T. J. Sergiovanni & J. H. Moore (Eds.), *Schooling for tomorrow: Directing reforms to issues that count* (pp. 213–226). Boston: Allyn & Bacon.

Sergiovanni, T. J. (1992). *Moral leadership: Getting to the heart of school improvement.* San Francisco: Jossey-Bass.

Standards and accountability. (2006, January 5). *Education Week, 25,* 80–81.

Toffler, A. (1980). *The third wave.* New York: Bantam Books.

Name Index

Subject Index